ULYSSES S.
GRANT

Books by Brooks D. Simpson

Advice after Appomattox: Letters to Andrew Johnson, 1865–1866
(with LeRoy P. Graf and John Muldowny)

*Let Us Have Peace: Ulysses S. Grant and the Politics of War
and Reconstruction, 1861–1868*

The Political Education of Henry Adams

America's Civil War

Union and Emancipation: Essays on Race and Politics in the Civil War Era
(coeditor with David W. Blight)

Think Anew, Act Anew: Abraham Lincoln on Slavery, Freedom, and Union

The Reconstruction Presidents

*Sherman's Civil War: Selected Correspondence of William T. Sherman,
1860–1865*
(with Jean V. Berlin)

Gettysburg: A Battlefield Guide
(with Mark Grimsley)

Ulysses S. Grant: Triumph over Adversity, 1822–1865

The Collapse of the Confederacy
(with Mark Grimsley)

The Civil War in the East: Struggle, Stalemate, and Victory

The Civil War: The First Year Told By Those Who Lived It
(with Stephen W. Sears and Aaron Sheehan-Dean)

The Civil War: The Third Year Told By Those Who Lived It

ULYSSES S. GRANT

TRIUMPH OVER ADVERSITY, 1822-1865

BROOKS D. SIMPSON

ZENITH PRESS

First published in 2000 by Houghton Mifflin. This edition published in 2014 by Zenith Press, an imprint of Quarto Publishing Group USA Inc., 400 First Avenue North, Suite 400, Minneapolis, MN 55401 USA.

ISBN: 978-0-7603-4696-9

Library of Congress Cataloging-in-Publication Data

Simpson, Brooks D.
Ulysses S. Grant : triumph over adversity, 1822-1865 / Brooks D. Simpson.
pages cm
"First published in 2000 by Houghton Mifflin Company"–T.p. verso.
Includes bibliographical references and index.
ISBN 978-0-7603-4696-9 (sc)
1. Grant, Ulysses S. (Ulysses Simpson), 1822-1885. 2. Presidents–United States–Biography.
3. Generals–United States–Biography. 4. United States. Army–Biography. I. Title.
E672.S614 2014
973.8'2092–dc23
[B]
2014012661

Book design by David Ford
Maps by Jacques Chazaud
Interior photographs courtesy Library of Congress

Cover design by Andrew Brozyna
On the front cover: Portrait of Grant by Alexander Gardner, ca. 1865
On the frontis: General Ulysses S. Grant in military uniform, photographed in 1865 by
M. B. Brady & Co. National Photographic Portrait Galleries. *Library of Congress*

Printed in the United States of America

10 9 8 7 6 5 4 3 2 1

For
Rebecca,
Emily,
and Olivia

Acknowledgments

●

I want to thank the people who assisted me at the Huntington Library, the Library of Congress, the National Archives, the Newberry Library, the Chicago Historical Society, the Illinois State Historical Library, the Rutherford B. Hayes Presidential Center, Morris Library (Southern Illinois University), Doheny Library (University of Southern California), Alderman Library (University of Virginia), and Hayden Library (Arizona State University). Thanks also go to my other editors and publishers, who waited patiently for their turn (and in some cases are still waiting): Dan Ross, Fred Woodward, Lew Bateman, and Andrew and Linda Davidson.

Two people with a particular interest in Ulysses S. Grant, John Y. Simon and William S. McFeely, are in some sense partly responsible for this book. Ably assisted by a skilled staff, John is into his fourth decade of editing Grant's papers for publication, and the result has eased my labors. At a very early stage in my career Bill took me aside and suggested that the best way for me to say what I wanted to say about Ulysses S. Grant was to write my own book.

In following this advice I have encountered good people who have given generously of their time and of themselves. Terry Winschel reviewed the chapters on Vicksburg; Gordon Rhea shared insights and some of his own work concerning the campaign from the Wilderness to the crossing of the James; Charles Dellheim read the early chapters and helped in many ways during the past several years. Pam Sanfilippo shared with me her research on White Haven, and the whole crew at the Ulysses S. Grant National Historic Site have been wonderful and welcoming to me in my visits. Also offering assistance and information were Jim Epperson, Chuck Ten Brink, Jeff and Janet Davis, Leah Berkowitz, and Dave Smith, who took me on a tour that included stops at Georgetown and the gravesite of Grant's parents.

Mark Grimsley, Candace Scott, and Roger Bridges read the entire manuscript, correcting errors, questioning arguments, and offering useful suggestions and constant encouragement. That's nothing new for Roger, who's been a boon companion and adviser for a decade. Among those friends who have been especially supportive, I want to thank Joan Cashin, Len and Bill Riedel, Frank Scaturro, Tom Schwartz, Michael Burlingame, Herman Hattaway, Ed Bearss, Al Castel, Trevor Hall, Lew Tambs, Rachel Fuchs, Noel Stowe, David Wilson, Wendy Venet, and Steve Woodworth. Dick Sewell and Al Bogue have continued to be as professional colleagues what they once were as mentors — models of what to do and how to do it.

Gerry McCauley has offered me good advice and counsel as we went through the process of contracting with a publisher. Harry Foster has served as my editor and, along with Katie Dillin and especially Liz Duvall, has guided me through the preparation of the manuscript; Charlotte Saikia's discerning pencil sharpened my prose and raised good questions; Jacques Chazaud prepared the maps.

For this paperback edition I have Elizabeth Demers to thank. Her hard work and patience did much to see this project through, as did the folks at Zenith/Quarto. As for those close to me, this book could never have been done without the love and support of my parents, who did all they could to foster a young boy's interest in American history, whether it was going to museums, visiting battlefields, or buying books. Nor could it have been done without the patient tolerance of my sister, Joy, who had to put up with her brother's interests but always reassures me that she finds them interesting, too. My wife, Cheryl, now knows more about Ulysses S. Grant than she ever cared to discover and made most memorable a trip to White Haven by asking our tour guide if she could see Julia's bed, because she was quite curious about the bedpost she named after her Ulysses. Finally, there are my three daughters, Rebecca, Emily, and Olivia, who like anything to do with the Yankees. No father could be prouder than I am of them.

Contents

●

Maps

•

Foreword

●

Gary W. Gallagher

Ulysses S. Grant offers a compelling example of why it is important to understand the difference between history and memory. Grant played a profoundly important role during the Civil War, presiding over military operations that placed him alongside Abraham Lincoln as one of the two individuals most responsible for suppressing the Confederate rebellion and restoring the Union. The loyal citizenry of the time understood this, and they celebrated Grant as a soldier, twice elected him president, and honored him in death with the most impressive tomb in the Western Hemisphere. Over time and for various reasons — some linked to efforts by former Confederates and Copperhead Democrats to denigrate him — Grant fell in the public estimation. Often characterized as a butcher who understood little about strategy but benefitted from overwhelming advantages of manpower and resources as well as a drunk and a corrupt president, Grant became, in historical memory, a figure far removed from nineteenth-century reality. Popular misconceptions about Grant have complicated the work of scholars seeking to present a fair, unvarnished treatment of him as a man, a general, and a political figure.

Since the early 1990s, Brooks D. Simpson has done as much as anyone to recover the historical Grant, to assess him in ways that give full credit to his strengths while also examining his weaknesses and failures. Simpson's *Let Us Have Peace: Ulysses S. Grant and the Politics of War and Reconstruction, 1861–1868* (1991), among the first books that sought to reframe interpretations of Grant, heralded the arrival of a most promising historian and whetted appetites for more on Grant. Simpson delivered with this book, the first edition of which was published in 2000 to wide praise. This new edition, the first in paperback, brings a superb book to a wider audience.

Simpson's mastery of sources and analytical acuity render this book a splendid place for readers to explore Grant's life and career from his birth in Point Pleasant, Ohio, through the end of the Civil War. It is an admirably rounded portrait that accords full attention to Grant's relationship with his family, his personality, his military training and service, his political skills, and his quite remarkable ability to overcome disappointments, both before and during the Civil War, that would have crushed many others. The principal focus is on the great challenge of preserving the Union. As Grant put it in his official report at the end of the war: "From the first, I was firm in the conviction that no peace could be had that would be stable and conducive to the happiness of the people, both North and South, until the military power of the rebellion was entirely broken." For Grant's accomplishment of that goal, as *Harper's Weekly* put it in April 1865, "the country pays now, and will forever pay, the homage of its unqualified gratitude to his genius and his spotless character."

By telling in detailed and often gripping fashion how Grant carried out his central part of the effort to salvage the Union, Simpson helps us recover why the editors at *Harper's Weekly* predicted long-term fame for the nation's preeminent Civil War soldier.

May 2014

Preface

●

William T. Sherman never hesitated to say what he thought to anyone who would listen, and he was not afraid to pass judgment. But he admitted that on one subject he was unable to offer an answer. He could never quite figure out Ulysses S. Grant. He marveled at his friend's self-confidence, his equanimity, his resilience and determination; but he could not explain the secret of his success: "I knew him as a cadet at West Point, as a lieutenant of the Fourth Infantry, as a citizen of St. Louis, and as a growing general all through the bloody Civil War. Yet to me he is a mystery, and I believe he is a mystery to himself."

If Sherman could not provide the answer, why should anyone else try? That is the question one must ask of any biographer of Ulysses S. Grant. It does not help that Grant often kept his thoughts to himself; no wonder he was called "the American Sphinx." To some extent, he remains what a newspaper reporter once called him, "an unpronounceable man." There are no simple answers to the riddles of his character and personality, no single threads that hold everything together; biographers who claim otherwise are either deluding themselves or misleading others. And yet Grant's life is as fascinating as it is important. As Owen Wister noted a century ago, "None of our public men have a story so strange as this." A seemingly ordinary man who accomplished extraordinary tasks, Grant deserves our attention and our understanding for who he was and for what he did; both his successes and failures can teach us much about his America and ours.

Grant has not fared well as a biographical subject in the past fifty years. A massive multivolume effort begun by Lloyd Lewis and continued by Bruce Catton carried the story to Appomattox, but Catton was happy to hear that he need not go further. In the past twenty years, despite the flood of literature about the Civil War, only two single-volume biographies have appeared, by William S. McFeely and Geoffrey Perret, as well as a few ᴏᴛʜᴇʀ ᴀttempts at explaining Grant's life; the publication of a comprehensive edition of his papers continues under the supervision of John Y. Simon. Each of these endeavors has its merits and offers compelling arguments, but there is more than enough room for an extended examination of Grant the soldier, the president, and the man. This first volume takes his story from birth through the Civil War; a second volume will continue the tale through the two decades after Appomattox to Grant's death in 1885.

I have no interest in becoming Grant's advocate or antagonist, in either elevating or denigrating him. Like anyone else, Grant had his strengths and weaknesses, his virtues and his vices; if parts of his character and personality are praiseworthy, one must also concede that he was far from flawless. In short, he was human. People who search for perfect heroes reveal much more about themselves than about their subjects; so do those who make their subjects scapegoats for an age. The tendency of some people to categorize biographers as being "for" or "against" their subject has always struck me as being simplistic and somewhat simple-minded (and occasionally self-serving). If there is much to admire in Grant, there are also areas where he should be subject to scrutiny and criticism. In treating Grant with empathy, I have guarded against becoming too sympathetic, let alone apologetic, although those readers who hold a negative assessment of him may disagree. Grant could be petty, vindictive, stubborn, overly sensitive, and partial to favorites; in dealing with troubling issues he sometimes was too eager to compromise principle in pursuit of pragmatic practice and too willing to accept things as they were. Yet he also displayed bravery, integrity, determination, persistence, generosity, gentleness, and a self-confidence that if not as unshakable as is commonly portrayed was nevertheless astonishing. Critics who question his military renown fail to appreciate just how valuable common sense, character, courage, intuition, and the ability to cope with circumstances are to the making of a great commander. Grant may not have carried himself as did Robert E. Lee, embraced the pomp and circumstance of war as did George McClellan, or expressed himself in William T. Sherman's colorful language of blunt realism and relentless logic; he may not have framed brilliant plans in the headquarters tent emphasizing elegant maneuvers or elaborate tactics — but generals are defined not by how they look or what they say but who they are and what they do.

In reading, writing, and thinking about Grant, I have been guided by one of his own wishes, expressed in his *Memoirs*, that he would like "to see truthful history written." Here and there I have drawn on sources that shed new light on Grant's life and career, but as I examined documents and read accounts I discovered that perhaps the toughest task facing a biographer is trying to get the story right. It was not so much uncovering new material as it was carefully rereading old sources that led me to cast a critical eye on traditional accounts and unexamined assumptions. I was surprised by what I learned about the Lincoln–Grant relationship, Grant's drinking habits, and the general's understanding of war and politics, including emancipation and reconciliation. If it became important for me to take a closer look at his performance as general-in-chief in 1864–1865, I was equally engaged in learning more about his personal struggles and his devotion to his wife and children. But, more than anything else, I found Grant's ability to keep moving on, to overcome obstacles, to prevail somehow, some way, testament to some inner strength that weathered periods of difficulty, depression, and self-doubt.

Perhaps it was no accident that three of the greatest American authors of Grant's time were drawn to him. Mark Twain's relationship with him is well known; Herman Melville came away from an encounter in 1864 intrigued, an impression that found expression in his observation, "Meekness and grimness meet in him — The silent General"; Walt Whitman observed, "In all Homer and Shakespeare there is no fortune or personality really more picturesque or rapidly changing, more full of heroism, pathos, contrast." But it may have been young Theodore Lyman who best expressed the fascination some people have about Grant when he observed in 1864, "He is the concentration of all that is American."

And this man wins in the end.
—Stephen Vincent Benét,
John Brown's Body

●

1

"My Ulysses"

●

JESSE GRANT exemplified what America was all about. A man of restless ambition striving to make his own way in the world, he was not shy about sharing his dreams, his hopes, and his accomplishments with anyone who would listen. Behind his drive was an understanding of what it meant to fail. Descended from good colonial stock, Jesse had watched his father, Noah Grant, fall short of the family standard. Noah's claims to military glory as a captain during the American Revolution find no support in existing records; he was overly fond of alcohol and frittered away opportunities and money. He had two sons by a first wife before she died; with his second wife, Rachel, whom he married in 1792, he had seven more children, including Jesse, born in 1794. Ten years later Rachel died in a cabin in Deerfield, Ohio. Noah was unable to hold things together, and before long the family broke up. The two youngest children went with their father to Maysville, Kentucky, where Peter Grant, Noah's son by his first marriage, was operating a tannery. The three middle children were parceled out to other families. Jesse, who was eleven, and his older sister Susan were set loose on their own.

The boy knew it would take a lot of work to make his way up in the world, but he was dead set on doing just that. For three years he scrambled to stay afloat. At fourteen he gained a job working on the farm of Judge George Tod, a member of the Ohio Supreme Court. He learned something about what might lie ahead for a hardworking lad when he saw the china bowls and silver spoons that the Tods used. Mrs. Tod did what she could to build the boy's ambition and talents, lending him books to read and urging him to find a calling at which he could prosper.[1]

Jesse took the advice to heart and at sixteen decided to learn the tanner's trade. He apprenticed with his half-brother Peter, then worked at several tanneries in Ohio, including one owned by Owen Brown, whose son, John, openly denounced the "peculiar institution" of slavery. Jesse

1

agreed with John's sentiments, explaining later that he had left Kentucky because "I would not own slaves and I would not live where there were slaves and not own them." In 1820 he moved to Point Pleasant, on the banks of the Ohio River, some twenty miles upriver from Cincinnati, and commenced working at Thomas Page's tannery in order to accumulate enough capital to open his own business. He also wanted a wife. Page pointed him in the direction of Bantam, ten miles to the north, where John Simpson and his family, migrants from Pennsylvania, had settled on land purchased from Page. Jesse was soon courting Hannah Simpson, "a plain unpretending girl, handsome but not vain," as her suitor remembered in later years. Moreover, she was quiet, allowing the voluble Jesse to hold forth uncontested. Although John Simpson was not too sure about Jesse's prospects, his wife, Sarah, loved to discuss books with the young man; having ingratiated himself with his prospective mother-in-law, Jesse found it easier to achieve his objective of matrimony. As Jesse's savings grew, John Simpson's reservations faded, and on June 24, 1821, Jesse Grant wed Hannah Simpson. The newlyweds returned to Point Pleasant, where Jesse had rented a simple white frame house next to the tannery.[2]

When he was not scraping or tanning hides, Jesse Grant spent his hours reading and writing. Always willing to share his opinions with others — and never doubting his own wisdom — he liked to set down his thoughts on politics for the local paper. Hannah quietly kept house, attended the local Methodist church (bringing Jesse with her), and before long discovered that she would soon have new responsibilities. In the early hours of April 27, 1822, she gave birth to a boy, weighing ten and three-quarters pounds, with rich red-brown hair, blue eyes, and fair skin. For nearly a month the newborn went nameless: when Hannah was well enough to travel, Jesse drove his family up to Bantam, where several Simpsons had gathered to help select a name. Hannah wanted to name the boy Albert, after Pennsylvania's Albert Gallatin, who had played a prominent role in Jeffersonian politics as a diplomat and secretary of the treasury. One sister seconded the choice; another preferred Theodore. John Simpson spoke up, offering "Hiram, because it is such a handsome name." When Sarah Simpson, fresh from reading Fénelon's *Telemachus* and thrilled by its dramatic description of Greek heroes, opted for Ulysses, Jesse, seeing yet another opportunity to please his mother-in-law, endorsed the suggestion (perhaps he had a hand in making it, for he had lent the book to Sarah). Aware of the growing political nature of the discussion, however, and determined to offend no one, he decided to leave the choice to chance. Anne Simpson, Hannah's youngest sister, drew a slip from a hat bearing the name Ulysses. Looking to swing one more deal, Jesse then declared that the boy's name would be Hiram Ulysses — a decision designed to delight both in-laws. Fate eventually triumphed over politics: the boy would always be known as Ulysses — or, as his father would put it, "my Ulysses."[3]

By the following year Jesse had accumulated enough money to strike out on his own. He moved his family inland to Georgetown, the county seat, set up his own tannery a block east of the town square, and soon settled with Hannah and their son in a new brick two-story home. The structure was an impressive sight among the log cabins and plaster walls of other residences in the small town known for the propensity of its residents to drink — no surprise in light of the two dozen distilleries in Brown County. No matter, thought Jesse — he was now set up to make a living in an area that provided a ready supply of tanning bark. He befriended the justice of the peace, Thomas L. Hamer, who shared his political preferences for Andrew Jackson and a more democratic polity, and commenced working and writing to make a name for himself. But at times his offspring stole center stage from his father. Just as Ulysses neared his second birthday, a small circus came to town. The toddler, adorned in petticoats, was fascinated by a trained pony; when the ringmaster invited members of the audience to ride the animal, Ulysses begged and implored his father until he got his way. Lifted onto the horse's back and held in place by an adult, he circled the ring several times, "manifesting more glee than he had ever shown before." Several months later, a neighbor with an odd sense of curiosity wanted to see how the child would respond to the noise of a pistol shot. As Jesse held Ulysses, the boy tugged at the trigger. Finally the weapon went off: delighted, Ulysses demanded, "Fick it again! Fick it again!" The next year, however, when the toddler heard the local physician prescribe powder to remedy an ailment, he cried out, "No, no, no! I can't take powder; it will blow me up!" Family members retold the story for years to come.[4]

By the time he was three, Ulysses was joined by a brother, Samuel; later came several more brothers and sisters, until by 1839 the Grants had three boys and three girls. Jesse added to the house as he added to the family: he bought books, read newspapers, and continued to make money and broadcast his opinions. As the eldest child, Ulysses got his own room on the second floor — but just about all he could see from his bedroom window was the tannery. He did not enjoy the view. The process of tanning hides as well as the stench that resulted turned his stomach. He hated doing chores. Whenever he could, he preferred to be with living animals, especially horses, for whom he soon developed a passion. As a small boy he liked to go out in the stable and sit beside his four-legged friends. Aware of the damage an errant hoof might cause, a neighbor shared her alarm with Hannah Grant. Calmly, Hannah smiled: "Horses seem to understand Ulysses."[5]

And Ulysses seemed to understand horses. He was only five years old when he learned how to stand on the back of a trotting horse, using the reins to keep his balance. At six he harnessed horses to haul brush, much to his father's surprise; when Jesse opened a small livery business, it was Ulysses who often drove passengers or carted wood. At nine he had saved up enough money to buy his first horse; local townsfolk brought him horses to break and train, and marveled as he raced through town or hugged the neck of an uncooperative colt as it bucked, kicked, and reared up on its hind hooves. When a horse had distemper, its owner would bring it to Ulysses to ride, for the best way to cure the ailment was by running the horse at a gallop to burn out the disease. Other boys tried to imitate him, sometimes prodded on by Ulysses, who teased them that their horses were too slow: one unfortunate youth was crushed to death when his mount suddenly shied and fell on him. Although Ulysses's reaction to the boy's death went unrecorded, thereafter he drew closer to the boy's mother, Mrs. Bailey, who lived just up the street. In turn she thought he was "exceedingly kind and amiable."[6]

Two stories about the boy and horses suggested something deeper about the character of Jesse Grant's eldest son.

Ulysses was eleven when another circus visited Georgetown. Once more the ringmaster brought out a trained pony; once more Ulysses mounted it. This time, however, the ringmaster barked orders for the pony to throw its rider while galloping at full speed around the ring. Ulysses simply dug in his heels. Undeterred, the ringmaster brought out a monkey: it scrambled on board, grabbed Ulysses by the hair, and stared down at the boy's face. People laughed; then they grew astonished when they saw that Ulysses stayed on. There was no quit in this boy. In a similar episode young Grant earned five dollars for hanging on to a particularly slick mount.[7]

And yet the boy's love of horses could also lead to embarrassment. He was only eight years old when he set his heart on buying a colt owned by Robert Ralston, a farmer who lived just west of town. Jesse, needing to expand his stable, entrusted his son to make the purchase, but only after instructing him in the fine art of negotiating, for he did not want to pay Ralston's asking price of twenty-five dollars. Accounts differ in the details of what happened next, but all agree that when Ralston asked the boy what his father would pay, Ulysses blurted out, "Papa says I may offer you twenty dollars for the colt, but if you won't take that, I am to offer twenty-two and a half, and if you won't take that, to give you twenty-five." As he later dryly remarked, "It would not require a Connecticut man to guess the price finally agreed upon."[8]

This tale soon made the rounds of Georgetown. Fathers and sons alike guffawed and laughed at the business acumen of "my Ulysses"; for once Jesse was forced to listen. Ulysses Grant later recalled that the story "caused me great heart-burning . . . and it was a long time before I heard the last of it."

Biographers looking to find the man in the boy have read much into the incident. It was an early sign of his naivete in business; it illustrated his determination to gain his objective; it epitomized his guilelessness and gullibility. But Grant put his own stamp on the story. "I certainly showed very plainly that I had come for the colt and meant to have him," he recounted: Jesse's desire to cut a deal would not deter his son from what he wanted. Additional information about the aftermath tended to place the incident in a better light. Nearly four years later, the horse now nearly blind, Ulysses sold him for twenty dollars — not a bad price; two years after that, he spotted the Ralston horse "working on the tread-wheel of the ferry-boat." Nevertheless, he never forgot the teasing: "Boys enjoy the misery of their companions, at least village boys in that day did, and in later life I have found that all adults are not free from the peculiarity."[9]

Horses were more honest than people, or so Ulysses seemed to believe, for he gave himself to them as he never did to his friends. He trusted them, and they responded to him. Nor was his compassion limited to horses. He showed little interest in hunting; as for his father's tanning trade, he frankly "detested it," preferring to work his father's fifty-acre farm on the outskirts of town or do anything else involving horses. He hauled and plowed; he transported passengers, sometimes as far as Cincinnati and once to Toledo, some 250 miles away; he often paid other boys to do his work at the tannery, then hired out his services as a horseman to people in the community, pocketing the difference. For fun he fished in the summer and skated in the winter, played ball with the boys, and took the girls on sleigh rides. He enjoyed swimming in White Oak Creek, which ran just west of the town, although once he nearly lost his life when he fell off a log into the creek, then flooded as a result of recent rains, and found himself being dragged away by the current; only the alert actions of his chum, Dan Ammen, rescued him from drowning. At school he was well-behaved, usually escaping the schoolmaster's switch; his schoolmates found him quiet, a bit shy, and not particularly studious.

"He was a real nice boy," one of the girls later remembered, "who never had anything to say and when he said anything, he always said it short." Another playmate noted that while Ulysses "was up to any lark with us," he "went about everything in such a peculiarly businesslike way. . . . I don't remember that I ever saw him excited." Perhaps he was a quiet boy because as Jesse's son he did not want to call more attention to himself — except when he mounted a horse, when he mixed flair with an occasional willingness to show off. Had it not been for this skill (and the burdens that came with being Jesse Grant's son), Ulysses would have led an unremarkable childhood.[10]

By the 1830s Georgetown was well on the way toward shedding its frontier origins. In 1827 a Methodist church opened across the street from the Grant residence; two years later the children started attending school in a newly opened brick building, the successor to the subscription school just a few dozen yards from the Grant house. Other homes appeared, including several that reflected the influences of the Greek Revival movement, complete with columns. What was once little more than a clearing was now beginning to look worthy of the name of county seat.

Jesse gained prominence in Georgetown's political affairs. His early preference for Andrew Jackson eroded in the 1830s, and he became a staunch advocate of the rising Whig party, with its plans for integrated national growth and development. Jesse never espoused an opinion halfheartedly, however, and one casualty of his new political loyalty was Thomas Hamer, who now represented Georgetown in Congress as a Democrat. Jesse's blunt editorials and poetry in the columns of the appropriately named *Castigator* placed him on the front lines of political controversy. He won his reward in 1837 when, in the aftermath of economic distress for which voters held Democrats accountable, he was elected mayor of Georgetown.[11]

Jesse's antislavery proclivities were becoming more pronounced as well, reflecting the rising intensity of the debate over slavery in the United States. However, his commitment paled beside that of the Reverend John Rankin, who lived by the Ohio River in Ripley. More than rumor had it that the reverend's house sheltered fugitive slaves, including a family of three who had made their way across the river by navigating floating pieces of ice. Although Jesse could claim no such fame, he was visible enough in business and political affairs, and it was this, to say nothing of his bragging about Ulysses, that sometimes led others to focus on the son in retaliation against the father. One of the reasons two brothers, Carr and Chilton White, had spread the Ralston horse story with such glee was that their father, the local schoolmaster, was a Democrat.

Hannah Grant went about her chores and responsibilities quietly, so much so that one must search carefully for her traces. Dan Ammen recalled that she was "a cheerful woman, always kind and gracious to children." But affection — or at least open displays of it — were rare in the Grant household. Ulysses told Ammen that he never saw his mother cry. Nor did Hannah brag as was her husband's custom: she was modest, retiring, and restrained. Unlike Jesse, she "thought nothing you could do would entitle you to praise," as one observer recalled; indeed, "you ought to praise the Lord for giving you an opportunity to do it." Such a demeanor obscured that Hannah was fairly well educated, something that inspired Jesse to learn as much as he could about reading and writing. The house contained a small library of several dozen books, perhaps the largest such collection in the town.[12]

The Grants loved their children and took great pride in their accomplishments. In turn Ulysses loved and respected his parents, although signs of friction with his father remained evident, and he said little about his mother, who remains something of an enigmatic presence. Yet the extremes of a boastful father and a reserved mother offered lessons for later life: as a parent Ulysses would never leave his children starved for affection.

As the Grant household continued to grow, so did the extended family. Eventually Ulysses could count thirty-nine cousins: thirteen in Ohio and twenty-six more in the slave states of Kentucky and Virginia. Jesse once remarked of the latter "that they had depended too much on slave labor to be trained in self-reliance, whereas his children had to wait upon themselves even so far as to black their own shoes." Responsibility led to prosperity in Jesse's mind, and he was in earnest about giving his children the right tools and character to succeed. He prized education and hard work, and his boys got a good helping of both. Ulysses may have been embarrassed by his father's boasting and uneasy about his drive to succeed in business; however, he appreciated the opportunities that his father's success made possible, and respected his commitment to educate his children as well as prepare them for life. But he would never follow his father into the tanning business. Nor was he exactly enthusiastic about his father's preference to call him Ulysses. Boys liked to taunt him with "Useless," an especially humiliating label in light of his father's principles: the boy inscribed his books "Hiram U. Grant."

Ulysses was not especially athletic, nor even healthy, despite his skill as a horseman. At times he suffered from ague and fever. More threatening was the cholera outbreak that swept across the region in 1833. Jesse Grant traveled to Kentucky to purchase a remedy. He brought back two jugs.

One contained a supposed cure; the other was filled with blackberry cordial, to stop the diarrhea that came with cholera. One Sunday morning, with his parents at church, Ulysses and his playmates, heated after some strenuous activities and convinced that a stomachache was the first sign of the dreaded cholera, hustled down to the basement to cure themselves with generous portions of medicine — and the cordial. The boys liked what they tasted and, believing that an ounce of prevention was always in order, often returned, as one recalled, "to have a pull at the cholera medicine. I don't know whether we took it right or not, but certain it is that we did not take the cholera."[13]

Fortunately, this story did not make the rounds of the town. Jesse, however, never missed an opportunity to recount tales of his eldest boy's determination, calmness under pressure, and resourcefulness. One time, Ulysses was taking two young ladies to Georgetown when his buggy encountered a flooded ford. He plunged straight ahead. The water rose: when it reached the waists of his passengers, they began to scream. Ulysses turned around. "Don't speak!" he shouted. "I will take you through safe." And so he did. His hauling exploits became legendary. Once he devised a method to load logs onto his wagon, aided only by his horse, by wrapping them in a chain and dragging them up a half-felled tree that served as a ready-made incline to the wagon bed. And for years to come townspeople would marvel at how Ulysses, then fifteen, hauled a massive stone from the banks of White Oak Creek up a steep and winding road for a doctor who wanted it placed at the front door of his new house.[14]

Jesse wore the stories out in the retelling, never letting listeners forget that he was speaking about "my Ulysses." At last a few townsfolk saw another chance to get even. A traveling phrenologist arrived at Georgetown, boasting of his ability to predict a person's future by feeling and assessing the shape of his or her head. At a public lecture the phrenologist offered to conduct a reading blindfolded: Ulysses, no doubt red-faced, was ushered to the stage. As the phrenologist's fingers played over Ulysses's head, the analyst exclaimed, "It is no common head! It is an extraordinary head!" People in the audience smirked and giggled. Jesse watched intently. At last the phrenologist reached the climax of the performance, declaring, "It would not be strange if we should see him President of the United States." It was a standard routine often used to mock a parent's pride in a child; once again, Ulysses had to suffer the consequences of his father's bragging.[15]

This uneasiness between father and son became more apparent as Ulysses entered adolescence. He continued to show no interest in entering the family business. Tannery practices repelled him so much that he could not stomach seeing any blood on his plate, preferring his meat to be cooked until it was nearly burnt. To some observers he seemed "more like a grown person than a boy," as quiet and serious as his mother. Aside from horses, however, he possessed few marketable skills or visible interests. He was ambivalent about entering any kind of business. Although he had shown some shrewdness in earning money and doubtless wanted to prove that he could be self-sufficient, his father's way of doing things was too sharp and brash for Ulysses. Surely there was a better way to be prosperous. In school he cared little for writing and even less for reciting: one of his teachers recalled that Ulysses found public speaking "unbearable," seldom spoke, and did so only "by the greatest exertion." Only in mathematics did he display any real talent. Solving problems had always been one of his most apparent skills, and the logic of mathematics came as second nature to him. But where this ability could lead remained elusive. Two pursuits that had crossed the boy's mind — becoming a farmer or a river trader — were unacceptable to his father, who suspected such occupations would cultivate habits of laziness, even shiftlessness. Lacking alternatives, and always looking for a good deal, Jesse investigated the possibility of sending Ulysses to the United States Military Academy at West Point.[16]

In considering West Point, Jesse did not necessarily envision a military career for his son. The Academy was the nation's leading engineering school: mathematics would prove useful in that field. Other boys from Georgetown had attended West Point, including Jacob Ammen, Dan's older brother. And, with the arrival of more children — and a hint of an economic chill in the air — money was an issue: West Point was free. So in 1836 Jesse sent Ulysses to a prep school in Maysville to bone up for admittance exams (he stayed with Uncle Peter's family). There the boy joined a local debating club, where he espoused the impracticality of immediate abolition and supported the proposition that intemperance was a greater evil than war. The following year the boy attended a local subscription school, followed by a year at a school in Ripley headed by the Reverend Rankin. Local rumor had it that Jesse redoubled his efforts to get his son into West Point when he heard that a neighbor's boy, Bartlett Bailey (brother of the boy killed while trying to emulate Ulysses's horsemanship) had just secured an appointment to the Academy. The Baileys lived up the street from the Grants, in a house with columns that more than rivaled Jesse's own sturdy but simple brick structure; in this case up the street also meant uphill, figuratively as well as literally. Jesse looked on Dr. George Bailey as competition, and he was determined not to lose.[17]

There was only one problem. Members of Congress selected candidates for examination for admission to the Academy. At first, Jesse thought that a fellow Whig, Senator Thomas Morris, could provide the nomination. But Morris had bartered it away to another congressman. That left Jesse's congressman — Thomas Hamer. It was not an auspicious alternative. For several years the once-close friends had been at odds over politics, and Jesse's mouth and pen had often gotten the better of him, aggravating the disagreement. Hamer fought to protect slaveowners' rights; Jesse supported Morris's efforts to end slavery and had sent Ulysses to the Reverend Rankin's academy.

A slot was open. Despite two tries at making it through the first year, Bart Bailey had failed his exams, news his father had tried to keep under wraps. However, Mrs. Bailey had shared the story with Ulysses when the boy, home from Ripley during Christmas break, walked up the street to get a quart of milk. Bart's resignation in the fall of 1838 was Ulysses's — or Jesse's — opportunity. When Jesse, brandishing a letter from Morris, broached his plan to Ulysses, the boy was not pleased. "But I won't go!" he protested. As he later recalled, his father "said he thought I would, *and I thought so, too, if he did.*"

But it would not be so easy. Officials flatly rejected Jesse's attempt to bypass Hamer by applying directly to the War Department for a nomination. So, on February 19, 1839, Jesse sat down, swallowed his pride (no doubt with some difficulty), and wrote to Tom Hamer to ask him to nominate Ulysses to West Point. Rumor had it that Hannah Grant visited Hamer's wife in an attempt to patch things up. The letter reached Hamer on the last day of his term as a congressman: he had decided to quit the House to attend to his private affairs. Hurriedly Hamer made out the request, although for a moment he was stumped trying to remember the boy's precise name. The deed done, he responded to Jesse's request: "I received your letter and have asked for the appointment of your son, which will doubtless be made. Why didn't you apply to me sooner?" The mails being what they were, Hamer actually arrived in Georgetown ahead of the letter and wondered when Jesse would show his gratitude. In due time the letter arrived, and all was well once more between Jesse Grant and Tom Hamer.[18]

Several townspeople looked askance at Ulysses's appointment. There was nothing exceptional about the lad — except for his way with horses. One disgruntled fellow, still smarting from the time Ulysses had named a horse after him, grumbled, "I'm astonished that Hamer did not appoint someone with intellect enough to do credit to the district."[19]

So Ulysses prepared to travel to the school on the Hudson River. "I really had no objection to going to West Point," he recalled years later, "except that I had a very exalted idea of the acquirements necessary to get through. I did not believe that I possessed them, and could not bear the idea of failing." He had seen what happened to Bart Bailey — and he could well imagine what would happen to Jesse Grant's son if he returned home in disgrace. He made the rounds of relatives and friends, did some last-minute studying, and packed his belongings. To identify his trunk, he and his cousins hammered in his initials, but it took only a moment to see that "H. U. G." would not do: Ulysses was not going to be the butt of any more jokes if he could help it. From now on he would be Ulysses Hiram Grant. On May 15, 1839, he bade farewell to his parents and four siblings (with a fifth on the way). As he passed the Baileys' house, Mrs. Bailey came out, crying, and kissed him. In light of all that had happened, the young man was both startled and grateful. "Why, Mrs. Bailey," he responded. "They didn't cry at our house."[20]

Up by steamboat to Pittsburgh, then by ferryboat to Harrisburg, and finally by train to Philadelphia, Ulysses Hiram Grant made his way east. He spent five days in Philadelphia — the first truly large city he had ever visited — staying with his mother's cousins, the Hare family. One of them described the newcomer as "a rather awkward country lad, wearing plain clothes and large, coarse shoes as broad at the toes as at the widest part of the soles." Then it was on to New York, where he encountered another Academy aspirant, Fred Dent of Missouri. Together the two westerners traveled up the Hudson River to West Point, some eighty miles north of New York City. Grant was not eager to reach his destination; he would have been perfectly content had an accident en route or some other misfortune forced him to return to Ohio, honor intact. But it was not to be, and so, as he later put it, "I had to face the music" (an especially pointed turn of phrase, for music made him cringe). Arriving on May 29, he secured a room at a local hotel, then presented himself at the adjutant's office, where he signed the register "Ulysses Hiram Grant." The adjutant firmly informed him that there was no appointment waiting for such a person. Two Grants were scheduled to arrive: Elihu Grant from New York and Ulysses S. Grant from Ohio. Apparently Congressman Hamer, in his rush to make out the papers of nomination, had mistakenly affixed an S (Hannah's maiden name was Simpson) to serve as a middle initial after the name by which the boy went — Ulysses. Try as he might to explain the mix-up, Ulysses confronted for the first time the reality that rules were rules, at least at West Point. He could agree to be Ulysses S. Grant or he could go home. Faced with this choice, Grant, who had never had much use for Hiram anyway, agreed to yet another name change — this one with memorable consequences.[21]

At the time, however, the switch proved significant primarily because it foiled Grant's effort to avoid mockery. As the cadets scanned the list of incoming candidates, their eyes fell on "U. S. Grant." Well, who was that? United States Grant? Uncle Sam Grant? One senior, a redheaded Ohioan, was among the leaders in this guessing game. William Tecumseh Sherman knew firsthand about name changes, for the William was slapped on after a priest refused to baptize a baby named after an Indian warrior. Grant explained what had happened, but it was no use. He was now Ulysses S. Grant. Before long his friends started calling him Sam, just as Sherman went by Cump; another cadet, James Longstreet of South Carolina, was known as Pete.[22]

Over the next month the cadet candidates, called "Things" by cadets, learned the basics of parade ground drill as they awaited entrance exams on July 1. Grant, lacking any sense of rhythm, struggled to keep in step and winced when bands played, an odd reaction for one whose voice was often described as musical. But he was better prepared for the practical jokes practiced by upperclassmen, having carried with him a letter of introduction — perhaps from one of the Baileys — to one cadet, who shared the secrets of some common pranks with the newcomer. Late one night, someone resembling an officer entered Grant's room and directed Grant and his roommate to memorize twenty pages of a textbook: they would be tested in the morning. When the impostor left, Grant went back to sleep, while his roommate fell for the ruse. However, Grant was the victim of another prank: some mischievous upperclassman ordered him to stand guard over a pump, and he remained at his "post" until thirdclassman William S. Rosecrans finally put an end to the joke. It was one of the few times someone got the better of him. He refused to be intimidated by his peers: once he knocked down a larger "Thing," the son of an officer, after his antagonist had shoved him out of line during drill. Meanwhile, he studied. The exams proved no obstacle — the schooling had paid off — and he joined fifty-nine others in making up the initial class of 1843. Eventually the class swelled to seventy-seven in number before the inevitable attrition began.[23]

Whatever exultation Grant felt at his success was soon tempered by his return to the parade ground for more drilling and field exercises, which he found "very wearisome and uninteresting." The monotony of such training was broken only by the visits of the academy's commandant,

Charles F. Smith, and the commanding general of the United States Army, Winfield Scott. Smith looked every inch the magnificent soldier; Scott, a bit older and thicker, was a national hero who looked the part in a rather ornate uniform. Grant was impressed. In his mind's eye he imagined himself in Scott's place, surveying the corps of cadets. It was best, he decided, to keep this fantasy to himself, lest he open himself to ridicule.[24]

For someone who was reluctant to attend West Point, Grant soon came to enjoy some aspects of "this prettiest of places." He waxed effusive about it to a cousin. "So far as it regards natural attractions it is decidedly the most beautiful place that I have ever seen." From his window he could see the Hudson, "that far famed, that beautiful river with its bosom studded with hundreds of snow white sails," he scrawled, revising as he wrote. All around him were reminders of the American Revolution and its heroes and its villains, including the house of Benedict Arnold, "that *base* and *heartless* traiter *to* his country and his God." All in all, "I do love the *place*. it seems as though I could live here ferever if my friends would only come too." But the school regimen was a different matter. Over the summer he did not sleep on a mattress for two months; he had been laboring away at algebra and French, the latter proving especially difficult; he had yet to see "a single familier face" nor had he *"spoken* to a single lady." He cared little for the tight-fitting uniforms ("if I do not walk *military,* that is if I bend over quickly or run, they are very apt to crack with a report as loud as a pistol") and less for the demerit system of penalizing cadets for infractions to preserve discipline. He denied that he was homesick (although the tone of the letter suggested something different), reported that he had laid eyes on various "big bugs," including Scott, President Martin Van Buren, and Washington Irving, and remarked that when he returned home in uniform, he hoped his friends "wont take me for a Babboon."[25]

"On the whole I like the place very much, so much that I would not go away on any account," Grant told his cousin. "The fact is if a man graduates here he is safe fer life, let him go where he will." He intended to "study hard and stay here if it be possible. If I cannot — very well — the world is wide." However, September's optimism faded with fall; by year's end Grant was bored. He rarely reviewed his lessons, preferring to explore the academy library to read the fiction of James Fenimore Cooper, Sir Walter Scott, and Washington Irving. He found mathematics easy and French excruciatingly hard, so that he needed but little time to study the former and despaired of making any sense of the latter, to the point that it seemed a waste of time to study it. Through the newspapers he avidly followed a debate in Congress over a bill that would abolish the academy, seeing in its passage an honorable way to return home. Jesse kept a close eye on his progress, and soon learned that his son had survived the January 1840 exams.[26]

With the new year Grant reassessed his desire to leave West Point. At last he was making friends. Roommate Rufus Ingalls of Maine was a fun-loving, mischievous cadet: it was he who was responsible for Grant's sole visit to the off-limits tavern known as Benny Havens, a favorite cadet haunt. Then there was William B. Franklin of Pennsylvania, New Jersey's Samuel G. French, fellow mathematics whiz Joseph J. Reynolds of Indiana, New Yorker Frederick Steele, and the Missourian Dent. Ingalls remembered that despite his roommate's dislike for extended study, "he was so quick in his perceptions that he usually made very fair recitations even with so little preparation." Grant found memorizing material difficult (especially the conjugation of French verbs), and in scientific subjects he never built on his natural knack for them with patient study. Mathematics, however, was a different story: as he later explained, "The subject was so easy to me as to come almost by intuition." At the end of the year, with the class back down to its original size of sixty, Grant ranked sixteenth in mathematics and forty-ninth in French; his fifty-nine demerits contributed to his class rank of twenty-seventh.[27]

Sophomore year was better, in part because the academy decided to introduce a course in horsemanship. Grant volunteered to break in the more troublesome mounts, succeeding, as Ingalls observed, "not by punishing the animal he had taken in hand, but by patience and tact, and his skill in making the creature know what he wanted to have it do." Roommate George Deshon of Connecticut was adept at sneaking food into quarters, although once a planned feasting on a turkey captured by fellow cadet Nathaniel Lyon was nearly cut short when an officer of the day burst in unannounced. Grant and Deshon snapped to attention, shoulder-to-shoulder, in front of the fireplace, shifting back and forth to conceal their prize from the inspecting officer (who probably ignored the prevalent aroma, satisfied that he had made his point). Grant tried to learn how to dance, but the experiment proved ill-fated, for how could he move in time to the music when he had a tin ear? He made new friends in the upper classes, including James Longstreet and Georgian Lafayette McLaws. Longstreet thought Grant modest, taciturn, and honorable to a fault: he and Ingalls agreed that Grant's fellow cadets often turned to him to settle a dispute. He also recalled that Grant was "the most daring horseman in the Academy," and no one disagreed. In private the cadets smoked — Grant gave it up when he became sick — and at times drank, although Grant swore off liquor when a classmate proved vulnerable to it.

Grant's studies were more diversified his second year. Once more he excelled in mathematics, and he showed promise in philosophy. Most surprising was his skill in drawing: one sketch demonstrated his feel for horses, while others reflected insight into human interaction. French remained a disaster, as did ethics — a catch-all term for grammar, writing, rhetoric, and geography. At least he would not have to take any more languages after he completed his second year of French. But it was not his success in class but his ability to make friends and ride horses that led Grant to reconsider his initial distaste for the school. By year's end he thought it might not be a bad idea to stay on at West Point on the instructional staff, and become a college professor — and then return to Georgetown in retirement.[28]

At the end of a cadet's second year he was rewarded with a ten-week furlough. "This I enjoyed beyond any other period of my life," Grant recalled. He returned to Ohio (the Grants had moved to Bethel, a dozen miles from Georgetown), where his family greeted him with so little emotion that it startled the boy who had driven him home. Jesse had expanded the family tanning business, forming a partnership with E. A. Collins, who opened a general store in far-off Galena, Illinois, along the Mississippi River in the northwest corner of the state. Jesse looked to employ his younger sons, Simpson and Orvil, in the business, for they did not share Ulysses's hatred of the tannery. He also had reason to be proud of his eldest son, who now stood twenty-fourth in his class. Even the endless hours of drill had left their mark. "Ulysses, you've grown much straighter!" Hannah Grant exclaimed on seeing her soldier son — to which he dryly replied, "Yes, that was the first thing they taught me."[29]

All summer Grant visited his friends, riding a young horse his father had set aside for him. There were stories that he was interested in a young woman — although it was unclear whether the target of his supposed affections was Kate Lowe, a relative of Bethel resident John Lowe, or Mary King, the recipient of one of his drawings. A comrade later recalled that Grant had someone on his mind during his days at West Point, and talked about getting married; but he never mentioned the name of his intended bride.[30]

The furlough came to an end all too quickly. Grant returned to the academy to find himself elevated to the rank of cadet sergeant, only to be overwhelmed (or uninterested) by the promotion, for he proved unequal to the responsibilities that came with the position. This year he had no classes in mathematics; he produced more sketches and watercolors; and he achieved average grades in chemistry. He became more unruly, and at

one point was confined to quarters for two weeks for speaking disrespect-
fully to a superior officer: at year's end he did not retain his rank, revert-
ing to private. Senior year was better, if for no other reason than it was the
last year Sam Grant would be a cadet. Yet it was the incoming class of 1846
that seemed to draw much of the attention. Cadets were impressed with
newcomer George B. McClellan, who at fifteen had already attended the
University of Pennsylvania for two years; Grant found Thomas J. Jackson, a
rough-hewn but determined and straightforward Virginian, also worthy of
interest.[31]

Grant's roommate his senior year was Fred Dent. It was rumored that
the two cadets had come close to blows in an argument over slavery until
Grant broke out laughing. From these unlikely beginnings grew a close
friendship. Other stories also circulated about Grant. Just before an engineering class one day, jovial Frank Gardner exhibited a large silver-cased
timepiece to his friends. Grant received it just as the cadets entered the
classroom and quickly jammed it inside his coat. Moments later he was at
the board, working out a problem. As he commenced explaining his solution to the class, a great clanging, "a sound not unlike a Chinese gong,"
as a cadet described it, echoed throughout the room. Only two people
knew what it was: Gardner, who was stifling a guffaw, and Grant, who felt
his chest pound as the timepiece's alarm banged away. Without missing
a beat, he coolly continued his recitation over the racket, waited until
the watch wound down, and only then took his seat — by which time it
seemed that the bemused instructor was the only person in the room not
aware of what had happened.[32]

Grant had little enthusiasm for his classes in ethics (which now covered
constitutional and international law, moral philosophy, and logic), geol-
ogy, military science, and tactics. More engaging were his extracurricular
activities. The cadet literary society elected him its president; he also belonged to a secret group, "Twelve in One," whose mission remains obscure, although its members wore rings that they pledged to give to their
future wives. And there were always the horses. One cadet recalled, "It was
as good as any circus to see Grant ride." After he broke a particularly re-
bellious dark bay, his classmates "would stand around admiring his wonderful command of the beast and his graceful evolutions." It comes as
somewhat of a surprise to note that in March he was confined to his room
for maltreating a mount.[33]

In June 1843 Grant brought the whole audience to its feet during the
final exercises at the academy riding hall. After a cadet exhibition of various riding skills, the riding master, a grizzled sergeant, raising the jumping bar above his head, announced, "Cadet Grant!" People looked to the

end of the hall, where a smallish, slight cadet was mounted on York, a huge sorrel. His fellow cadets had warned Sam Grant that York would kill him (to which he had replied, "Well, I can't die but once"). Now York galloped toward the bar. Grant felt the sorrel gathering for the jump; then the two made the leap with such grace that it seemed to one observer "as if man and beast had been welded together" as they cleared the bar. But it was second nature for the cadet, who had just established the academy's high-jump record. It would stand for over twenty-five years, by which time Grant was known for other things.[34]

Later that week Sam Grant graduated from West Point. He stood twenty-first in a graduating class of thirty-nine, a deceptive ranking when one recalled that at its largest the class numbered seventy-seven cadets. Indeed, he had never really exerted himself to do much better, although Rufus Ingalls, for one, thought that had he done so, he would have ranked much higher. Roommate Fred Dent ranked thirty-third, just behind Ingalls; William B. Franklin stood at the head of the class, followed by Grant's friend George Deshon.

Given his class rank, Grant had little choice when it came to selecting a branch in the service. He requested to be assigned to the Dragoons — a logical choice for a horseman — followed by Infantry. He had grown six inches in four years, although illness over the previous several months had brought his weight back down to 117 pounds. He went home to Bethel; for months he feared he might die of consumption, just as had two of his uncles. In midsummer he found out that he would join the Fourth Infantry — apparently the Dragoons had no vacancies. A month later he donned his new uniform. He had been impatiently awaiting this moment. Now he could show off to all the townspeople, especially the girls, and remind people that he had made it. Once more, however, he was the butt of other people's jokes. Riding to Cincinnati in uniform, he came across a little urchin, wearing just pants held up by a single suspender, who taunted him: "Soldier! will you work? No, siree; I'll sell my shirt first!" At least that was away from home. Returning to Bethel, he wondered why people were smirking. It did not take long to find out. Across the street from Jesse's house there was a stage tavern that employed a "rather dissipated" stable hand. When Grant came upon him, the man was dressed in sky-blue trousers with a strip of white cotton down the outside seams — a homemade replica of Grant's uniform trousers. From that day forward the new brevet second lieutenant never liked wearing a full-dress uniform. The memory of being laughed at — even by a menial laborer — never quite faded away. It was time to be something other than Jesse Grant's son.[35]

2

The Dashing Lieutenant

◉

AT THE END OF SEPTEMBER 1843, Brevet Second Lieutenant Ulysses S. Grant reported for duty with the Fourth United States Infantry at Jefferson Barracks, Missouri, just outside St. Louis. He did not intend to stay long. After he had served out his four-year commitment, he planned to seek out a professorship of mathematics and settle for the comfortable life of a college instructor, a position that would be challenging but not too demanding.

One of the reasons Jefferson Barracks appealed to the young officer was that it was not far from the plantation of Fred Dent's family. Dent himself was far away with the Sixth Infantry, but he had told his folks so much about his West Point roommate that it seemed as if they already knew him. The Dents called their home White Haven: it was just ten miles south of St. Louis, although visitors had to travel over a rugged road to visit the farm. Nevertheless, they came: the Dent children met such heroes as Governor William Clark (of Lewis and Clark fame) as well as "Colonel" Frederick Dent's old Pittsburgh associates.

Frederick Dent had been a merchant in Pittsburgh. In 1816, two years after marrying Ellen Wrenshall, he moved to St. Louis; about a decade later, just after the birth of his daughter Julia, he purchased a thousand-acre farm south of the city and christened it White Haven. Although it was originally intended to serve as a summer residence, Dent lost interest in business — he once complained that Yankees with their sharp ways had ruined it for him — and began to enjoy the life of a gentleman planter. Somewhere along the line he acquired the title of "Colonel" as well. Ellen Wrenshall Dent found her isolated life on the farm less attractive. The daughter of a merchant who had immigrated to America from England when she was young, she craved the amenities of the city, and felt that perhaps she had given up too much to come west. The self-sufficiency and creativity of western women intimidated her and her responsibilities were heavy. The Dents had four boys before Julia was born; it had been the family's increasing size (three more children, all girls, would arrive over the next decade, although one died in infancy) that had led Dent to look for a larger house.[1]

Julia Dent was her father's favorite daughter. She loved life at White Haven: she remembered childhood as harmonious and idyllic. Her mother read her stories and provided her with an armchair for school so that she would not have to sit on a backless bench; her father doted on his little princess; she idolized her brothers and played with her sisters and the servants. It never struck her that others might not share her delight in plantation life. Eighteen slaves tended the plantation: six men, five women, seven children. "I think our people were very happy," she remarked in later years. "At least they were in mamma's time, though the young ones became somewhat demoralized about the beginning of the Rebellion, when all the comforts of slavery passed away forever" — a revealing turn of phrase. The slaves played on old man Dent's coddling of his eldest daughter, often using her to seek favors from the master. When little Julia walked outside, several slave girls ("if they were very neat") followed her; if she chose to fish, they carried buckets with which to bring home her harvest of minnows.[2]

Julia was not quite eleven when her parents sent her to boarding school in St. Louis. The headstrong young lady soon made it clear that she would only study what she liked, and refused either to recite or practice her numbers. Rather, she read whatever she could. For seven years she resisted the efforts of others to educate her: at last in June 1843, just as Ulysses Grant was graduating from West Point, she left the school for the final time and returned to White Haven to see her brother Fred on leave. That fall she went to St. Louis, where she would stay with the O'Fallons, family friends of some repute in local society. Their daughter Caroline was deemed quite a catch by St. Louis bachelors who eyed the family fortune; Julia found herself overshadowed for once. Still, there were dances and parties enough, each with their share of young officers from the nearby barracks. Julia lacked classic beauty — for one thing, she suffered from strabismus, so that her right eye often looked upward — but she was lively and personable. Because she was barely five feet tall and had small hands, she appeared at first glance to be fragile and petite, but she was adept with horses and loved the outdoors. White Haven was her natural habitat, and she returned there in the spring.[3]

Ulysses S. Grant had no time for parties. He could not dance, and he was working hard on his mathematics in preparation for his hoped-for return to West Point as an instructor. But he had visited White Haven. The plantation was a mere five miles from the barracks, and many officers had made the journey. Six-year-old Emmy Dent thought the young lieutenant was "as pretty as a doll"; she soon developed a crush on him, as did her older sister, Nellie. "His cheeks were round and plump and rosy; his hair was fine and brown, very thick and wavy," Emmy recalled. "His eyes were a clear blue, and always full of light. His features were regular, pleasingly molded and attractive, and his figure so slender, well formed and graceful that it was like that of a young prince to my eye." Before long Grant was coming twice a week, sometimes staying for supper; Ellen Dent took a liking to him, in part because he held his own in discussions about politics with the colonel. These could be lively encounters, especially on the eve of a presidential contest. Ulysses had inherited his father's Whig inclinations, while Frederick Dent was a Jacksonian Democrat. While the old man held forth in dogmatic fashion, Grant calmly offered counterarguments, never raising his voice as he set forth his opinion in a lucid manner. Other members of the family listened as the two debated politics, especially the wisdom of annexing Texas. "That young man will be heard from some day," Ellen Dent declared. "He has a good deal in him. He'll make his mark."[4]

Julia Dent met Ulysses Grant during one of the lieutenant's visits. At first there seemed to be nothing out of the ordinary going on, for two of Grant's friends, James Longstreet and Robert Hazlitt, often came along. But then Emmy Grant began to notice that her sweetheart was coming over more frequently; he was riding off alone with her big sister Julia all too often; he found it easier to stay for supper if not longer. Perhaps he was simply happy to find another good rider: Julia could keep up with him. One slave recalled that Julia needed only slight assistance from Ulysses to alight on her mount "like a bird flitting from one tree to another." Who needed dancing?[5]

Emmy finally realized the truth. One day, as she was walking to school, Julia and the lieutenant rode up behind her and offered Emmy a ride. As the trio approached the schoolhouse, Grant spotted the children looking out the window at them. "They're looking at us, Emmy," he kidded. "They're saying, 'Look at Emmy Dent! Here comes Emmy Dent and her beau!'"

Emmy had heard and seen enough. "You're more like my sister Julia's beau," she exploded, adding a few choice words to indicate the depth of her disgust.[6]

Despite Grant's distaste for music, the couple attended dances often enough that when Julia showed up without him Captain Charles Hoskins struggled to hide his laughter as he inquired, "Where is the small man with the large epaulets?" They also went out with other couples, once getting caught in a thunderstorm. Bob Hazlitt grabbed a tarpaulin and offered himself as a human tent pole to keep the young women dry. Grant lingered so long and so often at White Haven that he sometimes did not make it back to camp in time for dinner at the officers' mess. The penalty for tardiness, imposed by the president of the mess, Captain Robert Buchanan, was a bottle of wine; when Grant flippantly mentioned that in light of his frequent late arrivals many more such fines would bankrupt him, Buchanan brought him up short, snapping: "Grant, young people should be seen and not heard!"[7]

Spring came to an abrupt end in April when orders arrived for the Fourth Infantry to move to western Louisiana. Grant seized a last chance to go on leave to visit his family before the transfer. Before he left St. Louis, however, he had one other piece of business to transact at White Haven. He asked Julia to wear his class ring; Julia, aware that in Ulysses's mind this was tantamount to an engagement, declined, explaining that her mother would not approve. The lieutenant "seemed rather put out at this and soon after took his leave," she later remembered, "lingering near me and asking me if I would think of him in his absence." Julia thought little of this: only when she learned, days after Ulysses had left for Bethel, that the regiment's date of departure had been moved up did she realize that she might never see him again. Bob Hazlitt had informed her that if Grant did not return to St. Louis by mid-May, he would be unable to visit for some time to come. The day Hazlitt indicated came: Julia rode out to Jefferson Barracks. But there was no sign of her lieutenant. The best she could do was to return home and wait. In the meantime, she named a bedpost after her absent friend and dreamed that he would return.[8]

Julia Dent was not the only one longing for a reunion. Grant had left just before news came of the accelerated schedule for the Fourth; a fellow officer quickly mailed him a letter, warning him not to open any dispatches from headquarters that might cut short his leave. Grant received his fellow officer's letter soon after he arrived at Bethel. Its contents brought matters into focus at once. For some time he had kept a journal of his thoughts as well as his lessons, containing information for his eyes only. But he had never come to terms with them. Now he did. "I now discovered that I was exceedingly anxious to get back to Jefferson Barracks, and I understood the reason without explanation from any one." He was in love.[9]

Grant decided to observe the exact terms of his leave, which required him to report to Jefferson Barracks twenty days after he left. On his return, post commander Richard S. Ewell gave Grant his orders to join his regiment in Louisiana. Grant then secured a few additional days of leave from Ewell to attend to some unfinished business. He grabbed a horse and set off for White Haven.

The trip turned out to be more challenging than usual. Gravois Creek ran across Grant's route. Usually it was so shallow that it was not worth notice. Recent rains, however, had turned it into a full-fledged river with a rapid current. Grant pulled up. "One of my superstitions had always been when I started to go any where, or to do anything, not to turn back, or stop until the thing intended was accomplished," he later recalled. In the past he had refused to retrace his steps when lost, managing to forge his way ahead to his destination. So rider and horse plunged into the creek, and, after some struggle, emerged on the other bank — the rider drenched but otherwise not worse for wear. Grant made his way to the house of Julia's brother John, borrowed a dry suit, and with John continued on to his destination. When he arrived, the family laughed, for John's clothes were "flopping like rags" over his slender frame. Grant smiled, then made his way toward his objective, slowly but surely. It proved a trying experience. For days he said nothing about his mission; neither did Julia reveal her sentiments. A trip they made to St. Louis to attend a wedding brought matters to a climax. Ulysses lent his horse to John Dent in exchange for the chance to drive Julia to the wedding in a buggy. As they approached another creek, the pair saw that it, too, was flooded, to the point that the water lapped against the bridge. Julia was concerned; Ulysses "was very quiet." She offered to go back; he promised to take her through. Just as the buggy reached the bridge, Julia declared, "Now, if anything happens, remember I shall cling to you, no matter what you say to the contrary."

"All right," Ulysses calmly replied. He drove the buggy across the torrent without a problem. Then he smiled and turned to a relieved Julia. Now was the time. He began asking questions. Did she mean that she would cling to him? Would she do so for all time? Would she marry him?

Consummate strategist that he was, Ulysses S. Grant was a master at timing. She said yes.[10]

Courting Julia Dent required more than tactical deftness. Her father might be willing to see his son in the army, but his girls were not going to marry army officers — that was no way to get ahead — especially when there were so many fine young men with excellent business prospects in

St. Louis for the asking. If this reminded Ulysses a bit of his own money-driven father, he kept such thoughts to himself. It would take time to wear down the parental objections to the match: for the moment, Ulysses and Julia decided to keep their engagement a secret. She accepted his class ring as a temporary engagement band. Anything more would have to wait: Grant had to rejoin his regiment, now based at a place called Camp Salubrity. He arrived at the beginning of June 1844.

Camp Salubrity was located on the Red River, a few miles from Natchitoches, Louisiana. It was supposedly so named because it was one of the healthier army posts, although conditions there were far from ideal. Grant and his regiment spent just over a year there encamped in linen tents — "our linen Mansions," as Grant put it — posted on a ridge near a pine forest; these lodgings did little to shield the men from the summer heat and the heavy rains that drenched their quarters. The food was bad; the cost of living was high; bugs and ticks infested the camp. There was nothing to do but sit and wait — although one had to sit on the makeshift bed, for there were no chairs. "So much for Camp Salubrity," Grant wryly remarked.[11]

Grant spent some of his time exploring the surrounding area; he also kept up a fairly frequent flow of letters to White Haven. He missed Julia: her failure to match him letter for letter left him depressed. "You don't know Julia with how much anxiety and suspense I await their arrival," he told her. Their engagement remained a secret, although Grant suspected that people were already aware of it. She had his class ring ("the strongest evidence I could have given you . . . of the depth and sincerity of my love for you," he wrote); he treasured a lock of her hair. At one point he asked her to find some name beginning with an "S" to stand duty for his middle initial, for he claimed he didn't know what it stood for. He read and re-read her rare responses, which told of Mrs. Dent's refusal to take the news of the engagement seriously and of gossips who insisted that the young lieutenant was committed to another young woman in St. Louis — rumors that infuriated Grant so much that he would not commit his remarks to paper. He reassured Julia, however, that he thought of her at every sunset: "At that time I am most always on parade and no doubt I sometimes appear very absent minded." At last he managed to request her parents' assent to the correspondence — thus putting in a claim for her hand — although he was embarrassed by the whole procedure ("You must not laugh at it Julia," he remarked, as he sent the letter in an unsealed envelope to her) and worried about their response. Imagining that the Dents would raise "all kinds of objections," he readied a response to whatever they might say. "Youth and length of acquaintance I feared might be brought against us," he told his beloved, "but assure them my dear Julia that the longest acquaintance, or a few years more experience in the world could not create a feeling deeper or more durable." Meanwhile he waited impatiently for her replies.[12]

Grant's letters reveal that he was an awkward but sincere suitor, utterly smitten by Julia. They also suggest that he had never before been in love, certainly not as he was now. In opening up to her he was revealing parts of his inner self long concealed from others — a lesson learned from childhood. Julia gave him the emotional support he lacked as a child from the demanding, gruff, and boasting Jesse and the all-too-reserved Hannah. As such he was vulnerable to the vicissitudes of courtship, with the everpresent dread that he would be humiliated far more profoundly than he had been by the snickers of Georgetown's residents. Ulysses Grant not only loved Julia Dent but also needed her and her love. She had become fundamental to his existence: when the two were separated and Grant was not working or otherwise occupied, her absence became all the more depressing.

Grant was not the only bored soldier at Camp Salubrity. With his fellow officers he traveled to Natchitoches to bet on the horses; he exchanged visits with the officers at nearby Fort Jesup. Some officers sought escape through the bottle: Grant reported that his classmate Edward Jarvis became so intoxicated at the races that he tumbled over benches and chairs. The lieutenant also became an avid card player, although he lost more than one game because he assumed that his fellow players were above cheating. James Longstreet noted that Grant was "the soul of honor . . . his hatred of guile was pronounced, and his detestation of tale bearers was . . . absolute." That Grant had so much time on his hands was something of a surprise to those who knew of his desire to return to West Point as an instructor, but when months passed without receiving orders detailing him to a faculty position, his hopes faded.[13]

Grant's mind always returned to White Haven and his beloved Julia. The Dents failed to answer his request for permission to correspond with Julia as a suitor; Julia herself was not always a faithful writer. Grant worried: yet he kept on writing. Unskilled in the language of wooing, he finally declared that such flattery was pointless: why use it "when we have spoken so much more plainly of our feeling for each other?" He waited to secure a leave so that he could go to St. Louis and present his case in person. Finally, in April 1845, he got his chance.[14]

Grant was correct in surmising that there was trouble at White Haven.

Ellen Dent had her doubts about the proposed match between the young lieutenant and her daughter, but they paled beside the strong objections of the colonel. "You are too young and the boy is too poor," he explained to Julia. "He hasn't anything to give you." Julia, fully aware that behind the plantation facade was a family in deep economic trouble — which helped explain Fred's presence in the army — retorted that she was just as poor and had nothing to give him. This point was lost on her father, who believed that his favorite daughter was a very marketable marriage prospect.

Ironically, however, Dent's very need to settle business back east gave Ulysses Grant a tactical advantage. On a Sunday morning in April, White Haven's piazza was filled with visitors wishing the colonel a safe journey on the morrow, when up rode the lieutenant, mounted this time on a dapple gray. Intent on accomplishing his mission, he hurriedly dismounted, rapidly walked up the stairs (giving Julia only the briefest of greetings), and commenced his campaign for her hand, cornering the colonel in the parlor as the rest of the family listened from the porch. Once more Dent objected that Julia was not fit to be a soldier's wife; Grant countered by saying that he would resign from the army and accept a position as a mathematics professor at a college in Hillsboro, Ohio. Checked here, the colonel then made a most astonishing proposition — why not marry Nellie instead? But the lieutenant would not be deterred by this odd diversion: at last he gained permission from the colonel to court Julia through the mails, although he would not give final consent to the match just yet. Persistent yet patient, Grant agreed; the next morning, he accompanied the colonel to St. Louis, doubtless continuing to plead his case, then returned for a most enjoyable two weeks with Julia, away from her father. She gave him a ring with her name inscribed on the inner surface.[15]

Grant's visit to White Haven came just in time. Trouble was brewing with Mexico over Texas. Whether the United States should acquire the Republic of Texas had been a dominant issue of the 1844 presidential contest: Democrat James K. Polk of Tennessee, who had pledged his support for territorial expansion, beat out Whig Henry Clay (one of Jesse Grant's favorites) as well as third-party candidate James G. Birney, who espoused abolitionist sentiments as the Liberty Party nominee. Jesse took special interest in the contest because Birney's running mate was old Tom Morris of Ohio, the senator whom Jesse had originally solicited for Ulysses's appointment to West Point. Polk's victory rendered the acquisition of Texas a foregone conclusion: the outgoing president, John Tyler, helped push through Congress a joint resolution for annexation just before Polk took office. The Mexicans, refusing to accept Texan claims that its boundary with Mexico lay on the Rio Grande, dispatched a military force to the area to contest that assertion. In response, the Polk administration directed General Zachary Taylor, in command of a makeshift "army of observation," to transfer his men to New Orleans, preparatory to a move into Texas when the republic ratified annexation. Grant returned to Camp Salubrity only to find out that he would be leaving again, this time for a far different destination.

As the soldiers packed, the officers looked forward to the prospect of war. They knew that their best chance for advancement lay in combat, although it was also a grim truth that promotions were often made to fill vacancies left by their comrades' deaths. Grant dismissed such morbid speculation but kept tabs on exactly where he stood in the great chain of advancement. He wondered whether a promotion in the not-too-distant future might result in reassignment nearer St. Louis. He seemed more anxious about Julia's inability to keep up her end of the correspondence; already the stay at White Haven was but a fond memory. But Julia's presence was a constant in his mind. Rumors of rivals for her affection, spread by the same mischievous woman who had once told tales about him, disturbed the lieutenant, as did Colonel Dent's continuing resistance to the match. Not exactly a romantic writer himself, Grant gave up trying to express his sentiments in elaborate prose, reminding Julia how he had fumbled in telling her of his love. But her response was all that he needed. "In going away now I feel as if I had someone els than myself to live and strive to do well for," he remarked — a rather remarkable comment, in light of the pressures of being Jesse's boy. "You can have but little idea of the influance you have over me Julia, even while so far away. If I feel tempted to do any thing that I think is not right I am shure to think, 'Well now if Julia saw me would I do so' and thus it is absent or present I am more or less governed by what I think is your will."[16]

The regiment's stay in New Orleans was relatively uneventful, although Grant had a few memorable experiences. The elderly commanding officer of the Fourth Infantry, Colonel Josiah H. Vose — who had forever earned Grant's gratitude when he had authorized the lieutenant's leave to visit St. Louis — collapsed and died on the parade ground after attempting to put his regiment through its paces in drill. William Whistler, Vose's replacement, was sixty-five years old and proved to have a serious drinking problem: when he went to court to face charges of public drunkenness, Grant escorted him; at the courthouse the pair encountered a squad from the lieutenant's own company ready to liberate their regimental commander from the local authorities. Finally, the young officer acquired a servant, "a black boy" named Valere, who spoke English, French, and Spanish. Grant and his close friend, Robert Hazlitt, paid eight dollars a month for his services.[17]

In September the Fourth Infantry received orders to travel to Corpus Christi, Texas, in the wake of Texas statehood. There it would join the Third Regiment and move south toward the disputed border with Mexico. While the bulk of the Fourth left on the steamer *Dayton,* Grant stayed behind with the remainder of his unit to await the arrival of a second transport before traveling up the Nueces River. Several days later, the *Dayton* exploded while crossing the bay: eight men, including two lieutenants, died. One of the officers was Thaddeus Higgins, who had transmitted letters between Ulysses and Julia; Higgins had married Julia's gossipy friend Fanny Morrison — the same woman who had spread stories designed to drive a wedge between Ulysses and Julia. Grant noted the disaster with sadness, but then observed that with the "vacancies that have lately occured" he was next in line for promotion and possible transfer.[18]

Grant liked Corpus Christi and began to think about asking Julia to join him. The camp was healthy; the climate delighted him; he loved riding over the plains. He believed that the chances of war with Mexico were fading: before long he might well be transferred elsewhere. It was time to try to conclude his personal campaign for Julia's hand. "Dont you think it time for us to begin to settle upon some plan for consumating what we believe is for our mutual happiness?" he asked her. He remained prepared to resign, although he was growing to like army life — especially since his promotion to second lieutenant was now assured (in part due to the *Dayton* tragedy). "I do not think I will ever [be] half so well contented out of the Army as in it," he remarked. Nevertheless, the life of a college professor had its own appeal. Grant was seriously contemplating a teaching offer. He wanted to be back with Julia; he also had little interest in annexation, and told his fellow officers as much. His father seconded the notion of a teaching career: it was time for his boy to get out of the army, especially if the alternative was to go to war against Mexico — a prospect that Jesse Grant's Whiggism probably found unacceptable. But there was another father for Ulysses Grant to consider. When Julia informed him that the colonel remained opposed, Grant began to press the matter even more, going so far as to suggest that perhaps Julia should defy her father.[19]

Grant was reluctant to leave the army because at last he found himself at home in it, surrounded by good friends in an interesting place. The area was plentiful with food, including one of his particular passions, oysters. He explored the countryside, encountering two wolves who made so much noise that Grant thought there must be a pack of twenty, and traveled to San Antonio as part of a month-long excursion. He was a failure as a hunter; he preferred watching birds fly to shooting them. Besides, he possessed other enviable skills. Once, in front of the entire regiment, Grant purchased a fractious stallion for twelve dollars (an extravagant price), then proceeded to break it in, although the stallion put up such a good fight that horse and man disappeared for three hours after putting on an exhibition in front of an assembled audience. The lieutenant was less successful when it came to another form of entertainment. To relieve boredom, some officers had constructed a theater; before long they were casting Shakespeare's *Othello*. Lieutenant Theodoric Porter was to play the title role; James Longstreet was the initial choice to play opposite him as Desdemona, but was too tall for the part. Grant, shorter and slender, was then recruited, but he failed to exhibit "the proper sentiment" for the role, which remained unfilled until the officers secured the services of a New Orleans actress.[20]

Grant continued to worry about Julia, who remained reluctant to confront her father. The young officer continued to urge her, promising to come to St. Louis whenever she set the time, either by securing another leave or by resigning — an extreme step he would take if necessary to gain her as his bride. Finally Julia made it clear that she did not want Ulysses to give up his commission; she would live with him on a post. However, she still hesitated to discuss their future with her parents. Meanwhile, Jesse continued to pressure his son to resign, unaware that Julia had already cast the deciding vote in that matter. In any case, as Grant soon realized, to resign now in the face of possible hostilities was out of the question. He reassured Julia that all was fine at Corpus Christi despite reports of sickness and immoral behavior among the soldiers. Nevertheless, life in Texas seemed to toughen one: Grant grew a beard for the first time. Between the camaraderie he enjoyed with his fellow officers and his willingness to defy Jesse Grant and Frederick Dent to get his way, Ulysses S. Grant was becoming his own man, intent on having Julia Dent as his wife.[21]

In March 1846 Grant's regiment joined the American forces under Taylor near Matamoros at the mouth of the Rio Grande. Now the Americans were squarely on disputed soil: but Grant's initial prediction that war seemed as likely as not soon faded. Nothing came of the few confrontations between Taylor and his Mexican counterparts. The Mexicans were long on talk but short on action: Grant agreed with others "that all they are doing is mere bombast and show, intended to intimidate our troops." Rumors circulated through camp that negotiations would settle the matter. Grant looked forward to returning to St. Louis in several months, "and then my Dear Julia may I hope to claim you as my partner for life." His thoughts remained fixed firmly on marriage. "Evry thing looks beliggerent to a spectator but I believe there will be no fight," he concluded in late April.[22]

He was wrong.

3

A Man of Fire

◉

IN LATER YEARS Ulysses S. Grant would judge the Mexican-American War to be "one of the most unjust ever waged by a stronger against a weaker nation." Such protests are absent from his correspondence at the time, but so is the sort of spread-eagle nationalism that was at the heart of the notion of "manifest destiny." At the time, he probably grumbled that the war had taken him away from his dear Julia. Even so, he cared little for annexation and even less for President James K. Polk's way of looking for trouble by stationing the American army in harm's way between the Nueces and the Rio Grande. As Grant later put it, "We were sent to provoke a fight, but it was essential that Mexico should commence it," so that Polk could proclaim that he was simply acting in self-defense and thus avoid the constitutional requirement of a congressional declaration of war.[1]

The Mexicans did not disappoint the American president. Just as Grant began to believe that perhaps the threat of war had passed, they decided that the time for "mere bombast and show" was over. Mexican forces captured American detachments; several American officers and enlisted men were killed. Taylor responded by marching his main force toward Point Isabel, his major supply source, which was threatened by the Mexicans, while leaving a smaller one to garrison Fort Texas, just across the Rio Grande from Matamoros — prompting the Mexicans to assail the latter force.

Grant realized that war was about to begin, and with it the possibility that he might die on the battlefield. In the distance he could hear the Mexican artillery fire away. He dreaded combat, and admitted to Julia that his life would be in danger. Lest she think that he was a coward, however, he hastened to add: "Don't fear for me My Dear Julia for this is only the active part of our business. It is just what we come here for and the sooner it begins the sooner it will end and probably be the means of my seeing my dear Dear Julia soon."[2]

After securing Point Isabel from attack, Taylor doubled back to relieve the American garrison at Fort Texas. Blocking the way back was a Mexican army that slightly outnumbered his own force of just over two thousand men. The two antagonists met on a wide plain near Palo Alto at midday on May 8. After deploying into line, Taylor decided to refresh his men, for it was a hot, dry day; back went canteens to be filled from a nearby stream. The Mexicans cooperated, waiting for the Americans to advance before committing to battle. Their artillery proved relatively ineffective, cannon-balls bouncing through the tall grass as the Americans opened ranks to let them through. The superior range of the American artillery allowed them to pummel the enemy. The duel continued for several hours, broken only by an attempt to put out a fire between the lines. Looking on from his position on the far right flank, Grant had time to wonder about how Taylor — or anyone else — could handle the burdens of command. Finally, as dusk approached, the Mexicans, having failed to assail the American line, prepared to fall back. Taylor pushed forward his right, and Grant came under fire. At closer range the Mexican artillery proved more effective: one shot ripped through the line just next to Grant, decapitating an enlisted man and striking the jaw of Captain John Page. Bone, blood, and brains spewed forth, knocking down several soldiers as Grant watched. He never forgot the sight. Still, Taylor achieved what he had set out to do; the Mexicans withdrew under cover of night.[3]

The next morning Taylor resumed his march. Aware that the chaparral ahead offered the Mexicans an excellent opportunity to ambush his columns, he sent forward a picked company to discover the enemy's position. Grant's captain went along with this expedition, leaving the young lieutenant in charge of his company. Reconnaissance revealed that the Mexicans had established a prepared position behind a series of ponds at Resaca de la Palma. Taylor decided to attack. Finding himself yet again on the American right, Grant led his company through the thickets until he came rather close to the enemy position without knowing it, drawing fire; the company hugged the soil and concealed its location until the Mexicans turned their attention elsewhere. The lieutenant then tried to redeploy to more favorable ground; at last he found a clear space and ordered his men forward against a group of Mexicans led by a wounded colonel — only to find out that they were capturing men who were already prisoners of war, for elsewhere Taylor's advance had driven the Mexicans away. That evening an advance column marched to the relief of the garrison at Fort Texas and broke the Mexican siege.[4]

Two days later, using a captured drumhead as his desk, Grant wrote Julia about his first experience under fire. He admitted that his near

h death at Palo Alto had unnerved him, as much by what he saw
realization that he could have just as easily been the one who was
ted. "It was a terrible sight to go over the ground the next day
and see the amont of life that had been destroyed," he continued. "The
ground was litterally strewed with the bodies of dead men and horses."
Since there had been fewer than sixty American casualties, such a comment reflects how deeply Grant was impressed by what he saw — and that
he counted among the horrors of war the dead on both sides. Nor was the
battlefield of May 9 an improvement: he described the wagons carrying
bodies to burial grounds. Despite these sickening sights, Grant was surprised to discover that he had not flinched under fire. "There is no great
sport in having bullets flying about one in evry direction but I find they
have less horror when among them than when in anticipation," he told
Julia. He added that "in the thickest of it I thought of Julia."[5]

In the letter there was no bragging about great exploits or descriptions
of personal heroism; if Grant passed over the incident of recapturing prisoners, he did not exaggerate his achievements. But he did choose to
shield some of what he had seen from Julia. Six weeks later he reflected on
the battle to an old Ohio friend, John W. Lowe. Again he recounted the
flight of that ball at Palo Alto, and this time offered a far more graphic image of Page's wound: "The under jaw is gone to the wind pipe and the
tongue hangs down upon the throat. He will never be able to speak or to
eat." Once more he mentioned the dead and the wounded on the field of
battle; once more he reflected on his discovery that he could weather
combat: "You want to know what my feelings were on the field of battle! I
do not know that I felt any peculiar sensation. War seems much less horrible to persons engaged in it than to those who read of the battles." And yet
Grant was willing to accept that it was horrible enough — he was far more
amazed at his own response, although he also knew that to admit any
weakness to someone who resided among the folks back home might well
bring him into disgrace.[6]

For the moment the fighting ceased. Taylor occupied Matamoros and
then decided to wait for reinforcements from the newly raised volunteer
regiments. Their arrival might offer Grant an opportunity for advancement, since among the officers in command of the volunteers was none
other than Thomas Hamer, who promised to appoint the lieutenant to a
position on his staff. In the meantime Grant continued to woo Julia in correspondence, attempting to ascertain what her parents were thinking,
while mentioning that he would probably resign at war's end and move to
Galena, in the northwestern corner of Illinois, at his father's urging (apparently the professorship was not now an option).[7]

Matamoros was an inhospitable place to spend the summer. Disease, wet weather thinned the American ranks; leaky tents provided little shelter; mail delivery was sporadic. Grant found Mexican society reprehensible: "The better class are very proud and tyrinize over the lower and much more numerous class as much as a hard master does over his negroes, and they submit to it quite as humbly." A good number of the poor residents "are either pure or more than half-blooded Indians, and show but little more signs of neatness or comfort in their dwellings than the uncivilized Indian." Some of the poverty he attributed to the influence of the Catholic Church, with what he believed to be its emphasis on myth and superstition and the maintenance of ignorance. But he expressed contempt for the Texans, who, along with some of the volunteers, enjoyed committing acts of violence (even murder) against local residents.[8]

Grant also had time to reflect on his commanding general. Zachary Taylor was not a stickler for regulation uniforms and parades. Nor did his plan of battle look particularly elaborate. What he did have, and in abundance, was a quiet confidence under fire. "No soldier could face either danger or responsibility more calmly than he," Grant later recalled. "These are qualities more rarely found than genius or physical courage." The general did what he could with what the administration had given him instead of demanding more; indeed, he gave those short-term volunteers who wanted to leave the opportunity to do so. In contrast, newspaper reports played up the battlefield exploits of several officers, much to Grant's disgust.[9]

After several months of refitting and receiving reinforcements, Taylor shifted his command westward to Camargo, some 100 miles upriver along the Rio Grande. He went to work to prepare a base of operations. Professional soldiers smiled and laughed when they heard that one of the new volunteer generals, Gideon Pillow from Tennessee, dug a ditch on the wrong side of a breastwork. That Pillow owed his job to his Democratic leanings and his friendship with Polk did not endear him to West Pointers. But Grant did not smile for long. In mid-August he received orders to serve as the quartermaster of the Fourth Infantry. It was an important position: quartermasters took care of pay, supplies, and transportation, and if Taylor was to move into the Mexican interior, it was essential that he pay more attention to logistics. At the same time Grant took over the duties of the commissary officer. The appointments reflected great credit on Grant's abilities as an organizer as well as trust in his talents, but they would also take him out of the front line. They also came close to making a businessman of Jesse Grant's soldier son: the lieutenant protested his assignment, but to no avail. When Taylor prepared to venture forth from

Camargo at the end of August, Grant issued orders not to infantrymen but to mule drivers.[10]

Taylor's objective was Monterrey, some 125 miles away to the southwest, where a Mexican army awaited him. The volunteers seemed eager for combat, but Grant did not share their enthusiasm. Although he had no doubts about the prospects for an American victory, he added, "Wherever there are battles a great many must suffer, and for the sake of the little glory gained I do not care to see it." He wanted an end to the war so that he could see Julia again: "If we have to fight I would like to do it all at once and then make friends." In the meantime Grant managed his balky mule train as best he could, seldom with the cooperation of the mules. Even the level-headed, calm lieutenant admitted that it was a trying experience. "I am not aware of ever having used a profane expletive in my life," he later remarked; "but I would have the charity to excuse those who may have done so, if they were in charge of a train of Mexican pack mules at the time."[11]

For all the talk about Palo Alto and Resaca de la Palma, Monterrey would prove to be the first serious battle of the Mexican-American War. The fortified city was held by over seven thousand soldiers. To the north was a citadel known to the Americans as the Black Fort. After approaching the outskirts of the city on September 10, Taylor spent ten days probing and scouting to determine the most effective way to deploy his force of 6,000 men. He settled on a double envelopment, with one of his divisions, under the direction of General William Worth, sweeping northward to come in from the west toward town while the main army advanced from the east; he set his plan in motion on the afternoon of September 20.

The plan did not come off as Taylor had envisioned. As Worth attacked the western edge of the city on the morning of September 21, Taylor ordered his men into action. First off was Grant's brigade, under the command of his old colonel, John Garland. From the rear Grant watched. Impatient and anxious to see action, at last he slowly rode forward to the front. Suddenly he heard officers barking orders for a charge. This was no place for the quartermaster, but Grant, "lacking the moral courage to return to camp," as he later put it, decided to join in. The charge was a mistake — and a costly one. Garland's men were caught in a crossfire, hit on the right flank by the guns of the Black Fort; before long the column, much cut up, moved away back toward the American position. Even worse, Taylor, in an attempt to help Garland, sent the Fourth Infantry forward, but three lead companies strayed into a direct assault on the easternmost Mexican fort and were cut down, losing a third of their force in minutes. In the middle of the action Grant had lent his horse to regimental adjutant Charles Hoskins, he of the query to Julia Dent about the small man with the large epaulets. Not long afterward word came that Hoskins was dead — and that Grant should serve as adjutant. The Mexican fort fell later in the day, but by nightfall Taylor had made little progress. Garland's brigade was assigned to hold the day's gains. Grant looked for Hoskins's body; coming upon it, he straightened out the dead man's arms and legs before turning to give a wounded man a drink. Elsewhere wagons moved bodies to the rear, including the remains of some of Grant's dearest friends.[12]

Taylor did not renew the attack the next day: he planned to move forward on the 23rd. In anticipation of further combat, the Mexican commander consolidated his forces inside Monterrey's inner defenses. On September 23 the American forces advanced block by block in a bloody urban brawl. As adjutant, Grant stayed at the front. Before long news came that the infantrymen of the Fourth were running low on ammunition; it would be difficult to get word back for more, in light of the heavy firing, but it was imperative to try. Grant volunteered; to minimize his personal risk, he took advantage of his skills as a horseman. Mounting a gray horse named Nellie, Grant hooked his legs around the animal's side, shielding himself from enemy fire as he grabbed hold of the mare's neck. Away they went, dodging from intersection to intersection without a scratch from the bullets whizzing by. The lieutenant made it, but his mission proved abortive, for Taylor ordered his men to pull back from the center of town. This decision had tragic consequences, for Grant had come across a house filled with wounded American soldiers and promised to get help. The withdrawal left them in enemy hands.

As night fell, the tired lieutenant took an opportunity to write Julia once more. He said nothing about his daring under fire, resting content with the admission that he "passed through some severe fireing." She still remained on his mind; so did his dead and wounded friends, as he listed their names for her. "I am geting very tired of this war, and particularly impatient of being separated from one I love so much." That night a white flag appeared, hoisted by Monterrey's defenders. The next day commissioners from both sides arranged for the surrender of the city on September 25. The Mexicans left the city under arms and marched southward; both sides pledged not to advance across a line drawn some fifty or so miles south of the city.[13]

Taylor's army settled down to the duties of an army of occupation, secure in the belief that it had completed its mission of driving the Mexicans away from Texas. When possible, the Americans treated the Mexicans with a gentle hand, aware that such behavior would alleviate the burdens of occupation for both soldier and civilian. As quartermaster, Grant paid local farmers a good price for their food; he patiently built up the regimental fund by setting up a bakery and selling bread to other commands. When rancheros attempted to interfere with his responsibilities, Grant did not hesitate to pursue them, sometimes becoming engaged in firefights; once he captured six rancheros after first rallying a squad of runaway soldiers. So long as the local citizens were willing to behave, so too was Grant: but resistance brought retaliation. Beneath the pleasant disposition resided an iron will.[14]

These adventures provided but minor respites from boredom and a trace of depression. Grant missed Julia; he also could not shake the memories of those friends who had lost their lives at Monterrey. Foremost among them was Lieutenant Robert Hazlitt, one of Grant's West Point classmates. Bob Hazlitt had been among those officers who had paid court to the Dent girls; he had known much of Grant's dreams and desires, including his intention to marry Julia. Two weeks before the battle of Monterrey, Grant had assured Julia, "Mr. Hazlitt is very well."[15] Now he was dead, a victim of Garland's bungled assault.

Ulysses Grant was never adept at expressing his emotions (he came closest in his letters to Julia), but he deeply mourned Hazlitt's death. He hoped for an early end to the conflict, "for fighting is no longer a pleasure" — not that he had ever said that it was. Hazlitt's passing brought home to him the cost of war. "How very very lonesome it is here with us now," he told Julia in mid-October. "I have just been walking through camp and how many faces that were dear to the most of us are missing now." He reminisced about those wonderful days at White Haven, when he had his dear Julia by his side — and Bob Hazlitt was still alive — in an effort to drive away "what you call the Blues." A month later, the feeling of loss had not subsided, for Grant told Hazlitt's brother that Bob and he had been "intimate friends and rather confidential ones and no one but his relations can feel more harshly his loss than myself."[16]

During these months, Grant drew even closer to Julia and to his old army friends — and further away from his family. He was annoyed to learn that his father had gotten a newspaper to publish one of his letters; henceforth, he pledged, "I intend to be very careful not to give them any news worth publishing." Newly arriving officers, including Cadmus Wilcox and Dabney Maury, found Grant's quarters a welcome place. Wilcox noted that Grant was "quiet, plain and unobtrusive . . . of good common sense

. . . and much esteemed among his immediate associates for kindly disposition and many excellent qualities." Maury seconded this opinion: "Grant
was a thoroughly kind and manly young fellow, with no bad habits, and
was respected and liked by his fellow officers, especially by those of his
own regiment."[17]

But year's end brought another tragedy. Thomas Hamer may have been
a political appointee, but his commitment to taking soldiering seriously
and his concern for his men won him respect from both professionals and
volunteers. When he had arrived at Taylor's camp, he had sought out his
West Point nominee to learn what he could about war and command. As
the two men surveyed an open field, Grant discussed hypothetical battles,
placing Hamer and himself in the position of opposing generals; just
as Hamer was ready to give up, Grant showed him a way out of his situation. The solution led to Grant's defeat, whereupon the lieutenant acted
out a surrender ceremony, even to the point of offering his sword to the
amused soldier-politician. Hamer was impressed by this "most remarkable
and valuable young soldier. . . . His capacity for future military usefulness
is undoubted." But Hamer fell ill with dysentery soon after he arrived in
Mexico; in late November, after he had seemed to be recovering, he sank
rapidly and died on December 2. Grant was among those who buried him
the next day. It fell to the lieutenant to break the news to Hamer's wife,
and he did so, concluding: "Personally, his death is a loss to me which no
words can express."[18]

By the end of 1846, Ulysses S. Grant had seen enough of war. It was time
to go home. He could not figure out why Taylor's army remained at
Monterrey, "playing war a thousand miles from home." The Americans
had gotten what they came for; if they were supposed to do more, then it
was time to get going instead of waiting for the authorities at Washington
to make up their minds what to do next. Little did he know that in fact
James K. Polk had come to a decision. The Democratic president had
found himself in a difficult position, for his two best generals, Winfield
Scott and Taylor, were both Whigs. At first, Polk had set Scott aside in favor
of Taylor; however, in light of Taylor's victories, the man known by his soldiers as "Old Rough and Ready" (in contrast to Scott's sobriquet, "Old
Fuss and Feathers") was now a hero, despite some grumbling about the
high cost of Monterrey and the truce that followed. Grant himself was
among Taylor's admirers, for the general was a quiet, confident leader,
combining an easygoing personality and relaxed attire with a determination to win. But Taylor's victories had not brought the Mexicans to their
knees; and so Polk reluctantly turned to Scott, who had worked long and

hard at mapping out a plan to take first Vera Cruz and then Mexico City. To support Scott's plan, Taylor dispatched his regulars to the Texas coast, where water transportation awaited them.

Thus the war would keep Ulysses and Julia apart a little longer. Grant reluctantly accepted his fate; he grumbled when a thief stole the chest containing the regimental fund.[19] It was time to leave Monterrey.

The Fourth Infantry reached Palo Alto on January 23, 1847; two weeks later it transferred to Camp Page — most probably named after the grievously wounded Captain Page of Palo Alto fame — along the Gulf of Mexico. From there the regiment boarded transports for the trip to Vera Cruz. It was a busy time for the quartermaster, who had to supervise the loading of equipment and check on the availability of supplies. Although Grant was confident that Scott would triumph, he was growing less sure exactly what it would take to end the war. "I fear though that there is so much pride in the Mexican character that they will not give up even if we should take evry town in the Republic," he told Julia.[20] Such a prospect seemed intolerable, for it would keep him apart from her.

By early March, the flotilla was off Vera Cruz; after several days of scouting, Scott chose a landing area, and on March 9 the regulars moved ashore. Much to their surprise, the Mexicans failed to contest the landing, choosing instead to hole up in the fortified city. Scott responded by ringing Vera Cruz with cannon in preparation for a bombardment: there was no need to assault the city with infantry in what would have been a bloody operation. Nevertheless, Grant once more narrowly escaped death. Unwilling to stay in the rear with his mules and supplies, he ventured forward with a lieutenant of engineers, Pierre G. T. Beauregard, to scout the enemy fortifications, while several other engineers, including young George McClellan and a Virginian, Robert E. Lee, watched. Beauregard and Grant made their way to an adobe house; seconds later, a Mexican shell crashed through the house's roof and exploded inside. Somehow the two Americans survived, emerging from the ruins coughing and sneezing.[21]

Scott's determination that Vera Cruz would not be another bloody Monterrey paid off. After several days of bombardment, the garrison's commander decided to abandon the city. On March 27, he and Scott reached an agreement. Instead of shipping the captured Mexicans back to the United States — or allowing them to draw on already precious supplies in a local prison camp — Scott paroled them; he also allowed forty officers to go free, convinced that their accounts of the siege would demoralize other Mexicans. On the 29th, the day of the formal capitulation, the Mexicans marched out. Officers retained their side arms and horses. The victorious Americans refrained from taunts and jeers. Why humiliate the defeated when allowing them to save face might pay dividends later? The occupiers were under strict orders to respect citizens and property — it was better to pacify the residents than to anger them. So vanished an opportunity for more heroics in battle. Grant sourly observed that his most important contribution during the siege was "to see to having the Pork and Beans rolled about"; longing to see Julia, disappointed with recent politically inspired appointments made by Polk, he once more thought of resigning.[22]

Vera Cruz was a great and relatively bloodless victory for Scott — only 67 casualties — but it was a prelude to larger challenges. Next was a march into the interior toward Mexico City, some 250 miles away, along the same route taken by Hernando Cortés centuries before. Grant gathered his wagons and animals for the long march to come. On April 13, Scott's column moved west. Soldiers fell by the wayside, thirsty and tired; Grant had to provide for these stragglers, either by wedging their bodies in the wagons or by moving them into the shade. Other soldiers discarded some of their heavy equipment, although sooner or later they would need the missing gear and call on the quartermaster for replacements. Grant coped with these challenges well enough to gain the title of permanent quartermaster (he had been acting quartermaster), a mixed blessing for someone who wanted to see action and who chafed at suggestions from, among others, Julia's father, that quartermasters never saw combat.[23]

It did not take long for Scott's column to run into its Mexican counterpart under the command of Santa Anna. The Mexican commander chose to contest the American advance at a pass through the mountains named Cerro Gordo. After several days of scouting and skirmishing, the battle opened on April 18. From the rear Grant watched the assaulting columns with awe intermixed with concern: "While it was a most inspiring sight," he remarked after the battle, "it was a painful one to me," for he thought the cost of the assault would be high. He was wrong. Santa Anna had positioned his men on the steep slopes in such a way that they could not bring effective rifle and artillery fire to bear on the Americans as they scrambled upward. Scott's victory was complete: at a cost of little more than 400 men, he had inflicted over 1,200 casualties and captured another 3,000 men — as well as Santa Anna's personal baggage, including the general's wooden leg.[24]

With victory came more challenges. Aware that the yellow fever season would soon hit Vera Cruz, Scott decided to withdraw the garrison there, leaving his supply link to the sea unprotected. Grant had no problem with that reasoning: he had told Julia that he was far more afraid of disease than of the Mexican army even though Scott's army would have to live off the land, placing even more responsibility on the shoulders of the quartermasters. Grant also had to wrestle with guerrilla bands who took swipes at wagon trains and stragglers left behind. Meanwhile a growing number of Americans were traveling eastward as some 90 percent of Scott's volunteers chose to return home rather than enlist for the duration of the campaign. What the general lost in numbers, however, he gained in discipline and reliability — and he would have fewer mouths to feed.

As May turned to June, Scott probed westward, his force augmented by new volunteers and other reinforcements. Enchanted by the region, Grant claimed that if he could bring Julia along he might well want to live there. But he was growing weary of war itself. "You say you would like to hear more about the war," he wrote John Lowe. "If you had seen as much of it as I have you would be tired of the subject. . . . Tell [the people of Bethel] I am hartily tired of the wars."[25]

The full campaign got under way in August. Once more Grant was to be found among the mules and wagons, those symbols (and stubborn realities) of a quartermaster's existence. His efforts to gain reassignment to a combat unit failed. And yet it should have been apparent to him that in light of Scott's plan of campaign, a good quartermaster was at least as important as a dashing infantry company commander to the American prospects for success. Still, battle represented the test of manhood, the stuff of romance (although Grant no longer believed in the romance of combat, with its dismembered bodies and bloodshed) and the opportunity for promotion as a reward for gallantry. He felt compelled to share the danger of battle with his friends; he found it difficult to accept that he had escaped the fate that befell Bob Hazlitt and Charles Hoskins. Death, it seemed, was a matter of chance: having narrowly avoided it in the fields of Palo Alto, the streets of Monterrey, and outside Vera Cruz, Grant had to wonder whether he led a charmed life.[26]

Perhaps he did. After all, he had already won another difficult battle. At last it appeared that Julia would indeed be his — although when remained a matter of some concern. Colonel Dent had dropped his objections to the marriage, in part because he was engaged in costly litigation that threatened to consume his savings and property — thus both eroding his leverage over Julia and making her a less attractive acquisition for those men who wanted more than a woman when they sought a wife. Aware of this diversity of male motives, Julia offered to release Ulysses from the engagement, but he would hear nothing of it. Nevertheless, from that day forward the lieutenant knew that his prospective father-in-law was helpless to prevent the marriage.[27]

Resigning from the army was no longer necessary for Grant to get married. Julia would have to accept that her future husband wanted to remain in uniform. Half in jest, he remarked: "My dearest dont you think a soldiers life a hard one!" When peace came — whenever that might be — Grant would find himself stationed in some army post: "I will be satisfied with any place wher I can have you with me. Would you be willing to go with me to some out-of-the-way post Dearest? But I know you would for you have said so often." In such ways he told Julia and others that despite an occasional threat of resignation, he wanted to stay a soldier.[28]

But this soldier was tired of war in general and of the part he continued to play in this particular conflict. Quartermaster responsibilities might be important, but Grant could not escape the feeling that he was thus shielded from danger. He left his mules and wagons for the front whenever possible: as James Longstreet recalled in later years, "You could not keep Grant out of battle."[29] Even as he recoiled from the horrors of the battlefield, he felt compelled to prove himself in combat. The coming campaign against Mexico City promised him plenty of opportunities to come under fire once more.

In the early days of the campaign, Grant accompanied the Second Dragoons on a reconnaissance toward the city. After several days of similar expeditions Scott decided to approach the city by the south — although Grant, who had been studying the approaches to the city, thought it would be better (and far less costly) to swing around to the north and advance forward on solid ground against weakly defended areas. He looked on as Scott opened his attack by taking Contreras, on the outskirts of the southern defenses. Then it was on toward the Churubusco River, where Grant's regiment came under fire from a convent that stood at the key point of the Mexican line. Looking for a fight, General William Worth, Grant's division commander, ordered his men forward, although the Mexican position was vulnerable to a flanking march along roads to the west. Fortunately for the Americans, the Mexicans ran low on ammunition — evidence of the importance of supply — just as Worth directed one final charge. The Mexicans retreated, the Americans proclaimed victory but failed to pursue the retreating enemy, in part because they had sustained heavy losses of nearly a thousand men.[30]

Grant shook his head at what he saw at Churubusco, remarking, "Too much blood has been shed." And yet the campaign was far from over;

the fortifications of Mexico City beckoned. He pondered whether there might be some way to approach Mexico City "without meeting such formidable obstructions, and at such great losses." Scott might have shared these sentiments, for during the next two weeks he declared a truce, believing that the Mexicans would now surrender rather than risk another defeat. He was wrong: Santa Anna used the respite to reinforce his position at the fortress of Chapultepec and a nearby group of buildings known as El Molino del Rey, where, if reports were to be believed, the Mexicans were casting new cannon. Again, frontal assaults against fortified positions promised heavy casualties. The operation got underway in the early hours of September 8 when Worth's division slammed into El Molino del Rey. The heavy fire from the Mexicans cut down many Americans until Worth pounded the position with artillery; then Fred Dent led four companies in a charge, followed by Grant and the Fourth Infantry. Lieutenant Dent captured a cannon, then disappeared from view. Moments later Grant came across him, wounded in the thigh, lying against a stone wall. He lifted his future brother-in-law onto the wall so that the litter-bearers could find him (although Fred rolled back off a few minutes later, suffering even greater injury in the form of broken bones). A Mexican rushed the two men, then turned his attention elsewhere; at the last moment Grant shouted a word of warning to a fellow officer who thus narrowly escaped being bayoneted in the back. Commandeering a wagon, Grant propped it up against the wall of a building; a squad followed him onto the roof, where they took charge of some captured Mexicans who had surrendered to a single American private.[31]

By midmorning the battle was over. Worth was under orders not to pursue the fleeing Mexicans into Chapultepec, so he did not exploit the hole he had punched in the Mexican line. Nor were any cannons being cast at Molino del Rey. It thus became even more difficult to justify the expenditure of life on a position that could have been reduced primarily by artillery fire. Scott shrugged off the result and turned to the main fortress. This time, however, he decided to use his cannon to effect, opening fire on September 12 before ordering the infantry forward the next day. Grant would be with Worth's division once more, but this time it was to swing north and east to San Cosme, three miles away, at the northwest corner of Mexico City. Much to everyone's surprise, Chapultepec proved an easier position to take than had Molino del Rey; San Cosme provided a more serious challenge. An aqueduct ran down the middle of the paved road to the gate, offering some cover to the attackers, until fire from the gate itself pinned down Garland's lead brigade. But Grant was not to be deterred. He made his way alone to the front, undetected by the Mexicans, until he discovered a way to assail their rear. Quickly he scampered back to share his findings with Garland's lead elements. If Grant could direct a small body of volunteers to the vulnerable area, they could swarm down on the defenders just as Garland's main force charged forward. It seemed like a daring plan, but Grant was sure he could pull off his part. Very well, then, responded the column's commander, Lieutenant John Gore: the attack would be made.

Grant and a squad of volunteers crossed the highway under fire and began to make their way forward when they encountered a group of American artillerymen in a ditch, who were armed with muskets. They agreed to follow Grant after he explained his plan to their commander, Captain Horace Brooks, who had been on the West Point faculty when Grant arrived there in 1839. The converging columns crashed into the Mexicans, who fled back along the road, with the Americans in hot pursuit until the Mexicans wheeled two cannon into place just under the main gate. To move forward now would be suicide, for what the cannons did not hit, the riflemen scattered on top of roofs and along the walls would surely strike. At that moment, orders arrived to fall back and prepare for a second chance. Grant's genius had gone for naught.[32]

Within a short time a second assault, this time supported by artillery, commenced. Once more Grant helped take the outlying position; once more the Mexicans fell back to the main gate. Again the lieutenant set off on his own, confident that the Mexicans would yet again leave their flanks unprotected. He was right: there was a way to go around the enemy left by taking over a church located some three hundred yards from the main gate. With another column of men and a disassembled mountain howitzer, Grant made his way over to the church, where he overcame the priest's initial reluctance to open the door by warning him that one way or another the American soldiers were coming in. The men then hauled the howitzer up to the church belfry, reassembled it, and then began dropping shells on the surprised Mexicans.

Such initiative did not go unnoticed. Worth sent an aide, Lieutenant John C. Pemberton, to bring Grant back to him. Grant went reluctantly, muttering that perhaps he had gone too far this time and was now under arrest. Worth warmly congratulated him and wanted to send another gun up the tower — although, as Grant noted, it could only hold a single cannon. But another officer, Raphael Semmes, followed Grant's lead and established another rooftop howitzer. Infantry units began chopping away at houses surrounding the gate; another artilleryman, Henry J. Hunt, eeled a cannon up the road to blast down the main gate itself. Worth's men surged forward, overcame resistance at the barricades, and took the gate. Before them lay Mexico City. Worth prepared to renew the assault in the morning; during the night Grant helped infantry tunnel through buildings to bypass the remaining barricades.

It was not necessary. The next day, local authorities sought to surrender the city; when sporadic firing continued (Colonel Garland was hit by one shot), the Fourth Infantry led the way into the heart of the capital itself, where Worth encountered another division already in control of the Grand Plaza and National Palace. For several days to come, there would be some nasty skirmishing, but Mexico City had fallen.

Two of Grant's friends, Sidney Smith and Calvin Benjamin — who had seen Grant care for the wounded and the dead at Monterrey — were dead; another, James Longstreet, was wounded. Smith's death opened up a first lieutenancy for Grant; he gained brevets (a form of honorary promotion) as first lieutenant and captain for his bravery in this final week of the campaign. Longstreet observed that Grant was "always cool, swift, and hurried in battle . . . as unconcerned as if it were a hailstorm instead of a storm of bullets." Garland himself remarked, "There goes a man of fire."[33]

With the campaign seemingly at an end Grant sat down to write Julia all about it. Modestly he remained silent about his own exploits, adding that he cared little for newspaper accounts of heroism all too often manufactured by the self-styled heroes themselves. The triumph was bittersweet, he thought: "The loss of officers and men killed and wounded is frightful." For years to come he would wonder if there had not been a better way to gain the Mexican capital. Fred was recovering nicely from his wound, but he was one of the few familiar faces left from St. Louis days. Only three other officers of the Fourth were still with Grant. It would be some time yet until he could return home, for the Mexicans still had not given up, forcing the Americans to become an army of occupation. "So you see it is not so easy to get out of wars as it is to get in them," he reflected to Julia.[34]

The brevet captain enjoyed life in Mexico City. He befriended an English family, the Greens, who lived across the street from Grant's makeshift barracks in a convent. In later years young Sarah Green recalled that he was "so good-natured, and full of his jokes"; another visitor to the Greens noted that Grant enjoyed listening to conversation and sought company. Meanwhile he went about his duties, buying food and providing for the men of his regiment, a little careless of his appearance (he now had long hair and a full red beard), and with a fondness for chewing tobacco and an occasional smoke. One observer noted that he "never drank to excess nor indulged in the other profligacy so common in that country of loose morals" (although exactly whose morals were loose the observer did not say); however, after encountering Grant in May, John Lowe (who had left his legal practice in Bethel to become a captain of Ohio volunteers) confided in a letter home his fears that the lieutenant "drinks too much but don't you say a word on that subject."[35]

Grant remained astonished at the beauty of Mexico and critical of the failure of its people to use their country's ample resources. "With a soil and climate scarsely equaled in the world she has more poor and starving subjects who are willing and able to work than any country in the world," he told Julia. "The rich keep down the poor with a hardness of heart that is incredible." With his fellow officers he explored caves and mountains; at other times he rode about by himself. Once he actually spurred his mount into Chapultepec itself: when a colonel asked how Grant proposed to remove the horse, the young officer rode him back down the stairs. Looking for another way to escape boredom, he attended a bullfight. What he saw shocked him: "I could not see how human beings could enjoy the sufferings of beasts, and often of men, as they seemed to do on these occasions."[36]

Grant was well liked by his fellow officers and had many friends. He seemed to gravitate to Southern-born associates, such as Longstreet, Cadmus Wilcox, and Henry Heth. Among his fellow mountain climbers were Simon Buckner, Henry Silbey, and Richard Anderson — Southerners all. He harbored no prejudices toward Southerners, nor indeed toward slaveholders, for he was very much in love with a slaveholder's daughter. If Grant had little use for President Polk — especially Polk's willingness to slight the regular army to advance his own political agenda — he admired both Winfield Scott and Zachary Taylor. Of the two, Taylor was his favorite because of his simplicity, lack of pretension, and directness of expression. Scott, in contrast, believed in wearing "all the uniform prescribed or allowed by law" during reviews, and in elaborately worded reports was "not adverse to speaking of himself, often in the third person, and he could bestow praise upon the person he was talking about without the least embarrassment." Still, both men fought well; as Grant put it, "Both men were pleasant to serve under — Taylor was pleasant to serve with."[37]

As Grant contemplated his commanders, he also reflected on what he had learned about war. Leadership and morale were essential to military success. The Mexican soldiers were brave enough, but they were poorly led and did not always seem to have their heart in the cause for which they were fighting. Courteous treatment by occupation forces served to weaken still more the enemy's will to resist. Neither fortified positions nor advantageous terrain were quite the obstacles they seemed to be: after all, Cerro Gordo had been a smashing American victory, despite the strength of the Mexican position. Unless an army was well-trained and well-led, fortifications could become a handicap, for inexperienced soldiers tended to flee whenever a lodgment was made in a defensive position, leading to a major breakthrough. That was a logical lesson drawn from the battles around Mexico City. Offensive tactics won the day again and again, although Grant still preferred maneuver to frontal assault. If he warmed more to Taylor than to Scott, he nevertheless respected Scott's ability to work with the navy at Vera Cruz and his calculated daring in marching toward Mexico City without maintaining a continuous line of supply.

At least of equal value was what Grant had learned about events behind the lines. Being a quartermaster might not bring one glory, but it was nevertheless important. Soldiers needed to be clothed, fed, and cared for. Disease killed more men than did bullets. A healthy, well-fed, and well-clothed army was more likely to win battles. The lieutenant had also observed the politics of war and civil-military relations. Partisan concerns had shaped the administration's appointments; both Taylor and Scott had chafed under Polk's directives, but kept their opinions to themselves. That Grant heard often from his Whig father about such matters — and that he agreed with his father — simply reinforced his initial distaste for the Polk administration, whatever Colonel Dent's sympathies might be. Still, orders were orders, and the only way to retain command was to respect one's civil superiors and bite one's tongue.

Finally, Grant learned something about himself under fire. Horrified as he was by bloodshed and death, he was not unnerved by the experience. He kept his cool, performed brave deeds, and displayed initiative as bullets and shells whizzed by. Aware that he might be hit and perhaps even killed, he accepted those chances as a functioning of fate. He remained the same quiet, unassuming fellow he had always been, although he knew that he had passed the test of combat.

Although Grant enjoyed his travels around Mexico City, all was not fun for the quartermaster. The soldiers who had discarded clothing in the spring now demanded warm attire for the winter, and Grant had to make arrangements with local people to sew new uniforms. To cover this drain on the regimental fund, Grant resumed his bakery business. And it seemed as if the army would never leave Mexico, even as news came that peace was finally at hand. "If you were here I should never wish to leave Mexico," he told Julia, "but as it is I am nearly crazy to get away." It was time to go home.[38]

Finally in May 1848 word came that the American army would leave Mexico within a month. The news had not come a moment too soon for Grant. He could not wait to claim Julia as his own; "I am so impatient that I have the *Blues* all the time," he told her. Just as frustrating was the frequency of theft; on June 16 someone stole his quartermaster funds, totaling a thousand dollars, that he had placed in the locked trunk of another officer. Grant would be held responsible for the money although a board of inquiry found him innocent of negligence. Only an act of Congress could relieve him of his obligation.[39] For the moment, however, this worry faded in light of the reality of going home at last.

4

Forsaken

◉

LIEUTENANT GRANT finally secured his long-awaited leave as soon as the Fourth Infantry returned to the United States in July 1848. He headed first to St. Louis, where, after securing a room at the Planter's House, a local hotel, he made his way to the Dents' city residence. The Dents rushed out to greet him. Emmy, with the critical eye of a twelve-year-old who knew about such things, noticed that the object of her girlhood crush had changed. Bronzed by the Mexican sun, he was "sturdier and more reserved in manner." War stories were the order of the day: only now did Grant tell of his ride across the streets of Monterrey aboard Nelly, and one of the Dent slaves, Mary Robinson, remarked that "he appeared to look upon Nelly's conduct as more courageous than his own." The colonel and his wife were eager to hear how Grant had rescued their son outside Mexico City — an act that did much to reconcile the old man to the marriage of the young officer and his eldest daughter. Grant pushed for getting married as soon as possible; he planned to visit his folks first, then return in time for the ceremony.[1]

Wedding plans in place, Grant traveled up the Ohio to Cincinnati, where he boarded a stagecoach for Bethel. He shared the coach home with a classmate of his sister Virginia; when the pair disembarked outside the Grant home in Bethel, some people mistook the young woman for Julia. "See how easy it is in a country vilage to give a report circulation!" Grant observed, all too aware of the truth of that remark. With them was Gregorio, a young body servant presented to Grant by a Mexican gentleman in gratitude for some unrecorded reason. Apparently the boy was willing to serve as the officer's valet in exchange for payment of his passage to the United States, clothes, and schooling. Gregorio proved adept with the lariat, roping everything in sight; Jesse declared he would make the boy what he could not make Ulysses — a tanner. Townspeople also wanted to hear about the war, and the once-shy Grant willingly shared his stories. But his mind and heart were elsewhere; he told his fiancée how much he looked forward to returning to St. Louis and his wedding, adding, "After my arrival Dear Julia I hope we shall never be so long separated again."[2]

On August 22, 1848, Ulysses S. Grant married Julia Boggs Dent. The ceremony took place in St. Louis at the Dent home on Fourth and Cerre Streets, a two-story brick residence, at eight o'clock in the evening. Present at the ceremony were James Longstreet, who had recovered from his wounds, and Cadmus Wilcox, who recalled later that Emmy's antics made her "a most pestiferous little nuisance." One guest described the groom as "brown . . . dignified and quiet"; his gift to Julia was a daguerreotype of himself. The next morning Grant then took his bride to Bethel to meet his family. It was her first trip away from St. Louis (as well as her first boat trip), and Julia was enchanted by it all — especially the steamboat's "breathing, panting, and obedience to man's will. I was really greatly impressed with the power of man." The journey seemed "like a dream to me and always pleasant." The marriage was off to a good start.[3]

After a stop in Louisville to visit some relatives, Ulysses brought his bride to Bethel at the end of August. The Grants turned out in force for this meeting; even Grandmother Simpson (in actuality John Simpson's second wife, for Hannah's mother had passed away) was there to greet the newlyweds. Julia's concerns about winning acceptance soon faded. She was favorably impressed by Jesse, but reserved her strongest praise for Hannah, "the most self-sacrificing, the sweetest, kindest woman I ever met, except my own dear mother." Over the next several weeks Ulysses and Julia made the rounds of the relatives; the lieutenant obtained an extension of two months to his leave, so that the two could return to St. Louis prior to their departure for Grant's new assignment in Detroit, Michigan.

For Grant had decided to stay in the army. Resignation seemed impossible now that he had a wife to support. For Julia, marriage would be a great transition, with no slaves, no White Haven, no doting father to care for every need. But the teaching position Grant had once sought was no longer available and his Louisville relatives ignored hints that he might be willing to resign if he could find a business opening. The lieutenant, in fact, had never set his heart on resigning. He enjoyed the camaraderie of army life, even if he dreaded the monotony of duty on a peacetime post. At least now he would have Julia by his side.[4]

Or so he thought. The return visit to St. Louis was difficult for the couple. Although Julia had enjoyed her travels, she missed her father, White

Haven, and St. Louis. The prospect of leaving them to go to Detroit was too much. Julia began sobbing at the mere thought of the idea. Grant did not know what to do. For four years he had struggled to make Julia his — and not her father's — and now, just when it seemed that he had won, Julia was wavering. Grant did not want to see Julia unhappy, but he was upset by her behavior. The colonel, always ready to seize an opportunity to confirm that he was the most important man in Julia's life, offered to let her stay with him. "You can get a leave of absence once or twice a year and run on here and spend a week or two with us," he told his son-in-law. "I always knew she could not live in the army."

There was a challenge in this offer to both Ulysses and Julia. Perhaps Julia was too spoiled to be an army wife. Perhaps Ulysses could never provide for Julia as had her father. Perhaps their love for each other was not as strong as they once thought. Ulysses chose not to demand his rights as a husband but to trust Julia's heart. He left it up to her, reminding her that they would be apart once more. Julia immediately realized what was at stake. "No, no, no, Ulys," she sobbed; "I could not, would not, think of that for a moment." And so it was settled: Grant had won the battle — for the moment, anyway.[5]

In the fall of 1848 the Grants traveled to Detroit, where he received new orders assigning him to Sackets Harbor in New York. He was not happy with the appointment: as the Fourth's quartermaster he thought it proper to be stationed with regimental headquarters in Detroit. The trip to the New York post proved expensive and exhausting as well as inconvenient, an inauspicious way to introduce his bride to army life. In winter, covered by snow, Sackets Harbor was isolated and the post showed signs of age and disrepair. Sometimes Grant traveled to Watertown, some ten miles away, where he played chess and checkers; he also befriended a lawyer, Charles W. Ford, and challenged him to race horses. The newlyweds stayed in Sackets Harbor until springtime, their home life made more interesting by Julia's efforts to run a household for the first time: she discovered that it was difficult to get along without a cook and servants and that she did not share her husband's mathematical abilities when it came to keeping house accounts. Just as the couple was starting to settle down and await the advent of warmer weather, which promised to improve their surroundings, Grant received orders to return to Detroit: his superiors agreed with his complaint that he had been the victim of unjust treatment.[6]

Grant liked his new assignment. The duties of a quartermaster were routine but not onerous. When Julia visited St. Louis, he missed her, and on his birthday he wrote her that Detroit was "very dull. . . . I have nothing atal to do here." It was left to his sergeant to defend his superior when a clerk wondered why Grant had been assigned to his position, since he showed no talent for paperwork. Sure, the sergeant admitted, the quartermaster was "not much good" at such matters, "but when you get to the soldier part of it, drill, manual of arms, and so on . . . he can handle the regiment as well, if not better, than any other fellow in it." The lieutenant found other concerns to occupy his time. In a neighborhood near his fellow officers on East Fort Street, he rented a house that had grapes, plums, and peaches growing in abundance in the yard. He went fishing with his friends and instructed a soldier to prepare a garden for Julia to tend on her return. He teased his absent spouse that he "would be quite a gallant" with the ladies, "but as I see no one that I like half as well as my own dear Julia I have given up the notion." In truth he sorely missed her; eventually he joined her in St. Louis and they went back to Detroit together.[7]

Detroit proved a pleasant place for the Grants. There were some awkward moments: Gregorio, encouraged by some local citizens who perhaps thought his status comparable to that of a slave, decided to go out on his own, and Grant let him go without asking to be reimbursed for debts still owed him. But Julia loved the "snug and convenient" frame house, with a large kitchen "for me to make my culinary experiments." Her husband played cards, smoked a pipe, and seemed rather quiet and easygoing — except when racing horses and buggies down the Detroit streets past a local sutler's store where officers gathered for a drink now and then. Sometimes Grant, fresh from a victory on the streets, treated everyone to a nip.

Town society proved wonderful; between parties, rides on steamers, and dances it seemed domestic bliss. One observer noted that while the quartermaster seemed shy at parties, he was "always very devoted and tender to his wife." A fellow officer thought Grant "came out of his shell in her presence. They were two people who hitched well together, they fit like hand to glove"; if anything, the lieutenant was "overly attached to his wife." In the fall Julia announced that she was pregnant; this event, which might have drawn the couple even closer, instead forced another separation. On the advice of Charles Tripler, the regimental doctor, Julia returned to her father's home and on May 30, 1850, gave birth to Frederick Dent Grant — a name that in itself suggested the continuing tension in the Grant marriage.[8]

Fathers (and fathers-in-law) had thus far figured prominently in Ulysses Grant's life; now he was a father himself. Immediately on hearing of his son's birth he secured a leave to journey to St. Louis for "urgent family reasons."[9] His wife and son returned to Detroit with him. Although many nineteenth-century fathers tended to distance themselves from their children, Grant would have none of that, and instead commenced a career of indulgent parenting filled with play and love — a marked contrast to the relationship he had enjoyed with his own father. Little Fred's arrival made the possibility of parting with Julia again all the more painful, redoubling the lieutenant's determination to do what he could to provide for their needs. Perhaps the army was not the best place for the three of them.

Life in Detroit had its ups and downs. Dr. Tripler's wife, Eunice, admired how Julia worked hard at home, directing matters "with a great lump of a baby in her arms." But Grant found his duties monotonous, and he was not always on good terms with the local citizens. In January 1851 Grant and his fellow officers, after slipping and sliding on the sidewalks of Jefferson Avenue, brought charges against homeowners for failing to clear ice and snow from their sidewalks. Among those so charged was the city's mayor, Zachariah Chandler. Chandler snapped that if army officers lost their balance walking, it was due to inebriation, not slippery walks. In the end the plaintiffs carried the day, but it was a token victory, for Chandler just had to pay court costs and a fine of six cents. Even more embarrassing was a masquerade ball that Julia and the wife of Major John H. Gore put on one winter evening. Although local ministers warned their congregations that this was frivolous behavior, unworthy of good Christians, the ball was quite a success. Julia appeared as a tambourine girl, but Ulysses refused to go as anything but himself — an army officer. Nevertheless, the criticism surrounding the event stung.[10]

Grant thus welcomed the news that the army planned to shift the headquarters of the Fourth Infantry. Initial orders called for headquarters to be located at Fort Niagara, but in light of that installation's small size, he anticipated returning to Sackets Harbor. "Wont this be pleasant," he remarked to Julia, who was once more spending spring at White Haven, after a visit to the Grants at Bethel. "My hope is that they will let us remain there long enough to enjoy it." Julia's trips told on him, as did the absence of his year-old son. By now Fred was "todeling along by himself and looking up and laughing as though it was something smart"; his father asked Julia to teach him to say "papa," but added that he should not learn any bad words. Once more Julia's failure to correspond frequently and promptly irritated him, especially when he heard that Fred was ill. "I feel a constant dread lest I shall hear bad news," he told Julia. "I know I shall be afraid to open the first letter I get from you." He wanted her to come east as soon as possible. It seemed almost as difficult for him to keep Julia by his side in peace as in war.[11]

Grant's second tour at Sackets Harbor promised to be a vast improvement on the first. Although the town, which had changed little in the past two years, was "as dull a place as can be immagined," the Grants would now be part of regimental society; before the end of the year a newly built railroad would be able to take them to New York City in fourteen hours. Grant looked forward to any sort of activity; as one of his fellow officers noted, "he was regarded as a restless, energetic man, who must have occupation, and plenty of it, for his own good." He hated the drudgery of completing forms and filling his time with aimless activities. Moreover, Julia still had not returned from White Haven, and it soon became evident to Ulysses that she would not come for some time, because travelers risked contracting serious illnesses when journeying on the rivers in midsummer. He did not hear from her for over a month; when he did he remarked that it seemed as if she was too busy making the rounds of St. Louis society to write. In the meantime he passed the days fishing and sailing on Lake Ontario; in July he traveled first to Montreal and Quebec, then to West Point and New York. Of his visit to the military academy he remarked, "I really felt very glad to get back to the old place where I spent, what then seemed to me, an interminable four years." He wanted to be stationed there, alongside several of his old classmates who were now on the instructional staff. But his thoughts always returned to his wife and son. "I expect he wont know me when he sees me again," he wrote, a reminder of how long it had been since he had last held his boy.[12]

Ulysses Grant disliked being apart from his wife for any length of time. He felt incomplete without Julia; friends did not compensate for her absence. Little Fred's absence compounded his misery. He wanted so badly to be the sort of father who spent time with his boy, walking and riding about — the father he never had. Grant also worried about the influences surrounding his wife in St. Louis. Doubtless Julia's father would try to keep his little princess to himself as long as he could; certainly St. Louis and White Haven seemed more attractive places than an army post in upstate New York. Julia's letters, when they did come, said little in response to his missives. Finally, he chided her: "I have seen nothing from you that shows whether you know that I have ever taken a trip since comeing to Sacket's Harbor. . . . I have asked you so many questions which you never answer." Did Fred have any teeth yet? Was Ellen (who had once set her heart on him) getting married? When was Julia coming back? Not until mid-August did he learn that his wife was at last prepared to return to him.[13]

Grant enjoyed summer at Sackets Harbor, despite Julia's absence, but the onset of fall weather reminded him of the post's shortcomings. Before long he wished he could return to Detroit. Instead, he and Julia spent another winter off Lake Ontario. The two attended church; Grant joined the Sons of Temperance, taking the pledge to cease drinking, and soon became an officer in the organization. Fred was the center of everyone's attention; Julia became expert at bowling. The Grants went off on sleigh rides to dinners and parties; there was ice sailing in winter and the promise of hunting and fishing as spring came. But those pleasures were not to be. Grant had once remarked that the army always waited until someone was comfortable before sending that soldier somewhere else; such was the case in the spring of 1852 when the Fourth Infantry received orders to go to the Pacific coast.[14]

The news could not have come at a worse time for Grant. Julia was pregnant again: it would be impossible for her to accompany him — although in any case the journey would not have been an easy one. Some companies of the Fourth would circle below South America; others, as well as the regimental quartermaster, would brave a crossing of the Panamanian isthmus in midsummer. Orders were orders, however, and Grant saw Julia off for Bethel and St. Louis once more, although this time it looked as if Julia would give birth in Ohio. In mid-June Grant accompanied his regiment down to New York and prepared for the expedition; at month's end he hurried to Washington, D.C., in a futile attempt to seek relief for the thousand dollars stolen from him in Mexico — a debt now four years old. When he arrived at the capital, he found all public business suspended as the city mourned the death of Henry Clay. Unable to meet with members of the House Committee for Military Affairs, he could not resolve the matter, although he was confident that the committee would support forgiving the debt if he could present his case.[15]

Grant had hoped to secure a few weeks' leave to go to Bethel and be present at the birth of his second child. But no sooner had he returned to New York than he discovered that his regiment was about to depart. "We sail directly for the Isthmus," he reported to Julia on July 5. "I never knew how much it was to part from you and Fred. until it come to the time for leaving. . . . Our seperation will not be a long one anyway. At least let's hope so. Good buy dear dear Julia. Kiss Fred. a thousand times. A thousand kisses for you dearest Julia."[16]

On July 5, 1852, Grant, along with eight companies of the Fourth Infantry, left Governor's Island in New York Harbor aboard the steamship *Ohio* and headed to Panama. It did not promise to be a pleasant trip. The commanding officer, Lieutenant Colonel Benjamin Bonneville, cared little for Grant (the origins of his apathy, supposedly rooted in some incident in Mexico, remain obscure) and had sought the appointment of another officer as quartermaster, but Grant's fellow officers stood behind him, and Bonneville dropped the matter. Accommodations were tight aboard the overcrowded vessel, adding to the quartermaster's discomfort. And he missed Julia. Day and night he paced the deck, "silent and solitary," smoking a pipe. Arriving at Aspinwall (now known as Colón), Colombia, on July 16, Grant quickly encountered more difficulty, for arrangements to move the regiment had collapsed, leaving him to help improvise an alternative. The regiment would split into two parties, with Grant in command of the band, civilians, the sick, and the regiment's baggage, including weapons, while Bonneville remained in charge of the main body. Everyone was anxious to get out of Aspinwall, for the city streets were flooded by summer rains, which stopped just long enough to allow "a blazing, tropical summer's sun" to add to the discomfort. "I wondered how any person could live many months in Aspinwall," Grant later remarked, "and wondered still more why any one tried."[17]

Grant's group boarded several dugout boats and made its way into the interior along the Chagres River. The travelers distrusted their boatmen, who got drunk every night and during the day got into knife fights. Arriving at Cruces, Grant discovered that there were no mules to hire from the authorized army contractor for the next stage of the journey. It would not do to tarry, for between wet weather, insufficient shelter, and cholera, Cruces was not a safe place for anybody. The lieutenant did what he could to get his column going, paying exorbitant prices for mules to continue the journey to Panama City. Although the trek took only a few days, it seemed to the participants to go on forever. The trails were rocky and uneven; no one could drink the water from springs along the way, no matter how hot it was, because it was likely that the springs were contaminated. Stricken by cholera, men, women, and children died, left to be buried in shallow graves. When all was said and done, a third of Grant's party did not survive Cruces and the crossing. Other members suffered greatly, especially those women who were unprepared for such physical exertions and discomforts. It was horrible. Grant was thankful that Julia and Fred were somewhere else: "My Dearest," he remarked, "you never could have crossed the Isthmus at this season."[18]

Nor did the regiment's troubles end when it reached Panama City. Grant might be able to obtain blankets, but he found it much more difficult to battle cholera. Witnesses noted how he tried to take care of both the ill and the well as he struggled to contain the epidemic — although old man Bonneville had foolishly loaded everyone onto the vessel that would transport the regiment to San Francisco. An old ship became a temporary hospital: Grant helped nurse the stricken, rarely sleeping for long. Yet, as one observer recalled, "his work was always done, and his supplies always ample and at hand. . . . He was like a ministering angel to us all." More members of the Fourth succumbed, as did women and children: at week's end the total number of dead from the crossing neared one hundred, including twenty children as young or younger than two-year-old Fred Grant. That mortality rate approached one in seven members of the entire expedition. Among the dead was Major Gore: Grant had to send his grief-stricken wife and their child back across the isthmus, accompanied by an officer. Grant heard later that a newspaper in Panama City placed much of the blame on him for the disastrous crossing, although members of the traveling party knew differently. "I will say however that there is a great accountability somewhere for the loss which we have sustained," he told Julia.[19]

Finally the regiment made its way to San Francisco. Grant put thoughts of the nightmarish journey out of mind during an exciting evening in town, where he won enough money at a faro table to buy a good dinner for himself and a fellow officer. During a four-week stay in California, he paid a visit to Julia's brothers John and Lewis, who were operating a mining camp, hotel, tavern, trading post, and river crossing at Knight's Ferry, east of Stockton along the Stanislaus River. He remained duly impressed by what California had to offer, how much it cost to live there, and the colorful and chaotic nature of a boom and bust society. Then it was on to Fort Vancouver, at the mouth of the Columbia River.[20]

The quartermaster hated to be away from his family. He wanted to hear all he could about his children: he had yet to learn whether his second child had been born, and he imagined Fred scampering about, talking to everyone. "Does he ever say anything about his Pa?" he asked, almost afraid to hear the answer; "Don't let him forget me dearest Julia." He was depressed when mail arrived (as it did every other week) without a letter from his wife. "No person can know the attachment that exists between parent and child until they have been seperated for some time," he remarked. "I am crazy sometimes to see Fred. I cannot be seperated from him and his Ma for a long time." All he could do for the moment was to share his memories with others; through the summer and into fall no letter arrived from Julia. It was not until December 3 that Grant learned that on July 22 his wife had given birth to a second child. "If it is a girl name it what you like," he had directed months before, "but if a boy name it after me" — a clear reminder of what had happened with his first child's name. Sure enough, the boy was named Ulysses S. Grant, Jr., although people soon took to calling him "Buck" because he was born in the Buckeye State.[21]

Grant was amazed by the opportunities that California offered. "There is no reason why an active energetic person should not make a fortune evry year," he told Julia. John and Lewis Dent seemed to be doing well in their new enterprise. "For my part," Grant continued, "I feel that I could quit the Army to day and in one year go home to with enough to make us comfortable, on Gravois (White Haven), all our life." However, he dared not give up the security of the army.[22]

With resignation out of the question, Grant turned to other ways to make money to reunite his family. He was struck by the natural beauty of the region, and thought it a good place to live. Dismissing reports of Indian troubles, Grant told Julia, "[they] are the most harmless people you ever saw. It is really my opinin that the whole race would be harmless and peaceable if they were not put upon by the whites." He especially deplored "those blessings of civilization, whisky and Small pox." Oregon, he thought, "opens the richest chances for poor persons who are willing, and able, to work." Like other army officers, he soon sought ways to augment his army pay, hoping to clear enough money to bring his family west. He bought a farm on which he planned to raise potatoes, sell wood to steamboats, and rent out dray horses. But spring rains washed away the farm and the wood had to be moved to avoid being swept away, costing Grant more money. An effort to sell cattle and pigs also fell through, although the sow he gave to the drum major produced a dozen pigs each worth forty dollars — to the drum major. A plan to sell chickens in San Francisco turned to disaster when the chickens died en route. Loans he made to other officers were not repaid. Even Grant's hope that he might upon his promotion to captain go to Washington to settle his accounts (and thus bring his family back with him) was only an illusion.[23]

Repeated failures began to tell on Grant. "I am doing all I can to put up a penny not only to enable you an our dear little boys to get here comfortably," he told Julia, "but to enable you to be comfortable after you do get here." But none of these efforts met with success. Grant grew more depressed. Lonely, he missed his family. When Julia sent him a lock of Buck's hair entwined with her own, he treasured the memento. He paced back and forth on the porch of his quarters, thinking and smoking, for hours; he took long rides through the woods and along a nearby river; at night he told anyone who would listen stories about his wife and children. He showed one enlisted man a tracing of the hand of the son he had never seen, trembling before finally turning away. A sergeant's wife recalled that at one point he looked up from Julia's letters, tears in his eyes, and remarked, "Mrs. Sheffield, I have the dearest little wife in the world, and I want to resign from the army and live with my family." In such circumstances, it was not surprising that he broke his temperance pledge and began drinking again.[24]

Grant suffered in other ways as well. His body ached in the wet winter weather; at times he could eat little more than tea and toast. As spring came, however, and he went to work on his farm, he grew stout, and once more he grew a beard. A summer cold came at a bad time: he was assigned to outfit two survey expeditions, including one headed by George B. McClellan. Whether it was to improve his health or to forget his situation, one night Grant had too much to drink. McClellan saw him in a drunken state and never forgot it.

Grant was glad when the expeditions left the fort. He especially hated the burdens of quartermaster duty on the Pacific coast, where he shouldered far more responsibility at no increase in pay. Riding horses provided a short respite: once he guided his mount over the hurdles offered by a battery of cannon "as easily and gracefully as a circus rider." At other times he told war stories, dissecting military operations with such precision that one listener exclaimed, "How clear-headed Sam Grant is in describing a battle! He seems to have the whole thing in his head." Perhaps that was because his mind was occupied with little else except for worry about his wife and children.[25]

Officers who before had thought nothing of Grant's drinking now noticed his slurred speech after he lifted a glass. "Liquor seemed a virulent poison to him, and yet he had a fierce desire for it," recalled Robert MacFeely, one of his fellow officers. "One glass would show on him, and two or three would make him stupid." Sometimes he went on brief "sprees," and then pulled himself together when other officers, worried about Grant's depression and what might happen, tried to cheer him up. Many officers had fallen victim to alcohol: there seemed nothing terribly out of the ordinary about Grant's behavior except that he could not handle nearly as much liquor as did some of his harder-drinking peers.[26]

With fall came news that Grant had at last advanced to the rank of captain. Promotion entailed with it a small raise and a reassignment — this time as commander of Company F, stationed at Fort Humboldt, some 250 miles north of San Francisco on the California coast. To reach his post, he had to travel first from Fort Vancouver to San Francisco, which he found still prospering in boom times — a speculator's paradise. The sight encouraged him to make yet another investment, this time by joining several officers in leasing the Union Hotel and turning it into a billiard room. Once more poor management, dishonest managers, and Grant's poor business skills led to disaster and made it even less likely that he could send for his family.

So when Grant arrived at Fort Humboldt on January 5, 1854, he came alone. The post was situated on a bluff overlooking a fine bay and the villages of Bucksport and Eureka. It had been established to protect the area's settlers from angry local tribes. Whatever Humboldt's future as a port, it offered opportunities for lumber and mining, as well as plentiful game. There was little else to do there, especially in winter, leaving Grant plenty of time to think about home and drive himself deeper into depression. As if that wasn't enough, the post commander was Robert C. Buchanan — the same officer who, at Jefferson Barracks, had once told Grant, "Young men should be seen and not heard." "Old Buck" was the sort of fellow who never gave up a grudge. As another officer noted, "He seemed to take delight in wounding the feelings of those under him, and succeeded pretty generally in making himself unpopular amongst the citizens as well as in the army."[27]

Grant passed the days going into town, playing cards, and stopping for a drink at a local saloon and James T. Ryan's general store. When he had nothing better to do, he could be found sitting on Ryan's porch, looking off into space, or walking the streets clad in a canvas jacket and pants, wearing a straw hat that almost hid the pipe in his mouth. People liked the quiet man who missed his family and who enjoyed riding his horses fast. Although he appreciated the view of the Pacific Ocean from his quarters — as far as the eye could see — he had no one with whom to share it. Before long, he fell sick, compounding his misery. Life at Fort Humboldt alternated between monotony and boredom, broken only by outbreaks of loneliness and depression. It was a bad place for Grant to be.[28]

All winter there was no word from Julia. Grant did not know what to make of her apparent silence, although he realized that her letters might have gone astray. "You do not know how forsaken I feel here!" he declared in anguish. Still, he feared the worst. "The state of suspense that I am in is scarsely bearable," he told her as February began. "I think I have been from my family quite long enough and sometimes I feel as though I could almost [desert and] go home 'nolens volens.'" He wondered about his sons, especially the one he had never seen. Did Ulysses talk yet? How was

Fred doing? There was plenty of time to engage in such melancholy. "I do nothing here but set in my room and read and occasionally take a short ride on one of the public horses," he moped. There were others on the post in the same situation, he noted, remarking that "misery loves company." Moreover, he was still in pain from the complications of a tooth extraction.[29]

Although Grant coped with his misery on occasion by turning to alcohol, what exactly happened at this time is encrusted in myth and rumor. He admitted that he drank when he was depressed, and at Fort Humboldt he was often depressed. His reaction to alcohol was erratic and apparent; as one early biographer noted, "with his peculiar organization a little did the fatal work of a great deal." Moreover, he often drank to offset the impact of ill health — a constant problem during his time at Fort Humboldt, in marked contrast to most of his stay at Fort Vancouver. Migraine headaches sometimes came close to incapacitating him; the cold, damp weather and the pain caused by his pulled tooth added to his misery. A local physician, Dr. Jonathan Clark, tended to the ailing officer. Many people of the time believed a drink could serve "medicinal purposes," but alcohol may have simply compounded Grant's ailments. However, it wasn't his drinking that got him into trouble — it was that Old Buck had it in for the new captain.[30]

By March Grant's letters to Julia were pathetic in their loneliness, and still no letters arrived from her. He missed his family desperately; bringing them west seemed impossible. Perhaps it was time to make a change. "I sometimes get so anxious to see you, and our little boys, that I am almost tempted to resign and trust to Providence, and my own exertions, for a living where I can have you and them with me," he told his wife. "It would only require the certainty of a moderate competency to make me take the step. Whenever I get to thinking upon the subject however *poverty, poverty,* begins to stare me in the face and then I think what would I do if you and our little ones should want for the necessaries of life." Despite promotion, his pay had actually dropped in the past year and life at Humboldt was expensive.

In his frustration, he came close to snapping at Julia. Even if she came to California, she could not have a servant, something Grant remarked she could not do without. But perhaps she was not eager to come out in any case, for "you never complain of being lonesome so I infer you are quite contented." He even dreamed that she had ignored his arrival at a party to dance with someone else while their boys watched.[31]

The arrival of spring did not alleviate his depression. "How very anxious

I am to get home once again," he told Julia. "I do not feel as if it were possible to endure this separation much longer. But how do I know that you are thinking as much of me as I of you? I do not get letters to tell me so." Since he had arrived at Humboldt, he had received "just one solitary letter . . . and that was written about October of last year." Life in the fort was featureless; although his health had improved, with little to do he did not stray far from his room — and there was a rumor that the army might give up this post for an inferior one inland.[32]

Grant was bored, hurting, and almost heartbroken in his homesickness. It was only a matter of time before something gave way. And it did.

On April 11, 1854, Ulysses S. Grant sent two letters to Washington. One indicated that he had received and accepted his commission as captain; the other contained his resignation, effective July 31. He also requested and secured a leave of absence from Fort Humboldt to allow him to get his financial accounts in order.[33]

Exactly why Grant took these steps remains in dispute. Certainly he had spoken of resignation as the only way to reunite his family. But others insisted that there was more to the story — that Grant had too often overindulged in alcohol, and he had been under the influence while on duty on payday, enabling Buchanan to finally force him out of the army under the threat of a court-martial. What exactly happened between Grant and Buchanan remains unclear (there are no contemporary documents extant to support the court-martial story). It would not have taken much, however, for the post commander to take action against Grant, especially if a growing problem with alcohol had compounded his already shaky health. Had Buchanan liked Grant, he might have been willing to overlook any minor transgressions — after all, many officers drank to excess (as would Grant's replacement at Fort Humboldt, Henry Judah). However, Old Buck didn't like him, and any slip gave the post commander the opportunity to make Grant's life even more of a hell than it already was. After all, as Rufus Ingalls later declared, Buchanan "was prejudiced against Grant & was an infernal old martinette & a d — a old S. of a B."[34]

Gossip being what it is, officers likely embellished the story in repeating it, until the image of a drunkard drummed out of the service (possibly under the threat of a court-martial) was firmly fixed in the minds of many people, most of whom had never met Grant. He never shook the stories; they would haunt him for the rest of his life. Whatever action Buchanan took or threatened to take, if any, he didn't have to try very hard to persuade Grant to do what he had long contemplated in any case.[35]

Resignation forced him to come to terms with the need to make a living. What was he going to do? After sending in his resignation, he fell ill once more: post returns listed him as "sick" for the month, and he continued ill until early May, with Dr. Clark supervising his recovery. Then he sent Julia a short letter reporting that he was soon to be on his way home; he did not mention his resignation or any reason for his departure from Fort Humboldt — just that he had a leave of absence.[36]

And so Grant squared his accounts and made ready to return to his family. He had no regrets: as he told a friend, "Whoever hears of me in ten years, will hear of a well-to-do old Missouri farmer."[37]

5

Hardscrabble

❂

GETTING HOME was as great a challenge for Grant as his journey west. He traveled to San Francisco, expecting to collect on some outstanding loans; when the borrowers defaulted, he sought assistance from Major Robert Allen, an old army buddy, who obtained free passage for Grant on a mail steamer. The exact state of Grant's finances at this time is a matter of dispute: several people later claimed that they loaned Grant money, whereas Grant, according to a St. Louis acquaintance, insisted that he had two hundred dollars in gold coin after expenses — although he gave two of the twenty-dollar coins to one old soldier and divided another one between two ailing miners. On reaching New York, he approached another old friend, Simon Buckner, to help pay for a trip to Sackets Harbor to confront Elijah Camp, a post storekeeper who owed him eight hundred dollars — only to discover when he arrived that Camp, having received Grant's letter notifying him of the purpose of his visit, had taken to his yacht to avoid repayment. Back in New York, Grant turned to Buckner for enough money to tide him over until his father could wire funds east. Buckner, afraid that Grant might spend money on alcohol, decided instead to vouch for his comrade until the funds arrived, along with brother Simpson. Then it was back to Bethel, where Grant planned to board a steamer at Cincinnati and head to St. Louis.[1]

Jesse Grant was not pleased with his Ulysses. He had attempted to forestall the captain's resignation by explaining to War Department officials that all his son needed was a leave of absence, but Secretary of War Jefferson Davis refused to reconsider. It was not as if he was financially unable to help his eldest son. Jesse's business ventures had expanded beyond tanning to embrace a store in Galena, Illinois, and he could provide for his other children. Rather, Jesse knew that his eldest son lacked business sense. He trusted people with large sums of money and bad luck haunted his attempts at enterprise. A disgusted father could not hide his disappointment as he greeted Ulysses with the sour comment: "West Point spoiled one of my boys for business." The ex-captain replied, "I guess that's about so."[2]

Grant finally made it to White Haven in August. As he came up the road in a buggy, he saw two little boys playing on the porch of White Haven. The younger one had blond curls; the older one, about four, had a round face. The two boys did not recognize the bearded man who ran toward them and swept them up in his arms, while a female slave ran into the house and shouted his arrival. Whatever problems he had encountered in getting home then seemed a small price for returning to Julia, Fred, and little Ulysses, whom he finally saw for the first time. Julia chided him for his naive business transactions, but she was glad to have him back — and glad that he was thinking about farming a parcel of land her father had given her at the time of her wedding. For the moment, at least, she could be near both her father and her husband. Before Grant could settle down to work, however, news came that Jesse wanted to see his son. So the family boarded a river steamer and made its way up to Covington, Kentucky, just across the Ohio from Cincinnati, where Jesse had relocated, suggesting that perhaps he was not such an abolitionist that he could not bear to reside in a slave state. As the Grants debarked, Julia noticed that the sunny sky had suddenly turned overcast. Having a superstitious nature, she wondered whether it was an omen.[3]

It was. As Julia later recalled, "There are no pleasant memories of that visit." After a few weeks of muttering, Jesse finally came up with an idea. Ulysses, he remarked, could work at the general store in Galena and become part of the family business with Simpson and Orvil, thus bringing together the three Grant boys again. Ulysses, who had entertained this notion before, was at first amenable to the proposition. Then, however, Jesse dropped his bombshell: Julia and the children would stay with the Grants in Covington. This would have been a remarkably insensitive, even stupid, proposition in the best of times, for Jesse was well aware of his son's desire to be with his family; but to offer it in light of present tensions and discomforts showed how dense and cruel the old man could be. Ulysses, as Julia recalled, "positively and indignantly refused his father's offer." It was back to St. Louis.[4]

Colonel Dent made a compelling counteroffer. He had given Julia sixty acres of land on his estate at the time of her marriage. Perhaps he could help his son-in-law make a go of it as a farmer. Grant had used a plow in his boyhood; what had happened to his potato crop in Oregon was the sort of bad luck that could happen to anyone. Since Julia's brother Lewis planned to remain in California, the Grants could live in his villa, Wish-ton-wish. The house was surrounded by oaks and situated just a mile and a half south of White Haven. Thus the colonel would have Julia nearby. The captain needed to do something about earning a living, for before long Julia was pregnant again. He prepared to make good on his promise to become a well-to-do Missouri farmer.[5]

In 1855, Grant's first full year as a farmer, he worked side by side with the Dent slaves putting in a crop of wheat and corn. Eventually he would also grow other vegetables, including (yet again) potatoes. Slowly he shook his depression; as Emmy noted, "He was a man whose whole nature demanded work." On July 4, Julia gave birth to a baby girl. Ulysses wanted to name the child Julia, but eventually the child was christened Ellen, after Julia's mother.[6]

The first year of farming provided mixed results. Although Grant secured higher yields than did his father-in-law, prices went down, and so he struggled. Donning his faded army overcoat, he supplemented the family income by hauling wood to town. Hauling, however, took him away from farming, limiting what he could make at it. And there were constant reminders that he needed money. Occasionally he would receive notices about funds due the government from his service as commissary officer and quartermaster: at one point these sums reached nearly ten thousand dollars. Nor did Grant like being under Colonel Dent's supervision. The colonel's predictions about Julia's husband seemed to have come true. Surely she could have done better. Grant now had daily reminders of his father-in-law's desire to keep his daughter close by, and of Julia's devotion to her father and White Haven. Perhaps one reason he liked hauling wood was to get away from the plantation and go to the city, where he might run into some old army buddies who were based at Jefferson Barracks or passing through town. A local physician, Dr. William Taussig, who disliked Colonel Dent but took care of the Grant children when they were ill, noted that Grant "chafed under this condition of things."[7]

As 1855 drew to a close Grant decided that he wanted to build his own house. It would be a way to exert his independence from Julia's family although it was little more than a symbolic protest, for the house would, after all, reside on land given Julia by her father. Although he wanted to build a frame house, the colonel "most aggravatingly" pressed for a log cabin, claiming it would be warmer. He cleared the land and hewed logs, setting them aside to be seasoned. Julia was not pleased by his effort. She liked living at Wish-ton-wish, even if it was a little distance from the farm. Finally, in the summer of 1856, it was time for the house-raising.

Julia later remarked that a frame house could have been built in a far shorter time. Grant, with a sense of humor about his situation, named the cabin Hardscrabble.[8]

Julia did not care for the log house. "It was so crude and so homely I did not like it at all, but I did not say so," she recalled years later. She tried her best to make the house a home but remained unhappy and despaired of ever attaining as Julia Grant the heights she had enjoyed as Julia Dent. Her husband tried to be more hopeful. Although tension remained between father and son, he assured Jesse at the end of the 1856 season: "Evry day I like farming better and I do not doubt but that money is to be made at it. So far I have been laboring under great disadvantages but now that I am on my place, and shall not have to build next summer I think I should be able to do better." However, short of cash, he hinted that a loan of five hundred dollars "would be of great advantage to me." Jesse seems to have ignored this last remark. In early December Ulysses had stopped by the Planter's House in St. Louis and there saw "J. R. Grant, Ky." entered in the register. Somehow, however, Jesse could not find it in himself to visit his son; weeks later Ulysses was reduced to asking, "Was it you?"[9]

Early in 1857 Grant tried again to gain his father's assistance. Jesse had once offered his son a thousand dollars; now Ulysses tried to revive this offer, in part "because there is no one els to whom, with the same propriety, apply." He worded his request to suggest how much he disliked asking for support: "It is always usual for parents to give their children assistince in begining life (and I am only begining, though thirty five years of age, nearly) and what I ask is not much. I do not ask you to give me anything. But what I do ask is that you lend, or borrow for, me Five hundred dollars, for two years, with interest at 10 pr. cent payable anually, or semmi anually if you choose, and with this if I do not go on prosperously I shall ask no more from you." He could not continue to farm without this infusion of cash; he was now prepared to sell the farm (having secured Colonel Dent's permission to do so — a reminder to Jesse that at least someone was willing to help him out) "and invest elsewhere."[10]

Grant eventually secured a bank loan (his father's role in this transaction, if any, remains unclear) and attempted once more to make ends meet by farming — something that was becoming ever more difficult. Julia's mother died at the beginning of the year, and the colonel persuaded his daughter to move the family to White Haven — not exactly a difficult task, given Julia's unhappiness at Hardscrabble. There would be fewer trips hauling wood to St. Louis, for now Grant had to supervise all the family farms. At first glance, this would not seem to be too difficult, for Colonel Dent owned a good number of slaves (the precise number at this

time is not known, although the 1850 census reports thirty D
split between White Haven and the family residence in St. Louis). How
ever, because most of the Dent slaves at White Haven were house servants,
Grant had to hire field hands.

Grant proved a poor manager of slave labor. A neighbor smiled as he recalled that the ex-captain "was helpless when it came to making slaves
work." Louisa Boggs, the wife of one of Julia's cousins, agreed: "He was no
hand to manage negroes. He couldn't force them to do anything. He
wouldn't whip them." He did not fare better with hired help. One of his
workers, an old free black named Uncle Jason, remarked: "He used ter
pay us several cents more a cord for cuttin' wood than anyone else paid,
and some of the white men cussed about it, but Cap'n he jis' kep' right on
a-paying for er work just er same." Uncle Jason decided that Grant "was
the kindest man he ever worked for." A white neighbor complained that
Grant paid his black workers too much, "a-spoiling them, sir, spoiling
them." Grant respected his fellow workers as he labored beside them. He
had no problem paying them and treating them like men; he could not
treat them as slaves, and the fact that they were slaves made him feel
ashamed. Never in his letters to his father could he admit that he worked
with slaves, preferring the term servants. Emma recalled that he opposed
the institution of slavery, yet added, "I do not think that Grant was such a
rank abolitionist that Julia's slaves had to be forced upon him" — a sign of
exactly how confused he was about the peculiar institution and the contradictions it presented to him.[11]

These philosophical issues faded in importance, however, compared
with his continuing struggles to make a living. His hopes for success in
farming crashed with the Panic of 1857 and the ensuing depression. Income from hauling wood could not redress the balance. Elijah Camp continued to avoid repaying his loan. Jesse was willing to help, but on his
terms. "Ulysses," he reportedly declared, "when you are ready to come
North I will give you a start, but so long as you make your home among a
tribe of slaveholders I will do nothing." That offered little solace. Depressed, sometimes he dawdled in St. Louis with his old army chums, although he told them that he no longer drank; despite his poverty, he insisted on honoring old debts whenever possible. Once he forced Pete
Longstreet to accept repayment of a five-dollar loan that had been outstanding for some fifteen years. He joked that he was "solving the problem
of poverty," but that was far from the truth. By Christmas he was so
strapped for cash that he pawned a gold hunting watch for twenty-two dollars. More responsibilities loomed ahead: Julia was pregnant once more.[12]

As 1858 began, Ulysses S. Grant was in trouble. He scrambled to repay old debts; he worried so much about how to survive financially that when Julia gave birth to their third boy on February 6, he named the child Jesse Root Grant — as if by doing so he could gain favor with his own father, for who would abandon a namesake grandchild? But the bad luck continued. Dogged by sickness, daunted by the continuing economic downturn, he continued to fall behind. His ventures in farming seemed doomed to fail. As fall came, Jesse Grant offered his son another business proposition. He picked the right moment to do so: Ulysses was suffering from malaria, with chills following fevers in regular succession, and little Fred had fallen so seriously ill that his father worried for his life. In such a situation, it would have been hard to concentrate on farming even if Ulysses had been physically up to the task. Furthermore, the two older boys now needed to start school, creating yet another demand on the former captain's income. With this in mind, Jesse invited his eldest son to come to Covington to help out in the family business.[13]

This time Ulysses gave in. He reminded his father that he wanted "the prospect of one day doing business for myself," adding that he did not want a salary: "There is a pleasure in knowing that one's income depends somewhat upon his own exertions and business capacity, that cannot be felt when so much and no more is coming in, regardless of the success of the business engaged in or the manner in which it is done." Of his diligence there was no question; of his business capacity there was sufficient doubt. Jesse would attempt to teach him the family business without entrusting him with it. At this time Jesse encountered George Bailey of Georgetown. The doctor, who remembered all too well Jesse's crowing about Ulysses in years past, now listened as Jesse talked about his plans to bring Ulysses home and "to make him over again, as he had no business qualifications whatever — had failed in everything — all his other boys were good business men, etc., etc." Bailey, who had long believed that Jesse Grant "is the greatest brag I have ever met with," tired of such bombast: "The truth is that U. S. is the only one of the family that has any soul in him."[14]

Ulysses, who saw no other option, prepared for the journey; Julia, however, was "bitterly opposed" to the arrangement, as she later admitted. Apparently, the Grants thought that Julia's extravagance was responsible for Ulysses's impoverishment, although Grant himself assured his father that he spent very little on the family. Julia, on the other hand, believed the Grants knew all too dearly the worth of a dollar because they were loath to let one go. Still, Grant sold his horses, farming tools, and crops in anticipation of the move. Somehow his sisters put a stop to this project. Exactly why they did so is unknown, but it was one of the few times they made Julia happy.[15]

Faced with necessity, Grant soon hit on a different idea. One of Julia's cousins, Harry Boggs, had a real estate business in St. Louis. He agreed to accept Ulysses as a partner. The Grants would have to move to St. Louis, but Julia would not be far from her father. In later years Julia questioned the wisdom of this agreement. She had long accepted that her husband was no good when it came to business, precisely because he was too trusting and generous. How could such a man collect rents and debts? Mrs. Boggs noted that her husband's partner was in despair. "He was gentle and dignified and uncomplaining, but it was pitiful to see him sitting silently in the cold, bare little room which he rented of us," she remembered. "He was sober and willing to work and he *did* work, but in those disturbed times he found it difficult to find employment."[16]

Grant initially left his family at White Haven; after renting a house, he finally brought them to St. Louis. Eventually he traded Hardscrabble for another house in town, gaining a note for $3,000 (payable in five years); Hardscrabble's new owner remained obligated to pay off a $1,500 mortgage that remained on the city house, and secured that debt with a deed of trust on Hardscrabble. But working with Boggs frustrated him. He grew irritated when his partner gossiped about his clients' business affairs; he disliked collecting rents, and if someone was unable to pay — and this happened often in the current dismal economic climate — he could not bring himself to evict them. Once he amused neighbors when he unknowingly rented a residence to a prostitute, who used the house as her place of business. Moreover, Grant's health continued to suffer, and at times he was not steady on his feet.[17]

Yet Grant could impress others. Boggs shared a building with three lawyers, who enjoyed talking with the Mexican-American War veteran about politics and affairs in Europe, especially the fighting in Italy. They liked his stories and were intrigued when he pointed to a newspaper map to offer his own opinions on the progress of the Italian conflict. At such moments Grant was not depressed; it was obvious, however, that he was not cut out for the real estate business, especially when the firm was not pulling in enough income for two people. During this financial crisis, he was delighted to receive a small windfall from the soldier who had borrowed forty dollars from Grant during the captain's return east in 1854: the principal — plus ten dollars interest. He was astonished. "It seems odd to get fifty dollars for forty dollars loaned," he told the lawyer who delivered the money. He added, with a touch of self-deprecation, "I believe this is the first interest I ever received in my life, and I didn't know I was a capitalist before."[18]

Grant found it hard enough to provide for his four children and his wife, but Julia's four slaves added to his expenses: a household of ten placed great demands upon him. They were house servants, and by now, they were all teenagers. Grant thought of renting one out if the family came to Covington, although he also thought he could teach him the "farrier's business" under Jesse's eye, for "he is a very smart, active boy, capable of making anything."[19]

Grant was well aware of the political debate over slavery and its expansion westward. During his first year of farming in 1855 he doubtless heard about the strife in "Bleeding Kansas" between pro- and antislavery forces, because many Missourians were involved in that struggle. The following year an abolitionist named John Brown — son of the Owen Brown who had once taken in Jesse Grant — retaliated for the proslavery attack on Lawrence, Kansas, by executing five slavery supporters. The year 1856 also marked the first time Grant voted in a presidential contest. There was no more Whig party: in its place two new tickets had emerged with strong appeal in St. Louis — the antislavery Republican party and the anti-Catholic, anti-immigrant Know Nothing party. The Republicans nominated John C. Frémont, "the Pathfinder," and the son-in-law of Missouri senator Thomas Hart Benton, a friend of the Dent family. The Know Nothings put forward former president Millard Fillmore; the Democrats countered with James Buchanan of Pennsylvania, long a prominent party leader. Grant cared little for Buchanan and less for Fillmore, but he was alarmed lest Frémont win, for his abolitionist supporters were sure to provoke extreme responses from secessionists and fire-eaters in the South. With these thoughts in mind, Grant decided to cast his ballot for Buchanan, hoping to stave off sectional conflict.

Early in 1857 newspapers reported that the Supreme Court by a majority vote decided that a Missouri slave named Dred Scott remained a slave even though his owner, an army surgeon, had brought Dred into a free state (Illinois) and a free territory (Minnesota). Chief Justice Roger B. Taney declared in his opinion that blacks "had no rights which white men are bound to respect." Taney went on to rule the Missouri Compromise unconstitutional on the grounds that the federal government had no power to prohibit slavery in the territories — an explosive contention when the westward expansion of slavery was the central issue of national politics. Grant could not help but follow the controversy. Missourian Taylor Blow, whose family had once owned Dred, was a key supporter of

Scott's suit for freedom; he knew the Dents and Ulysses Grant. Captain Henry Bainbridge, whose sister-in-law was married to Dred's owner, was a friend of Ulysses and Julia: he had delivered a letter to Julia from Ulysses in 1849 and had been stationed at Jefferson Barracks along with Grant in 1843 — just before he obtained use of Dred for several years. Grant and Scott may have met when the lieutenant visited the captain. Several months after the Supreme Court handed down its decision, Taylor Blow purchased Dred and his wife and freed them.[20]

The Supreme Court's decision and the issue of slavery, both in the territories and in general, continued to fuel partisan politics. In 1858, Grant read about the debates in Illinois between United States Senator Stephen A. Douglas, a Democrat, and his challenger, Republican Abraham Lincoln. As a nominal Democrat, Grant admired Douglas's effort to carve out a position between abolition and the extreme beliefs of proslavery Southerners, but he admitted, "It was a nice question to say who got the best of the argument." Neighbors, remarking that the former captain was "thoroughly informed" on the issues of the day, recalled that he was "opposed to slavery on principle. . . . against its further extension," but "deplored the agitation of its abolition." The mere idea of secession, however, infuriated him. "I could not endure the thought of the Union separating," he said later. "It made my blood run cold to hear friends of mine, Southern men — as many of my friends were — deliberately discuss the dissolution of the Union as though it were a tariff bill." A local lawyer noted that Grant, after reading the daily paper, would look off in the distance, depressed by what was happening.[21]

Grant seldom discussed his feelings about slavery, perhaps because his beliefs were compromised by his marriage. Neither Colonel Dent nor Julia saw anything wrong with slavery; after all, they did not break apart families by sale or treat their workers cruelly. Grant debated politics and slavery with his father-in-law, and neighbors noted that these disagreements contributed to already strained relations at White Haven. One of the Dent slaves, Mary Robinson, recalled that the former army captain made it clear (within earshot of the house slaves) that "he wanted to give his wife's slaves their freedom as soon as possible." Yet emancipation was easier said than done, for manumitted slaves who stayed in Missouri had to post bond for their good behavior, and neither the slaves, Dent, nor Grant had sufficient funds.[22]

Nevertheless, Grant entered a protest against the peculiar institution soon after he moved to St. Louis. On March 29, 1859, he filed documents in circuit court setting free William Jones, a thirty-five-year-old mulatto male just a shade shorter than himself. He had never mentioned Jones (at least by name) in correspondence; he did not mention him (or the fact that he had owned a single slave) later in life; Julia passed over the incident in silence in her own recollections. Exactly when and how Grant acquired ownership of a slave remain something of a mystery. The manumission document stated that Grant purchased William, although in later years it was understood that William had been presented to him as a gift. Since a thirty-five-year-old male slave could fetch upward of a thousand dollars on the auction block, Grant's decision to manumit William meant that he gave up the opportunity to obtain some dearly needed cash (and it is not known whether William posted bond or left the state).[23]

The sectional crisis made itself felt in his life in other ways. His father continued to denounce slavery and that "tribe of slaveowners," the Dents; he was convinced that Julia's extravagance was due to her being a slaveholder's daughter and was dragging down his son. Old Colonel Dent continued to preach the proslavery gospel, assailing anyone who questioned his Democratic beliefs. This family feud held larger implications for Grant. Many residents of St. Louis were suspicious of him because of his Northern birth — and manumitting William could not have helped his standing among such defenders of Southern ways. Antislavery advocates, however, could not forget that he was Colonel Dent's son-in-law, and thus he could not be trusted. As a result, Grant's chances to earn a living suffered. In August he applied for the office of county engineer, offering in support of his candidacy the names of a number of leading citizens belonging to various political parties including Taylor Blow. However, Grant feared that the board of commissioners, with a three-to-two margin in favor of the Republicans, would "make strict party nominations for all the offices under their control." To humor his wife, he went to a fortuneteller, only to return with the news that she agreed with his own prognostication. Whether it was his hard-headed political analysis or the fortuneteller's foresight, the prophecy was fulfilled; moreover, he was disgusted to learn that a German immigrant — not a native-born citizen — won the position. Just as disheartening, however, was that one of Grant's friends on the board, Dr. Taussig, admitted that he had withheld his vote from Grant because of the latter's kinship with the Dents. On a much larger scale, events at Harpers Ferry, where John Brown's abortive effort to spark a slave rebellion had shocked the nation, reminded Grant how high the stakes of politics might go.[24]

As 1859 ended, Grant got a job in the customs house, but held it for only a month; his hopes that he might get another shot at being county engineer in February 1860 were dashed. At the same time he learned that the old owner of their St. Louis home could not pay the mortgage due on the house: that meant the bank would repossess the residence and Grant would have to sue to regain Hardscrabble. Julia urged him to go to Covington, reminding her husband that his father "had always been not only willing but anxious to serve him (in his own way, to be sure)." This time Jesse Grant came to the rescue — although not without a good reason of his own. Ulysses's brother Simpson had been in poor health, and it was unclear whether he would live much longer. Not only was this a crucial time for Ulysses to learn the business; it was also a chance for him to earn his inheritance.[25]

Ulysses journeyed to Covington in March; when he arrived, he was suffering with a severe migraine. Transportation delays had made him late, and his father was not at home. One sister was also away (much to his relief; it seems that friction still remained from the last time Jesse had offered his son a job); other family members peppered him with questions as he sat in the dining room, his head "nearly bursting with pain." For hours he simply sat and waited, passing the time by writing to Julia. Several days later he accepted his father's offer to work under his brothers in Galena until he learned enough to become a partner.[26]

Ulysses and Julia hired out her slaves — the colonel had reminded Julia that if they accompanied the Grants to Galena, the slaves would be free, and that should things not work out, she could not reclaim them. Grant disliked this arrangement, but they were not his slaves; to secure the best treatment possible for them, he went so far as to offer to hire them out to local Republicans, a peculiar if well-intentioned idea.[27]

In April, the family boarded the steamer *Itasca* and headed north on the Mississippi to Galena. When the vessel tied up at dock, Grant debarked, a chair in each hand, followed by Julia and the children. He had managed to leave St. Louis, White Haven, Colonel Dent, and slavery, but only because of his father's willingness to take over as family provider.[28]

A river divides Galena; houses dot the hills (some rather steep) rising from the river. The family settled into a brick house high on the western hillside; from the front door one looked out over the downtown business district. Every day after work Grant walked up a flight of several hundred wooden stairs to make his way home. Julia had a servant to help with the cooking — always a problem for Julia — and the housekeeping. At the dinner table Fred described his day at school, complete with playground tussles, while Buck pressed to have his curls cut off, something Julia had refused to do, although Buck complained that he looked like a girl (the youngster eventually prevailed). Nellie found herself overshadowed by all these boys, but her father made sure she had her own share of attention. By far the most personable and mischievous of the children was little Jesse. Once, he attempted to put on his father's boots, only to tumble down the stairs, emerging rather shaken and with his front teeth broken off. The accident did not deter him from regularly challenging his father to wrestle. Grant would look down at his diminutive foe and announce, "I do not feel like fighting, Jess, but I can't stand being hectored in this manner by a man of your size." Jesse would flail away at his father's knees; before long the two would be rolling on the ground; until Jesse secured his opponent's surrender, he would ignore his father's warning that it was not fair to hit someone who was down. Afterward, with the children off to bed, the parents would settle down in the living room, Ulysses reading the paper or a book out loud to Julia (who found reading made her eyes hurt) while she did her sewing. It was the peaceful life Grant had always imagined.[29]

Grant proved adequate at best at the general store. Simpson's health continued to sink; Orvil seemed a little too much like his father's son, at least to some residents of the town, who characterized him as "an uninhibited sharper, and rather arrogant and conceited as well." The former captain felt out of place as a clerk, and he showed little aptitude at conducting transactions. Nevertheless, he would settle for what he could get. "I have evry reason to hope, in a few years, to be entirely above the frowns of the world, pecuniarily," he told an old St. Louis friend. Nevertheless, the family still welcomed any money Julia's father sent to her, and Grant borrowed from the firm to pay off old debts. He spent little on himself. Every day people could see him walking to work in his old army overcoat and slouch hat, a quiet man except when it came to telling stories of the Mexican-American War or of the Pacific coast. Some whispered stories about his past, but observers noted that Grant neither drank nor showed any liking for alcohol. Ely S. Parker, a civil engineer who had supervised the building of Galena's federal customshouse and post office, found him quiet at first, but once the captain got to know someone, he became not only "companionable but possessed of a warm and sympathetic nature." Perhaps this was because each man brought something unusual to Galena, for Parker was the son of a Seneca chief who had enjoyed prominence as a tribal leader. The two grew even closer after Parker helped Grant out of a tight spot at a local saloon, where the army captain had come under attack as the result of a heated discussion.[30]

Since 1860 was a presidential election year, there was a great deal of talk about politics. For the first time someone from Illinois would run for president; in fact, two residents of the state, Republican Abraham Lincoln and

Democrat Stephen A. Douglas, were among the four candidates. Grant tried to stay out of the discussions about the contest. "I don't know anything of party politics, and I don't want to," he declared. Aware that the Republicans stood an excellent chance of winning, he was deeply disturbed both by the breakup of the Democratic party and increasing talk of secession. Although the lawyer who handled the legal affairs of the general store, John A. Rawlins, was the town's leading Democrat, he did not sway Grant's feelings. Rawlins was a Galena native, who had worked his way up by selling coal to support his family, a responsibility he had to shoulder because his father was an alcoholic. He counted Parker among his friends; it was testimony to his skill that Jesse Grant, by now a passionate Republican, would allow his sons to entrust the store's legal business to a Democrat.

Rawlins liked Grant more for the captain's stories about the Mexican-American War than for his insights into current politics. Indeed, what Grant heard during political discussions shook his lightly held Democratic allegiance. When someone urged him to vote, Orvil Grant, a Republican, discouraged the idea, saying that the captain would cast his ballot for Douglas. Grant demurred. "I don't quite like the position of either party," he remarked, adding that in any case he had not met the residency requirement. He refused the Douglas Club's request to drill their marchers; but one evening as he walked home, he noticed the Republican "Wide Awakes" struggling to parade in unison and offered some advice.[31]

By November it was apparent that the Republicans would elect their man, Abraham Lincoln, the next president of the United States. Many Galenians were pleased with this result, for the town's congressman, Elihu B. Washburne, had been a Lincoln man and would have influence with the new president. Julia, who had defended the Democrats, watched as the torchlight procession of Republicans made its way to the courthouse. On election night Grant somewhat reluctantly helped host a little celebration at the general store. When one partier laughed off the notion that some Southern states might respond to the news of Lincoln's victory by leaving the union, Grant curtly responded, "The South will fight." The discussions of secession in St. Louis had convinced him that the threat was a serious one.[32]

As events in the South became daily topics of discussion at the store, Grant was a regular participant in the discussions, although he did not indicate how national events might affect him. He was becoming accustomed to his work, enjoyed it, and looked forward to becoming a partner and prospering at last. At home he read the papers out loud to Julia, who offered the contradictory opinion that secession was acceptable but that the federal government should prohibit it, even if it had to resort to force. Her husband could only smile at this. "It is hard to realize that a State or States should commit so suicidal an act as to secede from the Union," he observed, "though from all the reports, I have no doubt but that at least five of them will do it." Buchanan, once his choice for president, was now a "granny of an executive" because of his failure to act decisively. Yet he doubted that secession enjoyed widespread support: "It does seem as if just a few men have produced all the present difficulty."[33]

Nevertheless, Grant accepted the possibility of war. When William R. Rowley, clerk of the circuit court, declared, "There's a great deal of bluster about the Southerners, but I don't think there's much fight in them," Grant replied that he was mistaken: "There *is* a good deal of bluster; that's the result of their education; but if they once get at it they will make a strong fight. You are a great deal like them in one respect — each side under-estimates the other and over-estimates itself."[34]

In December Grant traveled on business throughout southern Wisconsin, southeast Minnesota, and Iowa. Everywhere he went, he heard more about the prospect of war — and people wanted to hear what he had to say. Back in Galena, people also sought out his analysis of the worsening crisis. No one could doubt where his sympathies lay. In late February a local Democrat known for his pro-Southern sympathies entered the general store and announced that representatives of the seceded states had met at Montgomery, Alabama, adopted a new constitution calling into existence the Confederate States of America, and named Jefferson Davis president. Grant first shook his head in disbelief, then declared that Davis and his associates deserved the hangman's noose.[35]

On March 4, 1861, Lincoln took office as the sixteenth president of the United States. Whether he would be the last chief executive to preside over that entity remained to be seen. For nearly six weeks the residents of Galena watched and waited, paying especial attention to the fate of the federal garrison stationed in Charleston Harbor at Fort Sumter. South Carolina had been the first state to secede; would it also be where war broke out? On April 13, 1861, the news arrived: the Confederates had fired on the fort. Two days later the townspeople learned that the garrison's commander, Major Robert Anderson, had surrendered and evacuated the fort. Flags went up; crowds filled the streets; there would be a meeting at the courthouse the next evening.

As Galena's residents gathered in the courthouse at sundown on April 16, most of them knew that the previous day President Lincoln had issued a call for 75,000 militia to serve ninety days. Elihu Washburne scanned the assemblage: he wanted to show that his hometown stood behind the president. Galena's mayor, a Democrat, opened the meeting with some weak words about compromise, implying that the Republicans had caused the war; Washburne retorted that partisanship was out of place at this time, and called on the assemblage to pass a series of resolutions to form militia companies in support of a war of reunion. Then John A. Rawlins took the platform. That he was a Democrat did not matter to him now: as he had walked to the courthouse, he had rejected a friend's characterization of the assemblage as a Republican gathering. Eyes ablaze, he proclaimed, "There can be but two parties now, one of patriots and one of traitors!" Sounding a great deal like his hero, Stephen A. Douglas, he ended a patriotic declamation of some forty-five minutes with the statement, "I have been a democrat all my life; but this is no longer a question of politics. It is simply country or no country. I have favored every honorable compromise; but the day for compromise is passed. Only one course is left for us. We will stand by the flag of our country, and appeal to the God of battles!"[36]

The speech moved many in the crowd, including Grant. Seeing a politician rise above politics at this moment of supreme crisis inspired the old army captain. As he walked home with Orvil, Grant pondered how to apply Rawlins's message in his own life. Before long the answer emerged. It was time to do what he had been trained to do. "I think I ought to go into the service," he finally remarked. Orvil agreed.

Grant would never again work at Jesse's general store.[37]

6

Off to War

◉

ON APRIL 18 Galena's citizens again gathered in the courthouse — this time to raise volunteers in response to President Lincoln's proclamation. Prior to the meeting, Elihu Washburne conferred with Augustus Chetlain, a Republican grocer who had headed the town's Wide Awakes, to select a presiding officer. They settled on the retired army officer who had seen action during the Mexican-American War, and whose Democratic leanings would go far to assure that this recruiting meeting would transcend partisanship. That evening, as the audience crowded the courthouse, John E. Smith, the county treasurer (and a Republican), called the assemblage to order. Immediately someone moved for the nomination of a presiding officer, naming the army veteran. The proposal met with a chorus of approval, and Ulysses S. Grant moved to the front of the room. "With much embarrassment and some prompting," as he put it later, "I made out to announce the object of the meeting."[1]

What followed were the usual round of speeches and declarations of patriotism. When the time came to call for volunteers, Chetlain, primed for the opportunity, headed the list. Rawlins could not go: his wife was dying of consumption. Nor did Grant volunteer — although he intended to seek a commission as a colonel. In his travels to Cincinnati as a boy, he had encountered another boy, William Dennison, who was the son of the manager of Dennison House; now Dennison was governor of Ohio. Surely he would offer Grant a regiment. Washburne countered with the proposal that Grant seek a command from Illinois governor Richard Yates, promising to recommend Grant for a place.[2]

The next day Grant, still inspired by the events of the past week, shared his sentiments with his proslavery father-in-law. "I know it is hard for men to apparently work with the Republican party," he wrote the colonel, "but now all party distinctions should be lost sight of and evry true patriot be for maintaining the integrity of the glorious old *Stars & Stripes,* the Constitution and the Union." He also reflected on the larger consequences of this oncoming conflict. "In all this I can but see the doom of slavery," he remarked. "The North do not want, nor will they want, to interfere with the institution. But they will refuse for all time to give it protection unless the South shall return soon to their allegiance. . . ." Other sources of cotton would emerge, he predicted, and the decline of King Cotton in the South would "reduce the value of negroes so much that they will never be worth fighting over again." The chaos of war would achieve what abolitionists had long desired.[3]

Over the next week Grant, Rawlins, and Rowley worked to raise more volunteers in the towns outside Galena. The former captain drilled the makeshift volunteer company for several days, supervised the making of uniforms, and laid out the blueprint for a flag. Its members offered to elect him captain in return, but he declined, and Chetlain assumed the post. Eager though he might be to serve, Grant wanted to go to war as a colonel at the head of his own regiment. This ambition reflected both self-confidence and pride — he had left a company command seven years ago; it would be humiliating to return to military service at the same rank. Meanwhile his patriotic fervor continued to grow. "Whatever may have been my political opinions before I have but one sentiment now," he told his father. "That is we have a Government, and laws and a flag and they must all be sustained. There are but two parties now, Traitors and Patriots and I want hereafter to be ranked with the latter, and I trust, the stronger party."[4]

Colonels were appointed, not elected; to head a regiment Grant had to make his ability known to Governor Yates. Thus he welcomed the opportunity to go to Springfield with Washburne and his newly drilled company. As the volunteers made their way to the train station on April 25, Grant followed them, wearing the now-familiar slouch hat and old army overcoat, a carpetbag at his side. Arriving in the state capital the next day, he soon saw his hopes of gaining a commission evaporate. Unimpressed with the former captain, Yates ignored him; an aide to the governor remarked that Grant's "features did not indicate any high grade of intellectuality. He was very indifferently dressed, and did not at all look like a military man" — especially to someone who looked for gold braid, brass buttons, and heroic posture as the prime requisites of military leadership. It seemed as if Grant had wasted his time, and the rain and mud of the next few days did little to elevate his spirits. Washburne convinced the captain to stay for several days while the legislature deliberated over the raising of regiments and the appointment of officers; finally Yates told Washburne that Grant could be of use drilling those volunteers not yet organized into regiments. This seemed like a good idea; but when the legislature passed a bill appointing three drill officers, Grant's name was not among them.[5]

With Galena's company now enlisted as part of the Eleventh Illinois Infantry, Grant made plans to return home on April 28. Yates had not noticed him, and so Grant ate his last dinner at the hotel, and left while Yates remained seated at the table. But for some reason — perhaps looking for one more chance — Grant loitered at the front door. Finally Yates came out. Calling Grant "Captain," he asked him to stay on that night and visit him the next day. The next morning Grant eagerly accepted the governor's offer of working in the adjutant general's office. Cheered by his success, he wrote his sister Mary that he had been "detained" by the governor to help organize Illinois volunteers.[6]

If Grant's letter to the folks at Covington seemed a bit vague as to exactly how he was going to help the governor, perhaps it was because he believed that he would be entrusted with great responsibilities. But he was not. His first job was to inspect the state armory and report on the number of usable weapons available. Way down in Vicksburg, Mississippi, so the story goes, a newspaper reported the results: "Captain Grant had, by great diligence, found *sixty-four* old muskets and *one* damaged six pounder." Before long, however, he spent most of his time performing fairly routine tasks, such as ruling sheets of paper in the absence of printed forms. Grant put his experience as a quartermaster and adjutant to good use, although he made no pretense of being a master of organization. "The only place I ever found in my life to put a paper so as to find it again was either a side coat-pocket or in the hands of a clerk or secretary more careful than myself." He told Yates that his "bump of order is not largely developed and papers are not my forte," but he did his best.[7]

Just as Grant was getting ready to return home in early May, Yates assigned him the task of mustering in new regiments as they arrived at Camp Yates, replacing an old West Point associate, John Pope. This was something, but it was not the colonelcy Grant wanted. "I find all those places are wanted by politicians who are up to log-rolling," he told his father (who knew more than a little about such matters), "and I do not care to be under such persons" — which could have been either an unintended rebuke or a call for Jesse to practice his talents along that line in Ohio. Nevertheless, his new position might open the door to more opportunities. "I imagine it will do me no harm the time I spend here," he told Julia, "for it has enabled me to become acquainted with the principle men in the state. I do not know that I shall receive any benefit from this but it does no harm."[8]

Grant's responsibilities extended beyond Springfield. He traveled southward to Mattoon, then west to Belleville, near St. Louis, and then to Anna to muster in three regiments. Arriving at Belleville ahead of the volunteers, he decided to visit friends in St. Louis. For some time now he had been following the struggle in Julia's home state. Missourians were truly a divided people. Unionists and secessionists sought control of the state; both sides believed possession of St. Louis to be of the utmost importance. "The state of affairs is terrible and no doubt a terrible calamity awaits them," he remarked. "Stationing Ill. Troops within striking distance of St Louis may possibly save the city." Only the quick action of Captain Nathaniel Lyon in seizing the contents of the federal arsenal before secessionist forces could get their hands on the weapons had prevented a major confrontation.[9]

Grant arrived in St. Louis just as tensions between unionists and secessionists reached a climax. For some weeks a pro-secession militia had been assembling outside the city at Camp Jackson. After transferring weapons from the arsenal to Illinois, Lyon gathered a force to march out to the camp. Frank P. Blair, the namesake son of Andrew Jackson's old political adviser, had formed his own regiment to support Lyon. Storefronts were empty, a sign of the city's economic struggles. Many slaves were "stampeding already"; secessionist masters were taking their people with them southward; before long, Grant predicted, Missouri would become a free state.[10]

On the morning of May 10, Grant watched as Lyon and Blair marched toward Camp Jackson. Introducing himself to Blair, Grant wished him luck then went on to visit the Dent plantation, where he found both Colonel Dent and his son John virtually committed to the Confederate cause. As he returned to the city, he heard shouts. Camp Jackson had been captured without a shot. Local unionists, who until now had maintained a low profile, hauled down a Confederate flag that had been hoisted above a secessionist enclave on Pine Street, a few blocks away from Grant's old real estate office. When an ardent secessionist protested, Grant snapped back that while he had yet to see a secessionist executed by hanging, "there were plenty of them who ought to be."[11]

Grant greeted Lyon and Blair on their return to the arsenal. They accepted his congratulations but offered little encouragement when Grant suggested that he might be able to help out. The same disheartening news came from his friends in town. St. Louis still had no place for him. In these times of crisis, when was he going to receive his chance? Certainly it would not come so long as he was mustering in regiments. The prospect depressed and frustrated him. Moreover, he thought the war would be "of short duration"; a few victories would smash the rebellion, slaves would fall in value, and the peculiar institution would collapse. "The nigger will never disturb this country again," he predicted to his father. However, he worried that the slaves might well rise up against their masters. If this happened, the forces gathering in the loyal states might have to suppress a different sort of rebellion, and Grant thought "they would go on such a mission and with the purest motives." On a lighter note, he teased Julia that before long her father and the other white residents of White Haven "will be left to themselvs at the mercy of Mary and the rest of the darkeys."[12]

Right now, however, mustering in regiments would have to do; Grant traveled back to Illinois, swearing in one regiment at Belleville and two at Mattoon. There he must have made an impression on the men, for the members of the Seventh District Regiment christened their quarters Camp Grant. But those in authority did not share the recruits' assessment: when Grant returned to Springfield, no commission awaited him. The war was passing him by. Perhaps old rumors about his past were in circulation: one of his colleagues in the adjutant general's office described him as "a dead-beat military man — a discharged officer of the regular army." Yet he did not take advantage of Captain Pope's offer to lobby some state officials on his behalf. "I declined to receive endorsement for permission to fight for my country," he recalled somewhat curtly years later. Perhaps he had already missed his chance.[13]

Grant left Springfield for Galena on May 23, disappointed in his quest for a colonelcy. The following day he forwarded to the adjutant general in Washington an application for a commission, expressing the notion that he felt "competent to command a regiment." But there was nothing to do at Galena; feeling "all the time as if a duty was being neglected that was paramount to any other duty I ever owed," an anxious Grant returned to Springfield at the end of the month, only to discover that all the state's regiments had been mustered into service and Yates was away in Washington. Grant picked up a rumor that he might yet get his long-sought regiment, but he was too restless to wait long, especially after Yates returned and failed to make an offer. He made a visit to Covington, then crossed the Ohio to look up George McClellan, now a major general of volunteers with headquarters in Cincinnati. He got as far as McClellan's outer office, where he was told that the general was out for the moment. For the next two days Grant waited and watched as staff officers worked away, writing with quill pens. Perhaps he thought that McClellan would remember him, although McClellan's last impression of him — as a tipsy officer on the West Coast — would not have helped much. Finally, he left Cincinnati and visited J. J. Reynolds, his old West Point classmate, in Indiana.

Reynolds had tried to help out Sam Grant in the past; perhaps he would do so again.[14]

At Lafayette Grant had an unpleasant encounter. A colonel of Ohio volunteers was holding forth on his political convictions. This war had nothing to do with slavery, he declared. Why, should he be about to engage the enemy when news came of a slave insurrection, he would join the rebs in putting down the uprising. Although Grant himself had speculated that many other officers would respond the same way, he was not one of them. Incredulous, he could not let the remark pass. "I don't wish to hurt your feelings, or disturb the harmony of our meeting," he told the colonel, "but I *must* say that any officer who can make such a declaration is not far from being a traitor!" Those present had to make sure that the two men did not come to blows.[15]

Grant insisted that he was not seeking a position. He told his father that he was "perfectly sickened at the political wire pulling for all these commissions." But Jesse Grant wasted no time in trying to pull strings. Off went letters to Attorney General Edward Bates and General Winfield Scott extolling his son.[16] Nothing happened.

In later years Grant would cite with approval the maxim that the man does not seek the office; the office seeks the man. Of course, it doesn't hurt if the man makes it easy for the office to find him. Such was Grant's situation. The men of the Seventh District Regiment — the regiment mustered in by Grant at Mattoon — had elected Simon Goode as their colonel. The officers now realized that Goode was unable to create a regiment from a mob of men. The colonel drank and was fond of quoting Napoleon, going so far as to declare, "I never sleep," to sentries at night. Neither, apparently, did his men, who busied themselves by committing acts of mischief, hanging around local saloons, and causing so much chaos that people dubbed them "Governor Yates's Hellions." Grant himself had recommended a capable young man with two years of West Point under his belt as drillmaster, but this was not enough to discipline the raw recruits. It had become an impossible situation; Yates ordered the regiment brought back to the state fairgrounds outside Springfield. Passing through town, George B. McClellan reviewed the regiment and pronounced himself satisfied. The junior officers knew better. The regiment needed a new colonel, they told the governor. They had someone in mind — the fellow who had mustered them in several weeks ago. On June 15 (the same day McClellan inspected the command) Yates named Ulysses S. Grant colonel of the Seventh District Regiment.[17]

When Grant arrived at Camp Yates, the men he encountered resembled an armed gang far more than they did a regiment. Dressed in worn civilian garb topped by a damaged hat, the new colonel was also less than imposing. As rumors spread that their new colonel was about, the men turned to examine this unprepossessing figure. They laughed. "What a colonel!" "Damn such a colonel!" One particularly brash fellow began to shadow box behind Grant's back until another volunteer shoved the pretend pugilist so hard that he hit Grant between the shoulders. But Grant remained unruffled. He greeted the adjutant and modestly announced that he "guessed he'd take command." The ruffians apologized, and one explained that "it was all in fun, and hoped the new Colonel wouldn't get mad about it."[18]

Grant had no time to get mad: but it was soon evident that he found such behavior simply unacceptable. On June 18 he officially announced his assumption of command; the next day he directed that only passes approved by him would be honored, although soldiers were free to leave camp from reveille to retreat — so long as they did not miss any roll calls for drill — replacing Goode's system of surrounding the camp with guards armed with clubs to keep the recruits away from the local womenfolk. There would be three daily drill periods (two on Sundays); those soldiers who failed to attend would find themselves in confinement. At first the soldiers did not respond to these new regulations, and offenders crowded the guardhouse: as they learned that the new colonel meant what he said, however, they began to comply with his directives. When several members of the night guard abandoned their posts, Grant chose not to impose the full punishment for this offense ("In time of war this punishment is death," he reminded them) but to let them off with a stern warning.[19]

Grant might not yet look the part of a colonel (he rushed home to Galena, and with a loan from his father's former business partner, E. A. Collins, made arrangements for a uniform, a horse, and suitable accoutrements, before returning with eleven-year-old Fred in tow), but he meant business. When roll call came late one morning, he simply sent his men back into quarters without waiting for a morning report — which was required to issue rations. He reminded officers as well as men of their obligations and duties. Some recruits were slow learners. A local roughneck who went by the name of Mexico showed up at drill one day with a hangover. When Grant sentenced him to the guardhouse, Mexico vowed that for every minute of his incarceration, "I'll have an ounce of your blood." That earned an order to gag him; several hours later, as the men watched, Grant personally undid the gag and released Mexico. Those expecting an explosion were disappointed or astonished when Mexico simply walked away. Grant had tamed this man, just as he had tamed horses and intended to tame the regiment — quietly but firmly. "We could not exactly understand the man," recalled one enlisted man. "He was very soon called 'the quiet man' . . . and in a few days reduced matters in camp to perfect order."[20]

Weeks of drill and discipline followed. His command "embraced the sons of farmers, lawyers, physicians, politicians, merchants, bankers and ministers, and some men of maturer years who had filled such positions themselves," he later recalled. For the most part he was pleased with his regiment, although he complained that he could not play cards with his field officers: "One is a preacher and the other a member of Church." With time on his hands, he sent for George B. McClellan's report on the Crimean War to study up on tactics and warfare.[21]

Before long the new colonel faced his first serious challenge. When he had mustered in the Seventh District Regiment at Mattoon, it was as state militia for thirty days. Although the men had pledged their willingness to enter federal service (for a three-year stint, unless the war ended sooner), they had yet to do so; slightly less than half of the 1,250 recruits had extended their service in the state militia by a month just after Grant arrived. There was no telling what might happen now that a new man was in charge. Anxious to do what he could to promote reenlistment, Grant accepted the offer of Democratic congressmen John A. Logan and John A. McClernand to visit his camp and address the regiment. He did so with some reluctance, for although Logan was an eloquent speaker, many people in Illinois questioned his loyalty and commitment. On June 19 the regiment heard out both men; Grant was surprised and moved by the power of Logan's patriotic pronouncements, which removed all doubt as to his sentiments. When Logan introduced Grant to the men, however, all the new commander could say was: "Men, go to your quarters!" Perhaps the quiet colonel, uncomfortable with public speaking, knew it would be better to leave well enough alone after Logan's stirring oration. After all, over the course of the next week he would introduce himself to his men and officers by instituting a regime of discipline, drill, and order. The regiment had nearly collapsed under Goode's lax regime; would the men now reject the new man's methods?

The moment of truth came on June 28. As Grant watched, the men of the Seventh District Regiment, almost to a man, signed up for three years of service in what would now be known as the Twenty-first Illinois. Yet there was a discordant note. Just as the swearing in was taking place, one of Grant's cousins galloped into camp, not on the horse Grant had purchased when last at Galena but on "a showey Livery horse hired for the occation," much to the colonel's disgust.[22]

The ceremony done, the crisis past, Grant could address new concerns. Already heavy rains and bad water were leading to sickness among the men. The colonel had a solution. He had just received orders to move his regiment to Quincy, located on the Illinois shore of the Mississippi River, some one hundred miles west of Springfield. He turned down the possibility of transport by rail, arguing that the march would be good for his command's discipline and health. The march got underway on July 3. Concerned that some of his men might break ranks to stop at farms and grab food, he "kept such a watch on them, and punished offenders so, that I will venture that the same number of troops never marched through a thickly settled country like this committing fewer depridations." As the regiment crossed the Illinois River, Grant learned that his men might be needed at Ironton, Missouri; however, the steamer that was dispatched to take his men down the river to St. Louis ran up against a sandbar, and by the time it was ready to move, new orders changed Grant's destination once more. An Illinois regiment was in danger of being surrounded by Rebels west of Palmyra, Missouri. Speed was of the essence: Grant's men would take the train after all to Quincy before marching across the Mississippi.[23]

With a battle apparently in the offing, Grant decided that war was no place for his young son, and he sent Fred home. Then he did some hard thinking about what was likely to come next. In later years he admitted to being anxious, not because of any concern about his own fate — he had been under fire frequently during the Mexican-American War — but because of the burdens of command. Thus he was relieved to learn that the endangered regiment had made its way back to Quincy on July 11. There would be no battle after all, at least not yet. Later he mused that both sides had simply run away.[24]

Over the next two days Grant moved his men across the Mississippi River to West Quincy, Missouri, and deployed several companies along the railroad to Palmyra, although he was suffering from a severe migraine — probably a sign of the tension he was under. "Secessionests are thick through this part of Missouri," he reported; but they restricted themselves to burning railroad bridges and tearing up track as well as attempting to pick off unwary Union detachments. Eliminating such pesky raiders became a priority, and Grant's regiment joined several others in attempting to track down a band of secessionist home guards under the command of

Colonel Thomas Harris, encamped at Florida, Missouri, some twenty-five miles south of the camp of the Twenty-first Illinois. As he prepared to march, he reflected on the region in which he was to campaign. Northerners and Southerners vied for control of the state; although Missouri had its share of antislavery advocates, many slaveowners also opposed secession. Whether they would continue to do so should slavery come under direct attack was an open question. It would not take too much aggressive behavior by Northerners to push the state toward greater sympathy with the South. With that in mind, Grant wanted to make sure that his soldiers behaved. Discipline would pay off on the march as well as on the battlefield: his men would give civilians no cause of complaint.[25]

On July 17 Grant's command moved out. The colonel kept his men in line, determined not to give offense, but many of the houses along the line of march were already deserted, their residents having fled at word that the Yankees were coming. At night he halted the column for a few hours' rest, and made ready to move out early the next morning toward the creek bottom where Harris's command was reportedly encamped. Grant felt his new responsibility most keenly. It would be the first time since the Mexican-American War that he would lead men into action; as he himself recalled, he had never before exercised formal top command in combat.[26]

At the first light of dawn, his men began the march. Grant was nervous. "As we approached the brow of the hill from which it was expected we could see Harris's camp, and possibly find his men ready formed to meet us," he later recalled, "my heart kept getting higher and higher until it felt to me as though it was in my throat. I would have given anything then to have been back in Illinois, but I had not the moral courage to halt and consider what to do; I kept right on." Finally his men reached the crest, and Grant came forward to have a look. What he saw startled him. "The place where Harris had been encamped a few days before was still there and the marks of a recent encampment were plainly visible, but the troops were gone," he remembered. "My heart resumed its place. It occurred to me at once that Harris had been as much afraid of me as I had been of him. This was a view of the question I had never taken before; but it was one I never forgot afterwards. From that event to the close of the war, I never experienced trepidation upon confronting an enemy, though I always felt more or less anxiety. I never forgot that he had as much reason to fear my forces as I had his. The lesson was valuable."[27]

Harris had indeed fled southward; after one day Grant ordered his men to return to camp. On the march back he discovered that his earlier insistence on discipline had paid off. "When we first came there was a terrible state of fear existing among the people," he told his wife. "They thought that evry horror known in the whole catalogue of disa[sters] follwing a state of war was going to be their portion at once." Well-disciplined and well-mannered soldiers created a different impression: civilians "find that all troops are not the desperate characters they took them for," despite some incidents of misbehavior. On the way back from Florida the regiment passed once more by local residences. This time, however, people came out to greet the Illinois volunteers. Grant felt vindicated: "I am fully convinced that if orderly troops could be marched through this country, and none others, it would create a very different state of feeling from what exists now."[28]

Reports of Grant's effectiveness in maintaining discipline spread so quickly that he soon found himself in command of several troublesome regiments at Mexico, Missouri. Recruits had been jostling local residents for food and drink; they enjoyed confronting civilians and forcing them to take the oath of allegiance under pain of arrest. Grant immediately halted unordered arrests and restricted soldiers to camp unless people invited them into their homes. These measures helped reassure local residents that Union forces intended to maintain order, not spark disorder. The community appreciated the colonel's actions: "I received the most marked courtesy from the citizens of Mexico so long as I remained there," he later recalled.[29]

Grant assessed the temper of secessionist sympathy while he was at Mexico. Many Missourians, accepting disunion as a fact, believed that "nothing is left for them but to choose between two evils" — secession and abolition. "You can't convince them but what the ultimate object is to extinguish, by force, slavery," he observed. Grant's efforts to explain otherwise met with little success. "They are great fools in this section of [the] country and will never rest until they bring upon themselvs all the horrors of war in its worst form," he concluded. "The people are inclined to carry on a guerilla Warfare that must eventuate in retaliation and when it does commence it will be hard to control." What kind of war would be waged depended in large part on whether Confederate civilians blurred the distinction between combatant and noncombatant: guerrilla warfare would seriously hinder reconciliation and the restoration of the Union. Meanwhile, Grant struggled with learning modern battle tactics; at last he discarded the movements that had evolved since his days at West Point in favor of simple orders that reflected common sense and were easily learned by his men. "I do not believe that the officers of the regiment ever discovered that I had never studied the tactics that I used," he remarked.[30]

One August morning when the regimental chaplain arrived with the morning paper from St. Louis, Grant was shocked to read that he had been promoted to brigadier general of volunteers. "I had no suspicion of it," he told the chaplain. "It never came from any request of mine. It must be some of Washburne's work." And so it was. Lincoln had instructed Illinois's congressional delegation to offer four names for promotion in an ordered list. The congressmen met and discussed several names. Among them were Stephen A. Hurlbut, who had been a Republican state legislator with previous military experience in the Seminole War; Benjamin Prentiss, a lawyer and a militia colonel; and John McClernand, whose military experience included the Black Hawk War and the state militia, although it was his political credentials as a leading Democrat in the state that compelled attention. All were more prominent than Grant; all therefore had enemies as well as friends. Washburne, using both his political clout and the fact that there was no strong opposition to Grant, advanced his name to the head of the list, making him senior to the others. But Grant had also impressed his superiors. General John Pope, Grant's district commander, judged him "thoroughly a gentleman & an officer of intelligence & discretion."[31]

The promotion was gratifying to Grant. At long last he was making progress on his own merits, or at least without actively advertising them. Soon afterward he marched his old regiment down to Jefferson Barracks, where he had been posted as a brevet second lieutenant some eighteen years before; he also returned to St. Louis, where he encountered Harry Boggs. "He cursed and went on like a Madman," Grant told Julia. "Told me that I would never be welcom in his hous; that the people of Illinois were a poor misserable set of Black Republicans, Abolition paupers that had to invade their state to get something to eat." Grant could not restrain himself: he told his old "pittiful insignificant" associate that he couldn't even get mad at him, whereupon Boggs roared with profanity. Both men knew that it was not so long ago that it was Grant who had been "pittiful insignificant."[32]

New rank brought with it new responsibilities. Before long Grant had assembled his first staff, selecting former St. Louis lawyer William Hillyer and Clark B. Lagow, a lieutenant in the Twenty-first Illinois, to assist him. But Grant saved his most important appointment for John A. Rawlins. For the past several months Rawlins had watched his wife slowly sink away; although he accepted Grant's offer, he did not join Grant's command until after her death at the end of August. Rawlins had always been a good friend; Grant appreciated his patriotism at the outbreak of the war and he had seen enough of his legal skills to believe him up to the responsibili-

ties of administration. Just as important, however, were two other characteristics. First, Rawlins was aware of the political aspects of this conflict,
and Grant could rely on him to help firm up his relationship with Congressman Washburne, for now he was well aware of Washburne's usefulness. Second, Rawlins was someone with whom Grant could talk — and to
whom he could listen: the lawyer was always full of ideas and opinions and
not afraid to share them.

Some observers later speculated that Grant's invitation had another
purpose: the lawyer hated alcohol. His father had been a heavy drinker,
and John Rawlins attributed his impoverished childhood to the liquor
problem — although the father's sin more often seemed to be laziness
than intoxication. From an early age, Rawlins had shouldered a great deal
of responsibility and demonstrated passion and drive. He first considered
becoming a preacher, then pursued a career in law and politics. But he
could never let go of the fear that he, too, might succumb to the lure of
the bottle. In light of Grant's past habits, some observers believed that
Rawlins's main staff function was to keep Grant sober. Or so they liked to
argue. If that was so, however, it would be hard to explain why Grant
waited until then to find a watchdog. Before long, however, Rawlins would
take it upon himself to perform that function as well as his other duties.[33]

The staff was more notable for its loyalty to Grant than for its military
knowledge; as a result, Grant continued to do much of his own work in
composing orders and reports. It would be some time before professional
military men would arrive to undertake duties more properly relegated to
a staff. Others noted that the new brigadier general packed away his colonel's garb and dressed in whatever felt comfortable until his new uniform
arrived, as if to emphasize that the man made the uniform, not the other
way around. One officer came across him wearing a felt hat and a blue
flannel suit lacking any insignia of rank, wielding not a sword but a clay
pipe. Perhaps he recalled how another quiet man — Zachary Taylor —
had displayed a similar distaste for uniform.[34]

No sooner had Grant heard of his promotion than he received new orders, transferring him to Ironton, Missouri, some seventy miles south of
St. Louis. Once more he had to bring several regiments under control by
stopping the random firing of weapons and empowering the post commander at nearby Pilot Knob to close all drinking establishments. Grant
could make little sense of the behavior of local residents. "Send Union
troops among them and respect all their rights, pay for evrything you get
and they become desperate and reckless because their state sovereignty
is invaded. Troops of the opposite side march through and take evrything
they want, leaving no pay but script, and they become desperate seces-

sion partisans because they have nothing more to loose." When circumstances warranted, however, he interrupted mail, confiscated secessionists' horses, and arrested several Confederate sympathizers to prevent them from passing information about his command. In taking these actions, Grant noted that he had neither orders nor copies of recent federal legislation which might govern his actions.[35]

Grant did not remain long at Ironton. In the aftermath of the Confederate victory at Wilson's Creek, Missouri, on August 10, 1861, General John C. Frémont — the man Grant had not trusted to be president — trusted Grant enough to put him in command of Union forces in central Missouri with orders to counter a Confederate advance. Although he disliked the new assignment, because it took him away from the Mississippi Valley, which promised to become a major theater of war, Grant traveled to Jefferson City. Once again, he found himself battling recalcitrant Missourians. When Confederate civilians fired into a troop train, Grant scoured the countryside to find them. "The party in pursuit will subsist off of the community through which they pass," he informed headquarters, although he added that foraging parties would follow strict rules. Still, he was prepared to take stern measures. Confederate raiders were "driving out the union men and appropriating their property"; Grant decided to mount local militia on horses confiscated from secessionists "who have been adding and abetting the southern cause." Although he opposed "indiscriminate plundering," he authorized local commanders to hold secessionist citizens hostage and to take all property used to assist Confederate forces. Other orders provided for the confiscation of the printing press and type of a local secessionist newspaper and the seizure of bank deposits. "Give secessionists to understand what to expect if it becomes necessary to visit them again," he instructed his subordinates.[36] Grant calibrated the behavior of his command toward civilians to match the latter's behavior, especially when those civilians came close to becoming combatants.

Grant also struggled to train raw recruits. "Drill and discipline is more necessary for the men than fortifications," he declared, an attitude that would surface time and again over the coming year. Besides, he added, he lacked an engineering officer and had forgotten much of what he once knew about entrenchments. Ammunition, clothing, and other equipment were more pressing needs. Too many of his colonels gave out leaves. Local militia — known as Home Guards — proved troublesome to command, until he declared that he was "prodigiously tired" of them. At one point he grew so frustrated at the chaos that he requested that his old regiment be transferred to him.[37]

Despite these irritants, command suited Grant. Although he could not fall asleep until the early hours of the morning, "I stand it first rate . . . and never enjoyed better health in my life," he told his wife. "The fact is my whole career since the beginning of present unhappy difficulties has been complimented in a very flattering manner. All my old friends in the Army and out seem to heartily congratulate me." However, something in one of Julia's letters disturbed him: "You should be cheerful and try to encourage me. I have a task before me of no trifling moment and want all the encouragement possible."[38]

At the end of August, Frémont reassigned Grant yet again, this time to Cape Girardeau, Missouri, with orders to take the offensive against Confederate forces under Jeff Thompson who were creating havoc in the southeastern part of the state. Grant, back on the Mississippi, welcomed the change. No sooner had he arrived at his new command on the afternoon of August 30 than he issued orders for an advance.[39]

"All I fear is that too much may be expected of me," Grant mused. Before long he faced his first challenge — but it was not from the enemy. Benjamin Prentiss, who was in charge at Cape Girardeau when Grant arrived, insisted that he outranked Grant and reacted churlishly to orders from his new commander. Grant snapped at Prentiss, ordering his men to move out; Prentiss responded by leaving his command and going to St. Louis to plead his case, which stalled the contemplated offensive against Thompson's raiders. Frustrated, Grant established his permanent headquarters at Cairo, Illinois, and waited for whatever would come next.[40]

He was not idle for long. Frémont's order directing Grant to take command looked toward the eventual invasion of Kentucky and the capture of Columbus, situated on a bluff along the east bank of the Mississippi. Such a move promised serious consequences, for Kentucky still professed to be neutral; whichever side first violated that neutrality by setting foot in the Bluegrass State risked alienating enough Kentuckians to drive the state into the enemy camp. Several days later, acting on information provided by a black man, Grant prepared to move on Columbus on September 5. Before he marched out, however, he learned that Confederate forces had already entered the once-neutral state and were approaching Columbus. After complying with Frémont's directive to cross into Kentucky and fortify the riverbank opposite Cairo, Grant turned his attention to Paducah, located at the mouth of the Tennessee River. A spy informed him that a Confederate column under the command of Gideon J. Pillow was on its way to the city. Reacting quickly, Grant notified Frémont that unless he heard otherwise he would follow Frémont's suggestion to take the city, then commenced his movement before any dispatch could arrive to restrain him.[41]

Before midnight on September 5, Grant embarked two regiments and a battery of artillery on transports; he then accompanied the makeshift force on its forty-five-mile trip upriver to Paducah. As the town came into view in the morning sun, Grant noticed that Confederate flags were flying in anticipation of Pillow's arrival. People were surprised, then chagrined, by the appearance of the bluecoats: "Men, women and children came out of their doors looking pale and frightened at the presence of the invader." Grant's force deterred Confederate forces from seizing the town. To meet the greater challenge of pacifying Paducah's residents, Grant issued a proclamation: "I have come among you, not as an enemy, but as your friend and fellow-citizen, not to injure or annoy you, but to respect the rights, and to defend and enforce the rights of all loyal citizens," he began. "I have nothing to do with opinions. I shall deal only with armed rebellion and its aiders and abetors." He elaborated in instructions to General Eleazer Paine, whom he left in command of a small occupation force. "You are charged to take special care and precaution that no harm is done to inoffensive citizens. . . . Exercise the strictest discipline against any soldier who shall insult citizens, or engage in plundering private property."[42]

It was a good morning's work: Grant returned to Cairo by afternoon. Days later Paducah came under the command of General Charles F. Smith, who had been commandant of cadets at West Point during Grant's years there. Smith moved upriver to take Smithland, at the mouth of the Cumberland River, giving Union forces control of yet another crucial river junction.

Grant's Paducah directives stood in stark contrast to Frémont's proclamation of August 30, placing Missouri under martial law and emancipating secessionists' slaves. Grant instructed his subordinates in Missouri to enforce Frémont's order, but it soon became the source of much controversy, particularly because of the emancipation clause. Grant's declaration at Paducah quelled fears that Frémont's directive would be applied to Kentucky, a most critical question at a time when the state's loyalty to the Union hung in the balance; several weeks later Lincoln forced Frémont to rescind his order. Stories circulated that the president was pleased with Grant's handiwork at Paducah, both in taking the town and in issuing his conciliatory proclamation.[43]

Within three months of receiving his commission as colonel of the Twenty-first Illinois, Ulysses S. Grant had demonstrated a rare understanding of the responsibilities of command. He stressed discipline and training to turn recruits into soldiers. He understood the wider implications of military movements and behavior, especially as they might affect civilians' loyalty to the Union. If he had yet to command a force in combat, he had learned much about how he would respond when that time came — and he had gained some valuable lessons while displaying insight and initiative. The results of this learning process made it now seem incredible that he had once struggled to obtain a commission. Before him lay the Mississippi River. He was ready to move south.

7

What I Want Is to Advance

●

WITH THE FLAG of the United States flying over Paducah, Grant pondered his next move. Clearing southeast Missouri of Confederates vied with securing control of the Mississippi as his primary concern. Expeditions to Columbus, Kentucky, and Belmont, Missouri, across the river from Columbus, resulted in skirmishes, leading Grant to conclude that Confederates were concentrating in the area. "The rebel force numerically is much stronger than ours, but the difference is more than made up by having truth and justice on our side, whilst on the other they are cheered on by falsehood and deception," he told his sister. Such a declaration, patriotic though it might be, represented a peculiar sort of analysis. His next statement reflected a more straightforward assessment of the situation: "This war however is formidable and I regret to say cannot end so soon as I anticipated at first."[1]

"Truth and justice" by themselves do not forge an effective fighting force. Training and discipline help; so does the proper equipment. Grant's experience as a quartermaster and commissary officer proved invaluable. He drilled his men and secured working weapons, transportation, and supplies. When Confederates arrested unionists, Grant retaliated by seizing secessionists as hostages; civilians who traded with the enemy also found themselves incarcerated. Black informants passed on news about weapons secreted away by Confederate sympathizers. He organized his command into brigades and elevated McClernand, already commander of the post, to head one of the new units. When soldiers protested that they were tired of firing blank rounds in target practice, Grant issued live rounds, and volunteers cheered as they mowed down weeds and perforated a target named Jeff Davis. And it was an odd moment when he encountered artillery officer John Page, son of the first man Grant had seen killed in Mexico some fifteen years earlier.[2]

Washburne returned from a visit to Cairo impressed by what he had seen. Grant, he told Secretary of the Treasury Salmon P. Chase, "is doing wonders in bringing order out of chaos. He is as incorruptible as he is brave." As Augustus Chetlain put it, "General Grant is doing wonders in and about Cairo in his quiet way." Once matters were settled, Grant would send for his wife and children; until then, he suggested to Julia that in light of Congressman Washburne's interest in his career (apparently the representative was already pushing to promote Grant yet again to the rank of major general) it might be wise for her to pay Mrs. Washburne a visit at her Galena home. Rumors of another promotion flattered him, but for the moment he was satisfied with his present situation, remarking, "Let service tell who are the deserving ones and give them the promotion." Yet Grant also looked over his shoulder at the possibility of being replaced, for plenty of officers of higher rank held inferior commands or were not assigned to any duty at present.[3]

Grant itched to move against the enemy. At headquarters he pored over maps, smoke from his meerschaum pipe encircling his head as he examined various routes southward. Columbus always attracted his attention. Located on a bluff at a bend in the Mississippi, it blocked Union efforts to launch an offensive down the river. Grant began to push for a blow against the city. "If it was discretionary with me with a little addition to my present force I would take Columbus," he hinted to Frémont. Rebuffed by silence, he could only complain. "I am very sorry that I have not got a force to go south with, at least to Columbus, but the fates seem to be against any such thing," he sulked, adding, "What I want is to advance." Yet he was unable to secure either the means for such an advance — his command remained ill-supplied — or the permission to undertake one. Delay proved costly, as the Confederates worked hard to secure what became known as the "Gibraltar of the Mississippi." By early November, Grant observed, "it was so strongly fortified that it would have required a large force and a long siege to capture it."[4]

Ironically, Grant had no sooner filed his complaint than he received an opportunity to move. Frémont sent several columns into motion to flush out Confederate forces under Jeff Thompson in southeast Missouri. As part of this offensive, Grant dispatched several detachments into the region; Smith was to move southward from Paducah. Grant, meanwhile, would block Confederate reinforcements from crossing the Mississippi into Missouri by threatening various points along the river. It wasn't quite the aggressive advance he had in mind, but it would have to do. Aware that the sympathies of southeast Missourians remained uncertain, he instructed a subordinate to prohibit foraging: "It is demoralizing in the extreme and is apt to make open enemies where they would not otherwise exist." As the expeditions set out, Frémont was relieved of command — leaving the department without a head, for all intents and purposes, for several critical days.[5]

As Grant finalized plans to launch his "expedition to menace Belmont," he contacted Smith on November 5, asking him to support the move by launching an overland thrust of his own from Paducah toward Columbus. An advance into Kentucky might make Confederate commander Leonidas Polk think twice about reinforcing the Missouri hamlet, allowing Grant to drive the Rebels out of Belmont and block any efforts to transfer Confederates across the Mississippi. The next evening Grant steamed downriver at the head of five regiments (four from Illinois and one from Iowa), a six-cannon battery, and two companies of cavalry, accompanied by two gunboats. Few knew the objective of the mission: Grant had said little to his subordinates, but officers and men were anxious for action. So was their commander. Although Frémont's orders clearly did not contemplate an attack against Confederate forces, Grant believed that if he did not do something, his men would become disheartened, even disorderly.[6]

So it was with some eagerness that Grant received a report early in the morning of November 7 that Confederates were indeed crossing the Mississippi from Columbus to Belmont, perhaps with the intention of moving on Oglesby. He had wanted to turn the demonstration into a battle all along, and now he had his chance. If he was thus exceeding his orders, he believed that changing circumstances gave him that right. Besides, a clash would season his men (and himself) under fire, and prick Confederate overconfidence. The misgivings he had once held on the eve of battle were gone. Quickly he decided to land his men on the Missouri shore with orders to attack the Confederate camp at Belmont, which was under the command of Gideon Pillow. Grant could not have planned to do much more because Belmont, located as it was below the bluffs of Columbus, was untenable without also seizing Columbus — an operation that Grant knew was beyond his resources. He had little more in mind than a hit-and-run dash against Belmont to disrupt Rebel operations. It was a decision, however, based on faulty information, for neither Thompson nor his fellow Confederate Sterling Price had received reinforcements.[7]

It was eight o'clock in the morning when Union steamers reached a landing, three miles above Belmont, located on a bend in the river that served to conceal it from Columbus. Quickly the soldiers debarked. As Union gunboats engaged Confederate batteries on the opposite shore, Grant formed his regiments in column, leaving five companies as a re-

The Western Theater, 1861–1862

serve to protect the transports, and moved forward. If he was nervous, he did not show it. By midmorning he had deployed his men along a road under a line of trees behind a strip of marshy ground, where they opened fire against the Confederates positioned on a low ridge to the east. Grant motioned his men forward; four regiments made their way toward the Confederate center, posted in a cornfield, while another regiment, the Twenty-seventh Illinois, swept around Grant's right, veered away from the main advance, and happened on another road that led directly to the Rebel camp, allowing the Yankees to outflank their foe. Grant's remaining units made their way though heavy timber, peering ahead to discover the Confederate position, guided as much by the sound of firing as by what they saw; in turn, however, the woods shielded them from Confederate bullets until they were almost on top of the enemy line.

Grant could do little more than to offer general directions: he watched from his horse as bullets whizzed by him. The Confederates were firing at will, and most of their shots passed over the heads of the advancing Union infantry — although a mounted figure was still vulnerable. This uncontrolled firefight soon bore serious consequences: before long the two northernmost Confederate regiments ran out of ammunition and gave way in some disorder before John A. Logan's Thirty-first Illinois. The battle in the center was more heated, as the cornfield afforded the Rebels a far better field of fire; however, Pillow preferred to throw his men forward piecemeal in bayonet attacks, whereupon Union riflemen ripped through their ranks with a volley. Finally, Yankee artillery began to make itself felt. Tennessee and Arkansas soldiers, disorganized and confused, seeing blue-clad units advancing right and left, abandoned their line for the safety of their encampment. In hot pursuit came Illinoisans and Iowans, determined to drive the enemy into the river.

Grant rode along behind the Union lines with his staff, encouraging his men, making sure that they did not waste ammunition — "Don't fire till you see somebody, and then take good aim," he once screamed — but could do little more. A bullet struck his horse, and Hillyer gave him another mount. There was bravery in all this, but little real command of events: Grant's staff officers functioned more as a headquarters escort than they did as instruments of command. Even his body servant, Bob, was along for the ride. Having made his "demonstration," Grant now realized that events were moving beyond his initial plan; he could not yet withdraw. Instead, he watched as his regiments pressed on toward the Confederate camp and scattered its defenders.[8]

It seemed a magnificent victory. Grant's forces had captured several hundred Confederate soldiers and six cannon as well as the camp and its contents. Their foe had fled, with many Rebels seeking protection by the banks of the river. It was exactly at this moment of triumph, however, that Union prospects began to unravel. Instead of finishing off their assignment and returning to their transports, the soldiers celebrated. Bands played as John McClernand addressed his men about their great triumph; soldiers ransacked the camp in search of booty and souvenirs. Grant had lost control of his men. And the battle was far from over.

For the Confederates were not finished. As the Yankees celebrated their triumph, Pillow rallied his broken regiments, while Leonidas Polk gathered a counterstrike force in Columbus. Prodded by his surgeon, Grant looked toward the river. He could not believe what he saw. Two transports, packed with Rebels, were making their way across the river. Captain Henry Walke's gunboats failed to deter the enemy flotilla; before long Grant's men found themselves under attack. Shells from Confederate cannon in Columbus flew across the heads of the Union soldiers; the sight of the reinforcements stopped the celebrants in their tracks.

Immediately Grant took charge. Whatever he felt inwardly about this turn of events — which reflected poorly on his ability to control his men — outwardly he projected the image of a calm and collected commander. First he tried to direct his men to turn their cannon on the Rebel steamers, but the Yankees were already beginning to panic. As the Confederates debarked, Grant, worried that they would seize the roads leading back to the landing, decided that it was time to leave. Ordering his men to set fire to the captured camp, he then directed them to return to the transports. Confederates emerged to contest their safe passage. Panicked privates shouted that they were surrounded: Grant responded that as they had cut their way in, they could cut their way back out. Most of the Yankees made their way back, a bit demoralized, a bit panicked, and very tired. The Twenty-seventh Illinois demonstrated an independent streak once more: in the end it would never make it to the landing, but continued marching on (at dusk it would be rescued upriver). In the rush to retreat Grant left behind a saddle (from his disabled horse), a mess chest, and a gold pen, as well as two horses. Rawlins galloped toward the transports, but Grant's servant, Bob, mounted on a captured horse, beat the captain to safety. Already on board were the five companies Grant had counted on as a reserve: they would not be able to contest the Confederate advance as he had hoped.[9]

At the steamboat landing, Grant supervised the boarding of his men, trying to make sure that the wounded were not abandoned (although in the end some 125 wounded Union soldiers fell into Confederate hands), and then rode forward to find out whether the Confederates were in close pursuit. They were nearer than he thought. He found himself alone on horseback in a cornfield as Rebel riflemen approached. General Polk, noticing Grant, declared, "There's a Yankee, if you want to try your aim." Suddenly Grant realized that he was in peril of losing his life. For a moment thoughts of his wife and family flashed through his mind. It was time to go. He signaled to one steamer that he was ready to leave — and none too soon, for by this time the riflemen were beginning to find their range. Grant galloped back to the landing and, as lead elements of the enemy began to fire on the transports, guided his horse down the bank and up a plank onto a steamer just as the flotilla debarked. He was the last man to leave the field.

Exhausted, Grant dismounted, entered the captain's quarters, and stretched out on a sofa. Soon he heard gunfire. The Confederate infantry was peppering the steamers as they pulled away, and enemy artillerymen might well be wheeling cannon into line. Grant arose from his sofa to watch; the artillery never did open fire, and before long the rifle fire died away as the flotilla moved upriver. With the battle over, Grant returned to the cabin to get some rest. As he entered, he saw that one bullet had come through the cabin and was lodged in the sofa where his head had been moments before.[10]

Slowly the flotilla made its way back to Cairo. At first, Grant remained inside his cabin, quiet and contemplative. Eventually he came out on deck to direct oncoming boats to take care of his wounded. He shouted the news of a victory to a newspaper correspondent aboard a boat that went out to greet the returning expedition. Although he judged the operation a success, he hastened to pull back other columns from southeast Missouri. Then it was time to take stock of his losses. Of the 3,114 men who started out with Grant, somewhat less than 600 were listed as casualties; in contrast, of the 5,000 Confederates engaged, 642 became casualties. For the rest of his life Grant persisted in the belief that he had saved his other detachments from destruction. Seeing no transfer of Confederate columns across the Mississippi, and mistakenly convinced that they had been in the offing, he was confident that he had halted them.[11]

Grant was pleased with both the battle and his soldiers. "I feel truly proud to command such men," he exulted the day after the battle. Certainly he was satisfied with what they had done. "We burned every thing possible and started back having accomplished all that we went for, and even more," he told his father, reminding him that to retain Belmont while the Confederates remained in Columbus was impossible. "The object of the expedition was to prevent the enemy from sending a force into Missouri to cut off troops I had sent there for a special purpose, and to prevent reinforcing Price." But the results went beyond that. "It has given me a confidence in the Officers and men of this command, that will enable me to lead them in any future engagement without fear of the result." He thought highly of McClernand's performance on the field of battle, and refrained from commenting on his speech-making. As weeks went by and Grant learned more about how the South reacted to the news of the battle, the impact of the clash continued to grow in his mind. "The battle of Belmont, as time passes, proves to have been a greater success than Gen. McClernand or myself at first thought," he reported to Washburne. "The enemies loss proves to be greater and the effect on the Southern mind more saddening."[12]

Both Confederates and Yankees celebrated victory at Belmont, although on each side there were dissenting opinions. The very nature of the hit-and-run operation, combined with the chaotic withdrawal in the face of a counterattack, understandably led many observers, especially in the North, to judge it a Union defeat. Among the general's critics was one of his own subordinates, William H. L. Wallace. Grant had explained to Wallace his reasoning for engaging the enemy: "He thought after he landed that if he embarked again without fighting he never would have been able to convince his volunteer soldiers that he was not afraid to fight." Wallace dismissed the explanation: "He had not the courage to refuse to fight. . . . I see that he & his friends call it a victory, but if such be victory, God save us from defeat." Grant withstood the criticism although he became more defensive about the battle, and several years later authorized the writing of a second report of the battle, predating it November 17, 1861. He also became far more aware of the importance of appearances in public assessments of military performance. "There is a desire upon the part of the people who stay securely at home to read in the morning papers, at their breakfast, startling reports of battles fought," he snapped. "They cannot understand why troops are kept inactive for weeks or even months. They do not understand that men have to be disciplined, arms made, transportation and provisions provided."[13]

Belmont was a learning experience in other ways as well. Grant discovered that he could lead men into battle. His personal courage under fire had never been in doubt, as witnesses of his exploits during the Mexican-American War could testify. But exercising command in battle was a different matter altogether. When Grant later spoke of the importance of

Belmont in giving his men combat experience, he neglected to add that it was also important to his own development. He had lost control of his men during the attack; his officers were not sufficiently apprised of his desire to mount a hit-and-run operation; he did not employ his staff officers skillfully, although in any case they were not yet equal to the tasks before them. Nevertheless, he had reacted well to adversity, improvised in response to changing circumstances, and was calm under fire. He also learned that he had to work harder to coordinate his moves with those of the gunboat commander, for Walke's failure to prevent Polk from reinforcing Pillow had proved critical in shaping the outcome of the clash.

Yet Grant failed to learn one of the lessons offered by Belmont. After flushing out Tom Harris's band in Missouri, he had realized that the enemy had as much reason to be afraid of him as he had to be worried about them. As a result, however, he often minimized concerns about possible enemy actions at crucial moments, allowing his self-confidence to exercise too much play over his decisions. Although Gideon Pillow's performance at Belmont was undistinguished, even flawed, holding him in such contempt left Grant unprepared for the Confederate counterattack precisely because he thought Pillow incapable of such an act — forgetting that Leonidas Polk was in charge. In concentrating on what he wanted to do, Grant risked overlooking what the enemy might do. Thus, the self-confidence that made him aggressive also left him open to surprises. It would be some time before he would realize the difference between being immobilized by fear of what the enemy might do and paying no heed to his opponent's options.

A few days after Belmont, Grant learned that he had a new superior officer. Henry W. Halleck, known to some wags as "Old Brains" because of his elaborate studies of military strategy, replaced Frémont as department commander. He would take a new approach to dealing with slavery. Frémont's August order, with its abortive emancipation clause, had sparked much controversy about the conduct and aims of the Union war effort. Halleck intended to remedy that. General-in-Chief George B. McClellan gave him explicit instructions "to impress upon the inhabitants of Missouri and the adjacent States, that we are fighting solely for the integrity of the Union, to uphold the power of our National Government, and to restore to the nation the blessings of peace and good order." Halleck quickly complied with McClellan's directive, barring fugitive slaves from Union lines — although the House of Representatives had already passed resolutions criticizing such action. Grant relayed Halleck's instructions to his subordinates. "I do not want the Army used as negro cat[c]hers," he admitted, "but still less do I want to see it used as a cloak to cover their escape," especially when Unionist masters were involved. A few weeks later, however, Grant revealed different priorities when asked to resolve a case involving a secessionist master. "It certainly is not the policy of our Army to, in any manner aid, those who in any manner aid the rebellion," he remarked. "The slave, who is used to support the Master, who supported the rebellion, is not to be *restored* to the Master by Military Authority."[14]

Such instructions comported with his own feelings about slavery's place in the war. "My inclination is to whip the rebellion into submission, preserving all constitutional rights," he declared. "If it cannot be whipped in any other way than through a war against slavery, let it come to that legitimately. If it is necessary that slavery should fall that the Republic may continue its existence, let slavery go." But it was too soon to attack the peculiar institution as a matter of policy. He knew that embracing emancipation at this early date would erode support for the Union among many residents of the border states while escalating Confederate resistance. He wanted "to visit as lightly as possible, the rigors of a state of war upon noncombatants." Such reasoning also guided Grant's marching orders for an expedition in January 1862. Soldiers should not take it upon themselves to interpret and execute the confiscation legislation passed by Congress, for the resulting behavior "makes open and armed enemies of many who, from opposite treatment would become friends or at worst noncombatants."[15]

At times Grant's concern about his men's behavior reached extremes. Once he instructed a colonel: "In cases of outrageous marauding I would fully justify shooting the perpetrators down, if caught in the act. I mean our own men as well as the enemy." But when civilians aided the Confederate cause, Grant responded with the same intensity. He ordered his subordinates to break up trade between Kentuckians and Confederates, authorized the arrest of civilians suspected of complicity in the practice, and threatened the imposition of martial law. Reports from Bird's Point, Missouri, suggested that secessionist civilians were firing on Union pickets; Grant instructed General Eleazer A. Paine to clean out the surrounding countryside with the warning "that all citizens making their appearance within those limits are liable to be shot" — creating a Civil War version of a free-fire zone. Soldiers should round up local residents and detain them at Bird's Point, "and require them to remain, under pain of death and destruction of their property until properly relieved." However, when Paine proposed to execute "the guilty parties on very short notice," Grant indicated that they should be tried by military commission. Once the emergency was over, Grant ordered Paine to release the prisoners and restore all property to them, including slaves. He did not want to alienate Southern whites without cause.[16]

Grant made sure to protect loyal citizens whenever he could; however, he concluded that in southeast Missouri "there is not a sufficiency of Union sentiment left in this portion of the state to save Sodom." In retaliation for raids on loyalists by secessionist citizens, he imposed a levy on Confederate sympathizers for the support of loyalist refugees — and taxed those secessionists "of Northern birth and education" an additional 50 percent, a sign of the intensity of his disgust with such people.[17] He wanted to keep the present conflict a war between armies, but he was learning that it was also a war between peoples.

Far more traditional were discussions with Confederate counterparts under flags of truce. Since October representatives of both sides had met aboard steamers on the Mississippi to discuss various military matters, including the exchange of prisoners. After what Grant brazenly termed the "skirmish" at Belmont (Polk declared, "Skirmish! Hell and damnation! I'd like to know what he calls a *battle*"), it was time for another meeting. Polk thought Grant looked grave and uncomfortable at first, although this gave way to smiles and pleasant conversation: "I was favorably impressed with him; he is undoubtedly a man of much force." After arranging for the exchange of prisoners, the two generals chatted away, agreeing that there was no place in this war for pillaging and plundering: it should remain a war between armies. But even in such meetings there were less serious moments. It had become somewhat of a tradition to conclude each conference with a drink. Before Belmont, Polk had proposed a toast to George Washington; only after his Union counterpart raised his glass did he add, "The first rebel." Grant now sought to even the score. He raised his glass, declaring, "Equal rights to all." Polk smiled, lifted his glass, then sputtered as Grant added, "White and black." Later stories would circulate that the drinking went beyond toasts, although Grant was not present at these bashes.[18]

The lull after Belmont allowed Grant time to get better acquainted with Charles F. Smith. During Grant's years at West Point, Smith had been the commandant of cadets, and the brigadier general had not outworn the cadet's admiration for the commandant. At first Grant found it difficult to issue orders to Smith, until Smith made it clear that there should be no awkwardness between the two men. Nevertheless, as much because of these old emotional ties as because Smith was a combat-hardened professional soldier, Grant relied on him. Smith provided a welcome respite from the often eager, always ambitious, and sometimes fault-finding John McClernand, although Grant had praised the Illinois politician's performance under fire at Belmont.[19]

Halleck's appointment thwarted a plan by Grant and McClernand for unifying the area south of Cairo and Paducah with an eye toward offensive operations; a month later, however, Halleck redrew the boundaries of Grant's command to achieve the same end, retitling it the District of Cairo. To help handle his new responsibilities, Grant significantly enlarged his staff. The most important addition was Colonel Joseph D. Webster, a former artillerist, who so impressed Grant both at Belmont and as an engineer that the district commander appointed him as chief of staff. There were also efforts to remedy other long-term problems. After returning to Washington from his October visit to Grant's headquarters, Washburne lobbied for more attention to be paid to Grant's needs. Even McClellan inquired about the general's "wants & wishes." Grant thanked his patron, promising to repay his efforts by exerting "my utmost ability to the end that you may not be disappointed in your appreciation." But the shortcomings in supply, transportation, and clothing persisted.[20]

Grant asked Julia to bring the family for a visit: they arrived soon after Belmont. The general set up comfortable quarters for them in a house that Julia, however, thought resembled a large barracks. Cairo seemed desolate to her, surrounded as it was by water; nevertheless, she enjoyed the reviews and even traveled on flag-of-truce boats. Most of all, she detested the length of her husband's beard, which Grant had allowed to grow several inches below his chin, where it was trimmed straight across. Julia persuaded him to have it closely cropped; never again would he allow it to grow far off his chin.

If Grant acceded to this request, he did not honor several made by his father. Jesse took some satisfaction in his son's progress. "I know that Ulyss was never worth anything in business," he told an associate; "it's because he's all soldier, Ulyss is." However, he was always on the lookout for new opportunities to make a buck. He tried to use his son's new prominence to secure contracts for harnesses. Ulysses put an end to that, arguing that "it is necessary both to my efficiency for the public good and my own reputation" that he not extend favors to his father. Nor would he share plans for forthcoming military operations with Jesse, who relied too much on dubious newspaper reports for information.[21]

Soon Grant encountered difficulties of a more serious sort. Suppliers, eager to enrich themselves by negotiating contracts, were infuriated at his decision to let quartermasters and commissary officers purchase goods on the market to reduce costs. Steamboat captains were not pleased with the activities of Captain William J. Kountz, sent west to arrange for new arrangements for transportation; before long Grant could understand why. Kountz always wanted to discuss matters with the general, although he had full authority to act on his own. It was not a good time to bother Grant: he was trying to outfit his command and provide for shelter and medical care, all the while battling a return of the ague — which had become so bad that his doctor prescribed alcohol to keep its effects in check.[22]

What happened next was a typical example of problems that would recur in the years ahead. Grant, tired of Kountz's distractions, finally took his work to Julia's room. Rawlins stepped in and ordered the captain to leave the general alone; when Kountz refused, Rawlins threw him out. Kountz retaliated by spreading stories that Grant was a drunk. The captain was picking up on rumors spread by local contractors, already upset with Grant, and by people whose trading practices had come under suspicion at Grant's headquarters when evidence surfaced that some people were trading with the enemy.[23]

These stories of Grant's intemperance had reached Washington even before Kountz began to spread them. One Galena resident returned from a trip to St. Louis in mid-December and told Washburne that perhaps it was time to check with Rawlins. Washburne did so. Replying at length, Rawlins heatedly denied the charge. On several occasions he had seen Grant take a glass of champagne in company with friends, adding that before Belmont a physician had advised him to drink two glasses of beer or ale daily to counter the ague — a treatment Grant judged ineffective: "But no man can say that at anytime since I have been with him has he drank liquor enough to in the slightest unfit him for business, or make it manifest in his words or actions." Rawlins told Washburne that he had become completely devoted to Grant ("I love him as I love a father," he wrote, a particularly revealing passage in light of Rawlins's attitude about his actual father), but should the general "at any time become a intemperate man or an habitual drunkard," he would leave Grant's staff or resign. Before Rawlins mailed the letter, he showed it to Grant, who responded, "Right; exactly right. Send it by all means."[24]

This letter probably arrived just in time to ease Washburne's mind, for by the beginning of 1862 the rumors had reached the ear of the president. William Bross, an editor for the *Chicago Tribune* who was disgruntled by

Grant's treatment of him, forwarded allegations to Secretary of War Simon Cameron, who in turn passed them on to Lincoln. To read reports that Grant had been intoxicated on flag-of-truce boats was bad enough; but the underlying motive for these accusations became apparent in the anonymous letter that accompanied the editor's missive: "Until we can secure pure men in habits and men without secesh wives with their own little slaves to wait upon them, which is a fact here in this camp with Mrs. Grant, our country is lost." The president told Cameron to refer the package to Washburne.[25]

And so Ulysses S. Grant realized he would never fully leave his past behind him. Any time he offended someone, that someone was sure to whisper that the general was a drunkard. In fact, although Grant occasionally consumed alcoholic beverages, there was no cause for alarm. At best his spells of sickness (and the treatments prescribed for them) lent some credence to such tales. Rawlins, whose fierce commitment to abstinence was already becoming legendary, expressed no objection to the medicinal use of alcohol. However, he concluded that henceforth he must protect Grant from the temptations of alcohol, because even a drink or two would tend to substantiate rumors of a bender — and Lincoln and other top administration officials would keep an ear open to such reports.

Local boatmen found it impossible to deal with Kountz. Because Grant needed as much water transportation at reasonable rates as he could secure, the captain's behavior threatened the continued progress of military operations. Finally, Grant placed Kountz under arrest.[26]

The incident highlighted Grant's problems in outfitting his command for action. He still lacked transportation; the weapons issued to his command proved flawed or inferior; there were not enough uniforms to clothe his men properly, and what they did wear was substandard. Investigations revealed that a quartermaster was engaged in suspicious activities; Grant had to look into such matters.[27]

Throughout January Grant impatiently waited to advance. Halleck, however, seemed content with employing his forces to feint at enemy positions, thus diverting attention from the advance of one of Don Carlos Buell's columns, under the command of George H. Thomas, into central Kentucky. Grant carried out his mission without a hitch, threatening Confederate positions in western Tennessee. He dictated misleading dispatches to the newspapers, secure in the knowledge that enemy spies would report such information, and rode across the countryside assessing terrain with future operations in mind. He wondered out loud what Halleck would think if he just happened to stumble into another skirmish just big enough to capture Columbus; he believed that "sloshing about in mud, rain, sleet and snow" to no apparent purpose "is not war."[28]

Information gleaned from these expeditions suggested to Grant the possibility of exploiting the river network to strike a blow at the Confederate center. The Tennessee and Cumberland rivers flow rather close together as they cross the Kentucky-Tennessee border on the way to emptying into the Ohio River to the north. To fend off Union offensives along these rivers, the Confederates had erected two forts. Fort Donelson, on the west bank of the Cumberland, was just north of the town of Dover, while some ten miles to the west Fort Henry stood on the east bank of the Tennessee. A third fort, Fort Heiman, was under construction across the river from Fort Henry. Although these forts were placed to defend against a Union offensive along the rivers, their presence also drew attention to that area.

A successful offensive against these forts would mean that instead of taking Columbus by direct assault, Union forces would outflank it, forcing the Confederates to give it up without a fight. This, in turn, would open up the Mississippi for future advances southward toward Memphis. Union occupation of these forts would also render Nashville vulnerable to capture, which in turn would force Confederate forces in central Kentucky to evacuate the state or risk being cut off. Thus, with one blow, Grant could achieve two objectives, each hitherto the target of separate offensives that had yet to get off the ground because Halleck and Buell, each reluctant to cooperate with the other or to move out on their own, were struggling to gain the upper hand with McClellan and the administration. After reviewing the correspondence between Buell, Halleck, and McClellan, Lincoln could not conceal his exasperation: "As everywhere else, nothing can be done."[29]

Returning from his foray down the Tennessee, Smith reported that Heiman and Henry were vulnerable to attack. Grant, who put great store by his old commandant's suggestions, grew eager for a fight. "I believe there is no portion of our whole army better prepared to contest a battle . . . and I am very much mistaken if I have not got the confidence of officers and men," he told his sister. Noting that his army now was larger than any force under Winfield Scott's command in Mexico, he told the folks in Covington that he might not be able to write much for a while, but that Julia and the children might soon come for a visit — leaving Grant to concentrate on preparing for the offensive. Then he traveled to Halleck's headquarters in St. Louis.[30]

Grant was not the only person to look longingly on the trio of Confederate forts. Halleck had long contemplated a thrust down the rivers, but only when he was ready. Grant was ready. When he met with Halleck, however, the icy and uncomprehending stare and utter disdain of his superior unnerved Grant, who proceeded to stumble through his proposals before Halleck cut him off "as if my plan was preposterous." Halleck took the bumbling interview as additional evidence that Grant was not the man for the job, but Grant persisted in his requests to advance. Returning to Cairo on January 28, he immediately telegraphed Halleck, asking permission to attack Fort Henry; the next day he sent a longer letter arguing that a move south would boost the morale of his men — and (although he did not say it) his own. He persuaded his naval counterpart, Flag Officer Andrew Hull Foote, to make a similar suggestion, evidently hoping that Halleck might pay more attention to a veteran seadog than to a discredited army captain.[31]

He was right. Halleck gave Grant the go-ahead, in part because Lincoln, frustrated at the inertia of the Union armies, had just issued an order calling on all armies to advance by Washington's birthday. Of even greater urgency was a report from McClellan (an incorrect one, as it turned out) that P. G. T. Beauregard, the hero of Fort Sumter, was on his way west at the head of fifteen regiments. (In fact, Beauregard alone was heading to Columbus, although his transfer west suggested its importance to the Confederacy.)[32]

Halleck's permission arrived just in time. Grant had returned to Cairo to discover that Captain Kountz was trying to haul him up before a court-martial on charges of drunkenness the previous December. John McClernand seemed to be acting on Kountz's behalf, lending a certain darkness to the whole affair: it was widely rumored that McClernand was trying to pull strings with his friend the president to secure an independent command. Kountz's lurid charges were rooted in malice and revenge; his connection to McClernand might prove most illuminating, but now was not the time to respond. Instead, Grant hastened to complete his preparations, eager to escape the intrigue, scandal, and corruption of the Cairo area and do what a soldier was supposed to do: fight.[33]

Grant hoped to start south on February 2, but delays set his timetable back a day, and the expedition did not depart until the evening of February 3. As the headquarters boat made its final preparations for departure, Rawlins noticed that Grant seemed uncharacteristically anxious. There was still time, after all, for Halleck to change his mind and call off the entire operation. But no courier came, and before long the boat moved off upriver. As Cairo faded out of sight, Grant's spirits rose. He was on his own now. "Now we seem to be safe, beyond recall," he told Rawlins, clapping him on the shoulder — a most unusual thing for Grant to do. "We will succeed, Rawlins; we must succeed."[34]

Halleck had been uneasy from the start of Grant's expedition. He had dispatched to Grant's headquarters an engineering officer, James B. McPherson, a lieutenant colonel with a bright record at West Point and much promise. Halleck hoped that McPherson would keep an eye on Grant (and provide Halleck with any information regarding Grant's "habits") and furnish some of the skills Grant supposedly lacked. No sooner had Grant left than Halleck began to receive reports that the Confederates were reinforcing Fort Henry. Grant's columns might well be overwhelmed, and now Grant was out of contact. Perhaps Polk would shift his focus from Columbus to reinforce the forts, or even cut off Grant; perhaps Confederate forces in Kentucky would march westward to drive back the advance. Buell, however, stiffly rejected a suggestion to send a column toward Bowling Green to divert the enemy. Halleck believed the expedition was premature; he had wanted to wait; he would have preferred a different commander. Now it was up to Grant. Old Brains braced himself for news of a repulse.[35]

Matters were less exciting on the river although the expedition had encountered some obstacles, chief among them floating torpedoes. Foote had his men fish one out of the water. A sailor, attempting to dismantle the torpedo, suddenly heard the hissing of escaping air. All those on deck, including Grant and Foote, feared that it was about to explode. As others jumped in the water, the two officers scrambled up a ladder to the top deck, Grant beating Foote to the top. Then the two men looked at each other. There had been no explosion. Relieved, Foote turned to Grant, a smile barely visible. Why had the general moved so quickly? Grant, poker face intact, wryly replied that the Army would not let the Navy get ahead of it.

After sailing back to Paducah on February 4 to move more men up (he told Julia that being away from the forces downriver caused him great anxiety), Grant set forth his plan of attack. Based on Halleck's initial instructions, it was simple yet effective. McClernand's division, some eleven regiments strong, would land on the east bank of the Tennessee. McClernand would first secure the road between Henry and Donelson to cut off the escape route of the Confederate garrison, while Smith's column, debarking on the river's west bank, would march southward along the river bank, overrun the still-unfinished Fort Heiman, and then bombard Henry, supported by Foote's gunboats. Grant would stay behind to coordinate his columns. "I do not want to boast but I have a confidant feeling of success," he told Julia.[36]

Impressive as this plan might be, Grant never got a chance to see if it would work. The Confederate commander opposing him, Brigadier General Lloyd Tilghman, had decided that Fort Henry, flooded as it was, was indefensible. He decided to send most of his men to Donelson; a token force would stay to buy some time for their escape. The plan succeeded. On the night of February 5 rains reduced the road over which McClernand would march into mud, even as it worsened conditions inside Henry. Whatever chance existed for a synchronized attack sank into the muck. The next morning, Foote's gunboats approached the fort far in advance of the struggling columns of Union infantry. They exchanged shots with the fort's cannon; before long Henry was down to four guns. At that point Tilghman sent off his infantry, struck his flag, and surrendered to a cutter that, because of the high water, found itself able to row into the fort itself. This time the Navy had gotten in ahead of the Army. Before long a somewhat chagrined Grant arrived, joined Foote in dining with the captured Confederate officers, and then wired headquarters. "Fort Henry is ours," he informed Halleck, giving Foote the credit for the capture. Then, almost as an afterthought, he added, "I shall take and destroy Fort Donelson on the 8th and return to Fort Henry."[37]

Although Halleck undoubtedly was relieved to hear that Henry had fallen, he could not fail to note that Grant, now out of his control, was improvising on his own. His orders envisioned the capture of Henry alone; Donelson simply was not as important. For the moment, Halleck showed little concern about this, mainly because most in the Union high command thought Henry a harder nut to crack than its twin on the Cumberland. Nor did it seem as if he would keep Grant in command for long, for his proposals to McClellan about expanding and restructuring his command failed to mention Grant.

Grant did not anticipate any difficulty in taking Donelson. He urged a reporter to stick around for a couple of days for a better story than the fall of Fort Henry; when the reporter asked if the general knew how many Confederates were there, Grant replied, "Not exactly, but I think we can take it; at all events, we can try." But his intention to capture Donelson on February 8 proved overly optimistic. Foote took his gunboats back to Cairo for repairs, heavy rain continued to fall, the roads were still muddy, there was much to be done at Henry, and the men were simply not ready to move. More men arrived from Paducah, and, to expedite matters,

Halleck dispatched one of his favorites, just recovering from a severe case of the jitters, to take charge of matters there — William T. Sherman. Halleck instructed Grant to make Henry secure from attack; entrenching tools were on the way for that purpose. That achieved, he directed Grant to move east to take Donelson and "run any risk" to destroy a railroad bridge spanning the Cumberland River near Clarksville, east of Donelson and Dover, to sever Confederate communications. Some of these messages made their way to Grant quickly; others, including the instructions about entrenching, were delayed in transit. By the time they arrived, circumstances had changed.[38]

"I intend to keep the ball moving as lively as possible," Grant assured his sister. He seemed to be thriving. "You have no conception of the amount of labor I have to perform," he continued. "Your plain brother however has, as yet, had no reason to feel himself unequal to the task and fully believes that he will carry a successful campaign." After consulting with his commanders, he decided not to wait for more reinforcements, but to push on, declaring, "Let us go by all means; the sooner, the better." He awaited the return of Foote's gunboats before he set out for Donelson; in the meantime he welcomed his son Fred for a short visit, assuring Julia that he would not "take him into danger."[39]

It was not until February 12 that the expedition got under way. The soldiers welcomed the return to dry land, and as the weather grew warm, they discarded blankets and overcoats. Grant rode in front, his personal baggage consisting of a toothbrush and a clean collar; with Gideon Pillow in command of the Confederate forces, this campaign would not take long. When an army surgeon's horse, straining against his rider, attempted to move ahead of the commanding general, Grant called on the rider to hold up: "Doctor, I believe I command this army, and I think I'll go first."[40]

By dusk Grant's columns had reached the outskirts of Fort Donelson. He planned to encircle the fort, let Foote's boats blast away, and be on hand for the inevitable surrender to follow. But it would not be that easy. Contrary to reports, Fort Donelson was a strong position, its guns commanding a good field of fire northward on the Cumberland. And it was growing stronger every minute, for the Confederate high command had decided to make a stand here. Reinforcements arrived daily, and by the morning of February 13 more Rebels than Yankees were in the vicinity. They were commanded, not by Pillow, but by John B. Floyd, once James Buchanan's secretary of war, a man accused of transferring federal weapons to Southern arsenals on the eve of the war; Pillow was second in command. Awaiting Foote's return, Grant directed his divisions to complete their investment of the fort, and tried to divert the Confederates by asking the commander of the gunboat *Carondelet,* Henry Walke, to shell the Confederate position as he had done at Belmont the previous November. That night it snowed, and the once-carefree soldiers, now without their coats and blankets, shivered throughout the night. Only the news that Foote had finally arrived cheered their spirits. It seemed obvious to all that Donelson was doomed.

Grant arose on the morning of February 14 in a good mood. He joked with his soldiers, bringing up short one who was bragging about his skill in subduing a Confederate cannon crew by asking if he had hurt anyone. Only the twinkle in the general's eye gave away the jest. There would be no need for earthworks, so confident was he of the imminent collapse of the Confederate resistance. However, Grant was impressed by the formidable Rebel works; aware that most of his men lacked combat experience, he decided not to attack. That the enemy might attack him never crossed his mind; he was too intent on what he was going to do to give much heed to what Floyd and Pillow might be thinking. They had far more reason to be concerned about him than he about them; his contempt for Pillow was never more evident or less justified. As Foote's gunboats opened fire, Grant must have believed that it was only a matter of time before the Confederates surrendered, and, unlike the scene at Fort Henry, this time he planned to be present.[41]

Then things began to go wrong. As Foote's gunboats inched closer to Donelson, they came under heavy fire. Cannon balls pounded the gunboats, and before long all four boats were damaged. Eventually they limped out of range, with Foote wounded. If Donelson was going to fall, it would have to fall to Grant. Throughout the day he worked to direct reinforcements to the front, green troops all, while McClernand, stationed on Grant's right, stretched his command in an effort to cut off a final escape path for the Confederates in the lowlands near the river, where a road ran south from Dover toward Clarksville. Lew Wallace's untested recruits would hold the Union center, while crusty Charles F. Smith retained command of the left flank opposite Donelson itself. Grant had established his headquarters at a farmhouse to the rear of Smith's lines, in part so that he could communicate more easily with Foote upriver, although it left him a good distance from McClernand's division. He would have done better to have remained closer to McClernand while leaving Smith on his own, but perhaps Grant welcomed Smith's proximity and recalled McClernand's capable performance at Belmont. The deployment, however, would have consequences for the morrow. Night came, bringing with it more freezing cold. It would not be so easy to take Donelson after all.[42]

On the morning of February 15, in response to a dispatch from Foote, Grant rode over to a landing and boarded Foote's flagship to discuss what to do next. The general expected a long siege, for he was reluctant to throw raw recruits against fortifications. He could hear gunfire in the distance, but dismissed it as incidental; sure that the Confederates would not attack, he had told his division commanders to stay in place until his return. Foote had bad news. Offering Grant a cigar, the naval commander informed him that the flotilla must return to Cairo for repairs. Grant, he suggested, should lay siege to Donelson and await the return of the gunboats in several weeks. The general responded that this would not do. Before long the two men worked out a compromise, whereby Foote would leave two of his gunboats with Grant, who would entrench and await reinforcements before attacking.

At noon Grant got in a rowboat and made his way back to the landing. There he encountered Captain Hillyer, who brought him most unsettling news. The Confederates had attacked McClernand; the Union position on the right was giving way.[43]

Grant galloped over to his right flank, his teeth clenching Foote's cigar. His headquarters staff knew little of the situation; Smith, who was sitting under a tree when Grant rode by, hardly stirred himself as he promised to move at a moment's notice. At last Grant arrived at a clearing where McClernand and Wallace were trying to pull things together. "This army wants a head," McClernand, shaken and bitter, muttered; Grant, catching the comment, snapped back, "It seems so." As he heard out his generals, Grant's face grew red, and he crumpled some papers in his hand. But when he finally spoke, the words came out calm and controlled. "Gentlemen," he announced, "the position on the right must be retaken."[44]

Grant rode forward. There seemed to be a lull in the fighting, as if both sides were pondering what to do next. One of Grant's staff officers, stripping a captured Confederate of his haversack, showed it to the general. It was filled with food. That could only mean one thing: the Confederate attack was designed to spearhead a breakout and eventual escape from Donelson. Both sides, Grant concluded, were demoralized and a bit dazed, much as they had been at Belmont months before. Whoever attacked first would win the day, he told a staff officer, "and the enemy will have to be in a hurry if he gets ahead of me." Such had been the lesson at Belmont, where it had been the Confederates who had seized the initiative at a similar moment. Now Grant would show what he had learned.

Reasoning that to concentrate for an attack on his right, the Confederates must have stripped forces opposing his left, he immediately decided to order Smith to smash the weakened Rebel right. Meanwhile, Wallace would launch a counterthrust at the Confederates, assisted by as much force as McClernand could rally from his broken regiments. Even the gunboats could make a contribution, for a few shells from the river just now would buoy his men's spirits while dampening those of the enemy.[45]

As he issued his directives, Grant appeared calm and self-possessed. Only the wording of a hastily composed note to Foote betrayed his anxiety, for he confided that "all may be defeated" if Foote failed to order his gunboats to open fire: "I must order a charge to save appearances." The general rode along the lines, telling his men that the Confederates were retreating and that it was time to attack. He galloped over to tell Smith to drive ahead, then returned to the right, rallied more men, and urged Wallace and McClernand to press forward. The confused and tired Confederates, unable to exploit their hard-won opportunity, slowly pulled back; soon news came that Smith had breached the works in front of Donelson, taking them away from Confederates who had hastily returned after receiving orders that countermanded previous instructions to move southward along the escape route.[46]

Although preoccupied with stabilizing his lines and preparing a counterattack, Grant was not blind to the carnage around him. When he saw a wounded Union lieutenant struggling to offer the Confederate lying next to him a drink from his canteen, he borrowed a flask of brandy from a staff officer, dismounted, and gave each man a drink. The Confederate whispered his thanks; the officer struggled to salute. Grant secured stretchers for both of them, ordering the stretcher bearers to take care of both men. Then he rode on, passing more dead and wounded soldiers. Finally, he could stand it no longer. "Let's get away from this dreadful place," he told his staff. "I suppose this work is part of the devil that is left in us all." Watching the wounded as they made their way back to the rear, he was moved to recite a line from Robert Burns: "Man's inhumanity to man/makes countless thousands mourn." Finally he returned to headquarters to see what tomorrow would bring.[47]

Tomorrow came early for Grant. He passed the night at a farmhouse behind Smith's lines and struggled to get some sleep, but was foiled by repeated interruptions. First he interrogated the captured servant of a Confederate officer, who told him that groups of Confederates were leaving Donelson. In response, Grant directed Smith to attack at dawn. Then he went back to bed, but only for a moment. Just after three in the morning,

Smith rode up to the farmhouse with something for the general. Outside a Confederate courier, bearing a white flag of truce, waited. Grant pulled on his clothes, then read what Smith had handed him. It was a dispatch, signed by his old friend, Simon Buckner, who was now in command of the garrison at Donelson. However puzzled Grant may have been by this (where were Floyd and Pillow?), he was pleased by the contents of the note. Only twelve hours earlier all had seemed lost for the Union, and now Buckner was requesting an armistice until noon and asking Grant what terms he would offer for the surrender of Fort Donelson. "What answer shall I send to this, General?" Grant asked his old instructor.

Smith's answer was swift and to the point: "No terms to the damned Rebels!"

Smiling, Grant sat down to compose a reply. When he was finished, he read it to Smith and the other officers present. How would this do?

> Sir: Yours of this date proposing Armistice, and appointment of commissioners, to settle terms of capitulation is just received. No terms except unconditional and immediate surrender can be accepted. I propose to move immediately upon your works.

Smith, noting the ability of his former student to turn a phrase, heartily approved, whereupon Grant recopied it. Smith handed the reply to the waiting Confederate courier. No sooner had the message bearer ridden away than Grant went back to work to prepare to attack at daybreak. Time was of the essence, for already there was a noticeable flow of escapees from the Confederate lines. But there was no need for more bloodshed, for Buckner notified Grant that he would "accept the ungenerous and unchivalrous terms which you propose." White flags went up along the Confederate lines. Fort Donelson had fallen.[48]

In the morning Grant met Buckner at a village tavern in Dover. The Union commander smoked as he chatted with his Confederate counterpart. It had been eight years since the two had last met, under very different circumstances, in New York. Grant allowed his new prisoners to draw rations. While he agreed to permit Confederate officers to take with them those slaves who served as their personal body servants, he told Buckner that other black slaves were now contraband of war: "We want laborers. Let the Negroes work for us." Then Grant inquired about the whereabouts of Floyd and Pillow. Buckner related a hilarious account of how both men, afraid of what might happen to them if they should fall into Union hands, had hurriedly handed over command to Buckner before making their escape. Grant must have smiled: it was just like Pillow. Both generals then returned to their commands to implement the terms of the surrender. Several hours later, Buckner boarded Grant's headquarters steamer to discuss final arrangements. As the meeting broke up, Grant drew Buckner aside and, remarking that Buckner might be in need of assistance, offered his prisoner what was in his purse. At once what remained of Buckner's hostility evaporated: Sam Grant never forgot either a favor or a friend in need.[49]

There was no formal surrender of the Confederate garrison. Grant believed that such a ceremony, with Buckner handing over his sword, would needlessly humiliate the defeated. After all, he hoped that someday they could be countrymen again. Moving the prisoners north took days; Grant made sure that his men did not mock the captives. Surrender was punishment enough.

As the news of the surrender spread, the reaction of several of Grant's superiors might have reminded an observer of the adage that while defeat was an orphan, victory had a thousand fathers. People, including McClellan and Halleck, scrambled to take credit for it just as Floyd and Pillow had fallen over each other trying to leave Donelson. In later years, who exactly devised the plan to attack the river forts became a point of controversy. Many would claim to have been the first to single out their significance, as if this alone was sufficient to earn the credit for their capture. In fact, the importance of the region was patently obvious to everyone, including the Confederates, who had built the forts for precisely that reason and thus ironically attracted notice to the area. Whatever the merits of this discussion, it was essentially moot. Grant's desire to move against the forts was original with him, he was the one who pressed to put it into operation, and it was he who directed the operations that resulted in the surrender of the Confederate garrison. He was Useless Grant no longer: now the malleable initials stood for "Unconditional Surrender" Grant.

8

Under a Cloud

●

GRANT HAD LITTLE TIME for celebration. Prisoners had to be shipped north; his command needed to be refitted; provisions had to be made to take care of the wounded. News arrived that the Confederates had evacuated Clarksville, some twenty-five miles east of Dover, and less than fifty miles northwest of Nashville itself. Grant had advanced on the former with an eye on the latter, and hinted to Halleck that he was ready to push southward. It looked as if the Confederacy was beginning to crumble. "My impression is that I shall have one hard battle more to fight and will find easy sailing after that," he told Julia. "No telling though."[1]

Grant was now a hero. Throughout the Midwest, people celebrated and cheered the man they had nicknamed "Unconditional Surrender." Newspaper accounts described Grant directing the battle with cigar, not sword, in hand. Many readers expressed their gratitude by showering the new hero with more boxes of cigars than Grant knew what to do with; eventually he pragmatically decided that the only way to get rid of them was to smoke them, and before long a cigar replaced his pipe as a favored means of relaxation. Old enemies were discredited: McPherson, back in St. Louis, informed Grant, "You will not be troubled any more by Kountz. His character is found out and I think he will be dismissed." And old rumors were laid to rest, at least for the moment; as one Galenan told Congressman Washburne, "Grant made a pretty fair fight for a Drunken man." From his post at Cairo William T. Sherman told his brother, Senator John Sherman, "Grant's victory was most extraordinary and brilliant — he was a plain unostentatious man, and a few years ago was of bad habits, but he certainly has done a brilliant act." And, as Grant soon learned, victory brought other rewards — notably his elevation to major general of volunteers. This time he took pride in the advancement, for it was earned. He even gloated a bit, injecting a note of sarcasm into a letter to Julia that betrayed years of humiliation: "Is father afraid yet that I will not be able to sustain myself?"[2]

Grant received reinforcements during the campaign, to the point that by the time of Donelson's capitulation he commanded 27,000 men. He reorganized his command into four divisions, headed by McClernand, Smith, Wallace, and newcomer Stephen A. Hurlbut. He was sure Julia was so tired of reading about Fort Donelson that "I shall write no more on the subject. Hope to make a new subject soon." The promise was father to the act. When William Nelson's infantry division, which Buell had sent to reinforce Grant, arrived at Fort Donelson on February 24, Grant sent it on to Nashville, convinced that the Tennessee capital would fall into Union hands on the appearance of bluecoats. But the fall of Nashville would only be a prelude to future operations. "'Secesh' is now about on its last legs in Tennessee," he wrote Julia. "I want to push on as rapidly as possible to save hard fighting." Memories of the wounded and dead still fresh on his mind, he added, "These terrible battles are very good things to read about for persons who loose no friends but I am decidedly in favor of having as little of it as possible. The way to avoid it is to push forward as vigorously as possible." It was time to move south. "I am growing anxious to know what the next move will be," he telegraphed headquarters.[3]

And Grant was becoming more curious about what role he would play in that next move. Would his promotion result in a change of command? It did not matter, he told Julia, so long as he was able to "remain in the field and be actively employed. Whatever is ordered I will do independantly and as well as I know how." He would even continue in a command inferior to his present rank — which implied that he knew he might well advance upward the chain of command. Although he thought he had done about as well as he could, he was aware that he had attracted his share of critics. He could not explain why two papers in Cincinnati, the *Gazette* and the *Commercial,* assailed him (although the *Commercial* had recently praised his generalship and highlighted his popularity in his army); he claimed unconvincingly that he was not "disturbed" by such remarks. Nor was that the only place where he might come under fire, he told Julia: "I am anxious to get a letter from Father to see his criticisms."[4]

Pressing forward, Grant hustled down to Nashville, arriving February 27. He expected to find Buell already there; the two generals finally met as Grant prepared to return to Donelson. It was not a pleasant encounter. Grant was eager to prepare for another offensive, while Buell fretted about holding on to Nashville. That, Grant replied, would be no problem: the Confederates seemed eager to leave the area as quickly as possible. Much would depend on the next move; Grant returned to Donelson to prepare for it. He also answered complaints from St. Louis about his use of steamers as temporary barracks, noted he needed more transports and wagons, looked to discharge soldiers who were judged disabled for one reason or another, and pressed for better rations. Not even poor health — he had been suffering from a severe cold for weeks, and as March began another headache struck — could stop him. "I have done a good job at Forts Henry and Donelson," he told Julia, "but I am being so much crippled in my resources that I very much fear that I shall not be able to advance so rapidly as I would like." And he was beginning to chafe at his inactivity. "I do hope that I will be placed in a seperate Department so as to be more independent," he declared, before quickly adding that he did not find fault with Halleck: "there are not two men in the United States who I would prefer serving under to McClellan and Halleck."5

Henry Halleck and George McClellan did not return the favor. While Grant had been marching and fighting, Halleck had been telegraphing, beseeching McClellan for a general of his own choosing to supplant Grant. He had settled on Ethan Allen Hitchcock, a respected veteran, but Hitchcock hesitated to return to the field, then thought it unseemly to supplant Grant after Donelson's fall. Halleck had responded to Grant's victory by rushing to take credit for it. Renewing his demand that the Western armies be consolidated under his command, he wired Washington: "Make Buell, Grant and Pope major-generals of volunteers and give me command in the west. I ask this for Forts Henry and Donelson." But Halleck could not offer what he had not accomplished, and his repeated efforts to bestow credit on others (and himself) to the exclusion of Grant proved unsuccessful. Lincoln submitted only one name for promotion. When the Senate confirmed Grant's elevation to major general of volunteers, Halleck discovered to his chagrin that Grant now outranked everyone in Halleck's command except Halleck himself.6

Chastened by Lincoln's refusal to recognize his greatness, Halleck became disgruntled. He began grumbling about Grant. As February came to a close he claimed that he had received no word from his errant subordinate in days (the records of the Department of the Missouri, however, contain several letters from Grant), and there was no response to his request that Grant gather his forces in anticipation of marching into West Tennessee (although Grant was doing just that). Meanwhile McClellan was pestering him for information about the location and size of forces. Halleck, growing impatient at what he believed was Grant's willful insubordination, fumed, "What is the reason that no one down there can obey my orders?"7

When Halleck heard that Grant had gone to Nashville, something snapped. Off went another telegram, this time to McClellan. "I have had no communication with General Grant for more than a week. He left his command without my authority and went to Nashville. His army seems to be as much demoralized by the victory of Fort Donelson as was that of the Potomac by the defeat of Bull Run. It is hard to censure a successful general immediately after a victory, but I think he richly deserves it." He had received no reports from Grant about his command, Halleck snapped: "Satisfied with his victory, he sits down and enjoys it without any regard to the future. I am worn out and tired with this neglect and inefficiency." Perhaps Charles F. Smith could straighten matters out.

McClellan might have problems setting an army into motion, but the words "neglect and inefficiency" were enough to stir him into action. He authorized Halleck to place Grant under arrest "if the good of the service requires it," replacing him with Smith. Secretary of War Edwin M. Stanton, who so recently had celebrated Grant's victories, gave his approval. Halleck welcomed the authorization and acted on it. Off went a wire to Grant, instructing him to place Smith in command of the expedition and to remain at Fort Henry. Then came the barb: "Why do you not obey my orders to report strength and positions of your command?" But this was not enough for him. McClellan would surely be interested in one more piece of information. Halleck telegraphed Washington, "A rumor has just reached me that since the taking of Fort Donelson General Grant has resumed his former bad habits."[8]

Grant was unaware of this last wire when he opened Halleck's dispatch placing Smith in command of the advance column. He showed it to Smith "in utter amazement, wondering at the cause, as well he might," as Smith later remarked. Puzzled by Halleck's complaint — after all, he had made such reports — he outlined his present situation and assured his superior of his willingness to follow orders "in every particular to the very best of my ability." But the contents of Halleck's missive left him in "a very poor humor"; he told Julia, "It may be allright but I don't now see it." That his father happened to be present at headquarters when he received the dispatch didn't help. Soon puzzlement gave way to pain. As he showed a friend Halleck's dispatch, his eyes grew wet with tears. "I don't know what they mean to do with me. . . . What command have I now?"[9]

Crestfallen, Grant carried out Halleck's directive. He sent Smith and his command up the Tennessee River toward the Tennessee/Mississippi border to destroy bridges; afterward, Smith was to establish a base on the river and prepare for future operations. Meanwhile more telegrams from Halleck chastising Grant arrived. Halleck twisted what had happened by explaining to Grant that it had been McClellan who had complained about Grant's behavior. This last charge hurt Grant deeply. He repeated to Halleck that he had made daily reports of his situation; furthermore, "I have done my very best to obey orders, and to carry out the interests of the service. If my course is not satisfactory remove me at once. I do not wish to impede in any way the success of our arms." He concluded, "I must have enemies between you and myself," and asked to be relieved from duty under Halleck.[10]

"You are mistaken," Halleck replied. "There is no enemy between you and me." In a way, he was right. Although eventually an investigation would reveal that a disloyal telegraph operator had disrupted communications between Halleck and Grant, nevertheless it was Halleck who had instigated this untoward series of events. Now Grant would not budge. "I have always been ready to move anywhere, regardless of consequences to myself, but with a disposition to take the best care of the troops under my command. I can renew my application to be relieved from further duty." Halleck tried to shrug this off, but when Grant received yet another missive from Halleck, this one delayed several days in transit, complaining about "the want of order & discipline, and the numerous irregularities in your command" in recent weeks — allegations offered in an anonymous letter to Lincoln's close friend, David Davis — he had taken enough. "There is such a disposition to find fault with me that I again ask to be relieved from further duty until I can be placed right in the estimation of those higher in authority."[11]

While Grant smarted under Halleck's rebukes, he did not suspect that his immediate superior was the author of his troubles. Instead, he believed "those higher in authority" were responsible — including, one gathers, Lincoln himself. Over the past several months Grant had offended several close associates of the president. Leonard Swett grumbled when Grant's crackdown on corruption at Cairo caught his friends; McClernand filled his letters to Lincoln with aspersions against his commander; now Davis, renowned as Lincoln's campaign manager in 1860, was passing on unsigned letters. Grant also recalled how his directives concerning fugitive slaves had come under criticism. As he had filed reports, he reasoned, surely a snafu in communications could not be the real reason for Halleck's action.[12]

As Grant waited for Halleck's reply, he pondered his future, "greatly mortified," as one officer put it, at Halleck's treatment of him. Once more rumors circulated that the real reason behind Halleck's action was that Grant had taken to drink again. The charge infuriated Colonel Webster. "It is a vile slander, out of whole cloth," he explained in a letter home.

"During all my acquaintance with him I have never seen him drink anything intoxicating but once, & then he put a little brandy into some medi-
cation to disguise the taste." Nor was Webster the only loyal friend. One afternoon a delegation of officers came aboard his headquarters boat. They
had something for him — a presentation sword. Four men, including two
named in the anonymous letter about irregularities forwarded by Davis,
had chipped in to buy it. Colonel C. C. Marsh of the Twentieth Illinois,
speaking for the group, commented that the sword had been some weeks
delayed in coming, but that this had proven fortuitous, "because at this
moment when the jealousy caused by your brilliant success has raised up
hidden enemies who are endeavoring to strike you in the dark it affords us
an opportunity to express our renewed confidence in your ability as a
commander." This proved too much for Grant. Never a master with the
spoken word, he choked up, then left the room to hide his tears. When he
returned, the sword was still there in its case, its ivory handle mounted in
gold. Grant looked at Dr. John H. Brinton, the army's surgeon, who had
found him on deck. "Doctor, send it to my wife. I will never wear a sword
again."[13]

But he would. Halleck soon found out that "those higher in authority"
were becoming curious about the hero of Donelson. Finally Lincoln instructed Stanton to ask Halleck for proof of his charges. The request came
in the wake of decisions to remove McClellan as general-in-chief and to
unify the armies in Tennessee under Halleck. Having secured what he really wanted all along, Halleck now hastily moved to exculpate Grant, reassuring "those higher in authority" that it was all a misunderstanding and
an accident. Then he wrote to Grant. "You cannot be relieved from your
command. There is no good reason for it. . . . Instead of relieving you I
wish you as soon as your new army is in the field to assume the immediate
command and lead it on to new victories."[14]

Grant had forced the issue by using his Washington connections.
Washburne possessed copies of the correspondence between Grant and
Halleck; the congressman's brother informed him that he suspected that
personal jealousy was at the root of Halleck's behavior. So did several of
Grant's staff officers. But there were also solid reasons for the mishap, including erratic communications and the intercepted messages. However,
Halleck had stretched the truth when he claimed that he had addressed
daily inquiries to Grant, for no record of such requests exist. Lacking trust
in Grant, Halleck had indulged his predilection for offering lectures and
issuing reprimands. Now, however, Old Brains had what he wanted. Lincoln had stripped McClellan of his position as general-in-chief; in the re-

organization Halleck rose to command of the West. In the wake of this triumph he wanted to avoid close scrutiny of his correspondence with Grant.[15]

Grant accepted Halleck's explanation with relief. He had thought highly of Halleck before their run-in and did not blame him for the circumstances behind the incident, especially after Halleck left Grant with the impression that he had shielded Grant from critics in Washington. Grateful for the reprieve — and convinced that it was Halleck who had saved him — he made ready to join his men upriver. Yet he also heeded Halleck's criticisms. He reorganized his staff and specified each officer's responsibilities. Dispatches became more businesslike and complete. And he began looking into what might be going on at Fort Henry. Grant had issued orders against pillaging and pilfering in the aftermath of the capture of Donelson, but as he moved south toward Nashville he was unable to supervise affairs in his rear. Although displeased by reports that captured goods had disappeared from Fort Henry, he realized there was truth to them; new orders that Grant issued after rejoining his army made clear that such behavior would not be tolerated. Nevertheless, he thought such accusations exaggerated, and pointed to "jealous and disappointed persons" as the source of much of his troubles.[16]

Grant soon found himself tangled in other difficulties. In the wake of Donelson's surrender he had authorized McClernand to make use of slave labor to fortify his new position. One expedition went far beyond Grant's intentions, seizing old men, women, and children while wantonly destroying property. Such acts violated Halleck's orders, and the captives were soon returned. Grant lectured McClernand: "It leads to constant mistakes and embarassment to have our men runing through the country interpreting confiscation acts and only strengthens the enthusiasm against us whilst it has a demoralizing influance upon our own troops." In the meantime he reminded his command that Halleck's orders concerning fugitive slaves remained in effect. Those slaves who had previously worked on Confederate fortifications would now labor for the Union. Nevertheless, the problem of refugees and their masters persisted. Some soldiers and officers alike disobeyed the order, while others remarked that if this war was to become an abolitionist conflict, "they would lay down their arms and return home." Newspapers criticized Grant for complying with Halleck's directives — at a time when Halleck was assailing Grant for his failure to do so in other matters.[17]

Already reeling from Halleck's reprimands, Grant had little patience with these new allegations. He had followed both administration directives and Halleck's orders. By sealing his lines, he had hoped to put an end to the fugitive problem; at the same time he had refused to return slaves who had been employed by Confederate forces, thus complying with the provisions of confiscation legislation passed by Congress in 1861. "So long as I hold a commission in the Army I have no views of my own to carry out," he informed Washburne. "Whatever may be the orders of my superiors, and law, I will execute. No man can be efficient as a commander who sets his own notions above law and those whom he is sworn to obey. When Congress enacts anything to[o] odious for me to execute I will resign."[18]

Congress responded to these reports and others on March 13, when it instructed Union commanders not to return fugitive slaves to their masters. Grant accepted the ruling without protest although it complicated the advance southward. More irritating was the continuing critical press coverage of his actions. Letters from Jesse offered a running commentary on the war and newspaper opinion. As the Cincinnati papers seemed to find fault with Grant at every opportunity, the general learned to accept it. At first he pretended that he was impervious to the barbs of reporters and editors; later he remarked, "I say I dont care for what the papers say but I do," for the "barefaced falshoods" had to bother Julia.[19]

Besides, Grant was suffering in other ways. He had been ill during the past two weeks, suffering from chills, fever, and "diaoreah." Discord between Julia and his sisters, as well as Jesse's behavior, also irritated him. "I feel myself worse used by my own family than by strangers and although I do not think father, of his own accord, would do me injustice yet I believe he is influanced, and always may be, to my prejudice." When it became apparent that Julia's sisters-in-law were mistreating her and complaining about how little she was contributing toward household expenses and rent, Grant, fed up with their "unmittigated meanness," directed her to leave — even though he had asked several times in vain about whether she had received money from him.[20]

Grant did not need these distractions as he prepared to join his command, convinced as he was that the Confederacy was already showing signs of weakness. "Great numbers of Union people have come into see us and express great hope for the future," he observed days after the fall of Donelson. "They say secessionests are in great trepidation some leaving the country, others expressing anxiety to be assured that they will not be molested if they come in and take the oath." He declared martial law in the region as a form of civil government and sought to protect the men against Confederate conscription. He noted with pleasure that several Tennesseans were joining the Union forces.[21]

Such signs of resurgent loyalty encouraged Grant to believe that the Confederacy was struggling to survive. "With one more great success I do not see how the rebellion is to be sustained," he mused.[22] With that in mind he headed south, determined to do what he could to close out the conflict.

On March 17, Grant rejoined his men. "I have just arrived, and although sick for the last two weeks, begin to feel better at the thought of again being along with the troops," he told Sherman. Others shared that view. William H. L. Wallace, who eventually would take charge of Smith's division, had come a long way in his opinion of Grant since he had censured his performance at Belmont. "Gen'l Grant came up yesterday & has command," he told his wife. "I am glad of it." Within days William R. Rowley, now a staff officer, reported to Washburne: "The Genl is in fine spirits and confident of our ability to go in & thrash them as soon as the weather and our orders will permit."[23]

Grant was happy to see that Sherman had joined his command at the head of a division of raw recruits. He recalled with appreciation how during the Donelson campaign Sherman had promised to do whatever he could to help Grant, and offered to place himself under Grant's direction, waiving any question of rank. "Command me in any way," he concluded. Perhaps Grant heard of the rumors that Sherman had crumbled under the strain of command the previous year in Kentucky, but he put those stories aside. Although he had not served alongside Sherman in the prewar army, Grant knew him from their year together at West Point — Sherman was one of the leaders of the Class of 1840, the senior class at the time Grant entered, and took credit for bestowing the nickname Sam — short for "Uncle Sam" (those malleable initials yet again) — on the young Buckeye plebe. The two men had run into each other again in the 1850s, at a time when both were struggling to survive outside the army. Nor was Grant oblivious to the political connections Sherman enjoyed. Sherman's brother, John, served in the Senate; his foster father and father-in-law, Thomas Ewing, Sr., was a venerable old Ohio Whig leader who still wielded political influence. They had made sure that Sherman encountered no difficulty in securing first a colonel's commission and then advancement to brigadier general. That had almost led to his undoing. After Bull Run, where Sherman performed adequately at best, he secured a transfer to Kentucky as second-in-command to General Robert Anderson, the hero of Fort Sumter. When Anderson proved unable to continue in command, Sherman found himself in charge. The pressure proved too much. Convinced that he was outnumbered, he called for reinforcements and begged to be relieved. Several observers (and a few reporters) decided that he was cracking up; rumors circulated that he was insane. Finally, after securing a transfer to Halleck's command, Sherman's nerves got the better of him, and he was sent home to get a grip on himself. Only now was he well enough to return to duty, eager to show everyone that he had conquered his fears (although he himself was not so sure).[24]

It was good to have a fellow professionally trained officer as a division commander. With Smith ailing — the result of an accident — Grant needed someone he could trust. He found McClernand irritating, and there was reason to doubt his loyalty — and no one could forget how he had panicked at Donelson. Added to that was the arrival of a new subordinate, Benjamin Prentiss, whose rift with Grant over rank and seniority the previous year was not forgotten by either man. The contrast with Sherman's willingness to wave seniority for the good of the cause was obvious. And both Lew Wallace and W. H. L. Wallace had much to learn about heading a division. For the moment, Grant kept McClernand's division downriver from the main encampment so that Sherman could remain in charge of the majority of Grant's combat forces.

The first thing Grant did when he arrived at the front was to acquaint himself with his army's location. Smith and Sherman had selected a relatively open area by a steamboat landing on the west bank of the Tennessee as an ideal place to assemble an army. It was located about midway down a loop in the Tennessee, some twelve miles in length, with another steamboat landing — Crump's — six miles downriver, where the loop turned eastward toward Savannah. A wide creek protected its western flank and emptied into the Tennessee just north of the landing, known as Pittsburg Landing, forming a funnel. Grant, trusting the judgment of Smith and Sherman, set up headquarters at Savannah in a mansion owned by a unionist. There he planned to wait for the arrival of Don Carlos Buell's 35,000 men. That seemed imminent, for on March 20 Buell's lead columns were just 60 miles away. Once the two armies merged, Halleck planned to take the field and lead an offensive against Corinth, a rail junction in the northeast corner of Mississippi. There the Confederates under Albert Sidney Johnston were massing a force of unknown size, although rumors placed it at over 150,000 men.[25]

Halleck placed Grant under strict orders not to bring on an engagement. The directive was designed to keep Grant in check, for no sooner had Grant rejoined his army than he started to drop hints about an advance on Corinth. This was all too familiar a pattern, and Halleck tried to make sure that his eager subordinate stayed put, for Grant reported that the Confederate army assembling in Corinth was in low spirits. He predicted that the town would be far easier to occupy than was Donelson. Halleck told him to stay where he was, wait for Buell, and fortify before moving forward. Such instructions curtailed efforts by scouting parties to discover what might be happening south of the Union encampment, and effectively ended notions of authorizing a reconnaissance in force to learn more about Confederate deployment, strength, and intentions.[26]

Grant was so anxious to move forward that he gave little thought to what might happen if the Confederates attacked. He concurred in Sherman's and Smith's decision not to entrench, deciding that the time would be better spent in drilling the men. This was no small concern: Sherman's and Prentiss's raw recruits had never seen combat. They might well cower behind entrenchments, and break at a run should their line be breached — at least Grant's experience during the Mexican-American War suggested as much. More serious was his failure to patrol the perimeter of his camp and to gather information about Confederate activities. Rather, Grant relied on haphazard rumors, passing much of what he overheard on to Halleck. Worried about the need to secure the river, he detached Lew Wallace's battle-tested division to protect Crump's Landing, located midway between Savannah and Pittsburg Landing. Meanwhile, Buell was taking his time to make the march from Nashville to Pittsburg Landing. Halleck tried to hurry him along while warning Grant not to take off on his own. No one was talking about what the Confederates might do; in fact, Halleck and Grant both believed that one more blow might shatter the Rebels' already fragile morale.

So Grant watched and waited. There was plenty to do at Pittsburg Landing. Soldiers were still violating directives concerning fugitives, much to his consternation; discipline was still suffering in other areas as well. Nevertheless, he was optimistic. "What you may look for is hard to say, possibly a big fight," he told Julia. "I have already been in so many that it begins to feel like home to me." As March drew to a close, he remarked, "A big fight may be looked for someplace before a great while which it appears to me will be the last in the West."[27]

On April 2, Grant reviewed his men at Pittsburg Landing, and he liked what he saw. Within days Buell would arrive; then it would be time to advance. That Halleck would be in the field did not seem to disturb Grant. But not all was well. There were reports of enemy movements, and Grant grew concerned that Lew Wallace's division might be attacked. Anticipating battle, Grant, having received more news about low Confederate morale, was confident of victory, so much so that he felt "as unconcerned about it as if nothing more than a review was to take place. Knowing however that a terrible sacrifice of life must take place I feel conserned for my army and their friends at home." Then on April 4 he visited Pittsburg Landing once more to check out reports of enemy movements. Assured that all was calm, he began to make his way back to the landing in a rainstorm, when his horse slipped, tripped over a log, and fell, slamming Grant's leg to the ground and severely injuring his ankle.[28]

On April 5, as Grant hobbled about headquarters in Savannah, he continued to receive reports of skirmishes outside his lines. Reports from Sherman made light of these incidents, and the division commander did not anticipate an attack. Grant, who may have heard stories of his subordinate's past propensity to exaggerate enemy strength and intentions, accepted his assessments at face value; they reinforced his own belief that the Rebels were still cowering at Corinth. Messages from Buell suggested that his lead division, under General William Nelson, would be up within a day; once Buell arrived, Grant was confident he could repel a Confederate thrust. Meeting advance elements of Nelson's command, he appeared "indifferent" as to exactly when Nelson should arrive, adding that he had plenty of men on hand. A colonel noted that it appeared that "if the fight was not monstrous," Grant was willing "to take all the glory himself" — a sign of just how frosty relations had become between Grant and Buell. But there was no doubt that the hero of Fort Donelson was feeling good about himself. "I have scarsely the faintest idea of an attack, (general one,) being made upon us," he telegraphed Halleck, "but will be prepared should such a thing take place."[29]

On the morning of April 6, Grant arose, sorted through his mail, and finalized plans to move headquarters down to Pittsburg Landing. It was imperative to do so, for he had just received news that McClernand had been commissioned a major general of volunteers, meaning that he now outranked all other officers at the encampment. Breakfast was at six o'clock, but no sooner had Grant sat down to eat than from the south came the muffled sound of cannon fire. Looking up from his cup of coffee, Grant listened, then got up. "Gentlemen, the ball is in motion," he declared. "Let's be off." He scribbled two notes — urging Nelson to move forward to the landing and notifying Buell of the attack. "I have been looking for this, but did not believe the attack could be made before Monday or Tuesday," he told Buell, suggesting either that initially he thought Lew Wallace's detached division might be under fire or he had anticipated the possibility of a more general assault, but had badly miscalculated when it might happen. Such notions ran counter to his belief that Confederate morale was low. Once more Grant's confidence, reinforced by Sherman's reports, had led him to overlook that the enemy might display some initiative. Instead of worrying too much about his foe, he had worried too little. Again he was away from his army when it came under attack.[30]

Grant and his staff quickly boarded the steamer *Tigress* and headed south to Pittsburg Landing. As the vessel passed Crump's Landing, where Lew Wallace was posted, Grant, seeing that Wallace was not under attack, ordered him to be ready to march at a moment's notice. Arriving at the landing at 9 A.M., Grant, crutch strapped under his saddle, rode ashore. He found a confusing and chaotic situation ripe for panic and defeat. Stragglers were making their way to the landing, some wandering in a daze, others running; when Sherman, attempting to rally one of his privates, had asked him why he was running, he barely caught the reply: "Because I can't fly!" Men huddled around the bluff above the landing; to all intents and purposes it seemed as if Grant's entire force had just run away. The Rebels had struck hard, catching many of the Yankees at breakfast and sending them reeling through the woods. Here was a disaster in the making. It would be up to Grant to stem it.

Swinging into action, Grant directed ammunition to be forwarded to the troops still fighting; he sent a staff officer back to Crump's Landing to hurry forward Lew Wallace; he did what he could to stop further straggling by policing his rear. Then he went to the front to organize his lines. This would be none too easy. Many in his regiments had never before heard a shot fired in battle and had broken within minutes; those who stood fast were finding it difficult to hold on. Moreover, the battlefield was rather flat, with fields and farms breaking up the woods: there was no single place from which anyone could make sense of the action, especially in the smoke and haze of battle. Grant made his way from division commander to division commander, cigar in hand, wearing a sword and sash. He looked anxious, reported one officer, "yet bore no evidence of excitement or trepidation"; other observers commented on his "coolness & bravery" under fire. One aide remarked that Grant looked "as though he was simply reviewing the troops." For the moment all seemed relatively under control: Sherman, already wounded, had finally rallied most of his men after his lines had given way around Shiloh Church. Other divisions were offering stiff resistance; only McClernand appeared "fussy and flurried." Noticing that Benjamin Prentiss's division was deployed in a sunken road with a good field of fire against the attackers, Grant ordered

Prentiss to hold on at all hazards. The general continued to ride back and forth, offering assistance and issuing instructions. "We'll find him where the firing is heaviest," Rawlins told another officer as they rode up from the landing to find Grant, and so they did.[31]

But where was Lew Wallace? Where was Nelson? Where was Buell? Immediately Grant dispatched staff officers and couriers to find out. A report that Wallace had arrived heartened him until he found out it was false. Meanwhile the firing around him increased, until an understandably anxious staffer burst out, "General, we must leave this place. It isn't necessary to stay here. If we do we shall all be dead in five minutes." Grant, concerned about other things, looked about. "I guess that's so," he finally replied. Several staff officers breathed far more easily as he led them to another position. But there was no safe haven near the front. As he galloped along, one shell fell to his front, while another passed under his horse; a bullet struck his sword scabbard.[32]

Aware that his lines would continue to fall back, Grant laid out a defensive position near the landing, and directed Colonel Webster to line up cannon and siege artillery hub to hub to blow away any final Confederate assault. He placed several regiments on guard by a bridge over which Wallace's command would cross, then directed other regiments forward to plug several holes in his line. Nevertheless, Sherman and McClernand continued to give ground. As noon came, the situation was not promising. Another message went out to Nelson urging him forward: "The appearance of fresh troops on the field now would have a powerfu[l] effect both by inspiring our men and disheartening the enemy," Grant explained, adding that it might "possibly save the day for us."[33]

Early in the afternoon Grant met Buell at Pittsburg Landing. Not setting his columns into motion until after noon, Buell then had come down to the landing ahead of his men. Looking at the swarms of stragglers, he sensed defeat. What were Grant's plans for retreat? Torn between relief at Buell's arrival and astonishment that he had taken so long in coming, Grant replied that he still believed he could win; if not, the men could scamper across the Tennessee on a makeshift bridge created from boats. It was a brief conversation, for Grant had other things on his mind, and Buell's condescending demeanor was particularly unwelcome.

Repeated Confederate assaults gradually pushed the Union lines back toward the landing. But Prentiss's men held on, and the bullets flew so thickly where they made their stand that the position was dubbed the Hornet's Nest. Grant visited Prentiss once more and repeated his orders. Then it was back to the landing to continue forming a final line of defense, although he speculated that it would not be tested. "I think they have done all they are going to do," he told Augustus Chetlain, who was now commanding a regiment. "We have fresh troops coming, and tomorrow we'll finish them." Yet there was no sign of Nelson or Wallace, and Grant failed to rally many stragglers. Prentiss could not hold on forever; but the Confederate offensive suffered a lull after Albert Sidney Johnston was wounded while urging his men forward against Union forces posted in a peach orchard at the extreme left of Prentiss's position. The wound proved mortal; P. G. T. Beauregard took command.[34]

Grant's concern would have been alleviated by the appearance of long-awaited reinforcements. Anticipating their arrival, he had decided to stand and fight. However, Buell's men had yet to appear, while Wallace's continued absence had become something of a mystery. Their absence became all the more pressing as the news came that the Hornet's Nest had finally given way before a final assault ordered by Beauregard, with Prentiss deciding to surrender what remained of his command. Webster's bank of cannon was ready; two gunboats, the *Tyler* and the *Lexington,* were also flinging shells in the general direction of the Confederate advance. There was time for a final assault. Did the battered attackers have enough stamina left in them to make it? Grant sat on his horse, watched, and waited.[35]

"Do you think they are pressing us, General?" Rawlins queried.

"They have been pressing us all day, John, but I think we will stop them here," Grant replied.

At long last, just as some Confederate brigades were scrambling to deliver a final blow, Nelson's lead brigade — commanded by Grant's childhood friend, Jake Ammen — appeared opposite the landing. Before long the men were being ferried across to the battlefield. Nelson rode up to Grant, saluted, and declared that while his soldiers were not yet trained, "if you want stupidity and hard fighting, I reckon we are the men for you." Grant wryly replied that he had seen enough of both this day.

Nelson's rookies were not necessary to check the Rebels; Webster's cannonade saw to that. But there was more blood to be spilled. A cannonball whizzed toward Grant. It smashed into the head of an aide, splattering Grant with blood and brain. The general, without flinching, kept his eyes fixed forward.

As the Confederates faded away, a lieutenant thought he heard Grant speak. He rode over to the general and awaited orders. But Grant simply stared straight ahead. "Not beaten yet by a damn sight," he muttered.[36]

With the day's engagement over, Grant began planning for the next day's battle. Earlier he had told Sherman that at Donelson the battle had been determined at just such a point of mutual exhaustion: whichever side attacked first would carry the field. With that in mind, he directed Sherman to prepare to attack the next day. After all Grant had been through, that order might seem remarkable, but he saw his opportunity and moved to seize it. "They can't force our lines around these batteries tonight," he remarked. "It is too late. Delay counts everything with us. Tomorrow we shall attack them with fresh troops and drive them, of course."[37]

As night came, so did a steady rain. Grant and his staff huddled around a fire. McPherson offered his grim report of the day's events, then waited for Grant's response. When none was forthcoming, McPherson spoke up, asking whether he should make plans for a retreat. Grant stirred and looked up at his aide. "Retreat? No. I propose to attack them at daylight and whip them."[38]

There was reason for optimism. Reinforcements continued to arrive during the night. Buell's men came across the river and took up position to Grant's left, while at long last Lew Wallace and his tired columns arrived. The *Tyler* and the *Lexington* periodically peppered the Confederates, but the occasional explosions did little except keep the men awake, forcing them to hear the moans of the wounded and the dying.

The night was an especially difficult one for Grant. At first he sought rest under an oak tree, but the rain and his pain drove him to seek shelter in a cabin on the bluff. Originally designated as army headquarters, it had been turned into a temporary field hospital, and long into the night surgeons performed amputations on wounded men with shattered limbs. Grant, his ankle throbbing, huddled there, slumped in a broken chair, resting his head on his arm. But what he saw and heard in the cabin sickened him, and so he hobbled back outside and made his way back to the tree, where he stood, a lantern in his hand, puffing away at a cigar as the rain came down. Sherman, still pondering the possibility of retreat, appeared. One look at Grant convinced Sherman that it was best to put aside his query; instead, he offered: "Well, Grant, we've had the devil's own day, haven't we?"

Grant looked up. Water dripped from his hat. "Yes," he replied, followed by a puff. "Yes. Lick 'em tomorrow, though."[39]

Early on the morning of April 7, Grant ordered his men to push forward. Buell's men did the same. The Confederates fell back at first, but rallied by midday along what had been the camps of Sherman and Prentiss. Once more Grant, his ankle so swollen that he had to be lifted into the saddle, directed regiments into battle near Shiloh Church. Some accounts even held that he led a charge, although Grant later dismissed such stories; he did, however, direct regiments to advance and rode just behind the front lines. Before long Beauregard had seen enough, and by midafternoon the Rebels withdrew. At first Grant contemplated a pursuit, but he soon decided his men were too weary; Buell hesitated to order his men forward although his forces were relatively fresh; and Grant seemed unwilling to issue orders to Buell, for fear he might not obey — an accurate assumption as it turned out. Besides, Grant knew that Halleck would not favor another engagement. A half-hearted effort by Sherman ended abruptly but a few miles south of Shiloh on April 8, leaving the Confederates to make their way back to Corinth unmolested.[40]

As the Union soldiers returned to their camps, what they encountered was sickening. Bodies of men and horses covered the field; rain turned the ground into mud. Grant later noted that one could cross an open field by walking on corpses. During the next several days, as soldiers returned to their commands, burial details struggled with an overwhelming task. Care as soldiers might about giving their comrades proper burials, when it came to the Confederates it was decided to dispose of them in deep trenches. The atmosphere was polluted by the smells of decomposing bodies. As they dug, dragged, and dumped, Grant's soldiers grumbled about their commander; members of Buell's command bragged that they had saved their buddies from destruction. When he arrived two weeks later, fresh from his triumph at Island No. 10 along the Mississippi, John Pope noted the "great bitterness of feeling and of expression" among the officers and men.[41]

Concerned about the condition of Grant's force, Halleck hurried down to Pittsburg Landing. "Avoid another battle if you can 'till all arrive, we shall then be able to beat them without fail," he told Grant. He seemed far more pleased with Sherman than with Grant and pushed for Sherman's promotion to major general of volunteers. As for Grant, the old criticisms soon reappeared. Although Grant took steps to restore order to his encampment, Halleck complained about the lack of discipline and compliance with established regulations and procedures. Civilians filtered in and out of camps, as did some soldiers; officers alarmed by the sound of gunfire discovered that soldiers were simply discharging their weapons. "This army is undisciplined and very much disorganized," Halleck observed on his arrival, and he held Grant responsible. "Immediate and active measures must be taken to put your command in condition to resist another attack by the enemy," he warned. Over the next several weeks a series of directives sought to bring order to the encampment as Halleck contemplated his next move; the general soon snapped that Grant did not comply "with the promptness of the commanders of the other Army Corps." One soldier saw Halleck aboard a steamer, pacing back and forth, "scolding in a loud and haughty manner" while Grant "sat there, demure, with red face, hat in lap, covered with the mud of the field, and undistinguishable from an orderly." Nevertheless, by month's end Grant thought Halleck "one of the greatest men of the age," perhaps because the department commander did not join in the louder chorus of public criticism leveled at Grant.[42]

As one battle of Shiloh ended, another one commenced. Between the lengthy casualty lists and the events on April 6, there was much to criticize; stragglers and panicked soldiers concealed their behavior by pointing fingers elsewhere. "I will come in again for heaps of abuse from persons who were not here," Grant predicted to Julia. He was right — but he also had critics at Shiloh. "Never was an Army more thoroughly & completely surprised," remarked one observer; another, one of Grant's officers, admitted that "there can be no doubt of our army being surprised . . . it was worse we were astonished." Back in Galena, local citizens discussed Grant's responsibility for the debacle. So did relatives of the dead and wounded throughout the Midwest; so did several politicians and newspapers. Among the charges circulating soon after the battle was one that claimed he had been drunk. Such charges were easily refuted. Staff officer William R. Rowley branded the story "an unmitigated slander"; others also reported that Grant was sober.[43]

With the benefit of hindsight, people would later say that Abraham Lincoln stood behind Grant at this critical juncture. "I can't spare this man; he fights," he reportedly told Alexander McClure, a Pennsylvania politician. But a cursory investigation of McClure's account of this conversation reveals it is a creative exercise bearing at best a tangential relationship to fact. The truth is that Lincoln most likely never uttered such a remark, for the administration was equivocal in its response to the rising chorus of charges against Grant. On April 23 Stanton telegraphed Halleck that Lincoln wanted to know "whether any neglect or misconduct of General Grant or any other officer contributed to the sad casualties that befell our forces on Sunday." Halleck might not be happy with Grant, but by now he had heard enough, probably from Sherman, to dismiss what had passed for newspaper reports of the battle. According to one of Grant's staff officers, "the conduct of the battle *and* all the *details* meet *his entire* approbation." Instead, Halleck blamed poor performances by some regimental officers, rejected reports that Grant had been surprised, and reminded Stanton that battles inevitably led to casualties. "General Halleck says the talk of surprise is sheer nonsense," reported one of Grant's staff officers.[44]

Certainly Grant did not believe an attack was imminent, and the intelligence offered by Sherman suggested little cause for concern. Halleck's telegrams prior to the battle indicated he was far more worried about Grant striking forward on his own than about the possibility of an offensive by the Confederates, whom he portrayed as demoralized. To be sure, Grant might have put aside his reservations and ordered Buell to pursue Beauregard after the battle; but Buell was doing his best to evade orders, and Halleck as well as Grant had hesitated to urge him on.

Several sources fueled the criticism. Newspaper reporters, led by Whitelaw Reid of the *Cincinnati Gazette,* had filed reports more notable for their color and drama than for their accuracy. Their dispatches emphasized the opening stages of the battle and faulted Grant and Sherman for allowing the Confederates to catch them unawares. A few stories went so far as to speak of soldiers bayoneted in their tents. Soldiers who broke at first fire echoed these reports to shake charges of cowardice, and were seconded by home politicians seeking to salvage the reputation of the boys at the front. Sherman snapped at "the dirty newspaper scribblers" and engaged in a heated exchange of correspondence with Ohio's lieutenant governor, Benjamin Stanton. Jesse Grant thanked Washburne "for your timely, truthful, and *able* defense of a brave & patriotic, but much slandered general." But the criticism continued for weeks. "It was a most reprehensive surprise followed by an awful slaughter," declared Joseph Medill, the editor of the *Chicago Tribune.* "I admire your pertinacity and steadfastness in behalf of your friend," he told Washburne, "but I fear he is played out. The soldiers are down on him."[45]

Grant soon grew tired of the criticism. It hurt to have his competence questioned, and the drinking stories embarrassed him (he told Julia that he was "sober as a deacon no matter what is said to the contrary" — itself an admission that Julia might have reason to suspect otherwise from previous experience). He was glad to have Halleck in command. "I hope the papers will let me alone in the future," he told Julia. "If the papers only knew how little ambition I have outside of putting down this rebellion and getting back once more to live quietly and unobtrusively with my family I think they would say less and have fewer falsehoods to their account. I do not look much at the papers now consequently save myself much uncomfortable feeling." He was sure that eventually everything would "come out all right," but it seemed like an eternity for a few weeks.[46]

In responding privately to criticism, Grant tried to claim that there had been no surprise at all. The papers "are giving me fits," he remarked; then he pointed out that he was outnumbered (which was true, although not nearly to the extent he thought) and insisted, "We could not have been better prepared had the enemy sent word three days before when they would attack," clearly an overreaction to the contention of utter surprise. However, he admitted to his father that he had not believed "that they intended to make a determined attack." These statements were somewhat consistent with his actions before the battle, and yet they betrayed his awareness that perhaps he was not as prepared as he might have been. Once more, in his eagerness to attack the enemy, he had overlooked the possibility that the enemy might attack him. It was the unlearned lesson of Belmont and Donelson.[47]

Writing to Jesse was a mistake. The old man saw to it that both his son's letter and those of staff officer William S. Hillyer appeared in the Cincinnati newspapers. Readers might scoff at the general's unsupported assertion that he had "the confidence of every brave man in my command"; they rejected the notion that only cowards were critics. Hillyer claimed that there was a conspiracy to besmirch Grant's name, and echoed his chief's characterization of his assailants and denial of a surprise attack. Other letters from Hillyer reviewed Grant's conduct during and after Fort Donelson although someone thought better of prolonging discussion of these issues in the press. As it was, what did appear sparked more criticism.[48]

Jesse's behavior angered his eldest son, who had no desire to issue rebuttals in the press: "Dont he know the best contradiction in the world is to pay no attention to them?" Grant was furious to discover that Jesse had shared private letters with the press. "This should never have occurred," he muttered.[49]

In the weeks after Shiloh Grant's trusted friend Charles F. Smith was gradually succumbing to the infection that had developed after his accident in March. Grant had missed Smith at Shiloh; he now realized that he might never again have his old commandant to rely on. Smith had defended Grant during the dispute with Halleck after Donelson. "Grant is a very modest person," he observed. "From old awe of me . . . he dislikes to give me an order and says that I ought to be in his place." On April 25, the day Smith died, Grant mourned, writing that "a better soldier or truer man does not live." Informing Smith's widow of the general's death, he spoke of his "great worth as a soldier and friend." He sent to Julia what he believed to be Smith's last letter. "He was a gallant soldier and one whos esteem was worth having," he noted. Grant still had someone to whom he could turn, however: "In Gen. Sherman the country has an able and gallant defender and your husband a true friend."[50]

For if Grant was losing someone to whom he had looked up as the model soldier, he was gaining a new friend, one who would look up to him and demonstrate absolute loyalty. Sherman's supportive dispatches to Grant during and after the Fort Donelson campaign stood in stark contrast to Halleck's hectoring missives; Grant knew that Sherman was even then just emerging from the shadow of newspaper criticism about his tenure in Kentucky in 1861, when charges that he was crazy became the stuff of editorials. As Sherman knew, the public was fickle (he once offered "vox populi, vox humbug" as his assessment); nevertheless, the attacks stung.

Sherman was reborn at Shiloh, handling his division brilliantly. In the back of his mind, however, he knew that much of the initial Confederate advantage in that battle was due to his underestimation of the enemy threat — overcompensating, no doubt, for his earlier statements about the large force required to conquer the Confederacy. He was forever thankful that Grant did not try to divert the flood of criticism directed at him toward the subordinate whose reports had contributed to near catastrophe. Returning the favor, Sherman defended his commander, denying that the Confederate attack came as a surprise and praising Grant's courage on the field. Grant was most appreciative. If the foundation of their friendship was laid before and during Shiloh, it was rendered firm by what followed.

Despite obvious differences in personality, appearance, and outlook, the two men had several things in common. Both had struggled to evade the shadow of dominating fathers who sought to control their lives: in Sherman's case his foster father was also his father-in-law, complicating an already difficult relationship. Both had resigned from the army and struggled in civilian life; both had finally found stability on the eve of the conflict, for Sherman had landed a position as the head of a military academy in Louisiana in 1859, only to leave it on that state's secession. Both had lived in the South; neither could be identified as an abolitionist, although Sherman's racial attitudes were far more defined and clearly prejudiced than were those of Grant. Both men had offered their services to the United States in 1861, yet they had held out for colonelcies. Political connections had resulted in each man's promotion; nevertheless, Sherman must have smiled in approval when Grant wrote him, "I care nothing for promotion so long as our arms are successful, and no political appointments are made."[51]

The new alliance was politically advantageous to both men. In posing as his friend's steadfast defender, Sherman doubtlessly appreciated Grant's decision to pass over the understated reports of enemy activity; Grant realized that Sherman had several powerful defenders in high places, including his brother, Senator John Sherman of Ohio, and his foster father, Thomas Ewing, Sr. As Grant had done his best to cultivate Elihu Washburne, he was not unaware of the need to have friends in Washington. Still, Sherman might never have attained such a close relationship with Grant had Smith lived.

Grant needed all the friends he could get. What he didn't need was a subordinate with ambitious designs of his own — a description that fit John A. McClernand. Early in the war the two men had cooperated, although once in a while Grant was treated to one of McClernand's lectures disguised as a dispatch. Now, however, McClernand, perhaps sensing that Grant was out of favor with higher-ups, began to present himself as the inspiration for Grant's successes. Grant was not blind to this. When he finally received McClernand's report about Fort Donelson, he was displeased with it, noting that it was "a little highly colored as to the conduct of the first Division"; moreover, McClernand claimed that he had told Grant to launch a general attack on Saturday, a conversation Grant did not recall. Grant noted similar mistakes in McClernand's report about Shiloh, adding that its comments about the performance of other divisions dealt with matters far from the division commander's field of vision and contradicted the accounts of those on the scene. Staff officers recalled that when Grant had visited Halleck to make the case for attacking Fort Henry, McClernand, who as the ranking officer took over for Grant, used his temporary status to issue orders and write letters offering his own opinions on what to do next. After the capture of Fort Henry McClernand had managed to describe the battle to Lincoln without mentioning Grant. When Smith had won promotion to major general and assumed control of the southward column in the wake of the Halleck-Grant fracas, McClernand had protested, unsure whether Smith had won promotion; otherwise, he declared, he ranked the veteran.[52] Coming within weeks of Sherman's generous offer to waive rank, and aimed as it was against a general whom Grant felt uneasy commanding, this protest struck a sour — and alarming — note. McClernand would bear watching.

In later years Grant would assert that after Shiloh, "I gave up all idea of saving the Union except by complete conquest." His remarks immediately after the battle suggest less pessimism. "I am looking for a speedy move, one more fight and then easy sailing to the close of the war," he told Julia in mid-April. He hoped that there would be no need for another battle like the one he had just endured, certainly not in the Mississippi valley. In anticipation of such a move, Halleck reorganized his command into wings at the end of the month. Four of Grant's old divisions would constitute the right wing, under the command of George H. Thomas, one of Buell's old division commanders. Buell retained command of three divisions, styled the center, while recently arrived John Pope and his four infantry and one cavalry division formed the left wing. McClernand took charge of a reserve of three divisions, including two of Grant's veteran units. Grant found himself named second-in-command of this arrangement, with the right to command the right wing and the reserve — a somewhat puzzling description of his responsibilities. Halleck ordered him to stay close to army headquarters.[53]

Grant viewed this nominal promotion as a way to shelve him. He termed his new position "anomylous" and believed that he was being punished, for "my position differs but little from one in arrest," a familiar feeling. If he was not given a field command, he wanted to be relieved from duty. Not that he blamed Halleck: Grant speculated that he "may be acting under instructions, from higher authority, that I know nothing of." After all, he had already earned his share of enemies. Just as important was that for the first time during the war he was operating under the direct and constant supervision of a superior officer. It was a new feeling for him — although in a sense it was just like having Colonel Dent or Jesse Grant looking over his shoulder. No wonder he felt uncomfortable.[54]

Whatever improvement there had been in Grant's spirits after he had withstood the first weeks of criticism about Shiloh was dashed by his new position, which seemed to confirm the attacks. "I am thinking seriously of going home, and onto Washington, as soon as the present fight or footrace is decided," he told Julia. "I have been so shockingly abused that I sometimes think it almost time to defend myself." In thanking Washburne for the congressman's support, he remarked that the only reason he had not written sooner was that he did not want to counter the increasing volume of criticism. Still, it hurt: "To say that I have not been distressed at these attacks upon me would be false, for I have a father, mother, wife & children who read them and are distressed by them and I necessarily share with them in it." He denounced his critics as disappointed battlefield scavengers, adding, "No patriots . . . would base their enmity on such grounds." It was as if people were telling the Ralston horse-purchase story all over again. Grant might appear to be impervious to criticism, but inside he was hurt and humiliated — and others knew it. "I should like to go to New Mexico, or some other remote place, and have a small command out of the reach of the newspapers," he remarked. His letters to Julia betrayed his frayed spirits. He snapped at her request for funds, then chided her for failing to write — although she was trying to correspond frequently.[55]

Halleck gruffly rejected Grant's protests. "For the last three months I have done everything in my power to ward off the attacks which were made upon you," he claimed, in what must surely rank as one of the most disingenuous statements of the entire war. "If you believe me your friend you will not require explanations; if not, explanations on my part would be of little avail." Buell and McClernand also announced their unhappiness. No matter: Halleck had things just the way he wanted them, and it was now on to Corinth to destroy Beauregard.[56]

Corinth was some twenty miles from Pittsburg Landing; Halleck should have reached its outskirts in a matter of days. Instead, it took over four weeks. Every evening the men threw up entrenchments; every day Buell expressed concern that his men were going too fast. Halleck accepted without question reports that Beauregard's force was growing exponentially. The entire advance gave new meaning to the term methodical; Grant later wrote that it was "a siege from the start to the close," although he was far less critical at the time. "No pains will be spared to make our success certain and there is scarsely that man in our army who doubts the result," he remarked. However, Grant himself had little to do with the operation. John Pope recalled later that the second-in-command found his "advice neglected and sneered at by those in authority," who made it clear that they wished Grant was elsewhere. At least on the last point Grant felt the same way. He would visit Pope's headquarters "and spend almost the entire day there, sitting about and lying on a cot," thoughts of resignation floating through his mind and sometimes escaping into conversation.[57]

By the end of May, with his army finally outside Corinth, Halleck readied to attack — when Beauregard, under cover of darkness, evacuated. At first Halleck and his generals did not believe it; Pope was convinced that he was about to be attacked on the very morning that lead elements of his force entered the empty town. "It is a victory as brilliant and important as any recorded in history," enthused Sherman. Grant agreed. "There will be much unjust criticism of this affair but future effects will prove it a great victory." He would not always feel thus. Later he recalled that "the trophies of war were a few Quaker guns, logs of about the diameter of ordinary cannon, mounted on wheels of wagons and pointed in the most threatening manner towards us."[58]

Grant had been making noises about taking a leave of absence after the fall of Corinth; members of his staff were beginning to inquire whether the general might be more useful elsewhere. Perhaps he would go to the Atlantic coast; perhaps he would be stationed somewhere in the occupied South; perhaps he would simply go on leave. He was worn out and depressed: "A few weeks relaxation would be hailed with a degree of pleasure never experienced by me before." To a Galena minister he remarked, "It has been my good fortune to render some service to the cause and my very bad luck to have attracted the attention of newspaper scribblers." Even his health began to suffer. Halleck had ignored his recommendations during the campaign; Grant recalled that once "I was silenced so quickly that I felt that possibly I had suggested an unmilitary movement." Grant was furious. After struggling to retain his composure, he sulked for hours. It was time to leave.[59]

He deliberated between seeking a new command and taking a leave of absence. Finally the latter won out. Halleck tried to talk him out of it; so did Sherman. Hearing from Halleck about Grant's imminent departure, Sherman hurried over to Grant's tent, where men were packing equipment and the general was sorting through papers. "Sherman, you know," Grant responded to his friend's query about why he was leaving. "You know I am in the way here. I have stood it as long as I can, and can endure it no longer." To dissuade Grant from leaving, Sherman insisted that "some happy accident" would soon restore him to prominence.[60]

Halleck provided the "happy accident." With Corinth safely in Union hands, he decided to consolidate his gains. On June 10 he returned Thomas to the command of his division, and restored Grant to his old command. "Necessity however changes my plans, or the public service does, and I must yeald," Grant explained at first to Julia. Only later did he mention that "there was quite a feeling among the troops, at least so expressed by Gen. officers below me, against my going." Once more he declared his gratitude toward Sherman for the division commander's behavior at Shiloh, perhaps an oblique way of acknowledging Sherman's role in Grant's decision, but to Washburne he chose instead to cite Halleck as the major influence behind his change in plans — although no doubt the promise of an independent command clinched the deal. When Sherman heard that Grant had decided to stick around, he told his friend, "You could not be quiet at home for a week when armies were moving, and rest could not relieve your mind of the gnawing sensation that injustice had been done you."[61]

Perhaps this was true, but at the moment the armies were not moving. With Halleck's permission, Grant established his new headquarters in just-occupied Memphis, after eluding capture by a Confederate cavalry detachment out looking for him. He had long observed with sympathy the impact of war on local civilians. "Soldiers who fight battles do not experience half their horrors," he told Julia. "All the hardships come upon the weak, I cannot say inoffensive, women and children. I believe these latter are wors rebels than the soldiers who fight against us." Before long, however, white refugees who had fled before the invaders began to return, "and seem to think the Yankees a much less bloody, revengeful and to be dreaded people, than they had been led to think." Pacification of secessionist civilians would be far easier, he thought, if their leaders could be silenced. "The feeling is kept up however by crying Abolitionest against us and this is unfortunately sustained by the acts of a very few among us." Soldiers stripped plantations of slaves, even though their owners were loyal unionists, thus alienating yet another white Southerner. Only through strict observance of the difference between loyalist and secessionist slaveholders could this problem be corrected; the occupation of the region by Union soldiers while restoring services such as mail delivery and implementing directives to conciliate the white population would regenerate loyalty. Most Confederate civilians, he told Washburne, were motivated more by fear of the consequences of defeat than by any love for the Confederate government.[62]

Such questions were presently being debated in Congress. Many Republicans were beginning to push for harsher measures against slavery and slaveholders. Aware of this, Grant took pains to make clear his own position to Washburne: "It is hard to say what would be the most wise policy to pursue towards these people but for a soldier his duties are plain. He is to obey the orders of all those placed over him and whip the enemy wherever he meets him." He stressed that soldiers' private opinions about policy should never affect the execution of their duties. Perhaps Grant recalled the criticism he had received about his decision to return slaves to plantations after Donelson; he did not want to be singled out as an opponent of such policies should Congress move beyond them.[63]

Grant would have a chance to test his views in Memphis. His early impressions of the city suggested that reunion might be further away than he had hoped. "Affairs in this city seem to be in rather bad order, secessionists governing much in their own way," he reported to Halleck. Before long he sought to impose his own order. After issuing detailed instructions for the proper behavior of soldiers to avoid giving offense to residents, he clamped down on contraband trade and established regulations for civil government, although he admitted to Halleck that he was acting in such matters without the guidance of governing directives. Several days later he warned the editor of the *Memphis Avalanche* not to publish articles critical of the Union occupation force; eventually Grant decided that newspaper editors had to take an oath of loyalty to the United States before they could continue publication. In reaching these conclusions Grant was far less concerned about the "freedom of the press" than he was about the ability of newspapers to shape public opinion — something he was keenly aware of from his recent personal experiences. On July 3, however, he went even further. Angered by persistent guerrilla warfare, which endangered his communications and rail lines as well as his men, he directed that secessionists in local communities would compensate the army for losses inflicted by guerrillas; any guerrillas captured would not be treated as prisoners of war. This sparked a predictable response: one Mississippian, infuriated by Grant's "fiendish policy," promised to retaliate: "Henceforth our motto shall be, Blood for blood, and blood for property."[64]

Such behavior caused Grant to reconsider his position on conciliating civilians. Perhaps there were a larger number of devoted Confederates than he had anticipated. It would not be easy to regain their sympathy; in fact, one might first need to crush their will for independence. These recalcitrant civilians and the sustained guerrilla operations, not the Confederate attack at Shiloh, persuaded him that perhaps this war would go on longer than he had anticipated and would require stern measures instead of conciliatory offers to break Confederate will. That he was willing to take such measures became apparent when he directed that families of Confederate soldiers and officeholders be removed from the city unless they signed a parole stating that they would offer no assistance to the Confederate cause. By gathering blacks to put to work on fortifying the city, he took another step away from conciliating whites who wanted slavery left undisturbed.[65]

Memphis whites were not Grant's sole source of irritation. Halleck had resumed lecturing him whenever possible. Grant warmed under the collar when he read one dispatch in particular. In reply to Grant's report of nearby enemy activity, Halleck, misreading the missive, claimed he could not locate the hamlet in question, chided Grant for failing to send out a reconnaissance, and concluded, "It looks very much like a mere stampede. Floating rumors must never be received as facts." Grant's curt response reflected his frayed ego. Halleck had not read the telegram closely enough; Grant had sent out reconnaissance parties; he did not heed "floating rumors," he reminded Halleck that "stampeding is not my weakness," and asked why Halleck was issuing orders directly to units under Grant's command, in some cases countermanding his. The blunt response stunned Halleck. Sternly stating that he would issue orders to Grant's command when the occasion required it, he added, "I must confess that I was very much surprised at the tone of your dispatch and the ill-feeling manifested in it, so contrary to your usual style, and especially toward one who has so often befriended you when you were attacked by others." More critical telegrams followed, and on July 11 Grant must have wondered what was up when he received the following: "You will immediately repair to this place and report to these headquarters."

If Grant expected another dressing-down, he was to be disappointed. Halleck announced that he had been elevated to the position of General-in-Chief and would soon leave for Washington. Grant would take over command of the forces in West Tennessee. He had not been Halleck's first choice: quartermaster Robert Allen, a boyhood friend of Grant, turned down an offer to take command. With Halleck away, perhaps Grant could breathe easier.[66]

In the spring of 1862 Ulysses S. Grant had proved once more that he was a survivor. He had overcome his mistakes at Shiloh and helped to turn disaster into victory. In the aftermath of the battle he had weathered criticism and stuck it out under Halleck, although just barely. If he was still under a cloud, at least the rain had stopped.

9

Enemies Front and Rear

●

ON JULY 17, 1862, Grant formally assumed command of the District of West Tennessee, a jurisdiction that extended from Cairo south to northern Mississippi. Although monthly returns indicated that some 78,870 officers and men were serving in the department, they were scattered throughout the region. "You must judge for yourself the best use to be made of your troops," Halleck lectured him, adding that Grant should be ready to reinforce Buell's army in middle Tennessee should the Confederates move north from Chattanooga.[1]

Establishing headquarters at Corinth, Grant reorganized his defensive perimeter while keeping an eye on enemy movements. Offensive operations seemed out of the question. The demands of occupation duty left time for little except chasing guerrilla bands, responding to civilian complaints, and restoring order. Inevitably this involved policing civilians' activities. When army authorities detected that one of Corinth's residents, Francis Whitfield, was receiving correspondence from the Confederate army, Grant placed him under arrest; when Whitfield declined to take an oath of loyalty to the United States, Grant sent him north to Alton, Illinois, to ponder his choice within a penitentiary's walls. He established headquarters in Whitfield's house, and Julia and the children soon joined him. Before leaving, Whitfield asked Grant to send a group of enslaved women and children south, where Whitfield's cousins would assume responsibility for them. As the slaves in question were neither adult males (and thus potentially military laborers) nor fugitives (already covered by previous legislation), Grant was uncertain as to government policy; previous criticism left him loath to act without instructions.[2]

Government policy toward slavery and secessionists was changing in the summer of 1862. On the day of Whitfield's arrest, July 17, Congress passed and Lincoln signed a second confiscation act, far broader than the first. It declared free all slaves belonging to Confederate sympathizers who escaped to Union lines or were seized by Union soldiers; all other property belonging to secessionists was liable to confiscation. Elihu Washburne informed Grant of the changed sentiment in Washington that spurred such legislation: "This matter of guarding rebel property, of protecting secessionists and of enforcing 'order No. 3' [issued by Halleck in November 1861] is 'played out' in public estimation. Your order in regard to the secessionists of Memphis taking the oath or leaving, has been accepted as an earnest of vigorous and decided action on your part."

Many Northerners, impatient at the pace of military operations, wanted action, especially now that George McClellan's campaign to take Richmond had met with defeat at the end of June. Washburne wrote to acquaint Grant with the lay of the political terrain. "The administration has come up to what the people have long demanded — a vigorous prosecution of the war by all the means known to civilized warfare," he explained. "The negroes must now be made our auxiliaries in every possible way they can be, whether by working or fighting. That General who takes the most decided step in this respect will be held in the highest estimation by the loyal and true men in the country. . . . If the constitution or slavery must perish, let slavery go to the wall."[3]

Grant's endorsement of the measure reflected his pragmatic bent. Confiscation would help break the rebellion; his experiences in Memphis led him to question the efficacy of reconciliation. "I have no hobby of my own in regard to the negro, either to effect his freedom or to continue his bondage," he explained to his father. "If Congress pass any law and the President approves, I am willing to execute it." Within days he authorized the use of blacks as laborers and provided for the impressment of secessionists' slaves. He instructed his subordinates to scour the countryside to secure blacks owned by secessionists. Before long he observed that if slavery was not yet doomed, it was certainly in trouble. "The war is evidently growing oppressive to the Southern people," he told his sister. "Their *institution* are beginning to have ideas of their own and every time an expedition goes out more or less of them follow in the wake of the army and come into camp. . . . I dont know what is to become of these poor people in the end but it [is] weakning the enemy to take them from them."[4]

Grant also cracked down on civilian behavior. He ordered the arrest of a *Chicago Times* reporter for filing an article "false in fact and mischievous in character." The correspondent joined Whitfield in confinement at Alton. He reminded his subordinates that should Confederate citizens prove troublesome, they were subject to arrest or expulsion, and that their property might be seized. Grant questioned whether these people should be treated as noncombatants: he reported, "Many citizens who appear to be quiet non combatants in the presence of our forces are regularly enrolled and avail themselves of every safe opportunity of depridating upon Union men and annoying our troops where in small bodies." At the same time, he did not want his own men mistreating innocent civilians. As he was riding about with his staff one day, he heard screams from a nearby dwelling; the cavalcade discovered a woman and her daughter fleeing from a Union soldier who was brandishing his musket and intent on mayhem or worse. Grant jumped down from his horse, grabbed the miscreant's musket, raised it above his head, and clubbed the assailant. "I guess you have killed him, General," Rawlins remarked, to which Grant replied, "If I have, it has only served him right."[5]

Wrestling with enemy activity was not nearly so easy. "Guerrillas are hovering around in every direction getting whipped every day by some of my command but keeping us busy," Grant observed in August. Guerrilla activity endangered communications, supplies, and occasionally lives. Determined to stop such behavior, Grant tightened security within his lines and restricted civilian movement. "I am decidedly in favor of turning all discontented citizens within our lines out South," he told Halleck; the new general-in-chief concurred, advising Grant to "clean out West Tennessee and North Mississippi of all organized enemies." Imprison or banish troublemakers: "Handle that class without gloves and take their property for public use."[6]

Forceful words, these; but while they bespoke a change in attitude, other policies conveyed different messages, especially when it came to trading with the enemy. Most infuriating were cotton speculators, whose efforts to buy bales opened up sources of specie, medicine, and contraband for the Rebels. "We cannot carry on war & trade with a people at the same time," Sherman, in charge at Memphis, declared. Grant agreed. He protested the practice to Washington, pointing out to Secretary of the Treasury Salmon P. Chase, "Our lines are so extended that it is impossible for any military surveillance to contend successfully with the cunning of the traders, aided by the local knowledge and eager interest of the residents along the border." Memphis proved a magnet for such activity. Buying cotton with inflated greenbacks was bad enough; purchasing it with specie, which would be far more useful to Confederates looking to trade with Europe, proved that the speculators' "love of gain is greater than their love of country." Out went orders directing the arrest of specie-paying speculators and those who refused to accept greenbacks in payment for Confederate products. As early as July 26, Grant had instructed a rear area commander to examine the baggage of all "speculators" who sought to come south, turning back those travelers with specie in their possession and arresting those who were carrying medicine and contraband articles: "Jews should receive special attention."[7] Eventually the assumptions embodied in this last directive would receive special attention.

The authorities at Washington were of a different mind when it came to cotton. Supplies of raw cotton were important for northern textile manufacturing; as stock ran low in English mills, owners and workers might press for British recognition of the Confederacy unless they could find alternative sources of cotton. Thus the administration revoked directives prohibiting the purchase of cotton with specie; Halleck notified Grant of this decision in the same letter that spoke of handling Confederate sympathizers "without gloves." Grant, aware of the contradiction in these instructions, protested to no avail.[8]

As if this was not enough to aggravate Grant, there was always his father. Jesse had advice about everything, from how to respond to newspaper criticism (Jesse was willing to do it himself, just as in the old days, by blundering into print) to how to bring up the children. Finally Grant wrote him to keep his opinions to himself. "You must not expect me to write in my own defense nor to permit it from any one about me," he told his father. His men liked him, and that was enough. "I do not expect nor want the support of the Cincinnati press on my side. Their course has been so remarkable from the beginning that should I be endorsed by them I should fear that the public would mistrust my patriotism." Nor did he care to reply to charges that he did not support the administration's new policy toward slavery. As for the children, they were not falling prey to secessionist influences or the evils of camp life, but resided comfortably with their parents in Whitfield's house.[9]

In mid-August Confederate forces began to shift location, a sign of possible future offensive operations. The respite from combat was coming to an end. In central Tennessee, Don Carlos Buell learned that Braxton Bragg was accumulating men and supplies at Chattanooga; as he fell back to cover Nashville, he called on Grant for reinforcements. This proved easier said than done. Grant had already sent one division to Arkansas; to forward two more divisions to Buell would leave his own command vulnerable to attack. Nevertheless, Grant moved quickly, although not quickly enough to suit an increasingly panicky Buell. As he thinned out his defenses, Grant, anticipating an attack, sent Julia and the children back to St. Louis — just in time for the school year — and focused on countering enemy moves. Five staff members were absent, while a sixth, Rawlins, was recovering from a serious operation. Guerrilla activities — including reports that steamers were being fired on from shore — demanded attention, as did Confederate raids on rear areas.[10]

Early in September Grant found his resources stretched to the breaking point. He had to disperse his command to cover a large territory; Halleck was calling on him for more troops; he remained short several staff officers, although Rawlins, still ailing, had returned to duty. To make matters worse, reconnaissance revealed that the enemy, under General Sterling Price, was massing near Iuka, some twenty miles southeast of Corinth, for an attack on Grant's lines in northern Mississippi. Hastily Grant responded to the threat, staying up through the night as he digested reports and wrote orders to his subordinates. He was sure that the grand Confederate offensives, stretching from his front to the Potomac, constituted a desperate last bid for victory. Within a week he was able to report to Julia, "I am concentrated and strong. Will give the rebels a tremendous thrashing if they come."[11]

It was not clear exactly what Price intended to do. Some reports had him moving into Tennessee to join Bragg's forces; others claimed that he intended to draw Grant from Corinth, leaving the city vulnerable to an attack from another Confederate column under Earl Van Dorn. Estimating that Van Dorn could not reach Corinth in under four days, Grant on September 15 set into motion an ambitious plan featuring a two-pronged attack to eliminate Price before turning on Van Dorn. One column, under Edward O. C. Ord, would sweep down on Iuka from the northwest and strike Price; a second column, led by William S. Rosecrans, would drive up from the southwest, catching the Confederates in a pincers movement. If Rosecrans could secure control of the road from Iuka south to Fulton, the Rebels might well be crushed.

The plan was too clever: it required precise coordination and synchronization. Rain impeded Rosecrans's advance; Grant hoped Ord would pin Price in place and distract his attention from Rosecrans coming up from behind. Time was important. Should Van Dorn move in earnest on Corinth, Grant would abandon his strike in favor of defending the city. He also tried to wear down Price in other ways. On the evening of September 18 word arrived of a smashing Union victory near the town of Sharpsburg, Maryland, promising the destruction of Robert E. Lee's Army of Northern Virginia. Grant passed the word along to Ord, who secured his superior's permission to share the information with Price in an effort to secure the foe's surrender. Indignant, Price rejected the ploy; he certainly could not verify the report of Lee's defeat and he was not likely to accept the word of a Yankee (the report proved greatly exaggerated).[12]

By evening it was obvious that Rosecrans would not be in position to at-

The Mississippi Valley Region, 1862–1863

tack until early the following afternoon. Grant then reversed his plan: Rosecrans, not Ord, would strike first. A dispatch went out to Rosecrans explaining the change in plan; two of Grant's staff officers rode to his headquarters. On the morning of September 19 Ord's men approached the outskirts of Iuka. They heard what they took to be a minor skirmish in the distance. Grant had told Ord to hold back his attack until he heard the sounds of battle between Price and Rosecrans, and so Ord waited . . . and waited. At about 6 P.M., a division commander reported seeing smoke in the direction of Iuka. Ord remained in place, believing that the Confederates were burning stores; he could hear nothing resembling a battle. But a battle there was: Rosecrans's men had gone into action earlier that afternoon. Fighting desperately, the Confederates held on to their position around Iuka; in reinforcing his attack, Rosecrans was forced to leave uncovered the road to Fulton. That proved unfortunate for the Federals, for when the Rebs evacuated Iuka in the early morning hours of September 20, they took to that road to make good their escape. It was a bad ending to a frustrating battle for Rosecrans: during the night he had exclaimed, "Where in the name of God is Grant?"[13]

In this interrogatory lay the seeds of a dispute. Rosecrans had assumed that Ord would open the action; Ord waited for the sound of Rosecrans's guns before moving. That he heard nearly nothing was later attributed to an acoustical shadow, an odd atmospheric condition that deadens noise. But that did not answer the question of who was supposed to open the attack. Despite Grant's change in plans, Rosecrans acted as if the original idea was still in force, going so far as to ignore one of Grant's staff officers, Clark B. Lagow, who had urged Rosecrans to attack in compliance with Grant's new orders. His dispatches and behavior clearly indicate that he thought that Ord would engage Price, allowing him to move into position athwart Price's rear; Grant's orders to Ord were predicated on Rosecrans initiating combat. Had Ord pressed forward, he might not have trapped Price, but he surely would have been able to help Rosecrans. Nor did Rosecrans convey to Grant the news that circumstances had forced him to leave the Fulton Road uncovered.[14]

On learning early on the morning of September 20 of Rosecrans's battle the previous afternoon, Grant urged Ord forward. He brushed off Rosecrans's testy dispatches, which took a most insubordinate tone, reading as if Rosecrans commanded Grant and not the other way around. But Price was gone; a pursuit proved fruitless. Grant chose not to blame either Ord or Rosecrans for what happened (and did not happen). It was time to turn back to Corinth.

Revived by the offensive and frustrated that it did not accomplish all that he had intended, Grant looked for a new opportunity to strike. He traveled to St. Louis to confer with his counterpart in Arkansas, Major General Samuel Curtis, about using Curtis's army to sweep eastward from Helena, Arkansas, on the Mississippi's west bank, and threaten the Confederate rear. Perhaps the trip would improve his health, which had been lagging for the past few weeks, in part due to stress and overwork in the absence of staff officers.

Grant was not the only general contemplating his options. Price, unable to help Bragg's invasion of Tennessee and Kentucky, received orders instead to link up with Van Dorn at Ripley, Mississippi. Together the generals decided to turn the tables on Grant. They would march north to Pocahontas, Tennessee, just north of the Mississippi state line a dozen miles west of Corinth, giving the appearance of threatening Grant's reserve under the command of Stephen Hurlbut at Bolivar, a dozen miles or so to the north. Instead, however, they would turn east and strike Rosecrans at Corinth. With 22,000 men, they hoped to overwhelm Rosecrans's 15,000, although Corinth was heavily fortified with lines built by both Confederate and Yankee spades.

As Grant was still at St. Louis, it would be up to Rosecrans to hold the Rebels in check. He did so with skill, concentrating his forces and increasing his strength until he actually outnumbered the Confederate column; at the same time he secured intelligence that disclosed the true target of the enemy advance. As the two sides met north of Corinth on October 3, Grant, back in Tennessee, ordered Hurlbut to advance in the hope of recreating his pincer offensive. He hurried reinforcements forward while urging Rosecrans to advance if he was not under attack: "Fight!"[15]

For a moment what had failed at Iuka seemed to be working outside Corinth. Rosecrans repulsed Price and Van Dorn in two days of heavy fighting; the Confederates retreated northward, where they encountered the lead elements of Hurlbut's column. "I cannot see how the enemy are to escape without losing everything but their small arms," Grant remarked. "I have strained everything to take into the fight an adequate force and to get them to the right place." However, Rosecrans failed to press his advantage promptly, once more leaving open an escape route for the Rebels, who fled south to regroup at Holly Springs, Mississippi.[16]

Concerned about the high number of wounded in Hurlbut's command, aware that Hurlbut needed to replenish his supplies, and realizing that the moment had passed to shatter the disorganized Confederates in retreat, Grant called off the pursuit, much to the disgust of Halleck and Rosecrans. "Why order a return of your troops?" Halleck wired. "Why not reinforce Rosecrans & pursue the enemy into Miss, supporting your army on the country?" Grant could have been excused for raising an eyebrow as he read this missive: Halleck excelled at telling other people to do what he found so hard to do himself. As for Rosecrans, had he been more alert earlier, there would have been no need for a pursuit. Within days he, too, was crying for forage and supplies. The men were worn out and hungry; they were not equipped to press onward. To order a pursuit in such circumstances would risk too much.[17]

Although Grant did not achieve all that he had set out to do, the victories at Iuka and Corinth improved his standing in Washington. Halleck commented that he wished that other generals would do as well — a slap at the inert McClellan and the lethargic Buell; Lincoln telegraphed his congratulations. Betraying unwarranted optimism, Grant declared, "It does look to me that we now have such an advantage over the rebels that there should be but little more hard fighting." But friction between Grant and Rosecrans intensified. Increasingly willing to second-guess Grant, Rosecrans acted as if he were exercising an independent command. When Grant informed him of the rumors circulating about his critical remarks, he protested that Grant "had no truer friend no more loyal subordinate under your command than myself." Grant thought otherwise. So did members of Grant's staff, who went so far as to ask Julia Grant to talk to her husband. She did. "Do not trouble yourself about me, my dear little one," Ulysses replied. "I can take care of myself."[18]

Rosecrans wasted no opportunity to promote his own fortunes at Grant's expense. Proof of this appeared when *Cincinnati Commercial* correspondent William D. Bickham, long one of Grant's enemies in the press and a favorite at Rosecrans's headquarters, composed several columns exalting Rosecrans and attacking Grant and Ord, including an implication that Grant was drunk at Iuka. Angered by such reports, Grant treated Rosecrans roughly when he filed his second report on Iuka. It omitted the praise Grant had showered on his subordinate immediately after the battle and countered Bickham's press dispatches. After Rosecrans informed Halleck of the controversy, the general-in-chief averted an open breach between the two generals by selecting Rosecrans to replace Don Carlos Buell, who had been fired by Lincoln for failing to pursue Bragg after checking the Confederate thrust into Kentucky at Perryville.[19]

Without knowing it, Halleck had just rescued Grant from himself, for Grant was on the point of requesting Rosecrans's removal or transfer from command. Coming less than three weeks after the victory at Corinth, such an act would have reminded people of Halleck's own efforts to displace Grant after Fort Donelson and might have sparked charges that Grant was jealous of his subordinate's success. Moreover, Rosecrans would have been

all too happy to contest such a request and take the opportunity to criticize Grant. Instead, he got the independent command he wanted; likewise
Grant was glad to see him go. Putting the best face on a deteriorating relationship, he generously told Rosecrans: "I predict an important command
where in the course of events we may cooperate." However, newspaper reports celebrating the achievements of the new commander of the Army of
the Ohio, complete with sideswipes at Grant, irked him. "It is a great annoyance to gain rank and command enough to attract public attention,"
he told Ord. "I have found it so and would now really prefer some little
command where public attention would not be attracted towards me."[20]

Friction between Julia and Grant's family also continued. So did his father's voluble misbehavior, until Grant refused to divulge his plans, noting, "You are so imprudent that I dare not trust you with them; and while
on this subject let me say a word. I have not an enemy in the world who has
done me so much injury as you in your efforts in my defense. I require no
defenders and for my sake let me alone." Jesse's remarks about other generals circulated through Cincinnati and its environs, "and the inference
with people naturally is that you get your impressions for [from] me." No
doubt such remarks had fueled the clash with Rosecrans. Jesse had increasingly become a professional as well as a personal liability.[21]

Finally Grant asked Julia to bring the family down to join him in what
Julia described as "a straggling old country house." When headquarters
shifted to LaGrange in early November, Julia found herself in a more impressive residence, where the only problem she encountered was a station-
ary washstand. She complained to Ulysses, who replied that she disliked it
because she had to go to the washstand instead of having it brought to her
— a none-too-subtle reminder of her past dependence on servants. Julia's
presence reduced the family friction, at least for the moment. Grant knew
who was to blame. "All that comes from you speaks so condescendingly of
every thing Julia says, writes, or thinks," he told his father in November.
"You without probably being aware of it are so prejudiced against her that
she could not please you. This is not pleasing to me." When he learned
that Jesse would repeatedly reprimand his grandson Fred, Ulysses, perhaps with his own childhood in mind, explained that Fred's health was not
always the best and that scolding made him diffident and quiet. Once
more the old man was being his overbearing self. Now, however, his son
knew how to stand up and lash back.[22]

After Iuka and Corinth, Halleck elevated Grant's command to department status. Wondering whether the decision had any deeper significance, Grant queried Halleck about future operations. Observing that he

had no idea what his fellow department commanders might be contemplating, Grant argued that at present he lacked sufficient forces to do more than hold on to what he currently occupied. However, if he could consolidate his position by abandoning Corinth (after rendering it useless as a rail junction), he would then advance southward toward Vicksburg. Located along a string of bluffs on the east bank of the Mississippi at a point where the river swung north, then south in a hairpin, the city provided an excellent location for the Confederates to block Union efforts to gain control of the entire river. Although a halfhearted Union effort to take the city in the summer of 1862 had failed, it had alerted the Confederates to the need to fortify the area. With New Orleans and Memphis now in Union hands, all eyes turned to Vicksburg as the logical target of future operations.[23]

Grant's effort to rouse Halleck met with no response. Left on his own, he decided to press southward into Mississippi, targeting Holly Springs, some fifteen miles south of the Tennessee state border along the Mississippi Central railroad, as his objective. Once taken, it would provide an ideal location for a supply depot to assist penetrations farther south. Two columns would first converge on Grand Junction, Tennessee, then head toward Holly Springs; Sherman would mount a diversion from Memphis.[24]

The Confederates short-circuited any chance of a battle when Lieutenant General John C. Pemberton ordered the evacuation of Holly Springs on November 9. Encouraged by news from Halleck that reinforcements were headed down the Mississippi, Grant looked to expand the scope of his campaign, although he remained ignorant of any overall plan requiring cooperation between departments. However, he also heard rumors that some of the reinforcements he anticipated were to report to McClernand. Perhaps the report simply referred to McClernand's work recruiting regiments in the Old Northwest. He decided to ask just what was going on. "Am I to understand that I lay still here while an Expedition is fitted out from Memphis or do you want me to push as far South as possible?" he wired Halleck. "Am I to have Sherman move subject to my orders or is he and his forces reserved for some special service?" Bad enough that Halleck had not divulged any grand plans of operations for the Mississippi Valley; now Grant was confused about affairs in his own command. Already discomfited by the news that Leonard Swett, with whom he had feuded back in Cairo in 1861, was to join the administration in some capacity, Grant wondered whether he would come under attack from Washington.[25]

Grant need not have worried about Swett — the reports proved false —

but his concern about McClernand was justified. McClernand had long sought his independence from Grant. Several testy exchanges with his superior had revealed that their relationship was deteriorating. In July, he had asked Washburne to seek his reassignment to the Army of the Potomac, only to have Halleck reprimand him for failing to make his request through proper channels. Now the troublesome Illinois Democrat had taken advantage of his leave to lobby Lincoln for permission to recruit new regiments from the Midwest and to lead them in an expedition on Vicksburg independently of Grant. The president was receptive because Midwestern governors (perhaps prompted by McClernand) were pointing out the importance of reopening the Mississippi.[26]

Lincoln, frustrated by the slow pace of military operations in the East (McClernand had accompanied him on a visit to McClellan's headquarters in October) and aware of the political as well as military benefits that might accrue from McClernand's plan, was willing to give it a try. Stanton also embraced the idea. Promising naval support was David D. Porter, who preferred the earnest McClernand to "self-sufficient, pedantic, and unpractical" West Pointers. But not everyone was enthusiastic about McClernand. Halleck, who had little if anything to do with developing the plan, had seen enough of McClernand to judge him more of a politician than a general; even Lincoln, despite thinking that McClernand was "brave and capable," told Secretary Chase that he was "too desirous to be independent of every body else." These reservations resulted in the drafting of orders that gave McClernand far less than the free hand he desired. After raising his new regiments and forwarding them according to Halleck's directions, he would assume command of his expedition — but only after "a sufficient force not required by the operations of General Grant's command" was available. Halleck would determine what exactly constituted "a sufficient force" and Grant's own needs; the recruits would be "employed according to such exigencies as the service in his judgment may require."[27]

One cannot blame Lincoln for endorsing McClernand's proposal, coming as it did when so many of his other generals seemed lethargic. It was doubtless also encouraging to see a Democrat who was still enthusiastic about prosecuting the war when other generals with Democratic affiliations, namely McClellan and Buell, questioned the wisdom of administration measures concerning emancipation. Nevertheless, the command structure envisioned by the operation contained flaws that guaranteed trouble. Lincoln seemed dimly aware of all this, and yet he allowed McClernand to go forward. By failing to take Halleck or Grant into his confidence in planning the move, the president left the department commander with less than full control over his ostensible subordinate; the wording of the orders offered Lincoln the chance to evade responsibility for ensuing events. That might make for slick politics but was unworthy of the commander-in-chief.

Furthermore, the project was a clear sign that Lincoln's faith in Grant was conditional and qualified. If the president had resisted demands to remove him after Shiloh, he did not now do anything to help him. Lincoln's actions this fall suggested that if he could not exactly spare Grant, he was not going to rely on him, instead fueling the ambitions of a rival who lost no chance to chastise his superior officers. It did not help that a report was circulating in Washington that Grant had been intoxicated in St. Louis during his visit in late September. At least one cabinet member (Attorney General Edward Bates) heard of the incident; Halleck forwarded the report to Grant for comment. It was reasonable to suppose that there must be something to all these stories. Perhaps, Lincoln concluded, it was time to give someone else a chance.[28]

For the moment Grant knew virtually nothing of McClernand's mission. Responding to his inquiry, Halleck artfully answered: "You have command of all troops sent to your Dept., and have permission to fight the enemy when you please." That this said exactly nothing about McClernand gave good cause for suspicion, but Grant decided to take those words and run with them. It helped to know at last what other department commanders were doing — there would be movements directed at the Mississippi Valley from Arkansas and New Orleans. However, Halleck, who had previously objected to his plan to rip up the rail network around Corinth, raised objections to his present idea to use the railroad from Memphis to supply his army in northern Mississippi as he prepared to move south through the interior. Those railroads would not be rebuilt. "Operations in northern Miss. must be limited to rapid marches upon any collected forces of the enemy, feeding as far as possible on the country," Halleck declared. "The enemy must be turned by a movement down the river from Memphis as soon as a sufficient force can be collected."[29]

Grant probably was bewildered, if not angry, when he read this wire. First he had asked Halleck whether there was an overall plan of campaign in the West, so that he would not draw up plans in isolation or ignorance — only to be ignored. Then Halleck had waited until Grant's offensive was well under way before announcing, almost as an aside, that he preferred a different line of approach. Instead of directing strategy or coordinating armies to achieve general objectives, the general-in-chief simply offered observations and objections. Finally, he was less than forthcoming about McClernand, apparently hoping that Grant would take Vicksburg before McClernand was ready to do so.[30]

Rather than voicing objections, Grant developed a slightly different plan, although he remained wedded to an overland offensive southward through Mississippi. Sherman would join him from Memphis with three divisions; Union forces based at Helena, Arkansas, would advance on Grenada, Mississippi (Grant had finally gotten his way on controlling troops stationed at Helena). A move employing river crossings required active assistance from the navy. Grant decided to confer with Admiral Porter, who headed the flotilla north of Vicksburg. This meeting was long overdue. Porter had often complained about the aloofness of West Point–educated generals — until the administration had assigned him to cooperate with McClernand's operation. At first the tandem seemed to be ideal, for both men nursed a grudge against army professionals, but Porter soon saw that McClernand was a glory-seeking politician with an inflated sense of his talent. Nevertheless, the naval officer's aversion to West Pointers remained. Even though Grant had worked with the navy before, so far this fall he had ignored it, leaving Porter to exclaim, "I don't trust the Army. It is very evident that Grant is going to try and take Vicksburg without us, but he can't do it."

Knowing how much emphasis West Point generals placed on pomp and appearance, Porter donned his best dress uniform. Thus when he greeted Grant, he was surprised to find himself shaking hands with a man wearing a plain brown coat and gray trousers, dusty from a long journey. Although Grant disdained wearing his dress uniform except for ceremonial circumstances, his present outfit rendered him nearly anonymous. Perhaps he was dressing down to counter Porter's concerns; more likely he did not want to attract attention to his movements on the eve of a major campaign.[31]

Somewhat taken aback, Porter guided his guest to a side table, where the two men sat and talked. The naval commander may have been pleased that Grant had forsworn the trappings of command, but he also had to admit that his army counterpart did not exactly look like a general. As the two men talked, however, Porter decided that he sounded like one. Grant's "calm, imperturbable face" concealed any anxiety; what came across instead was the man's determination to do something. Nothing of the West Pointer was evident in the general. He was not arrogant; he did not assume an air of superiority; he spoke to Porter as an equal; he set forth his plan of campaign in a straightforward manner that made sense. Porter recognized that Grant, not McClernand, was the man to take Vicksburg.[32]

After conferring with Sherman on November 21 at Columbus, Kentucky, Grant returned to his headquarters. Before long, he told his father, "I will again be in motion. I feel every confidance of success but I know that a heavy force is now to my front."[33]

As Grant wrestled with preparing an offensive against Vicksburg, he confronted several other issues. Maintaining security and order within occupied Tennessee demanded time, energy, and continuous attention. Guerrilla forces were at best an annoyance and at worst a serious threat to army communications and supply while also disrupting efforts to pacify the civilian population; raiding cavalry columns added to destabilization. Between the destruction of railroads and the impact of foraging by both sides, many people lacked food and clothing. Grant laid assessments on secessionist sympathizers and redistributed the supplies and funds collected to deprived civilians; he ordered the arrest of anyone who aided enemy raiders and guerrillas.[34]

Grant also worried about the behavior of his own soldiers. The advance on Grand Junction offered renewed evidence of the need to control their behavior. "Houses have been plunder'd and burned down, fencing destroyed and citizens frightened without an enquiry as to their status in the Rebellion," Grant observed; livestock had been slaughtered or driven off in defiance of standing orders on civilian property. The general reminded his men that violators were subject to the death penalty, explaining that such activities impaired discipline and alienated the citizenry. Such instructions assumed renewed importance as Grant advanced southward into Mississippi, for he found the residents subdued and cordial to his men.[35]

Lincoln's preliminary Emancipation Proclamation on September 22 was an attempt to encourage the revival of unionism in the South by promising that the administration would allow slavery to continue in areas where citizens elected representatives to Congress. Believing that many Southern whites would thus act "to avoid the unsatisfactory prospect before them," the president instructed military governors and generals to provide for the holding of elections whenever they could do so. Grant doubted that these measures would succeed in West Tennessee, for secessionist crowds mobbed unionist speakers while guerrilla bands terrorized the countryside and disrupted Union military operations, sometimes by firing on unarmed steamers carrying civilians. In retaliation, Grant expelled secessionist families from Union lines; Sherman burned the town of Randolph, Tennessee, to set an example of what was in store for Southern whites persisting in such activities. The reestablishment of loyal Union governments seemed premature in such circumstances, but Grant, obeying orders, issued a proclamation on December 9 calling on Tennessee voters to hold congressional elections before the end of the year.[36]

The number of black refugees grew as Grant pushed forward, because many secessionist slaveholders fled, leaving their slaves to migrate toward Union lines. Before Grant could concentrate on military matters, he had to provide for and control these displaced people. Previously he had sent black refugees to the North, having heard that some Northerners were willing to employ black women as servants; however, the Lincoln administration, sensitive to Democratic charges that emancipated blacks would swarm over the North in search of jobs — a frank and effective appeal to the racist sentiments of many Northern whites — put a halt to that.[37]

Grant finally devised a solution that was at once humanitarian and pragmatic. Realizing that the continued flood of refugees into his lines promised to overwhelm his command, tax his resources, spread disease, and inhibit discipline, he decided to establish encampments for black families. Blacks would earn wages and work toward providing for themselves by harvesting cotton and corn from the surrounding abandoned plantations. Union authorities would supervise these workers. Although Grant gave no indication of having studied the methods other Union commanders had used to address the same problem, his solution resembled that implemented along South Carolina's Sea Islands earlier that year. His idea was shaped in large part by expediency rather than profound thought about the process of emancipation. Grant's major responsibility was to defeat the Confederacy, not to direct a social revolution.

Grant placed Chaplain John Eaton of the Twenty-seventh Ohio in charge of his program. Not exactly a willing volunteer, Eaton sought out Grant, hoping to be excused from the responsibility. The general would have none of that. He calmly explained his thinking behind the matter, admitting that his proposal attempted to satisfy the demands of military necessity and "the dictates of mere humanity," as Eaton phrased it. Many whites, Grant argued, believed that blacks would not work of their own free will. His own experience in Missouri suggested otherwise; it also suggested that the best way to counter racist stereotypes was to provide concrete examples of how freed blacks would respond to opportunity. Give blacks the chance to earn a living, either by helping the military authorities or by working on plantations, and they would prove to whites that they would work on their own, eroding racist assumptions. Then whites might accept the idea of blacks in military service; once blacks demonstrated that they would fight for their freedom, whites might go so far as to contemplate blacks as citizens, maybe even voters.

As Eaton listened, he was persuaded of the merits of Grant's idea and the rationale behind it. "Never before in those early and bewildering days had I heard the problem of the future of the Negro attacked so vigorously and with such humanity combined with practical good sense," he recalled. Grant might not see himself as a committed abolitionist, but his plan for an orderly and supervised transition from slavery to freedom could establish a firm foundation for emancipation by helping blacks adjust to their new status while challenging white stereotypes. If he had not imbibed at full strength his father's antislavery principles, neither had he subscribed to the prejudices of his father-in-law. If he had been a slaveholder, it had not been as a planter presiding over a large plantation of faceless workers, but as a small farmer working alongside blacks. He knew from personal experience that blacks would work; all they needed was the chance to do so and the incentive to do well. Nevertheless, he believed it would be heartless to thrust blacks into freedom without any guidance or assistance. To expect that former slaves could immediately function on an equal basis in a free society would contradict abolitionist claims that the peculiar institution scarred its victims.

Grant's plan embodied the important assumption that the only way to challenge racism was to repudiate stereotypes and ignorance. It may have reflected paternalistic notions, especially in its insistence that whites oversee newly freed blacks, but it solved immediate problems of subsistence and survival and served the needs of the Union military. It was another example of applied common sense, something in short supply. Moreover, it was Grant's idea. Only after he had implemented it did he inform his superiors what he had done.[38]

If Grant responded thoughtfully to this problem, in addressing another one he proved that he could also be captive to old attitudes. For months he had protested the restricted reopening of trade in areas under his command, arguing that this practice prolonged the war by funneling specie and valuable supplies into the Confederacy. Speculators and traders were not above bribing military officers (and some of the officers had a hand in such business as well). Administration representatives, members of Congress, and other prominent Northerners all eyed the main chance. Grant was disgusted by such activity. Even as he revoked an order by a subordinate that banned "All Cotton-Speculators, Jews and other Vagrants" from

Union lines on December 9, he snarled that the patriotism of speculators was "measured by dollars & cents." His anger became more evident eight days later, when he issued General Orders No. 11: "The Jews, as a class, violating every regulation of trade established by the Treasury Department, and also Department orders, are hereby expelled from the Department." Any Jewish residents who refused to leave would be imprisoned.[39]

This infamous directive as well as Grant's correspondence before and after its release singled out Jews for avarice connected with cotton trading and other unsavory activities. Although he protested that he was not an anti-Semite, some of his statements were clearly anti-Semitic. Many of Memphis's most prominent merchants were Jews, as were some of Cincinnati's leading businessmen, and they drew on preexisting trading relationships to exploit the present opportunity. But there was a significant difference between assailing people for what they did and attacking them because of their religious faith, and Grant crossed this line. While he questioned stereotypes about blacks, he failed to subject his beliefs about Jews to similar scrutiny. Attitudes toward work and business lay at the core of both reactions, suggesting that Grant had thought much about how people got ahead in the world. Blacks deserved a chance to work hard and make something of themselves (much as Grant had struggled to do in the 1850s); Jews, he believed, were too greedy, too sharp in their dealings, and measured all worth in terms of money (much like Jesse).

Grant's anti-Semitism, however much it may have shaped the wording of his order, did not induce him to issue it, nor was he alone in explicitly mentioning Jews in complaints about the cotton trade. What sparked him to act was his belief that Jewish cotton traders were more successful than were other "unprincipled" traders: "The Jews seem to be a privileged class that can travel any where. They will land at any wood yard or landing on the river and make their way through the country." The War Department had just forwarded to him a complaint that Jews were carrying large amounts of gold into Kentucky and Tennessee, presumably to purchase cotton. And, if many of the merchants in Memphis were Jewish, so were the partners in Mack and Brothers, a Cincinnati firm that had just employed Jesse Grant to secure a permit from his son in exchange for a quarter of the profits. Once more Jesse was trying to meddle in his son's life; once more he was looking to make a buck. His son, who was bitterly opposed to such transactions, may have found it too much to take — although it would have been more appropriate to vent all his anger on his father.[40]

What created the uproar was not Grant's decision to exclude from Union lines those Jews who were involved in cotton trading; it was the attempt to ban *all* Jews from the boundaries of his command. That this was not his intention soon became apparent when headquarters expressed no objection to the continued presence of Jewish sutlers. But others did not so understand the order. Throughout the Department of the Tennessee post commanders moved to eject Jews, and one Jewish officer resigned in protest. Protests about the directive reached Washington, and on January 4 Halleck ordered Grant to revoke it. The following day one of Halleck's staff officers privately explained to Grant that it was the all-inclusiveness of the order that had rendered it objectionable: "Had the word 'pedler' been inserted after Jew I do not suppose any exception would have been taken to the order." Halleck reinforced this interpretation several days later, adding that even Lincoln would not have objected to a more precisely framed order. Others were less kind. From Paducah petitioners denounced "this enormous outrage on all law & humanity"; in Congress Democrats introduced resolutions condemning the order, although they were tabled. Washburne defended Grant, also attributing the difficulty to the order's sweeping coverage. In later years the general would express regret over the whole incident and protest that he had been misunderstood. But the affair would long haunt him and encourage his critics; years later even Julia would castigate "that obnoxious order."[41]

General Order No. 11 appeared just as Grant was reaching the critical point in operations against Vicksburg. Despite all the problems presented by hungry black refugees, cotton speculators, recalcitrant secessionists, and lukewarm unionists, the major challenges confronting him remained the Confederates in his front and McClernand in his rear. For weeks he had been directing operations and improvising responses, under pressure to achieve something quickly. Just as the campaign got under way, a telegram from Halleck sought information on the size of his command with specific reference to the number that could be sent down the Mississippi. This implied that McClernand was about ready to move; however, when Grant explained that he was already embarking on his own campaign, Halleck wired back: "Proposed movements approved. Do not go too far."[42]

Grant might have been excused for wondering what exactly Halleck meant by "too far"; better to move now and ask questions later. Yet success depended on coordinated movements between two separated forces, always difficult to achieve. The weather was bad; McClernand was on his way south; Grant knew that his advance left his lines vulnerable. There was, he remarked, "an immence number of lives staked upon my judgement and acts"; he was tired of reading critical comments in the press and from "people at home . . . who never heard the whistle of a hostile bullet."[43]

Initially, Grant had favored marching straight down along the rail lines into central Mississippi to the state capital at Jackson, some forty-five miles due east of Vicksburg, but heavy rainfall in early December hampered his movements. Before long he doubted the wisdom of continuing southward past Grenada, for his supply lines would grow too long and vulnerable. Perhaps it would be better to follow Halleck's suggestion and send a force down the Mississippi to take Vicksburg. After all, raiders might cut a railroad, but they could not dam a river. Grant revised his plan of attack. Sherman would descend from Memphis along the Mississippi, debarking his command of some 32,000 above Vicksburg along a string of bluffs on the Yazoo River. From there he would penetrate inland to cut the railroads between Vicksburg and Jackson, then turn on Vicksburg itself. Grant would draw Pemberton's attention away from Vicksburg by continuing his advance into north central Mississippi.[44]

Grant met with Sherman at Oxford on December 8 to map out the campaign. As Sherman and Porter had long exchanged letters on the subject of army-navy cooperation along the Mississippi River, it seemed only fitting that Grant would now give the two men a chance to work together. Moreover, all three officers had a common desire to take Vicksburg, thus denying that opportunity to McClernand. If all went well, Vicksburg would already be in Union hands by the time McClernand arrived.[45]

Such haste had its costs, and in retrospect it appears that this operation was troubled from the outset. It seemed almost more important for Grant and Sherman to deprive McClernand of Vicksburg than to take it from the Confederates. Once Sherman was off, it would be difficult for Grant to coordinate the two columns, let alone communicate changes if something went awry. Yet Grant's plan called for his column to move according to circumstances, reacting to Confederate movements. He was ignoring the lessons about cooperation and coordination offered by Iuka and Corinth. Perhaps Grant believed that the only problem there had been entrusting Rosecrans and not Sherman with command of one column.

Actually, Grant was having problems with managing his expanded responsibilities. He now admitted to Halleck that some of his past problems were "due to having an entire Staff of inexperienced men in Military matters." That situation had improved with the arrival in November of James H. Wilson, an engineer, and several other officers; of his personal staff he regarded Rawlins and Theodore S. Bowers as "absolutely indispensable." Worried that James B. McPherson's promotion to major general might be thwarted, he impressed Halleck with the former staffer's value; expressing satisfaction with his other leading subordinates, he dreaded the assignment of less capable men with senior rank to his command. "I am sorry to say it but I would regard it as particularly unfortunate to have either McClernand or Wallace sent to me," he told Halleck. "The latter I could manage if he had less rank, but the former is unmanageable and incompetent."[46]

Yet Grant's greatest fear was realized when Halleck, responding to his plan to direct Sherman to travel downriver to take Vicksburg, wired: "The President may insist upon designating a separate commander." Grant also learned that McClernand was ready to come south and assume command of the waterborne column. He telegraphed Halleck that Sherman had already departed, adding that the expedition "would be much safer" under that general. Lincoln did not agree. Back came instructions to organize his command into four corps, with McClernand in charge of the expedition now commanded by Sherman. Off went a letter — not a telegram — from Grant to McClernand notifying the latter what was being done and inviting him to take charge of the expedition against Vicksburg. It was critical to act before McClernand received the dispatch.[47]

It was left to the Confederates to deliver the final blows to Grant's offensive. On December 18 Confederate cavalry under Nathan Bedford Forrest crossed the Tennessee River and looked to sever Union lines of communication and supply. Unworried, Grant hoped to punish Forrest. Although Forrest temporarily severed one of Grant's supply lines, his raid's major achievement was the disruption of the elections to assess the revival of loyalty in West Tennessee. Moreover, by breaking Grant's lines of communication, Forrest blocked the transmission of his letter to McClernand.[48]

What seemed like a momentary setback grew in magnitude when news arrived of additional cavalry columns coming from the south. Although Grant alerted his subordinates, he was helpless when the commander of the garrison at Holly Springs folded in the face of Earl Van Dorn's raiders, who accepted the Yankee's surrender before destroying the Union supply depot. Without those supplies, the push southward could not continue. It was time to fall back; Grant's men, placed on half rations, foraged to make up the difference. That they were able to do so with ease surprised the general; with better planning, he might have taken advantage of the bulging barns and available livestock to feed an army. But he was clearly disappointed at being forced to withdraw. It could have been worse, for Julia and little Jesse evaded capture by leaving Holly Springs just before the Confederates arrived (illustrating the danger of having one's family at the front). They arrived at Oxford while Grant was attempting to corner Van Dorn by dispatch. The general, relieved, hurried out to meet their wagon, quickly hugged that "little rascal" Jesse, kissed Julia, and then ducked back into his office.[49]

At first Grant still believed that he might salvage his campaign. Otherwise, Sherman's column would face far more Confederates than anticipated with no help in sight. However, rumor had it that Vicksburg had already fallen to forces from the south; later reports claimed that Sherman had taken the city. Those reports were in error. Sherman and his men suffered a bloody repulse at Chickasaw Bayou north of Vicksburg on December 29. On New Year's Day, 1863, Grant heard that Vicksburg was still in enemy hands; after some uncertainty he finally learned that Sherman's attack had failed, although it was not until January 9 that he received confirmation. By that time McClernand had arrived and had superseded Sherman in command of the river column.[50]

Undeterred by the December setback, Grant commenced planning another drive to take Vicksburg. Arriving at Memphis on January 10, he began investigating various possibilities but was hampered by his ignorance of McClernand's situation and needs. "This expedition must not fail," he declared. "If there is force enough within the limits of my controll to secure a certain victory at Vicksburg they will be sent there." Whatever frustration he felt about McClernand's role was submerged in his desire to do what he could to achieve a victory. What he learned the next day, however, tried his patience to the breaking point. Instead of preparing to renew the offensive against Vicksburg, McClernand had decided to direct his command (and Porter's gunboats) up the Arkansas River to Arkansas Post, where the Confederates had established Fort Hindman. Grant exploded. He drafted a dispatch to inform McClernand that he did not approve of the operation, arguing that it would not contribute to Vicksburg's fall: "Unless you are acting under authority not derived from me keep your command where it can soonest be assembled for the renewal of the attack on Vicksburg." In disgust he wired Halleck that McClernand had "gone on a wild goose chase." Halleck authorized him to remove McClernand; orders were drafted to do just that.[51]

It was fortunate for Grant that he held off relieving McClernand. On January 13 he learned that McClernand had taken Fort Hindman on January 11; acknowledging the receipt of McClernand's dispatch announcing the victory, Grant, instead of offering his congratulations, again suggested that he return to the vicinity of Vicksburg. Miffed, McClernand grandly declared, "The officer who, in the present strait of the country, will not assume a proper responsibility to save it, is unworthy of public trust." Off went another complaint to Lincoln about the "clique of West Pointers" who blocked his path to greatness.[52] Left unmentioned by McClernand (and still unknown to Grant) was that it had been William T. Sherman, USMA 1840, who had actually proposed the expedition to Arkansas Post.

Grant, distrusting McClernand, had already decided to take personal command of the Vicksburg expedition. He believed that by now the city was "very strongly garrisoned and the fortifications almost impregnigable." Encountering McClernand at Napoleon, Arkansas, just below the mouth of the Arkansas River, on January 18, Grant put aside his distaste for his erstwhile subordinate as he conferred with McClernand, Sherman, and Porter on what to do next. Perhaps it was time to revive attempts to dig a canal across the peninsula opposite the city to divert the course of the Mississippi and render Vicksburg vulnerable to assault. One conclusion was clear: Grant would have to direct the operation in person. Neither Sherman nor Porter thought McClernand could be trusted with independent command. They also told Grant that the trip up the Arkansas River had been Sherman's idea. That the discovery caused Grant to reevaluate his previous assessment of the campaign demonstrated it would be hard for McClernand to do anything right in his eyes.[53]

All in all, it was not a good time for Grant. General Cadwallader Washburn reported that the general was "pretty blue"; Rawlins remarked that if he was in Grant's place he would resign. Instead, Grant decided to do what he could with the material at hand, accepting things as they were. After putting matters in order around Memphis and northern Mississippi, he left for the front on January 27, and headed south to Young's Point, Louisiana, just upstream from Vicksburg on the river's west bank. The travel had done him some good: his depression had lifted. "He looks well & feels pretty well," observed Washburn, "but feels that he has got a heavy job on his hands."[54]

10

Struggle and Scrutiny

●

EARLY ONE SPRING MORNING in 1863 a steamer carried three men up the Yazoo River to look at the terrain northeast of Vicksburg. The ship wound its way through curves and past the high ground on the river's east bank. Intent on making a close examination of the area, the three men transferred to an ironclad, leaving twelve-year-old Fred Grant behind on the steamer. The boy's disappointment paled in comparison with the feelings of the three men on the gunboat after they stared long and hard at Haynes' Bluff, bristling with enemy cannon protruding from elaborate fortifications. William T. Sherman and David D. Porter, veterans of the tragedy at Chickasaw Bayou, believed that an assault on such a position was tantamount to suicide. Reluctantly Ulysses S. Grant agreed, sadly concluding that "an attack upon Haines Bluff would be attended with immense sacrifice of life, if not with defeat."[1]

For some nine weeks Grant had explored ways to transfer his army to dry land east of the Mississippi River preparatory to an advance on Vicksburg. His men had waded through swamps and dug ditches in the deltas in an effort to open up a water passage for transports or to divert the course of the Mississippi itself. None had succeeded. An assault on Haynes' Bluff represented the last chance to turn the Confederate right north of Vicksburg.

But Grant still had one card left to play. "In two weeks I expect to be able to collect all my forces and turn Enemy's left," he wired Halleck. It was a move fraught with risk, for although he might be able to shift his troops across soggy roads to a point south of the city, the only way to cross the river would be for Porter to run his gunboats and army transports past Vicksburg's batteries on the bluff. The bend in the river and the slowness of the current would give the Rebel gunners an excellent opportunity to render the flotilla into splinters. Yet it represented Grant's last chance for capturing Vicksburg and remaining in command. Newspaper columns reported that his command was dying of diseases contracted in the wetlands west of the city; rumors circulated that the general was off drinking again. And Grant had no doubt that John A. McClernand was doing all he could to regain the command that he insisted was rightfully his by order of the president. Should this final bid for victory fail, the politician-general might well get his wish.

The next day, after setting his plan in motion, Grant took Fred for a horseback ride along the banks of the Mississippi. After months of frustration and failure, he needed to get away from headquarters. That evening he sat down to write Julia, who was at White Haven. "It is hard to tell when the final strike will be made at Vicksburg," he scribbled. "I am doing all I can and expect to be successful."[2]

From the time he arrived at Young's Point on the evening of January 28, Grant had believed that the best way to approach Vicksburg would be to shift his army south of the city and cross the Mississippi River. "As I understand it," J. Russell Jones, a Galena acquaintance who accompanied Grant on his trip downriver, remarked to Congressman Washburne, "the only hope of getting Vicksburg is in being able to get below & in behind. If that can be done we are all right, if not, it is doubtful." However, the levees were wet, and some were under water: they would not be usable as roads for a while. Grant decided to test alternatives. It was better than doing nothing, and the activity would promote the health of his men. Should something turn up, all the better. "I hope yet to fool the rebels and effect a landing where they do not expect me," he told aide William Hillyer. "Once on the East bank of the river, on high ground reaching Vicksburg, there will be a big fight or a foot race." He ordered gunboats and scouting parties to explore several possible avenues of approach. "I am pushing everything to gain a passage — avoiding Vicksburg," he assured Halleck.[3]

At first John A. McClernand, his head still filled with ideas of commanding his own army, did not fully understand that circumstances had changed with Grant's arrival. He was stunned to learn that Grant had issued orders to units McClernand believed were still under his direction. Misreading (or intentionally misinterpreting) Lincoln's original directive, McClernand insisted that he remained independent of Grant's control: "The question should be immediately referred to Washington, and one or the other, or both of us relieved." Lincoln, McClernand believed, would stand behind him, especially after comparing the record of the two generals over the past month. "One thing is certain: two Generals cannot command this army, issuing independent and direct orders to subordinate officers and the public service be promoted."[4]

Grant agreed. In response, he formally assumed command of operations against Vicksburg, leaving McClernand in charge of the Thirteenth Corps, thus reaffirming the instructions he had received from Washington in December. Sherman headed the Fifteenth Corps; Hurlbut, back in Memphis, would command the Sixteenth Corps; McPherson took over the Seventeenth Corps. McClernand sullenly acquiesced, but he requested that Grant forward a copy of their correspondence to Washington, so that Halleck, Stanton, and especially Lincoln could see what was going on along the west bank of the Mississippi. Grant complied: in a cover letter to Halleck he indicated his lack of trust in McClernand's ability "to conduct an expedition of the magnitude of this one successfully." He reported that his fellow generals concurred in that assessment. "It is due to myself to state that I am not ambitious to have this or any other command," he added. Whatever his superiors decided, "I will cheerfully submit to and give a hearty support." Meanwhile McClernand, pulling on his own strings to the White House, asked Lincoln for permission to undertake a separate expedition into Arkansas, thus demonstrating that he lusted to exercise independent command much more than he desired to take Vicksburg (and that he had no qualms about circumventing the chain of command, for he bypassed Grant and Halleck). He received no reply from the president and Grant remained in command, which should have alerted him that something had changed. Instead he went on plotting Grant's removal.[5]

Grant realized the delicate situation presented by McClernand's scheming. He dared not remove him outright in the aftermath of the Arkansas Post episode; the telegram authorizing Grant to act, after all, had been based on Grant's initial characterization of that operation as a "wild goose chase." Moreover, the president was suitably impressed by McClernand's accomplishment (especially as he learned of it in part from McClernand's own facile pen). When staff officers pressed Grant to take action, Grant simply replied that he could not afford to feud with a general he was compelled to command.[6]

Absent a major blunder by McClernand, the only way Grant could nullify him would be by taking Vicksburg — no easy task. Whatever the merits of moving southward, it would be impossible before spring to reach a suitable crossing point, for much of the land was under water or too soggy to sustain the weight of men, cannon, horses, and wagons. Sherman, tired of waging war in the swamps and bayous, urged him to take the entire army back to Memphis and advance on Vicksburg from the north. Grant disagreed. The Northern public would regard a retrograde movement, no matter how prudent, as a retreat after a defeat. In turn, criticism of that move would turn into cries for Grant's removal, just what McClernand wanted. Never could Grant overlook that his replacement was in the wings: it would always influence his thinking about Vicksburg. He knew he must tread carefully. "Vicksburg will be a hard job," he told Julia. "I expect to get through it successfully however."[7]

The Mississippi River took a hairpin turn west of Vicksburg, cutting northeast, then swinging southwest just before it passed by the city proper. The previous summer, Union soldiers had commenced digging a trench across the base of the peninsula formed by the turn hoping that the resulting canal might furnish a new channel for the Mississippi, rendering Vicksburg vulnerable to assault. When Grant arrived, Sherman's men were at work on this canal. Grant thought little of this particular effort, but the idea of cutting waterborne passages through the swamps west of Vicksburg appeared to have merit. If nothing else, the project would keep the men active. During the next several months, canal-digging became a less-than-favorite pastime of Grant's men as the rising waters lapped up against their campsites and threatened to wash away the earthen banks they had just raised.[8]

Grant explored other ways to approach Vicksburg. Two lay to the north. The first, through the Yazoo Pass, nearly 100 miles upriver, required destroying a levee to reopen a water route, while the second, through Steele's Bayou, was a score of miles north of Vicksburg. In both cases it would take time to create channels for transports and ironclads, and heavy rains during February made things worse. Two other routes pointed south. Lake Providence, west of the river near the Arkansas-Louisiana border, might serve as a passageway to transfer Porter's gunboats and the transports south of Vicksburg without exposing them to fire from the city's cannon, although that route would also take Grant and his men far afield from Vicksburg. Finally, Grant could march his men south along the stretch of land from Milliken's Bend, just west of Vicksburg, to New Carthage, and there look for a place to cross the Mississippi — if the transports survived their trip past Vicksburg's batteries. It would not be until spring that he could take advantage of that route; Grant hoped that one of the four alternatives might succeed. None did.[9]

The ensuing setbacks and delays were disappointing to Grant, but none constituted a disaster. To some extent, the efforts to dig canals curried presidential favor, for Lincoln, drawing on his experiences as a riverboat man, reportedly thought highly of such enterprises. The Northern public, however, did not view recent operations in the same light. The story circulated that the editor of the *Chicago Times* had ordered his correspondents,

"If there is no news, send rumors!" Other reporters, anxious to win credit for breaking stories, sent news of army movements to their newspapers, heedless of the consequences. Military commanders did what they could to silence such reports, including forbidding the circulation of papers in army lines, only to be criticized for denying freedom of the press. Yet when Grant directed the commander at Memphis to rescind an order prohibiting the circulation of the Democratic *Chicago Times,* he was assailed by the editor of the rival Republican *Chicago Tribune,* Joseph Medill. "Your man Grant has shown his cloven foot and proves himself to be little better than a secesh," Medill growled to Elihu B. Washburne. The *Times* was a Copperhead organ, out "to breed more mutiny and demoralization" among Grant's troops. The general's act would not go unnoticed by the *Tribune.* "No man's military career in the army is more open to destructive criticism than Grant's," Medill reminded the congressman. "We have kept off of him on your account. We could have made him stink in the nostrils of the public like an old fish had we properly criticized his military blunders." If Grant continued to allow such Democratic dissent to continue, "we shall not be so tender on him in the future."[10]

Grant agreed with Medill on the impact of press reports on army morale. "My confidance in taking Vicksburg is not unshaken . . . if our own people at home will give their moral support," he told Julia. "At present however they are behaving scandalously." The impact of such criticism was evident. Soldiers on leave deserted, and Democrats defended their action. "I want to see the Administration commence a war upon these people," he snapped. "They should suppress the disloyal press and confine during the war the noisy and most influential of the advocates." However, he would not do so on his own (and risk coming under even more criticism). Meanwhile, newspapermen reported, "The confidence of the army is greatly shaken in General Grant, who hitherto undoubtedly depended more upon good fortune than upon military ability for success."[11]

Soon reports circulated that Grant's men, exposed to the swamps, were sick and dying at an alarming rate. These stories had a slim foundation in fact. Between cramped quarters aboard river transports and the cold, damp environment, many men had fallen ill by the end of January. In mid-February even Grant admitted that with the rain and mud conditions were none too good, although the well-being of the men had improved over the past two weeks. Still, he denied the exaggerated accounts that appeared in Northern papers. The health of his soldiers was "as good as any previous calculation could have prognosticated," he told Halleck. "I believe too there is the best of feeling and greatest confidence of success among them." Inspectors arrived to examine conditions and confirmed Grant's assessment. "In fact the health of the army, tho' not quite as good as that of the army in general, is amazingly good," Frederick Law Olmsted of the Western Sanitary Commission reported after a visit in March. "You cannot conceive how well and happy the men in general looked. . . . If I were young and sound, I would like nothing so well as to be one of them."[12]

Other matters disturbed Grant. Cotton traders drove him to distraction. He ordered McPherson to exclude all civilians from his lines; to another general Grant remarked that it would be fine by him if cotton speculators risked the same treatment accorded to soldiers or civilians who crossed the picket line — being shot — adding that they "are more damaging than the small pox or any other epedemic." Noting the rising number of resignations on the grounds of disability, he speculated that their true ailment might be called "cotton on the brain." Even a direct protest to Secretary of the Treasury Salmon P. Chase did little good. For the moment Grant had to be satisfied with the administration directives regulating trade. There were personal problems as well. The general lost his false front upper plate after his body servant mistakenly took the washbowl in which they rested and cast the contents into the Mississippi. Once more Julia was having trouble with the Grants, and Grant had to intervene. Finally, Jesse was sticking his nose in his son's military plans, writing Congressman Washburne to suggest that either the recently displaced Ambrose Burnside or Grant's West Point classmate, William B. Franklin, be sent west to consult with Grant. The meddlesome father worried that his son might well lose his command and drift away once more from the army and back into the family business. That would not do, Jesse realized: "I am satisfied the army is the place for him."[13]

Day and night, Grant pondered what to do next. Mary Livermore, a representative of the United States Sanitary Commission, once came upon the general, "sitting at the table, wearing his hat, a cigar in his mouth, one foot on a chair, and buried to his chin in maps, letters, reports, and orders." Aboard a steamer one evening, as a military band played, Grant examined maps while staff officers and other generals relaxed and sipped the night away. McPherson approached his commander. "General, this won't do, you are injuring yourself," he began; then, with glass in hand, he invited Grant to "join us in a few toasts and throw this burden off your mind." Grant smiled. "Mac, you know your whiskey won't help me to think; give me a dozen of the best cigars you can find, and, if the ladies will excuse me for smoking, I think by the time I have finished them I shall have the job pretty nearly planned." And so, as the partiers slowly slipped off to bed, they left the general, smoking away, thinking and planning.[14]

John A. McClernand was a frustrated man. His plan to head his own army had gone awry somewhere. Were Stanton and Halleck conspiring against his advancement? Certainly Lincoln would not betray him; but even the president, after looking over a rather pungent missive from McClernand charging Halleck with "wilful contempt of superior authority" and "utter incompetency," asked his man on the Mississippi to avoid *"family* controversies" and work together with his fellow generals.[15]

Undeterred, McClernand soon decided that the best way to gain what he so dearly coveted was to charge that Grant was drinking again. Reporters covering the Thirteenth Corps began circulating stories, inspired, David Porter believed, by McClernand himself. But the corps commander did not rely on the newspapers alone. He soon made common cause with one of Grant's old foes, William J. Kountz, who had reappeared along the Mississippi that winter after exchanging letters with McClernand. From Kountz, the general learned that Stanton was in his corner. McClernand soon gave Kountz a more important mission than supervising river transports. He immediately sent Kountz back to Washington with a letter of introduction to the president that characterized the courier as "an honest and reliable gentleman." Kountz carried with him a story that Grant had been "gloriously drunk" on March 13, and offered to substantiate his report. He left just in time, for Rawlins, always on the lookout for troublemakers, had contacted McClernand with instructions to order Kountz to report to army headquarters.[16]

Other rumors were circulating about Grant's drinking. In February, another general, Charles S. Hamilton, confided to Senator James R. Doolittle of Wisconsin, *"Grant is a drunkard.* His wife has been with him for months only to use her influence in keeping him sober. He tries to let liquor alone — but he cannot resist the temptation always." Hamilton described how he and a friend encountered a "beastly drunk" Grant in Memphis, took him in hand, denied him any more to drink, and called for Julia. At the time Hamilton was seeking his own command, perhaps by displacing McPherson, which may have colored the accuracy of the report. Frustrated in his efforts, he soon resigned, much to Grant's relief.[17]

Most sensational — and quotable — were the charges by Murat Halstead, editor of the *Cincinnati Commercial.* Grant had long struggled with the Cincinnati press. It had been Halstead's paper that had carried the headline "General Sherman Insane" in 1861; in 1862 it had criticized

Grant after Shiloh to the extent that Grant felt compelled to commit the mistake of replying with a letter. It did not help matters that Sherman had just attempted to court-martial a *New York Herald* reporter who wrote critically of the general's performance at Chickasaw Bayou, lending support to the idea that generals on the Mississippi had something to hide. When reporter Joseph B. McCullagh fed Halstead stories about Grant's drinking, the editor decided to take up the matter with his chief friend in Washington, Secretary Chase.[18]

Halstead was blunt: "How is it that Grant who was behind at Ft. Henry, drunk at Donelson, surprised and whipped at Shiloh and driven back from Oxford, Miss., is still in command?" he thundered. "Our noble army of the Mississippi is being *wasted* by the foolish, drunken, stupid Grant." The editor elaborated in a second letter, declaring that Grant was "a jackass in the original package. He is a poor drunken imbecile. He is a poor stick sober, and he is most of the time more than half drunk, and much of the time idiotically drunk." This was a remarkable set of observations for someone residing several hundred miles away from Grant's headquarters. "About two weeks ago," Halstead continued, relaying the latest story circulated by McClernand, "he was so miserably drunk for twenty-four hours, that his staff kept him shut up in a state-room on the steamer where he makes his headquarters." The conclusion was inescapable. "Grant will fail miserably, hopelessly, eternally. You may look for and calculate upon his failure in every position in which he may be placed, as a perfect certainty."[19]

Chase forwarded Halstead's letter to Lincoln, observing, "the reports concerning Gen. Grant, similar to the statements made by Mr. H., are too common to be safely or even prudently ignored." Another newspaper correspondent, bemoaning "how hopeless our cause is in the hands of Maj Genl Grant," told Chase that the general's "mind is too often rendered imbecile by whiskey," and relayed how he had come upon Grant — and Rawlins! — passed out. Bishop Charles P. McIlvaine also passed on rumors of Grant's intoxication and recalled that similar stories had floated about Cairo in 1861 — when Kountz (coincidentally, of course) had first come into the spotlight. But Chase and several of his correspondents had little interest in promoting McClernand's fortunes. They wanted Lincoln to reward William S. Rosecrans, commander of the newly named Army of the Cumberland, with reinforcements from Grant's command. It had been Rosecrans who had whispered tales of an intoxicated Grant to another *Commercial* reporter the previous fall. Old Rosey had spent much of the early months of 1863 pressing Lincoln to send him men; Halstead thought they should come from Grant. Chase, having fastened on Rosecrans and Joseph Hooker as his generals of the moment, shared these letters with Lincoln as he pressed for the proposed reinforcement of Rosecrans. By April it was whispered about the War Department that Grant's men would be sent to Tennessee.[20]

The motives behind the reports of Grant's drinking were transparent. But was there something to them? Rumors circulated throughout Grant's command about his habits. There was excessive drinking going on at Grant's headquarters, but it seemed to involve some of Grant's staff officers. In March, Rawlins, either in response to an actual incident or because he was worried about what might happen in the future, secured from Grant a pledge not to touch alcohol. Other observers denied reports of the general's inebriation. Mary Livermore came away from an encounter with Grant convinced that he was no drunkard. Frederick Law Olmsted, who arrived at Young's Point in late March, later recalled that a woman who interrupted his conversation with the general later spread stories that he had been intoxicated during the interview, despite Olmsted's testimony to the contrary.[21]

People who were supposed to be among Grant's steadfast supporters raised more serious doubts about operations around Vicksburg. Cadwallader Washburn was among the skeptical. "I fear that Grant won't do," he informed his brother the congressman in mid-March. "He trusts too much to others, and they [are] incompetent." Only Rawlins stood out as a man of ability. Washburn lashed out at "the contempible imbecility that characterizes the management of this whole army." Before long, he had given up hope. "The truth is, Grant has no plan for taking Vicksburg & is frittering away time & strength to no purpose," he concluded. "The truth must be told even when it hurts. You cannot make a silk purse out of a sow's ear." Reading such reports, Elihu Washburne grew distressed. Was Grant played out? He shared his brother's letter with (of all people) Chase, with permission to show it to Lincoln. Chase later informed Washburne that Lincoln "seemed much impressed" by the letter, although what may have left the greatest impression was that it had been Washburne who had forwarded it.[22] Even Grant's old patron had lost faith in his man.

Whether Grant would keep his job had long been a topic of discussion. Of the three men entrusted with directing army operations, only Henry W. Halleck seemed to be in Grant's corner, even though his earlier criticisms had once jeopardized Grant's future. Nevertheless, one of McClernand's staff officers informed him that "Halleck is a bitter enemy of yours" who would "oppose any appointment to an independent command." However, Secretary Stanton was open to suggestions. So was Abraham Lincoln. Stories in later years described how the president stood by Grant during these trying times — even Grant accepted them as true. Most famous was the tale of how Lincoln fended off a delegation of ministers who protested the retention of a drunkard in command; the president countered by asking what brand of whiskey Grant consumed, so he could send a barrel to each of his other generals (something that would not have been necessary in the case of the commander of the Army of the Potomac, Joseph Hooker, who knew his way around a bottle). Privately, however, Lincoln worried. Repeatedly he sought information about matters in the West, once inquiring, "Do Richmond papers have *any thing* about Vicksburg?" He considered sending Benjamin F. Butler to the Mississippi to report on the situation — and a week later Stanton drafted orders directing Butler to supersede Grant.[23]

In March, the administration decided on a course of action. Lacking reliable and disinterested sources of information about Grant and his command, Lincoln and Stanton decided that if they could not see things for themselves, they could choose someone to serve as their eyes and ears. Charles A. Dana, a former newspaper editor who was now a troubleshooter for the War Department, seemed ideal for the task. Stanton sent him west on the pretense that he would be investigating how paymasters performed in the West: Grant had already complained that his men were not being paid on time, so the general might not suspect the true import of Dana's mission. Receiving his orders on March 12, Dana immediately headed to Memphis.[24]

Although the president might have been concerned about Grant's drinking, the flurry of reports on that problem descended on Washington *after* he and Stanton had sent Dana off. More important to them were stories that Grant and his generals were lax in their commitment to emancipation. These accounts were not altogether untrue, at least as it concerned generals such as Sherman. However, when senators heard that another general, Frederick Steele, was returning fugitives to their masters in violation of congressional directives, they held up his confirmation as major general of volunteers. Grant protested in strong language; eventually Steele got his commission. But reports of hostility to emancipation and freed blacks among the officers and men of the Army of the Tennessee persisted. In fact, Grant had barred refugees from his lines, for the blacks (mostly children and the elderly) who were abandoned by planters were too much of a burden for him to handle. The army would use contrabands where needed, but otherwise it would be better for blacks to remain where they were and seek wage-paying work. "Humanity dictates this policy," he explained, although the real problem was the impossibility of supervising both the revolution wrought by emancipation and operations against Vicksburg.[25]

Had Grant been winning battles, reports of his failings, coming in the wake of the protest over General Orders No. 11, might have proved less damaging. However, he had little to show for the past several months of campaigning. Holly Springs and Chickasaw Bayou counted against him, while the president credited McClernand with the victory at Arkansas Post. Thus, at the same time Dana learned of his mission, Stanton decided to send Adjutant General Lorenzo Thomas to the Mississippi Valley to supervise the raising of black regiments. That mission pleased Lincoln: "The bare sight of fifty thousand armed, and drilled black soldiers on the banks of the Mississippi, would end the rebellion at once," he told the military governor of Tennessee, Andrew Johnson. "And who doubts that we can present that sight, if we but take hold in earnest?"[26]

The letters and reports about Grant's rumored intoxication and alleged incompetency fueled the doubts already circulating in Washington. Lincoln and Stanton waited for word from Dana and Thomas before acting. The president remained anxious. Just a week after Dana's departure, he wired the commander at Memphis: "What news have you? What from Vicksburg? What from Yazoo Pass? What from Lake Providence? What generally?"[27]

Ironically, Grant's best friend in Washington may have been Henry Halleck. The general-in-chief had grown frustrated with military affairs in the East, in part because the president, despite requesting Halleck's military expertise, often took it on himself to hire and fire generals and pass judgment on plans of operation. He had bypassed Halleck when consulting with McClernand; he did so again in allowing Joe Hooker to contact him directly. Meanwhile, Halleck was losing patience with Rosecrans's repeated excuses for procrastination. Matters got so bad that in March Halleck notified Hooker, Rosecrans, and Grant that there was a vacant major general's commission in the regular army which would be awarded to whoever won a major victory — a blunt offer of a reward for action.

Grant, who had once been a source of endless concern for Halleck, was trying to do his best without complaining, and Halleck returned the favor by keeping Grant informed about affairs at Washington. Although he still lectured his subordinate about the need to keep him posted about events at the front and occasionally chided him about the principles of strategy,

Halleck was trying to be supportive. "The eyes and hopes of the whole country are now directed to your army," he told Grant. "In my opinion the opening of the Mississippi will be to us of more advantage than the capture of forty Richmonds. We shall omit nothing which we can do to assist you." Lincoln was "rather impatient about matters in Mississippi," he warned Grant. Something had to happen — and soon.[28]

"I will have Vicksburg this month or fail in the attempt," Grant promised Halleck at the beginning of March. But March came and went, and Vicksburg remained in Confederate hands. It was not due to Grant's lack of trying. Rains and high waters repeatedly thwarted his canal operations. Grant sent McPherson and a combined army-navy force to Yazoo Pass with orders to clear out the river and create a passage for transports and ironclads, but Confederate cannon at a hastily constructed earthwork called Fort Pemberton blocked the way to the Yazoo River. Next came an expedition traveling through Steele's Bayou, north of Vicksburg, to reach the Yazoo by the Sunflower River, avoiding Fort Pemberton. However, Porter's gunboats became entangled in a web of felled limbs and winding roots, and only the quick response of Sherman's men saved them from capture. And when Grant considered the utility of the Lake Providence route, which he had once thought was "the most practicable route for turning Vicksburg," he realized that he lacked sufficient transports to move his force. Thus he had contemplated an all-out assault against Haynes' Bluff in desperation, well aware that it might prove costly.[29]

Failure after failure, disappointment following on disappointment — it never seemed to end. "I am very well but much perplexed," he told Julia as the month drew to a close. "Heretofore I have had nothing to do but fight the enemy. This time I have to overcome obstacles to reach him." If he could simply set foot on dry land on the east bank of the Mississippi, "I think the balance would be of short duration." But time was running out. "This campaign is being badly managed," Cadwallader Washburn told his brother Elihu. "All of Grant's schemes have failed. He knows that he has got to do something or off goes his head."[30]

Even before he had joined Sherman and Porter to examine the feasibility of an assault at Chickasaw Bayou, Grant had turned his mind to the possibility of swinging southward and crossing the Mississippi. If he could move several corps southward to the west bank of the Mississippi and arrange for gunboats and transports to meet them there, he could cross the river and send McClernand and his men south to meet with Nathaniel P. Banks's army in Louisiana, and the joint force would reduce a Confederate garrison at Port Hudson, Louisiana, a hundred miles downriver from Vicksburg. Afterward, reinforced by McClernand and a detachment from Banks, Grant could move on Vicksburg.

Grant crafted his plan with an eye toward his superiors. He knew that the president favored uniting his army with Banks's command between Vicksburg and Port Hudson with the hope of taking each city in turn. What he did not know (but perhaps suspected) was that Lincoln was, according to one observer, "rather disgusted" with the lack of progress so far. Halleck had displayed little enthusiasm about Grant's previous attempts to approach the city, once asserting that in the process Grant was dispersing his command in such a fashion as to render it ineffective to strike a decisive blow. Perhaps now he would offer more support.[31]

The success of Grant's new plan depended on several factors. First, much would rest on whether Porter could move a sufficient force south past the batteries at Vicksburg. There was a chance he would refuse; there was a chance that the guns would batter the flotilla into uselessness. Much also depended on whether Grant could get Banks to cooperate. Delays in communication by themselves rendered coordinated movements difficult if not impossible, and by now it was evident that Banks was prone to change his mind with alarming frequency, which might well doom any movement.

Aware of the risks, Grant acted. At the end of March he ordered McClernand to begin moving his corps southward toward New Carthage, downriver from Vicksburg. It would take some time for the men of the Thirteenth Corps to get there, for they had to repair the road network as they went to facilitate the subsequent movement of additional men and supplies. Other soldiers would dig one more ditch, connecting the river to a bayou to facilitate the movement of men and supplies by barge. Porter promised to support the movement, but reminded Grant that "when these gunboats once go below we give up all hopes of ever getting them up again," the warning that had spurred Grant to take a careful look at Haynes' Bluff before abandoning it as a line of operation.[32]

Running the batteries was not quite as daring as it sounded. It had been done previously elsewhere on the western rivers. Several times in February Porter had sent a steamer down the river past Vicksburg; one was later captured by the Confederates, leading to a campaign to destroy the makeshift Rebel flotilla. Should disaster strike Porter's flotilla, Grant could still return north to Memphis.[33]

Yet, even if the gunboats and transports succeeded in passing Vicksburg, Grant knew that Pemberton could well foil an attempted crossing of the Mississippi if he concentrated his command at the appropriate point.

Something had to be done to distract and confuse the foe. In February Grant had speculated about the impact of a raid through central Mississippi by "500 picked men" under the command of cavalryman Benjamin Grierson. The raiders could sever the rail lines around Jackson; although the operation "would be a hazardous one . . . it would pay well if carried out." Conflicting orders from Memphis delayed implementation, until at last Grant issued a clear directive to fit out the expedition. On April 3 he gave Grierson the go-ahead. Pemberton would have to keep an eye on his rear and attempt to catch the raiders; should Grierson succeed in disrupting rail connections, the Confederates would have more to worry about. Perhaps the Confederates would disperse their men just as Grant was concentrating his command for a strike across the river.[34]

When Grant outlined his plan to his generals on March 30, Sherman shook his head in disbelief. He still preferred returning north to Memphis and coming down the overland route through central Mississippi. McClernand took notes. "The next day or day after that," Porter recalled, "McClernand wrote to Grant, and proposed the same plan, giving all Grant's reasons. This letter he dated two days before the council, meaning to claim the credit if the plan succeeded, and say nothing about it if he failed." Thus Porter was astonished to learn that Grant had entrusted McClernand with spearheading the march south. Why, Porter demanded to know, was McClernand in the lead? Grant explained that Sherman had opposed the plan, while McClernand had supported it (and would even try to take credit for it). Besides, Grant would be alongside McClernand, looking over his shoulder; Sherman, ever reliable, needed no such scrutiny.[35]

Yet Sherman was not quite as steadfast as Grant thought. "Grant is brave, honest, & true, but not a Genius," he had concluded earlier that month. He still favored the original plan of the previous December. To anyone who would listen, he recited his doubts about running the batteries and coming at Vicksburg from the south, ending with the almost fatalistic rejoinder that he would obey orders. Believing that Grant was down to his last chance, he distanced himself from his friend's proposal even as he professed his loyalty. Nevertheless, he distrusted McClernand even more. He advised Grant to call another meeting of corps commanders to place McClernand's sentiments about the campaign on record before it commenced and handed Grant his own written protest against the operation. "Whatever plan of action he may adopt will receive from me the same zealous cooperation and energetic support as though conceived by myself," he concluded.[36]

Grant took the protests of Porter and Sherman in stride. Such ideas meant little in the long run. It would do no good to point fingers should he fail once more to take Vicksburg. Whatever might be said of the performance of others, it was his job that was on the line.

It was a daring plan, made no less daring by the failure of alternatives. It was also a plan shaped by concerns not purely military. Grant knew that even the appearance of a setback might cost him his job. He was confident his plan would work. It had to work.

For all the illness among Grant's men, the general himself had enjoyed good health that winter. Now, just as he prepared to put his plan into motion, he fell sick. "I am sorely afflicted at this time scarsely being able to sit, lay, or stand," he wrote Julia on April 6. "Biles are the matter."[37] That day two visitors arrived at Grant's headquarters. Neither seemed likely to improve his disposition.

Grant and his staff officers had long expected Charles A. Dana. They were not fooled by the ostensible purpose of his visit: they knew a spy when they saw one. Several staff officers fumed. One suggested throwing him in the Mississippi (which would have caused the very thing they most feared, Grant's removal). Rawlins suggested that the best policy would be to keep Dana under control until the campaign got under way. The representative from the War Department was to be given everything possible to make him feel welcome — an armed guard, his tent pitched next to Grant's — all of which would also allow Grant and Rawlins to keep an eye on him. Nevertheless, everyone was aware of his presence: as Sherman informed his brother the senator, "Mr. Dana is here I suppose to watch us all."[38]

Although Grant was aware of Dana's real mission, he remained undisturbed. If anything, Dana could provide Washington with the daily dispatches that Grant found an annoyance. The general immediately took Dana into his confidence and explained his plan of campaign so clearly that Dana promptly embraced it. Sherman and Porter also realized the importance of cultivating Dana and getting him to accept their point of view. This entailed disparaging McClernand at every opportunity, often with a touch of artfulness. In Dana's presence they reiterated their objections to Grant's decision to entrust command of the lead column to McClernand; Grant would respond by reminding them that McClernand had supported the plan from the first and that it would unnecessarily disrupt the deployment of his army to place someone else in front. It was such a perfect performance that Dana never discerned its manipulative purpose. In complaining as they did, Sherman and Porter — the two officers in the best position to observe McClernand in action at Arkansas Post — made the case against McClernand's competence (and countered stories that credited McClernand with the victory) so successfully that Dana accepted their argument. By keeping McClernand in the lead, Grant demonstrated that personal differences would not obstruct military operations. At the same time he was informing Dana that McClernand agreed with the plan, so that if it did fail, McClernand could not claim that he would have done something else.[39]

The other visitor required equally careful handling. Newspaper reporter Thomas W. Knox, the target of Sherman's wrath the previous February, had returned to seek reinstatement of his credentials to cover Grant's operations for the *New York Herald*. Although several observers found Sherman's insistence on court-martialing the correspondent curious if not embarrassing, Knox's willful distortion of what happened at Chickasaw Bayou offended all but the most devoted of Sherman's enemies. Knox had traveled to Washington to present his case to Lincoln, carrying with him a letter from none other than McClernand, who dismissed Sherman's charges as representing nothing more than technicalities. If Lincoln was not willing to accept this explanation at face value, neither was he willing to ignore Knox, who worked for one of the nation's most influential papers. Instead, he decided to ask Grant to consider the matter in hopes that he would revoke the sentence of banishment imposed by Sherman's court.

Grant, aware of McClernand's influence with the president, nevertheless noted that the president had left the matter up to him. He decided to allow Knox to return only if Sherman consented, to which the redhead fired back, "My answer is Never." Grant then sent Knox on his way, but "knowing the propensity of persons to misrepresent grounds taken in matters when they are personally interested" (a nudge at McClernand as well as Knox), made sure to forward the relevant documents to Lincoln. Several days later Grant himself took some steps to silence the press, ordering Stephen Hurlbut, commanding at Memphis, to review all press dispatches with an eye to military information. When news of prospective operations began to leak out anyway, Grant issued even more definite instructions: "Suppress the entire press of Memphis for giving aid and comfort to the enemy by publishing in their columns every move made here by troops and every work commenced."[40]

Other visitors soon arrived. Elihu Washburne came at Grant's invitation, although he did so with his brother's skeptical words fresh in his memory. Governor Richard Yates also appeared; he was willing to accept

McClernand as Grant's replacement "if anything happened."[41] Finally, Adjutant General Lorenzo Thomas reached headquarters one morning.

Halleck had warned Grant of the import of Thomas's visit. "It is the policy of the government to withdraw from the enemy as much productive labor as possible," he explained in a lengthy letter outlining administration policy toward the former slaves. The enlistment of blacks in the Union army would increase manpower and free whites from garrison duty: "It certainly is good policy to use them to the very best advantage we can." Reports had reached Washington that Grant's generals were subverting the process of emancipation and enlistment. Soldiers had to obey orders, regardless of their personal opinions; it was up to Grant to "use your official and personal influence to remove prejudice on this subject, and to fully and thoroughly carry out the policy now adopted and ordered by the government."

The general-in-chief patiently explained the underlying reasons for these new policies. "The character of the war has very much changed within the last year. There is now no possible hope of a reconciliation with the rebels. The union party in the south is virtually destroyed. There can be no peace but that which is enforced by the sword. We must conquer the rebels, or be conquered by them." He hastened to add that this was an "unofficial letter," and that he was writing "simply as a personal friend, and as a matter of friendly advice." Nonetheless, its import was clear. Those generals who did not support administration policy would find it difficult to retain command, especially in the absence of battlefield success. Grant needed to protect himself from these attacks.[42]

On the day Thomas arrived, Grant responded to an inquiry from General Frederick Steele concerning the fate of refugee blacks. "Rebellion has assumed the shape now that it can only terminate by the complete subjugation of the South," he hastily wrote. Union commanders should "use every means to weaken the enemy by destroying their means of cultivating their field, and in every other way possible." Taking in blacks deprived the Confederates of laborers; in turn, they could prove useful as soldiers. Grant advised Steele to "encourage all negroes, particularly middle aged males to come within our lines," adding that Thomas was raising black regiments.

Grant offered the adjutant general every assistance. Out went orders instructing officers to "especially exert themselves in carrying out the policy of the administration, not only in organizing colored regiments and rendering them efficient, but also in removing prejudice against them." When several officers expressed their disagreement by handing in their resignations, Grant recommended their dismissal from the service. "At least three of my Army Corps commanders take hold of the new policy of arming the negroes and using them against the rebels with a will," he reassured Halleck. "They at least are so much of soldiers as to feel themselves under obligations to carry out a policy (which they would not inaugerate) in the same good faith and with the same zeal as if it was of their own choosing. You may rely on my carrying out any policy ordered by proper authority to the best of my ability."[43]

Thus Grant skillfully defused another threat. While he certainly recognized that recruiting blacks would increase his army and free white soldiers on occupation duty for combat, his vigorous implementation of the directive also impressed Thomas, making the adjutant general a useful ally instead of a critic. "This army is in very fine shape, unusually healthy, and in good heart," Thomas told Stanton, quelling whatever remained of the stories of a disheartened and disease-plagued army. Before long he admitted that he was "a Grant man all over." And at last the land was beginning to dry out. "The embarrassments I have had to contend against on account of extreme high water cannot be appreciated by anyone not present to witness it," Grant told Halleck. "I think however you will receive favorable reports of the condition and feeling of this Army from every impartial judge, and" — here he might well have smiled — "from all who have been sent from Washington to look after its welfare."[44]

On April 11 (the day Thomas arrived) Grant learned that the Navy Department had instructed Porter to transfer his squadron south of Vicksburg in the near future. It was time to move. Two days later engineers opened the canal connecting the Mississippi to the bayous north of New Carthage. It would take a few more days to clear obstructions along the water route, but the main task was achieved — or so it seemed. Soon rising waters rendered the route unreliable for vessels. Porter would have to run these unarmed transports as well as gunboats by the Vicksburg batteries. Grant hurried to make sure that as many transports and barges as possible would make the trip. Sailors and soldiers stacked sandbags and bales of cotton and hay to cushion the walls of the vessels against direct hits, and loaded barges with coal, forage, and equipment for McClernand's corps, which had reached New Carthage. All was ready for the operation to commence on the evening of April 16.[45]

The scene at Grant's headquarters boat that night was oddly domestic, for Julia had just arrived at headquarters with Buck in tow to join Fred. Generals and staff officers crowded the deck. Grant sat, watching; Julia, sitting next to him, held his hand; Buck climbed aboard a staff officer's lap, while Fred scrambled around the deck searching for the best view. It was as if the family was taking in the fireworks at a Fourth of July celebration. Dana and Thomas looked on, knowing full well that Grant's fate might be determined this night.

Just before ten o'clock the flotilla commenced its hazardous journey. Those aboard the steamer could barely make out a series of black shapes moving slowly down the river, quietly floating, all engines off. Here and there one could see a light astern, shielded from the view of the Confederates across the river. No one expected the enemy to be taken by surprise: everyone waited for the batteries to open fire. As the head of the flotilla made its way around the bend in the river just north of the city, the bombardment began. Grant quietly watched, "an intense light in his eyes." The Confederates soon set fire to several buildings in hopes of illuminating the dark shapes. Buck cowered, frightened of the noise and flashes of light, until his father told him to go to bed. Sometime after midnight the cannon got the range on a steamer, and smashed it into flaming bits; other vessels also took hits.[46]

Between the darkness and the distance it was difficult to determine exactly what had happened. The fires along the riverbanks offered no assistance, for they soon burned out. Grant decided to see for himself. Mounting his horse, he raced down to New Carthage, arriving the next morning. The news was fairly good. Of the three transports, one had run aground, while another was damaged. The barges had come through, as had Porter's gunboats. Grant also noticed that much work remained to be done to dig a navigable canal route. But he was relieved at having cleared the first hurdle.[47]

Before long new obstacles presented themselves. When McClernand's men found that the poor roads hampered movement, Grant considered moving his men by water, only to discover that the water level was sinking rapidly. A new road, requiring the building of bridges and significantly lengthening the march route to Grand Gulf, seemed the best alternative. On April 20 Grant issued his final orders for the movement. Soldiers and officers would have to travel light; only a few tents, serving to shield rations from rain and to house regimental, brigade, and division headquarters, would accompany the column. The men would need more food; McClernand called for more barges and transports. On April 22 a second fleet of transport steamers loaded with rations ran the batteries. Once again Grant stood on the deck of a vessel, "cool and collected," puffing away on his cigar, "anxious, without doubt, but apparently quite unconcerned," as an observer later recalled. Although Vicksburg's cannon succeeded in disabling only one steamer, the *Tigress* (of Shiloh fame), the loss was serious because it was carrying the medical stores that would be so sorely needed after a battle.[48]

At first Grant hoped to cross the Mississippi above Grand Gulf at Davis Bend — site of Jefferson Davis's plantation — but the lack of high dry land on the east shore made this impossible. So the general turned to the appropriately named Hard Times, "a cluster of tumble-down cabins" twenty-two miles downriver, almost due west of Grand Gulf. The usually calm general could be seen galloping from point to point, "wrought up to the last pitch of energy." Porter observed: "Grant works like a horse . . . and will wear himself out." But he did not. He knew that much depended on what happened in the next few weeks. "I never expect to have an army under my command whipped unless it is very badly whipped and cant help it," he told his father, "but I have no idea of being driven to do a desperate or foolish act by the howlings of the press." If he was removed, so be it.[49]

Although Grant was making progress, the march was taking more time than he had anticipated. Needing to keep Pemberton in the dark, he asked Sherman, still opposite Vicksburg, to launch a feint against the city. Well aware of Sherman's skepticism about his plan and of the role so far assigned him, Grant did not order Sherman to make the demonstration, but instead requested it, stressing that he would understand if Sherman preferred not to weather the press criticism that would follow an apparent repulse. Grant knew Sherman would resent any hint that what he did was influenced by how newspapers would report it. He was right. Sherman gleefully complied with the request — the press be damned. Nevertheless, he privately maintained that the entire operation was "one of the most hazardous & desperate moves of this or any war. . . . I have no faith in the whole plan." Grant, he insisted, had caved in to political and popular pressure.[50]

McClernand remained far more troublesome. His new wife accompanied him, and where she went her servants and baggage must go as well, a violation of Grant's order directing that officers' baggage be left behind. Instead of instructing his men to commence crossing the river, he turned out an Illinois brigade for review by Governor Yates, complete with a cannonade, in direct violation of Grant's explicit instructions to conserve ammunition for the campaign ahead. As McPherson's lead regiments arrived, they found McClernand's men blocking the way. While the soldiers shivered in the rain, McClernand sought warmth in the arms of his bride.

Grant, fuming, composed a letter of reprimand; but when he arose on the morning of April 27 — his forty-first birthday — he saw to his surprise that McClernand was up and ready to go. Grant pocketed the letter, then issued orders directing McClernand to be ready to move at a moment's notice, adding that his previous directive concerning private baggage must be observed.[51]

The critical moment of forcing a crossing was at hand. McClernand's and McPherson's men assembled at Hard Times, opposite Grand Gulf, while Porter's gunboats shelled Grand Gulf's batteries. Grant watched from the deck of a tugboat. By his side was Fred, who had remained with his father when Julia returned north with Buck. The Confederates held firm, inflicting significant damage on Porter's flotilla, including a direct hit on the admiral's flagship. As Grant boarded the vessel to confer with Porter, he was sickened to see "mangled and dying men" strewn across the deck. It was a sight that remained with him to the end of his life.[52]

Thwarted at Grand Gulf, Grant searched for yet another crossing point. At first he settled on Rodney, some nine miles downriver, where a road led to Grand Gulf. An aged black told Grant that a crossing at Bruinsburg, closer to Hard Times, would save time and offered a high dry road inland. The transports ran the batteries at twilight (the setting sun hampered the vision of Confederate cannoneers), while soldiers marched across a levee. As Grant rode in the night, his horse stumbled, and Dana, half expecting to see the general pitched off his mount, was surprised to see him stay in the saddle and ride on as if nothing had happened. When dawn broke on April 30, Grand Gulf's defenders saw the blue columns and Porter's fleet disappearing downriver.[53]

That afternoon Union soldiers began crossing the Mississippi at Bruinsburg. No Confederates waited on the east bank. Sherman's feint had succeeded in confusing Pemberton. As Grant watched his columns set foot in Mississippi, he felt "a degree of relief scarcely ever equaled since." True, Vicksburg was not yet taken, and much hard campaigning and fighting remained. "But I was on dry ground and on the same side of the river with the enemy. All the campaigns, labors, hardships, and exposures . . . that had been made and endured, were for the accomplishment of this one object."[54]

11

Triumph at Vicksburg

●

SHORTLY AFTER MIDNIGHT on May 1 lead elements of McClernand's corps, pressing eastward from Bruinsburg, encountered a Confederate force under John S. Bowen outside Port Gibson, a half-dozen miles south of Grand Gulf, on the south branch of Bayou Pierre. Badly outnumbered, Bowen carefully deployed his soldiers along the road network west of the town. The terrain complicated efforts to launch an assault. Ridges sliced the field from east to west, forcing attackers to stay close to the roads atop the ridges and the adjoining slopes lest they become entangled in the underbrush that filled the ravines. Grant remarked that he never saw such rough ground. McClernand pushed forward, deploying his corps on two roads, one division advancing northward while the other three continued eastward — away from the first division.[1]

The advance soon stalled. Grant rode forward to see what was the matter. Along for the ride was Governor Yates. The group of horsemen came under fire; the governor, uneasy in his saddle, began to bob and weave. Grant looked at the spectacle, then remarked, "Governor, it's too late to dodge after the ball has passed." But something else could be done to calm Yates's nerves. Out went a request for Porter to open fire on the shore batteries back at Grand Gulf, perhaps in the hope of diverting possible Confederate reinforcements. At last the superior Union numbers began to tell. To the north the defenders began to disperse, but only after Grant had directed McPherson to send some brigades in support; to the east the enemy held its ground a bit longer. Late in the morning the initial Confederate line pulled back; McClernand and Yates rode forward to savor the triumph, and just as at Belmont, the general seized the opportunity to address his men about the victory they had gained. Grant watched briefly, then silently pointed to the east, where the Confederates were forming a second line of defense. Efforts to pierce that line continued throughout the afternoon, as McClernand opted for a straightforward

191

drive that weakened as the men traversed rough terrain. Eventually the Confederates yielded. There were simply too many Yankees to stop. Bowen wisely ordered a withdrawal. Grant told Porter that his men had "utterly routed the enemy"; he asked the admiral's assistance in handling the Confederates captured that day, for "we expect to take more prisoners tomorrow." He instructed McClernand to "push the enemy" into the night, then prepare to "renew the attack at early dawn and if possible push the enemy from the field or capture him." Riding over to a field hospital to grab a cup of coffee, he looked up and was startled to see his oldest son; he had assumed Fred was back aboard Porter's flagship.[2]

The victory at Port Gibson was a tribute to the success of Grant's diversions against Pemberton. As ably as Bowen had conducted his defense, he would have had a much better chance of keeping McClernand at bay with sufficient numbers at hand. In responding to raids and feints, however, Pemberton had dispersed his command, enabling Grant to achieve local superiority — and not for the last time. Whether Grant would be able to retain his advantage remained uncertain. As the sun rose on May 2, Bowen was gone, Port Gibson was empty, and several bridges north and west of town were destroyed. Unwilling to let the moment slip, McClernand dispatched an aide, Colonel Henry Clay Warmoth, to inform Grant that he had taken Port Gibson. So circuitous was Warmoth's route that by the time he tracked Grant down the general was in the town. Although it seemed rather pointless, the colonel announced: "General Grant, I am sent by General McClernand to inform you that we have Port Gibson." Even Grant had to join in the laughter.[3]

Grant did not tarry to savor his victory. Immediately pioneers and work details from McClernand and McPherson's corps, under engineering officer James H. Wilson's supervision, commenced building new bridges. By afternoon the first one was completed; another would be ready for use early next morning. Grant prodded his soldiers forward, telling them to "push right along — close up fast." One brigade forded the river and captured a large Confederate commissary depot bursting with bacon, while another traded shots with a Rebel rearguard. As McPherson's men pressed to the northeast, the Confederates evacuated Grand Gulf. Anxious to keep the pressure on, Grant turned down Bowen's request for a truce to take care of the dead and wounded from Port Gibson, adding that Union and Confederate casualties would receive equal treatment. Picking up a local paper, he read that Grierson's raid had created havoc in the Confederate rear. He smiled at the sight of Fred and Dana, mounted on two large white horses with aging saddles and bridles, but then reminded himself that he also was mounted on a borrowed horse with minimal equipment.[4]

On May 3 Grant learned of the evacuation of Grand Gulf; he rode over to take a look at the town's defenses, confer with Porter, send off dispatches, and refresh himself. He had not had a change of clothing since his birthday on April 27; the only piece of personal baggage he had carried with him was a toothbrush. He felt much better after bathing, changing his underclothes, and eating a warm meal aboard Porter's flagship. There was also mail for him. Banks, replying to a dispatch Grant had penned in late March, anticipated a juncture between the two armies. Much had changed since then — Banks's reply was dated April 10 — and the delays in communication suggested just how difficult it would be for the two men to coordinate their movements. Moreover, Banks could only offer Grant twelve thousand additional men for the Vicksburg campaign and would release them only after he had taken Port Hudson, which he believed he would not reach until May 10.

After reading this message, Grant decided to improvise. Cooperating with Banks was too awkward. Instead of sending McClernand south to join Banks as he had planned, he would order McClernand and McPherson to move eastward into Mississippi. "The road to Vicksburg is open," he told Sherman; "all we want now are men, ammunition and hard bread — we can subsist our horses on the country, and obtain considerable supplies for our troops."[5]

Grant composed a dispatch to Halleck explaining present circumstances and his decision about what to do next. He knew that his superior might frown on the change in plans, but he was determined not to pass up the opportunity before him. Moreover, he reasoned, it would take some time for a courier to carry his dispatch back to Young's Point, where it would make its way upriver to Cairo, where it would be transmitted by telegraph to Washington. Add the return trip, and it might be eight days before he would open the general-in-chief's response. "You can do a great deal in eight days," Grant later remarked.[6] *USG sees an opportunity, does not want Halleck to forbid him from doing it*

The move was not without risks. Vicksburg's cannon could wreak havoc on river-borne supplies, while Confederate general Richard Taylor might turn his attention from Banks to strike from the west and south. But Grant did not hesitate. "The country will supply all the forage required for anything like an active campaign, and the necessary fresh beef," he wired Halleck. "Other supplies will have to be drawn from Milliken's Bend. This is a long and precarious route, but I have every confidence in succeeding in doing it." Sherman was to gather together a supply train filled with bread, bacon, salt, sugar, and coffee and then march his command down to Grand Gulf, which would now be Grant's supply depot. Other messages directed commanders on the west bank of the Mississippi to find shorter and faster ways of moving supplies forward and shifting units south to replace Sherman's men. Dispatches to Halleck indicated what to expect; finally he wrote a letter to Julia. "Fred is very well, enjoying himself hugely. He has heard balls whistle and is not moved in the slightest by it." Fred's father was also having a good time. The victory at Port Gibson, he declared, "is a most important one. Management I think has saved us an immense loss of life and gained all the results of a hard fight." Unable to hide his satisfaction, he continued: "I feel proud of the Army at my command. They have marched day and night, without tents and with irregular rations without a murmur of complaints." His correspondence done, Grant made his way back to the front, riding through the night to reach his men in the early morning hours of May 4.[7]

During the next several days Grant rested his men as he waited for Sherman. Having seized control of a flatboat bridge across the Big Black less than twenty miles due south of Vicksburg, he could now threaten to take that city. Sorties explored routes to Vicksburg and Jackson, the state capital, gathering information while confusing Pemberton as to Grant's next move. Meanwhile he hurried Sherman along and tried to hasten the movement of supplies; his orders crackled with impatience and eagerness to press his advantage. "Everything depends upon the promptitude with which our supplies are forwarded," he reminded an officer as he urged him to expedite shipments of rations and forage. "Movements here are delayed for want of Ammunition and stores," he complained. "Every days delay is worth two thousand men to the enemy." No longer would he risk running Vicksburg's batteries.[8]

Over the next two days Grant mapped out his plan. He would continue to penetrate into central Mississippi. As he advanced northeast, his columns could threaten both Vicksburg and Jackson, forcing the Confederates to cover both or abandon one. He had thirty thousand men under McPherson and McClernand; Sherman would bring another thirteen thousand or so. But he had to move quickly, for he had received reports that the Confederates were sending reinforcements to Mississippi to bolster Pemberton. It was critical to meet and defeat each Confederate force before they could unite. There was no time to see whether Halleck or Banks would agree to his plan; Grant had to do this on his own.[9]

Grant's men rested, refitted, and foraged for food and supplies. "Rations now are our only delay," he informed Hurlbut, back at Memphis.

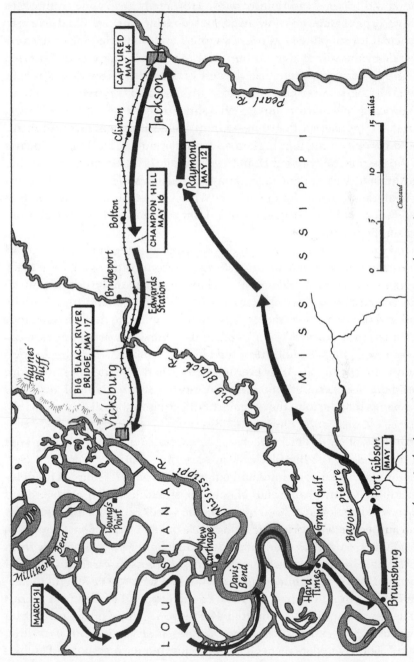

The Vicksburg Campaign, March–July 1863

MARCH 31

Milliken's Bend

Young's Point

New Carthage

Davis Bend

Hard Times

Bruinsburg

Port Gibson, MAY 1

Bayou Pierre

Grand Gulf

LOUISIANA

Mississippi

Haynes' Bluff

Vicksburg

BIG BLACK RIVER BRIDGE, MAY 17

Big Black R.

Edwards Station

Bridgeport

Bolton

CHAMPION HILL MAY 16

Raymond MAY 12

Clinton

Jackson

CAPTURED MAY 14

Pearl R.

M I S S I S S I P P I

Chazaud

0   5   10   15 miles

One dispatch betrayed his impatience: "How many teams have been loaded with rations and sent forward? How many have gone to the 13th Army Corps? I want to know as near as possible how we stand in every particular for supplies. How many wagons have you ferried over the river? How many are still ready to bring over? What teams have gone back for rations?" Sherman marched south and crossed the Mississippi at Grand Gulf; McPherson pushed eastward; McClernand pressed northward, threatening the railroad linking Vicksburg to Jackson and points east. Sherman complained that unless Grant issued instructions, traffic jams would develop along the single road from Grand Gulf to Willow Springs on the way to Grant's army. Doubtless he read Grant's reply with some astonishment: "I do not calculate upon the possibility of supplying the army with full rations from Grand Gulf. . . . What I expect, however, is to get up what rations of hard bread, coffee, and salt we can, and make the country furnish the balance."[10]

Grant was not completely cutting his supply line: the countryside could not provide ammunition, medical stores, and some other goods. But as far as possible, his men would live off the land — a plan made possible by the failure of local planters and farmers (or Confederate authorities) to deny food and forage to the invaders. When Sherman finally arrived on May 9, he shook his head. This was all against the rules. But Grant was ready to go. In several days, he told Julia, the fate of Vicksburg would be decided on the battlefield. "No Army ever felt better than this one does nor more confidant of success," he announced. Almost as an afterthought, he finally told Banks that the joint move against Port Hudson was off.[11]

As Grant waited, so did Pemberton. The Confederate commander kept his men west of the Big Black River, reasoning that if he ventured east, Grant might strike northward and cut him off from Vicksburg. This delay played into Grant's hands. On May 11 he issued his orders. McClernand was to advance northward to Fourteen Mile Creek, some six miles south of the railroad between Vicksburg and Jackson and east of the Big Black River. Once there, he would shield Grant from a possible attack from Vicksburg. Sherman would join him there. McPherson was to push toward Raymond, Mississippi, fifteen miles west of Jackson. "We must fight the enemy before our rations fail, and we are equally bound to make our rations last as long as possible," Grant told McPherson. "Upon one occasion you made two days' rations last seven. We may have to do the same thing again." The Confederates detected the movement; in response Pemberton finally directed his command to march eastward, protecting the rail-

Is this why USG goes to Jackson?

road. It looked as if the Confederates would make a stand at Edwards Station, five miles east of where the rail line crossed the Big Black.[12]

B. of Raymond

The next day McPherson encountered stiff resistance outside Raymond. It was his first real opportunity to handle a corps in battle, and he fumbled it. Nevertheless, after several hours of fighting, his sheer numbers overwhelmed the defenders. Although Sherman and McClernand also engaged in several firefights with Confederates, Grant decided to leave Pemberton alone for now while he followed up McPherson's victory with a drive on Jackson. Having learned that Joseph E. Johnston was gathering a force at the state capital, he decided to break it up before it could pose a serious threat. Moreover, occupying the city would allow Union forces to destroy its usefulness as a rail junction, hindering any future efforts by Johnston to concentrate in the area. Meanwhile, McClernand would shield the rear of the attackers from Pemberton. Once more Grant shifted in response to events; once more it would pay off.[13]

On May 13, as McClernand shifted to Raymond to keep an eye on Pemberton, Sherman and McPherson marched their men through the rain toward Mississippi's capital. Late the following morning, as the rain eased, lead elements of the two Union corps ran into a makeshift defense west and south of the city. Johnston had hastily assembled some six thousand men in an effort to conduct a delaying action. Sherman came up from the

B. of Jackson

southwest and struck the Confederate left, while McPherson, bearing down from the west, smashed the Rebel right. Within several hours the defenders abandoned the city. Entering Jackson, Grant met McPherson and Sherman at a hotel near the statehouse. Fred beat his father there, and later reported that he had seen the United States flag raised over the capitol dome.[14]

As the generals conferred, Grant opened two critical dispatches. McPherson handed him the first, which had been delivered by a courier dressed in Confederate gray, who was in fact a Union agent. The message contained instructions from Johnston to Pemberton to march his men east along the Vicksburg-Jackson railroad to effect a juncture with Johnston's growing force. Charles Dana gave him the second dispatch. Signed by Edwin M. Stanton and dated May 5, it authorized Grant "to remove any person who, by ignorance, inaction, or any other cause, interferes with or delays his operations." Written in response to Dana's report concerning McClernand's laggard behavior in late April, it made clear once and for all who was boss — and added that Grant would be held responsible "for any failure to exert his powers."[15]

If the latter message provided Grant with some relief, the former

USG keeps McClern in a position? a

alerted him both to danger and opportunity. Johnston, thrown off balance by Grant's attack, was regrouping at Canton, several miles north of Jackson, where he awaited reinforcements. To the west Pemberton waited. Under no circumstances could the two Confederate columns unite. Now was the time to strike Pemberton — hard. "Time is all-important," Johnston had told Pemberton; Grant could not agree more. Within minutes he started issuing orders. McClernand was to do an about-face and march westward, stopping at Bolton; McPherson would join him as quickly as possible. Together, they would attack Pemberton. Sherman would stay at Jackson to keep an eye on Johnston while rendering Jackson and its rail network useless to the enemy. Once the orders went out, Grant turned in, sleeping in the same hotel room that Johnston had used the previous night. When the proprietor inquired about payment the next morning, Dana thrust forward a hundred dollars — in Confederate money.[16]

On May 15, as McClernand and McPherson moved westward, Grant and Sherman supervised the destruction of war stores and factories at Jackson. They came across one mill where the workers were still busy making duck cloth for tents with "C.S.A." woven in each bolt. The owners protested in vain that the primary purpose of the factory was to supply employment for women and poor families; after the workers left, the factory went up in flames. Also destroyed was an arsenal, an iron foundry, a carriage factory containing caissons and limbers for artillery, and sundry other businesses. After Grant left, the soldiers, some of whom had been drinking, took matters into their own hands, destroying a church, two hospitals, a bank, and several public buildings. Sherman tried in vain to stop the havoc, noting that it would "injure the morals of our troops, and bring disgrace on our cause." Winds spread the flames, causing even more destruction.[17]

As smoke rose from Jackson, Grant rode west, stopping for the night at Clinton, some eight miles east of Bolton. He knew what he wanted to do and how to do it. Not so with his counterpart to the west. It had been a difficult three weeks for John Pemberton. Raids by Grierson and Abel Streight had distracted him as Grant moved south to cross the Mississippi; the following week he waited in vain for Grant to strike northward from his beachhead toward Vicksburg, slowly shifting his lines east to Edwards Station. As the three Union corps swung eastward, Pemberton crossed the Big Black hoping to intercept Grant's line of communications and supply, although Grant had virtually severed the former and relied on convoys for what his men could not gather through forage. Now came Johnston's dis-

not communicating w/ Halleck? or Hurlbut back in Memphis?

patch to move eastward and join forces (Johnston had sent three copies). Pemberton was understandably a bit frustrated and confused. Nevertheless, his men (some 23,000 in all) marched along the railroad past Edwards Station, across Baker Creek, and onto Champion Hill, which dominated the terrain just west of Bolton. The field featured three east-west roads, two of which eventually converged at Edwards Station; the third linked these two routes, then curled eastward at the base of Champion Hill and headed toward Jackson, twenty miles away. Pemberton made camp for the night, anchoring his left on the hill. *Johnson tells Pemb to move E + join forces w/ him*

Just before dawn on May 16, Grant learned that Pemberton was on the move. Immediately he notified his corps commanders. McClernand was to place his men in line, "feel the enemy," but refrain from bringing on a general engagement "till we are entirely ready." McPherson was to press forward; Sherman was to send another division westward with "great celerity." Grant eagerly awaited battle. "The fight may be brought on at any moment — we should have every man on the field," he told Sherman.[18] *swiftness*

Grant was not to be disappointed. After his lead division encountered Confederate skirmishers along the roads south of Champion Hill, McClernand deployed three divisions in a north-south line and waited, complying with Grant's order not to bring on a general engagement prematurely. To the north, a fourth division, under the command of Alvin P. Hovey, left Bolton and ran head-on into the Confederates on the hill, just at the bend in the road. Two of McPherson's divisions came up in support; so did Grant, prodded to hurry by a plea from McPherson: "I think it advisable for you to come to the front as soon as you can." Otherwise, McClernand would be in charge.[19]

After looking over the field, Grant decided that the bulk of Pemberton's army opposed McClernand. He hesitated to order McClernand forward, however, even after McClernand inquired whether he should now bring on the long-awaited general engagement. Better, Grant thought, for McClernand to await reinforcements. He directed Hovey to advance, with one of McPherson's divisions in support; McPherson's other division, commanded by John A. Logan (known as Black Jack because of his jet-black hair and mustache) would swing around Hovey's right and attack the hill from the north.

The battle opened in earnest; before long Hovey was heavily engaged. If McClernand advanced, Pemberton's position would collapse. But the corps commander did not move, contenting himself with exchanging skirmish fire with the enemy. This was partly Grant's fault, for dispatches from headquarters clearly implied that McClernand should be cautious. More-

*B of Champion's
14.7|*

over, Grant had already seen McClernand struggle in conducting offensive operations on several battlefields, most recently at Port Gibson. Now it was difficult to get word to McClernand on what to do and unrealistic to hope that he would demonstrate initiative by acting on his own, especially in light of previous messages from Grant. It was not until just after noon that Grant finally told McClernand to move forward against the enemy "and attack him in force if an opportunity occurs." Before long he sent several staff officers over to repeat the same message.[20]

Perhaps Grant should have paid more attention to McClernand, but he already had his hands full opposite Champion Hill. At first Hovey carried the summit after a furious firefight. On his right Logan pressed forward in pursuit; Grant, watching him advance, let show a glimmer of pride as he instructed a staff officer, "Go down to Logan and tell him he is making history to-day." But Pemberton, feeling little pressure from McClernand, rushed reinforcements to his left just in time to throw back the attack and regain the crest. The Union line wavered, and looked like it would break. There, watching, was Grant; Fred was close by. The general thought that the attackers had probably spent themselves: "If we can go in again here and make a little showing, I think he will give way." Expecting at any moment to hear that McClernand had joined the battle, he saw little cause for concern. Meanwhile, he ordered Logan to bear to the east to help Hovey out, while Marcellus Crocker's division solidified Hovey's line. Even McClernand's inactivity had its benefits, for Pemberton could not move too many men to the hill without opening up a path for Yankees on his right.[21]

B. of Champion's Hill

Eventually the Yankees checked the Confederate counterattack; before long the Rebels gave way. Only now did McClernand advance; Pemberton's men scrambled westward, and some took the opportunity to leave the war altogether. Grant, not completely satisfied, ordered McPherson to hurry westward in pursuit.

On the face of it Champion Hill was a smashing victory. Pemberton lost nearly four thousand men and twenty-seven cannon; most of the remainder of the Confederate force was retreating to Vicksburg. However, as Grant arranged for the treatment of the wounded and the burial of the dead, he saw that he had missed an opportunity to do more. In asking Logan to help Hovey, he had diverted Black Jack's division from a position astride Pemberton's line of retreat. What ifs began to race through his mind. If McClernand had pressed forward earlier . . . if Grant had known about the road network . . . and so on. Nevertheless, there was glory enough for one day. "I am of the opinion that the battle of Vicksburg has been fought," he informed Sherman. "We must be prepared however for whatever turns up." With that he ordered Sherman to abandon Jackson and rejoin him: "Get to Black river as soon as possible."[22]

As evening came, Grant and his staff rode on, pushing the pursuit forward with such ardor that at last the party found itself alone in the dark, ahead of McPherson's columns. Reluctantly Grant retraced his steps and made camp for the night next to a Confederate field hospital, where the sights, smells, and sounds disturbed him, as at Shiloh. One delirious wounded man, whose brains were protruding from a wound, wandered about screaming and yelling. "While a battle is raging one can see his enemy mowed down by the thousand, or the ten thousand, with great composure," Grant later observed; "but after the battle these scenes are distressing, and one is naturally disposed to do as much to alleviate the suffering of an enemy as a friend."[23] *— not a butcher*

At this campsite a dispatch from Halleck finally caught up with him. Dated May 11, it read: "If possible the forces of yourself & of Genl Banks should be united between Vicksburg and Port Hudson so as to attack these places separately with the combined forces." Perhaps Grant smiled as he pocketed the message. Circumstances had changed. The directive described a situation that no longer obtained. There would be no turning back.[24]

As the sun rose on May 17, Eugene Carr's division of McClernand's corps met up with Confederate troops at Big Black River. Most of the Rebels were already headed for Vicksburg, but Pemberton had stationed three brigades just east of two bridges (a railroad bridge and a makeshift boat bridge). North of the bridges, the river angled eastward, apparently protecting the Confederate left; a lake shielded the defenders' right. The only reason Pemberton had defended the bridges was that he hoped one of his divisions, led by William W. Loring, which had not joined in the retreat from Champion Hill, would find its way back to Vicksburg — but Loring, in fact, had deliberately decided to take his men elsewhere, in part because he could not stand Pemberton. Thus the dramatic battle that followed was pointless. As Grant looked on, Michael Lawler's brigade inched around the Confederate left, then burst upon the Rebels and shattered their line. Some of the Confederates fled across the bridges, only pausing to set them on fire; many others raised their arms high in surrender. As Lawler reported his accomplishment, Grant listened with pride. "When it comes to just plain hard fighting," he once remarked, "I would rather trust old Mike Lawler than any of them." Perhaps his joy would

B of Big Black River

have been tempered had he known at the time that Fred, who had let a boy's natural curiosity get the better of him, had ventured close enough to the firing to be hit in the right thigh, leaving a slight but painful wound.[25]

Just as Lawler led his men forward, an officer rode up to Grant. It was General William Dwight, one of Banks's staff officers, with a copy of a message from Halleck to Banks, also dated May 11, urging Banks to take the same course of action Halleck had recommended to Grant, adding that united action would render success "almost certain." Dwight, interpreting these messages as orders, implored Grant to break off his campaign and comply with Halleck's wishes. Grant declined. No one was going to stop him from taking Vicksburg. In later years he would confuse the arrival of Halleck's dispatch to him with that carried by the staff officer, and report that he had chosen to ignore what he termed an "order." Much has been made of this statement, although Grant himself said that Halleck had issued his directive under a misapprehension of the situation. Grant's act of defiance, such as it was, had occurred two weeks before at Grand Gulf; it was then that he had rejected the idea of uniting with Banks, for perfectly good reasons, as he explained to Halleck, who appreciated that Grant was in the best position to judge for himself.[26]

That afternoon and through the night, work crews labored to build three bridges. Grant rode to Bridgeport, on the east bank of the Big Black River just a few miles north of Edwards Station, where Sherman's command was crossing on a pontoon bridge. By the morning of May 18 rebuilt bridges elsewhere across the Big Black groaned under the weight of Union soldiers marching westward. Vicksburg, some thirteen miles away, seemed within Grant's grasp. Sherman directed his men toward the Yazoo; at last he stood on the ground he had so desperately and fruitlessly sought the previous December. There he met Grant. As the two men surveyed the area, Sherman finally burst forth, half in joy, half in astonishment. Turning to Grant, he exclaimed: "Until this moment I never thought your expedition would be a success; I never could see the end clearly; but *this* is a campaign, — this is a success if we never take the town."[27]

But Grant was not finished. Vicksburg still awaited him. He ordered his three corps forward against the city's fortifications on the afternoon of May 19. He thought the city might fall almost of its own accord: surely Pemberton's demoralized men would not put up much of a fight. To his surprise, the Confederates repulsed the attack. Initially he attributed the setback to lack of preparation. There was some truth in this, for only Sherman's corps was in proper position that afternoon, while Mc-

[handwritten annotation: bc of a rushed camp'n?; should USG have moved a little slower to keep these men?]

Clernand was too far away to be of much help. However, the Confederates opposite Sherman had not been at Champion Hill or Big Black River, so they had little cause to be demoralized. The assault had been too hasty, too improvised, and based on too much optimism. Grant shrugged off the setback. On May 21, as he made arrangements to protect the wounded soldiers who had been left behind (and were now in enemy hands) during the previous three weeks of battle ("My only desire is to know that there is no unnecessary suffering," he remarked), he also issued orders for a second assault for the morning of May 22.[28]

In years to come Grant would explain that the primary reason for the second assault was his belief that his men would not have enough patience to accept a siege until they had proof it was necessary. It is more likely that it was Grant who was reluctant to settle for a siege. It would be difficult to keep his men healthy during the summer months as they sat in their trenches around Vicksburg; the besiegers might have to fend off a relief expedition from either Jackson or Louisiana. "If prossecuted with viger it is confidantly believed this course will carry Vicksburg in a very short time and with very much less loss than would be sustained by delay," he scribbled, indifferent to spelling. And his men were so tired of their diet over the past week that Grant had to still cries of "Hardtack! Hardtack!" with the promise that loaded wagons were on the way. So, as supplies arrived and soldiers constructed roads behind Union lines, commanders looked for the best places to break the enemy line.[29]

An assault would be no easy task. Confederate engineers had taken full advantage of the rolling terrain and bluffs east of the city to build elaborate field fortifications anchored by a series of redoubts and forts. Attackers would have to make their way across open ground sliced with ravines, through abatis, and up steep slopes to reach the enemy; in preparation several Union engineers supervised the building of ladders to ease the way forward. Instead of a cannon signaling the start of the assault, the corps commanders synchronized their watches. At ten o'clock the blue line surged forward.

Sherman's attack bogged down within minutes; several brigades failed to make it to their jump-off positions on the right. McPherson's brigades also stalled. To the south, however, McClernand's men enjoyed more success, reaching the Confederate parapets in several cases and actually entering one redoubt. Nevertheless, Grant, observing the progress of the assault from a Union artillery position on high ground behind McPherson's lines, believed that little more could be accomplished — until McClernand sent him a message claiming that if McPherson launched a diversionary attack to relieve pressure on the Thirteenth Corps, his men could break the enemy's position.

Grant did not agree with McClernand's analysis. True, McPherson's men were not doing much of anything now, but it was unlikely that they could mount the sort of attack McClernand envisioned. Grant first instructed McClernand to draw on his own command for reinforcements, which was nearly impossible, for in deploying his men for a broad front attack, McClernand had stripped himself of almost all reserves, and the rest of his command was already engaged. Still, he was convinced he was on the verge of a breakthrough. Misinterpreting the presence of several flags on the parapets as a sign that large parts of the enemy line had been overrun, he told Grant, "A vigorous push ought to be made along the entire line."[30]

Grant initially reiterated that McClernand should look elsewhere, perhaps to units still approaching the battlefield — an impracticable suggestion revealing his reluctance to comply with his subordinate's request. Sharing the dispatch with Sherman, he muttered, "I don't believe a word of it." Sherman argued that Grant had to renew the assault. If Grant failed to act, McClernand would blame lack of support for his failure to achieve victory, confirming his previous protests about the West Point conspiracy against him. Sherman would order his men to attack again; Grant should do likewise with McPherson's forces.[31]

Grant gave way. He allowed his fear of political repercussions and a nagging feeling that perhaps he was too eager to disparage McClernand to overrule his own assessment of the situation. The men renewed the assaults; they got nowhere. As dusk came, the Yankees started to pull back. Many men died that afternoon because Ulysses S. Grant did not stand his ground; later he would estimate that of the three thousand men who were killed or wounded that day, half of them were victims of the assaults undertaken in response to McClernand's request. Grant blamed McClernand for the losses: he should have blamed himself for listening to Sherman. And he had no one other than himself to blame for what happened after the assault. For several days the dead and wounded lay between the lines; the odor led Confederates to joke bitterly that having failed to drive them out by force, Grant now intended to stink them out. It was left for Pemberton to propose a ceasefire to remove the dead and wounded late on the afternoon of May 25. There was no excuse for Grant's behavior. One might take an unwillingness to accept defeat too far.[32]

Grant played down his setback in his report to Halleck, seriously underestimating his losses and contending that his men "simply failed to enter the works of the enemy." He now determined to take Vicksburg by siege. "There is no doubt of the fall of this place ultimately," he told Porter, "but how long it will take is a matter of doubt," although he initially speculated that Pemberton could not last more than a week. He was convinced that direct assaults would produce little result. "The place is as strong by nature as can possibly be conceived of and is well fortified," he informed Halleck. Engineers began laying out trench lines and identified promising areas for mining or approaching the Confederate fortifications. Grant watched their progress, sometimes too closely for comfort: once, a soldier cried out, "See here, you damned old fool, if you don't get off that mule you'll get shot." At first he thought that Banks might move up the river to help finish the job, but the Massachusetts general had focused his efforts on taking Port Hudson. Not even instructions from Halleck could drag him away; he actually asked Grant for reinforcements. Politely but firmly, Grant refused the request.[33]

Grant also realized that the Confederates might mount a relief operation. Word soon reached him that Joe Johnston was attempting to assemble an army at Jackson with just that aim in mind. The Confederate commander, surprised by the speed with which Grant had moved, doubted Pemberton could hold out long. In response, Grant ordered expeditions to scour the countryside east of Vicksburg, identifying routes over which a relief force might approach. The destruction of the railroads around Jackson complicated Confederate efforts to supply such a force, but Grant remained on guard. In late May he directed cavalry units to sweep eastward from Vicksburg to strip the countryside of forage, livestock, and slaves and to destroy all railroad bridges they encountered; later he augmented this force with several brigades of infantry with orders "to clean out any force" between the Big Black and Yazoo rivers.[34]

Finally, there was still the problem of McClernand. Grant no longer worried about losing his job, but McClernand undoubtedly would continue to disparage him as often as he could. Moreover, in the aftermath of the May 22 assault Grant was now convinced that McClernand was incompetent. "He is entirely unfit for the position of Corps Commander both on the march and on the battle field," he told Halleck. "Looking after his Corps gives me more labor, and infinitely more uneasiness, than all the remainder of my Dept." Left unsaid was that exactly those considerations should have shaped Grant's responses to McClernand's messages on May 22. At first he contemplated removing McClernand, but decided instead to wait until after Vicksburg fell to persuade him to take a leave of absence. Meanwhile, he would keep a careful eye on the commander of the Thirteenth Corps, although he established his headquarters behind Sherman and not far from McPherson.[35]

As May gave way to June, Grant's concerns about a relief expedition grew. Reports of as many as 45,000 Confederates assembling under Johnston filtered back to Union headquarters. Although Grant was skeptical about these rumors, he called for reinforcements. It looked as if Johnston might concentrate at Canton, some twenty miles north of the state capital and thirty miles east of the Yazoo River. A Confederate attack on Haynes' Bluff, located on the east bank of the Yazoo a dozen miles northeast of Grant's headquarters, appeared to offer the best chance of threatening Grant's position. Anticipating such a move, Grant sent forces up the Yazoo toward Satartia and Mechanicsburg, some thirty miles northeast of Vicksburg, to block a potential advance.[36]

While worrying about the prospects of a relief operation, Grant fell ill. The weather around Vicksburg had turned hot; remaining hopes for a quick end to the siege evaporated. Work on constructing regular approaches continued, moving ever closer to Confederate lines; perhaps the siege would come to a close sooner than expected. Headquarters took on an air of anticipation: stuffed away inside a tent was a case of wine and spirits to celebrate the eventual victory. But that soon changed. On June 4 Grant received word that Johnston had taken Yazoo City, some fifteen miles northeast of Satartia. At first he ordered advance forces in that region to pull back from Satartia and Mechanicsburg; then he decided to inspect the situation himself. On the morning of June 6, he boarded a steamer headed north along the Yazoo for Satartia. With him was Charles Dana.

It was a sick man who left headquarters that morning, although it is unclear exactly what was the problem. Perhaps it was a migraine brought on by stress. Others, looking to offer him some relief, had proffered a glass or two of liquor. It was bad enough that Sherman's doctor had proposed wine as a remedy, but Rawlins exploded when he encountered Grant on the evening of June 5, chatting with several staff officers who were sipping wine and asking him to join them. Rawlins retreated to his tent to prepare yet another temperance lecture in the form of a lengthy letter. "The great solicitude I feel for the safety of this army leads me to mention what I had hoped never again to do — the subject of your drinking," he began. Perhaps his suspicions were "unfounded," but when the general, "because of the condition of your health if nothing else, have been in bed," chose in-

USG's drinking temptations

stead to chat away while alcohol circulated, it was time to worry. Moreover, the chief of staff believed that "the lack of your usual promptness of decision and clearness in expressing yourself in writing tended to confirm my suspicions." Rawlins admitted he might be wrong, but he wanted to make sure that Grant adhered to his March pledge of total abstinence. According to one account, Rawlins gave Grant the letter the next morning, just before Grant's departure; although there is no record of Grant's response, Rawlins must have been reassured, for he did not accompany the general aboard the steamer.

What happened next has become the source of great discussion and even greater mythmaking. In all probability, Grant sought relief from his pain by downing a glass of liquor; when that, far from doing the trick, made him feel worse, even woozy, he retreated to his cabin. As the steamer approached Satartia, two gunboats hailed it, reporting that Union forces had abandoned Satartia and it was no longer secure. Dana notified Grant of this; still reeling from his headache, Grant left it up to Dana what to do next. Dana decided to return to Haynes' Bluff. The next morning, Grant arose, discovered where they were, and ordered a cavalry detachment to ride over to Mechanicsburg to see what was going on. Dana, satisfied that Grant was better, accompanied the detachment; Grant returned to Vicksburg.

In years to come, this was not what people read and repeated. What emerged instead was a story charging that Grant got drunk on a joyride up the river. Dana himself gave credence to this story, writing in 1887 that Grant was merely on "an excursion" on the Yazoo "during a dull period in the campaign," which allowed him to get "as stupidly drunk as the immortal nature of man would allow." Even richer was the story of newspaperman Sylvanus Cadwallader, who concocted an account featuring his heaving bottles out of the steamer's stateroom before locking the intoxicated general up — followed the next day by yet another Grant spree, capped by a wild horseback ride through the woods in which he was saved from certain disaster by a combination of luck, fate, and Cadwallader. That Dana, who surely would have heard the ruckus on the steamer described by the reporter, denied that Cadwallader was present was only the most serious of several contradictions between the two accounts, which they and James H. Wilson tried to reconcile in 1890 by concluding that there must have been *two* trips! By that time, both Cadwallader and Wilson agreed that Grant was highly overrated (and their own contribution to his success, as well as that of Rawlins, was very underrated); Dana had become disillusioned with the general.

about USG's drinking (?)
while going up Yazoo to
Satartia

Key components of the tale woven by this trio unravel in the face of a careful reading of the evidence; nevertheless, many fine scholars, always on the lookout for a colorful story or two to enliven their narratives, and desperate for a good account of Grant actually drinking, have embraced it without batting an eyelash. They have even cited Rawlins's letter in confirmation of the story although it was prepared *before* Grant left; they ignore the endorsement appended by Rawlins: "Its admonitions were heeded, and all went well." How could Rawlins have said that if Cadwallader's report is accurate? To accept this fable, one would have to believe that an ailing Grant, alarmed as he was about the security of his lines, nevertheless decided to board a steamer headed for the threatened area just to get away from Rawlins so he could drink in private — and that he knowingly invited along for the ride a representative from the War Department whose assignment was to report on his private habits and fitness for command. Tucked away in a draft of his biography of Rawlins was Wilson's admission of what really happened — Grant "fell sick, and thinking a drink of spirits would do him good, took one with the usual unhappy result."[37]

Grant returned to headquarters from his trip up the Yazoo confident that he could hold his ground. He would fortify Haynes' Bluff to check any attack. Word arrived that reinforcements were on their way from Memphis to strengthen the new line. Adding to his confidence was the news that black recruits drilling at Milliken's Bend had fended off a Confederate attack on June 7. In forwarding a report of the action to Washington, Grant praised their behavior as "most gallant and I doubt not but with good officers they will make good troops." It soon became apparent that one reason the blacks fought so well was that they learned that the attacking Confederates advanced under the black flag of no quarter; less noticed was the role Porter's gunboats played in checking the attackers.[38]

Although hopes for a short siege were gone, Grant now believed his lines were secure. "My position is naturally strong and fortified against an attack from outside," he told his father. "I have been so strongly reinforced that Johnston will have to come with a mighty host to drive me away." Still, he speculated that if the May assaults had succeeded, he might have "made a campaign that would have made the state of Mississippi almost safe for a solitary horseman to ride over." Now, by the time the city surrendered, it would be too hot to undertake a large-scale campaign. "The fall of Vicksburg now will only result in the opening of the Miss. river and demoralization of the enemy. I intended more from it." Still, he could

USG defends F attack by Johnston by:
fortifying Mayne's Bluff,
eventually Sherman surveils
Johnston, at end of June
p 209

afford to relax and was feeling better; his mind turned to more personal concerns. Off went a letter to Julia asking her to bring the family to headquarters: "I want to see you very much dear Julia and also our little children." Fred was enjoying himself; his wound no longer bothered him and Grant claimed that both of them had "enjoyed most excellent health" during the campaign. A week later he modified that statement to admit that he and Fred had just suffered a bout with dysentery. Meanwhile he solidified his defenses against a possible relief expedition. More reinforcements arrived, including two divisions, some eight thousand men strong, from Ambrose Burnside's Ninth Corps in Kentucky. They occupied the fortified line along Haynes' Bluff, now ready to repulse any Confederate threat from the east. Work on reducing the Vicksburg garrison continued; again Grant exposed himself to enemy fire. Once, as he perused the enemy position through field glasses, he told division commander Alvin P. Hovey to take cover. Hovey objected. Grant was the one who should take cover, he claimed, pointing out it would be "easy to fill my place, but with you, sir, it's different." Another time the general ascended a tower built a short distance from an enemy redan along McPherson's front. As he peered through his field glasses, he made for an excellent target. Unaware of the identity of the unwary Federal, a Confederate soldier yelled that he ought to duck lest he get his head shot off; his superior officer, recognizing that the Federal was an officer, reprimanded the soldier for using disrespectful language toward an officer; Grant took advantage of the respite offered by the exchange to descend the tower. He liked what he saw: by the middle of the month he remarked that the Confederates "cannot show their heads without being shot at a short enough range to kill a squirrel." Periodically he bombarded the city; so did Porter's gunboats. Soldiers lobbed hand grenades into enemy lines.[39]

Each day Grant went out to see how the siege was progressing. A newspaperman described him walking about, "with his shoulders thrown a little forward of the perpendicular, his left hand in the pocket of his pantaloons, an unlighted cigar in his mouth, his eyes thrown straight forward, which, from the haze of abstraction that veils them, and a countenance drawn into furrows of thought, would seem to indicate that he was intensely preoccupied." As he strolled though his army's camps, the men rose to their feet: "They do not salute him, they only watch him . . . with a certain sort of familiar reverence" as Grant passed by, "turning and chewing restlessly the end of his unlighted cigar."[40]

Just when it seemed that things could not get better — short of Vicksburg's capitulation — they did. For Grant at last found a way to get rid of

John A. McClernand. Relations between the two generals had reached a boil in the aftermath of the May 22 assaults. McClernand denounced rumors that his command had not performed its assigned task (it would have been more correct to say that Grant, Sherman, and McPherson thought that McClernand had misled them as to his command's accomplishments that bloody day). The corps commander once snapped that he would be damned should he comply with any more of Grant's directives, speaking with such heat that James Wilson, who had delivered the order, told him to apologize or face the engineering officer in a fist fight. Attempting to recover, McClernand explained: "I was simply expressing my intense vehemence on the subject matter, sir, and I beg your pardon." When Grant heard this, he smiled; afterward, when people complained to him about Rawlins's swearing, he would explain, tongue-in-cheek, "He's not swearing — he's just expressing his intense vehemence on the subject matter."[41]

Soon there was more reason for Rawlins to display his intense vehemence — this time in chorus with Sherman and McPherson. On June 17 Grant learned that four days earlier a Memphis newspaper had reprinted a congratulatory order from McClernand to his corps for their service on May 22. Before long a second copy surfaced, this time from a Missouri paper. Somehow McClernand's staff had failed to forward a copy of it to Grant's headquarters; perhaps, however, that was no accident. For the commander of the Thirteenth Corps had decided to announce that his corps alone deserved credit for the success of the campaign; Sherman, McPherson, and their men had fallen short. Neither corps commander would tolerate such a lie: both forwarded letters to Grant protesting the contents of the order and asking for an investigation.[42]

It was not just that McClernand had gone too far this time: in Grant's estimation he had gone too far many times. A peculiar combination of circumstances, however, allowed Grant to respond as he had long desired to do. Knowing that Vicksburg was doomed and that he could fend off a relief effort, he no longer needed to worry that McClernand might seize on some defeat to renew his campaign for Grant's job. Moreover, Edward O. C. Ord had just reported for duty and was a qualified replacement as a corps commander. Finally, in failing to forward a copy of his order to army headquarters prior to its publication, McClernand had violated regulations, rendering himself vulnerable to removal.

On June 18, Grant had Rawlins draw up an order relieving McClernand from command and naming Ord to replace him, "subject to the approval of the President." Rawlins wanted it delivered immediately; Wilson, who

had once been a McClernand favorite, volunteered to hand it to Mc-
Clernand personally, and so off he went into the night, in dress uniform,
with an escort headed by the provost marshal. It was two o'clock in the
morning when the colonel reached the Thirteenth Corps; he discovered
that the general was not quite ready to receive him. When at last Wilson
entered McClernand's tent, he found the general in full uniform, sword
on the table, as if he knew something was up. McClernand unfolded the
dispatch, read it, and exclaimed, "Well, sir! I am relieved!" Taking a deep
breath, he added, "By God, sir, we are both relieved!"[43]

McClernand left, but he did not plan to go quietly. Questioning Grant's
authority to remove him, he pursued his case with higher authorities; off
went a letter to Lincoln asking for a hearing. None of this surprised Grant,
who notified Halleck that McClernand's order was "calculated to create
dissention and ill feeling in the Army," implying that had he felt free
to act, "I should have relieved him long since for general unfitness for his
position." Dana confirmed that assessment, highlighting McClernand's
"repeated disobedience of important orders . . . general insubordinate
disposition . . . palpable incompetency for the duties of his position" and
the fear that, should anything happen to Grant, McClernand would assume command. Ultimately, Lincoln, Stanton, and Halleck would determine McClernand's fate. For the moment, however, Grant could rest secure in the thought that the only fire in his rear would come from Joe
Johnston. Almost as if in celebration, he ordered a general bombardment
of Vicksburg on June 20.[44]

As June drew to a close, Grant tightened the noose around Vicksburg.
Information from deserters alerted him to the defenders' increasingly
desperate situation; hungry and tired, they talked about attempting to escape by climbing aboard rafts and making their way across the Mississippi.
He responded to every report of a possible Confederate attack by redoubling preparations to check a relief column; eventually he ordered
Sherman to take over surveillance of Johnston with an eye to driving him
off once Vicksburg fell. No longer was he worried about an attack; he now
itched to crush Johnston. Meanwhile McPherson and Ord kept creeping
closer and closer to the city; on June 25 Grant ordered the detonation of
the first of two mines to crack the enemy line. He watched as the mine exploded; however, assaulting troops were unable to seize the crater, and the
Confederates repaired their line to the rear. Nevertheless, the operation
convinced Grant that the end was near. Several days later he predicted to
Julia that the garrison would capitulate on July 4 or 5; she should start
making plans to visit him. It was time to consider where the children

would go to school the next year. Perhaps Julia could find a place that would enable her to spend some time with him, "when I am still. I do not expect to be still much however whilst the war lasts."[45]

Meanwhile Grant responded to reports that Confederate officers had ordered the execution of several dozen black soldiers and their white officers captured at Milliken's Bend. He contacted Richard Taylor, commander of Confederate forces in Louisiana, ostensibly to ascertain the truth of these reports, but in reality to warn him that such behavior would not be tolerated. "It may be you propose a different line of policy toward Black troops and Officers commanding them to that practiced towards White troops?" he asked, adding, "If so I can assure you that these colored troops are regularly mustered into the service of the United States. The Government and all Officers under the Government are bound to give the same protection to these troops that they do to any other troops." It was the color of the uniform, not the color of the skin of the man wearing it, that mattered to him. Taylor denied the charges although the stories lingered; in the future Grant would have to ponder the possible consequences of putting black soldiers in combat zones, for Taylor observed that the captured blacks would be turned over to state authorities instead of receiving the same treatment as white prisoners of war.[46]

As July came, Grant contemplated one last push. Another mine went off on July 1; mortar fire from Porter's gunboats inflicted serious damage on the Confederate river defenses. Determined to bring things to a head, Grant began issuing orders to prepare for an assault on July 6. However, on the morning of July 3, under cover of a flag of truce, a Confederate courier delivered to Union lines a message from Pemberton requesting an armistice and a conference. Pemberton somewhat gruffly asserted that he was acting "to save the further effusion of blood," although he still believed that he would be able "to maintain my position for a yet infinite period." Grant promptly replied that he had no interest in appointing commissioners to negotiate a surrender: "The useless effusion of blood you propose stopping by this course can be ended at any time you may choose, by an unconditional surrender of the city and the garrison . . . I have no terms other than those indicated above." That might have brought all talk of a surrender to an abrupt end, but one of Pemberton's generals, John S. Bowen, already stricken with deadly dysentery, urged Grant to meet Pemberton at three o'clock in the afternoon between the lines of the two armies on McPherson's front. Bowen and Grant had known each other before the war in St. Louis. Grant, thinking that a conversation might do some good, acceded.[47]

At three o'clock in the afternoon the two commanders met on the Jackson road between the lines, just south of where McPherson had exploded his mine on June 25. Pemberton, who was late, was in full uniform, while Grant remained in field dress, although for this occasion he sought to smooth the way to a productive discussion by bringing a demijohn with him. He might have saved himself the effort. Neither man wanted to begin the conversation; at last Pemberton announced that he was there in response to Grant's request for an interview, thus inadvertently revealing that Bowen had misled him. Startled, Grant replied that he had made no such request; Bowen was left to explain himself to both men. When Grant reiterated that he would not soften his demand for unconditional surrender, the Confederate commander huffily declared that then there was no need to continue talking, and added ominously, "I can assure you, sir, you will bury many more of your men before you will enter Vicksburg." Grant, silent, merely puffed on a cigar; frustrated, Pemberton then proclaimed that he had sufficient supplies to hold out indefinitely.[48]

This was all bluster, and Grant knew it. Better, he thought, to see if Pemberton's subordinates were more amenable to reason. Either Bowen or Grant suggested that the two army commanders should step aside and let their generals try to work something out. Pemberton, seeing in this some semblance of the proposed conference of commissioners, agreed, and the two men sat down together. Pemberton tried to control his temper; Grant quietly pulled at tufts of grass, an unlit cigar in his mouth. But the other generals did no better at structuring an agreement. Grant rejected Bowen's proposal to allow the garrison to march out, complete with small arms, artillery, and all the honors of war. Pemberton concluded that the question of terms was up to Grant; Grant replied that he would contact Pemberton that evening.[49]

Back at headquarters, Grant called his corps and division commanders together. Although he rejected Bowen's proposal, it was evident that to ship some thirty thousand men to prison camps in the North might be more than the Union navy could handle (Pemberton knew this as well, for he had intercepted pertinent communications between Grant and Porter). And it was doubtful that an assault would be worth the cost, especially as in the end one would still have to decide what to do with the surviving Confederates. The only alternative appeared to be to parole the garrison; that is, disarm it and send it away with the assurance that these men would not return to duty until exchanged just as if they were prisoners. Grant reasoned that many of the surrendered Confederates had seen enough of war for one lifetime, and they might infect others with their disaffection.

Later he added that he believed that "consideration for their feelings would make them less dangerous foes during the continuance of hostilities, and better citizens after the war was over." In the end, Grant gave in to his subordinates; he sent off the proposal to Pemberton and waited. Several hours later, he had his reply. After reading it, he sighed, then said calmly, "Vicksburg has surrendered."[50]

True to form, Pemberton tried to wriggle a few concessions. He wanted his men to stack arms in a formal ceremony; more importantly, he wanted all officers and private citizens to retain their personal property (which, of course, meant slaves). Grant rejected these amendments (although he was willing to have the Confederates stack arms before returning to their camps to await the parole process) and gave Pemberton a deadline of 9 A.M. on July 4. The answer came when Union officers saw the white flags go up along the Confederate lines. Three divisions marched into the city to take possession; Grant followed, and made his way to a large house where the Confederate high command watched the proceedings from the porch. Irritable to the end, Pemberton failed to offer Grant a seat and gave him the cold shoulder; when Grant asked for a drink of water, someone remarked that he could go to the kitchen and get it himself. Before long Grant and his staff mounted and rode away; when officers complained of their frosty reception, Grant smiled: "Well, if Pemberton can stand it, under the circumstances, I can." The Union entourage rode on to the courthouse to witness the raising of a United States flag, then boarded Porter's flagship for a reunion with their naval ally. As officers from both services toasted each other with wine provided by Porter, the admiral saw Grant sitting calmly, seemingly unaffected by the celebration.[51]

So ended one of the war's great campaigns — the greatest triumph to that date secured by a Union general. Vicksburg was now in Union hands; when Port Hudson fell five days later, so was the Mississippi River. Some thirty thousand Confederate soldiers took their paroles, and many went home (however, thousands more rejoined the Confederate army without being properly exchanged). Thousands of black slaves gained their freedom, and more than a few prepared to fight to preserve it. All of this was the product of Grant's skill, determination, and perseverance in overcoming obstacles of terrain and climate, with enemies to his front and at his rear seeking to defeat him.

The outcome secured one other objective. On July 5, before news of the surrender reached Washington, Abraham Lincoln visited Daniel Sickles, who had been severely wounded at Gettysburg. Talk soon turned to events out west and the man in charge. What did the president think of Grant now? "He doesn't worry and bother me," Lincoln replied. "He isn't shrieking for reinforcements all the time. He takes what troops we can safely give him . . . and does the best he can with what he has got. And if Grant only does this thing down there — I don't care much how, so long as he does it *right* — why, Grant is my man and I am his the rest of the war!" Two days later he learned of Vicksburg's surrender.[52]

For months Abraham Lincoln had wondered whether Grant was the best man for the job. However, what Grant did in May astonished him: as the siege got under way, the president judged the campaign "one of the most brilliant in the world." And so on July 13, as he worried about whether George Meade would snuff out the Army of Northern Virginia at Williamsport, Maryland, he sat down to write Grant the first truly warm personal note he had ever penned to the general. The two men had never met, but it was time, the president decided, to offer Grant "a grateful acknowledgment for the almost inestimable service you have done the country." But that was not all. The president explained that from the start he had believed that the only way for Grant to take Vicksburg was to cross the river south of the city; only the notion "that you knew better than I" checked his skepticism about the other attempted routes. However, once Grant had crossed the river, Lincoln was disappointed that the general did not turn south to unite with Banks, and feared that in advancing toward Jackson, Grant had erred. What followed was at once graceful in itself and an admission that carried a broader application: "I now wish to make the personal acknowledgment that you were right, and I was wrong."[53]

strategy?

12

The Heights of Chattanooga

●

IT TAKES TIME to parole thirty thousand men. It was necessary to issue the proper paperwork; ensure that each prisoner sign a parole as a reminder of his obligation; march the Confederates out of Vicksburg; and establish an occupation force to maintain order. Grant blocked attempts by Pemberton and others to renegotiate the terms of the surrender by reinterpreting them. As the paroled Confederates finally departed a week later, he directed his own men "to be orderly and quiet" and to refrain from making "offensive remarks." Fostering resentment to counteract the Confederates' demoralization would not help the Union cause. Although those blacks who wanted to accompany their masters were allowed to leave with them, Grant had no intention of prolonging involuntary servitude: "I want the negroes all to understand that they are free men"; he had already instructed his commanders to gather up all the black men they could find and put them to work.[1]

Even as he opened negotiations with Pemberton, Grant, anticipating the final result, had ordered Sherman to move eastward toward Jackson: "I want you to drive Johnston out in your own way, and inflict on the enemy all the punishment you can." He sent several divisions to assist that effort. Another division was earmarked for Port Hudson until news arrived that it had fallen to Banks on July 9. Grant then directed that division to capture a Confederate post at Yazoo City. Sherman's expedition against Jackson turned into a full-fledged campaign; after driving Johnston away, the Yankees completed the destruction of railroads, factories, and buildings that had commenced in May. It was time to rest and refit — although not for long. During the respite Grant pushed for promotions for Sherman and McPherson; he learned that he was now a major general in the regular army.[2]

Grant's confidence in his subordinates was reciprocated in full. Neither Sherman nor McPherson had embraced Grant's April plan; both did what

when did USG embrace total war?

they could to make it work. Frank Blair came away from the campaign simply amazed by what he had seen. Visiting Washington in August, he shared his astonishment with his sister Elizabeth. Grant had taken great care to avoid mishap; the implementation of the operation reflected that hard work, and the result, concluded Elizabeth, "has evidently uplifted their general in the hearts as well as heads that he should look ahead so much to prepare for their comforts as well as safety."[3]

Nor was he yet done. To bolster his army's strength, Grant turned with new energy to the recruiting of black regiments. His recent triumph had left him with new areas to garrison, and he believed that the black recruits were ideal for the task. Armed with the weapons captured at Vicksburg, they could patrol the city and the surrounding plantations. Nevertheless, he complained that some of commissioners appointed to supervise work on those plantations were doing "a great deal of harm"; even Captain Abraham Strickle, whom he termed "honest and enthusiastic in the cause that he was serving," was "probably influenced by old theories of abolishing slavery and elevating the negro." Exactly how Grant thought the commissioners should do their jobs remained unclear; implied was the observation that the experiment in free labor required constant and close supervision — and Strickle's death made things worse. Reports that recruiting parties were impressing former slaves off the plantations of unionist planters irked him, although when further investigation suggested that the planters might have misrepresented the state of affairs, he let the matter drop. At the same time Grant acknowledged that some of his own white soldiers had provoked clashes with the blacks, and he defended Colonel Isaac Shepard, in charge of the black recruits, for punishing the miscreants when their own commanders failed to exercise discipline. By the end of July he could report: "The negro troops are easier to preserve discipline among than our White troops and I doubt not will prove equally good for garrison duty. All that have been tried have fought bravely."[4]

Matters were quiet in the aftermath of Vicksburg's fall. Julia and the children spent much of the summer at army headquarters, a large white house that was home to William and Ann Lum. So did Grant's staff, including John Rawlins. For once he was not preoccupied with Grant: it was the Lums' Connecticut governess, Mary Emma Hurlbut, who had all his attention. He had now been a widower for nearly two years and was attracted to the young woman, who blushed whenever she approached him to ask a favor. If Grant noticed, he said nothing. Instead, he waited for orders from Washington. He wanted to mount a campaign against Mobile, Alabama; Banks, although in agreement, also wanted to advance into Texas, while in Missouri, John M. Schofield looked to clean out Arkansas. Grant detached men to help both generals, but kept pressing for Mobile. Halleck held him off for the moment. "Before attempting Mobile, I think it will be best to clean up a little," the general-in-chief observed; it would take some time for Washington to settle on a course of action.[5]

Among the messes Grant had to clean up was the continued threat posed by John McClernand. On the day after Grant received formal notification of his promotion to major general in the regular army, he reviewed McClernand's report of the operations of the Thirteenth Corps during the Vicksburg campaign. It was one thing to give the men and officers of the corps the credit due them for their part in the campaign; it was quite another to let McClernand's "pretentious and egotistical" report go forward uncontested, and fruitless to comment on its misstatements without rewriting the entire document. Yet Grant suspected (correctly) that the disgruntled general had already furnished Lincoln with a copy of this exercise in self-defense; indeed, McClernand had requested a court of inquiry covering the period between Belmont and the May 22 assault. Grant had to end McClernand's meddling once and for all.[6]

Grant had already taken steps to enhance his relations with the top brass. By befriending Dana, he had turned a possible critic into a staunch ally whose messages criticizing McClernand buttressed the case for his removal. Now the envoy from the War Department was back in Washington, reassuring all who would listen — including Lincoln and Senator Henry Wilson of Massachusetts — that Grant was committed to emancipation (and that he was not a drunkard). Dana believed him to be "the most modest, the most disinterested, and the most honest man I have ever known." Lorenzo Thomas, also in Washington, shared with others his favorable impression of Grant's views on emancipation and black enlistment. And just before Vicksburg fell, Grant sent John Eaton (the chaplain in charge of black refugees in northern Mississippi and West Tennessee) to meet with Lincoln. But Grant still wondered whether McClernand's skills at self-promotion and distortion would affect the president's thinking. Thus he decided to send Rawlins to Washington to hand-deliver his own report of the Vicksburg campaign, confident that the lawyer-politician could more than hold his own in providing a damning indictment of McClernand. In a skillfully worded letter of introduction, Grant told Lincoln that Rawlins "has not a favor to ask for himself or any other human being. Even in my position it is a great luxury to meet a gentleman who has no 'axe to grind' and I can appreciate that it is infinitely more so in yours."[7]

Rawlins reached Washington on July 30 and first met with Halleck, who assured him that the high command "have finally decided to hand McClernand out to grass," although a promised order to muster him out of service never materialized. The next day the chief of staff was the featured guest at a cabinet meeting. Secretary of the Navy Gideon Welles praised Rawlins's "frank, intelligent and interesting description of men and of army operations. . . . The unpolished and unrefined deportment of this earnest and sincere patriot and soldier interested me more than that of almost any officer whom I have met." Nevertheless, Welles discerned that Grant had "sent him here for a purpose" — to dispose of McClernand. Rawlins argued persuasively that McClernand was "an impracticable and unfit man, — that he has not been subordinate and intelligent, but has been an embarrassment, and instead of assisting has really been an obstruction to, army movements and operations."

Welles was won over, concluding that "McClernand is at fault," although he added: "Grant evidently hates him, and Rawlins is imbued with the feelings of his chief." Rawlins's presentation also succeeded in persuading the president. McClernand's requests for a court of inquiry were first ignored, then turned down; his attempts to revive them, colored by dark insinuations about Grant's conduct and personal habits, also achieved nothing. The president, who formerly had allowed McClernand to pass on complaint and innuendo without reprimand, now informed him that he would never gain the vindication he sought, observing, "This is a case . . . in which I could do nothing without doing harm." If forced to choose between Grant and McClernand, the president left little doubt which way he would go (although, blinded by his egotism, McClernand failed to get the message).[8]

One sign of Grant's popularity was a movement to bring him east to replace George G. Meade as commander of the Army of the Potomac. Meade's laurels from the victory at Gettysburg, fought just as the siege at Vicksburg was approaching its end, started withering when he failed to bring Lee to battle again before the Confederates returned to Virginia in mid-July. Lincoln was unhappy; Meade snapped that if that was the case someone else could take over. Eventually tempers cooled, and the quest for a replacement subsided. Grant sighed in relief. The assignment would have caused him "more sadness than satisfaction. . . . Here I know the officers and men and what each Gen. is capable of as a separate commander. There I would have all to learn." Besides, the appointment of a

Westerner to command the main Eastern army would create problems "with those who have grown up, and been promoted, with it. . . . Whilst I would disobey no order I should beg very hard to be excused before accepting that command." Grant had already experienced enough criticism and second-guessing from Washington; why court more of it?

Grant's old critics were either seeking somewhere to hide or were stumbling over each other in their haste to assure the general of their support. Secretary of the Treasury Salmon P. Chase, as slippery as his given name might imply, did not even await the news of Vicksburg's fall to tell Grant of "my deep sense of your great services to our country. . . . It has given me great satisfaction to be somewhat useful in sustaining you here by laying before the President, from time to time the letters of Mr. Mellen (Chase's representative in the Mississippi Valley). . . . He . . . has constantly defended you against the assaults sometimes of slanderous malice and sometimes of mistaken honesty." The secretary conveniently omitted to mention the other letters he had shared with Lincoln charging Grant with drunkenness and advocating his removal or the transfer of his command elsewhere. Chase, always anxious to align himself with a winner, demonstrated which way the wind was blowing in Washington that summer.[9]

Even better was confirmation of Abraham Lincoln's faith in Grant. Curious as to why the general had not acknowledged the receipt of his letter congratulating him on the fall of Vicksburg (Lincoln had just observed, "Grant is a copious worker, and fighter, but a very meager writer, or telegrapher"), the president now wanted to explain why the administration wanted to postpone an expedition against Mobile. In addition, the president wanted to know more about the progress of raising black regiments. "It works doubly," he observed, "weakening the enemy and strengthening us." Lincoln did not mention either Rawlins's visit or McClernand's fate; he was simply trying to open up a direct line of communication to Grant and to reassure him of his confidence in the general.

Grant replied in a letter explicitly designed to cultivate the relationship. He graciously conceded that while he wanted to advance on Mobile, "I see however the importance of a movement into Texas just at this time." More important was his endorsement of administration policy toward black enlistment. He had given it his "hearty support," explaining: "This, with the emancipation of the negro, is the heavyest blow yet given the Confederacy." Slaves no longer labored hard for their masters, and this was undermining productivity; recruitment efforts would increase once his men cleared Rebel cavalry from the area. To counter previous complaints about his lack of support for black enlistment, he assured the president that he would give Lorenzo Thomas (who had just returned to the valley) "all the aid in my power." Even if he did not agree with the wisdom of administration initiatives, as an army officer he was pledged to implement them; in this case, however, he wanted to express his "honest conviction" that "by arming the negro we have added a powerful ally. They will make good soldiers and taking them from the enemy weaken him in the same proportion they strengthen us" — a neat paraphrase of Lincoln's own judgment. Lincoln was so pleased with Grant's response that he shared it with others and referred to it in public statements.[10]

Elsewhere Grant sounded the same themes. After escorting Julia and the children as far as Cairo on their way to St. Louis, he returned to his command. He stopped at Memphis, where he allowed himself to be honored by that city's loyal citizens — a sign of how much had changed in a year. In response, Grant, in a document apparently prepared under his approval, declared that he was pleased to see that the "miserable adherents of the rebellion . . . are being replaced by men *who acknowledge human liberty as the only true foundation of human government.*" Others found it more memorable that at a second banquet for Grant, the mayor, having imbibed more than enough, first dumped a plate of soup into Lorenzo Thomas's lap and next showered him with champagne; the mayor then beat a quick retreat before Thomas could respond in appropriate fashion — highlighting the wisdom of Grant's decision to turn his wineglass upside down and decline anything stronger than water. Later that evening, chatting with John Eaton, he recalled his life on the West Coast, remarking that "the vice of intemperance" encountered by so many officers there "had not a little to do with his decision to resign."[11]

At the end of August Grant shored up his political flanks in a letter to Elihu Washburne. Once more he expressed relief that he had not been transferred east to command the Army of the Potomac; he preferred to remain out west, where he knew "the exact capacity of every General in my command to command troops, and just where to place them to get from them their best services." Then he turned to larger issues. "The people of the North need not quarrel over the institution of Slavery. What Vice President Stevens [Alexander Stephens, the Confederacy's vice president] acknowledges the corner stone of the Confederacy is already knocked out. Slavery is already dead and cannot be resurrected." That was all to the good: "I never was an Abolitionest, not even what could be called anti slavery, but I try to judge farely & honestly and it become patent to my mind early in the rebellion that the North & South could never live at peace with each other except as one nation, and that without Slavery. As anxious as I am to see peace reestablished I would not therefore be willing to see any settlement until this question is forever settled."[12]

In agreeing to postpone an attack on Mobile in favor of a strike into Texas, Grant showed his willingness to bow to his civilian superiors when necessary. The Lincoln administration had good reason to pay attention to the Lone Star State. There was some concern that the Texas coastline might provide a welcome haven for ironclad rams being built in Liverpool; the French in Mexico offered both support to the Confederacy and a threat to the integrity of the borders of the United States. Halleck had already ordered Grant to reinforce Banks with an eye to a movement into Texas; he told both Grant and Banks that there were "important reasons why our flag should be restored in some point of Texas with the least possible delay." Both Banks and Grant still preferred to operate against Mobile, and the two had discussed such an operation when Banks made a quick trip to Vicksburg on August 1. Now they had to confer again to determine the best strategy for achieving the administration's objective. At the end of the month Grant headed south to New Orleans, arriving on September 2.[13]

Banks made lavish preparations to receive Grant. On the night of his arrival there was a reception at the St. Charles Hotel, but once again Grant refused to address the assembled throng (he was developing a considerable talent in avoiding such requests). The next morning he took Banks about town in a carriage, putting the horses through their paces; Banks returned the favor that evening by hosting a levee. Finally, on September 4, Banks took Grant out to Carrollton, upriver from the city, to review two corps: the Vicksburg veterans of the Thirteenth Corps and the Nineteenth Corps, headed by one of Grant's West Point classmates, William B. Franklin. After galloping past the troops, Grant remained mounted as they marched by. Then it was time for another celebration, complete with wine, music, and singing — not exactly an ideal entertainment, given Grant's tin ear and problems with alcohol. When the party made its way back to New Orleans that afternoon, Grant's mount, a large and spirited horse, grew unmanageable, and Grant, just as when he was a boy, let it loose. That in itself presented no problem, although Grant later described the horse as "vicious and but little used." When rider and horse approached a railroad, however, an oncoming locomotive sounded its whistle; the horse panicked, shied, and fell, taking Grant with it, crushing his left leg and knocking him unconscious. "We thought he was dead," a bystander later remarked. Officers carried Grant to a nearby inn, where doctors hurried to his side. The general slowly regained consciousness and discovered that his left leg, from knee to thigh, was swollen, "almost to the point of bursting," continuing up his left side. "The pain was almost beyond endurance," he later recalled. There would be no more riding — or even walking — for a while.[14]

Grant had been the victim of a falling horse once before, in the mud at Shiloh. This time his confidence in his skill contributed to the accident because it encouraged him to take risks others would avoid. But that explanation did not satisfy those onlookers who concluded that Grant must have been drinking excessively at the luncheon table. Among them were Banks and Franklin. The former confided to his wife, "I am frightened when I think he is a drunkard. His accident was caused by this, which was too manifest to all who saw him" (Banks failed to explain how Grant's drinking caused the locomotive to blow its whistle or the horse to fall). Franklin, who loved to gossip about Grant (although Grant, for reasons still unclear, held Franklin in high regard), declared several months later that "Grant had commenced a frolic which would have ruined his body and reputation in a week." Franklin, however, remained silent on why he had done nothing to stop the process.

Other witnesses, including Cadwallader Washburn (who did not mince words about Grant) and Lorenzo Thomas, said nothing about drinking. There is a noticeable difference between downing a glass or two of wine and becoming intoxicated; Grant did not topple off the horse, but was thrown by it. Had the general been in the condition described by Banks and Franklin, no one could have failed to observe it; indeed, Banks and Franklin would have been derelict in their duty to allow Grant to ride in such a condition. Yet one wonders whether Grant, flushed by a drink or two, pressed the limits of his skill with horses to the breaking point, and nearly paid for it with his life.[15]

For nearly two weeks Grant remained bedridden; on September 14, he was carried aboard a steamer headed back to Vicksburg. Julia hurried down to his side; so did Rawlins, who got wind of the drinking rumors and accepted them at face value. The enforced rest had a positive aspect; it gave the general a chance to reflect on serious issues. During his stay in New Orleans he told a young officer that while he had once opposed enlisting blacks, he now favored it, and were he to enter the service now he might well apply for command of one of the new regiments. He also pondered the prospects for reconstruction in the Mississippi valley, and Halleck prodded him to contribute some reflections on the matter.

Grant's decision to parole the Confederate garrison at Vicksburg was shaped in part by his belief that the Rebel soldiers were dispirited and would spread their disillusionment with the Confederate cause to others. From Sherman came confirmation that many Mississippians were ready to abandon their quest for independence; several leaders had already inquired about the best way to erect new governments loyal to the old flag. To encourage resurgent unionism, Grant distributed food and supplies to civilians in the countryside to compensate for the impact of his operations. Orders went out directing soldiers to refrain from "molesting" citizens and to issue receipts for any goods they took; blacks were encouraged to negotiate work contracts with their former masters. "It should be our policy now to make as favorable an impression upon the people of this State as possible," Grant advised Sherman.[16]

One way to do this was by fine-tuning the government's policy toward the freed slaves to foster loyalty among whites. While Grant still wanted to raise more black regiments, he urged recruiters to distinguish between loyal and disloyal whites when stripping their plantations of black workers; it might be better not to disturb those blacks who worked for whites who now demonstrated a willingness to give up the fight. On the other hand, blacks working for disloyal planters should be impressed into federal service. However, he had little sympathy for those whites who continued to harass blacks, explaining that what appeared to be "signs of negro insurrection" usually occurred in retaliation for white efforts to intimidate blacks "by whipping and in a few instances by shooting them."[17]

Grant once more stated his opposition to trading with the enemy, especially through the Treasury Department's policy of issuing permits for individuals to buy cotton — even when such people included his brother-in-law. Such purchases might help furnish mills in the North and in England with raw cotton, but they also gave the Confederates funds to purchase munitions and supplies. At a time when the Union blockade and Grant's own campaigns were attempting to deny the Confederacy resources, dealing in cotton seemed counterproductive; it also offered both soldiers and civilians incentives for corruption. "The people in the Mississippi Valley are now nearly subjugated," he told Chase. "Keep trade out for but a few months and I doubt not but that the work of subjugation will be so complete that trade can be opened freely with the states of Arkansas, La. & Mississippi."[18]

With these thoughts in mind Grant, still laid up in Vicksburg, finally replied to Halleck's inquiry on September 19. Sherman had forwarded to him a lengthy document on reconstruction ultimately intended for Halleck, recommending the continued harsh treatment of white Southerners to break their spirit. For once Grant disagreed with his prize lieutenant, arguing that there was "a very fine feeling existing in the State of Louisiana, and in most parts of this state, toward the Union."[19]

Reconstruction, however, depended on the progress of Union arms; events in Georgia were threatening to deal a major setback to the chances of reunion. On the day Grant wrote to Halleck, William S. Rosecrans's Army of the Cumberland engaged Braxton Bragg's Army of Tennessee along Chickamauga Creek in northwest Georgia. For months, while Grant had operated against Vicksburg, Rosecrans had stayed put in central Tennessee, ignoring hints and requests from Washington to commence his own campaign. Only in July did he finally move forward, but once he was under way, he skillfully maneuvered Bragg's army out of Tennessee and forced the Confederates to abandon Chattanooga. At the same time, Ambrose Burnside, finally reunited with the Ninth Corps, moved into East Tennessee, capturing Knoxville. These triumphs, however, proved short-lived. On September 20, Bragg, reinforced by two divisions detached from the Army of Northern Virginia under the command of James Longstreet, drove Rosecrans back to Chattanooga. Within days Grant's old subordinate found himself virtually besieged.

On September 22 Grant received a week-old dispatch from Halleck referring to the need to reinforce Rosecrans. Realizing something was up, he immediately ordered two divisions to start eastward. Three days later Halleck's original request for assistance, dated September 13, finally arrived; Grant sent Sherman forward with two more divisions. The delays in communication were more annoying than costly, for none of Grant's command could have reached Rosecrans prior to the battle. Grant abandoned any notion of attacking Mobile, although he could not hide his disappointment. Nor was he happy with the possibility of losing Sherman as a subordinate should the administration appoint him to succeed Rosecrans. On a more positive note, he was out of bed by the end of the month, moving around on crutches, and regaining his stamina; before long he was riding again, although he needed help to mount or dismount.[20]

His recovery was timely. On October 5 Grant received a message from Halleck (dated September 29) suggesting that he come north to supervise the movement of forces to Rosecrans; five days later a second dispatch arrived requesting him to travel to Cairo as soon as he was able and await instructions from Secretary Stanton. Leaving McPherson in command of the Vicksburg region, Grant prepared to comply. Down went the headquarters tents outside the Lums' residence; Julia gathered together her luggage; by dark the general and his staff had left Vicksburg.[21]

Grant reached Memphis on October 14. Neither he nor members of his staff had any idea what awaited them at Cairo. The man most responsible for his trip was Charles A. Dana, who had been with Rosecrans at Chickamauga. The War Department envoy had come away with a very negative impression of the commander of the Army of the Cumberland. His telegrams to Stanton suggested just what sort of damage Dana could have done to Grant's career the previous spring. Dana questioned Rosecrans's competence, courage, and even his sanity; he raised fears in Washington that Rosecrans would abandon Chickamauga. Rosecrans's erratic behavior, alternating between confident prediction and expressions of hopelessness, fear, and timidity, did not help matters. Lincoln, who at first had tried to cheer up the defeated general, soon lost confidence in him and considered Dana's suggestion to place Grant in command. Sherman thought that this was the plan, and Halleck dropped a hint when he assured Grant, "You need not fear being left idle. The moment you are well enough to take the field you will have abundant occupation."[22]

Arriving at Cairo on October 16, Grant received new orders the next day to head for Louisville, Kentucky. Halleck directed him to bring his staff with him in preparation "for immediate operations in the field." The general, his wife, and the staff arrived in Indianapolis that evening; on the morning of October 18 the party prepared to leave for Louisville, where Julia Grant expected to meet old friends.[23]

The train was just about to roll out of the Indianapolis station when the word came to delay its departure pending the arrival of an important passenger. It was none other than the official from the War Department who had traveled west to confer with Grant — and it was not simply a paper-pushing functionary who climbed on board. Secretary of War Edwin M. Stanton made his way to Grant's car, saw a group of officers, and strode forward, hand outstretched. "How do you do General Grant? I recognize you from your pictures," he exclaimed. Unfortunately, the man he greeted so vigorously was not Grant but his medical director, Dr. Edward Kittoe. Abashed, Stanton got pointed in the right direction, while Grant struggled to conceal his amusement.[24]

Stanton carried orders appointing Grant to the command of three departments — his own as well as those of the Cumberland and the Ohio — now known collectively as "the Military Division of the Mississippi." He was thus in charge of army operations from the Appalachian Mountains to the Mississippi River, more or less. Two problems immediately confronted him: maintaining the Union's hold on Chattanooga and supervising the operations of Ambrose Burnside in the vicinity of Knoxville, some 135 miles northeast of Chattanooga. Stanton also presented Grant with the option of placing the reliable George H. Thomas in command of the Army of the Cumberland. The choice was not difficult, in light of Grant's previous friction with Rosecrans: he informed Stanton that Rosecrans often failed to obey orders. Thomas was a better general, although he would not necessarily have been Grant's choice to take over.[25]

The train carrying the general and the secretary reached Louisville that evening. Word went to Chattanooga that Rosecrans was out and Thomas was in. The Grants left to visit friends; Stanton took rooms at the Galt House. That evening, more alarming news came from Chattanooga; Dana's dire portrayal of conditions suggested that retreat was only a matter of days. Stanton sent for Grant. At last someone located the general, who hurried over to the hotel to find the war secretary, still clad in his nightshirt, pacing the floor. Grant did what he could to calm him down. "Hold Chattanooga at all hazards," he wired Thomas. "I will be there as soon as possible."[26]

Grant seemed in good health and spirits, although Stanton observed that the general "is still quite lame and moves with difficulty with a crutch." The general was cheered when he heard from Chattanooga. "I will hold the town until we starve," Thomas declared. In welcome contrast to Rosecrans's uneasiness, his successor's resolution was as steady as a rock. With that concern alleviated, Grant left Julia behind in Louisville and headed toward Chattanooga. Arriving in Nashville on October 20, he found himself dragged out to address a crowd that had gathered in front of his hotel. Although Grant evaded his task by remarking that he had "never made a speech in his life, and was too old to learn now," Governor Andrew Johnson, never at a loss for words, compared the general to Napoleon and Caesar.[27]

The next day Grant continued traveling by rail to Stevenson, Alabama. One observer noted that "he appeared almost sad as he looked vacantly without seeming to see anything that he was passing." As the train stopped, soldiers crowded around for a look at the general, only to see him making his way across the platform on crutches. "He wore an army slouch hat with bronze cord around it, quite a long military coat, unbuttoned, no sword or belt, and there was nothing to indicate his rank," one soldier noted. "His appearance would have attracted no attention had he not been General Grant." The men called on their general to make a speech; this time Grant could not even tip his hat because his hands gripped the crutches, a sign of the pain he was in.

Grant returned to his railroad car, where Oliver O. Howard paid a visit. Howard, who had lost an arm in 1862, now commanded the Eleventh

[handwritten: → O.O. Howard commands one of these — see prev. pg]

Corps, one of two corps detached from the Army of the Potomac, placed under the command of Joseph Hooker, and sent to Rosecrans after Chickamauga. A staff officer messenger interrupted the two generals to invite Grant to visit Hooker at his headquarters. This was typical of the bombastic Hooker; but Grant's reply was a pleasant surprise to Howard, who decided he liked his new commander. "If General Hooker wishes to see me," Grant quietly remarked, "he will find me on this train." Subordinates called on their commander, not the other way around. Hooker took the hint and appeared a short time later. Grant also met the relieved William S. Rosecrans. Rosecrans was bitter, but apparently he was not fully aware of Grant's role in his removal, for he conversed freely and without rancor as he outlined his plans. Grant found them impressive: "My only wonder was that he had not carried them out."[28]

[handwritten margin note: what were they? see memoir]

Grant and Howard journeyed from Stevenson to Bridgeport, Alabama, where the two men entered Howard's tent to talk. Seeing a flask of whiskey on the table, an embarrassed Howard hastily apologized and added, "I never drink." Grant, who seemed amused by all that might be going through Howard's mind, simply offered the deadpan response, "Neither do I." Howard was impressed. The new man, he later told his wife, "does not drink liquor and never swears" — in short, he was no Joe Hooker. "He is modest, quiet, and thoughtful. He looks the picture of firmness."[29]

At Bridgeport the railroad bridge across the Tennessee River had been destroyed; the Confederates blocked the line, and so from here to Chattanooga Grant would have to travel by horse. The next morning, Rawlins helped him into the saddle and off they rode. The party had to navigate a narrow, muddy road that wound through the mountains north and west of Chattanooga. Broken wagons and the carcasses of dead horses and mules marked the way. Rain and wind made the trek even gloomier, and Grant suffered more pain when his horse slipped and fell, bruising the general's sore leg. It was not until the evening of October 23 that the caravan reached Chattanooga, where Grant sought out Thomas's headquarters on Walnut Street.[30]

[handwritten: → & Dana was worried abt Chatt surrendering on Oct. 18 — see p227]

Thomas received his new commander rather coolly. Taken aback by the news of Rosecrans's removal, perhaps he suspected that Dana, a firm Grant supporter, had something to do with it (as indeed Dana did). He was also miffed by Grant's "at all hazards" wire. Although he offered his guest a seat and some food, he did nothing about securing dry clothes for the visitor. The best Grant could do for the moment was to draw his armchair up to the fireplace and pull out a cigar. A puddle of water soon spread outward from his muddy boots. At last, James H. Wilson, who had preceded his superior to Thomas's headquarters, burst out, "General Thomas, can't you get General Grant some dry clothing?" Thus prodded, Thomas responded, but Grant declined the offer.[31]

Grant was more interested in hearing about the state of affairs confronting the Army of the Cumberland than in analyzing Thomas's rude behavior. He listened as Thomas and his staff, led by chief engineer William F. Smith, set forth the positions of both forces and the supply problems they faced. The bad roads made it impossible to gather sufficient rations to feed the army; for the moment there was no way to feed Hooker's force as well. Only after something was done about the supply situation could anyone begin to think about how to raise the siege. Grant listened, then began asking questions. "So intelligent were his inquiries," recalled Horace Porter, a staff officer with the Army of the Cumberland who was encountering Grant for the first time, "that he made a profound impression upon every one by the quickness of his perception and the knowledge which he had already acquired regarding important details of the army's condition." Then he settled down to write a series of dispatches, announcing his arrival and preparing for what was to come. Dana summed it all up when he telegraphed Washington: "Grant arrived last night, wet, dirty and well."[32]

The next day, Grant, Thomas, and Smith rode west from Chattanooga to acquaint Grant with the lay of the land and to evaluate a plan Smith believed would restore a line of supply. The city, described by Doctor Kittoe as a "rough and wretched looking place," was located along a series of sharp bends in the Tennessee River. Flowing southward, the river made a right turn to the west for nearly a mile and a half, then resumed its southward flow before making a hairpin loop at the foot of the commanding heights of Lookout Mountain. The river then undulated westward until it approached Bridgeport, the Union railhead, where it resumed moving in a southwest direction. It might have reminded Grant of the way the Mississippi and Ohio curved around Cairo. Just east of Chattanooga the Confederates deployed themselves along the crest of Missionary Ridge, overlooking the city and the Army of the Cumberland; Bragg had also occupied Lookout Mountain and some of the heights west of the hairpin turn. Only one route remained open to Chattanooga — the horrendous wagon road over which Grant had just traveled.[33]

Smith focused attention on two points along the river: Brown's Ferry, a few miles west of Chattanooga, crossing the river just after it turned north, and Kelley's Ferry, some seven miles or so to the west. The two ferries were joined by a road that promised a more direct supply route to Chattanooga than the road Grant had just traversed. Union forces, moving downriver at night to conceal their movements from the Confederates, would seize Brown's Ferry, then secure the road running westward to Kelley's Ferry. In support of this movement, Hooker's command, marching east from Bridgeport along the rail line to Chattanooga, would arrive at Wauhatchie, just south of Brown's Ferry. From there they would march toward the Tennessee River and Lookout Mountain, thus driving the Confederates away from the newly opened supply line. Pontoon bridges would ease the transportation of supplies; soldiers would be able to contemplate real meals once more, instead of eyeing their hungry artillery horses for dinner.[34]

This plan resembled the one Rosecrans had outlined to Grant, although Smith claimed pride of authorship. Grant first wanted to see if it was practicable. The general dismounted and limped to the banks of the Tennessee River near Brown's Ferry, in full sight of Confederate pickets on the opposite bank — who honored an agreement struck with their counterparts across the water not to fire on each other. The terrain was as Smith described it; the plan was possible. Grant placed Smith in charge of the operation. Pleased with the assignment, Smith sought specific instructions. Grant had none to give, observing "that when he had confidence enough in the man to leave him in command of an army he had confidence enough to leave the details to him." Orders went out to hurry Sherman and Hooker forward, for Grant had received reports that Confederate reinforcements might be joining Braxton Bragg, enabling him to swing between Chattanooga and Knoxville with Nashville as his ultimate destination.[35]

The Union commander was not his usual optimistic self. It was becoming apparent that the Army of the Cumberland was in no condition to do much to save itself. If Bragg pushed northward, Union forces would be unable to follow him. In so clearly seeing how his opponent might exploit current circumstances, Grant overlooked that Bragg might not possess the same drive or information about the Union predicament. At the same time he wrestled with the problem posed by a feud between Hooker and Henry W. Slocum, commander of the Twelfth Corps, who refused to serve under Hooker. Grant found both men difficult; if it was up to him Howard would command the eastern contingent. However, the authorities at Washington refused to take action, leaving Grant to iron out the rough spots.[36]

For the moment, the most critical task was to get things in motion so that the Army of the Cumberland could eat again and revive itself. Orders went out to move wagons forward, repair railroads, and secure steamers. "We began to see things move," one officer later remarked. "We felt that everything came from a plan." Grant constantly rode about to study the terrain and the situation. "This is one of the wildest places you ever saw and without the use of rail-roads one of the most out-of-the-way places," he told Julia. The exercise did him good. Within days he was able to discard his cane and mount his horse unaided. Once, when Grant journeyed out to Chickamauga Creek to view the enemy position, the Confederate pickets, overhearing the officer in charge of their Union counterparts call out the guard for Grant, did the same, saluting the general. At another time Grant actually chatted with one of Longstreet's privates, although, he later insisted, "not with a view of gaining any particular information."[37]

By October 27 all was set to execute Smith's plan. Early that morning several barges teeming with soldiers floated down the Tennessee, wending past Lookout Mountain before debarking at Brown's Ferry and pushing back an undersized Confederate force there. The next day Hooker's columns advanced to Brown's Ferry from Wauhatchie, securing the route through Lookout Valley. Confederate attempts to drive them back failed. On the evening of October 28 Grant reported to Washington that the operation had been "iminently successful." Before long supplies were moving along the newly christened "Cracker Line" to Chattanooga. One Illinois captain recalled that the men did not much care who came up with the idea, saving their praise for the man who implemented it: "We voted the man of few words a trump card from the start."[38]

Much would be made of who was responsible for the idea of opening up the supply line to Chattanooga. Rosecrans, Thomas, and Smith each claimed the honor for themselves. However, it was left to someone else to make sure that it was implemented. John A. Rawlins knew as much. Writing to his beloved Mary Hurlbut, he remarked, "It is decisiveness and energy in action that always accomplishes grand results, & strikes terror to the heart of the foe, it is this and not the conception of great schemes that make military genius."[39]

With the supply crisis resolved, Grant turned to offensive operations. Sherman was en route to the city; Hooker could now bring up his two corps to the foot of Lookout Mountain. It would take time, however, to refit Thomas's men. Braxton Bragg further complicated matters. The Confederate commander dispatched two divisions to Knoxville under the command of James Longstreet. Disgusted with Longstreet's failure to thwart the Federal effort to open a new line of supply to Chattanooga,

Bragg decided to rid himself of a man with whom he had long feuded while keeping an eye on the Union forces gathering in East Tennessee.

About ten thousand Yankees were at Knoxville, led by Ambrose Burnside, who was conducting operations in the field for the first time since he had been relieved of command of the Army of the Potomac in early 1863. Whatever notions Burnside had of marching to Chattanooga vanished when he received reports that Robert E. Lee was sending more men westward; by the time he learned that these stories were greatly exaggerated (one brigade came west), Burnside had decided to hold on to what he had. (Although Grant had previously instructed Burnside to fortify his position and bring up supplies, he did not expect Burnside to remain totally passive.⁴⁰)

The idea of a Confederate counteroffensive against Knoxville was nothing new to Grant. Rumors about such a move had circulated among Union generals for several days. At the end of October Grant asked Burnside if a large Rebel force was advancing northward. Within a week he decided to send Wilson and Dana to assist Burnside — and to tell Grant what was really going on. William F. Smith, who had won Grant's trust, had shared with him stories of Burnside's incompetence, increasing Grant's concern. The general asked Smith to start thinking about how best to threaten Bragg's right along the northern section of Missionary Ridge.⁴¹

On the evening of November 6, a Confederate deserter informed his bluecoated captors that Longstreet was marching north as part of a major effort to oust Burnside from Knoxville. Grant responded immediately. Deeming a mere demonstration insufficient, he favored launching an attack against the northern end of Missionary Ridge to force Bragg to recall Longstreet. Orders went out to Thomas to prepare to attack; Grant wired Sherman to hurry up; another telegram reassured Burnside of Grant's intent to act. It was "imperative" to do something now.⁴²

Having outlined his plan, Grant waited for Thomas to implement it. Although Thomas had earlier participated in discussions about a demonstration against Bragg's right, he paled at the notion of a full-scale attack. He shared his reservations with Smith, who had urged Grant to order the attack. Together the two men rode out to examine the ground (something Smith should have already done in complying with Grant's earlier request to develop an attack plan). What they discovered proved sufficient to thwart the operation. Bragg's lines stretched so far north that Thomas could not hope to outflank him, and a frontal assault would prove costly. Smith broke the news to Grant; Thomas added that his command was in no condition to attack. This was true, at least to some extent: there were no animals to move artillery up into support, and Thomas's men were still recovering from their earlier travails. Better, Thomas argued, for Hooker to take Lookout Mountain and thus complete the reopening of his lines of communication to the west — although it was hard to fathom exactly how this would help Burnside. Faced with Thomas's objections, Grant called off the attack. He did not explain why to either Burnside or the authorities at Washington. Instead, he set forth Thomas's idea to Halleck while minimizing the possible threat to Burnside.[43]

Perhaps the most important consequence of this abortive advance was that it shattered a growing bond of trust between Grant and the generals of the Army of the Cumberland. Memories of his uncomfortable initial meeting with Thomas had dissipated in the aftermath of the successful effort to open the Cracker Line. At Grant's headquarters, a two-story brick house owned by secessionist James Whiteside, Grant and several of his old associates from West Point had spent their free time recalling the old days. Smith, Joseph Reynolds (Thomas's chief of staff), and Gordon Granger chatted away with their host; James Wilson marveled at "how perfectly harmonious this vast district is, what a perfect understanding and how far removed the leading men are from envy, distrust, or ill feeling." That was no longer the case. And if he found himself unhappy with Thomas, Grant was so displeased with Hooker's mixed performance in opening up the Cracker Line that he contemplated his removal. Looking for someone in whom he had complete trust, he telegraphed Sherman to come as soon as possible.[44]

As Sherman marched eastward, Grant waited. He scanned the newspapers gleaning explanations for his promotion and Rosecrans's displacement. "This time however I do not see myself abused," he told Julia. "I do not know whether this is a good omen or not. I have been so accustomed to seeing at least a portion of the press against me that I rather feel lost when not attacked from some quarter." He stayed awake past midnight, writing and answering dispatches and making preparations for what he hoped would be a decisive blow against Bragg's right along the northern part of Missionary Ridge. "Since Vicksburg fell this has become really the vital point of the rebellion and requires all the care and watchfulness that can be bestowed upon it," he told Julia. But conditions were improving. At night the general and his staff dined on roast beef, potatoes, and bread, with Grant doing the carving. Looking toward the future, he spoke of his children and his financial investments to one of Julia's cousins, William Wrenshall Smith, who arrived for a visit. Rawlins reported that the general "is all himself and in splendid health."[45]

At the same time Grant had to attend to housekeeping matters with his staff. Clark Lagow had been on Grant's staff since 1861, when Grant, just promoted to brigadier general, took Lagow from the ranks of the Twenty-first Illinois. Dana judged him "a worthless, whiskey-drinking, useless fellow" Rawlins and William Rowley, afraid that Lagow would tempt Grant to join him in a glass, had been working to get rid of him for some time. Some of Lagow's friends visited him at headquarters, and on November 14, Lagow started a round of poker over drinks. The game went on long and loud far into the night, until Grant himself broke up the carousing. Lagow was so embarrassed that several days later he tendered his resignation.[46]

Grant was impatient to do something, and soon. Smith's negative characterizations of Burnside as well as Burnside's own messages had eroded Grant's faith in the general's ability. "I do not know how to impress upon you the necessity of holding on to East Tennessee," he told Burnside on November 15; at worst the general should defend Knoxville.[47] *at best, go on offensive?*

That evening, William T. Sherman finally made his way to Chattanooga, much to Grant's relief. It had been some time since the two friends had worked close together. In marked contrast to the scene at Thomas's headquarters several weeks earlier, Grant pointed to a rocker, saying, "Take the chair of honor, Sherman." When Sherman remarked that his host was entitled to it, Grant, a twinkle in his eye, replied, "Never mind that. I always give precedence to age." With Thomas and Howard, the generals talked well into the night, cigars puffing away, mapping out the best way to attack Bragg. The next morning, Grant, Sherman, Thomas, and Smith rode out to look over the terrain. Sherman was amazed by what he saw, from what seemed to be a strong enemy position to the condition of Thomas's recovering command. "Why, General Grant, you are besieged," he remarked. "It is too true," Grant dryly replied.[48]

Sherman arrived

Grant had his own ideas on how to extract himself from the present situation. Smith still favored attacking the northern section of Missionary Ridge: he would simply use Sherman's men in place of Thomas's. The veterans of the Army of the Tennessee would remain north of the Tennessee River, then cross it above Chattanooga and bear down on the Confederate right, while Thomas threatened the enemy center. Some of Thomas's officers had grumbled about the plan; Thomas himself still preferred a blow against Lookout Mountain. Smith, holding fast to his desire to strike Bragg's right, sought to gain Sherman's and thus Grant's approval. Sherman and Smith climbed the same hill that Smith and Thomas had used to observe the Confederate position. After looking it over, Sherman con-

what were they?

planning the offensive

see p 232

P5

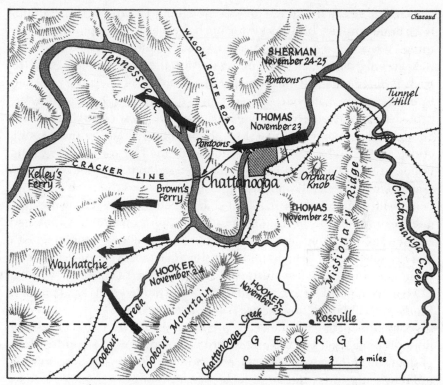

Chattanooga, November 22-25, 1863

cluded that he could take it. This was enough for Grant. But whatever was to be done must be done quickly for Burnside's sake: "I am pushing everything," Grant assured Halleck, "to give Gen. Burnside early aid."[49]

As evening came, Sherman, impressed with the need for haste, hurried back to his command. Grant, tired after a long day of exertion, returned to headquarters. Someone offered him a drink, which he gratefully accepted. Rawlins exploded when he learned of it. Lagow's drinking was bad enough; now demon rum might be about to trap Grant on the eve of a critical battle. To his fiancée, he denounced "the free use of intoxicating liquors at Head Quarters which last night's developments showed me had reached to the General commanding. I am the only one here (his wife not being with him) who can stay it in that direction & prevent evil consequences resulting from it." Apparently, Rawlins concluded, Grant had learned nothing from his New Orleans accident about "indulging with this his worst enemy." He drafted a passionate letter to Grant, asking him "to immediately desist from further tasting of liquors of any kind," adding: "Two more nights like the last will find you prostrated on a sick bed unfit for duty" — although no one else had noticed anything awry. Inspired by his commitment to temperance, he predicted that Grant would bring ruin not only on himself but also on his nation should he drink "another drop of that which unmans you." In the end, however, Rawlins decided to withhold the letter and to discuss its subject with Grant.[50]

Rawlins need not have worried. Grant was not about to embark on a binge that would have confined him to his bedroom. True, Julia's cousin had brought with him several bottles, including some Kentucky wine from Hannah Grant for her son, but Lagow and his buddies had polished off much of it. Just as important, the general had reason to be on his best behavior, for once more Washington had sent a visitor, General David Hunter, who arrived at Chattanooga on November 15. Grant offered to share his quarters with Hunter, giving him an excellent opportunity to observe him up close. The next day the two men engaged in a storytelling session. "Grant is in high spirits and tells a story admirably," William W. Smith, a member of the audience, noted. "In general he is extremely reserved, but with one or two friends he is very entertaining and agreeable." Hunter was also charmed. He later testified that Grant, far from falling prey to the bottle, had taken only two drinks during the three weeks Hunter was present. In their conversation Grant may well have promised Rawlins that he would abstain from further drinking of any sort (although Hunter's letter suggests he did not take his pledge literally); the whole matter seemed a tempest in a teapot. Nevertheless, as was his habit, Rawlins filed the letter away for future reference.[51]

[handwritten notes at top: has been ~ 1 mo. since USG arrived ... how has Burnside been holding out? – see P.3]

"One more week will decide a greatdeel here," Grant confided to his Galena friend and financial adviser J. Russell Jones on November 17. "Within that time either the position of the enemy will be greatly worse than at present or our[s] will not be so good." The next day he issued his orders for the battle. Sherman would attack Missionary Ridge at daylight on November 21 and carry the Confederate position as far as the railroad tunnel; Thomas would support the attack, looking to join with Sherman. As Grant put it, "I am tired of the proximity of the enemy and do not intend to stand it if it can be helped."[52]

Most plans of battle rarely survive first contact with the enemy. Knowing that, Grant remarked that he would await Bragg's reaction to the initial assault before deciding what to do next. But he did not make headway even with this plan. Heavy rains turned Sherman's route of march into mud. That in itself would have slowed anybody down, but Sherman made matters worse by marching his command division by division, each followed by its own wagon train. Wagons sank; livestock struggled; the movement bogged down. Grant took responsibility for what had happened, although he expected better from his prize lieutenant.[53]

Both Dana and Wilson, just returned from Knoxville, noted the commander's ill-concealed annoyance. In turn their arrival increased Grant's anxiety, for he had believed that they would remain with Burnside and compel him to hold on. There was no doubt that Bragg was up to something: on November 20 he notified Grant to evacuate noncombatants from Chattanooga. Judging the message an ill-disguised ruse, Grant offered no response. But the bad weather continued, and Grant soon conceded that he would have to postpone the attack, first to Sunday, then to Monday. The delays suited Thomas just fine: he showed little interest in the plan. To Rosecrans he wrote, "If we can hold out for a month longer, — *[handwritten: /6/]* our position will be entirely secure," not exactly the words of an aggressive fighter.[54]

Grant did not share such sentiments. Impatient over the delay and worried that Burnside would not hold on, he grew frustrated. "I have never felt such restlessness before as I have at the fixed and immovable condition of the Army of the Cumberland," he told Halleck on November 21. Sherman's force "is really the only one I can move" — and it was moving none too fast, for the next day Grant had to postpone the attack yet again to November 24. Meanwhile, he learned that more Rebels were on their way to reinforce Longstreet.[55]

Finally, on November 23, Grant decided that he had waited long enough. Early in the morning he read a wire sent to Halleck by Orlando B. Willcox from Cumberland Gap. Willcox, complaining that he had not

[handwritten at bottom: → N of Knoxville]

[margin, top right: ↘ Willcox reaches out to Halleck]

heard from Grant, had wanted to know whether Halleck would approve Willcox's "sacrificing all my cavalry" in an attempt to save Burnside. Something inside Grant snapped. For weeks he had been telegraphing Willcox orders on what to do, to no effect: "He has been retreating too fast to get them at the points to which they were directed." What concerned him more was Willcox's statement that he had heard firing at Knoxville. At the same time, Grant learned that a deserter had told his captors the Confederate forces were retreating. The moment of decision appeared to be at hand, even if Sherman was not. Unwilling to let Bragg off without a fight and determined to detain his opponent from reinforcing Longstreet, Grant ordered Thomas to advance against the first Confederate line along a rise due west of town known as Orchard Knob.[56]

[margin left: Union offensive opens ↓ along Smith's plan -see p 234]

That afternoon Grant, Thomas, and others went to Fort Wood, just east of Chattanooga, to watch the opening of the offensive against Bragg. Thomas drew up his divisions as if for a review — at least that is what the Rebels thought — and then ordered them forward. They brushed aside the skirmish line assigned by Bragg to hold the position, as the surprised Confederates scampered back to the protection of Missionary Ridge. The result was more than Thomas had ordered; he had intended a reconnaissance in force followed by a return to the original position. Quickly Grant and Thomas huddled; Rawlins chimed in, somewhat unnecessarily, that it would dampen the men's spirits if they had to abandon the position now and retake it later. Grant turned to Thomas with his decision: "Intrench them and send up support."[57]

Despite reports from Orchard Knob that Bragg's Confederates remained in force along the base and crest of Missionary Ridge, Grant wondered whether the enemy would retreat and thus elude his grasp. Events forced him to alter his plans yet again. Three of Sherman's divisions were in position to cross the Tennessee River the next morning, but a fourth, under Peter J. Osterhaus, remained stranded north of Lookout Mountain, for the pontoon bridge at Brown's Ferry had snapped. Grant had already shifted enough additional forces toward his left to support Sherman, so he decided to turn a problem into an opportunity. Osterhaus would now join Hooker's men in an advance against Lookout Mountain, long Thomas's wish.[58]

Sherman's opening move went well. In the early morning hours of November 24, his lead division made a cross-river assault patterned on Smith's Brown's Ferry operation. Within hours workers lashed together segments of a concealed pontoon bridge; Sherman decided to fortify his bridgehead, although as yet he had encountered no serious resistance.

By midday he was ready to move against Missionary Ridge. Meanwhile, Hooker prepared to move against Lookout Mountain, having decided to interpret Thomas's orders for a demonstration as authorizing a full-scale assault.[59]

Grant watched and waited. Believing that Bragg was reinforcing his right to counter Sherman, he told Thomas to be prepared to advance when Sherman attacked, then waited for news from his friend. None came. Anxious to see what was happening, Grant rode about, "smoking and appearing more like a farmer out looking at stock, than a General in a battle." Hooker, however, got his men into motion. At first they encountered no opposition; then they swept past the Confederate defenders and headed for the slopes of Lookout Mountain. After a sharp firefight, the Yankees overran a fortified line before broken terrain and stiffening resistance slowed them down. It came as a surprise when the Confederates, under orders from Bragg, abandoned the mountain to take up a new line shielding the Rebel left at Rossville Gap.

Feds take Lookout Mtn

As evening fell, Grant was optimistic. Sherman reported that he had already advanced as far as Tunnel Hill on Missionary Ridge, placing him in excellent position to crush Bragg the next morning. Informing Thomas of this fact, Grant instructed him to prepare to advance in the morning: "Your command will either carry the rifle pits and ridge directly in front of them, or move to the left as the presence of the enemy may require." The situation on Lookout Mountain, in the absence of definite word from Hooker, remained less certain. As night came, Grant and members of his headquarters looked southward toward that height's northern slope, the flash of skirmish fire reminding one observer of summertime fireflies. A full moon illuminated the entire valley. Finally, Grant turned in to get some rest. It would be a busy day tomorrow; perhaps Bragg was already preparing to withdraw.[60]

but a skirmish ---

November 25 dawned "clear and bright." Early risers were treated to a spectacular sight: sunrise revealed the Stars and Stripes on the summit of Lookout Mountain. The order for the day was simple. Hooker would press forward against Bragg's left, while Sherman crumpled the Confederate right. Grant and Thomas rode forward to Orchard Knob and established headquarters. Before long there was bad news. Sherman sent word that in fact he had not taken Tunnel Hill — a deep ravine just north of that location, which had escaped Union observation, served to give the Confederates an ideal defensive position. Seeing the terrain in front of him, Sherman hesitated; Grant told Thomas to wait and forwarded reinforcements to Sherman. For the moment, the Yankees had stumbled, but Grant be-

but Feds prevail in end

Sherman had taken the "wrong" hill

lieved that his trusted lieutenant would press forward; eventually the pressure on the flanks would compromise Bragg's position.[61]

By midday, as cold winds blew across Orchard Knob, Grant realized that nothing was going according to plan. Struggling to advance, Sherman looked for help, imploring, "Where is Thomas?" Hooker was doing no better. He took the better part of the morning to get his men into motion, only to find his advance thwarted by the destruction of a bridge over Chattanooga Creek that would take hours to replace. Moreover, the Confederates seemed willing to slug it out. Periodically, a cannon shell whizzed over the headquarters contingent. Still, Grant remained calm. Early in the afternoon he left the knoll to eat lunch and smoke a cigar. Patience would pay off.

But when Grant returned to the knob in midafternoon, nothing had happened. Hooker was still stalled; there would be no threat against Bragg's left. Grant looked toward Tunnel Hill. Not only had Sherman failed to take it, he was having trouble holding his own. Grant and others concluded from what they saw that Bragg was stripping his center to counter Sherman's attack. Whether this was in fact true (a point much to be debated in the years to come) is not nearly so important as that Grant believed it was true. He decided that if Thomas moved forward, Bragg would be forced to take away men now opposite Sherman. "Hooker has not come up, but I think you had better move, on Sherman's account," he finally remarked to Thomas.[62]

Grant had in mind a two-stage assault by Thomas's men. First, they were to take the rifle pits at the base of the ridge; only after re-forming were they to advance up the slope on Grant's order — perhaps in coordination with either Hooker or Sherman. It would not be an easy assignment. Until a few days ago, the rifle pits at the base of the ridge had been the heart of Bragg's center. Convinced that Grant would never order a direct assault up the ridge, Bragg had neglected its defenses along the crest. Only with the fall of Orchard Knob had the Confederate commander taken steps to fortify the crest beyond a few half-hearted trenches. In addition, Bragg had shuffled his units holding the crest, giving Grant the impression that he was shifting them elsewhere and leaving his center vulnerable.[63]

The idea seemed reasonable, although a frontal assault up a ridge might ordinarily be deemed suicidal. But then the same could have been said about attacking Lookout Mountain. Grant believed that Missionary Ridge was lightly defended, reducing both the risk and the cost of an attack. And, in any case, the initial move involved only an advance against the rifle pits. Should the situation change, he could call off the intended strike against the crest.

Nothing happened. Thomas objected to the idea, and when Grant failed to press his point, the commander of the Army of the Cumberland thought he had prevailed. He was wrong. Rawlins fumed, then roared. Why weren't the men moving out?[64]

Whether the target of Rawlins's wrath was Grant or Thomas was not clear, but the outburst jarred Grant into action. He told Thomas it was time to move. Still, nothing happened. Grant's patience ran out. Interrupting a conversation between Thomas and division commander Thomas J. Wood, Grant bluntly asked Wood whether he had received orders to attack. Surprised, Wood replied that this was the first he had heard of the idea. Turning to Thomas, Grant growled, "General Thomas, why are these troops not advancing?" Thomas explained that he had told Wood's immediate superior, corps commander Gordon Granger, to issue orders for an advance. Grant looked over to see Granger engrossed in the operations of an artillery battery. Struggling to control his temper, he ignored the pain in his leg as he walked over to pay Granger a visit. Confronting the corps commander, Grant inquired whether he had received orders to advance. Granger replied in the negative, evidence that someone in the Army of the Cumberland was lying to shift responsibility for forestalling an attack.

Grant had heard enough. To Granger he spoke sharply: "If you will leave that battery to its captain, and take command of your corps, it will be better for all of us." Then he took charge of Thomas's army, directing Wood to move forward. Staff officers relayed similar orders to the other division commanders.[65]

On Granger's personal command, six cannon shots fired in succession from his adopted battery on Orchard Knob signaled the advance. As the columns surged forward, Grant watched "with intense interest." What he saw was amazing. The Confederates quickly abandoned the first line of rifle pits. Union soldiers soon found themselves under fire from Rebel infantry posted on the crest of the ridge. They could not stay where they were, they could not go back without suffering serious casualties; but they had to do something, and they had to do it now. "Without awaiting further orders or stopping to reform," Grant recalled, the men continued up the slope. Several division and brigade commanders actually thought that they *were* acting under orders, for the crest of the ridge *was* the ultimate target.[66]

Grant watched, chomping down on his cigar as the ragged and uneven lines made their way toward the crest. He had intended for the men to regroup and advance by columns — on his order. Had Thomas ordered this assault? No, Thomas replied; he had long opposed an attack up the

[handwritten marginal notes: "things go different f plan (plan on p. 240)"; "see p 244"]

ridge until the Confederates were giving way elsewhere. Granger, still smarting from Grant's rebuke, also denied responsibility, although he added, "When those fellows get started all hell can't stop them." Very well, Grant remarked, as he turned back to the ridge; but somebody was going to be held responsible if things went wrong. As the lines bent back and forth and wavered, Thomas grew queasy with concern; Grant told him to calm down (it was too late to do anything, anyway), then resumed watching. The blue lines continued to surge upward. Suddenly Grant realized they were going to make it. Hurriedly he informed Sherman what was going on, betraying a bit of impatience at the performance of his favorite subordinate: "Thomas has carried the hill and line in his immediate front. Now is your time to attack with vigor. DO SO!"[67]

"The men swarm up, color after color reaches the summit, and the rebel line is divided," Montgomery Meigs, quartermaster general of the Union army who was among the generals on Orchard Knob, recounted. Within moments "the confused, astonished and terrified rebels fly this way and that to meet enemies, every way but down the rear slope of the ridge and by this way they mostly escape." Meanwhile, Hooker's columns were finally astride the ridge, sweeping northward; ironically, Sherman, who was busy bringing his operations to a close, did not participate in the attack that was designed to rescue him from his failure. Turning to an orderly, Grant shouted, "Bring my horse! I'm going up there."[68]

When he arrived at the crest, he found an astonishing scene. The Confederate line had been so poorly laid out that the defenders found it difficult to fire at the attackers, who hugged the folds in the ridge. When Thomas's men gained several footholds, the Confederate line disintegrated. Here and there pockets of resistance sought to stem the blue tide, and Grant directed his men to drive them away. As the Confederates fled, the victorious Yankees cheered their commander. Satisfied that Bragg's men had abandoned the field, the general returned to Chattanooga that evening, pondering what to do next.

At first Grant thought it best to concentrate on relieving Burnside. On reflection, however, he decided to press on after Bragg's scattered columns. His hesitation, combined with his decision to send Granger's corps away when it was in perfect position to spearhead an advance, impaired prospects for a successful pursuit. Besides, the men were tired, cold, and hungry after a long day's work. The next day Sherman pressed forward through the fog, but Thomas proved slow to implement Grant's directive to "follow [the enemy] with all your force." By November 27 Confederate resistance had stiffened at Ringgold in northern Georgia. Content with severing a rail link that supplied Longstreet's command, Grant called an end to the pursuit. He was disappointed. "If I had ammunition and horses I could now march to Mobile, Charleston and Richmond," he told a kinsman. Besides, he was well aware of the priorities at Washington. In wiring his congratulations for the fighting through November 24, Lincoln had concluded, "Remember Burnside." It was time for Grant to focus on Knoxville. He ordered Granger to start moving and instructed Sherman to turn northward. He also arranged for a copy of his message to Burnside informing him of the relief columns to fall into Longstreet's hands.[69]

Sherman marched to Knoxville, only to find that Burnside's men were no longer in danger. Longstreet had attacked the garrison on November 29, but the Federal position along Fort Sanders, just west of the city itself, proved too much for the assault force. Learning what had happened at Chattanooga, Longstreet prepared to move away; the captured missive from Grant to Burnside confirmed him in the decision to retreat eastward toward the northeast corner of Tennessee. When Sherman entered the city on December 6, Burnside treated him to a fine dinner of roast turkey. Sherman was chagrined; worn out from weeks of fighting and marching, he had hurried north because he thought Burnside's men were starving.[70]

The relief of Knoxville marked the end of the Chattanooga campaign. Lincoln's long-sought goal to liberate East Tennessee was at last achieved; Union armies were now poised to strike into the Confederate heartland. On December 7 the president called for a day of national prayer to thank God for the result: the following day he offered his thanks to the general who had achieved it. "Understanding that your lodgment at Chattanooga and Knoxville is now secure, I wish to tender you, and all under your command, my more than thanks — my profoundest gratitude — for the skill, courage, and perseverance, with which you and they, over so great difficulties, have effected that important object. May God bless you all."[71]

Grant was pleased with what he had achieved. "This Army has rendered a good account of itself in the last week, driving a big nail in the coffin of rebellion," he boasted at the end of November. To Washburne he declared that the panorama of battle "was grand beyond anything that has been, or is likely to be, on this continent. . . . Our troops behaved most magnificently and have inflicted on the enemy the heavyest blow they have received during the war." Yet he wanted to do more. He contemplated a campaign against Mobile; he even urged Sherman to start a column of cavalry into South Carolina.[72]

In later years Grant and Sherman would insist that Chattanooga had been fought according to plan, much as these two friends also insisted that there had been no surprise at Shiloh. But it is improbable that what became known as "the miracle of Missionary Ridge" was the result of conscious design — indeed, one would question the wisdom of ordering a frontal assault up such a steep and broken slope. Grant no doubt contemplated an assault by Thomas in support of Sherman; that he planned what happened strains credulity.

Nevertheless, neither was Chattanooga first and foremost a soldiers' battle. Grant's presence proved indispensable to the result. Others may have laid plans for reopening the supply line to the city, but Grant made sure that it was done. He worked hard to coordinate several commands and surmounted (although he did not ignore) friction among his generals. He also demonstrated that he could improvise on the battlefield in response to circumstances and contingencies and could exploit opportunities. Were it not for his concern about relieving Burnside, he might well have destroyed Bragg's retreating force.

Ely S. Parker, who had joined the staff in September 1863 at Rawlins's insistence after Grant had helped him win a commission, was astonished by the sight of Grant under fire during the battle of Chattanooga and the ensuing pursuit. Gone was the quiet clerk behind the counter of a general store. In battle Grant was "perfectly heedless of the storm of hissing bullets and screaming shell flying around him," because he was watching and reacting to what was unfolding around him. Once astride his mount, the general was a dynamo, pressing forward impatiently, and often without stopping to eat or rest. "Roads are almost useless to him, for he takes short cuts through field and woods, and will swim his horse through almost any stream that obstructs his way."[73]

What happened at Chattanooga secured Grant's future. David Hunter's report quelled any remaining qualms about the general's personal habits. "He is a hard worker, writes his own dispatches and orders, and does his own thinking. He is modest, quiet, never swears, and seldom drinks, as he only took two drinks during the three weeks I was with him. He listens quietly to the opinions of others and then judges promptly for himself; and he is very prompt to avail himself in the field of all the errors of the enemy." Grant knew of Hunter's mission: he remarked to Washburne that Hunter's continual presence made it difficult to write. But he also knew that now his position was indeed secure. Between Vicksburg and Chattanooga, he had done much to set the Union cause on the road to victory in the West. Whether he would be able to see it through to completion awaited events elsewhere.[74]

13

The Top Spot

●

[handwritten: interesting]

[handwritten: making it amphibious would?]

NOT CONTENT TO REST on the laurels he had garnered at Chattanooga, Grant soon itched to move forward again. He renewed his call for an amphibious assault against Mobile, which would deny the Confederates time to regroup. If he failed to capture the city itself, he would transform his foothold into a supply base and then push into Alabama and Georgia. At the same time Union cavalry would sweep into South Carolina and Georgia. Together these operations would shred the Confederate heartland, severing critical links in the rail net and hampering the movement of men and materiel. "It seems to me this move would secure the entire states of Alabama & Mississippi, and a part of Georgia or force Lee to abandon Virginia & North Carolina. Without his force the enemy have not got Army enough to resist the Army I can take."

[handwritten: Strategy]

Halleck held fast to a different set of strategic priorities. He insisted that Grant first solidify control of areas already seized during the past year. It was not enough to hold Knoxville: he wanted Longstreet driven completely out of East Tennessee. The logistical nightmares confronting any one who tried to undertake offensive operations in such rugged terrain during winter meant that Halleck's priorities amounted to doing nothing at all. Ranking just behind East Tennessee was the trans-Mississippi West. The general-in-chief explained that the president remained committed to an offensive that would drive the Confederates out of Louisiana followed by a possible invasion of Texas. Mobile would have to wait.[1]

Frustrated, Grant wondered why other commands could not achieve the objectives that stood in the way of the Mobile operation. Could not the Army of the Potomac force Longstreet out of East Tennessee by severing the railroads that connected the region with Virginia? Grant was not alone in questioning that army's inactivity. At the end of November, just as Grant was driving Bragg away from Chattanooga, Meade had crossed the Rapidan River in search of battle in central Virginia. Lee prepared for the encounter by establishing a fortified line at Mine Run. Meade's assault preparations fizzled when corps commander Gouverneur K. Warren judged the Confederate works to be too formidable. The Yankees pulled back. On hearing the news, Lincoln and others threw up their hands. The contrast between Chattanooga and Mine Run was almost too painful to contemplate. Rumors circulated that Meade would lose his job.

In Washington, Charles A. Dana pushed for Meade's replacement. He knew that Grant believed either William F. "Baldy" Smith or Sherman would be suitable successors. Yet neither was ideal for the post. Sherman's collapse under pressure in 1861 still counted against him, as did his willingness to express opinions at variance with those of the administration. Smith's previous career in the East was not exactly spotless, for in the aftermath of Fredericksburg he had informed Lincoln personally that he believed Ambrose Burnside was incompetent. Although that might well be true, Smith's action was unprofessional; observers wondered if his friendship with George McClellan had contaminated him. Nevertheless, both Stanton and Halleck preferred Smith, and Lincoln agreed. For the moment, however, nothing happened.[2]

Grant was the man who stood highest in Lincoln's estimation. On December 8, when he had learned that Knoxville finally was safe, Lincoln formally offered Grant and his men congratulations "for the skill, courage, and perseverance" with which they had triumphed "over so great difficulties." The previous evening he had shared with others his confidence in Grant, in a comment made with an eye on Tennessee and his mind on Meade and his men. After being briefed on the current situation in East Tennessee, Lincoln exclaimed, "Now, if this Army of the Potomac was good for anything — if the officers had anything in them — if the army had any legs, they could move thirty thousand men down to Lynchburg and catch Longstreet. Can anybody doubt, if Grant were here in command, that he would catch him?" In his solution, however, Lincoln revealed the difficulty: Grant could not be in two places at once. The president made clear where he preferred the general; "I do not think it would do to bring Grant away from the West."[3]

Lincoln was not alone in celebrating Grant. In fact, he was running a bit behind the crowd, and it was heading in a somewhat different direction. Near the head of the parade was Elihu Washburne, who on December 8 had introduced a joint resolution of thanks to Grant, complete with a special gold medal. But what he did the previous day, as the House of Representatives commenced its winter session, caused more talk: he gave notice that he would introduce a bill reviving the rank of lieutenant general. The

Washburnes role in USG's promotion

bill he presented a week later did more than that; it expressly recommended Grant for the new rank — thus attempting to circumvent the president, who possessed the authority to nominate generals.[4]

Washburne did not intend to slight Lincoln. Indeed, he hastened to remind Grant that the president had "stood like a wall of fire" against his critics after Shiloh. The congressman strongly favored a second term for Honest Abe. Others did not. Among the names they floated as possible successors was Ulysses S. Grant — and no one was louder than James G. Bennett, editor of the *New York Herald*. Bennett's constant shifting of opinion during the war matched that of his rival, the *Tribune*'s Horace Greeley, although on the whole Bennett embraced conservative assumptions whereas Greeley was widely known as an advocate of Radical Republican measures, including emancipation. Eager to push an alternative to Lincoln who would thwart the desires of Radical Republicans, Bennett settled on Grant as an ideal candidate. The lieutenant general bill was nothing more than an effort to "switch him off the presidential track."[5]

USG is sought for presidency

Before long Bennett sought to put Grant back on track. The general would be a man above party, committed to reform (defined as cutting expenses, reducing the debt, and ending corruption) and conservative principles — which meant a brake on emancipation and its consequences. "General Grant is the man for the people," an editorial cheered, "and now is their time to bring him out upon the course." Other editorials elaborated on the argument. The general was "free from any entangling alliances with the scheming party managers and trading spoilsmen of the country"; thus, he would promote men based on merit. "Let the independent masses of the people, who have had enough of their despicable managing party politicians, and their horrible, bloody and destructive work, proceed at once to bring out General Grant as their Presidential candidate, and they will surely cut out the politicians, set aside the incompetent and blundering administration, and carry the day." It succinctly concluded that "the whole country looks up to him as the great genius who is to end this war, restore the Union and save us from the dangers which the end of the war may bring upon us."[6]

Back at Chattanooga, Grant observed the growing interest in him. Although he appreciated Washburne's support, he wanted the congressman to understand that he did not lust for promotion: "I have been highly honored already by the government and do not ask, or feel that I deserve, any thing more in the shape of honors or promotion." Even more disturbing was talk of a presidential candidacy. The thought of running for president had never crossed Grant's mind. Such talk in the newspapers simply reminded him that fame was fickle. His silence, however, only fed the speculation. At last Grant felt compelled to respond to Barnabas Burns, chairman of Ohio's Democrats, who had written him for permission to place Grant's name in nomination before a meeting of prowar Democrats. "The question astonishes me," he replied. He wanted nothing to do with the presidency, and failed to see why he would be a suitable candidate. "Nothing likely to happen would pain me so much as to see my name used in connection with a political office," he declared. "I am not a candidate for any office nor for favors from any party. Let us succeed in crushing the rebellion, in the shortest possible time, and I will be content with whatever credit may then be given me, feeling assured that a just public will award all that is due." Nevertheless, the talk continued. How Grant would handle it would have a great deal to do with where he would be in the spring of 1864.[7]

Confounding Confederates, not parrying political inquiries, occupied Grant as 1863 drew to a close. He had established headquarters at Nashville so Julia could be with him, but before long he was on the move again. On Christmas he journeyed to Knoxville to check on Longstreet, who remained near the Virginia-Tennessee border. It proved an arduous trip, consuming three weeks. He returned convinced that a major winter campaign against his old friend would be difficult if not impossible: the cold weather, the terrain, and the lack of supplies all counted against the possibility of success. Even in Nashville there were signs of a harsh winter, as sick soldiers crowded local hospitals. Julia made the rounds, visiting soldiers, who attempted to use her as an intermediary to gain a discharge from her husband. Before long Grant put an end to the visits. "I hear of these all day long and I sent for you to come that I might have a rest from all this sad part," he explained. "I do not want you to know about these things. I want you to tell me of the children and yourself. I want and need a little rest and sunshine."[8]

That winter James Rusling, a colonel in the quartermaster's department, caught his first look at the hero of Chattanooga and was disappointed. Here was no shiny general with brass buttons, sash and sword, but a rather common-looking man, just like "a country storekeeper or a western farmer." The general was "evidently intent on everything but show." But when it came to giving orders, Grant came alive, his "clear and penetrating eye" and set jaw suggesting that he could "dare great things, and hold on mightily, and toil terribly" in pursuit of his objective. He might be a man of few words, but "he knew exactly *what* he wanted, and *why* and *when* he wanted it." Nearly every night the general could be found using the telegraph to keep tabs on his command (and the enemy), as he pondered the next move. Once, the colonel approached Grant with a requisition order authorizing large expenditures. Briefly reviewing the report, the general gave his approval, catching the colonel by surprise. Might the general want to ponder the matter a little longer? Was he sure he was right? Grant looked up. "No, I am not," he responded; "but in war anything is better than indecision. We *must decide.* If I am wrong, we shall soon find it out, and can do the other thing. But *not to decide* wastes both time and money, and may ruin everything."[9]

Grant looked everywhere for an opportunity to take the offensive. He instructed Sherman to return to Vicksburg, assemble a mobile column, and launch a large-scale raid into central Mississippi to strip the region of forage and war materiel, destroy the rail network, and deny the area to the Confederates as a base from which the Rebels could hinder a Union drive toward Atlanta or Mobile or even threaten to retake points along the Mississippi. The latter city was still very much on Grant's mind as he wrote Halleck to suggest future operations. Once Mobile was in Union hands, he argued, a Union army operating in concert with a second army based at Chattanooga could drive into the Confederate heartland, with Atlanta and Montgomery, Alabama, as objectives. This would slice the Confederacy yet again into smaller and smaller pieces by severing the logistical and transportation links between regions. It would be Vicksburg all over again, this time without the Mississippi River as an obstacle. Grant would command one column, while either Sherman or McPherson — two generals he trusted and who knew how to cooperate — would head the other one.[10]

In proposing this campaign Grant knew that he was challenging Halleck's preference for continued operations west of the Mississippi. Although the general-in-chief maintained that diplomatic reasons had justified Banks's abortive expedition into Texas, he still wanted to mop up Confederate resistance in Arkansas and western Louisiana. While success here would eradicate an irritating Rebel presence, it was less than clear exactly how such operations would contribute materially to Confederate collapse, especially when the electorate would be looking for signs that the Lincoln administration was winning the war. Aware of Halleck's stubborn adherence to trans-Mississippi operations, Grant even tried to outflank his superior. Baldy Smith and James Wilson, who viewed themselves as Grant's strategic planners, wrote Dana in support of the Mobile operation; Dana, no stranger to intrigue (and now assistant secretary of war), passed their dispatches on to Stanton.[11]

Halleck threw cold water on most of Grant's ideas. Clearing out East

Tennessee remained his top immediate priority. Lincoln and Stanton attached "the greatest importance" to the region for political as well as military reasons; recent Confederate activity there underlined the need to secure it. In contrast, he questioned the wisdom of undertaking a winter campaign in Mississippi. Grant, who had learned from his experience at Vicksburg the previous spring, directed Sherman to commence his offensive against Meridian before he received Halleck's response and was not surprised when Halleck renewed his objections to the plan and demanded that East Tennessee and Banks's operation receive priority. Even so, the general-in-chief's inability to issue direct orders thwarted his own idea: "I do not wish to change any instructions you may have given," he wired; such language allowed Grant to ignore Halleck's opposition.[12]

It was to be expected that Halleck and Grant would exchange ideas on what to do in the West. In one of his messages, however, Halleck opened another door by asking Grant to offer some thoughts on Union operations across the board during the coming year. Coming as it did after a brief discussion of affairs in the eastern theater, Halleck's remark gave Grant a chance to present his views on the proper course to pursue in the East. In conversation with Baldy Smith, he had listened as Smith outlined operations in the eastern theater over the past two years. Of special interest was a plan Smith and William B. Franklin had proposed in the aftermath of the debacle at Fredericksburg, featuring a thrust by a sizable Union army up the James River to cut Richmond's rail connections southward. Grant thought highly of Franklin, and he had been impressed by Smith at Chattanooga. Moreover, the idea resembled Grant's own musings about Mobile. He instructed Smith and Cyrus Comstock, a promising engineer and top West Point graduate who had joined the staff the previous year, to draw up a plan. The two officers did so, and on January 19 Grant forwarded the result to Halleck.[13]

The Grant/Smith/Comstock plan reveals Grant's thinking about how best to dislodge Robert E. Lee and the Army of Northern Virginia from the Old Dominion. In the previous two years, attempts to defeat Lee by advancing across the Rapidan-Rappahannock river network had failed four times (Second Manassas, Fredericksburg, Chancellorsville, and Mine Run) and had once not even gotten under way (Burnside's "Mud March" of January 1863). McClellan's attempt to use water routes to threaten Richmond from the east had also failed, and any effort to revive it would be rebuffed by the authorities at Washington, in part because success would raise the question of whether political influences had thwarted Little Mac.

[handwritten: in East ↑]

As a result, the two major field armies occupied virtually the sam[e posi-]
tion they had the year before; despite all the dramatic battles and clever
campaigns, stalemate prevailed. Better, Grant thought, to seek another
way to get at Virginia — by going around it. A Union army sixty thousand
strong, based in the southeast corner of Virginia, would strike at Raleigh,
North Carolina. Once that city was in Federal hands, Grant would shift
his base of supplies southward to New Bern, on the North Carolina coast,
and mount a second campaign against the port of Wilmington, North
Carolina. By threatening Lee's logistical links to the Confederate interior,
Grant hoped to pull him out of Virginia altogether; aware of Halleck's
continuing insistence to secure East Tennessee, Grant opined that the
Confederates would have to abandon that as well to muster sufficient
manpower to protect what was left of their rail net. The invaders could
forage liberally off the land, as at Vicksburg; their presence would ener-
gize the Unionist movement in North Carolina and would liberate slaves.
Finally, the campaign might break the Virginia stalemate: "It would
draw the enemy from Campaigns of their own choosing, and for which
they are prepared, to new lines of operations never expected to become
necessary." It might even be possible to commence operations at an early
date, for the climate was tolerable enough to contemplate a winter campaign. Of course, he added, Halleck would be the best judge of whether
the plan could be carried out. Reminding the general-in-chief that he
was responding to an inquiry, not volunteering unsolicited thoughts, he
concluded: "Whatever course is agreed upon I shall always believe is at
least intended for the best and until fully tested will hope to have it prove
so."14

[right margin handwritten: I think Rafuse also mentions this plan]

[right margin handwritten: USG suggests a plan to Halleck for E Theater]

If Grant found his boss's comments on his ideas about what to do next
in the West to be harsh, he must have been taken aback when he read
Halleck's objections to Grant's proposed North Carolina campaign. Apparently misunderstanding the thrust of Grant's comments, Halleck, following a line set forth by Lincoln, declared that the primary objective in
the East was not Richmond but Lee's army. The best way to fight Lee was
by choosing as the field of battle an area that did not unduly lengthen or
tax supply lines. A movement into North Carolina, he continued, was not
exactly a new idea. It would be impossible to raise the army to do it without reducing the Army of the Potomac from its present strength of seventy
thousand to about forty thousand, at which point it would be vulnerable
to an offensive strike by Lee, who would prefer going north to coming
south to check the North Carolina force.15

[right margin handwritten: Halleck's response]

A close examination of Halleck's analysis reveals why he and others

[bottom handwritten: read the letter in full]

had struggled without success to solve the Virginia stalemate. For Meade, even with just seventy thousand men, outnumbered Lee, who awaited Longstreet's return. In these circumstances, could he not afford to detach a portion of his command (perhaps as many as the thirty thousand Halleck suggested) and, along with the garrison outside Washington, keep Lee in check? Abraham Lincoln had asked the same question the previous September. "If the enemies sixty thousand are sufficient to keep our ninety thousand away from Richmond, why, by the same rule, may not forty thousand of ours keep their sixty thousand away from Washington, leaving us fifty thousand [Meade's army at that moment numbered ninety thousand] to put to some other use? . . . I can perceive no fault in this statement, unless we admit we are not the equal of the enemy man for man." As these statements appeared in a letter in which Lincoln reaffirmed his understanding that Lee's army and not Richmond should be the objective of operations, the president — like Grant — did not share Halleck's reasoning that a detachment was irreconcilable with defeating Lee.[16]

Moreover, there was more than one way to get at Robert E. Lee. Halleck assumed that Lee would never leave Virginia unless it was to invade the North; this matched Lee's own preferences, for just the previous month Lee had fended off an attempt to transfer him west to confront Grant. If the Army of the Potomac could hold Lee in check for a short period, the threat to North Carolina might well achieve that end — and in any case Lee would have to do something to provide for the security of the region. The implication of Halleck's reasoning was clear: he did not think that the Army of the Potomac could deal with Lee using even numbers, for Lee's army was better led. Nor was he willing to contemplate other ways to raise a force sufficient to carry out Grant's North Carolina operation, although there would be plenty of excess manpower once soldiers returned from reenlistment furloughs and recruiting trips.

The plan also reveals Grant's preferences in fighting this war. One looks in vain for the unimaginative slugger and butcher; instead, one finds a strategist who knew the importance of logistics, considered the wider implications of military operations, and was willing to try something different. Grant's plan was bold, imaginative, and achievable; it took a broad view of the eastern theater, transcending Virginia and surmounting the obsession with Lee; it promised a war of maneuver, not of bloody attrition. In combination with his proposed twin offensives against Mobile and Atlanta, it threatened to rip the Confederacy apart. Its only shortcoming was that it was not acceptable to Lincoln or Halleck. That alone proved to be an insurmountable — but not necessarily permanent — obstacle. For, as Halleck admitted, "the final decision of this question will probably depend, under the President, upon yourself."[17]

Politics were woven into everything that winter. Grant was compelled to take an active role in pushing for Senate confirmation of the promotions Sherman and McPherson had earned from the Vicksburg campaign. Off went a letter to Henry Wilson, who chaired the Senate's Committee on Military Affairs. Grant knew Wilson's politics; Dana had assured Wilson of Grant's commitment to emancipation. Questions remained, however, about the degree to which Sherman and McPherson shared that commitment (and justifiably so). Anticipating that objections would be political, Grant countered that both men "may be relied upon for an honest and faithful performance of their duties regardless of what may be their private views of the policy pursued. Neither will they ever discourage, by word or deed, others from a faithful performance of their duties." Had Sherman kept his skepticism about politicians in general and emancipation in particular to himself, instead of broadcasting his opinions freely in his correspondence and conversation, such a letter would not have been necessary, but it served as a reminder of the wisdom of maintaining good relations with one's civil superiors, even if that meant keeping one's mouth shut — something at which Grant excelled.[18]

It was becoming apparent that political considerations continued to shape deliberations over the lieutenant general bill. From Washington, where he had gone to run the Cavalry Bureau, James Wilson kept Grant informed of the rumor mill. Washburne, he reported, was attempting to gather support for the bill by claiming that its passage (and Grant's securing the promotion) would reward the hero of Vicksburg for not entering the field as a presidential candidate. Wilson judged that Washburne had gone too far in presenting himself as Grant's guardian, adviser, and confidant (all positions Wilson desired for himself). Nevertheless, Washburne's effort to force Grant's promotion failed: the Senate struck out the provision explicitly naming Grant to the new rank before sending it on to the House. The bill as it now stood, however, allowed the lieutenant general to take the field, countering claims that the promotion would chain Grant to a desk in the political thickets of the capital. Only one member of the Senate's Military Affairs Committee, William Sprague of Rhode Island, still objected to the revival of the rank, and Wilson attributed this to Grant's unwillingness to assist Sprague in the senator's efforts to engage in the cotton trade. Less satisfying was the news that Lincoln, citing "grave

Lincoln did

political considerations in Illinois," had <u>ordered McClernand to report</u> <u>for duty under Banks.</u>[19]

Questions about his own political ambitions plagued Grant. He fended off one inquiry by claiming that the only office he desired to hold was that of mayor in Galena, in order "to build a new sidewalk from my house to the depot." People chuckled when they heard that — except, perhaps, the current occupant of the mayor's office. But the talk continued. Grant fended off one inquiry from former Democratic congressman Isaac N. Morris, the son of Jesse's old friend, Thomas Morris. "I am not a politician, never was and hope never to be, and could not write a political letter," he declared. "My only desire is to serve the country in her present trials. To do this efficiently it is necessary to have the confidance of the Army and the people. I know no way to better to secure this end than by a faithful performance of my duties." In short, <u>he would not offer his own views</u> <u>on politics or dissent openly from administration policies,</u> whatever his private views: "In this respect," he added, "I know I have proven myself a 'good soldier.'" Turning to the presidency, he reiterated that it was "the last thing in the world I desire. I would regard such a consummation as being highly unfortunate for myself if not for the country." It would be best, he concluded, for Morris to treat this as a private letter, "because I want to avoid being heard from by the public except through acts in the performance of my legitimate duties."[20]

unlike Mc- Clellan

Jesse Grant confirmed to Morris his son's lack of interest in political office. "I am fully satisfied that he would not be a candidate for the Presidency under any circumstances," he wrote. "He went into the service avowedly to contribute his mite towards putting down this wicked rebellion without having any political ambitions after this was accomplished. He is now a Major General in the regular army, and will doubtless be placed at the head of it. And I believe that is the extent of his ambition." But he said nothing in this letter about not having it appear in print, and he filled it with stories of his eldest son as a child that highlighted Ulysses's ingenuity and determination. Eventually it made its way into the papers, courtesy of Morris.[21]

In light of Grant's remarks he was surprised that Washburne and J. Russell Jones would wonder whether the general had been seduced by talk of the White House. The congressman had hurried to remind his general that "when the torrent of obloquy and detraction was rolling over you, and your friends, after the battle of Shiloh, Mr. Lincoln stood like a wall of fire between you and it, uninfluenced by the threats of Congressmen and the demands of insolent cowardice." According to Washburne, many of the people who were currently using Grant's name as "a foot ball for the Presidency" were looking to serve their own agendas. Several of the people now "clamouring the loudest" for a Grant presidency "were the most bitter in your denunciation, eighteen months, or two years ago." Jones's letter was even more curious, for it revealed the outlines of a quid pro quo: Lincoln would support Grant's promotion if Grant supported Lincoln's reelection. "As things now stand," he warned, "you could get the nomination of the Democracy, but could not be elected as against Lincoln." To thwart that possibility, Washburne had already released to the press Grant's letter of the previous summer calling for the destruction of slavery as a prerequisite for peace, which deterred some Democrats from considering Grant. Rawlins suggested that Washburne and Jones need not worry, for Grant was "unambitious of the honor" and would not allow himself to be used to embarrass the Lincoln administration or its head.[22]

The general had more important things on his mind. On January 17 he learned that Fred, who was spending the winter in St. Louis, was seriously ill with typhoid. Grant, always a devoted father, recalled that Sherman had the previous year lost one of his own boys. Just as he prepared to depart for his son's bedside, word reached him of a possible Confederate offensive in East Tennessee. Torn between his worry about Fred and his lack of confidence in the ability of John G. Foster (who had replaced Burnside in command of the Knoxville garrison and surrounding forces) to keep the Confederates in check, a frustrated Grant sent Julia to St. Louis and traveled from Nashville to Chattanooga to induce Foster to attack — only to learn that Foster was too ill to take the field. At last Grant instructed Thomas to keep an eye on Longstreet and left for St. Louis. By the time he arrived, Fred was well on the way to recovery; Julia, however, reported that one of the Dent family slaves, also named Julia, who had remained with the Grants as a nurse after gaining her freedom, had decided not to risk reenslavement by returning to Missouri. Grant accepted an invitation to attend a dinner in his honor arranged by many of the same people who had once known him as an honest but unlucky farmer and real estate broker. It was a triumphant return to the scene of his frustrations and failures. People interrupted him to introduce themselves as he dined at the Planter's House; crowds gathered outside the hotel and serenaded him, although he refused their request for a speech by saying, "Making speeches is not my business" — testimony to what a good (and shrewd) soldier he was. But he had no problem listening to other people make speeches, especially if they were about him. Two hundred and fifty people gathered on the evening of January 29 to toast and celebrate his accomplishments. Among them was Colonel Dent, who was willing at last to be seen in public with his Federal son-in-law. The general, aware that he was now the subject of intense scrutiny, refused to touch any of the glasses of wine served with each course. He was equally guarded in his comments. Rising in response to a toast, he said simply, "Gentlemen, in response, it will be impossible for me to do more than to thank you."[23]

For Julia, what began as a family crisis had turned into a moment of triumph. At last her husband was the toast of St. Louis. She could set aside the loss of her nurse in such a situation. However, she now realized what lay ahead. The wife of the hero of Vicksburg and Chattanooga owed it to her husband "to try to look as well as possible," but she believed that her appearance was marred by strabismus. Although years ago a local doctor had assured her that a simple operation would correct the condition, the prospect had always scared her — until now. Yet when she mustered up the courage to inquire about having the operation, the same doctor told her that it was too late. She shared her disappointment with Ulysses. "What in the world put such a thought in your head, Julia?" he asked. When she replied that the operation might make her a little less plain — she had seen the pretty women flocking around her Ulys — he embraced her. "Did I not see you and fall in love with you with these same eyes? I like them just as they are, and now, remember, you are not to interfere with them. They are mine, and let me tell you, Mrs. Grant, you had better not make any experiments, as I might not like you half so well with any other eyes."[24]

Suddenly Julia understood something important. Others in St. Louis, even those who liked Grant, must have marveled at his rise to fame and wondered how it had come about. Oh, a few people had seen something special in him, including her mother. But most thought of him as a man who once was at best unlucky, at worst a failure: and now, somehow, he was the Union's most successful general. Why remained inexplicable to many. Yet Julia Grant knew that the major general who had just given her that order was at heart the same ex-captain who had come to St. Louis nearly a decade before to start life over as a farmer — so that he could be with his wife and children.

At last Grant returned to the front. Explaining to his father that he had no time to swing by Covington, he declared that he did not want to leave the South again until the war was over: "The attention I received whilst it is flattering, is to me very embarrassing." But no relief was to be had in Louisville; Grant wondered to Julia if he would have to find a "one company outpost out on the railroad where no body lives" for some rest. Nevertheless, he kept an eye on matters at Washington. Ever pragmatic, he knew that a promotion carried with it a pay increase that would furnish Julia with more spending money.[25]

As Grant traveled, the House of Representatives took up the lieutenant general bill. On February 1, it affixed an amendment designating Grant for the new rank, a reaction to rumors that Lincoln might name Halleck. There was some opposition. James A. Garfield, fresh from the field, thought it might make Grant a desk general (although, as one of Rosecrans's staff officers, he may have inherited his superior's dislike for Grant). Accepting the amendment, Washburne crowed that "this war would never be ended until we had a fighting general to lead our armies." However, the amendment did not survive the Senate, as several senators pointed out that in specifying Grant the bill infringed on Lincoln's constitutional powers. Washburne was ready to fight it out in a conference committee until he learned that Lincoln would nominate Grant.[26]

The president's approval of either the bill or Grant had never been certain. The administration had not lobbied on behalf of the measure; critics claimed that the chief executive might well reward Halleck, not Grant, with a third star. Much more important to Lincoln was knowing whether in promoting a general he was elevating a rival. He had already suffered through several generals who fantasized about replacing him in the White House. Even now George B. McClellan was readying himself for the Democratic nomination. Would Grant do likewise?

Lincoln looked for an answer. Grant, no slouch at this sort of political intrigue, decided to provide one. One of his generals, Frank Blair, was now a congressman. He wrote Grant to inquire about the rumors of his political ambitions. Grant, aware that Blair was working closely with Lincoln, shared his sentiments. "Everyone who knows me knows I have no political aspirations either now or for the future," he told Blair. He hated to see his name "associated with politics either as an aspirant for office or as a partizan." Then making it clear that he understood the purpose of the exchange, he warned Blair, "Show this letter to no one unless it be the president himself" — a rather ill-disguised hint to do just that. The president put out other feelers; Washburne advised him to consult with Jones, who just happened to have in his possession another letter from the general. "Nobody could induce me to think of being a presidential candidate," Grant had flatly declared, "particularly so long as there is a possibility of having Mr. Lincoln reelected." The president, secure in the knowledge that "the Presidential grub" had not been "gnawing at Grant," decided it

was time to back the lieutenant generalcy bill and elevate Grant to general-in-chief. The quid pro quo had been met.[27] *what were these?*

As February drew to a close Grant was ill: he told Julia that he had taken
enough quinine "to make my head buz." For the past month he had
worked to conduct several winter campaigns before turning his attention
to the big push in the spring toward Atlanta. At the same time he had
grown exasperated with all the talk about his presidential ambitions. "I
have always thought the most slavish life any man could lead was that of a
politician," he confided to his boyhood friend Daniel Ammen, who was
now a navy commander serving along the Atlantic coast. "Besides I do not
believe any man could be successful as a soldier whilst he has an anchor
ahead for other advancement." He hurried to dampen his father's interest
in the matter: "I am not a candidate for any office. All I want is to be left
alone to fight this war out. . . ." He would not issue a public letter; aware
that once more Jesse was stirring the pot, he asked his father to come visit
him — in part because he did not want to set forth his feelings on paper.[28]

At last word came that the lieutenant general bill had passed, and that
Lincoln had nominated him to fill the new rank. Days later came a telegram from Halleck directing him to report to Washington as soon as possible. Grant found a moment to send the news to Sherman — who had
returned from his Meridian expedition (which he deemed a success).
see p250
"Whilst I have been eminently successful in this War, in at least gaining the
confidence of the public, no one feels more than me how much of this
success is due to the energy, skill, and harmonious putting forth of that
energy and skill, of those who it has been my good fortune to have occupying a subordinate position under me," he scribbled, fumbling awkwardly
with his effort to be gracious. Then he hit his stride: "What I want is to express my thanks to you and McPherson as *the men* to whom, above all others, I feel indebted for whatever I have had of success. How far your advice
and suggestions have been of assistance you know. How far your execution
of whatever has been given you entitles you to the reward I am receiving
you cannot know as well as me." With those generous remarks, carrying
with them the implication that things would never be the same, Grant prepared to go to Washington.[29]

On the afternoon of March 8, 1864, a man in the worn uniform of a major
general entered Willard's Hotel in Washington, D.C. By his side was a thir-
teen-year-old boy. No one noticed the pair as they approached the front
desk to register; indeed, the sight of a major general in the hotel was so familiar that one wag ventured you couldn't hurl a rock though the lobby

without hitting several sets of shoulder straps bearing stars. The registration clerk looked at the new arrivals, mentioned that perhaps he could do something for them — say a room on the top floor — and shoved forward the register. Only when he flipped the book around to scrutinize the signature did his eyes widen. In fact, he sputtered, there was a fine suite of rooms open on the second floor. Nothing else would do for "U. S. Grant and son, Galena, Illinois."

Grant accepted the accommodations, and he and Fred went to freshen up. On his arrival at the B & O depot with Rawlins and Comstock, he had gone first to army headquarters and then to Georgetown to seek out Henry Halleck, but failed to find him; now father and son, more than a bit hungry, wanted to eat before going out again. But they found little peace in the hotel dining room. Other diners began to whisper and point at the new arrivals; finally someone stood up on a chair and announced to everyone that the Hero of Chattanooga was among them. People stood, cheered, and shouted Grant's name, pounding on tables until silverware, plates, and glasses danced. Finally the general struggled to his feet, wiped his mustache with his napkin, bowed several times, and then tried to return to the task at hand. Among those who observed him carefully was Theodore Lyman, a volunteer aide on Meade's staff, who was on his way north to enjoy a few weeks of leave. "He is rather under middle height, of a spare, strong build; light-brown hair, and short, light brown beard," Lyman wrote; "his eyes of a clear blue; forehead high; nose aquiline; jaw squarely set, but not sensual. His face has three expressions: deep thought; extreme determination; and great simplicity and calmness." Under the circumstances, Grant was remarkably calm — but not totally self-composed. No sooner had he finished dinner than a congressman took it upon himself to introduce Grant to all who wanted to shake his hand. As one newspaper put it, people "crowded around the blushing and confused object of this sudden ovation, and overwhelmed him with their admiring interest."[30]

Grant next decided to walk to the White House, two blocks away, to meet Abraham Lincoln. Some self-appointed guide — accounts differ as to his identity — pointed out that the president was holding a reception. Indeed, many people had turned out, not so much to see Lincoln (they had plenty of chances to do that) as to catch a glimpse of Grant, whose arrival had been rumored in the papers. Along the way Grant met Rawlins and Comstock, and the little group ventured into the Executive Mansion. They turned to their right and entered the East Room; the crowd gave way as Grant advanced, rather quietly, to the tall man at the other end of the room. Smiling, Abraham Lincoln extended his right hand and warmly greeted his visitor. "This is General Grant, is it not?"

"Yes," Grant replied.[31]

This initial encounter between the president and the general proved to be a short one: others gathered there also wanted to see the coming man. Secretary of State William H. Seward presented Grant to Mary Todd Lincoln; then the crowd demanded its turn. At last Grant, in danger of being trampled by swarms of admirers, was persuaded to stand on a sofa so all could see him. "He blushed like a girl," observed a correspondent for the *New York Herald*. "The handshaking brought streams of perspiration down his forehead and over his face. . . . He quite affects the plain and home-spun style of doing things, and acts it admirably, or else he is an extra ordinary example of unconscious freshness." One thing was clear: this was no McClellan. Nevertheless, his arrival electrified the room. "Ladies suffered dire disaster in the crush and confusion," recalled another reporter; "their laces were torn and crinolines mashed; and many got upon sofas, chairs, and tables to be out of harm's way or to get a better view of the spectacle. It was the only real mob I ever saw in the White House. . . . The little, scared-looking man who stood on a crimson-covered sofa was the idol of the hour."[32]

In time Seward and others escorted Grant out of the East Room and into a more private setting in the Blue Room where Lincoln and Secretary of War Stanton were waiting. The president informed Grant that he would formally present the general with his commission the next day; in the course of the ceremony the president would make a few remarks. Handing Grant a copy of his statement, Lincoln asked him to prepare a reply, expressing the hope that the general would "say something which shall prevent or obviate any jealousy of you from any of the other generals in the service" and "something which shall put you on good terms as possible with the Army of the Potomac."[33] The president had heard of Grant's reticence and was trying to avoid an embarrassing scene during the orchestrated event. At the same time, he seemed to be trying to dictate a response, although he added that the general need not be bound by those suggestions.

Grant said nothing. He returned to his hotel to work out his reply, Fred hovering over his shoulder. The next day, with Fred, Rawlins, and Comstock in tow, he made his way first to Halleck's office, then to Stanton's, and then back to the White House, arriving in time for the one o'clock ceremony. Awaiting him were Lincoln, Halleck, and the cabinet. Lincoln faced Grant, presented him with his commission, and then read his stiffly worded address: "General Grant: The nation's appreciation of what you have done and its reliance upon you for what remains to do in the existing great struggle are now presented with this commission, constituting you lieutenant general in the Army of the United States. With this high honor devolves upon you also a corresponding responsibility. As the country herein trusts you, so under God it will sustain you. I scarcely need to add that with what I here speak for the nation goes my own hearty personal concurrence."

Now it was Grant's turn. As all eyes turned to him, he took out a piece of paper with words scrawled in pencil — and found it trying to read in the dim light. "Mr. President," he began, peering at the page, manifestly uncomfortable. "I accept this commission with gratitude for the high honor conferred. With the aid of the noble armies that have fought on so many fields, it will be my earnest endeavor not to disappoint your expectations. I feel the full weight of the responsibilities now devolving on me and know if they are to be met it will be due to those armies, and above all to the favor of that Providence which leads both nations and men." Despite the formal prose, the response was all Grant, for he shared his moment with his men. John Nicolay, Lincoln's secretary, observed that Grant had failed to incorporate either of Lincoln's suggestions, although in fact Grant had done so — in his own way — by speaking of the "noble armies that have fought on so many fields," not of himself. The secretary added that the general "made rather sorry and disjointed work of enunciating his reply." But Grant had sent notice that he would be his own man.[34]

The next morning Grant set off for his first visit with the Army of the Potomac and its commander, George G. Meade — a visit Meade had been dreading for some time. Not long after Gettysburg, in the wake of Lee's successful retreat to Virginia, Meade heard that a disappointed Lincoln might replace him with Grant. Over the next several months as Grant recorded more successes while Meade merely held his own, the irritable commander of the Army of the Potomac kept an eye on his competition from the West. "I knew him as a young man in the Mexican war," he told his wife, "at which time he was considered a clever young officer, but nothing extraordinary. He was compelled to resign some years before the present war, owing to his irregular habits. I think his great characteristic is indomitable energy and great tenacity of purpose. He certainly has been very successful, and that is nowadays the measure of reputation. The enemy, however, have never had in any of their Western armies either the generals or the troops they have had in Virginia, nor has the country been so favorable for them as here."[35]

With Grant's elevation Meade prepared himself to be displaced, even as
he battled efforts of enemies led by Daniel Sickles, Daniel Butterfield, and
Joseph Hooker to deprive him of the credit for the victory at Gettysburg.
He had just returned from Washington, where he had testified before the
Joint Committee on the Conduct of the War about that campaign. What
he picked up along the way convinced him that Hooker and Sickles were
making some headway. Now it was time to face Grant, and Meade growled
to his wife that he might well be deposed: "I understand he is indoctri-
nated with the notion of the superiority of the Western armies, and that
the failure of the Army of the Potomac to accomplish anything is due to
their commanders."[36] Meade planned to forestall this humiliation by offering to step aside.

Grant arrived at Brandy Station in midafternoon on March 10. Although it was raining heavily, a regimental band played "Hail to the Chief"
as Meade's chief of staff, Andrew A. Humphreys, greeted him at the station. With Humphreys was one friendly face — that of Rufus Ingalls, once
Grant's West Point classmate and now the army's quartermaster. One observer was not impressed with Grant's appearance: "His dress is very plain,
eyes half closed, he takes little or no notice of anything." Trailing behind
him was Baldy Smith, who was brimming with anticipation that he was
about to inherit Meade's spot.[37]

Meade met Grant and ushered him to his headquarters. The ensuing
encounter proved a pleasant surprise to both men. While in Washington
Grant had encountered Sickles at dinner; he was also aware of the ongoing investigation into Gettysburg. He found the effort to depose Meade
distasteful (and perhaps he was reminded of the intrigue directed at displacing him prior to Vicksburg). So when Meade opened his conversation
by suggesting that perhaps Grant would like to replace him, and promised
to serve wherever Grant saw fit, the new lieutenant general smiled. Impressed with Meade's sense of selfless duty — far superior to that displayed by Hooker or Sickles — Grant decided to retain the present commander of the Army of the Potomac.

Grant also made a good first impression. "He had been very civil, and
says nothing about superseding me," Meade told his wife. Humphreys also
found himself "agreeably disappointed in Gen'l Grant's appearance," remarking that "he is good looking, with an intellectual face and head which
at the same time expresses a good deal of determination." Although Grant
was somewhat reserved with his new acquaintances, he greeted old friends
warmly, and was "cordial and demonstrative" with Meade. Nevertheless,
Humphreys added, there was something about the visit "that indicated

[handwritten margin note: Baldy Smith = USG's strategist aide, I think]

[handwritten margin note: replacing]

that it was the visit of a rival commander to a rival army." In light of the reception many of these generals had accorded the bombastic John Pope nearly two years ago when he arrived from the West to form a new army, this underlying tension was understandable. But Grant was no Pope, and as soon as the Army of the Potomac found this out, the atmosphere improved greatly. Still, a slight edge would remain for some time, a discomfort built of unfamiliarity and remnants of distrust and suspicion.[38]

Grant was always a quick study, and over the next twenty-four hours he made up his mind on several key issues. Before he came east he had intended to return west in time for the spring campaigns. Two nights in Washington, however, persuaded him "that here was the point for the commanding general to be. No one else could, probably, resist the pressure that would be brought to bear upon him to desist from his own plans and pursue others." Surely neither Sherman nor Baldy Smith would succeed in such an environment. Grant, however, was determined to command in the field, not from a desk. Thus, as he explained to Comstock, he would keep Meade, who was familiar with the capacities of the generals and men of the Army of the Potomac, in place; Grant would accompany him. Halleck would remain in Washington "as office man & military adviser" (which is what Old Brains had been doing for some time). Sherman would assume Grant's former job, and McPherson would take Sherman's spot as commander of the Army of the Tennessee. These decisions made, Grant returned to Washington. Meade accompanied him — a sign of the promising beginning between the two men. "I was very much pleased with General Grant," he remarked a few days later. "In the views he expressed to me he showed much more capacity and character than I had expected."[39]

Grant's second stay in Washington was even briefer than his first. He prepared to return to Nashville to confer with Sherman and his old generals. Lincoln wanted Grant to stay around for a few days. Next evening there was to be a dinner in his honor at the White House. The new general-in-chief begged out. There was much to be done, and no time to waste. "Really, Mr. President, I have had enough of this show business," he explained. Then he was off.

Sherman, whose suspicion of Washington knew no bounds, had wondered how his friend would weather the new environment. "You are now Washington's legitimate successor and occupy a position of almost dangerous elevation," he observed, "but if you can continue as heretofore to be yourself, simple, honest, and unpretending," all would be fine. However, he thought it would be best for Grant to leave Washington as soon as possible. "Halleck is better qualified than you are to stand the buffets of Intrigue and Policy. Come out West, take to yourself the whole Mississippi Valley. Let us make it dead sure, and I tell you the Atlantic slope and Pacific shores will follow its destiny as sure as the limbs of a tree live or die with the main trunk. We have done much, but still much remains to be done." Perhaps in his passion Sherman got carried away with his prose, for Grant had already done his share toward recapturing the Mississippi Valley. Mobile, Atlanta, and other points in the Confederate heartland were now the proper targets of military operations in the West. But the larger message was clear. "For God's sake and for your Country's sake come out of Washington. . . . Here lies the seat of the coming Empire, and from the West when our task is done, we will make short work of Charleston, and Richmond, and the impoverished coast of the Atlantic."[40]

Grant shared Sherman's reservations; however, he reached precisely the opposite conclusion. That he would stay in the East was the most important piece of news he carried westward with him. Arriving at Nashville on March 14, he gathered his old comrades for a conference. He described his meetings with Lincoln and Stanton and his visit to the Army of the Potomac, marveling at how well equipped and supplied it was compared with the armies of the West. However, he also noticed something else a little different about that army. Several old friends, while congratulating him on his new position, could not resist adding what was in the next months to become a deafening refrain: "You have not yet met Bobby Lee."[41]

To overcome this attitude, Grant wanted to import some of his old generals. Sherman, however, resisted, and in the end Grant got only one man: Phil Sheridan, who had distinguished himself as a fighter in several battles with the Army of the Cumberland. He would head up the Army of the Potomac's cavalry corps. Grant also tried to curtail Nathaniel Banks's Red River expedition, ordering Banks to take Shreveport in timely fashion, then return the men borrowed from Sherman. "I look upon the conquering of the organized armies of the enemy as being of vastly more importance than the mere acquisition of territory," he added, and hinted that the long-desired campaign against Mobile might finally be in the works.[42]

There was more than talk at Nashville. Grant took the generals on a courtesy call to Andrew Johnson, Tennessee's military governor; the group also attended plays, with Sherman offering pointed criticisms of the performances. Grant accepted a sword presented by the residents of Jo Daviess County (where Galena was located). Once more he was called on to make a speech: this time he pulled out a rumpled piece of paper and handed it to the head of the delegation to read. Sherman smiled. "His whole manner was awkward in the extreme, yet perfectly characteristic," he recalled, adding that he could not stop himself from laughing. Nevertheless, Grant was well aware of the circumstances confronting him. "The position I am now placed in I feel will prove to be a trying one, but by having an eye to duty alone I shall hope to succeed," he told an old Illinois friend. He planned to "move from one Army to another so as to be where my presence seems to be more required."[43] *like in East @ the moment*

Sherman watched and listened as his friend unfolded his plan on how to win the war. Inspired by what he saw — and glad that Grant had survived his initial encounters with Washington — Sherman recalled what he had written Grant a week earlier. Marveling at "the simple faith in success you have always manifested, which I can liken to nothing else than the faith a Christian has in a Savior" — something Sherman knew about from experience, for his wife was a devout Catholic — he believed that this was the key to Grant's success. "I knew wherever I was that you thought of me, and if I go in a tight place you would come if alive. My only points of doubt *huh* were in your knowledge of Grand Strategy and Books of Science and History. But I confess your common sense seems to have supplied all this." Grant had given Sherman confidence; now it was up to the new general-in-chief to do the same for the Army of the Potomac.[44]

After several days of conferences and discussions Grant was ready to return to Washington. He asked Sherman to accompany him to Cincinnati so that they could confer about the spring campaign with only Julia in earshot. On the train Grant explained that he would like to offer several generals new commands in an effort to reunite the army. Surely they could put talents of George B. McClellan to good use; even Don Carlos Buell, whatever Grant's personal reservations, might prove himself as a corps commander in the West. Perhaps these men had failed in independent command only because they had secured it too early in their careers. Sherman liked the idea, but nothing came of it. Grant was able to shuffle into slots several generals who were going to lose their commands in the East, but the plan of bringing McClellan back fizzled, while Buell wanted no part in the sort of war Grant and Sherman planned to wage. Grant never forgot Buell's refusal to serve, and it colored his evaluation of that general for the rest of his life. → *what is Simpson's source? for entire ¶* *total war ?*

Arriving at Cincinnati, the two men sat down in a room at the Burnet House and pored over maps. Years later Sherman, addressing veterans of the Army of the Tennessee at Cincinnati, would recall the meeting. Pointing to the Burnet House, he remarked, "He was to go for Lee and I was to go for Joe Johnston."[45] *war of emancipation ?*

building in Cincinnati

14

Planning the Grand Offensive

●

THE GRANTS RETURNED to Washington on the evening of March 22 after Julia had spent a day shopping in Philadelphia — she wanted to make sure that she wore clothes suitable for the wife of the lieutenant general. In some respects she had a better idea than did her husband of what awaited them. The next morning Grant encountered yet more show business. Although the general had posed for photographs several times during the war, the prints were not widely circulated. An etching of a rather overweight, balding fellow with a long beard purporting to be Grant had appeared in numerous news weeklies and books, along with pulp biographies of someone named "Ulysses Sydney Grant." The general could still make his way through a crowd unnoticed: when he stopped off at Cincinnati to visit his father at Covington, the old man had sent a driver and a carriage to pick up his famous son, only to see Grant walking home on foot, bag in hand, his uniform concealed by a plain overcoat.

To secure a new photograph of the general, Stanton (who now knew what Grant looked like) hustled the general down to Mathew Brady's studio on Seventh Street and Pennsylvania Avenue. Grant took up his position in front of the camera, his face barely revealing any emotion, and waited patiently. It was midafternoon, and Brady directed his assistant to go up on the roof to uncover the skylight. The assistant slipped; the skylight shattered. As Brady and Stanton watched in horror, shards of glass, each some two inches thick, cascaded around the general, each fragment potentially damaging if not lethal. As the last pieces hit the floor, the two men stared, astonished, at Grant, who sat unmoved and unhurt. He glanced up at the ceiling, then back at the cameras, as if nothing noteworthy had happened. Brady later called it "the most remarkable display of nerve I ever witnessed"; an excited Stanton, fearing rumors of an assassination attempt, swore the photographer to secrecy. Then the session went on.[1]

Image was everything during these months. Yet, for all the celebration on Grant's behalf, there was also some grumbling and renewed whispering about old ghosts. Rumors circulated that on the trip to Covington Grant had become intoxicated. Immediately supporters rushed to deny the story. Jesse assured one reporter that his son "had not drank a drop of liquor in ten years, except a very small quantity on one occasion, by order of a physician." By now the general's supporters and associates had heard enough of such stories. The previous December, an aide wrote home: "If you could see the General, as he sits just over beyond me, with his wife and two children, looking more like a chaplain than a general, with that quiet air so impossible to describe, you would not ask me if he drinks. He rarely ever uses intoxicating liquors; more moderate in his habits and desires than any other man I ever knew; more pure and spotless in his private character than almost any man I ever knew."[2]

Grant's stay in Washington was brief. After directing Halleck to provide for the transfer east of Philip H. Sheridan to head the Army of the Potomac's cavalry, the commanding general headed back to Culpeper, Virginia, where he had established headquarters. During the next several weeks he laid out his plans for the spring campaign, requesting maps and information from Washington as he sat and studied. He already had a good idea of the political terrain in which he would operate. The proposals he had forwarded to Halleck in January required revision in light of what he had encountered during his visits to the capital. Now he worked to frame an overall plan of operations and assemble the means to implement it.

→ see p250

Not since 1861 had the Union high command articulated its grand strategy. In the early months of the war General Winfield Scott had set forth what would become known as the Anaconda Plan. It called for the establishment of a blockade around the Confederacy followed by a major offensive to seize control of the Mississippi River Valley. In light of what happened from 1861 to 1863, many people have claimed that Scott pointed out the path to Union victory. However, both the establishment of a blockade and an offensive to recapture the Mississippi were obvious goals. Once these initial objectives were achieved, Scott would have had the Union armies sit and wait, slowly strangling the Confederacy to death, while the resurgence of unionism in the South would reintegrate the former Confederate states into the Union with a minimum of destruction and bloodshed. That vision had long since vanished.

The decision after First Bull Run to place George B. McClellan in charge of what became known as the Army of the Potomac — and not at the head of a column headed south along the Mississippi — reflected different priorities. The East became the focus of attention. In August 1861, McClellan presented his plan of operations calling for the defeat of enemy armies in the field in a decisive battle coupled with "a rigidly protective policy as to private property and unarmed persons." Although he acknowledged the strategic value of the Mississippi, he added a thrust at East Tennessee (a move Lincoln favored), some interesting ideas about campaigns in the trans-Mississippi West, and a major confrontation in Virginia. McClellan had the chance to implement this plan when he replaced Scott as general-in-chief in November 1861; but the only operation that took place, the East Tennessee campaign, proved a disaster. Circumstances, not the implementation of a master plan, led to initial Union triumphs in the West, notably those gained by Grant. Soon afterward McClellan lost his position as general-in-chief, and Lincoln waited until July 1862 to fill the position with Halleck. Old Brains, however, proved incapable of devising an overall strategy for implementing his sound observations about the difficulties of achieving decisive victories in the East. Ever ready to evaluate the plans of others, he never exercised the powers of his office with vigor, preferring to delegate military operations to subordinates on the grounds that they knew better than he what to do (although he always reserved the right to second-guess their decisions). The lack of overall control was most noticeable during the Vicksburg campaign, when Halleck failed to compel Grant and Banks to work toward a common end.[3]

Grant's approach to grand strategy emphasized coordination and cooperation. Unlike McClellan, he would not give short shrift to the West; unlike Halleck, he would issue directives instead of offering advice. The plan that emerged integrated elements of his January proposals with the preferences of others, including Lincoln. As he told Sherman, he intended "to work all parts of the army together and somewhat toward a common center." His approach toward the sector between the Appalachians and the Mississippi remained basically unchanged. Sherman's February raid toward Meridian, Mississippi, had rendered it difficult for the Confederates to mount a serious offensive from that area, although there remained the danger of Confederate cavalry using the region as a base of operations to mount forays against Federal supply depots, railroads, and other rear areas in Tennessee. A major field army under Sherman — really, an army group composed of three armies (the Tennessee, the Cumberland, and the Ohio) would drive deep into Georgia with orders to destroy the Army of Tennessee, now under Joe Johnston, and capture the railroad junction

Handwritten annotations at top: apparently USG's grand strategy was based on framework of his January suggestion to Halleck — for proof see p 268 ¶2 ¶269 + p269 ¶2 +4

↳ on p 250

of Atlanta. That achieved, Sherman would then penetrate deeper into the Confederate heartland, although circumstances would determine his target. Meanwhile, a second army drawn from Banks's command in Louisiana would move by sea against Mobile, then north toward either Selma or Atlanta. Ultimately these thrusts would slice up the Confederacy. → *[handwritten: than the W. which was unchanged]*

Grant made more significant adjustments to his January plan for operations in the East. Although he still toyed with the idea of launching an invasion of North Carolina with Ambrose Burnside's Ninth Corps, he now saw an easier way to challenge Lee by striking at his rear. The Union had long occupied Hampton Roads, Norfolk, and Fort Monroe, but to little purpose after McClellan's withdrawal from the James River in 1862. Grant would organize and augment the forces in this area to form a small field army — christened the Army of the James — with orders to advance up the James by water and land south of Richmond to cut off the Confederate capital from points south and perhaps even threaten the city itself. If this operation was less ambitious than the original plan to invade North Carolina, it could still accomplish some of the same ends. Over time Grant developed a similar plan for Union forces in the Shenandoah Valley and the Blue Ridge Mountains, with several Federal columns charged with severing rail links, pinning down Confederate forces, and denying Lee resources that either came from the area itself or were transported by rail through the region.) *[handwritten: USG grand strategy]*

[handwritten margin: USG creates A. of James ???]

That left the Army of the Potomac. It would engage Lee's army and force it out into the open, away from the prepared positions along Mine Run. If the other columns in Virginia were successful in their work, the Confederate commander would find himself caught between saving Richmond, preserving his supply lines, and fending off a numerically superior field army. Grant doubted Lee could do all three; if things went as planned, Lee might not be able to do any of them. The result would be the destruction of Lee's army, not by a battle of attrition, but by striking him on all sides and forcing him to react in difficult circumstances to Union initiatives.

[handwritten margin: like McPherson says]

[handwritten margin: the goal of USG's grand strategy]

Although this plan embodied some of the assumptions of Grant's January plan, it did not incorporate all the features of that proposal. The changes disappointed William F. Smith, who had helped frame the January plan, as well as Smith's new friend, James H. Wilson, who even now flattered himself as the brains behind some of Grant's greatest triumphs. Rawlins got wind of this when Wilson showed him a letter from Smith "in which all the selfishness of his nature is evinced," as Rawlins put it. Immediately he shared the letter with Grant, suggesting that perhaps Grant had overestimated Smith's abilities and overlooked less admirable qualities. Certainly the incident cemented Meade's standing as commander of the Army of the Potomac, although Grant still thought he could make use of Smith.[4]

On April 1 Grant arrived at Fort Monroe, Virginia, to confer with Benjamin F. Butler about the role Butler's Army of the James would play in the next campaign. With him were Julia, Rawlins, Washburne, Comstock, and Smith, still looking for a command. Butler was renowned primarily for his activities in occupied New Orleans, notably his order directing that women who harassed Union soldiers were to be treated as prostitutes. That he had improved the sanitary conditions in the Crescent City was mostly ignored; that family members may have profited from his tenure was more notorious (Butler himself earned the nickname of "Spoons" because of his alleged fondness for local silverware). He owed his position as a major general to political clout, a beneficiary of Lincoln's eagerness to woo Northern Democrats to support the initial war effort by awarding them military commissions. Because of his early commission date, Butler outranked far more competent generals, making his placement something of a burden. However, he had never commanded troops in the field; his skills on the battlefield had yet to be tested.

Some may have questioned Butler's military ability, but there was no doubt that he was shrewd. Like Grant, he saw the potential for offensive operations along the James River against Richmond; in pointing out the advantages of such a campaign, he impressed Grant as a like-minded leader who simply needed able subordinates with military expertise to carry out his plans. That it was April Fool's Day eluded everyone's notice, except, perhaps, Comstock, who concluded that Butler was "sharp, shrewd, able, without conscience or modesty — overbearing. A bad man to have against you."[5]

The mission Grant gave Butler seemed simple enough. The Army of the James was to strike at Richmond. Reinforcements from South Carolina would allow Butler to commit two corps to the operation, to be commanded by Smith and Quincy A. Gillmore, who had spent much of the war engaged in operations against Charleston. The army would move by water up the James River, seize City Point, located at the junction of the James and Appomattox Rivers, some ten miles east of Petersburg, and use City Point as a base from which to strike at Richmond. Eventually, Grant observed, the Army of the Potomac might arrive opposite Richmond, and in that case the two armies would work together.[6]

Over the next several weeks Grant provided Butler with refinements of this outline. Butler's replies suggested his willingness to cooperate, a welcome sign. However, Grant's insistence that Butler move on Richmond from the south bank of the James would be best achieved by establishing a base at Bermuda Hundred, not City Point (although it would be wise to occupy the latter in any case). Then Union forces could strike at the railroad that connected Richmond with Petersburg, some twenty miles to the south, just across the Appomattox River, before advancing on Richmond proper. Grant could have achieved much the same end (and made better use of City Point) by having the Army of the James first take Petersburg itself. But no written directive mentioned Petersburg, and it remains unclear whether it was mentioned in conversation. At the same time, Grant's letters explicitly discuss the "probability" of a juncture with Butler, suggesting that he did not then anticipate destroying Lee in battle south of the Rappahannock and Rapidan. Finally, Grant erred in deciding to leave Baldy Smith with Butler. Smith disliked his superior and had a reputation for being disagreeable and contentious. These qualities had cost him a previous field command, and apparently he had not profited from his experiences. He did not yet know that Butler would be a worthy foe in the struggle for control of the operation.[7]

Traveling to Washington, Grant outlined his plan to Lincoln, then gave Sherman his assignment. "You I propose to move against Johnston's Army, to break it up and get into the interior of the enemy's country as far as you can, inflicting all the damage you can against their War resources." How Sherman was to go about this, Grant would leave up to him. Out went a series of dispatches to Franz Sigel, followed by a visit from a staff officer, detailing operations in western Virginia. As Sigel owed his commission more to his political influence with German-Americans than to his military skill, he would bear watching. Returning to Culpeper, Grant framed Meade's orders, stating their underlying principle: "Lee's Army will be your objective point. Wherever Lee goes there you will go also." Meade and his chief of staff, Andrew A. Humphreys, would determine how to go after Lee. Several days later Grant journeyed to Annapolis to confer with Burnside about the role the Ninth Corps would play in the spring campaign by operating alongside Meade's army (although for the moment Burnside, who ranked Meade, would report to Grant).[8]

Sherman understood what Grant was demanding of himself as well as of others. "That we are now all to act in a Common plan, Converging on a Common Center looks like Enlightened War. Like yourself you take the biggest load and from me you shall have thorough and hearty cooperation."[9]

Grant sought the destruction of Lee's army in combat by forcing Lee out into the open under conditions favorable to a Union victory — whether that meant a Confederate attack against a larger Union army or a Union blow against the Confederate rear as Lee hurried to protect Richmond or his supplies. His orders called for relentless war, but not for a mindless struggle of attrition featuring repeated frontal assaults in which one traded casualties in accordance with a harsh calculus of war. Although no one questioned Grant's willingness to fight, the record suggested that he had been frugal with human life during his offensive operations (his most horrendous losses came when he was attacked at Shiloh). Nor did Grant fall victim to an oversight that Lincoln and Halleck shared: in shedding the fixation of capturing Richmond, the president and his chief adviser had gone to the other extreme of focusing so narrowly on the destruction of Lee's army in combat that they failed to recognize how they might use Richmond to secure that end. Grant appreciated that Richmond was a symbol, not only for Union armies to capture, but for Confederate armies to defend; he also realized that the city performed many of the same functions in Virginia that Atlanta did in the Confederate heartland. One could threaten Lee by threatening it, much as Lee had sought to control the operations of the Army of the Potomac by threatening Washington.

Such was the plan that Grant devised in March and April of 1864. Here and there he revised the details; circumstances forced on him other alterations or less than ideal compromises. But simply setting forth a plan was not enough. Grant had to prevail on Lincoln to accept his plan; he had to select subordinates who understood their roles and possessed the ability to execute their assignments; and he had to establish an administrative structure to oversee operations. These proved difficult challenges.

It was no secret by 1864 that Abraham Lincoln had developed troubled relationships with many of his generals, and that his judgment in selecting commanders was not faultless. The president often asserted that he was looking for a general who would accept the responsibility of command and exercise it (instead of offering excuses and looking for scapegoats), but the record showed that he often meddled in military campaigns. He did so with good intentions, and his instincts, honed by experience, were sometimes (but not always) on the mark. Vivid memories of the struggle with McClernand disturbed Grant when he learned that in February 1864 Lincoln had restored McClernand to command of the Thirteenth Corps, now in Louisiana. The general had also heard about Meade's troubles with the president and Halleck. That Lincoln still took an active interest in planning operations became evident when he presented to Grant an idea he had first offered Ambrose Burnside in November 1862 involving an amphibious strike to outflank the Confederate defenses along the Rapidan and Rappahannock rivers. Grant listened respectfully, saying nothing, but later revealed to a staff officer that the plan was seriously flawed. Thereafter the president, while claiming that he did not want to know the details of Grant's plan, kept himself informed of the overall approach. During one such meeting, when Grant outlined to Lincoln the workings of the supporting columns in his Virginia plan, the president grinned: "Oh, yes! I see that. As we say out West, if a man can't skin he must hold a leg while someone else does." (Grant liked the phrase so much he incorporated it in a letter to Sherman.)[10] *> Lincoln says it first*

By showing forbearance and refraining from criticism, Grant did not offend the president; in turn, Lincoln, seeing that Grant agreed with him about fundamentals — notably the concept of simultaneous, coordinated advances — allowed the general leeway in implementing them. At the same time Grant looked to end the practice of subordinate generals traveling to Washington to seek private audiences with the president in which they disparaged their superiors. Orders went out instructing that correspondence on military matters had to be transmitted through military channels, with violators subject to court-martial or dismissal. That was just the sort of measure Sherman desired; he had remarked with characteristic bluntness that he hoped that Grant would impose the death penalty on any congressman who crossed the Potomac. Grant had just seen Meade burned by such behavior in the congressional inquiry into Gettysburg. In turn, the lesson offered by Sickles and company on how critical subordinates can cripple civilian trust in commanders was not lost on the commander of the Army of the Potomac. (In the months to come he might grumble about Grant in letters to his wife, but he never shared his grievances with Lincoln.[11] *that's good ✓* *> Meade*

Grant worked long and hard to establish a solid relationship with Lincoln built on mutual trust and respect. Rarely did he criticize the president, even when suffering the impact of presidential decisions (especially the appointment of generals to commands to appease political constituencies). The contrast with McClellan was palpable. The new general-in-chief was "the quietest little fellow you ever saw," Lincoln told William Stoddard, one of his private secretaries; he could virtually melt into the background, calling no attention to himself. "The only evidence you have that he's in any place is that he makes things git! Wherever he is, things move." The thought excited the president. "Stoddard, Grant is the first

which commanders did Lincoln insist on using?

Sigel? Banks?

general I've had! He's a general!" The secretary sought elaboration. "I'll tell you what I mean," Lincoln replied. "You know how it has been with all the rest. As soon as I put a man in command of the army he'd come to me with a plan of campaign and about as much say, 'Now, I don't believe I can do it, but if you say so I'll try it on,' and so put the responsibility of success or failure on me. They all wanted me to be the general. It isn't so with Grant. He hasn't told me what his plans are. I don't know, and I don't want to know. I'm glad to find a man who can go ahead without me. . . . He doesn't ask me to do impossibilities for him, and he's the first general I've had that didn't."[12]

Yet Lincoln asked much of Grant in the appointment of subordinates, for 1864 was an election year. One way to gain and retain the support of constituencies was by appointing one of their favorites to independent command. Much has been made of the wisdom and necessity of commissioning so-called political generals. Critics who draw a hard and fast line between military amateurs and professionals forget that some of the professionals owed their opportunities to the politicians with whom they were linked. Grant knew that (and Elihu Washburne would have reminded him had he forgotten it); so did Sherman, member of the powerful Ewing family and the brother of a United States senator. Many generals educated at West Point had established relationships with politicians or even entertained thoughts of entering politics themselves. And Grant knew that not all generals who owed their commissions to political clout were as troublesome as McClernand. He thought highly of Frank P. Blair and John A. Logan, who had served under him. But offering commissions to politicians was one thing: placing them in charge of armies or departments, especially before they proved their worth, was another. Moreover, because Lincoln had made many of these appointments early in the war, these troublesome generals often possessed seniority over their more capable peers.) Grant would have to entrust them with carrying out major components of his plan.

Nathaniel P. Banks proved the model example of the ways in which presidential preferences and political needs modified Grant's wishes. Although Banks had been a somewhat difficult colleague during the Vicksburg campaign, Grant appeared to have had a cordial relationship with him — until the visit to New Orleans in September 1863. Grant left that encounter with more than just a badly bruised leg. Henceforth he questioned Banks's abilities as a general.

Still, Grant was willing to work with Banks in planning to move quickly against Mobile. It was left to Halleck to remind him that the president still gave priority to an advance up Louisiana's Red River. Lincoln had long believed that it was essential for Union forces to gain control of as much as Louisiana as possible while that state's unionists sought to erect a new state government. An advance westward toward Texas would also serve as a show of force against the French-supported regime of Maximilian in Mexico lest it get any ideas about retaking Texas, although Lincoln no longer emphasized this goal in correspondence with Banks. Perhaps the problem was that Banks was being asked to do too much at once; it did not help that the Massachusetts general harbored hopes of running for president should Lincoln's prospects fade. Under orders from Halleck Banks commenced preparations for the operation in January. He planned to move up the Red River toward Shreveport. Another column under Frederick Steele would support the movement by advancing south from Arkansas. The campaign got under way just after Grant took over as general-in-chief.

Grant did not embrace the operation he had inherited; he wanted to wrap it up as soon as possible so that he could implement his Mobile offensive. On March 15, he told Banks that as soon as he took Shreveport, he was to return the forces he had borrowed from the Army of the Tennessee in time to participate in the spring campaigns against Mobile and Atlanta. If he found himself too pressed for time to take Shreveport, then he should abandon the thrust up the Red River; the other operations took priority. Concerned that Banks would ignore the directive, he told Halleck that "it is important to have some one near Banks who can issue orders to him and see that they are obeyed." Several weeks passed without news that Banks had achieved anything. Grant repeated his instructions, directing Banks to consolidate his lines, abandon the Shreveport offensive if necessary, and concentrate some thirty thousand men for the Mobile operation: "It is intended that your movements shall be co-operative with movements of Armies els[e]where and you cannot now start too soon." Finally he sent David Hunter to Banks's headquarters to see what was happening.[13]

Within days of Hunter's departure, Grant heard from Banks. Loath to abandon operations in Louisiana, the Massachusetts general claimed that he needed over one hundred thousand men to counter the actions of an enemy army he conceded was no more than twenty-five thousand strong. Grant had heard enough. "I have been satisfied for the last nine months that to keep General Banks in command was to neutralize a large force and to support it most expensively," he wired Halleck. "Although I do not insist upon it I think the best interest of [the] service" demanded Banks's removal. Grant chose his words carefully, knowing that the general was a particular favorite with Lincoln, to whom Halleck would show the dispatch. The president hesitated, saying that he needed to know more.[14]

For days Grant and Halleck exchanged telegrams discussing how to reconstruct the command situation in Louisiana, but they did nothing about Banks. Halleck explained: "Genl Banks is a personal friend of the President, and has strong political supporters in and out of Congress. There will undoubtedly be a very strong opposition to his being removed or superceded, and I think the President will hesitate to act, unless he has a definite request from you to do so, as a military necessity, you designating his successor or superior in command. On receiving such a formal request (not a mere suggestion) I believe, as I wrote you some days ago, he would act immediately. . . . The President will require some evidence in a positive form to show the military necessity of the act. In other words he must have something, in a definite shape, to fall back on, as his justification." Some newspapers were already publishing editorials in support of Banks: "The administration would immediately be attacked for his removal."[15] *Lincoln is hesitant to remove Banks*

Arriving at Banks's headquarters on April 27, Hunter found matters near disaster. Delayed by his participation in setting up a loyalist government in Louisiana, Banks was disappointed when he learned that gunboats found it difficult to navigate the Red River; when his offensive was checked short of Shreveport by a series of Confederate victories, Banks withdrew, leaving the gunboats (commanded by Grant's friend, David D. Porter) stranded when the water level fell. By the time Hunter arrived at Alexandria, Louisiana, the whole campaign had unraveled and Banks was washing his hands of the whole affair. "The Department of the Gulf is one great mass of corruption," Hunter informed Grant. "Cotton and politics, instead of the war, appear to have engrossed the army," which had lost faith in its commander. Other correspondence confirmed Hunter's findings. Grant notified Halleck that Banks's "own report and these letters clearly show all his disasters to be attributable to his own incompetency."[16]

Grant accepted that it was now too late to get the Mobile operation under way in time to be part of his plan for simultaneous advances the first week in May. Preparations for the spring offensive demanded his attention. He would return to the Banks matter in due course. But the whole matter raised some interesting questions. Who *had* authorized Banks's expedition up the Red River? Not Grant: the orders were issued before he became general-in-chief. Banks disavowed the campaign to Hunter. That left Lincoln and Halleck. Why, at a time when the president claimed he had found the man who would implement his preference for coordinated, cooperative operations against a common center, was Banks advancing against Shreveport? Not only did this move deprive Grant of men essential to attack Mobile, but it also represented a major diversion undertaken for political and diplomatic reasons (and, one fears, to meet the hunger for cotton). And exactly how much evidence did Lincoln need before he would displace Banks? For Grant to insist on that general's removal would cause a confrontation with the president, highlighting the conflict between military and political priorities. Aware of the damage such an incident might inflict on his relationship with Lincoln, Grant offered tactfully worded requests rather than issuing demands. It was up to the president to appoint department commanders; it was up to him to weigh political benefits versus military costs.

The Banks affair also highlighted the evolving command structure Grant attempted to put in place in 1864. He had accepted the appointment as general-in-chief contingent on the assurance that he could make his headquarters in the field. This was no minor concession. In 1862 Lincoln had stripped McClellan of the position when Little Mac took the field and embarked on his campaign in Virginia. Despite occasional visits to the field, Halleck preferred to remain at his post in Washington. Initially Grant planned to stay in the West; only after he had witnessed the political pressures that proximity to the capital placed on the Army of the Potomac (as well as the temptations to ambition and intrigue that proximity offered both soldiers and politicians) did he conclude that he would spend much of his time in the East. Nevertheless, he still thought he would move from command to command as circumstances dictated. From a desk in Washington Halleck would transmit messages between generals; Grant also communicated with him on other topics, including appointments and removals.

Halleck continued to perform his self-assigned role as military adviser and interpreter. His record in this regard had been mixed: following Gettysburg he had so muddled matters in mediating between Lincoln and Meade that he had widened the rift between the two men. Moreover, Halleck could not quite get over that his former subordinate now ranked him. He continued to criticize plans; sometimes he second-guessed Grant and aired his objections to instructions instead of immediately transmitting them. Ironically, he would lecture the lieutenant general on the need to state what he wanted in blunt language when Halleck himself had tended to cajole and criticize others instead of taking charge during his tenure in the top spot. Despite his eagerness to advance his position in early 1862, he had never been comfortable exercising command or taking responsibility.

Grant also exchanged telegrams with Secretary of War Edwin M. Stanton. This was an uneasy relationship because of a long-standing disagreement over the exact chain of command that should be derived from the war secretary directing the staff departments while the commanding general headed forces in the field. Grant wrestled with this structure, appealing to Lincoln for total authority: the president declined to change the official delegation of responsibility, but added, "There is no one but myself that can interfere with your orders, and you can rest assured that I will not." In that spirit Lincoln ruled in favor of Grant over Stanton when it came to thinning out the forces defending Washington to build up the field armies: "You and I, Mr. Stanton, have been trying to boss this job, and we have not succeeded very well with it. We have sent across the mountains for Mr. Grant, as Mrs. Grant calls him, to relieve us, and I think we had better leave him alone to do as he pleases." It was a good story — and it concealed the truth that Grant could not always do as he pleased.[17]

Grant also made changes in his staff. Although Baldy Smith and James H. Wilson were not formally members of that body — Smith served as the Army of the Cumberland's chief engineer while Wilson was now assigned to the Cavalry Bureau — Grant decided that both men were entitled to field commands. During 1863 he had managed to attract to his staff several young and promising professionally trained officers. Just before Vicksburg Cyrus B. Comstock, a West Pointer who had returned to teach at the academy, joined the staff as Grant's chief engineer officer — a position once held by James McPherson. Now Grant added two more West Pointers, Orville E. Babcock and Horace Porter. Babcock had served on Ambrose Burnside's staff; Porter had held staff positions with the Army of the Potomac as well as the Army of the Cumberland before meeting Grant at Chattanooga. Both were skilled engineers who were happy to attach themselves to the Union's preeminent general.

The staff overhaul was necessary if Grant was to cope with his new responsibilities. The previous July Dana had characterized the headquarters group as "a curious mixture of good, bad, & indifferent. . . . a mosaic of accidental elements & family friends." True, Dana reported, Rawlins exercised "a great influence" over Grant, and reminded his superior to abstain from drinking "whenever he commits the folly of tasting liquor," but he was "too slow and can't write the English language correctly without a great deal of careful consideration." Several other officers, including the departed Clark Lagow, were worthless. But aide Theodore S. Bowers was a capable fellow, and Comstock, who at the time had just joined the staff, "will be the source of much improvement." More along those lines was essential. "If Gen. Grant had about him a staff of thoroughly competent men, disciplinarians, & workers, the efficiency & fighting quality of his army would soon be very much increased," Dana concluded. "As it is, things go too much by hazard & by spasms; or when the pinch comes, Grant forces through by his own energy & main strength what proper organization & proper staff officers would have done already." Apparently Grant agreed.[18]

Grant made several other minor appointments: his brother-in-law Fred was made an aide, and Adam Badeau an erstwhile novelist, writer, and intimate associate of Wilson, joined William R. Rowley, an old favorite, as the general's private secretary. The trio of Comstock, Porter, and Babcock, however, changed the atmosphere around headquarters. Rawlins, Bowers, and Ely Parker viewed the newcomers warily. Smith and Wilson still believed that they were members of the general's inner circle. Rawlins had always understood himself to be more of an associate than a subordinate, and more than once he betrayed anxiety over the consequences of Grant's rise. "I grow dizzy in looking from the eminence he had attained, and tremble at the great responsibility about to devolve upon him," he told Emma (whom he had married in December). The new men had not shared in that climb. Rawlins could not understand that Grant now required the advice and assistance of professionally trained officers. He became so protective of his relationship with Grant that he privately lashed out at Wilson, whose presumptuous behavior was evident in his dispatches from Washington.[19]

Grant intended neither to demote Rawlins nor to devalue his contributions, but to protect him from his own deficiencies in planning. If he occasionally found Rawlins overbearing and overprotective, he also knew that his friend meant well and that his obsessions, especially about alcohol, sometimes reflected personal demons. He also recognized Rawlins's assets, notably his loyalty and his willingness to speak bluntly and freely. When the Senate failed to confirm Rawlins's promotion to brigadier general, Grant was dismayed and intervened, telling Henry Wilson, who headed the Senate's Committee on Military Affairs, that Rawlins "comes the nearest being indispensable to me of any officer in the service." This was an exaggeration — most people thought Grant's most indispensable officer was Sherman (including Sherman) — but Grant needed to overcome arguments that this mere staff officer did not deserve a star on his shoulders (especially when Grant could look around and count the number of stars on the shoulders of Meade's staff). If Rawlins's lack of field command experience was the problem, fine: "he shall command troops at once." But it seemed a shame that he was being penalized for his service: "I shall feel, that by keeping with me a valuable officer, because he made himself valuable, I have worked him an injury." Other aides also lobbied Washburne, hinting that it was of "vital importance" for the promotion to go through, as if the failure to confirm Rawlins as a brigadier would lead to his departure from the army, followed by disaster on the battlefield.[20]

And yet it was these vague allusions to Rawlins's indispensability that made his confirmation a matter of discussion. The Senate had actually confirmed his promotion on April 1; however, Senator James R. Doolittle of Wisconsin immediately moved to reconsider the vote. One of Grant's aides thought there was "a screw loose somewhere." The senator never explained his reasons, but it had been just over a year ago that he had received a letter from General Charles Hamilton in which Hamilton, fuming that he was being passed over for promotion, revealed: "*Grant is a drunkard.*" That elsewhere Hamilton tarred a number of other generals with the same charge and that it came at a time when he was doing all he could to gain a promotion — a scheme that badly backfired when Grant accepted his resignation — meant little just now. What meant more was that James Wilson, in his own characteristically misguided way, was presuming too much about Rawlins's influence with Grant and claimed he was far more intimate with the general than the facts warranted. Rawlins himself fell victim to that behavior because Wilson then (and later) claimed Rawlins kept Grant sober and was essential to his success. Of course, Rawlins himself believed as much, telling Emma that senators understood "the wholesome influence I am supposed to exercise for his good, which is not unknown personally to several gentlemen of great influence in Washington." And yet the exact nature of this assistance was open to question, for if Rawlins had long sought Lagow's dismissal partly on the grounds of that man's fondness for the bottle, he said nothing when his good friend Ely Parker imbibed to excess. Grant's kinsman William Smith was on the mark when he observed after Chattanooga, "Rawlins sometimes acts ugly. Like General Wilson his sudden elevation has spoiled him." That was too bad, for, as Smith added, Rawlins "is invaluable to the General and I hope he may always prosper so long as he continues true to him" — a telling qualification.[21]

If Rawlins was Grant's guardian against drink, he had been less than a success, judging from the stories that circulated. Nor did the general succumb to his supposed weakness when Rawlins was absent. At the St. Louis dinner the previous January 1864, John M. Schofield noted that Grant refused to partake of the wine circulated rather liberally during the festivities. "I dare not touch it," he told Schofield. "Sometimes I can drink freely without any unpleasant effect; at others I could not take even a single glass of wine." Rawlins sweated when he read newspaper reports of the dinner, worried that something bad could have happened. "You are fully aware of my fears in all this," he confided to Emma. "I need not state them." But he could not refrain from alluding to them, even when he discovered he was wrong: for when Grant returned, Rawlins admitted, "His appearance has agreeably disappointed me and for once I have done him injustice in my thoughts." That Rawlins might commit the same injustice again — and had already done so countless times before — did not disturb a man who was intent on demonstrating to his new wife just how important he was.[22]

In the end, Doolittle withdrew his motion; Rawlins was confirmed on April 14. Perhaps Grant had attended to the matter once more on his way through Washington during a visit to Annapolis. In highlighting his role as the keeper of Grant's conscience, however, Rawlins unwittingly revealed that it was not because of his military expertise that he deserved promotion — which in turn explained why Grant turned to new officers, who understood both their profession and their role, as the campaign of 1864 grew near.[23]

[Handwritten margin note: ⟶ promoted to brig. gen. (see p 279)]

[Handwritten note: Rawlins is getting too big for his bridges?]

Devising a plan to bring down the Confederate war effort was a tremendous challenge. In mapping out and executing his plan, however, Grant also had to struggle with the weight of public expectations, the constraints placed on him by election-year considerations, and the ambivalence of the officers and men of the Army of the Potomac.

[Handwritten note: ⟶ like Lincoln's political missions + political generals]

A good many observers believed that the coming campaign would prove decisive. Grant's very vigor, reported the *New York Herald,* "inspires the public confidence to a reasonable anticipation of quick work and great results." It would be all or nothing this year. "If, with General Grant at the head and the struggle as it now is, we cannot put the rebellion down in the coming summer, we can never put it down," the *Herald* proclaimed, adding the next day, "If we do not end it now we never can." Other newspapers echoed these sentiments. *New York Tribune* reporter Charles A. Page looked forward to "the pivotal battle" in Virginia; the *New York Times* agreed that the spring campaign would bring "the decisive battles of the struggle."[24]

Lincoln's critics were ready to pounce on the administration with

[Handwritten margin note: Public expectations of USG + campaign are being raised. ✓ see p. 285]

charges of political interference should Grant not succeed. "Will General Grant be hampered and harpied by politicians, as General McClellan was, or will he be permitted to do what he thinks ought to be done?" demanded the *Herald*. Still casting about for alternatives to the incumbent, it succinctly set forth what was at stake for the president: "His political fortunes, not less than the great cause of the country, are in the hands of General Grant, and the failure of the General will be the overthrow of the President." If Lincoln wanted to win reelection, the paper observed, he had better not meddle with his general. An editorial headline predicted "The Certainty of Our Success if Grant Is Left Alone."[25]

The presidential election loomed over everything. The vast majority of Northern voters were committed to a successful prosecution of the war. Where they disagreed was whether the Lincoln administration could win the war. A good number of Republicans complained that the president was not waging war in earnest; an even larger number of Democrats thought that the president's insistence on abolition fueled defiance among many white Southerners. Although a significant number of Democrats were pressing for a negotiated settlement, and a smaller number were willing to accept Confederate independence, they did not control the party. The best way for Lincoln to retain the presidency would be to have Union armies claim victory on the battlefield — or at least make enough progress to persuade a majority of voters to give the administration four more years in power.

This meant that the pressure was on Grant to produce results that presaged ultimate triumph. Most Americans understood war in terms of dramatic battles and the capture of enemy cities, not in terms of logistics, manpower, and relentless combat. Grant had to win early enough and often enough to meet the demands of the election year calendar; he would always have to keep in mind how the Northern public would interpret military movements; and he would have to heed Lincoln's concerns about the political ramifications of military appointments and removals. "The weight of cares & of responsibility you and the government have put on the head of that man is fearful to think upon," one of Washburne's friends told the congressman. In short, Grant would not be left alone. Washington in general and Lincoln in particular would always be looking over his shoulder.[26]

Grant had seen what Meade had endured during the investigation of his conduct of the Gettysburg campaign and had little patience with such business; by making his headquarters in Virginia, Grant would "avoid Washington and its *entourage*," as Meade explained to his wife. However,

Grant would have to negotiate a relationship with Meade, who could be touchy about points of pride, easily irritated, and prone to explode when things did not go his way. Understanding this, Grant tried to allow Meade to manage his own affairs. When Meade decided to consolidate the army's five corps into three, Grant offered no objections. "He appears very friendly, and at once adopts all my suggestions," a pleased Meade reported. "I believe Grant is honest and fair, and I have no doubt he will give me full credit for anything I may do, and if I don't deserve any, I don't desire it." Grant shared his negative feelings toward Hooker, Sickles, and Butterfield, the leaders of the anti-Meade faction in the Gettysburg inquiry, and made light of demands for Meade's replacement, including one presented in the pages of the *New York Tribune* by Horace Greeley. Should Grant encounter Greeley, he assured Meade, he would "tell him that when he wanted the advice of a political editor in selecting generals, he would call on him." Nor would Grant countenance invidious comparisons between the two men. He laughed off reports that he had put an end to reviews, military balls, and various spectator sports, including horse races; he ignored news items revealing that he ate what the soldiers ate or that one sign that he would infuse the Army of the Potomac with a more aggressive spirit was his decision to establish his headquarters at Culpeper, placing him nearer enemy lines than Meade (who remained in Warrenton, some eight miles northeast).[27]

Doubtless Grant's sentiments were sincere ones — he well knew the fickleness of newspapers, having been a victim of their criticism — but he was also alert to Meade's sensitive ego. He did what he could to maintain the impression that Meade was as much in command of the Army of the Potomac as if Grant was still in the West. Meade noticed. "Grant has not given an order, or in the slightest degree interfered with the administration of this army since he arrived, and I doubt if he knows much more about it now than he did before coming here," he wrote home. "It is undoubtedly true he will go with it when it moves, and will in a measure control its movements, and should success attend its operations, that my share of the credit will be less than if he were not present. Moreover, whilst I have no doubt he will give me all the credit I am entitled to, the press, and perhaps the public, will lose sight of me in *him*." Yet, even as he complained about the impression the papers crafted of Grant, he offered a somewhat different and more sympathetic view of Grant in person. Noting that many visitors came away from an encounter with the general unimpressed, he observed, "Grant is not a striking man, is very reticent, has never mixed with the world, and has but little manner, indeed is somewhat ill at ease in the presence of strangers; hence a first impression is never favorable. . . . At the same time, he has natural qualities of a high order, and is a man whom, the more you see and know him, the better you like him. He puts me in mind of old Taylor, and sometimes I fancy he models himself on old Zac."[28]

Staff officers and commanders offered their estimate of Grant. Theodore Lyman, Meade's aide, liked what he saw. "Grant is a man of a good deal of rough dignity; rather taciturn; quick and decided in speech," he wrote his wife. "He habitually wears an expression as if he had determined to drive his head through a brick wall, and was about to do it. I have much confidence in him." Others were more skeptical. Charles Wainwright, artillery chief for the Fifth Corps, set down his impressions: "It is hard for those who knew him when formerly in the army to believe he is a great man; then he was only distinguished for the mediocrity of his mind, his great good nature and his insatiable love of whiskey."[29]

Well aware that he was under close scrutiny, Grant knew that it mattered what the soldiers made of him. During March and April he gave the army a chance to look at him (and he at it) in a series of reviews. It rained during the Fifth Corps review on March 29, adding to the depression already felt by many of the soldiers who were still grumbling over their transfer from the old First Corps. Among these grousers were members of the Iron Brigade, one of the best units in the entire Union army. The colonel of the Sixth Wisconsin, Rufus Dawes, had come away from previous encounters pleased with Grant: "He looks like a plain common sense man, one not to be puffed up by position nor abashed by obstacles." But this was a review, after all. One was supposed to be equal to the pomp and circumstance that attended such affairs. Instead, Dawes noted, Grant did not return the cheers offered by several regiments. Annoyed, the colonel ordered his men to offer a simple formal salute. The lieutenant general responded by taking off his hat and bowing. The Badgers were satisfied: "Grant wants soldiers, not yaupers."[30]

Perhaps the rain dampened everyone's ardor. Wainwright complained that Grant "rode along the line in a slouchy unobservant way, with his coat unbuttoned and setting anything but an example of military bearing to the troops. There was no enthusiasm." Conditions were better when the Sixth Corps passed in review on April 18. The lieutenant general's mount was "one of the handsomest I have seen in the army," Lyman noted. And the rider matched the horse, for Grant was decked out in full uniform, complete with sash and sword. "He is a man of a natural, severe simplicity, in all things — the very way he wears his high-crowned felt hat shows this:

he neither puts it on behind his ears, nor draws it over his eyes; much less does he cock it on one side, but sets it straight and very hard on his head." Lyman's scrutiny extended to the way Grant sat on his horse: "He sits firmly in the saddle and looks straight ahead, as if only intent on getting to some particular point. General Meade says he is a very amiable man, though his eye is stern and almost fierce-looking." An officer of the Second Rhode Island, Elisha Hunt Rhodes, filed a somewhat different report. "General Grant is a short thick set man and rode his horse like a bag of meal. I was a little disappointed in the appearance, but I like the look of his eye. He was more plainly dressed than any other general on the field." Such scrutiny told as much about the observer as the observed, although in this case Lyman and Rhodes both agreed that Grant was something unusual, perhaps even special. The general returned the compliment. "Grant expressed himself finely pleased, and is quite astonished at our system and organization," Meade boasted.[31]

The sun also shone on the review of the Second Corps on April 22. All morning regiments and batteries assembled on the review ground near Stevensburg. At noon an artillery salute announced Grant's arrival. The general-in-chief took a position opposite the center of the assembled corps; as he wheeled to face the long lines, a bugle sounded the call for present arms and thousands of muskets fell into place. With Second Corps commander Winfield Scott Hancock at his side, Grant then rode past the line; brigade bands broke out in a rendition of "Hail to the Chief" as he approached them. Once Grant returned to his initial position, the corps swept before him in line of march by brigades, each greeted by the lieutenant general, who raised his hat in salute.[32]

The observations of officers and men reinforced that people saw what they wanted to see in Grant; much the same could be said of observers' assessments of what the Army of the Potomac made of Grant. Some of Grant's supporters denied there was a problem. The *Herald* boldly announced that Grant was already "the idol of the Army of the Potomac"; its crosstown competitor, the *Tribune,* predicted: "The mass of the army will heartily welcome Gen. Grant as their commander, and we believe will fight under him as they have never fought before." A month later the *Tribune* declared that the next campaign "will substantially quell the Rebellion and end the war. The army is in the best possible condition and spirit. McClellanism has disappeared. Rivalries between commanders and corps are at an end. The army is at last a unit."[33]

Such reports overstated the case, but so did those that posited an intense conflict between the new general-in-chief and the army. Nevertheless, that division was evident. "We wanted to take his measure before we took any stock in him," recalled one battle-hardened veteran. "In fact, we were rather jealous at having a Western man made better than our own officers." Enlisted men and junior officers seemed more willing to give the new man a chance than did many senior officers. "General Grant is well liked," brigade commander Emory Upton noted, "and, as he is taking time to prepare his campaign, there is strong probability of his success." More discerning was the observation of Captain Charles Francis Adams, Jr., who took command of the headquarters cavalry escort at the beginning of May. "The feeling about Grant is very peculiar," he remarked in a letter to his father, the minister to the Court of St. James. There was "a little jealousy, a little dislike, a little envy, a little want of confidence — all in many minds and now latent; but it is ready to crystallize at any moment and only brilliant success will dissipate the elements. All, however, are willing to give him a full chance and his own time for it."[34]

Rufus Ingalls, who served as quartermaster of the Army of the Potomac, had once recalled that as a cadet Grant broke in all the new horses. "He succeeded in this, not by punishing the animal he had taken in hand, but by patience and tact, and his skill in making the creature know what he wanted to have it do." So it would also be with the Army of the Potomac. "The army has been turned and twisted over again," grumbled one veteran, "and now we will see how quick the Army of the Potomac will kill the reputation of 'Unconditional Surrender.'" A good number of these veterans were going home when their enlistments expired sometime that spring. It was uncertain how many of them would continue to give their all as they approached the end of their hitch. Replacing them would be conscripts, bounty-induced volunteers, and soldiers who had spent much of the war behind the lines on guard or garrison duty. Few of these men would be nearly as good as the veterans they were to replace.[35]

Although he heard the whispers and the rumors, Grant chose to emphasize the positive. "He spoke of the army as being in the most splendid condition, and animated by the best possible spirit," one friend reported. In the right circumstances, he was even able to smile at his current success. Among the Army of the Potomac's division commanders was John C. Robinson. Years ago in St. Louis the ex-captain had approached Robinson about a job in anticipation of a campaign against the Mormons. Now he asked Robinson if he remembered the conversation. Yes, Robinson replied; he remembered it very well. Pointing to the three stars on his shoulder straps, Grant remarked, "Well, old fellow, who, then, would ever have believed this?"[36]

Had Richard Henry Dana been asked that question, he would have shaken his head in disbelief. The novelist had observed Grant in the lobby at Willard's during the general's most recent visit to Washington. "He had no gait, no *station,* no manner," Dana complained. "Rough light brown whiskers, a blue eye, and a rather scrubby look . . . the look of a man who did, or once did, take a little too much to drink . . . a slightly seedy look, as if he was out of office on half pay, and nothing to do but hang around the entry of Willard's cigar in mouth." And yet it was Dana who was hanging around the lobby to watch Grant's every move. "He gets over the ground queerly. He does not march, nor quite walk, but pitches along as if the next step would bring him on his nose" (perhaps a sign that the general's New Orleans injury was still bothering him). Yet something about Grant kept Dana's attention. On second thought, he decided that the general's "face looks firm and hard, and his eye is clear and resolute, and he is certainly natural and clear of all appearances of self-consciousness." Once more someone was deriving character, personality, and intelligence from appearance — an exercise that revealed more about the observer than about the observed. After further scrutiny, the writer decided that Grant "had a clear blue eye and a look of resolution, as if he could not be trifled with, and an entire indifference to the crowd about him." How indifferent soon became obvious. Eager to say that he had exchanged words with Grant, Dana approached the general to engage him in idle conversation. Fishing for some sort of response characteristic of a great warrior, he remarked: "I suppose, General, you don't mean to breakfast again until the war is over."

Grant looked at Dana. Perhaps he had noticed that the writer's gaze had followed him wherever he went. It took him only a moment to size up both the situation and the inquisitor.

"Not here I shan't."[37]

South of the Rapidan, Robert E. Lee and his generals traded estimates of their new opponent. Lee himself showed little concern; he was confident that Grant, whatever his previous record, was beatable. So it had been with Grant's predecessors, who had come and gone in a process that was as predictable as it was remarkable. "I fear they may continue to make these changes," he once remarked, "until they find someone whom I don't understand." *true*

Perhaps no other Confederate possessed as much insight into Grant as did James Longstreet, his West Point buddy and groomsman. Unlike many of his fellow Rebels(Longstreet knew that the Army of Northern Virginia was in for a fight. "I tell you that we cannot afford to underrate him and the army he now commands," he warned a cocky officer.)"We must make

[handwritten top margin: when did he say this?]

up our minds to get into line of battle and to stay there; for that man will fight us every day and every hour till the end of this war."[38]

By the end of April Grant and Meade had agreed on the best course of action against the Army of Northern Virginia. The rugged terrain due south of the army's camps made a straightforward advance against Lee's center out of the question. It did not take long to dismiss notions of moving against Lee's left flank to the west. Although the terrain in the region between Culpeper and Orange, Virginia, was open and rolling, such an operation would depend on keeping open a single rail line, the Orange and Alexandria Railroad, to bring up supplies for a prolonged campaign. Confederate raiders could cut that line at any time; indeed, Grant himself had barely eluded capture by some of John S. Mosby's men when he traveled by rail to Washington in mid-April. Even a significant detachment to protect the line's security might not prove sufficient protection, and it would come at the cost of eating into the numerical superiority Grant required to launch a sustained offensive.[39]

[handwritten left margin: see memo.]

This left Grant and Meade with just one alternative — to march across Lee's right flank and cross the Rapidan and Rappahannock as in earlier campaigns, using the fords west of Fredericksburg. Supplying the army would be far easier, for munitions and provisions could move most of the way by water along the Potomac River and Chesapeake Bay. However, the terrain south of the rivers provided a challenge, especially the heavily wooded area known as the Wilderness. Memories of Chancellorsville were less than a year old; Meade's Mine Run operation of the previous fall had met with grief. But Meade's chief of staff, Andrew A. Humphreys, was determined to learn from that experience. He devised a plan by which one corps, the Second, would sweep south of the Wilderness and march westward with the intent of outflanking the Confederate works at Mine Run. Meanwhile, the Fifth and Sixth Corps would cross the river, then use the east-west roads that divided the Wilderness to move against Lee's front; Burnside's Ninth Corps would remain at Warrenton to cover the army's rear and its large supply train during the first days of the movement. Should the four Union infantry corps (along with the three divisions of cavalry) execute this move successfully, Lee might find himself in difficult circumstances unless he reacted quickly. Not only would the Confederate position along Mine Run be in danger of being turned, but the Union army could even position itself between the Army of Northern Virginia and Richmond, forcing the Confederates to take the offensive to regain the upper hand.

[handwritten left margin: why AofP went into wilderness]

[handwritten left margin: I thought Meade consolidated army into 3 corps p 283]

Grant was perfectly willing to fight it out with Lee in central Virginia,

[handwritten bottom: ooh, I see, 3 AofP corps plus Burnside's SEPARATE 9th corps]

pinning the Army of Northern Virginia in place while Butler threatened
Richmond, Sigel advanced southward through the Shenandoah, and Union columns in southwest Virginia destroyed railroads, bridges, and resources. But he knew that much depended on Lee's response to the
crossing of the rivers. "Should Lee fall back within his fortification[s] at
Richmond," he informed Halleck, he planned to "form a junction with
Butler, and the two forces will draw supplies from the James River. My own
notions about our line of march are entirely made up. But, as circumstances beyond my controll may change them I will only state that my effort will be to bring Butler's and Meade's forces together."[40]

When exactly the movement would begin depended on the weather. Although the Second Corps review on April 22 took place under clear skies
and on dry ground, some two days later a downpour turned the roads into
quagmires. Grant passed the time quietly, conversing with visitors to headquarters, including Herman Melville. The author listened as the general
described the charge up Missionary Ridge, remarking, "I never saw anything like it." Knowing Grant to be a man of few words, Melville concluded
that the comment was "equivalent to a superlative or hyperbole from the
talkative." The general also learned that he had won a sword at the New
York Sanitary Fair (a fund-raising event to help provide soldiers with sun-
dries and assistance), beating out none other than George B. McClellan.
Rumors circulated that the victory was a last-minute thing, with administration supporters piling on the dollars to buy enough votes to guarantee
the result; in the spirit of fair play Julia, who had visited the fair, cast the
vote she bought for McClellan. Meanwhile, her husband expressed satisfaction with what he saw around him. "The Army of the Potomac is in
splendid condition and evidently feel like whipping some body," he told a
Galena associate. "I feel much better with this command than I did before
seeing it. There seems to be the very best feeling existing." Only his frustrated efforts to remove Banks caused him any anxiety.[41]

On April 27 the general celebrated his forty-second birthday. "Getting
old am I not?" he asked Julia in a letter full with teasing remarks. "Don't
know exactly the day when I will start or whether Lee will come here before I am ready to move. Would not tell you if I did know." The next day,
however, he decided that the armies would start out on May 4. During the
last week he grew impatient; he wondered whether it was time for Julia to
head home to be with the children, and he looked for letters from them.[42]

There arrived at headquarters on May 1 a letter from Abraham Lincoln.
The president, mindful of what was about to take place, wanted to reassure Grant of his "entire satisfaction with what you have done up to this
time, so far as I understand it. The particulars of your plan I neither

know, or seek to know. You are vigilant and self-reliant; and, pleased with this, I wish not to obtrude any constraints or restraints upon you. . . . If there is anything wanting which is within my power to give, do not fail to let me know it. And now with a brave Army, and a just cause, may God sustain you."[43]

On the face of it, the president's letter was a kind message, reflecting his respect for and trust in Grant. However, it was not a complete representation of the situation. The retention of men such as Banks and Sigel constrained Grant's freedom of action. The general wanted Banks removed, but the president procrastinated. As Halleck complained, "It seems but little better than murder to give important commands to such men as Banks, Butler, McClernand, Sigel and Lew Wallace, and yet it seems impossible to prevent it." Yet these men were not the cause of all Grant's troubles. The day he received Lincoln's letter Grant had been reminded of the limitations of his authority when he opened a dispatch from William S. Rosecrans. Exiled to Missouri, Rosecrans was dragging his heels in response to directives to reinforce other commands, claiming that he needed every man he could lay hands on to suppress a potential uprising by a "secret society." Grant sharply replied that such a message "means that you must do as you please or be held in no way responsible." Comstock reviewed the exchange and shook his head. Rosey's request was a "model" for "disobedience of orders. If Grant had the power he would be mustered out of service." *If* Grant had the power . . . but he did not. The president did.[44]

And yet Grant knew that to highlight these contradictions between profession and practice would not do, especially not now. Nor would he set aside the president's letter, much as he had done with Lincoln's gracious admission of error in the aftermath of Vicksburg. No, if he wanted Lincoln's trust and support, he would have to reply in kind, overlooking whatever misgivings he might have or whatever memories he might harbor. And so he sat down and composed his response.[45]

Culpeper C. H. Va. May 1st 1864

The President,

Your very kind letter of yesterday is just received. The confidence you express for the future, and satisfaction with the past, in my Military administration is acknowledged with pride. It will be my earnest endeavor that you, and the country, shall not be disappointed.

From my first entrance into the volunteer service of the country, to the present day I have never had cause of complaint, have never expressed or implied a complaint, against the Administration, or the Sec. of War, for throwing any embarassment in the way of my vigerously prossecuting what appeared to me my duty. Indeed since the promotion which placed me in command of all the Armies, and in view of the great responsibility, and importance of success (I have been astonished at the readiness with which every thin[g] asked for has been yielded without even an explaination being asked. Should my success be less than I desire, and expect, the least I can say is, the fault is not with you.)

how. very gracious of

USG

Very truly
your obt. svt.
U. S. Grant
Lt. Gen.

By May 3 everything was almost ready. The army would commence its movement at midnight, hoping to elude detection by Confederates atop Clark Mountain, south of the Rapidan, for several critical hours. No trains would leave the army's camps once the movement got under way; the general had imposed a news blackout for the moment. That evening he briefed his staff on what he planned to do. Perhaps he would be able to meet Lee out in the open in central Virginia; he thought it just as likely, however, that the campaign would end in a siege. Walking over to a map, *huh* he drew a semicircle in the air with his finger from Richmond to Petersburg. "When my troops are there," he remarked, "Richmond is mine. Lee must retreat or surrender."[46]

The previous evening, as final arrangements were being made, Grant retreated to his quarters to write Julia one more time. He was well aware of the importance of the campaign that was about to commence. "I know the greatest anxiety is now felt in the North for the success of this move, and that the anxiety will increase when it is once known that the Army is in motion," he told her. Perhaps a little anxious himself, he sought to reassure himself by reassuring Julia. "I believe it has never been my misfortune to be placed where I have lost my presence of mind, unless indeed it has been when thrown in strange company, particularly that of ladies. Under such circumstances I know I must appear like a fool."[47] There was more to this than just an offhand remark. For the Army of the Potomac was also strange company. The infighting among officers, the whispered doubts about the new chief, the attitude of assumed inferiority to Bobby Lee's butternuts — this was not Grant's army, and he knew it. In the campaign to come he would be battling the officer corps of the Army of the Potomac as much as he was battling the Army of Northern Virginia. He could not beat Lee until he had won over his own men.

"Love and Kisses for you and Jess. Ulys."

15

No Turning Back

JUST AFTER MIDNIGHT on May 4, 1864, the Army of the Potomac and Ambrose Burnside's Ninth Corps, together some 118,000 strong, began their march toward the Rapidan River. Cavalrymen had hurried on ahead the previous morning to secure the crossing points; after the horsemen accomplished their mission, engineers began lashing together pontoons and constructed bridges across the river. Daylight was but a few hours old when Gouverneur Warren's Fifth Corps marched over the bridge laid at Germanna Ford, followed by John Sedgwick's Sixth Corps; Winfield Scott Hancock's Second Corps crossed the river at Ely's Ford on the way to Chancellorsville. At first Burnside's corps would remain in the rear to guard against a possible Confederate drive. Eventually it would follow Sedgwick. Two cavalry divisions would ride ahead of the line of march, while a third remained behind to protect the Union rear.

Not until morning did Grant and his staff join the caravan. Discarding his usual simple field dress, the general put on the uniform coat of a lieutenant general, with three stars on each shoulder strap, and completed the ensemble with sword, sash, and a pair of buff thread gloves. Riding at his side was Elihu Washburne, eager to witness what he doubtless believed would be the decisive moment of the war. Soldiers took one look at the congressman's black suit and cracked that the new commander had brought along his personal undertaker.[1]

Although it had been a wet April, the roads were now dry, and the army made good progress southward on this bright, clear spring day. Even better, Lee had decided not to contest the river crossings. To do so would have forced him to spread out his forces to cover a long front. Shortly after noon Grant and his staff rode across the bridge at Germanna Ford and set up headquarters outside a house on a bluff just south of the river. Meade's headquarters was nearby. When Grant saw the Pennsylvanian's personal flag, a silver wreath encircling a golden eagle on a lavender field, he remarked: "What's this! — Is Imperial Caesar anywhere about here?"[2]

292

[handwritten annotation: has USG ordered Butler, Sigel, etc into motion yet? — see P2 end]

The lieutenant general was in a good mood. To a reporter's query about how long it would take to get to Richmond, he replied that it should take only four days — if Lee cooperated. For the rest of the day he sat on the front porch of the house, watching Sedgwick's men tramp past. Union signal officers reported that they had intercepted Confederate messages, revealing that Lee, having spotted the advancing blue columns, was setting his own men in motion. Grant transmitted the news to Halleck, observing: "Forty Eight hours now will demonstrate whether the enemy intends giving battle this side of Richmond." Orders went out to Burnside to move south that night. Some of Grant's staff officers, jaunty at the prospect of combat, spoke freely of the whipping Lee was about to suffer. Members of Meade's staff shook their heads. They knew better.[3]

[handwritten annotation: see p 288]

Evening came. After eating dinner, Grant and his staff gathered around a campfire. Meade joined them, accepting the lieutenant general's offer of a cigar. Worried about the vulnerability of the army's lengthy supply train to attack, he had already modified the original plan of operations that called for the lead infantry corps to approach Lee's old defenses at Mine Run by the evening of May 4. Instead, the three corps had halted during the afternoon to allow the wagons to catch up. Now Meade informed Grant of another change in plan for the following day. To shield the trains against Confederate cavalry, he proposed to detach a second cavalry division for escort duty. That left James H. Wilson, who had never before commanded troops in combat, with the difficult job of providing a screen for the entire army as it prepared to wheel westward. Meade also decided to abandon the idea of outflanking Lee's Mine Run position to the south by a rapid march, preferring first to establish a line across three east-west routes that ran through the thick woods and undergrowth south of the Rapidan. Although this would consume valuable time, Grant allowed Meade to have his way. He had to attend to his other responsibilities. Messages arrived announcing that Sherman, Butler, and Sigel were all moving. It was a good day's work for the general-in-chief. Just before midnight he went to bed, aware that a battle might well be in the offing.[4]

[handwritten annotations: USG has given Meade authority to comm. A of P / Meade makes changes to the plan. USG approves (tacitly?)]

It was to be a short night's rest. At 3 A.M. people began stirring about headquarters, and breakfast was served an hour later. Ordering the headquarters train forward, Grant remained behind to await Burnside's corps. Just after 8 A.M. he sighted the head of the Burnside's lead division. Relieved, he sipped some coffee. Moments later, one of Meade's aides galloped up. The message he delivered came as no surprise. Lead elements of the Fifth Corps on the Orange Turnpike west of the Germanna Road had encountered Lee's advancing columns. Meade, convinced that all he faced was a delaying action, had ordered Warren to attack. Whether this would result in a short, sharp firefight or lead to a general engagement was unclear. Grant's reply was to the point: "If any opportunity presents itself for pitching into a part of Lee's Army do so without giving time for disposition."[5]

Grant seemed almost relieved at the news that Lee had come out to attack. At last he would be able to test the Army of the Potomac in combat, and he did not quite know what to expect. For this was not the Army of the Tennessee, whose generals and men he knew — and who knew him. Here there did not seem to be that mutual confidence between commander and men which made each act with assurance. The only way to learn about an army, Grant knew, was to command it in battle. He was far less worried about Lee and the Army of Northern Virginia. If anything, he was eager for the confrontation. For weeks he had heard the whispers that he had not yet faced Bobby Lee; now Grant would test not only Lee, but also the Army of the Potomac, just as he in turn would be tested by each.

For several minutes after learning of first contact Grant quietly continued to watch Burnside's men march across the pontoon bridge. It was as if he wanted to demonstrate to everyone that he trusted Meade to go ahead on his own. But he was never much good at waiting patiently when battle was imminent. Finally he rode forward to Meade's headquarters, located on a knoll at the junction of the Orange Turnpike and Germanna Road. An officer, watching the general and his staff pass by, noted that Grant "bore no evidence of anxiety about him."[6] Behind the passive expression was a general who wanted to see what was going on. When he arrived at Meade's command post, however, he learned to his chagrin that little had been done to pitch into Lee. Immediately he issued orders for an attack.

Grant's staff set up headquarters near Meade's tents, then waited for the sounds of cannon and rifle fire that marked the commencement of battle in earnest. Instead of pacing impatiently in anticipation of combat, Grant lit a cigar, sat down on a tree stump, took out his penknife, and commenced whittling away on a twig. To an unwary observer the general appeared cool and calm. The condition of the gloves told a different story: they went from nicked to shredded in a matter of hours. Reports soon reached headquarters that a battle was indeed under way. A Union brigade, after driving the Confederates across an open field north of the turnpike, had withdrawn in confusion when Rebel reinforcements, drawn from Richard S. Ewell's Second Corps, counterattacked. Obviously Lee meant to fight. Grant buckled on his sword, mounted his horse, and set out along the turnpike to get a glimpse of Warren's situation. It was hard to make much out between the trees, the tangled underbrush, and the smoke, but Grant was unwilling to postpone the confrontation a minute longer. Returning to headquarters, he began issuing orders with a rapidity that betrayed his eagerness to get on with a fight.[7]

The ensuing struggle took place primarily along two pikes running roughly east to west: the Orange Turnpike and, to the south, the Orange Plank Road. These roads joined several miles east of the Germanna Road, but west of that road they ran nearly parallel to each other, some two to three miles apart. The Germanna Road, over which Grant had advanced that morning, ran southeast from Germanna Ford, intersecting the Orange Turnpike five miles south of the Rapidan River (the junction where Grant and Meade had established their headquarters) and ending at the Orange Plank Road. Between the two turnpikes the Germanna Road met the Brock Road, which then crossed the Orange Plank Road as it headed south and east toward Spotsylvania Court House. These crossroads were among the few distinguishable landmarks in the heavily wooded terrain known to all simply as the Wilderness.

Meade's veterans remembered the Wilderness, although the memories were not fond ones. Its trees had shielded Stonewall Jackson's flank march at Chancellorsville a year ago. Lee, knowing the region well, believed that Grant would find it difficult to march rapidly through it. His attacks targeted the key crossroads in an effort to sever Grant's army. The narrow roads, dense undergrowth, and limited visibility — further curtailed by the smoke and haze of battle — made this a less than ideal place to fight; it would be hard to move troops or locate friend and foe alike. Artillery would be of little use, and superior numbers were by no means an advantage. Yet Grant did not hesitate to meet Lee's offer of battle. Warren and Sedgwick, whose men were just arriving, would check, then assault Ewell. Another of Sedgwick's divisions went into action on the Orange Plank Road, checking A. P. Hill's Confederate Third Corps just before the Rebels reached the junction of that road and Brock Road in an effort to cut Hancock's corps off from the remainder of the Union army. Hancock's men hastily doubled back, arriving at the crossroads to stabilize the Union left.

Grant did not have to wait long for his first taste of what it was like to fight a battle with the Army of the Potomac. Charles Griffin, whose division had recoiled in the face of the Confederate counterattack along the Orange Turnpike, rode up to headquarters at 3 P.M. to complain that his opening assault had failed for want of support. His colorful denunciation of his colleagues attracted attention. Rawlins thought Griffin insubordinate; an astonished Grant, not quite catching Griffin's name, turned to Meade. "Who is this General Gregg?" he asked. "You ought to arrest him!" Meade, no stranger to temperamental outbursts, knew Griffin all too well. Turning to Grant, he buttoned up the general's coat in almost fatherly fashion as he calmly replied, "It's Griffin, not Gregg; and it's only his way of talking."[8]

As the battle unfolded, people watched Grant closely. One of Meade's staff officers saw Grant sitting on the grass, still smoking (although now he was using a pipe), "looking sleepy and stern and indifferent"; a newspaper reporter described Grant's face "as peaceful as a summer evening, his general demeanor indescribably imperturbable"; Captain Charles Francis Adams, Jr., in charge of Meade's cavalry escort, called Grant "the coolest man I ever saw." But the commanding general was not indifferent to the news that Alexander Hays, one of Grant's old West Point classmates, had been killed as he led his brigade into action along the Orange Plank Road. Shaken, Grant struggled to gather his thoughts and feelings for several minutes before he responded in halting sentences that praised Hays's courage and character. Another friendly face was gone, and there were none too many for Grant in this army.[9]

As dusk fell, the battle quieted down. After hearing about the day's events from staff officers, Grant conferred with Meade to plan the morrow's action. Neither side had gained the upper hand in the opening engagement, which had moved back and forth along both east-west pikes. Grant decided to have Hancock renew the attack along the Orange Plank Road against the Confederate right under Hill at 4:30 A.M. Burnside, who was just coming up, would join the assault. As there had been no evidence yet of the arrival of Longstreet's First Corps, perhaps Hancock could smash Hill before Lee received reinforcements. Warren and Sedgwick would keep an eye on Ewell's butternuts astride the Orange Turnpike.

Meade returned to his headquarters to prepare for the attack, leaving a seated Grant gazing into the campfire. A newspaper reporter for the *New York Tribune,* eager to return to Washington to transmit a report of the first day's battle, interrupted his pondering. Did Grant have anything to say to the awaiting public? "You may tell the people that things are going swimmingly down here," the general deadpanned. The reporter, sensing a brushoff, walked away. Suddenly Grant got to his feet. Catching up to the correspondent, he engaged in a short conversation out of earshot of his staff. The reporter nodded, then continued on his way. Returning to his tent, Grant soon turned in for the night, remarking that tomorrow, May 6, would be a busy day.[10]

Grant had not been asleep for very long when a staff officer awoke him with a dispatch from Meade. After conferring with his corps commanders, Meade believed that between the "dense thicket" and "the fatigued condition of the men" it would be better to postpone the attack until daybreak to allow the proper placement of reinforcements. Left unmentioned was Burnside's behavior at the conference, during which he announced that he would put his men on the road thirty minutes later than Grant had ordered. Grant compromised, setting 5 A.M. as the time for the advance. Any later might allow Lee to take the initiative.

Grant awoke yet again at 4 A.M. He heard Burnside's columns making their way to Hancock's right flank, a sign that they would not be in position for the start of the scheduled assault. The general settled for a hasty breakfast (a cucumber doused with vinegar and some coffee) and then secured two dozen cigars for what he expected would be a good day's work. Puffing away, he paced back and forth, waiting for news. Initially there was cause for optimism, for Hancock drove the Confederates back in confusion. However, Burnside failed to get his men up in time, despite the best efforts of two of Grant's staff officers. At last Longstreet's corps appeared, first checking, then rolling back the Union attack. Hancock's line finally held, and when a stray Confederate bullet took down Longstreet with a wound, the Rebels pulled away to regroup. [11]

As Hancock and Longstreet grappled in the woods, Ewell's artillery kept bombarding Warren. At one point several cannonballs plowed the meadow not far from headquarters. When someone queried Grant about withdrawing to a safer spot, he calmly replied, "It strikes me it would be better to order up some artillery and defend the present location." Before long the artillery fire died away. By midafternoon the battle had reached a lull, as both sides consolidated their positions. Grant, still smoking "imperturbably as the Sphinx," called for yet another thrust by Hancock and Burnside, but Lee was quicker, directing Longstreet's men to renew their attack. This time the Confederates came close to breaking Hancock's lines, aided by a forest fire that blinded the bluecoats as it burned their breastworks. But the Yankees did not crack, and eventually drove the Rebels away. [12]

The reports of the fighting from Hancock's front alarmed many at headquarters. Grant issued orders to reinforce Hancock and get Burnside into the fray. "His speech was never hurried, and his manner betrayed no trace of excitability or even impatience," recalled Horace Porter. Appearances were deceiving. After issuing his orders, Grant returned to his whittling, slicing away at stick after stick as he made quick work of each (as well as of those gloves, which were now worn through). Meanwhile, he lit, smoked, discarded, and replaced a steady progression of cigars. The waiting, the inability to see his orders executed, frustrated him. "The only time I ever feel impatient is when I give an order for an important movement of troops in the presence of the enemy, and am waiting for them to reach their destination," he told Porter. "Then the minutes seem like hours." Several times he rode toward the front as if to hurry things along. Encountering wounded and dead soldiers, he looked away, but the pained expression on his face was visible to all. He gained some relief from tension by helping a driver of beef cattle shoo a stray steer back to the herd.[13]

Near dusk, just as it seemed that the fighting was over for the day, news arrived at headquarters of a fierce Confederate assault on the Union right against Sedgwick's Sixth Corps. The fading light obscured that the Confederates had attacked with only two brigades; in the darkness it seemed like more. Reports asserted that large portions of the Sixth Corps had been captured and the Confederates were poised to cut the army off from the Rapidan. Rumor after rumor foretold disaster. Grant, Meade, and a few others remained calm, but there were signs of panic. One hysterical officer cried that Sedgwick was dead and the entire corps scattered. "I don't believe it," Grant replied. Lee, he reasoned, could not have shifted many men to his left after fighting all day on his right and center. Meade and his chief of staff, Andrew A. Humphreys, moved to repair the damage to Sedgwick's front, while Grant issued instructions to protect his trains and a division of black soldiers.[14]

Then it happened. As Grant sat on a stool in front of his tent, listening to progress reports, a general, overwhelmed with excitement, nearly accosted him. "General Grant, this is a crisis that cannot be looked upon too seriously," he proclaimed, the words bursting forth in rapid fire. "I know Lee's methods well by past experience; he will throw his whole army between us and the Rapidan, and cut us off completely from our communications."

And so the crisis had come — not from Lee, but from the Army of the Potomac's fear of the Confederate leader. This, Grant realized as he stirred to his feet, was the moment for which he had been waiting. Removing a cigar from his mouth, he glared at the intruder. Then he exploded. "Oh, I am heartily tired of hearing about what Lee is going to do," he snapped. "Some of you always seem to think he is suddenly going to turn a double somersault, and land in our rear and on both of our flanks at the same time. Go back to your command, and try to think what we are going to do ourselves, instead of what Lee is going to do." Everyone at

crisis met & passed

headquarters turned to look as the dressed-down officer shrank away from Grant without a word.[15]

Grant had met and passed his greatest test — that of reminding the Army of the Potomac who was in command. Unfamiliar with both officers and men, tired of reviews and rumors, he had long waited to see how it would respond in battle. Not knowing that had made him anxious and impatient. His opponent in gray caused him no such concern. True, Lee had put up a terrific fight, as Grant freely acknowledged. This was no Pemberton or Bragg in his front; the intensity of combat reminded him of Shiloh. But facing Lee was far preferable to hearing about him from an officer corps spellbound by the Confederate's skills. Perhaps now he wouldn't hear any more from his own men about Bobby Lee. But of Grant's anxiety there can be no doubt. When Hancock visited headquarters that evening, Grant offered him a cigar, only to discover that it was his last one. Porter later estimated that during the day Grant, aside from the occasional pipe, had consumed some twenty cigars, "all very strong and of formidable size. But it must be remembered," continued Porter, "that it was a particularly long day." Never again would Grant indulge so intensely; never again would he need to so much.[16]

Before long couriers carried to headquarters the news that Sedgwick had stabilized his position. Then, and only then, did Grant finally give way, if only for a moment. He retreated to his tent, threw himself on his cot, face down, and "gave way to the greatest emotion." "I never saw a man so agitated in my life," remarked Charles Francis Adams, Jr.; Rawlins and Bowers had never seen Grant as they did now. But in a few minutes the commanding general pulled himself together, and before long he rejoined his staff "in a state of perfect composure." He soon decided it was time to turn in for the night, and when staff officers came to his tent with additional news, they found their commander peacefully asleep. But not for long. After others around the headquarters had also gone to bed, Grant, roused by a false report of an attack, sat by the campfire, thought about what had happened, and chatted with newspaper correspondent Sylvanus Cadwallader. Only as he rose to return to his tent did he remark on the rather sharp way Lee had received him. Ulysses S. Grant had survived his first battle with the Army of the Potomac.[17]

Fog and smoke from the forest fires wafted through Grant's headquarters as the sun rose on May 7. It had been a horrible night on the front lines. Fires had spread across the woods, flames consuming the screaming wounded left stranded between the lines, as if the Wilderness were hell itself. No one was eager to start in again. Despite some heavy skirmishing,

take defensive position

neither side renewed the battle. Lee's men had pulled back to their fortifications to await a Yankee assault. Assessing his losses, Grant noted that many of his wounded were but slightly so — although soldiers near the end of their tour of duty were more likely to give in to wounds they once ignored. He also believed that Lee's army had suffered at least as much as his. "At present we can claim no victory over the enemy," he telegraphed Halleck, but "neither have they gained a single advantage."[18]

Convinced that it would be difficult to achieve a decisive victory against an entrenched foe in this tangled terrain, Grant decided to swing south and east toward open country. Orders went out for a general movement toward Spotsylvania Court House, commencing after dark. That Grant found it necessary to trace out for Meade the routes each corps was to take suggested that he would no longer stand by and let Meade run the show unsupervised. When James H. Wilson, who had experienced a rough time of it in his first combat command as head of a cavalry division, rode into headquarters, Grant, reading the worried look on his face, announced, "It's all right, Wilson; the army is moving toward Richmond." For the rest of the day the general walked around, deep in thought, the ever-present cigar or pipe in his mouth. "To-night Lee will be retreating south," he quietly concluded as he puffed away.[19]

Many of the men in the rank and file of the Army of the Potomac believed that if any army was going to retreat, it would be theirs. "We have had the usual three days' fighting on this side of the river, and by about to-morrow night we will be back in our old camp," grumbled some Pennsylvania privates. Other soldiers remembered the retreat after Chancellorsville just over a year before. These gloomy predictions seemed confirmed when orders came to prepare to move out that evening. As the men fell into line and began to march away from the front lines, many of them thought that when they reached the next intersection, they would turn to the left and toward the north.[20]

But when the columns came to the crossroads, they did not turn north. They turned right. The weary soldiers immediately realized what that meant. They were headed south. They were advancing. "It flashed upon us, like lightning, that there would be no more 'falling back,' and the troops broke into the wildest enthusiasm," one officer recalled.

Things would never be the same for the soldiers of the Army of the Potomac. They had a general who demonstrated his faith in them not through boastful and florid proclamations, but through orders. Grant might amount to little during a review, but he could fight — and advance afterward. Much was yet to come; but the war would henceforth be different.

[margin annotations:]
move to Spotsylvania bc Lee is entrenched to get to open ground, to get closer to Richmond
also, Spotsylv is on Brock Rd (see Rafuse p14)
USG probly couldn't march due South bc there were no roads that way
as crow flies toward Richmond
source?

see p 301 P5

The men knew that. And when they saw Grant and Meade riding down the road surrounded by their staffs, they made sure that Grant knew they knew it. Cheers rose from the ranks as the riders passed behind Hancock's lines, the men swinging their hats and crowding toward Grant. "Pine-knots and leaves were set on fire," recalled Horace Porter, "and lighted the scene with their weird, flickering glare." Although the men were told to keep quiet, lest the noise give away Grant's plans, the celebration continued, causing edgy Confederates to open fire in anticipation of an attack. Grant smiled, remarking that these cheers were sufficient revenge for the Rebel ones of the previous night. "I was truly happy that we were advancing, which indicated that we had not been beaten," recalled one soldier. "The rank and file of the army wanted no more retreating." Rhode Islander Elisha Rhodes agreed. "If we were under any other General except Grant I should expect a retreat, but Grant is not that kind of soldier, and we feel that we can trust him." Elsewhere columns celebrated as they turned southward, and a band struck up the ditty, "Ain't I Glad to Get Out of the Wilderness."[21]

During the early hours of May 7 Abraham Lincoln anxiously awaited news of the battle. The previous evening Secretary Stanton had ordered the arrest of a newspaper reporter at Manassas Junction because he refused to tell the secretary what was going on until he had telegraphed an account to his paper, the *New York Tribune.* Lincoln intervened, allowed the reporter, Henry Wing, to send his dispatch, and then secured a special train to bring him to the White House. Ushered into the president's presence, the reporter recounted what he had seen to Lincoln and several others, then waited until the room emptied. Only then did Wing approach Lincoln with the personal message Grant had given him two evenings before. Lincoln perked up. What was it?

Wing gulped. "He told me I was to tell you, Mr. President, that there would be no turning back."

Smiling, Lincoln bent down and hugged and kissed the reporter. The president had found his general.[22]

As Grant, Meade, and their staffs made their way along the Brock Road, they encountered the head of Warren's Fifth Corps. To clear the route for the infantry, the cavalcade headed toward Todd's Tavern along some side trails, only to get lost in the night and nearly ride into enemy lines. Grant, at the urging of his staff, abandoned his usual superstitious refusal to retrace his steps lest it lead to disaster, and the riders returned whence they came. They then sought to grab a little rest in a field, Grant falling asleep

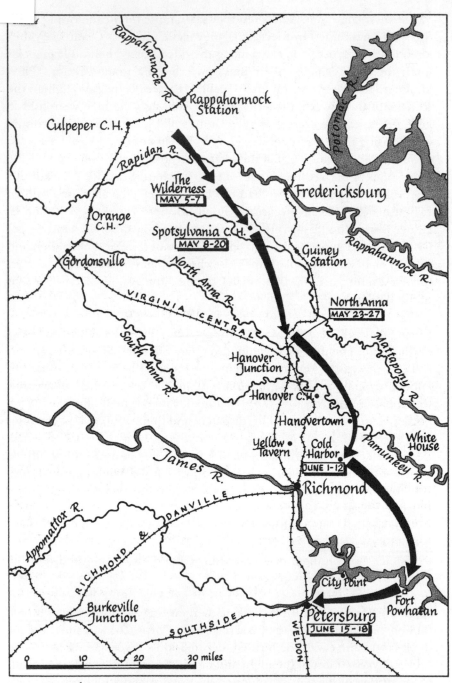

The Overland Campaign, May–June 1864

beside a campfire before an officer covered him with an overcoat. Not until the next morning did the party discover that they had chosen a pigpen for their campsite.[23]

The headquarters staff was not alone in stumbling through the woods on the night of May 7. Lee, uncertain whether Grant was retreating or moving by his left, had decided that in any case the best response was to slide his army toward Spotsylvania Court House. Fortune smiled on the Confederates: the Union advance had bogged down due to traffic difficulties between Meade's infantry and Sheridan's horsemen, while Lee's lead division, commanded by Richard Anderson, had pushed through the burning woods without halt just in time to come up in support of a cavalry skirmish line northwest of the courthouse at Laurel Hill. Once more Warren's Fifth Corps opened the battle, and once more they were held in check by the Confederates. Tired by marching, they failed to attack with any spirit, but at least this time the men could see their enemy.[24]

Ignoring signs of friction among Meade and his corps commanders, Grant telegraphed Washington late that morning that "the best of feeling prevails." He claimed that the fighting in the Wilderness "was decidedly in our favor"; only Confederate entrenchments and a cumbersome wagon train "rendered it impossible to inflict the heavy blow on Lees army I had hoped." Still planning to join Butler, he confidently remarked, "My exact route to the James River I have not yet definately marked out." It was as if he thought that Spotsylvania Court House would fall to him in at most a matter of days.[25]

By afternoon he would have reason to reassess this conclusion. Frustrated with the traffic tie-ups that had delayed the advance of the infantry, Meade, in a "towering passion," confronted Sheridan at midday. Didn't he know how to handle cavalry? Didn't he know that his troopers had blocked the line of march? Sheridan, whose temper matched Meade's, fired back that his men had reached the courthouse, only to fall back when the supporting infantry columns failed to arrive. Had Meade not countermanded his orders, all would have gone smoothly. If Sheridan had his way, he declared, he would take his men and whip Jeb Stuart's cavaliers in a moment. The exchange escalated, and one of Grant's staff officers observed that Sheridan's retorts were "highly spiced and conspicuously italicized with expletives."[26]

Meade probably had the better of the argument, for Sheridan's inexperience as a cavalry commander acting in coordination with infantry had been painfully evident over the past several days. Sheridan, however, had a friendly ear at headquarters, as Meade soon found out when he recounted the exchange to Grant. Hearing of Sheridan's declaration about Stuart, Grant responded, "Did Sheridan say that? Well, he generally knows what he is talking about. Let him start right out and do it." Grant's expressed desire to let Meade run the show was giving way in the face of signs that someone had to kick some sense into this army; yet it would be hard for Meade to exercise command confidently if the general-in-chief was ready to overrule him. Meade, who had hoped that Grant would reprimand Sheridan, seethed as he dictated the orders.[27]

Tempers also soon frayed in front of Laurel Hill. Sedgwick's Sixth Corps joined Warren's men in trying to push aside the Rebels. Warren, showing signs of stress and exhaustion, was not bearing up well under the burden of corps command. Ordered to cooperate with Sedgwick, he snapped: "You . . . can give your orders and I will obey them, or you can put Sedgwick in command and he can give the orders and I will obey them; or you can put me in command and I will give the orders . . . but I'll be God damned if I'll *cooperate* with General Sedgwick or anybody else." Little happened; Grant and Meade, growing impatient, rode over to see what was going on. The two generals and their staffs pulled up in a wooded patch near the front as skirmishers exchanged fire. "Bullets here and there came clicking among trunks and branches and an occasional shell added its discordant tone," reported Theodore Lyman. "I almost fancy Grant felt mad that things did not move faster, and so thought he would go and sit in an uncomfortable place." It was not until dusk that the Union line moved forward, only to be beaten back. The armies slugged it out through the evening, neither giving ground. "Time wasted until dark when it was too late to produce any result," grumbled Cyrus B. Comstock, Grant's aide. Meade fumed about the performance of his corps commanders.[28]

On the morning of May 9 Grant, eager to examine Lee's position, rode along the lines. No sooner had he left Sedgwick's command than the corps commander was cut down by a Confederate sniper. Grant, shaken, twice asked for confirmation of the report. Sedgwick was too good a commander to lose; he was more valuable than a division. Horatio Wright took over the Sixth Corps.[29]

Grant could not mourn for long. His reconnaissance revealed that Lee's lines wrapped around the crossroads, the northern apex of his position forming a salient. In response, Grant decided to extend his lines east and north around the Confederate right. Burnside's corps was coming from the north; he would test Lee's right flank north of Spotsylvania Court House. Hancock would throw several divisions across the Po River west of Laurel Hill and advance against Lee's left. Meanwhile, Sheridan's men mounted at daybreak to circle around Lee's right and head for the railroads in his rear, with the hope of drawing Stuart's troopers out for a fight. Their departure hindered Grant's ability to gather information about the location, strength, and intentions of the enemy across his front, although he rarely used cavalry for such purposes; instead he would act on educated guesses and fragmentary information. The horsemen left behind (including the cavalry attached to Burnside's corps) were not employed for reconnaissance. On the positive side, perhaps Sheridan could smash Stuart and wreak havoc in Lee's rear.[30]

It would not be easy to mount an attack at Spotsylvania. The wooded, rolling terrain was challenge enough, providing defenders with cover and nullifying Grant's advantage in artillery, but now both sides were becoming adept at digging in and erecting formidable field fortifications within a short period. One of Meade's aides marveled at the speed with which the Confederates readied their lines: "It is a rule that when the Rebels halt, the first day gives them a good riflepit; the second, a regular infantry parapet with artillery in position; and the third a parapet with an abattis in front and entrenched batteries behind. Sometimes they put this three days' work into the first twenty-four hours." Field returns revealed that Grant could muster only 75,000 effectives for action.[31]

Grant directed Burnside to test Lee's right covering Spotsylvania Court House. The Ninth Corps commander frittered away a chance to inflict a major blow, although at one point his men closed to five hundred yards of the courthouse itself. In response to reports that Lee was massing opposite Burnside, Grant pushed ahead with a plan to threaten the Confederate left. Hancock threw three divisions across the Po River in the afternoon, too late to mount a serious attack that day but early enough to alert Lee of their presence. All night the Confederate commander positioned his men to deliver a devastating blow. On the morning of May 10, Grant, realizing that the Confederate left was not weak after all, decided to pull Hancock back, although the process of extricating the three divisions proved taxing. "Enemy hold our front in very strong force and evince strong determination to interpose between us and Richmond to the last," he wired Halleck. "I shall take no backward step but may be compelled to send back to Bell[e] Plain for further supplies. . . . We can maintain ourselves at least and in the end beat Lee's Army I believe." In the meantime, however, Halleck was to send him all the infantry "you can rake and scrape" from the Washington defenses and elsewhere.[32]

Concluding that if Lee had shifted his forces to check first Burnside and then Hancock, he must have weakened his line elsewhere, Grant ordered

[handwritten margin note top: ok, smart...]

an attack against Lee's center. Warren was to renew his drive on Laurel Hill, with several of Hancock's divisions, weary from their adventure south of the Po, coming up in support. Responding to Warren's demand for a structured chain of command, Grant and Meade put Hancock in charge of this operation. Burnside was to press forward against Lee's right once more; Grant instructed him to scout out the enemy position, and if there was any chance to hit Lee to "do it with vigor and with all the force you can bring to bear."[33]

[handwritten margin note: all simultaneously? THAT might work if the corps comms don't screw up]

The highlight of the afternoon's operation was to be an attack by twelve handpicked regiments of the Sixth Corps under the command of Colonel Emory Upton, who had argued forcefully for a headlong rush toward Lee's center with the soldiers under orders not to halt to return fire until they reached the enemy's line. Grant and Meade liked the idea and wanted to encourage aggressive action after days of delays and procrastination. Upton's target was a smaller salient on the western side of what was now understood to be a large salient that formed the Confederate center. Gershom Mott's division of the Second Corps was to support Upton's assault.

[handwritten margin note: assault on salient planned]
[handwritten note in line: dang. knew it.]

What was to be a coordinated series of attacks disintegrated into several piecemeal thrusts, lacking coordination. Warren, overeager to restore his reputation, advanced ahead of schedule; ignorant of this last-minute change, Upton and Mott stayed in place, allowing the Confederates to repulse Warren. Disappointed at the setback, headquarters rescheduled the Upton/Mott operation for 6:00 P.M., an hour after the original time. Word of the change never reached Mott, who was already wrestling to reconcile conflicting orders that called on him to defend a two-mile front while concentrating his men for an attack: his men stepped off at 5:00 P.M. as originally planned. Instead of supporting Upton, they were left on their own, and Confederate artillery quickly broke up their advance. When Upton launched his attack an hour later, no other forces could exploit whatever success he gained. Thus his initial breakthrough, which vindicated Upton's tactical savvy, proved to be bittersweet. Horatio Wright, new to the responsibilities of corps command and confused by what was unraveling in front of him, turned to the lieutenant general for advice. Frustrated, Grant shot back, "Pile in the men and hold it" — which was not exactly the most constructive advice he could have offered. At last Upton withdrew. Not until this chance faded away did Hancock at long last strike at Laurel Hill — although his officers and men did so with great misgivings, being new to the ground and skeptical of success. Warren did nothing to support this last bid for victory on the right; one brigade broke

[handwritten note bottom: once again, good plans (coordinated assaults all along the line) but devil is in details → a BIG reason for campaign turning out the way it did = culture of AotP]

through, but retired when no one came up in support. Burnside received orders to attack at the same time, with little result.[34] Grant was disappointed. Another opportunity had been forfeited at great cost. After updating a reporter on the day's events, he remarked: "We have had hard fighting to-day, and I am sorry to say we have not accomplished much. We have lost a good many men, and I suppose that I shall be blamed for it." He paused, then continued: ("I do not know any way to put down this rebellion and restore the authority of the Government except by fighting, and fighting means that men must be killed. If the people of this country expect that the war can be conducted to a successful issue in any other way than by fighting, they must get somebody other than myself to command the army.")

Grant began to see that Meade was finding it difficult to implement his directives. The Army of the Potomac seemed unable to coordinate offensive operations; anything that could have gone wrong on May 10 did go wrong. And managing Burnside presented its own set of problems. The amiable general would procrastinate, ask for instructions, then act on his own; both Porter and Comstock had trouble persuading him to implement the lieutenant general's preferences. It was impossible for Grant to supervise both Meade and Burnside at the same time with any success. Unhappy that his previous plans had failed, he went to the front several times to see if he could push things along. Once a shell nearly decapitated a nearby horse, causing it to jump about. Grant remained with his eyes fixed to the front, surveying the scene with field glasses. He barely escaped death when a shell exploded in front of him while he was composing a dispatch. Momentarily interrupted, he glanced up, then resumed writing. Wisconsin infantrymen observed the scene; one remarked, "Ulysses don't scare worth a damn."[35]

The next morning Grant showed how unruffled he was. Elihu Washburne, about to return to Washington, asked Grant if he could carry any message back to Lincoln and Stanton. Grant remarked that while he was pleased with his progress so far, he didn't want to raise false hopes of an early success. He then entrusted the congressman with dispatches for Halleck and Stanton — the first time he had written the war secretary during the campaign. He puffed away at a cigar as he scribbled out his messages, his head almost enveloped in smoke before he paused to blow it away — a process that he repeated several times as he thought and wrote. "We have now entered the sixth day of very hard fighting," he began his message to Stanton. "The result to this time is much in our favor. Our losses have been heavy as well as those of the enemy. . . . I purpose to fight it out on this line if it takes all summer." The words were written without flourish; Grant buried similar language in his description of the situation to Halleck. Nor did they convey the sense that there had been missed opportunities to do so much more. Instead, they stood out to anyone who read the message as a statement of his deep determination to see the thing through. More important to Grant was the arrival of more good news from Butler and a message that Sheridan was ripping up rails.[36]

Grant pondered the lessons of May 10. Getting the Army of the Potomac to launch a coordinated attack was proving very difficult, making the confusion at Chattanooga mild by comparison. But all was not lost. Despite some bad moments, the Union forces retained the upper hand. Whatever the course of events to date, it was clear that Fredericksburg and Chancellorsville were not to be revisited. Meade, agreeing, thought his men "have gotten . . . decidedly the better of the enemy, though their resistance is most stubborn." Pleased at Upton's initiative, Grant recommended him for promotion to brigadier general; the assault had revealed the vulnerability of the Confederate center to a carefully planned and well-executed attack. "A brigade today — we'll try a corps tomorrow," he remarked on the evening of May 10. But he would have to wait a day. Rain came on May 11, halting operations for the moment. Everyone welcomed it. Generals, officers, and men alike were exhausted from the continuous fighting.[37]

As eager as he was to strike at Lee, the pause was good for Grant, too. During the past several days he had drawn up plan after plan based on hunches about the location of enemy forces, instead of settling on one plan and seeing it through; in the confusion he had failed to concentrate his force and supervise his generals effectively. Now he had time to think things through before giving orders for another attack. That afternoon he inspected his lines. Members of a Wisconsin regiment looked up as he visited Warren's corps. As skirmishing increased in intensity, he leaned forward on his horse and listened to determine the flow of the engagement, working at his cigar as he read and wrote dispatches.[38]

Grant returned from his visit with a better knowledge of the Confederate position and a better idea of how to crack it. Lee had shored up his flanks, but his center continued to protrude. Upton's men had pierced the west wall of the salient; Grant believed that if he massed Hancock north of the center of the salient, with orders not to fire until they hit the enemy line, he could smash the Confederates. "There is but little doubt in my mind but that the assault last evening would have proven entirely successful if it had commenced one hour earlier and had been heartily entered into by Mott's division and the 9th Corps," he told Meade. To add to the element of surprise and increase concealment for the attack, he concluded that it would have to take place in the early morning hours. If Burnside could strike the eastern flank of the salient while Warren and Wright stood ready to exploit any openings, the Confederates might crumble. Off went orders to Burnside to attack at 4:00 A.M.; staff officers Comstock and Orville E. Babcock were instructed to accompany him to "impress" the Ninth Corps commander "with the importance of a prompt and vigerous attack."[39]

Meade and his corps commanders also required Grant's closer supervision. Warren's haste in getting into action on May 10 was an uncharacteristic change of pace from his usual deliberate style. Whether that chance reflected a new attitude or was a momentary lapse remained to be seen. Theodore Lyman believed that the hero of Little Round Top was simply not equal to the responsibilities of corps command. The same might be said of Wright, but he had just been elevated to that role, and it would be unfair to expect him to have excelled at it under such circumstances.[40]

[margin note:] probs of AofP commanders

This left Winfield Scott Hancock as the most reliable corps commander in Meade's army. Even he was less than flawless. His aggressiveness concealed his inability to reconnoiter either the enemy's position or the ground over which he was to advance. Such had been the case on May 10, and it would be the same again. Before departing to join Burnside, Comstock picked out the place where Hancock would form his corps in preparation for the attack; however, neither Meade nor Hancock examined the terrain in front of them. In later years Humphreys would note that knowledge of the ground was at best sketchy; he did not explain what he, as chief of staff for Meade, did to remedy that shortcoming. Irritated by Grant's assumption of a more active role in army operations, Meade was "cross as a bear"; however, when given a chance to exercise command, he did not arrange for reconnaissance, and Hancock did little better. As one of his staff officers later admitted, "topographical insight was not one of Hancock's strong points." Division commander Francis C. Barlow complained that "no information whatever, as far as I can remember, was given to us as to the position or strength of the enemy, or as to the troops to be engaged in the movement (except that the 2nd corps was to take part in it), or as to the plan of attack, or why any attack was to be made at that time or place." Instead, after dusk the division commanders met with members of Hancock's staff, who described the ground as they pointed to a makeshift map drawn on the wall of a local dwelling. "I remember well the loudly expressed indignation of those officers at being sent to conduct

[margin note:] more probs

[margin note:] not good

[bottom handwritten note:] did USG know abt the dysfunction?

an important movement when they had no information whatever as to the position or strength of the enemy, or indeed upon any of the important points, and at times a sense of the ludicrous, of the absurdity of the situation, prevailed over the feeling of responsibility and indignation," Barlow recalled. Others more soberly recounted that Barlow thought he was on a suicide mission, for he entrusted his valuables to a friend.[41]

Frank Barlow excelled at finger-pointing, an activity that preoccupied all too many of his peers in the Army of the Potomac; even he had to tell two of his brigade commanders to stop complaining. He left it to his listeners to conclude who was at fault, but the responsibility rested on the shoulders of Meade and Hancock. Perhaps Meade did not realize that Grant injected himself more directly into managing the army because Meade failed to do his job, which included learning about the enemy's disposition and intentions. It would not be the first time that Meade, his staff, and his corps commanders performed poorly; it would not be the last time that they failed to prepare for an assault or to cooperate enthusiastically and heartily. In each case men paid for the result with their lives.

It was dark and foggy in the early morning hours of May 12. Before long the drizzle turned into rain. Four o'clock came and went. Grant, whose headquarters were located a mile west of Hancock's corps, waited to hear the beginning of a battle. Finishing his coffee, he wrapped himself in an overcoat and sat by a campfire as the rain came down. Gusts of wind blew the cape of his coat over his face as he sat and waited for reports from the front. At last artillery fire to the far left indicated that Burnside's advance was under way; moments later he heard rifle fire and cheers from Hancock's front. But it was an hour before the first reports arrived at headquarters. They brought good news. Hancock's men, belying Barlow's gloomy predictions, had punched a hole in the salient, and were pushing forward. Large numbers of Confederates had fallen prisoner. Before long Grant encountered one. Edward Johnson, a division commander, had fought alongside Grant in the Mexican-American War. Grant mentioned that it had been a long time since the two men had met; when Johnson replied that he had not expected to meet Grant "under such circumstances," Grant dryly replied, "It is one of the sad fortunes of war." Then he offered his prisoner a cigar. As the two men chatted, a courier delivered a dispatch from Hancock, declaring that he had "finished up Johnson, and am now going into Early." Grant, wishing not to offend Johnson, passed the message around instead of reading it out loud.[42]

Before long, however, news came that the Confederate resistance had stiffened. Grant sought to renew the attack, at times using a field telegraph to communicate with the corps commanders. Dispatch after dispatch went out to Burnside urging him into action. "Push the enemy with all your might," Grant urged. "That is the way to connect." Burnside, already irritated by the presence of Comstock and Babcock, chafed at such instructions, crumpling Grant's message into a tight wad. Although his divisions fought hard, they made little impression on the Confederate lines; at one point Grant grew so displeased that he snapped at Burnside, "See that your orders are executed." But Old Burn was not the only general to irritate Grant. Gouverneur Warren appeared reluctant to commit the Fifth Corps to the fray, and at one point Grant authorized Meade to relieve him from command. Riding forward, the lieutenant general moved from point to point to gain a better view of the battle with his field glasses.[43]

What he saw was opportunity beginning to slip away in the rain and mud of Spotsylvania. The attack had bogged down because no one had thought much about how to exploit the breakthrough. Simply piling in more men created confusion, especially when heavy rains created a bloody quagmire. The Confederates were building a new line at the base of the salient. And yet Grant had inflicted heavy damage. For once he had benefited from a Lee mistake, for the Confederate commander had ordered the removal of artillery from the salient, only to change his mind in time to allow the Yankees to capture the guns before they were back in place. Returning to headquarters late that afternoon, Grant apprised Halleck of the result. "The eighth day of battle closes, leaving between three and four thousand prisoners in our hands for the days work, including two General Officers, and over thirty pieces of artillery. The enemy are obstinate and seem to have found the last ditch."[44]

Grant worried that Lee might now retreat to the protection of the Richmond fortifications, thus saving his army. Reconnaissance reports, however, soon revealed that Lee had reestablished his line. Continuing rainfall rendered maneuver difficult, and so Grant rested his men and took stock of his situation. Off to Washington went his recommendations for promotions. Most noteworthy were his requests to elevate Meade as well as Sherman to the rank of major general in the regular army, a sign that he appreciated Meade's situation if not always his services thus far. Not all of his staff shared that sentiment. Several of Grant's aides advised their chief to take direct control of the army in the interests of efficiency and harmony. Meade's temper had flared several times and there was too much squabbling among his subordinates. Grant reminded his staff that he would be overburdened if he were to assume direct command of the Army of the Potomac in addition to his responsibilities as general-in-chief. To relieve Meade would most certainly spark even more resentment among those officers already unhappy with Grant's presence. This ended the conversation. Grant could have added that replacing Meade alone would not have remedied the command problem, given the subpar performance of several corps commanders.[45]

Grant was impressed by his foe. Lee was proving to be far more challenging than Bragg or Pemberton. The number of casualties concerned him, although he accepted it as a necessary price of combat. "Among the wounded the great majority are but slightly hurt but most of them will be unfit for service in this battle," he told Julia. Reinforcements would raise his men's morale. Still, there was much fighting ahead. "The world has never seen so bloody or so protracted a battle as the one being fought and I hope never will again," he remarked. "The enemy were really whipped yesterday but their situation is desperate beyond anything heretofore known. To loose this battle they loose their cause. As bad as it is they have fought for it with a gallantry worthy of a better."[46]

Grant's own command was having its troubles. There were many stragglers and slightly wounded men who had tried to prolong their stays at hospitals in Washington. The large number of the latter impressed observers, and reporter Whitelaw Reid soon had noted that of the wounded he had seen some two thirds were "so slightly wounded as scarcely to deserve being treated as disabled" — a sign that some men were not anxious to see action again so soon. However, reinforcements were on the way, drawn from the regiments of heavy artillery that had once garrisoned the capital's defenses. They were sorely needed. Comstock estimated that the Army of the Potomac's three infantry corps totaled some 31,000 effectives, plus Burnside's corps. Another headquarters estimate claimed that Grant had just over 56,000 men, excluding those regiments whose terms of service were about to expire. When Grant expressed regret at the tremendous cost in lives, Meade replied, "Well, general, we can't do those little tricks without losses." Rain continued to soak both armies over the next several days, bedeviling Grant's efforts to renew the offensive while buying time for Lee to perfect his fortifications. It was "a rest that the men on both sides were glad to have," Meade observed.[47]

Grant had not intended such a respite. Anxious to strike yet another blow, he looked to hit the Rebel right, swinging the Fifth and Sixth Corps from their position opposite the Confederate left to a position just east of Spotsylvania Court House. However, the columns bogged down in the rain and mud; by the time the two corps were in place to attack, it was late

> not willing to waste
> lives

morning on May 14. Believing that Lee had already shifted his men to check an advance, Grant called off the assault — although in fact the Confederates remained vulnerable much of the day.[48]

Here and there combat continued as the Union line shifted until it ran from north to south east of Spotsylvania. Grant personally directed the taking of a hill and was pleased by Warren's willingness to move rapidly to drive the Confederates away after the position had changed hands several times. The general also encountered wounded men at a farmhouse in the area. In one room he found a Confederate corporal who had been wounded in the right cheek. The general secured medical assistance for the soldier, then moved on. By the time he returned to headquarters that night, he was covered with mud. The following day, while inspecting the Sixth Corps' position, Grant found himself under artillery fire, but instead of scampering for cover, he simply rode on, oblivious to the "shower of debris" that fell on him.[49]

"We have had five days' almost constant rain, without any prospect yet of its clearing up," Grant informed Halleck on May 16. "The army is in the best of spirits, and feels the greatest confidence in ultimate success. . . . The elements alone have suspended hostilities." But the roads had become so impassable that Grant could not transport his wounded back to Fredericksburg. "There is a determination on all sides to fight it out, and have an end put to the war; a result which I think will most certainly be accomplished if we can overcome the army before us," observed Meade. But he added that the continuous fighting had worn down the men; the respite afforded by the rain had proven a most welcome one.[50]

While both sides waited for the rain to let up, elsewhere the war continued. Dispatches arriving at headquarters announced that Sherman and Butler were pressing forward; Butler had reached the railroad between Richmond and Petersburg, threatening a significant supply line. Even more important was news that Sheridan, wrecking railroads as he moved southward, had smashed into Confederate cavalry at Yellow Tavern; in the ensuing engagement Jeb Stuart fell mortally wounded. But Grant was uneasy about Sigel's progress in the Shenandoah Valley, and had brought David Hunter to headquarters to confer on what to do.

Sherm + Butler on the move,

On May 17 the weather began to improve. So did the spirits of Grant's men. "I am well and happy and feel that at last the Army of the Potomac is doing good work," remarked a Rhode Islander. "Grant is a fighter and is bound to win." Grant proposed to take the offensive the next morning, sending Wright and Hancock against Lee's left behind the site of the salient. A closer examination of the Confederate defenses, however, sparked second thoughts, as the initial assault columns were driven off. "Even Grant thought it useless to knock our heads against a brick wall," Meade remarked. On his way to survey the field, Grant noticed several wounded men along the side of the road. One soldier in particular, suffering from a chest wound, drew his attention. A staff officer rode by, splashing mud in the soldier's face. Grant winced. Horace Porter dismounted, wiped the injured man's face, and examined his wound, only to find that it was mortal. In a few minutes the soldier died. Grant, his face bearing "a painfully sad" expression, kept looking, first at the man, then at the galloping staff officer, who remained unaware of his callousness. The general did not speak for some time.[51]

More bad news awaited Grant on his return to headquarters. Butler had run into trouble between Richmond and Petersburg, and had pulled back from his position astride the railroad connecting those two cities. Equally disturbing was that Sigel had met with disaster at New Market on May 15, where he was driven away by a force half his size. "If you expect anything from him you will be mistaken," Halleck scoffed. "He will do nothing but run. He never did anything else." Of course, Grant had not placed Sigel in command in the first place: that honor belonged to Lincoln. Lee, far from worrying about how to counter three offensives, could now draw reinforcements from the victorious Confederates. Finally, from Louisiana came word of Nathaniel Banks's continued fumbling. It was time to risk presidential displeasure in the interest of military success. Immediately Grant replaced Sigel with Hunter. Repeating his desire to relieve Banks, he learned that Banks had already been displaced at last by Edward R. S. Canby.[52]

The news from Butler and Sigel forced Grant to reassess his campaign plan. During the past weeks he had sought to bring Lee to combat in the open field, reasoning that he could inflict far more damage at less cost in such an engagement than by assaulting Lee's men in their fixed positions outside Richmond. But Lee's men had proven masters at quickly constructing field fortifications; now, with Butler and Sigel out of the picture, Lee could reinforce his position around Spotsylvania without worrying about his rear. Grant decided to flank Lee's right with the eventual aim of joining forces with Butler. Perhaps Lee could be forced to come out and fight in the open (as he did on May 19, when he hit Grant's right flank, only to be checked by the heavy artillery regiments in a desperate clash).

The May 19 attack but momentarily delayed Grant's next flanking move. On May 20 Hancock's corps forged ahead in an effort to lure Lee into attacking, while the other three corps followed at a distance.

Butler's failure on James contributes to USG reassessing his plan

Grant established headquarters at Guiney Station, where Stonewall Jackson had breathed his last just over a year earlier. When an aide cautioned that perhaps they should pull back to await the arrival of Warren's corps, Grant responded that it would be better to hurry Warren forward. More disturbing was the continued inability of Butler to apply any pressure on Richmond and Petersburg. Among the Confederate prisoners captured were members of George E. Pickett's division, which had been assigned to defend Petersburg. "I fear there is some difficulty with the forces at City Point which prevents their effective use," Grant telegraphed Halleck. "The fault may be with their commander, or, it may be with his subordinates. Gen'l Smith, whilst a very able officer, is obstinate and is likely to condemn whatever is not suggested by himself." Left unsaid was that it had been Grant's idea to pair the two men; he had been mistaken in his faith that Butler, assisted by Smith, could achieve great things. If Butler could not pin down enough Confederates, it would be better to draw on his command for reinforcements. He asked Halleck to send someone down to report on the situation; the next day he thought it best to have Smith join him soon, as Lee was receiving reinforcements from Richmond.[53] *→ bc Butler isn't pressuring it*

USG .3 keeping Halleck posted often

Headquarters this day was next to a large plantation house owned by a Confederate colonel. His wife, a loyal Rebel, insisted that Sherman's men would make no headway against her husband and Joe Johnston. Grant patiently listened and then, in his quiet way, disagreed. Moments later the woman, overhearing him reading a dispatch announcing that Sherman had taken Rome, burst into tears. Her mother-in-law, however, gained some satisfaction at the expense of Ambrose Burnside. The courtly corps commander arrived at headquarters to report on his troops' movement. Bowing to the older woman, he remarked that he supposed she had never seen so many Yankees before. "Oh, yes, I have; many more," she replied. Startled, the curious Burnside inquired where she had encountered them. "In Richmond," she snapped back, obviously referring to Libby Prison. Even Grant laughed.[54]   *→ flanking move, I think*

Lee swept south to intercept Grant's advance, passing up the opportunity to strike at the elongated line of march offered by the dispersed Union corps. Grant took note of his foe's failure to attack. Perhaps the Confederates were wearing down. In turn the Yankees failed to lash out at one exposed Confederate corps as it tramped past Warren's men, for no one in the front lines thought it important enough to inform headquarters of the proximity of the enemy column. Instead, the two armies met again along the North Anna River. Hancock and Warren forced a crossing of the river on May 23, and Warren repulsed a Confederate effort to drive him off. Comstock noted that some of the division commanders, "too fearful of losing men," were not pressing forward vigorously.[55]

Early the next day Grant joined Meade at a church along the Telegraph Road. Initially he believed that he would push the Confederates aside with ease. "Negroes who have come in state that Lee is falling back to Richmond," he informed Halleck; perhaps it would be better to keep Butler's men where they were. Hancock's men pressed forward in force across the river three miles east of Warren; Burnside came up to connect the two corps, while Wright backed up Warren. But rumors of a Confederate withdrawal were in error (Lee was luring Grant into a trap by allowing the Yankees to advance.) The first sign of trouble was Burnside's inability to cross the North Anna. As enemy resistance stiffened, Grant realized that his forces were in a precarious position, with the center still north of the river while both wings were south of it. Lee might concentrate on either flank and deliver a deadly blow before Grant could shuttle reinforcements to the endangered section, a move that might involve two river crossings from flank to flank; formidable Confederate earthworks meant that any attack would be costly.[56]

Not all the news that morning was bad. Sheridan's horsemen were returning. The cavalryman himself showed up at headquarters, and Grant joked that he had exaggerated his accomplishments. Whether Meade, who must have had mixed feelings about the appearance of his antagonist, agreed was not reported. Moments later, matters worsened when Charles A. Dana eagerly shared with all a dispatch from Sherman — including the blunt message that if Grant could inspire the Army of the Potomac to do something the war might well come to a close. Meade exploded. He had heard enough about Grant, Grant, Grant. In a voice that sounded like "cutting an iron bar with a handsaw," he declared: "Sir! I consider that despatch an insult to the army I command and to me personally. The Army of the Potomac does not require General Grant's inspiration or anybody's else inspiration to make it fight!" Damn that "armed rabble" in the West; (it did not have to face Bobby Lee and his boys with Lincoln, the cabinet, Congress, and the newspapers looking over their shoulders.[57])

In this way the crisis between Grant and Meade over the management of the Army of the Potomac came to a head. It had been brewing for some time; it did not help that during the lull in combat after the May 12 assault Meade and his staff officers had read what the papers were saying about Grant. Reporters who thus distorted the truth, snapped one aide, "are the scum of creation." Grant had tried to handle Meade gingerly; he had flattered Meade's performance in dispatches and defended his performance to others. Yet it was also evident that he was intervening more directly in the operations of the army than he had originally intended. Now he pulled back in significant ways. First, he ended Burnside's career as an independent corps commander, placing him under Meade — a step long overdue. Between the collapse of Sigel's campaign in the Valley and growing concern about Butler and the Army of the James, Grant simply could not take the time to direct Burnside; doing so absorbed too much energy and was at best marginally effective. Second, he decided to let Meade manage his own army.[58]

Grant realized his position astride the North Anna was less than ideal. "The situation of the enemy," he told Burnside, was "so different from what I expected." Interviews with prisoners revealed that Lee was receiving more reinforcements — the Army of Northern Virginia was actually approaching parity with the Army of the Potomac in terms of absolute strength, if only until additional Union replacements arrived. Realizing that Butler had failed to pin many Confederates in place, Grant wanted to shift part of the Army of the James northward. Until either reinforcements arrived or Grant moved, however, matters would be precarious. Nor was he the only person to believe as much. That afternoon an elderly woman paid headquarters a visit. Confronting the general, she announced: "I believe you command all these h'yah Yankees that are comin' down h'yah and cavortin' round over this whole section of the country." When Grant bowed in acknowledgment, the woman continued: "I'm powerful glad General Lee has been lickin' you-all from the Rapidan cl'ah down h'yah, and now he's got you jes wh'ah he wants you." Only once did Grant come close to breaking out in laughter, when his inquisitor asked whether he had confronted Lee at Gettysburg. "Well, no," he replied; "I wasn't there myself. I had some business in another direction." Having mocked the Yankees long enough, the woman left; moments later she returned, seeking protection. Grant detailed an aide to perform the task.[59]

Grant's confidence grew when it became evident that the Confederates were not going to launch a major assault. Attacking Lee here was out of the question; making sure that he in turn did not attack either flank was an immediate concern; but should the next march be across Lee's right or left? If Grant's staff officers had their own opinions, they did not share them: an observer noted that they sat "in a circle all day. . . . & look[ed] at Grant." On the evening of May 25 the general-in-chief called together Meade's corps commanders to discuss what to do next. Warren and artil-

lery chief Henry Hunt made the case to turn Lee's left for the first time in
the campaign. Meade argued that it was time to slip around the Confederate right once more.[60]

Initially Grant, tempted by the thought that Lee might not expect to be
flanked on his left, sided with Warren and Hunt — and thus overruled
Meade. He soon reconsidered this decision; as Meade had explained, the
advantages of waterborne supply favored a move across the Confederate
right. (It was the only way to link up with elements of the Army of the
James, whereas a leftward move would involve crossing three streams, all
tributaries of the single stream the army would cross when advancing by
the enemy's right.) Moreover, if Grant was going to let Meade manage his
command, overruling him would once more undermine his subordinate's
authority just after Grant had tried to add to it. Thus that evening Grant issued orders for a move in accordance with Meade's preferences — but
only after a detachment destroyed a section of the Virginia Central Railroad, thus depriving Lee of yet another supply link.[61]

Extracting the Army of the Potomac from its present position proved a
challenge. Wilson's cavalry division rode westward, convincing Lee that
the whole army would follow, thus breaking the pattern of advances by the
left; the withdrawal began under cover of darkness on May 25 and continued the next evening. In the meantime Grant made sure that materials for
preparing pontoon bridges to span the James were ready for use. He
found Lee's failure to strike a blow revealing. Surely the Confederates had
missed a golden opportunity. Perhaps the campaign was wearing the Rebels down at last. "Lee's army is really whipped. . . . A battle with them outside of intrenchments cannot be had," he told Halleck. "Our men feel
that they have gained morale over the enemy and attack with confidence.
I may be mistaken but I feel that our success over Lee's army is already in-
sured."[62]

The soldiers shared Grant's confidence. For a moment they had appeared to be in a tight spot, but this time the Confederates somehow
failed to spring the trap. A week had passed since Spotsylvania, casualties
were down, and the army was moving forward again. One colonel noted
that "now we felt we had a leader in whom all felt the utmost confidence in
his ability and the certainty of his leading us to ultimate victory, though his
presence excited no enthusiasm." Charles Dana agreed. "Rebels have lost
all confidence, and are already morally defeated," he wired Washington.
"This army has learned to believe that it is sure of victory. . . . Rely upon it,
the end is near as well as sure." Here and there officers echoed the dismay
of Charles Wainwright, head of the Fifth Corps artillery, who expressed
disgust at yet another march by the left: "Can it be that this is the sum of

our lieutenant general's abilities? Has he no other resource in tactics? Or is it sheer obstinacy?" But other observers were impressed that the army had escaped and was on the move again. As Grant rode past a Pennsylvania regiment, the men lifted their caps. "Grant acknowledged the reception with a smile and salutation," noted a captain. "He looked calm, satisfied, and resolute. The cold relentless energy with which he is pursuing Lee is actually sublime."[63]

Even the tension that had pervaded relations between the staff of the two top generals appeared to have dissipated. On May 27 Lyman reported that the Army of the Potomac's staff was doing all the work, leaving Grant's staff with time on their hands. Perhaps that was why Grant came down with a bad headache that day. It was the first time Lyman had seen him suffering from one of his periodic "sick-headaches"; the lieutenant general applied chloroform to his head in an effort to gain relief.[64]

The armies pressed southward on May 28. Grant established headquarters at a house occupied by several "strongly sesech" women. Once more he found himself confronted by a feisty Confederate civilian, described by Lyman as "a conceited, curious, sallow, middle-aged woman, itching to 'tackle' a Northerner." Grant listened to her litany of grievances, complaints, and boasts, and replied in his usual dry, understated way, "whereat," Lyman continued, "she was plainly taken aback, as she looked for a volley of gasconade!" The general was far more concerned about the effort to push south from the Pamunkey River toward Hanovertown. Meade believed that eventually Lee would be forced to seek protection behind Richmond's fortifications, whereupon "the grand decisive fight will come off, which I trust will bring the war to a close, and that it will be victory for us."[65] → why would they want to fight Lee when he's in fortifications

As commander of the headquarters cavalry escort, Captain Charles F. Adams, Jr., was in an ideal position to see the lieutenant general at work. "Grant is certainly a very extraordinary man," he observed. "He does not look it and might pass well enough for a dumpy little subaltern, very fond of smoking. Neither do I know that he shows it in his conversation, for he never spoke to me and doesn't seem to be a very talkative man anyhow." An observer who looked for signs of greatness in his appearance would be disappointed. However, no "intelligent person could watch him, even from such a distance as mine, without concluding that he is a remarkable man. He handles those around him so quietly and well, he so evidently has the faculty of disposing of work and managing men, he is cool and quiet, almost stolid and as if stupid, and in a crisis he is one against whom all around . . . would instinctively lean."

Most impressive was Grant's ability to get people to work together. "He took command under the most unfavorable circumstances — jealousy between East and West; . . . that general feeling that the officers from the West were going to swagger over those here and finally that universal envy which success creates and which is always ready to carp at it," Adams wrote; "the materials were all ready for an explosion at the first mistake Grant made." Yet "now Grant had this army as firmly in hand as ever he had that of the Southwest. He has effected this simply by the exercise of tact and good taste. He has humored us, he has given some promotions, he had made no parade of his authority, he has given no orders except through Meade, and Meade he treats with the utmost confidence and deference. The result is that even from the most jealously disposed and most indiscreet of Meade's staff, not a word is heard against Grant. The result is of inestimable importance. The army has a head and confidence in that head. It has leaders and there is no discord among those leaders. We seem to have gotten rid of jealousy and all now seem disposed to go in with a will to win."[66]

Adams's estimate exaggerated the harmony at headquarters. But something had changed. For over three weeks the Army of the Potomac had wrestled the Confederates, never quite achieving victory but never backing down, either, as it made its way around Lee's left time and again. "The enemy, I think, outfight us, but we outnumber them, and, finally, within the last three days one witnesses in this Army as it moves along all the results of a victory, when in fact it had done only barren fighting," the captain observed. "For it has done the one thing needful before the enemy — it has advanced. The result is wonderful. Hammered and pounded as this Army has been; worked, marched, fought and reduced as it is, it is in better spirits and better fighting trim today than it was in the first day's fight in the Wilderness. Strange as it seems to me, it is, I believe, yet the fact, that this Army is now just on its second wind, and is more formidable than it ever was before." Meanwhile, Lee's men appeared to be losing their edge; they had not launched one of their trademark counterattacks for weeks. "They are now fighting cautiously, but desperately," Meade noted, "disputing every inch of ground, but confining themselves exclusively to the defensive."[67]

Reinforcements had arrived. Grant had placated Meade. Lee was no longer counterattacking. Richmond beckoned. The climax of the campaign might be only a few days away.

16

A Very Tedious Job

◉

AS THE ARMY OF THE POTOMAC pressed southward, its achievements excited and thrilled Northerners. Newspaper reports suggested that the beginning of the end was at hand — and that the end was not far off. The *New York Tribune*, drawing on Henry Wing's observations, proclaimed the first day of the Wilderness "a grand victory"; two days later a headline blared, "LEE DRIVEN AT ALL POINTS." On May 10 the *New York Herald* predicted "not only that Richmond will very soon be ours, but that hardly a remnant of Lee's defeated, exhausted and demoralized legions, as an organized body, will be left to tell the story." In the aftermath of Grant's May 11 dispatch pledging to "fight it out on this line if it takes all summer," the *Tribune* declared, "We have reason to believe that a very few days now will settle the fate of the rebellion. It is staggering to its fall from the crippling blows of Grant, and cannot survive the summer." The end of the war seemed to be at hand. "Every loyal heart is full of joy at the glorious tidings which continue to come up from the front," Noah Brooks reported, "and citizens everywhere are congratulating each other upon the near prospect of an end of this wasteful and wicked war. The 'coming man' appears to have come at last, and Grant is the hero of the war."[1]

It was not until after the two armies left Spotsylvania that citizens began to have doubts. "I begin to imagine that Grant is not going to beat Lee so easily as everybody seemed to suppose," one Washingtonian confided to his diary. "After having cheered ourselves hoarse over the success and prospects of successes by Grant and the Army of the Potomac," Brooks observed, "we find ourselves pausing to take breath and discovering that our successes are more prospective than immediate, at least so far as the campaign in Virginia is concerned." The disappointment was palpable. "The great public, like a spoiled child, refuses to be comforted, because Richmond is not taken forthwith, and because we do not meet with an unbroken success at every point," the reporter told his readers. By the beginning of June some observers sounded distinctly uneasy. From Washington, Gideon Welles, secretary of the navy, observed the growing anxiety. "Great confidence is felt in Grant," he noted, "but the immense slaughter of our brave men chills and sickens us all." Others, including the president, spoke in more positive terms. Replying to an invitation to attend a mass meeting of loyal New Yorkers, Lincoln replied that he had to remain in Washington. ("I approve, nevertheless, whatever may tend to strengthen and sustain Gen. Grant and the noble armies now under his direction. My previous high estimate of Gen. Grant has been maintained and heightened by what has occurred in the remarkable campaign he is now conducting; while the magnitude and difficulty of the task before him does not prove less than I expected." He called on everyone to support the general "and his brave soldiers," who were "now in the midst of their great trial."[2])

It was June 3.

As May came to a close, Union columns drew closer to Richmond. Despite the ("constant marching & fighting, such as the Army of the Potomac never experienced before," noted one soldier, the men seemed "spirited & confident of success." On May 29 they encountered Confederates at Totopotomoy Creek, a dozen miles northeast of the Confederate capital. But there would be no battle here. Refusing to assault Lee's works along the creek, Grant decided to continue to slide around the Rebel right. Meanwhile he learned that Baldy Smith with the Eighteenth Corps of the Army of the James was on the way to join him, moving by water to White House, a point along the Pamunkey due east of Cold Harbor. Grant hoped that Lee would take the bait and strike out at Smith, but instead the opposing armies raced toward the crossroads at Cold Harbor, south of the Totopotomoy. No one knew how Cold Harbor got its name. It was not particularly cool, and there was no harbor in sight. Confederate control of that road junction would block Grant's line of march southward toward the James. Although the Rebs won the race, they could not secure their gains, for Sheridan drove them off on May 31. When he learned that more Confederates were on the way, the cavalryman wanted to pull back, but Grant told him to dig in while he hurried reinforcements forward. Sixth Corps infantry arrived on the morning of June 1 just as Sheridan repulsed a second Confederate attack; later that day Smith's men appeared, their belated appearance due to an error in orders.[3]

It was a hot day, and soldiers choked on the dust kicked up by the

devil in the details

marching column. Yet the movement of armies meant that Lee's men could not hide behind earthworks. Grant urged Warren to attack, but once more that general dithered making meticulous preparations, and the opportunity was lost. Captain Adams noted that the lieutenant general "was thinking very hard and looking abstracted, pulling his beard, whittling and smoking" — signs that he was growing impatient. Even Meade was eager to do something, and Grant approved his plan to order Smith and Wright to attack. Wright's corps made some headway against Lee's lines, taking numerous prisoners. Confederate counterattacks elsewhere proved ineffective. Nevertheless, Emory Upton complained that the attack, made with insufficient preparations, was too costly: "Our men are brave, but can not accomplish impossibilities."[4]

Meade's temper began to show. He denounced Warren for acting without orders; then, as Lyman listened with some astonishment, he "said each corps ought to act for itself and not always be leaning on him." In the midst of this tirade, one of Baldy Smith's aides rode up to report that Smith needed ammunition and transportation, and "considered his position precarious." This proved too much for Meade, who exploded: "Then, why in hell did he come at all for?" He complained that Grant's dispositions spread the army out, making it difficult to concentrate to deliver a blow. Later he muttered, "The papers are giving Grant all the credit of what they call successes; I hope they will remember this if anything goes wrong."[5]

Meade is angry

of troops

Grant was more selective in choosing targets for his wrath. As he led his staff toward the Totopotomoy, he came upon a teamster who was beating a horse in a misguided effort to dislodge a wagon that was stuck in wet ground. The profanity that filled the air made Rawlins sound like an altar boy. Grant galloped up, raised his fist, and shouted, "What does this conduct mean, you scoundrel! Stop beating those horses!" The insolent teamster, undeterred, continued whipping the horse, snarling, "Well, who's drivin' this team anyhow — you or me?"

Even though Grant was infuriated at the man's behavior and insubordinate response, the teamster's retort may have struck a deeper chord that resonated with what Grant had endured for weeks. Immediately he ordered the teamster to be tied to a tree for six hours; the fellow showed no regret for his actions as soldiers led him away. The incident upset the general for the rest of the day.[6]

wow

Such disgruntlement, fatigue, and strained nerves did not augur well for coordinating offensive operations. Encouraged by the gains of June 1, Grant and Meade wanted to launch an attack on Lee's right flank early the

see how Overland Camp'n affects peoples' nerves

next day. Orders went out to shift Hancock's corps from the Union right to the left, opposite the point of attack. What seemed a promising opportunity soon dissipated as one of Meade's staff officers mishandled directing the corps to its new position; Hancock's men, exhausted by a night of marching and countermarching, were too tired to play their accustomed offensive role. Meanwhile, Smith insisted that he needed to replenish his ammunition and fodder. By midday it was obvious that the original plan would have to be scrapped. Headquarters rescheduled the attack first for 4 P.M., then an hour later, but by early afternoon Grant, convinced that the men were too tired and that any advance that afternoon would be repulsed, decided to postpone the assault until dawn on June 3. By then the men would be well rested and in position. As Meade had become sensitive about Grant's willingness to issue direct orders to corps commanders, Grant left the planning of the assault to the commander of the Army of the Potomac. Out went orders from Meade announcing the change in plan and instructing his subordinates to "employ the interim in making examination of the ground in their fronts, and perfecting the arrangements for the assault."[7]

These instructions were mere wishful thinking. The command structure was unraveling. Warren argued with his subordinates; Burnside and Meade exchanged testy messages; Smith still smarted from Meade's eruption. Grant contributed to the confusion when he turned down Meade's request to place Burnside subject to Warren's orders, citing Burnside's seniority. His preference — to direct the two corps commanders to cooperate — ignored Warren's protest about such arrangements. Neither corps commander responded vigorously to Confederate forays on their front, even though in advancing the Confederates left the cover of their entrenchments. Grant, greatly annoyed, remarked, "We ought to be able to eat them up"; he wanted generals to show some initiative and not merely repulse the Rebs. That Lee was emboldened to take action at all, contrary to Grant's insistence that he was reluctant to attack, was lost on the Union commander.[8]

Preparations for the major assault were sadly lacking. Meade issued no overall attack order, leaving his corps commanders to plan their advance and reconnoiter the ground. Inevitably this resulted in a failure to coordinate assault columns. When Smith, lacking direction from Meade, offered to work with Horatio Wright in developing a coordinated plan of attack, Wright replied simply that he planned to "pitch in." Corps commanders failed to conduct adequate reconnaissance, leaving the enemy position terra incognita. No one had apparently learned the lessons afforded by May 12.

In leaving matters in Meade's hands, Grant had let them slip altogether. The lieutenant general was so focused on delivering a major blow against his opponent that he ignored intelligence suggesting Confederate morale remained solid. And it was nothing short of stupid to overlook that Lee's men would take advantage of the twenty-four hours of delay to do all they could to improve their position. June 3 would not be June 2.

Many of the men had some inkling of what awaited them. Horace Porter observed soldiers "calmly writing their names and home addresses on slips of paper, and pinning them in the backs of their coats, so that their dead bodies might be recognized on the field." Union soldiers had done the same at Fredericksburg and Mine Run; likewise the Confederates at Gettysburg; these homemade dog tags were by now a standard ritual before battle. The soldiers may not have deemed the assault suicidal, but they knew it would be bloody.[9]

At 4:30 A.M. the Union infantry began moving forward. First reports were encouraging. One of Hancock's divisions actually seized the Rebel position in its front, complete with seventeen guns. But then some depressing reports filtered back. Several divisions reported that they could make no progress; others announced short-term gains followed by retreats. Hancock's triumph was short-lived, as a counterattack drove the bluecoats away. He notified Meade that he doubted that any more progress could be made; Smith requested assistance from Wright; Wright, overlooking the limp performance of his men, reported that he had taken a skirmish line. Meade ordered his commanders to renew their efforts; then he asked Grant for instructions in case things went wrong. "The moment it becomes certain that an assault cannot succeed, suspend the offensive," Grant replied, "but when one does succeed push it vigorously, and if necessary pile in troops at the successful point from wherever they can be taken. I shall go to where you are in the course of an hour."[10]

By midmorning Meade had lost control of the attack. In the face of Hancock's pessimistic reports, the army commander had allowed his subordinates to decide whether to renew the assault. Wright and Smith each argued that whether they would press forward would be up to the actions of the other corps commanders. Finally, Meade ordered Smith and Wright to attack without reference to each other; he instructed Hancock to try one more time. Hancock demurred; Wright and Smith remained in place.

Finally Grant took charge. Although he had promised to see Meade early in the morning, he remained at his headquarters for several hours, digesting dispatches. Meade's handling of affairs disturbed him, for when he finally decided to visit the front, he headed, not to army headquarters, but to the command posts of the corps commanders. Their reports convinced him to call an end to the attack. He did so at 12:30 P.M. in a message to Meade. The army was to consolidate what it had gained and remain in place to prevent Lee from retreating to the Richmond fortifications, for otherwise the Confederate commander might feel safe enough to detach units to counter Hunter's advance toward Lynchburg. A cousin saw him return from the front looking downcast and depressed, aware that what had happened was "bad — very bad." Just how bad, however, remained to be defined by the returns from the front. Attempting to put the best face he could on matters, he told Halleck that the attack had driven the Confederates into their entrenchments, and that Union losses were "not severe" — an estimate that was revised when Dana reviewed the returns. Yet the fighting was not over for the day. In the evening the Confederates launched another assault, only to be driven away by Hancock's men. As the Rebels retreated, the Yankees jeered, "Come on! Come on! Bring up some more Johnnies! You haven't got enough!"[11]

at least day ends on good note for Feds

It was a good question, however, whether there would be enough Yankees after a few more Cold Harbors. "I had immediate and entire command on the field all day," Meade bragged. Grant had left him alone through much of the battle, except for a visit at midday. Others concurred that this was Meade's fight. Charles Wainwright noted that after weeks of reading newspaper accounts "of Grant doing this and that, hardly ever mentioning Meade's name," during this battle Grant had remained out of sight, his name barely mentioned.[12]

Meade's willingness to take credit for the operation — almost to the point of boasting — suggested that not everyone at headquarters appreciated the magnitude of what had happened. Soon after the assault William R. Rowley wrote Washburne that the losses might not reach 3,500, and that, if anything, the results of the fighting so far were "in our favor" (Rowley later revised his estimate upward). Meade himself reported to his wife that the battle ended "without any decided results, we repulsing all attacks of the enemy and they doing the same"; the losses he estimated "about equal on both sides" — approximately 7,500 men. The perspective at army headquarters tended to obscure the reality of the day's events, until full reports came in. "There has been no fight of which I have seen so little as this," commented Lyman. But soon it became clear that the army had suffered a resounding repulse; by nightfall Lyman and others estimated that "we lost four or five to one." Wainwright characterized Meade's order directing each corps to act on its own as "absurd"; whoever issued it "had either lost his head entirely, or wanted to shift responsibility off his own shoulders." In keeping with his unsparing criticism of Grant, how-

see prev. pg

ever, he suspected it was really the lieutenant general's handiwork. "There is much feeling in regard to this murderous & foolish system of assaulting, without supports, reserves, or any adequate force to hold the works that may be carried," one officer growled. Lyman agreed. "I do think there has been too much assaulting, this campaign!" he exclaimed. Only the best men and officers could make such assaults, and they were cut down in droves. The grind of campaigning was beginning to tell. Warren was especially worn out. In exasperation he declared, "For thirty days now, it has been one funeral procession, past me; and it is too much!"[13]

The Second, Sixth, and Eighteenth Corps bore the brunt of the assault on the morning of June 3, although the image of 7,000 men falling within minutes overestimates the losses and underestimates the length of time of the action. Burnside's Ninth Corps had pushed forward in the morning, but Grant's order cut short a planned afternoon advance. Warren's Fifth Corps did little more than stand in place. As evening came, the Confederates launched a few minor attacks of their own, although Union headquarters exaggerated their scale. Confusion as to Confederate intentions continued into the next morning. Lee contracted his left flank, opposite Warren and Burnside, while on the right his men continued to exchange shots with the enemy. Union soldiers worked throughout the day at improving their makeshift fortifications. Both sides kept up a steady rate of artillery fire, and anyone who raised his head to peer over earthworks risked a bullet in the skull. For the moment it looked as if the battle might be renewed by either side.[14]

During the day (June 4) Grant reviewed reports from the front revealing the extent of the setback on the day before. Perhaps as a brief escape from his fearful responsibilities, he set aside time to write his daughter Nellie, thanking her for writing him. Julia had sent him a copy of a picture of Nellie as "The Old Woman in the Shoe," taken at a sanitary fair in St. Louis, showing the little girl wearing spectacles and surrounded by dolls. Only once did he allude to the bloody business before him: "We have been fighting now for thirty days and have every prospect of still more fighting to do before we get into Richmond. When we do get there I shall go home to see you and Ma Fred, Buck and Jess." After offering advice and describing what the family would do together once reunited, he closed the letter with typical fatherly advice: "Be a good little girl as you have always been, study your lessons and you will be contented and happy." Later that day he was entertained by stories of how his brother Orvil reacted when he came under fire during a visit to the front. Although several other civilian members of the party panicked as soon as they came under fire, Orvil, much like his brother, remained composed and calm, choosing to follow the lead of division commander John Gibbon.[15]

Firing continued on June 5. That evening Meade observed, "The enemy has tried his hand once or twice at the offensive, and in each case has been repulsed and severely punished." If firing was sporadic, it nevertheless remained frequent enough to hinder efforts to recover the wounded who remained between the lines. The overwhelming majority of these soldiers were Union wounded. Early that afternoon Hancock asked headquarters whether something could be done to recover these men. Meade forwarded the message to Grant, who authorized Meade to send forth a flag of truce; Meade replied that such a request would have to come from Grant, as the Confederates did not recognize him as being in command. And so Grant wrote Lee. "It is reported to me that there are wounded men, probably of both Armies, now lying exposed and suffering between the lines occupied respectively by the two armies — Humanity would dictate that some provision should be made to provide against such hardships. I would propose therefore that hereafter when no battle is raging, either party be authorized to send to any point between the picket or skirmish line, unarmed men bearing litters, to pick up the dead or wounded without being fired upon by the other party — Any other method equally fair to both parties you may propose for meeting the end designed will be accepted by me —"[16]

This was an awkward proposal. It was unlikely that firing would actually cease completely anywhere; there was nothing in the message about the display and recognition of flags of truce to signify a cease-fire. Lee realized this. "I fear that such an arrangement will lead to misunderstanding and difficulty," he replied. "I propose therefore instead, that when either party desires to remove their dead or wounded, a flag of truce be sent as is customary." It took time for these messages to make their way back and forth, and it was not until the morning of June 6 that Grant, reading Lee's reply, accepted his counterpart's proposal — or so he thought — and suggested that the recovery operation begin at noon and last for three hours. That should have been enough, but Lee wanted more. Specifically, he wanted Grant to first send forth a flag of truce *to request permission for a truce* to bury the dead and recover the wounded. Until then, he would instruct his men to turn back Union stretcher bearers and burial details.[17]

Lee had turned a muddled discussion over how best to recover the dead and wounded into an exercise in military protocol. Most of the dead and wounded belonged to Grant's command, and his initial proposal was inadequate. But to prolong the suffering between the lines in the name of propriety was <u>a bit much</u> — what harm could it have done to accede to Grant's second proposal? More than anything else, <u>Lee wanted the ac-knowledgment of defeat that accompanied a flag of truce.</u> Bowing once more to his foe's requirements, Grant, his impatience barely concealed, replied: "The knowledge that wounded men are now suffering from want of attention, between the two armies, compels me to ask a suspension of hostilities for sufficient time to collect them in, say two hours — Permit me to say that the hours you may fix upon for this, will be agreable to me and the same privilege will be extended to such parties as you may wish to send out, on the same duty, without further application." But the trag-edy was not yet over. Lee did not receive Grant's message until it was grow-ing dark; he set aside a two-hour period, starting at 8 P.M., for a cease-fire, *Yikes.* but that message did not arrive at Grant's headquarters until after the specified period had passed. Another exchange of correspondence was necessary before a cease-fire could be effected. Grant's exasperation showed as he closed his letter, expressing regret "that all my efforts for al-leviating the sufferings of wounded men, left upon the Battle-field have been rendered nugatory." When the armistice finally came, it was of little help, for by now most of the wounded not already recovered by their com-rades were dead, some riddled by bullets from firefights in the aftermath of the assault.[18]

Many biographers and historians have studied this exchange, probably reading too much into it about the character of the correspondents. That what happened was unfortunate is clear; that much of it was unneces-sary was obvious. Lee's final proposal on June 7 was no different from the one Grant had made the previous morning. And not all the dead and wounded between the lines were wearing blue uniforms, for in the confu-sion surrounding the proposed cease-fire on the evening of June 6 Union skirmishers picked up a handful of North Carolinians who were combing the ground for their comrades, including a colonel who had fallen on June 1. Neither general deliberately sought to prolong the human suffer-ing between the lines, and confusion, misunderstanding, and delays in communication contributed to the tragedy. Grant could have made things easier by asking for a truce instead of making his initial problematic pro-posal. Yet Lee seemed to take grim satisfaction in forcing Grant to follow the procedures he outlined.[19] → *in that it didn't go by military protocol*

That both sides needed to engage in such negotiations was due to the persistence of <u>firefights for days after the repulse of June 3.</u> Meade noted that the Confederates "made a furious attack" on the evening of June 5; he added, "we are pretty much <u>engaged all the time,</u> from early in the morning till late at night." Grant himself came under fire from Confederate artillery as he inspected the lines.[20]

Officers and men who had once been willing to do what they were told pondered what had happened at Cold Harbor. Division and brigade commanders freely questioned the actions of their superiors. "I am disgusted with the generalship displayed," Emory Upton snapped. "Our men have, in many instances, been foolishly and wantonly sacrificed. Assault after assault has been ordered upon the enemy's entrenchments, when they knew nothing about the strength or position of the enemy." Upton's comments actually applied, not to June 3, but to June 1, which he termed "a murderous engagement"; in the days that followed, his brigade remained in their rifle pits. Nowhere was the lack of preparation more evident, however, than on June 3, where the failure to have taken advantage of the postponement of the assault on June 2 was inexplicable. Meade might brag that the battle was his to fight, but he failed to prepare for it adequately or to instruct his corps commanders to do so. In turn, the corps commanders had repeatedly left preparations to others or failed to act at all. "Some of our corps commanders are not fit to be corporals," Upton concluded.[21]

And yet one may make too much of these protests. As much as the soldiers may have questioned what happened on June 3, they agreed that it was better to fight than to retreat. Many of them recalled what had happened the last time the Army of the Potomac was on this ground in 1862. "If McClellan were to visit this army now he would not be much flattered by the talk of the soldiers," Horace Porter, who had served under McClellan, noted. "They all say if he had not have retreated with them, himself leading the way, but stood and let them fight it out as Grant is doing they would have been in Richmond two years sooner. Grant is cheered at all points, and every soldier begins to appreciate his indomitable courage." The last statement suggests that perhaps Porter was a bit overoptimistic, as did what followed: "For a day or two we have been luring out the Rebels to attack us, and then driving them back with great slaughter." Still, he maintained that the army was confident and "as cheerful as when we first set out."[22]

In years to come Cold Harbor would become for many people the representative battle of the Overland campaign, a monument to the bloody futility of mindless frontal assaults against an entrenched enemy. Rawlins would supposedly claim that it was all due to the alleged ascendancy of Cyrus B. Comstock at headquarters, for the aide was often fond of proclaiming. "Smash 'em up! Smash 'em up!" But such assessments were wide of the mark (and Comstock's diary offers no support for Rawlins's reaction as reported by James H. Wilson). What happened on June 3 was by no means the bloodiest assault of the campaign or the war; it was not typical of the previous month's operations, which featured flanking and probing for weaknesses; and the repulse did not mark an end to operations or a final defeat for Grant's campaign. But that it was a disastrous failure was clear to all. Grant had taken two chances. Misinterpreting Lee's failure to attack at North Anna as a sign that the Confederates were worn down and ready to crumble, he gambled that one last blow might do the job; he also decided that he should allow Meade to reassert control of his army's movements. What happened demonstrated that Lee's army was still dangerous, even lethal, and that Meade and his corps commanders were not up to preparing for or conducting a major assault. James H. Wilson alluded to this in an unfortunate exchange with Meade: when the Army of the Potomac's commander snarled, "Wilson, when is Grant going to take Richmond?" Wilson shot back: "Whenever the generals and troops in this theater all work together to that end." Grant later admitted "that there had been a butchery at Cold Harbor, but that he had said nothing about it because it could do no good." Instead, he took responsibility for the defeat, and openly stated that he regretted ordering the last assault — not because of the blood shed, but because it was shed in vain to "no advantage whatever."[23]

If Grant was disappointed by the setback at Cold Harbor, the defeat did not shake his confidence in ultimate victory. His brother Orvil came away from a visit to headquarters convinced that "every thing looks favorable, the taking of Richmond is only a question of time." But time was not on Grant's side. At the end of May dissident Republicans assembled in Cleveland to put forth Grant's old superior, John C. Frémont, as a presidential candidate. On June 7, Republicans gathered in Baltimore to nominate Lincoln for a second term as rumors circulated about the setback at Cold Harbor. "We have had severe slaughter," grumbled Gideon Welles, who suspected that Grant was not so able after all. "Brave men have been killed and maimed most fearfully, but Grant persists." A delegation of Missouri Republicans in opposition to Lincoln actually cast their twenty-two votes for Grant as their nominee.[24]

Grant and his generals took stock: for weeks they had worried about the impact of expiring enlistments on the performance of some regiments. As one officer noted the day before Cold Harbor, it was too much to expect soldiers on the verge of leaving to do their job: "It makes all the difference in the world with the mens courage[. T]hey do dread awfully to get hit just as thier time is out." Now entire regiments began to leave, led by the famed Pennsylvania Reserves, Meade's old unit, which departed at the end of May. In the wake of departures and losses it was time to reorganize the units that remained, and the revisions went out in the wake of the June 3 assault. During the pause Grant reassessed his understanding of Lee and his army, for Cold Harbor made it clear that there was still a great deal of fight left in both. "I think Grant has had his eyes opened, and is willing to admit now that Virginia and Lee's army is not Tennessee and Bragg's army," Meade remarked in grim satisfaction.[25]

Meade was more right than he knew. Dana had already wired Washington that Grant had hoped to meet Lee on an open field, but his hope "has been spoiled by Lee's success in avoiding battle upon any equal terms." At first the general was inclined to ordering another assault, but by June 5 he had embarked on a different course. He announced his new tack in a letter to Halleck. "I now find, after over thirty days of trial, the enemy deems it of the first importance to run no risks with the armies they now have. They act purely on the defensive behind breastworks, or feebly on the offensive immediately in front of them, and where in case of repulse they can instantly retire behind them. Without a greater sacrifice of human life than I am willing to make all cannot be accomplished that I had designed outside of the city." He decided to pin Lee in place for a week to allow Sheridan to sweep north and west to cut the Virginia Central Railroad, leaving Lee dependent on his southward rail links for supplies. Grant would then target those lines by sweeping south, crossing the James River, and attacking Petersburg. If David Hunter's column in the Shenandoah could reach Lynchburg and destroy the James River canal to Richmond, all of Lee's supply lines would be cut, forcing him to come out and fight in open terrain — a battle Grant felt sure of winning.[26]

There was risk in Grant's plan. His men would have to disengage from close contact with the enemy and march over miles of roads and two unbridged rivers — the Chickahominy and the James. Lee might attack an isolated corps, or target Butler's men on Bermuda Hundred for an assault. Bridging the James would be no easy task, either, especially if the Confederates dispatched gunboats to the area. Grant would also have to shift his base of supplies. But he had contemplated such a move since the beginning of the campaign, and before Cold Harbor he had made sure that pontoons and bridging material would be waiting for him when he reached the James.[27]

In acting as he did, Grant rejected Halleck's preference that the army remain north of the James to shield Washington from a Confederate attack. To do so would leave his forces dependent on railroads for supplies (and guarding the railroads would drain his command of manpower); Lee would not have to worry about protecting his supply lines running south from Richmond. "My idea from the start," he reminded Halleck, "has been to beat Lee's Army, if possible, North of Richmond, then after destroying his lines of communication North of the James river to transfer the Army to the South side and besiege Lee in Richmond, or follow him South if he should retreat." That explained why from the beginning he had checked on the status of pontoons and siege artillery. Halleck's repeated objections to this line of reasoning were becoming irritating: Porter later recalled that the chief of staff "was rather fertile in suggestions, although few of them were ever practicable."[28]

Gone was any notion of a quick victory, or of a Confederate army about to crack. "This is likely to prove a very tedious job I have on hand," he wrote Julia, "but I feel very confidant of ultimate sucsess. The enemy keeps himself behind strong entrenchments all the time and seems determined to hold on to the last."[29]

On June 6 Sheridan took his horsemen westward to rip up rail lines. The same day Grant called Horace Porter and Cyrus Comstock to his tent and gave them an assignment: find out where the army could cross the James River. Both men were familiar with the region, having served together on McClellan's staff two years before. They scurried off to White House to catch a steamer for the James. As he waited for their return, Grant made plans to take up the railroad laid from White House to the Chickahominy so that the Confederates could not use the rails to repair broken lines elsewhere. Engineers began working on a series of fortified positions by the Chickahominy for protection should Lee attempt to attack. "Every thing is progressing favorably but slowly," he assured Elihu Washburne. "All the fight, except defensive and behind breast works, is taken out of Lee's army. Unless my next move brings on a battle the balance of the campaign will settle down to a siege."[30]

Grant also had to smooth the ruffled feathers of several subordinates. Meade was especially upset. Newspaper report after newspaper report praised Grant and ignored him. He told one officer that "he had worked out every plan for every move from the crossing of the Rapidan onward, that the papers were full of the doings of *Grant's* army, and that he was tired of it, and was determined to let General Grant plan his own battles." Yet what brought matters to a head was a newspaper report that mentioned Meade. On June 2 the *Philadelphia Inquirer* printed a dispatch from correspondent Edward Crapsey that spoke highly of the general: "He is entitled to great credit for the magnificent movements of the army

since we left Brandy [Station], for they have been dictated by him. In battle he puts troops in action and controls their movements; in a word, he
commands the army." However, Crapsey then repeated the (widespread
(and false) rumor that Meade had advised Grant to retreat on the evening of May 6; Grant overruled him and thus "saved the army and the nation, too."[31]

No newspaper article could have been better designed to light Meade's
admittedly short fuse. Crapsey had touched on the two most sensitive areas of the general's ego — that he was an advocate of retreat (echoes of
Gettysburg) and that it was Grant who deserved the credit for the army's
great accomplishments. Even worse, Grant knew Crapsey's family back in
Illinois — proof that the thrust of the article was no accident. Immediately Meade called Crapsey to his tent and demanded that he identify his
source. Sidestepping the inquiry, Crapsey replied that such had been the
talk of the camp — which only made Meade angrier. He decided to make
an example of the correspondent. On June 8, Crapsey found himself tied
up, placed backward on a mule, and exhibited around camp to the beat of
the "Rogue's March," with the words "Libeler of the Press" emblazoned on
a sign hung around his neck. Then he was sent back north. Marsena Patrick, who as provost marshal general had planned the show, thought it
would be "a warning to his Tribe."[32]

Worried about how the newspapers reported his actions, Meade's lashing out assured even worse treatment. "I fear the General will hurt himself
by this," Wainwright remarked, "for these newspaper fellows stick very
close by one another when an outsider attacks them." He was right. For
months reporters ignored Meade altogether, not even mentioning him in
their dispatches — which only made the sensitive Meade more miserable.
No sooner had Crapsey left than Ambrose Burnside proposed similar
treatment for the *New York Times*'s William Swinton. That reporter had offended both Burnside and Hooker; he had gained reentry into the army
by convincing Washburne to introduce him to Grant as a "literary man"
who was going to write a history of the war. Swinton deemed it research to
eavesdrop on private conferences, but Grant did not see matters in the
same light, especially after accounts of those conversations appeared in
Richmond newspapers, and so he ejected Swinton from headquarters in
May. Undeterred, Swinton eventually made his way to Burnside's headquarters and managed to offend Burnside again. Grant, suspecting that
Burnside would shoot Swinton as a spy, decided that it would be better if
Swinton followed Crapsey back home.[33]

Grant also tried to ease Meade's mind about the bulletins issued by the

War Department. He explained that he had composed only a handful of telegrams to Stanton (although he was in error when he said to Meade that he had "never" done so); Stanton drew on Dana's telegrams to compose his news summaries, which he released in the form of dispatches to Major General John A. Dix at New York. Meade was relieved because he had thought that Stanton did not mention Meade's contributions because Grant had not done so (one of Grant's few telegrams had, in fact, recommended Meade for promotion). For the moment, at least, the information tempered his remarks about Grant.[34]

Such incidents distracted the general-in-chief from the main business at hand. Most disturbing was that the Army of the James failed to exploit a wonderful opportunity to seize Petersburg even before Grant was ready to cross the James. It was not the first time that the Union high command had let such an opportunity pass by. At the outset of Butler's advance on Richmond, Smith and Gillmore had proposed to swing south to take Petersburg, but Butler had rebuffed them, preferring to move against the railroad connecting that city with Richmond. In late May Butler hoped to use Smith's corps to take Petersburg, only to lose it when Grant called for Smith to join his command prior to Cold Harbor. It did not help that Butler failed to share his ideas with Grant. Several more plans either to take the city or at least to rip up railroads and destroy bridges over the Appomattox just north of Petersburg proved abortive. When Butler took another stab at the city on June 9, it came as no surprise that it failed. Butler had not consulted with Grant or coordinated his movements with those of Meade and Smith. The hasty assault served only to alert the Confederates to the weakness of the Petersburg defenses, giving them time to shift forces southward.[35]

Grant took little notice of Butler's failure before Petersburg. Eager to take the initiative before Lee did, he decided that he could not wait for Comstock and Porter to return before setting his command in motion. On June 11, he informed Meade and Butler that the move would commence the following evening and laid out guidelines for the line of march. The objective was to cross the James and strike at Petersburg.[36]

Just after midnight Porter and Comstock reported back from their mission. Grant listened carefully to their report, puffing hard on his cigar, impatiently prodding the officers to tell what they knew, even though he had already decided to cross the river at Fort Powhatan, a dozen miles or so downriver from City Point. Porter was not surprised. "This is all part of the original plan explained to me the day before we left Culpepper," he wrote. Perhaps the two aides also discussed Butler's effort to approach Petersburg on June 9; at least they were convinced that Lee could not break the Union lines at Bermuda Hundred, located at the juncture of the James and Appomattox rivers.[37]

In the morning the general and his staff had their pictures taken by Mathew Brady. Grant "appeared with his moustache and beard trimmed close, giving him a very mild air — and indeed he is a mild man, really," observed Theodore Lyman. But when Brady posed the commanding general next to a tree in front of his headquarters tent, the mildness disappeared, to be replaced by a look of quiet but firm determination — the look captured in one of the most famous photographs of the war. That afternoon headquarters shifted southward. When the wagons carrying the tents did not appear that evening, Grant made a fire, and with a board for a mattress and a bag for a pillow, lay down to get some rest. Such simplicity struck Lyman. Grant's grammar might sound twisted to Lyman's Harvard-trained ear, "but he talks it naturally, as much as to say, 'I was so brought up and, if I try fine phrases, I shall only appear silly.'" His prose, "though very terse and well expressed, is filled with horrible spelling." Nevertheless, Grant "has such an easy and straightforward way that you almost think that he must be right and you wrong, in these little matters of elegance." "He is an odd combination," concluded the young Brahmin; "there is one good thing, at any rate — he is the concentration of all that is American."[38]

That night the move got under way. Smith's Eighteenth Corps returned to White House to board transports that would head for Bermuda Hundred. Four other infantry corps began their march. Before long the Chickahominy was bridged at two points. Grant watched as the regiments tramped across the bridges. He maintained his seat "with uncommon grace, controls him with one small gauntleted hand" as he rode forward. "All absorbed, all-observant, silent, inscrutable, he controls and moves armies as he does his horse." Someone reported that some wagons had capsized. Charles Dana began to swear; Grant, looking over, cut him off: "If we have nothing worse than this —" Before long he rode on to the James.[39]

Nothing worse happened. The Fifth Corps peeled off to face westward; the Second Corps pressed onward, followed by the Sixth and Ninth Corps. Late the following morning the head of the lead columns reached the James, where boats waited to ferry the soldiers across. Intelligence reports noted a shift in Confederate forces southward, but Lee's men remained north of the James. Pleased, Grant informed Halleck, "I will have Petersburg secured if possible before they get there in much force. Our movement from Cold Harbor to the James River has been made with great celerity, and so far, without loss or accident." Already that morning he had boarded a steamer and headed for Bermuda Hundred to confer with Butler, returning that afternoon to supervise operations. Meanwhile, work commenced on the pontoon bridge at Fort Powhatan. Late that night it was finished. What the soldiers saw fascinated them. A pontoon bridge, over two thousand feet long, spanned the river. Not a Confederate soldier or gunboat was in sight. "All goes on like a miracle," Dana informed Stanton.[40]

The crossing itself was a military masterpiece. Horace Porter left his readers with a memorable portrait of the general, standing on the north bank of the James on the morning of June 15, "watching with unusual interest the busy scene spread out before him," so much so that for once he was not smoking. What followed was more troubling. Although Hancock's corps was on the south side of the James by the morning of June 15, its rations had yet to arrive. Grant ordered Hancock to march halfway to Petersburg, then await the rations. Establishing headquarters at City Point, on the south shore of the confluence of the James and the Appomattox, the lieutenant general waited for news that Baldy Smith had commenced his attack against Petersburg. Before long he heard gunfire in that direction; the battle was under way.[41]

All day Grant waited for news of Smith's progress. Seeing that the Confederates were at last moving men to Petersburg, he ordered Hancock forward, rations or no. Another corps would be ordered up to bolster the attack. Soon he learned that Hancock's men were not in motion; new orders went out urging him on. The Second Corps commander later claimed that he had no idea that he was to join with Smith in an attack that day. Grant was beginning to sense that another opportunity might be slipping away. "If Petersburg is not captured tonight," he told Hancock, "it will be advisable that you and Smith take up a defensive position and maintain it until all the forces are up. It was hoped to be able to carry Petersburg before the Enemy could reinforce their garrison."[42]

Early on the morning of June 16 Grant rode forward to see for himself what was happening at Petersburg. Gone was the long uniform coat with the double-breasted brass buttons. In its place was a flannel blue blouse with a single row of four buttons; only shoulder straps with the three stars of a lieutenant general distinguished Grant from a private. He saw that Smith's men were in possession of impressive fortifications. If Union forces could build on that achievement, perhaps Petersburg might fall after all. What Grant did not know, however, was that those works had been but lightly held, and Smith, with memories of Cold Harbor still haunting him, had taken most of the day to do anything. Now Smith was sick, and Hancock, who had finally arrived with his corps the previous evening, was in intense pain from the aftereffects of his Gettysburg wound.

Aware that the Confederate defenders were receiving reinforcements, Grant ordered Burnside to bring his corps forward; he told Meade to "hurry Warren up" and to "get here to take command in person." He directed Hancock to consider attacking late that afternoon, and placed him in charge until Meade arrived — a questionable decision in light of Hancock's uncertain health. Then the lieutenant general made his way back to City Point to check on Butler. Encountering Meade, Grant shared what he had found. Encouraged by Smith's progress (he believed that the works Smith had taken were the strongest yet seen in the campaign), he urged Meade to launch an assault at dusk. More good news awaited him, for Butler reported that the enemy had evacuated the works in his front. Federal soldiers pressed forward, and by midday they had actually reached the Richmond and Petersburg Railroad.[43]

Once more, however, the bright light of opportunity dimmed during the day. To reinforce Butler, Grant diverted Wright's Sixth Corps from Petersburg. That weakened the force Meade could assemble for his attack: although he worked hard all day to accomplish something, his assault at 6 P.M. proved disappointing. Smith's gains were meager, and Hancock's corps could make little headway. "Our men are tired and the attacks have not been made with the vigor and the force that characterized our fighting in the Wilderness," Meade observed; "if they had been I think we should have been more successful." He directed Lyman to report the result to Grant. The aide found the lieutenant general, "in shirt and drawers," on the point of going to bed. Sitting on the edge of his cot, the general listened as Lyman detailed Meade's plans for a night attack. At last he allowed himself a smile: "I think it is pretty well to get across a great river, and come up here and attack Lee in his rear before he is ready for us!"[44]

When he arose on June 17, Grant remained optimistic that something could still be done. He ordered Butler to hold on to his gains, and issued instructions for Smith and Wright to swap places; he also approved Butler's request to remove one of his corps commanders, Quincy Adams Gillmore, who had botched the attempt to take Petersburg the previous week. Then he rode forward to consult with Meade and Hancock. Before long he learned that Confederate counterattacks had forced Butler to abandon the gains of the previous day. The news from Petersburg was equally disheartening. Although Burnside launched a successful morning assault, subsequent thrusts by Hancock and Warren did not exploit those gains. The men were tired and uninspired; they wanted nothing to do with assaulting earthworks and hit the ground when they came under fire. "You cannot strike a full blow with a wounded hand," Lyman mourned.[45]

Meade tried once more to take Petersburg on June 18. He would have to do so without Hancock, who was in such pain that he finally told David Birney to take over the Second Corps. Once more the Union attackers achieved early gains, although the result was misleading, for the Confederates had pulled back to consolidate their lines. Moreover, the exhaustion of the men was now palpable. In desperation Meade tried to make one last drive forward at midday. It sputtered. Frustrated, he reverted to the form he had displayed at Cold Harbor. Confessing, "I find it useless to appoint an hour to effect cooperation," he pleaded with Birney to try one more time, but by late afternoon the effort to take Petersburg had ground to a halt. *at least Union is close on P-burg, bc Confs pull back*

"The attack this afternoon was a fiasco of the worst kind," Wainwright observed that evening. "I trust it will be the last attempt at this most absurd way of attacking entrenchments by a general advance in line. It has been tried so often now and with such fearful losses that even the stupidest private now knows that it cannot succeed, and the natural consequence follows: the men will not try it. The very sight of a bank of fresh earth now brings them to a dead halt."[46] *A of P is exhausted* — *USG cannot capture P-burg in one swoop*

Grant did not seem too surprised. Perhaps he realized that he had gotten about as much out of his generals and men as he could reasonably expect — and he had always foreseen the possibility that his campaign would end in the siege it now appeared it would become. "I am perfectly satisfied that all has been done that could be done," he told Meade.[47]

Once more Grant's men had achieved some success; once more they had somehow wasted an opportunity to do more. "If we only *could* have been a little quicker and more driving, we might have had Petersburg at a mouthful," reflected Lyman. Again the command structure had come up short. By entrusting matters to Meade, Grant had taken a risk; despite Meade's best efforts, the result again highlighted his shortcomings in conducting offensive operations. "In all this fighting and these operations I had exclusive command," Meade told his wife, "Grant being all the time at City Point," except for two visits to the front on June 16 and 17. Yet Grant could not be everywhere at once. Between Butler and Bermuda Hundred, Petersburg, and the crossing of the James, he had much to manage, and he had to trust that his generals would do what they could to achieve success.[48] *Meade had command of the P-burg offensive*

Perhaps they did. The men were simply exhausted. "I have never seen the Army so haggard and worn, so worked out and fought out, so dispirited and hopeless, as now when the fall of Richmond is most likely," Captain Charles Francis Adams, Jr., remarked. "Grant has pushed his Army to the extreme limit of human endurance."[49] The same could be said of army, corps, and division commanders. The strain of continuous campaigning was affecting them. Ironically, the sacrifices the army made that spring had so depleted it physically and spiritually that it could not take advantage of the opportunity bought at such a great price. The losses suffered by the Second Corps, for example, were horrifying, ripping through both the ranks and the command structure. Grant had called on those soldiers once too often.

Whether one could be as charitable to the corps commanders was another question altogether. Hancock and Smith came under the most scrutiny. The commander of the Second Corps devoted so much attention to reports critical of his performance that one might wonder why he did not display the same vigor on the field. Hancock was simply too ill to exercise effective command, but the same cannot be said of Smith. "Unless I misapprehend the topography," he had informed Butler on the night of June 15, "I hold the key to Petersburg." However, he had already dropped it that afternoon, spending precious hours conducting a personal reconnaissance, just as in years to come he would spend much time defending his performance. Suffering from the effects of drinking contaminated water while he was at Cold Harbor, he failed to delegate any responsibility. Yet he was determined not to order his men forward until he had obtained a thorough understanding of the ground in front of him, regardless of the time lost in gaining such information through a personal reconnaissance. To avoid the shortcomings in preassault preparation that had marked Cold Harbor, he went too far in the opposite direction, and hesitated to order his men forward at a time when they could have walked into Petersburg. Nor did he improve on his performance the next day, when victory was still possible. Grant had misapprehended Smith's abilities as a combat commander, although he would be slow to realize it.[50]

At Petersburg Grant missed his chance to deliver a decisive blow. Uncertainty and confusion had marked the Confederate response to the crossing of the James. Lee knew that his foe might attempt such a move, but he lacked information about what was happening. Nor did he receive an accurate assessment of matters opposite Petersburg from Pierre G. T. Beauregard, who was in charge of that city's defenses. Nevertheless, Beauregard's skillful management of his small force combined with the hesitancy, procrastination, and confusion of the Union commanders opposite him staved off disaster. At least Lee could take satisfaction in the knowledge that Wade Hampton had checked Sheridan north of Richmond, thus preventing the Union cavalry from sweeping westward to wreak greater damage on Confederate supply lines.

And yet, if Grant had ample cause for disappointment, something had been gained. He had proven that he was not about to give up; setbacks such as that suffered at Cold Harbor simply redoubled his determination to try again. Soldiers might continue to complain about his tactics — and they did — but the vast majority of them did not think that they had failed or were defeated. "Grant will take Richmond, if only he is left alone," concluded Captain Adams from his vantage point at headquarters; "of that I feel more and more sure. His tenacity and strength, combined with his skill, must, on every general principle, prove too much for them in the end."[51]

Adams did not have to wait long for signs that Grant was determined to keep plugging away. Aware that Sheridan was on his way back to him, the lieutenant general decided to order the cavalry already present to embark on an operation to cut Lee's lines of communication south of Petersburg. James H. Wilson was to lead his cavalry on a swing south and west of Petersburg toward Burkeville Junction, forty miles west of Petersburg, where the Southside Railroad from Petersburg crossed the Richmond and Danville Railroad. If Union cavalry ripped up those rail lines, Lee would find it far more difficult to resupply his army. Joining Wilson and his 3,000 riders were another 2,400 cavalrymen from the Army of the James, led by August V. Kautz. They set out early on the morning of June 22. Meanwhile Grant looked to push his command forward so that Union fortifications would reach to the Appomattox River west of Petersburg, tightening the noose around the Confederates.[52]

It was just as well that the general continued to press forward, for on June 21 he received an unanticipated visitor. Abraham Lincoln had decided to see matters for himself. Only a week earlier he had been confident that Grant's crossing of the James would achieve great things. "I begin to see it," he wired Grant. "You will succeed. God bless you all." He had then traveled to Philadelphia, where, reminding an audience at a sanitary fair that Grant had promised to fight it "through on this line if it takes all summer," he added, "I say we are going through on this line if it takes three years more." The crowd cheered; privately, however, the president knew that people were wondering when the war would end. Was victory

Lincoln's visit has some purpose besides goodwill to USG...

imminent? Would it come before the fall elections? How many more battles would have to be fought? How many more men would be killed, wounded, or maimed? He was just as anxious as anyone else to receive answers to those questions, and he decided that the best way to get them was to visit the front. With his son Tad at his side he boarded a steamer and headed toward City Point.[53]

Grant and his staff were sitting outside the general's tent when Lincoln, in his typical black suit, "looking very much like a boss undertaker," in Porter's words, suddenly appeared. The president greeted his general with enthusiasm, for the moment setting aside a bout with seasickness. "I just thought I would jump aboard a boat and come down and see you," he explained. "I don't expect I can do much good, and in fact I'm afraid I may do some harm, but I'll just put myself under your orders and if you find me doing anything wrong just send me away." With a laugh, Grant replied that he would do just that; then he took the president out for a look at the army and a visit with Meade. Not everyone there was happy to see the visitor. "No one knows what he came for," Meade's son, an aide, complained.

The president got his first look at black soldiers in the field when he visited Baldy Smith's camp. "The black troops received him most enthusiastically, grinning from ear to ear, and displaying an amount of ivory terrible to behold," Porter observed. They cheered wildly, crowding around Lincoln, kissing his hand, brushing his coat or his horse so that they could tell others that they had touched the president. And Lincoln was touched. His eyes brimming with tears, his voice broke as he talked with the men; the encounter reminded everyone what was at stake. That night, back at City Point, the president unwound, telling stories, perhaps because Grant had reassured his superior that all was going well. "You will never hear of me farther from Richmond than now, till I have taken it. I am just as sure of going into Richmond as I am of any future event. It may take a long summer day, but I will go in." The next day the president visited Butler's command. Impressed by what he saw, he remarked: "When Grant once gets possession of a place, he holds on to it as if he had inherited it." Still, Lincoln felt a twinge of worry. "I cannot pretend to advise, but I do sincerely hope that all may be accomplished with as little bloodshed as possible." With that he returned to Washington; Attorney General Edward Bates concluded that the president was disappointed that not more had been accomplished.[54]

In fact, all was not going well. On the morning that the president made his appearance, Grant received word that David Hunter's column had been roughly handled at Lynchburg. News of the setback was fragmentary; Grant wanted Hunter "to save his army in the way he thinks best either by getting back into [his] own Dept or by joining us."[55] At the same time he and Meade were struggling to devise a plan to sweep yet again around the Confederate right.

Grant looked to prevent a stalemate by slicing one of Lee's primary supply lines, the Weldon Railroad, which connected Petersburg to North Carolina. Two corps — Hancock's Second and Wright's Sixth — would spearhead the drive. Lee's men were waiting; they exploited a gap between the two corps to inflict significant damage. "Troops did not fight nearly as well as when we started — best officers and best men gone — losses enormous," noted Comstock. "The men are refusing to assault anymore, and the Officers cannot or will not expose *themselves* as heretofore," observed Marsena Patrick. "So far as I can learn," Wainwright reported, "our men broke at once, behaving miserably." At first Grant did not appreciate the dimensions of the setback along the Weldon Railroad; only later did he report that the result "was much worse than I had hitherto learned."[56]

Fifty days of marching, fighting, and dying had taken their toll. Comstock estimated that losses since May 4 were between sixty and seventy thousand. Grant noted that the combat had been continuous. Writing during a lull in the fighting in the aftermath of Cold Harbor, he observed: "War will get to be so common with me if this thing continues much longer that I will not be able to sleep after a while unless there is an occasional gun shot near me during the night."[57]

"The siege of Richmond bids fare to be tedious," the lieutenant general concluded. He called on Halleck to send him more reinforcements from other fronts to enable him to "act offensively." There should be no more sideshows. Every available man should go to support the operations in Georgia and Virginia. And something had to be done to repair the damages to the Army of the Potomac. "As to the next step, I do not know," wrote Theodore Lyman; "Grant is as calm and as apparently sure as ever."[58]

Grant's confidence was remarkable. As if matters were not bad enough, Wilson's raid turned into a fiasco. At first the raiders did their job, burning freight cars and taking up track. However, once the Union horsemen began traveling along the Richmond and Danville line running southwest from Burkeville Junction to Roanoke Station, they encountered resistance. With his horses wearing out and his supplies dwindling, Wilson decided to return to Petersburg. The march was perilous, and at times it

seemed as if the pursuing Confederates would swallow up Wilson's men altogether. That, at least, is what people back at headquarters feared, although Grant remained confident. In the end, Wilson was lucky to return,
having been thrashed at Reams Station on the Weldon line less than ten
miles from Union lines. Wilson's raid goes poorly

The collapse of the Wilson raid marked yet another failure to cut Lee's
supply lines. Grant had hoped much from it; he also entertained notions
that Hunter might soon advance again toward Charlottesville and the
James River canal. Although he wanted to explore the possibility of moving between Petersburg and Richmond, it was becoming clear that the
campaign was evolving into a siege. The crossing of the James, while impressive, had not turned out to be the master stroke Grant had intended.
Nevertheless, the general could now commence waging his war against
Lee's links to the Confederate heartland.[59]

The Northern public did not appreciate the advantages gained over
the past several weeks. In the eyes of many observers, Grant had come up
short. Noah Brooks observed that people's "over-sanguine expectations
are dashed by the tardiness of the grand *coup* which was considered sure
to come." Richmond remained in Confederate hands, and the Army of
Northern Virginia was still ready to do battle. Yet, as Charles Francis Adams, Sr., noted from his post in London, some things had changed. "General Grant shows one great quality of a commander," he observed. "He
makes himself felt by the enemy as well as by his own troops." The once-
confident Confederates were now praying for the salvation of Richmond.
"The only cause of this change of tone is General Grant. If he will go on in
the same line for a while longer, there is no telling what may be the state of
mind to which he will bring them."[60]

A soldier agreed. Edward L. Cook had seen Grant on June 14, when the
general visited Bermuda Hundred as the Army of the Potomac crossed
the James. "He is very plain and unassuming and attracts no notice," he
told his parents. "He wore no sword or other outward trapping except his
buttons and plain shoulder straps. His pants were tucked inside of a pair
of long dusty boots and his whole attire looked dirty & travel stained."
Head forward, eyes looking down, the general "walks with a long slow
stride and slightly emphasized his left foot step" (apparently the result of
his New Orleans accident). "I associated with his appearance the idea or
similee of a huge ponderous iron roller (on a very slightly inclined plane)
which though hard to start yet when once fairly underway by its momen-
tum carried every thing before it and is almost impossible to stop."[61]

True enough. Yet that in itself was not sufficient. Robert E. Lee, who

see prev. pg

had long dreaded a siege, had concluded that once it was under way it would only be "a matter of time" before he had to abandon Richmond. But time was something Grant did not have in an election year. He needed not just to achieve results but to do so in timely fashion. "Our work progresses here slowly and I feel will progress securely until Richmond finally falls," he assured Julia. "The task is a big one and has to be performed by some one."[62]

17

Summer of Discontent

◉

BY THE END OF JUNE Ulysses S. Grant realized that he faced several problems that would tax all his skills as a general. Although he had driven Lee
back to Richmond and Petersburg after a costly campaign and was preparing to lay siege to those cities, many observers saw the result as little more
than a stalemate that could have been achieved with far less bloodshed. "I
fear that the truth is that all the fight is gone out of our men," grumbled
artillerist Charles Wainwright. "Grant has used the army up, and will now
have to wait until its morale is restored before he can do anything." Further direct blows seemed fruitless. People wondered whether the Union
was any closer to victory than when Grant took charge in March; Lincoln's
reelection prospects dimmed.[1]

Disharmony and incompetence, which had thwarted so many chances
for battlefield success, were still in evidence among Union generals in
both the Army of the Potomac and the Army of the James. Grant had
finally rid himself of Sigel and Banks, but to undo the damage their failures had inflicted on his strategic plan would take time. Finally, was Henry
W. Halleck proving more of a help or a hindrance to army operations?

As the days heated up, so did relationships between Grant's subordinates: something was seriously lacking in relations among the leading
officers of the Army of the Potomac. One needed only to look at George
G. Meade's performance to gain insight into the problems. The army
commander had long complained that the press had overlooked his contributions during the spring campaign and steamed when he believed that
Grant and his staff were meddling too much. However, he had failed to
distinguish himself on the battlefield. Several times he had neglected to
ensure that proper preparations were complete prior to launching attacks; after he had committed his men to battle, he lost control of his generals, occasionally throwing up his hands when he could not coordinate
their actions. The general's temper was legendary, and his relations with

346

all his corps commanders save Hancock were shaky.) He thought both
Horatio Wright and Ambrose Burnside were incompetent, and several
times had come close to requesting that Warren be relieved of command, most recently after the failure to take Petersburg. In turn, several
of Meade's subordinates openly questioned his ability. Marsena Patrick
grumbled about the general's "despicable Selfishness & indifference";
Wright cited his assault orders at Cold Harbor and Petersburg as evidence
that they had been ordered "without brains and without generalship." By
early July even Meade confessed that he believed reports that his staff
"would, all, gladly leave him, on account of his temper."[2]

Dissatisfied with Meade's performance at Cold Harbor and Petersburg, Grant knew that the general's high-strung, snappish personality had
caused rifts with his subordinates. Yet the corps commanders were far
from faultless. Even Hancock, who by most accounts was the best of the
lot, had been less than stellar, for he had failed to reconnoiter his front
prior to the assaults of May 12 and June 3 and had proved far too cautious
before Petersburg. It said much about the situation that the ailing Hancock was the least troublesome of Meade's corps commanders. Wright had
yet to show that he was equal to his new responsibilities: when Upton was
complaining about the deficiencies of corps commanders, Wright was his
superior; in the aftermath of the battles of June 22–23, Lyman concluded
that the overcautious Wright was "totally unfit to command a corps."
Much the same had already been said of Warren. Instead of carrying out
orders, he suggested what everyone else should do. Patrick found him "a
very loathesome, profane ungentlemanly & disgusting puppy in power"
(some people thought the same of Patrick). Finally, there was Burnside,
whose performance during the campaign was undistinguished at best. Although he had graciously submitted to Grant's decision to place him under Meade, by the beginning of July the two men were again at odds:
Meade had expressed reservations about a plan, approved by Burnside, to
construct a mineshaft under a portion of the enemy's fortifications, fill it
with explosives, and blow a hole in the Rebel position.[3]

Nor was the quarreling among generals limited to the Army of the Potomac. Ben Butler, Baldy Smith, and Quincy Gillmore were still pointing
fingers at each other for the generally mediocre performance of the Army
of the James — its failure highlighted by the subsequent siege of cities
that once were the army's for the taking. Butler, in fact, had squabbled
with Wright, just as Meade and Smith had exchanged words. In contrast,
Grant had good relations with Sherman and no longer feared that the
Confederates might transfer brigades from the Army of Tennessee to

shore up Lee's army: the Confederates could no longer supply a force of that size.[4] → *bc of the effects of what Union force?*

Although Grant was no stranger to friction among generals, what he saw in the East baffled him. (Victories had been sacrificed because these generals failed to cooperate with each other or to push forward aggressively.) The continuous combat had exposed the shortcomings of the command structure. Once, while the army was still north of the James, Grant asked James Wilson if he knew what was wrong with the Army of the Potomac. Thinking it would be a waste of time to list everything, Wilson instead offered a solution. Load Ely Parker up with whiskey and then let the Seneca chief loose with a scalping knife and a tomahawk with instructions to bring back the scalps of several generals. Grant, smiling, had but one question: which ones? Any six or so would do, Wilson replied; the act in itself would send the message.[5]

There was something to Wilson's suggestion, yet Grant would not easily find capable replacements for his commanders. Besides, (it was not all the fault of the generals. The men were exhausted.) Many soldiers were counting the days until they went home, casting doubt on whether they would give their all one more time. Day after day the men had marched and fought, risking their lives; the heavy losses would be hard to replace either in quantity or quality. (Grant had never put the Army of the Tennessee through such a campaign, nor had he ever faced such a talented and skilled opponent.) Moreover, (Grant sometimes had been too impatient, too optimistic, and a little too impulsive; perhaps he had unrealistic expectations for an army whose talents and shortcomings he was slow to recognize.[6]) → *USG's faults in camp'n*

And yet, despite missing opportunities and making miscalculations, and suffering severe losses, the forces under Grant's command had done much that spring. (The Army of Northern Virginia's casualty list had reached the neighborhood of 35,000 men, soldiers who would be hard to replace.) Although Lee might have several tricks still up his sleeve, he knew it would be very difficult to drive Grant away from Richmond. And, (if Grant had never faced as able an opponent as Lee, the opposite was also true.) Grant's respect for Lee may have grown, but he never allowed his foe to gain the upper hand psychologically, an advantage Lee had skillfully exploited against Grant's predecessors.

Thus if Grant had not achieved all he had set out to do that spring, he nevertheless had reason to be satisfied with what he had accomplished. "You people up North now must be of good cheer," he reminded J. Russell Jones. "Recollect that we have the bulk of the Rebel Army in two grand

right. rt past

Lee's casualties

true -

AofNV) Confs @ Atlanta

Armies both besieged and both conscious that they cannot stand a single
battle outside their fortifications with the Armies confronting them. The
last man of the Confederacy is now in the Army. They are becoming discouraged, their men deserting, dying and being killed and captured every
day. We loose to but can replace our losses. If the rebellion is not perfectly
and thoroughly crushed it will be the fault and through the weakness
of the people North. Be of good cheer and rest assured that all will come
out right."[7]

[handwritten: → does this cause USG to take unnecessary offensives + butcher his men?]

As Grant penned these words, he was pondering his next move against
Lee. Although he now accepted that he would have to commence siege
operations, (he still looked for a way to get the upper hand, either by
launching a direct attack on Lee's lines or by striking at Rebel railroads)

[handwritten margin: had wanted to take p-burg after crossing James]

It would not be easy to renew operations. The men were tired, the generals were bickering, and the weather turned beastly warm. In the absence
of rain, fine dust irritated men's eyes and throats and dirtied water. It was
particularly bad on June 29, when Grant visited his corps commanders to
learn more about the present situation. Ben Butler accompanied him. Arriving at the headquarters of Ambrose Burnside, a general well known for
his abundant supply of whiskey, Grant, suffering from a headache, helped
himself to a drink. Then Grant and Butler went on to Baldy Smith's headquarters. Although Smith claimed he kept no liquor at headquarters,
when Grant asked for another drink Smith served him — twice — first
from a bottle "which had been sent as a present sometime before and no
other," then from a second bottle "of very common brandy" which Smith
claimed was there because one of his generals was afraid of drinking contaminated water. Leaving Smith's tent, Grant made his way back to his
headquarters, but (so Smith said) the general vomited over his mount before arriving "in the most disgusting state."[8] *[handwritten: USG drunk]*

No one else ever mentioned the incident, although if Smith was to be
believed, it was a most public exhibition. And it did seem curious that
Smith attributed what happened to some elaborate blackmail plot by Butler — for it had been Smith who served Grant two drinks. After all, if Butler had guided Grant from corps headquarters to corps headquarters in
an effort to get him intoxicated, why did they visit Smith's tent if that general "kept no liquor"? Indeed, the only person who sought to turn the incident to his advantage was Smith. Eager to have Grant act favorably on his
request for a leave of absence, he notified Rawlins of what had happened
in his tent. The chief of staff replied stiffly that he appreciated Smith's
"friendly forethought" and interest in Grant, adding that "it is only what

one knowing your friendship for him might have expected." In light of Rawlins's suspicions about Smith's loyalty and trustworthiness, this was a loaded phrase. "Being thus advised of the slippery ground he is on, I shall not fail to use my utmost endeavors to stay him from falling. Your application for a leave of absence will be presented to the General for his favorable consideration." In short, Rawlins thought it might be a good idea if Smith went away for a while.[9]

As Smith himself later admitted, he provoked hostility in others: "I had a bad habit of saying what I thought and was in hopes that if I were away things might go on more smoothly." He demonstrated the necessity for the latter by engaging in the former. On July 2 he advised Grant to remove Butler from command and offered a critical assessment of the Army of the Potomac, adding that disharmony among his generals was "one of the causes of want of success." Of Butler he wrote: "How can you place a man in command of two army corps, who is as helpless as a child on the field of battle, & as visionary as an opium eater in council [?]"[10]

Grant had been contemplating what to do with Butler for some time. (He was convinced that the Massachusetts general lacked the ability to exploit opportunities and to work well with subordinates.) Yet changing Butler's assignment presented political problems. In late June Charles Dana visited Washington to discuss the Butler dilemma and to learn what Grant's civil superiors would permit him to do. Returning to City Point on July 1, he briefed Grant. The general then explained the situation to Halleck. "Whilst I have no diff[i]culty with Gen. Butler, finding him always cle[ar] in his conception of orders, and prompt to obey," he wrote, choosing his words carefully, "yet there is a want of knowledge how to execute, and particularly a prejudice against him, as a commander, that operates against his usefulness." If Butler stayed, Smith, who was — according to Grant — "one of the most efficient officers in service, readiest in expedients an[d] most skilful in the management of troops in action," would have to go. Perhaps Butler could be reassigned to a department where his skills at managing "a dissatisfied element" would be of use — somewhere far away from the front.[11]

Halleck's reply on July 3 carried with it echoes of his previous remarks about Nathaniel Banks. "It was foreseen from the first that you would eventually find it necessary to relieve Genl. B on account of his total unfitness to command in the field, and his generally quarrelsome character," he wrote. The possibility of reassignment had already been "a matter of consultation," but those who partook in such discussions (Halleck did not identify them) thought that the reassignment Grant had suggested would cause more trouble than it was worth. Halleck then offered his own idea. Why not reorganize the department so as to separate Smith and Butler? Grant could establish Butler's headquarters at Fort Monroe while creating an independent command, denoted the Eighteenth Corps, for Smith.[12] *Halleck does not approve Butler's removal*

Halleck's convoluted solution showed that he was confused about the structure of the Army of the James and Smith's present command (none other than the Eighteenth Corps). It would have been better to suggest removing the Army of the James from Butler's department and turning it into an independent field army, much like the Army of the Potomac. Instead, what Grant proposed on July 6 was to order Butler to his headquarters at Fort Monroe, leaving Smith in command of the troops in the field (the Tenth and Eighteenth Corps). Halleck failed to translate that intent into an order.[13] *reorganization, Smith now commands AofJ troops* *what Dept. is Butler head of?*

Absent from this discussion was any direct correspondence between Lincoln and Grant. The president distanced himself from the entire incident, with good reason. He had just accepted the resignation of Secretary of the Treasury Salmon P. Chase, a favorite among many Radical Republicans, and had decided not to sign the Wade-Davis Bill, which embodied the notions of many congressional Republicans about reconstruction. These acts sparked criticism of the administration, and several Republicans contemplated a call for a second presidential nomination. Perhaps Lincoln could be induced to step aside; if not, perhaps Radical dissidents could rally behind another man. In these circumstances, to offend Benjamin Butler could prove very dangerous to Abraham Lincoln's chances of reelection. Everyone at City Point was reminded of the interplay between political and military decisions when a delegation of senators and congressmen led by Benjamin F. Wade arrived on July 6. Wade (a Radical) chaired the Joint Committee on the Conduct of the War, an entity that had investigated the operations of the army before, most recently in the case of Gettysburg (as Meade remembered all too well); he was also the co-sponsor of the reconstruction bill Lincoln had just refused to sign.[14]

The politicians came at a particularly bad time. Meade was flailing away at everyone. He was angry when he learned that Grant wanted Marsena Patrick to assume the position of provost marshal for all the armies operating against Richmond (as a way of exercising control over Butler's administration of military justice) without removing him from his position with the Army of the Potomac. Meade snapped that Patrick was welcome to leave, but he refused to "share" Patrick with Grant. At the same time he

Meade / USG = disharmonious

picked a fight with James H. Wilson over the behavior of Wilson's troopers during their recent raid. And now the very senators who had questioned his generalship at Gettysburg were poking around headquarters.

Rumors circulated that the commander of the Army of the Potomac was "quarreling with all his subordinates." Grant pondered whether it was time to replace Meade with Hancock, a decision endorsed by Dana. "Grant has great confidence in Meade, and is much attached to him personally," the assistant war secretary told Stanton, "but the almost universal dislike of Meade which prevails among officers of every rank who come in contact with him, and the difficulty of doing business with him felt by every one except Grant himself, so greatly impair his capacities for usefulness and render success under his command so doubtful that Grant seems to be coming to the conviction that he must be relieved." Nor was this simply a matter of Meade's disposition. "His order for the last series of assaults upon Petersburg, in which he lost 10,000 men without gaining any decisive advantage, was to the effect that he had found it impracticable to secure the co-operation of corps commanders, and therefore each one was to attack on his own account and do the best he could by himself," Dana reported. "Consequently each gained some advantage of position, but each exhausted his own strength in so doing, while for the want of a general purpose and a general commander to direct and concentrate the whole, it all amounted to nothing but heavy loss to ourselves."[15]

Moreover, the generals' ongoing war against the correspondents had recently escalated. At the end of June Hancock, who was becoming all too aware of newspaper criticism of the Second Corps' performance at Petersburg, called Meade's attention to a report filed by William H. Kent with the *New York Tribune*. Fortunately for Kent, he had left the army before he could be ejected in style. Although Grant took note of the grievance, he could not let pass Meade's assertion that he had failed to inform Meade and Hancock of the plan for that day; he struck out a sentence which made that point explicit, for that would only add to the growing friction. The commanding general heard rumors that William Swinton had reappeared; out went orders prohibiting either correspondent from returning to the army. His generals seemed much better at reading newspapers than in following orders, and more concerned about protecting their reputations than in achieving the sort of victory that would render all criticism academic.[16]

Complaints that the newspapers got the story wrong were not new. However, Meade and Hancock in particular were sensitive to their criticism and worried that the performance of their men (and themselves) would be tarnished forever by bulletins from the front. No stranger to the barbs of reporters and editors, Grant had learned better ways to counter such coverage. It was no accident that Sylvanus Cadwallader of the *New York Herald* was a favorite at his headquarters and believed himself to be a trusted confidant of the commanding general. In turn, other commanders courted *Herald* correspondents, even including a seat at officers' messes. Cadwallader went a step further, opening up his own elaborate mess at City Point, complete with good food and cigars. Officers and couriers loved the treatment, and Cadwallader cultivated news sources and gathered information, secure in the knowledge that no one would eject him from Union lines.[17] →see p 351

In the midst of all this, (Grant's effort to restructure the relationship between Ben Butler and the Army of the James completely fell apart.) News of Halleck's flawed directive, known as General Orders No. 225, was leaked to Butler, who learned of it on July 9, only two days after it had been prepared. It called for the troops in Butler's command "serving with the Army of the Potomac" to be formed into the Eighteenth Corps, to be commanded by Smith, while Butler would exercise command over "the remainder of the troops in that department" from headquarters at Fort Monroe. → right.

Halleck, that skilled authority on military protocol, had so muddled the wording of the order as to make things worse. Oblivious to the presence of the Tenth Corps, the directive left it unclear whether it was to be merged with the existing Eighteenth Corps to form a new corps under Smith. Otherwise, the order made no sense at all, for the Eighteenth Corps already existed, and Smith already headed it. Instead of simplifying matters, the order complicated them; Lincoln and Stanton had reviewed it, but whether it had yet been formally issued was an unanswered question.[18]

It was a frustrating time for Grant. Meade, Butler, and their corps commanders were involved in both overt and covert controversy; Wade and his fellow committee members were sniffing around camp; now Halleck had botched his job. That there was a war on seemed to escape everyone else's attention. One might excuse the lieutenant general for deciding that perhaps it was time for a stiff drink. William B. Franklin, who was hovering around headquarters in hopes of gaining an assignment, told Smith that Grant was imbibing (Franklin loved to gossip about the general's personal habits). The next day the two men visited City Point, sought out Rufus Ingalls, who had taken charge of a large white house on the bluff, and asked for a drink. Ingalls told him he would hunt up some whiskey; Franklin and Smith entered the dining room, where they found "a pitcher, two tumblers, and a bottle" — evidence, Franklin said, that Grant had been drinking with his old West Point classmate. Grant appeared a moment later, followed by Ingalls; the lieutenant general helped himself to some brandy.[19] *USG drinking*

In later years Smith claimed that he was so angry at seeing Grant drink that he had to say something; however, he decided to hold forth, not on the general's drinking, but on Cold Harbor. Even Franklin thought his friend was rather severe. The next morning, July 9, Smith informed Rawlins that Ingalls was providing Grant with alcohol; then, in a moment of true inspiration, he declared: "I will support no one after I am convinced that we cannot win with him." This cast a new light on the nature of his concern. After all, the last time Franklin and Smith had joined forces, it was to intrigue against Ambrose Burnside after Fredericksburg — an act that led to their transfer elsewhere. Smith was already snarling about Butler and Meade; was Grant next? Smith chose to denounce Meade to Grant once more, explaining: "I wanted only to have General Grant act in such a way as to prevent disastrous results coming from the jealousies of small minded leaders whose first regard was for themselves and the second for the country perhaps." His mission accomplished (although not as he had intended it), Smith headed for New York to visit his sick wife.[20]

complicated army intrigue

Smith's performance played right into Butler's hands, for it raised questions about Smith's ability to get along with anyone. Perhaps elevating him would be premature. The next morning Butler, having been provided with a copy of General Orders No. 225 by an informant, met with Grant to discuss it. Butler wanted to know what was behind the order; Grant replied that it should not have been issued and immediately wired Halleck to suspend it. Better, he argued, to keep Smith in charge of the existing Eighteenth Corps, formally appoint a new man to head the Tenth Corps, and add the Nineteenth Corps (currently scheduled to be transferred to Virginia from Louisiana) to the Department of Virginia and North Carolina. Franklin (not Smith) would be assigned to command in the field under Butler's supervision. Pleased that he had thwarted both Halleck and Smith (and not associating Grant with the order), Butler left happy. He believed that Grant was on his side, and several days later assured Grant of his friendship. Nothing was said about Grant's drinking; Baldy Smith had done himself in.[21] *→ see above ¶*

AofJ reorg

One would never have guessed from Grant's struggles with Meade, Halleck, Butler, and Smith that anything else was going on. But there was.

lol so many people

Indeed, a crisis loomed that demanded Grant's immediate attention, for a Confederate column was approaching Washington.

Much was made of Grant's daring action in crossing the James, yet when he took that chance, so did Lee — by detaching Jubal Early and an entire corps from his army. Old Jube's first mission was to check David Hunter's advance, and he did so on June 18 at Lynchburg. But it was Hunter's decision to retreat westward, away from the Shenandoah (and everything else), that opened up an ideal opportunity for Early to pursue Lee's second objective — to disrupt Grant's offensive by crossing the Potomac and either invading the North or threatening Washington itself. Lincoln was always sensitive about Washington's security, and rightly so, especially in an election year; moreover, since Grant had drawn heavily from the forces garrisoning Washington for reinforcements, the capital was vulnerable to attack if Early arrived before the Union high command could react.

Grant knew that Early had left Lee's army to confront Hunter, but he assumed after Lynchburg that the Confederate expeditionary force had returned to the Richmond/Petersburg area. "Early's corps is now here," he declared on July 3; he was more interested in planning his next move against Lee. However, the next day intelligence reports located Early in the Shenandoah and predicted that he was headed north across the Potomac — perhaps toward Washington's weakened defenses. Although Halleck took satisfaction in having his forecast of a Rebel advance fulfilled, he was slow to assess the situation or call for troops.[22]

Finally Grant responded. On July 6 James B. Ricketts's division of the Sixth Corps departed for Washington, followed several days later by the rest of the corps. Next Grant decided to divert the Nineteenth Corps, earmarked for the Army of the James, to Washington. He had counted on those men to stretch Lee's lines below Petersburg to the breaking point; he had turned down suggestions to do it with the force on hand. Now he saw in Early's raid a chance to catch a significant part of the Army of Northern Virginia outside entrenched positions. "We now want to crush out and destroy any force the enemy have sent north," he told Halleck. "Force enough can be spared from here to do it."[23]

If Grant had to leave the Petersburg front for any reason, Butler, by virtue of his seniority in rank, would command both his army and the Army of the Potomac. Yet Lincoln, anxious to dispose of Early, wanted Grant to do just that. He suggested that his general-in-chief take charge of matters around Washington "and make a vigorous effort to destroy the enemie's force in this vicinity." That thought had crossed Grant's mind on July 9, but by the time the president's message arrived, Grant had met with But-

[handwritten margin notes: "no kidding — Butler would have probly messed up in USG's absence"]

ler and Smith. For the general-in-chief to leave now would be one command crisis too many. He decided to stay at City Point, informing Lincoln that "it would have a bad effect for me to leave here." Besides, he believed that with the force at hand "the enemy will never be able to get back with much of his force."[24]

Lee hoped that Grant might decide to counter Early's thrust by launching yet another attack on Lee's lines. Grant, however, had no intention of complying with his foe's wishes — although he almost did so on hearing a rumor that a second corps was on its way to join Early. One of the reasons he decided not to go to Washington himself was because he thought that was "probably just what Lee wants me to do."[25]

The Sixth Corps debarked in Washington just as Early's men, having pushed aside a patchwork defense force under Lew Wallace at Monocacy, Maryland, approached the outskirts of the capital from the north. After some fighting on July 11, Early pulled back, returning to Virginia on July 14. It had been a near-run thing. Aware how his own policy of stripping the Washington defenses of men and his belated discovery of Early's departure had contributed to the crisis, Grant displayed "considerable anxiety and uneasiness" as he awaited word from the capital. The opportunity to destroy the Confederates failed to materialize. Halleck was to blame. Confident that Early had been checked, Grant requested Halleck to place Wright in command of the pursuit force. "Boldness is all that is wanted to [drive the] enemy out of Maryland in confusion," he told Dana, now in Washington. But it was not to be. Once more Halleck was far more confident and free with advice as an armchair strategist than he was when any enemy forces were in proximity — at which times rumor had it that he sought to fortify himself with alcohol. Wright found it difficult to amass a force drawn from several commands and mount a pursuit while responding to directives from Washington telling him to shield the city; Grant could not do much from City Point; and Halleck would not take any initiative, resting content with promising to carry out Grant's directives (and doing a bad job of that). As Dana put it, "Gen Halleck will not give orders except as he receives them — The president will give none, and until you direct positively and explicitly what is to be done everything will go on in the deplorable and fatal way in which it has gone on for the past week."[26]

Just how obstinate Halleck could be became apparent after Early withdrew. Grant decided that Hunter's force — which had finally shown up after its roundabout retreat — would be sufficient to prevent another northward Confederate excursion. If the Sixth Corps and the Nineteenth Corps could get back to City Point, Grant might be able to do something

[handwritten: USG plan]

to Lee before Early arrived back in Richmond. To implement this plan, Grant sent staff officer Cyrus Comstock to Washington. Halleck welcomed him by asking, "in a rather sneering way, . . . when were we going to take Richmond." Once more the chief of staff presented his case for laying siege to the Confederate capital from the north in order to shield Washington. To send the two infantry corps down to City Point would simply invite Early to make a return visit. They would remain where they were until it was confirmed that Early had rejoined Lee. Accepting that, Grant found himself frustrated again when he directed that the forces around Washington advance toward Gordonsville and Charlottesville. Nothing happened. Someone had to coordinate military operations in the Washington area with the goal of destroying Early's force and taking the Shenandoah Valley out of the war. Until Grant resolved this situation, he would not be able to continue pressing against Lee.[27] *[handwritten: USG has to focus on Early's force]* *[handwritten right margin: thus ruining USG's plan]*

What happened around Washington affected Grant's efforts to revamp his command structure on the banks of the James. Instead of placing Franklin in field command of Butler's forces, he would put him in charge of the forces around Washington. Even that proposition was almost derailed when Franklin temporarily fell prisoner to Early's men (although he managed to escape). *[handwritten: woah]*

It would have been much better all around had the Confederates kept a better eye on their captive. Exactly why Grant was so confident of Franklin's abilities remains something of a mystery. Franklin had been Grant's classmate at West Point, and Smith had often spoken highly of him, but his record was at best mixed. At Fredericksburg his ineptitude had contributed to the Union defeat, and his most notable quality was an interest in intrigue that made him a perfect sidekick for Smith; Franklin had doubtless taken advantage of his recent visit to City Point to press his claims for a command. In later years people would make much of Grant's keen judgment in selecting generals. Franklin and Smith offer the discerning observer reason to pause.

However, if Franklin was to go elsewhere, there would be no buffer between Baldy Smith and Ben Butler. One of them would have to go. Perhaps Butler had told Grant that he would not go quietly; in any case, Grant had by now heard enough about Smith's critical remarks to decide that he could promote harmony by removing Smith from the scene.[28]

Baldy Smith had prepared the way for his own rapid fall from grace by talking too much about others and doing too little himself. Grant had entertained second thoughts about Smith's performance at Petersburg when he learned that the reason Smith had overrun a rather impressive set of earthworks was because they were thinly held. Had Smith pressed forward instead of pulling up, Petersburg might have fallen in June. Now Grant had to confront the fact that Smith had denounced both Meade and Butler as incompetent in language that implied the general-in-chief was a fool to retain them.[29]

Smith, aware that something was afoot, reported back for duty at City Point on July 19. Grant was waiting to see him. It was not a pleasant encounter. The lieutenant general told him that he was relieved of command. He offered a series of explanations, emphasizing Smith's talent for fostering disharmony. Smith remained unsatisfied. Finally, Grant spoke bluntly: "You talk too much."[30] *Smith relieved f command*

That this last retort was only too true was evident from Smith's reaction. Unable to see that it had been a combination of his own incompetence and his willingness to criticize others that had made him expendable, Smith concocted a series of rationalizations for his removal, each of which involved Grant's drinking. Perhaps, he argued, Butler had saved himself and secured Grant's removal by threatening to broadcast the fact that Grant had drank himself sick on his tour of corps headquarters. Perhaps Ingalls, smarting from a reprimand from Rawlins about providing the general with alcohol, had gone to the general and ratted on Smith. Butler denied the blackmail story (and Smith forgot that he, not Butler, had provided Grant with two drinks on June 29). Smith simply could not face that once more he had self-destructed, thanks in large part to his infinite capacity for intrigue and his compulsion to assail others. Ever since the beginning of June, Patrick noted, "he has quarreled with Meade & every one else, ending in an attempt to trash Grant over Meade's shoulders, for which Grant shut him up — The discovery that he has been plotting against Grant himself, within the last 20 days, has brought matters to a head."[31]

John Rawlins provided the most effective rebuttal to Smith's allegation that his removal was connected to Grant's drinking. He knew that Grant had taken a drink on June 29; indeed, if Smith was to be believed, Rawlins saw an intoxicated commander return to headquarters. Yet Rawlins approved of Grant's action in relieving Smith "because of his spirit of criticism of all military movements and men, and his failure to get along with anyone he is placed under, and his disposition to scatter the seeds of discontent throughout the army." Indeed, it had been Rawlins who had provided Grant with evidence of such fractiousness when he shared with Grant letters in which Smith had questioned Grant's campaign plans for 1864. Perhaps he sensed that Smith was one of those people who put him-

↳ see the letter

self first and the country second. As Lyman put it, "Thus did Smith the Bald try the Macchiavelli against Butler the cross-eyed, and got floored at the first round!"[32]

Bursting with confidence, Butler paraded around headquarters, claiming that the Democrats had asked him to run for president. Patrick remarked that the general "is playing everyone, to get some power over each individual." He had reason to do so. Whatever other intentions Grant had about reorganizing Butler's command soon fell by the wayside. Camp scuttlebutt had it that there were "complications at Washington." Grant had to rest content with providing new corps commanders (Edward O. C. Ord for the Eighteenth Corps and David Birney for the Tenth Corps) whose working relationship with Butler had to be an improvement on that of their predecessors. It would be up to Grant to keep a closer eye on Butler himself.[33]

Having decided what to do with the Army of the James, Grant returned to the issue of what to do about the situation at Washington. Hearing no response to his proposal to put Franklin in charge, Grant repeated it, whereupon Halleck replied that Franklin would not be satisfactory (Stanton had held up the appointment). Grant then took his case to Lincoln. It was necessary, he insisted, to secure unity of command of the forces outside Washington. Aware that Franklin was no longer a viable choice, he then suggested Meade, a move that might help resolve another one of his command problems. Patrick observed, "The jealousy on the part of corps commanders against each other and against Meade — especially the bad blood that exists between Meade & Burnside — prevents any unanimity of counsels, or concert of action, even among the troops belonging to the Army of the Potomac." Sending Meade to Washington would remedy that situation. Hancock would replace Meade; John Gibbon would take over the Second Corps. "Many reasons might be assigned for the changes here suggested," Grant remarked, "some of which I would not care to commit to paper, but would not hesitate to give verbally." He sent Rawlins to meet with Lincoln to elaborate on his reasoning.[34]

The confusion continued. Unable to get Halleck to take charge of the Washington forces — Halleck never quite got over that Grant was now the one issuing the orders — Grant prodded Stanton into directing Halleck to do so. Nothing happened. At the same time, signs of renewed activity by Early's command meant that the Sixth Corps and the Nineteenth Corps would not be sent to City Point. The president, taking Grant's hint, decided that it was time to talk with his general. Stanton proposed a meeting at Fort Monroe on July 30; Grant requested that the conference take place twenty-four hours later, for he would have to be at the front that day.[35]

Back on July 4 a soldier had scribbled in his notebook a remark attributed to Grant: "He says he could take Petersburgh and Richmond at any time but he would have to lose a great many men, and that he can take it a great deal easier by laying still and watching them." But Grant was never much for "laying still" for long, and a siege would look like a stalemate in the eyes of the Northern electorate. He began to probe for weak spots in Lee's lines, the idea of a full-scale assault preceded by elaborate preparation never far from his mind. If he could not change his commanders, at least he would make sure that they did their jobs. If he failed to penetrate the enemy trenches, Grant would have to swing around Lee's right yet again to sever his rail connections to the south and west.[36]

USG's plan

With these alternatives in mind, Grant considered Ambrose Burnside's proposal to blow apart the enemy lines — literally. Among the regiments of the Ninth Corps, the Forty-eighth Pennsylvania, under Colonel Henry Pleasants, was composed of coal miners from the western part of the Keystone State. They had been digging a shaft underneath the enemy trenches on their front with the intent of placing explosives at the end of the shaft. Meade and his staff officers dismissed the scheme as impractical, but Grant, who had mined Pemberton's lines at Vicksburg, was more receptive to the plan, especially when no one else had a better idea.

Burnside's mine plan took hold in part because flanking movements would require too many men. Moreover, Grant soon learned that Sherman's men were under attack outside Atlanta. It was of the utmost importance to make sure that Lee did not send men to reinforce the new Confederate commander there, John Bell Hood. Grant, who had taken Sherman's predictions of imminent success at face value, wondered what had stalled the progress of his favorite lieutenant, especially after Jefferson Davis replaced the cagey Joe Johnston with the aggressive Hood, who seemed all too eager to forgo the protection of fortifications. And then there was the staggering news that James B. McPherson had been killed on July 22. As Grant read the dispatch, "his mouth twitched and his eyes closed as if he were shutting out the baleful words. Then the tears came and one followed the other down his bronzed cheeks as he sat there without a word of comment"; for several days afterward he shared his recollections of his faithful lieutenant. Such reflections reminded him all the more forcibly of the contrast between his old comrades and his new associates.[37]

strategy

Grant realized that in the North the prevailing impression of Union arms was one of failure, defeat, and stalemate. Gone were the optimistic predictions of the spring, replaced by a sense of frustration and weariness with the struggle. Stanton and Halleck cited Early's raid as evidence that Grant had failed, and that the siege of Petersburg was a mistake because it left Washington vulnerable — a point that was sure to count for something with the president. There was talk that someone was going to have to pay with his job. Meade seemed the obvious choice. Grant himself had contributed to the situation by informing Lincoln during the president's visit to the front in June that he did not need any more men. That was before it was apparent that there would be a long siege. To break the stalemate now, Grant estimated that he required 50,000 men, an implicit admission that Lee's detachment of Early had derailed the arrival of reinforcements earmarked for Grant's command.[38]

Unwilling to rely solely on Burnside's project, Grant first wanted to see what would happen if he pushed against Lee's left north of the James. Once more he called on the Second Corps to spearhead the movement. Hancock's men would recross the James and advance north against Confederate fortifications at Deep Bottom, a position along the north bank of the river due north of Bermuda Hundred. If Hancock could drive the Rebels westward, he might open a part for Sheridan's horsemen to strike northward toward Richmond; otherwise, the Union cavalry might circle eastward before heading north with orders to destroy the railroads north of the enemy capital. Even if this move backfired, it might compel Lee to shift his forces to strengthen his left, rendering the lines at Petersburg vulnerable.[39] → USG plan

The Second Corps commenced marching on July 26, and the next day approached Deep Bottom. The Confederates were there in force. Although Hancock's men scored several initial successes, enemy reinforcements arrived promising a harder fight. Riding to the front to assess the situation, Grant decided that such a fight would prove too costly. Perhaps he also concluded that Hancock's command was not ready to make such a fight, for Comstock suspected that the men were still suffering the aftereffects of their rough handling the previous month near the Weldon Railroad. The following day Confederate resistance stiffened even more, while Sheridan's expedition fizzled. Nevertheless, something had been achieved. As expected, the strike north of the James caused Lee to shift men to counter it, leaving a smaller force to defend Petersburg. Grant was cheered by that information. "I am yet in hopes of turning this diversion to account so as to yeald greater results than if the first object had been accomplished," he told Halleck. It was time to spring Burnside's mine.[40]

What happened next was a tribute to the inability of the generals of the

author's summary of mine disaster

Army of the Potomac to set aside personal differences and to pull together to achieve a common goal. Patrick, aware of the friction between
Meade and Burnside, thought that it "will prevent Meade, probably, from
taking hold, with any vim, to carry out Burnside's idea." The provost marshal was right. *before it happened* To his credit, the Ninth Corps commander had pondered
long and hard on how to exploit the opportunity presented when the
mine breached the enemy's defenses. Simply to advance into the gap created by the explosion promised disaster. The detonation would destroy a
portion of the Confederate line that bent back, rendering any column
that rushed forward to occupy it vulnerable to fire on both flanks. The assault force would need to advance toward the edges of the hole created by
the mine's detonation, with orders to swing out and roll up the flanks of
the defending forces on both sides of the gap while other attackers continued forward to occupy a hill in the Confederate rear. The plan called for
training and rehearsal, and Burnside thought he had found the ideal
force for such a mission, a division of soldiers eager for action: the black
troops under the command of Edward Ferrero.[41]

The idea of using black soldiers to spearhead an attack in Virginia was
novel but not entirely new, for black regiments from the Army of the
James had participated in the early assaults on Petersburg and had acquit-
ted themselves well. Ferrero's men had spent their time in service guarding the vast Union supply train, and in that role had seen some combat in
fending off Confederate raiders during operations north of the James.
Moreover, their relative freshness and evident eagerness might prove an
advantage because white soldiers were jaded by previous setbacks. To ignore such a ready source of manpower when other divisions were struggling to regain their initial numbers seemed foolhardy, especially when
many of the black soldiers possessed more time in the ranks and higher
morale than the white replacements trickling in.[42]

As Hancock embarked on his swing north of the James, Grant checked
with Burnside to see whether the Confederates had yet discovered the
mine. Back came word that although the enemy was digging counter-
shafts, none had met with success. It would soon be too late to take advantage of the opportunity presented by Pleasants and his men. Convinced
that Lee, in countering Hancock, had thinned the defenses around Petersburg, Grant advised Meade to go ahead with plans to detonate the
mine: "The details for the assault I leave for you to make out."[43]

In directing Meade to supervise the execution of the plan, Grant allowed his eagerness to let his subordinate exercise command prevail over
his awareness of the troubled relationship between Meade and Burnside.

has USG not learned not to leave Meade in charge??

For Meade balked when he reviewed Burnside's proposal. First, he argued, it called for too much explosive powder — an argument that had merit, for the prevailing wisdom said that too much explosive might not produce the desired result. Much more controversial was his decision not to use Ferrero's men in the initial assault. His reasoning suggested that he had become captive to his sensitivity to criticism. Should the assault fail, Meade argued, he would come under attack from some Republicans (specifically those who had found fault with his performance at Gettysburg) for needlessly sacrificing the lives of black soldiers. Yet there was something else to Meade's decision: he was not yet convinced that black soldiers were ready to see combat. He was not alone. Back in May Theodore Lyman, observing Ferrero's men on guard duty, remarked: "We dare not trust them in the line of battle. Ah, you may make speeches at home, but here, where it is life or death, we dare not risk it."[44]

Burnside stood by his decision. So did Meade, who proposed to take the matter up with Grant. Burnside assented, entrusting Meade to make the presentation instead of accompanying his superior to headquarters. Thus Meade was able to offer his reasoning without fear of rebuttal and could make other unilateral changes in the plan. He instructed Burnside to remove the abatis composed of sharpened sticks, logs, and wire that had been placed in front of his lines to hamper a Confederate assault and to prepare the parapets in his front so that the attackers could make their way over them with ease and in good time. This would consume valuable time and energy and alert the Confederates that something was up. Finally, having stripped Burnside of his specially trained attack force, Meade also ignored the original plan to have the attackers peel off to the right and left to roll up the enemy flanks, preferring a straightforward punch once the men advanced through the gap created by the explosion.

Shortly after noon on July 29, Meade arrived at Burnside's headquarters armed with Grant's decision. Ferrero's men would not lead the assault. Meade had convinced Grant not to risk the political ramifications of failure. Disheartened, Burnside listened as his three other division commanders argued why their men should not lead the attack before deciding to let them draw straws. Fate decreed that James Ledlie, a poor excuse for a major general but a great drinker, would spearhead the charge. This done, Burnside salvaged what was left of his original plan. Ledlie's men would swarm around the hole left by the explosion and head for the Confederate rear; the other two divisions would perform the flanking functions originally assigned to Ferrero, who would follow in Ledlie's wake. Meanwhile Meade informed Warren and Ord of their roles in support of

Burnside's assault. Grant reviewed Meade's orders that afternoon and approved them "most heartily."[45]

With a new moon, the night of July 29–30 was pitch black. Originally the mine was scheduled for detonation at 3:30 A.M. That time passed, and thirty minutes later Grant rode up to Meade's headquarters post. He was puzzled. "What is the matter with the mine?" he asked. Meade speculated (correctly, as it turned out) that the fuse had gone out. The waiting continued. Finally, at 4:46 A.M., everyone at headquarters heard "a dull, distant explosion, like a heavy gun, far away." Dirt flew skyward; artillery opened fire.[46]

Spectacular as the explosion seemed, what followed was in its way even more astonishing. For Ledlie's lead brigade was composed, not of trained infantrymen, but of dismounted cavalry and heavy artillerymen. The men struggled up the parapet (which no one had torn down) and then headed, not along the sides of the crater, where they could either get through to the other side or begin rolling back the enemy flanks, *but into the crater itself*. Other brigades followed, and before long the massive hole in the earth was filled with thousands of soldiers, struggling to get out. As Ledlie drank in a rear area, his men botched their attack, and before long the rest of Burnside's command succeeded in arriving just in time to be part of the repulse. Ferrero's men joined the fray, but it was too late. Recovering from the shock of the explosion, the Confederates soon mended the breach in their line, and then started firing into the mass of men in the crater. The Rebels seemed especially eager to pick off the black soldiers, including some who were trying to surrender. The Union soldiers were helpless; they could not advance, and they were finding it hard to extract themselves.

Aware that something had gone badly wrong, Grant rode forward to see for himself. Horace Porter persuaded him to dismount lest he offer too inviting a target, and so on foot he scrambled toward Burnside's command post, blending into the scene with his plain private's blouse, and took a shortcut by jumping over the parapet and jogging across the dirt, exposed to enemy fire. By the time he reached Burnside, he had made up his mind. The opportunity was gone. It was time to pull back.[47]

This was easier said than done. It would be difficult for the jumbled regiments to retreat under fire, and Burnside was reluctant to abandon the operation. When he reported these circumstances to Meade, the two men lost their tempers; the resulting explosion rivaled the one at dawn. Meade bluntly inquired of Burnside whether his men were obeying his orders, which the corps commander took as an insult. In turn Burnside snapped

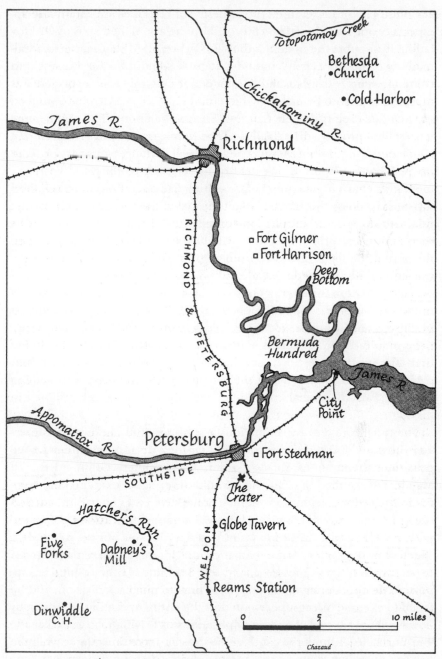

Richmond and Petersburg, 1864–1865

at Comstock, for he resented the presence of one of Grant's staff officers, especially one who thought so little of him; he also flailed away at Ord for failing to support the assault, although Ord retorted that matters had already become hopelessly confused. It took some time for Burnside to come to terms with what had happened. "I certainly fully expected this morning to go into Petersburg!" he remarked.[48]

The mine itself had been a success. The exploitation of the opportunity it presented proved a dismal failure. "Every thing was in our favor," Patrick concluded, "but nothing was carried out well." The reasons for this were many. Whatever opinion one held of the combat readiness of Ferrero's men, it was hard to imagine them botching the operation as had Ledlie's division. To revise the attack plan on the eve of the operation in conjunction with three reluctant division commanders did not augur well for its success. But the primary reason for failure lay in bad leadership during the assault. Ledlie failed to coordinate or supervise his division as it advanced; neither Burnside, Meade, nor Grant himself exercised sufficient oversight. "There were screws loose somewhere and the machine would not work," observed one of Grant's staff officers. The assault was pointless because it was headless. Nor did Burnside's men distinguish themselves. "The men did not fight hard enough," Lyman observed. He concluded that "the blacks seem to have done as well as whites — which is faint praise." Comstock opined that the assaults lacked the drive necessary to succeed. "We will never have another such opportunity," he scribbled in his diary.[49]

The usual round of recriminations and finger-pointing ensued. Meade and Burnside debated the impact of Burnside's decision not to make the preassault preparations Meade's orders had outlined. Grant sided with Meade. Determined that Burnside would never again exercise field command, he ordered a court of inquiry. Some two weeks later Burnside left the army on a leave of absence. He never returned.[50] "It was the saddest affair I have witnessed in this war," Grant concluded. "Such opportunity for carrying fortifications I have never seen and do not expect again to have." Yet he shared responsibility for the result. He supported Meade's decision not to employ Burnside's black division, and he failed to exercise direct supervision over the entire operation, although by now he should have known the implications of leaving matters to Meade and Burnside. "I think the cause of the disaster was simply the leaving the passage of orders from one to another down to an inefficient man," he later reflected. "I blame his seniors also for not seeing that he did his duty, all the way up to myself." Nevertheless, he had learned something.

(He concluded that "fortifications come near holding themselves without troops." From now on Grant would work against both ends of Lee's line, looking for an opportunity to outflank him, overextend him, or sever supply lines.[51])

Early on the morning of July 31 Grant traveled to Fort Monroe to meet with Lincoln. The failure of the Crater still weighed heavily on his mind: he would much rather have presented the president with a victory than with more disappointment. Now he needed to straighten out the confused command situation around Washington. (Both the president and the general-in-chief wanted to do more than to simply render the capital secure. A unified command under an aggressive Union commander could destroy a portion of Lee's army in the field, deprive Lee's army of resources from the Shenandoah Valley, and perhaps make it far enough south to destroy the Virginia Central Railroad.) Explaining that Franklin was unacceptable, Lincoln was lukewarm to the idea of transferring Meade, ostensibly because it would look as if he was being demoted, but probably in part because the president, recalling Gettysburg, did not see Meade as a general capable of conducting a vigorous pursuit. Ironically, he was willing to discuss the possibility of naming George B. McClellan to take charge — an option worth considering more for political than military reasons, for McClellan was a leading candidate for the Democratic presidential nomination. Although Grant had previously expressed an interest in offering McClellan an assignment, nothing came of this proposal. Grant then suggested Sheridan for the command — although Hunter would remain as head of the department. Lincoln agreed. "I presume our Father Abraham looks on his election prospects as waning, and wants to know if Ulysses, the warrior, if some *man* or some *plan* can't be got to do some *thing*," Lyman speculated. "In one word he wants to know — WHY THE ARMY OF THE POTOMAC DON'T MOVE."[52]

As the president returned to Washington, news arrived at Grant's headquarters that Early had once more crossed the Potomac River. There was no time to waste. Back at City Point, Grant informed Halleck that Sheridan was to receive instructions "to put himself south of the enemy and follow him to the death. Wherever the enemy goes let our troops go also." But once more Halleck proved obstinate. Questioning Grant's decision to put Sheridan in command of the Sixth Corps as well as the cavalry, he persuaded Sheridan to head only the cavalry. Then he again pressed for operations north of the James. At first Grant wavered. "Make such disposition of Sheridan as you think best," he responded. Halleck retorted

Halleck
:3
bad

that what Sheridan did was Grant's responsibility, neatly overlooking that it had been his second-guessing that had led to this exchange. Finally Lincoln intervened. Telling Grant that he approved of the initial directive, the president asked his general to "please look over the dispatches you may have received from here, even since you made that order, and discover if you can, that there is any idea in the head of any one here, of 'putting our army *South* of the enemy' or of following him to the *death* in any direction. I repeat to you it will neither be done nor attempted unless you watch it every day, and hour, and force it."[53]

This was enough for Grant. Lincoln's message came at a time when the general was still mourning the failure at the Crater. "So fair an opportunity will probably never occur again for carrying fortifications," he had told Meade upon his return to City Point. Pondering what could have been, he became depressed, then ill. Aide Theodore Bowers understood. "The chances of success were so great — the failure so utter — that all men who understand the whole matter are paralized and pettrified," he observed. Now Grant's efforts to resolve the command imbroglio at Washington were unraveling. Lincoln was right. Grant would have to see to it personally that his orders were executed. On August 4 he telegraphed Lincoln that he was on his way to Hunter's headquarters — although he did so without making a fuss, lest Lee choose this moment to attack.[54]

When Grant arrived at Hunter's headquarters at Monocacy, Maryland, on the evening of August 5, he encountered confusion. Cyrus Comstock noted that Hunter "was doing nothing & not knowing what [the] enemy was doing." Grant thought that the best way to find out the distribution and location of Early's forces was to consolidate Union forces and advance. He suspected that Early had detached a small raiding party for a northward excursion. After Union forces advanced up the valley, Grant wanted to make sure "that nothing should be left to invite the enemy to return. Take all provisions, forage and stock wanted for use of your command. Such as cannot be consumed destroy." Once more distinctions should be made between loyal and disloyal citizens: the former were entitled to vouchers for what the army took.[55]

The arrangement that Grant had constructed for Hunter and Sheridan resembled the one he had tried to impose on Butler; that is, Hunter would remain as titular commander of the department but Sheridan would control the forces in the field. Hunter, citing Halleck's lack of confidence in him, offered to step down. Such magnanimous behavior stood in stark contrast to Butler's tenacious efforts to retain his command. Grant was impressed. He named Sheridan acting department commander and handed him the orders that had been intended for Hunter. "What we want is prompt and active movements after the enemy," he added. "I feel every confidence that you will do for the very best and <u>will leave you as far as possible to act on your own judgement</u> and not embarass you with orders and instructions."[56]

Grant also left Sheridan with one other explicit directive: he was to take orders from no one <u>but Grant himself</u>. He had <u>grown tired of Halleck's interference</u>; it was time to put an end to the confusion attending the management of the defense of Washington. As he later put it, ("It seemed to be the policy of General Halleck and Secretary Stanton to keep any force sent there, in pursuit of the invading army, moving right and left as to keep between the enemy and our capital; . . . they pursued this policy until all knowledge of the whereabouts of the enemy was lost." By taking Early off the board, Sheridan would put an end to Grant's troubles, and at last achieve what Grant had long desired — taking the Shenandoah Valley out of the war altogether.[57]

It had been a <u>trying</u> summer. Time and again <u>Grant bent his preferences to political realities</u>. Seeking the military successes that would go far to secure Lincoln's reelection (and thus guarantee the prosecution of the war to a successful conclusion), he had wrestled with difficult subordinates. Yet in most cases political concerns had circumvented his solutions. Butler remained untouchable; Meade and his bruised ego continued in command of the Army of the Potomac. <u>Only with Sheridan's appointment did Grant finally get his way.</u> But few realized this. (In Washington members of the administration were becoming impatient with Grant.) "A nation's destiny almost has been committed to this man," moaned Secretary of the Navy Gideon Welles, "and if it is an improper committal, where are we?"[58]

18

Celebrations and Salutes

◉

AFTER INSTALLING SHERIDAN in command with orders to take Early and the Shenandoah out of the war, Grant hurried back to City Point, passing "through Washington so quietly that scarce any one knew that he was in the city," as a staff officer noted. Grant intended it that way. Others shared his wariness toward the capital. "Don't stay in Washington longer than is necessary to give impulse to events and get out of it," warned Sherman. "It is the center of *intrigue*." However, the scene at City Point on August 9, the day of Grant's return, made Washington look safe. Late morning found Grant sitting in front of his tent, staff officers in attendance, listening to a report of possible sabotage efforts by the enemy. Moments later an ordnance boat docked at the landing exploded. Shells, splinters, and debris flew through the air. Meade's aide Theodore Lyman reported that "it perfectly rained shells, shot, bullets, pieces of timber, and *saddles* (of the latter there was a barge load near by)." At first Grant did not move; then he walked to the wharf to see what had happened as everyone else headed in the opposite direction. "The only man who, at the first shock, ran *towards* the scene of terror was Lieutenant-General Grant," remarked Lyman, "which shows his kind of character very well."[1]

Although Grant escaped harm, others did not. One orderly was killed and several more were wounded, as was staff officer Orville Babcock. Eventually the count reached fifty-three dead and one hundred twenty-six wounded — the vast majority of them black laborers. Although investigators, failing to recover evidence of sabotage, concluded that the explosion was accidental, a Confederate operative later revealed that it was the result of a Rebel plot. From then on Grant's officers kept a quiet watch over him to protect him from assassination attempts.[2]

Grant had returned to City Point determined to prevent Lee from reinforcing Early. Intelligence reports soon suggested that perhaps as many as four Confederate divisions were earmarked for the Shenandoah. In re-

370

sponse, Grant approved a movement that would commence with an elaborate deception) The Second Corps (yet again) would board transports as if it was being transferred to Washington, only to be deposited at night at Deep Bottom, Virginia, in a revival of the July offensive. No one thought to see whether soldiers could actually debark at Deep Bottom, or whether steamers could make their way up the river; the charade consumed so much time it lost the secrecy needed to carry out the scheme. Moreover, the soldiers, already tired from marching, boarding, and landing, found the heat of the following morning overpowering, and the opening attack was feeble. Before long intelligence reports concluded that Lee had sent only a single division northward, an attempt to draw Yankees away from Richmond and Petersburg as the first step in shifting the campaign away from the James.[3]) *uh oh*

Grant, determined not to risk large losses in another attack on enemy earthworks, ordered Hancock to pin down the force assembled opposite him while Warren's Fifth Corps swung southward to snap the Weldon Railroad. When lead elements reached the railroad at Globe Tavern, less than three miles south of Petersburg, on the morning of August 18, they began ripping up the rails. Confederate efforts to drive them away failed. "It is touching a tiger's cubs to get on that road!" Lyman observed. Eager to seize any opportunity to kill Confederates out in the open, Grant directed Meade to tell Warren "not to stop when the enemy is repulsed, but to follow him up to the last." Although renewed Rebel attacks on August 19 caused some anxious moments when several Union brigades broke, Warren held his position, and the next day his men shattered another assault column. That was not enough for Grant. "It seems to me that when the enemy comes out of his works and attacks and is repulsed he ought to be followed vigorously to the last minute with every man," he told Meade. He wanted to strike again. Observing that Warren had fended off several Confederate divisions, he wired his generals opposite Petersburg to consider a counterblow: "There must be a weak point somewhere."[4] *→ good decision?*

To strengthen Warren and to build on his success, Meade sent the Second Corps, which had just recrossed the James River, south. This was a mistake: Hancock's men were exhausted and in no condition to do what was being demanded of them. On August 22 one division reached Reams Station, three miles south of Globe Tavern. Rebels soon appeared in the distance. Hancock shifted another division south, bringing the size of the Union contingent to some nine thousand men, approximately half of what Meade thought Hancock had on hand. Laboring under the impression that Hancock could hold his own, Meade did nothing to reinforce him, despite signs that Lee was massing men against him (something that eluded Hancock's notice as well). When the Confederates attacked on the afternoon of August 25, several Union regiments gave way, sometimes without offering much resistance. Those regiments that remained fought long and hard to prevent an effort to encircle them until a bitter Hancock ordered his men to withdraw as dusk came. "The enemy brought everything they could rake and scrape," he remarked a few days later. "We ought to have whipped them." But the noose was just a bit tighter around Richmond and Petersburg.[5]

Disappointed that more did not come of this effort, Grant grew even more irritated when he reflected on Henry Halleck's recent behavior. Theodore Bowers observed that the commanding general had "his eyes opened as to Halleck's position and conduct" during his trip to Maryland. Old Brains often criticized Grant's campaigns — to others as well as to Grant — and changed the intent of Grant's directives to others. Evidence that the chief of staff was cracking under the strain of the summer campaigns came when Halleck warned that Grant would have to shift forces northward to suppress civil disturbances that he believed were sure to follow the imminent draft call. Perhaps a new war would break out in the North, he speculated, as Democrats resisted conscription and attacked the administration. "Are not the appearances such that we ought to take in sail and prepare the ship for a storm?" he queried.[6]

Grant, busily engaged in supervising major offensive operations, responded in a message that betrayed his growing impatience with Halleck: "If there is any danger of an up rising in the North to resist the draft, or for any other purpose, our loyal Governor's ought to organize the Militia at once to resist it. If we are to draw troops from the field to keep the loyal states in the harness it will prove difficult to suppress the rebellion in the disloyal states." To comply with such a request would endanger Sherman's operations around Atlanta. Halleck had remarked in 1862 that one of Grant's telegrams suggested that he was being "stampeded"; it was obvious that such a description now fit Halleck far better.[7]

Nor was Grant alone in recognizing that fact. Four hours after his stern reply reached the War Department on August 17, Abraham Lincoln wired back, "I have seen your dispatch expressing your unwillingness to break your hold where you are. Neither am I willing. Hold on with a bulldog gripe [grip], and chew & choke, as much as possible." As Grant read the president's remarks that evening, a smile creased his face; then he laughed. To his astonished aides, he remarked: "The President has more nerve than any of his advisers."[8]

Halleck never regained his prominence in the chain of command. With army headquarters now firmly established at City Point, there was little need for anything more than a telegraphic relay station at Washington. Bowers recognized that in adopting the new command structure around the capital Grant effectively took care of Halleck. "He has settled Halleck down to a mere staff officer for Stanton," he informed Rawlins. ("Halleck has no control over troops except as Grant delegates it. He can give no orders and exercise no discretion. Grant now runs the whole machine independently of the Washington directory." In midmonth Grant went a step further, suggesting that Halleck take charge of the Department of the Pacific — about as far away as he could send him. Although in the end Halleck stayed in Washington, he never again enjoyed Grant's full trust.[9]

As August dragged on, the general-in-chief grew uneasy. Nothing was working. "Grant is not at all well," remarked Marsena Patrick, "and there are fears that he is breaking down." Such reports were exaggerated, but the lieutenant general was frustrated with his inability to do anything with the Army of the Potomac. In turn, a growing number of officers were muttering that their commander was a simpleton overwhelmed by the task before him. Dr. John H. Brinton, once Grant's medical director during the early campaigns in the West, observed that Grant "had not many friends amongst the Army of the Potomac men. They were all McClellan men, and insisted that Grant was only treading the same path followed by McClellan and that his bloody victories were fruitless. They did not like him and had no confidence in him." Gouverneur Warren was one of those McClellan men. "To sit unconcerned on a log, away from the battlefield whittling — to be a man on horseback or smoking a cigar — seems to exhaust the admiration of the country," he snarled; "and if this is really just, then Nero fiddling over burning Rome is sublime." Patrick, always with an ear for gossip, heard officers sympathetic to McClellan speculate on whether Lincoln would seek to negotiate a peaceful settlement to the war without emancipation as a precondition.[10]

Grant refused to be discouraged. "We must win if not defeated at home," he told Sherman. Desertion eroded Confederate strength; Grant worked hard to get every possible soldier to the front, stripping rear areas and urging Sherman to set aside his prejudices and employ blacks behind the battle lines. "I state to all Citizens who visit me that all we want now to insure an early restoration of the Union is a determined unity of sentiment North," he wrote Elihu Washburne. ("The rebels have now in their ranks their last man. . . . A man lost by them cannot be replaced. They have robbed the cradle and the grave equally to get their present force." Confederate victory could no longer be achieved on the battlefield. To Grant it was obvious that "the end is visible if we will but be true to ourselves." Only domestic unrest or a Democratic victory could revive their morale. Confederates "hope a counter revolution. They hope the election of the peace candidate. In fact, like McCawber, the[y] hope [for] *something* to turn up," he offered, referring to a character in Charles Dickens's *David Copperfield*.[11]

Yet it was Grant who felt a bit like Wilkins Micawber. He needed a victory to sway public opinion. "I never before saw Grant so anxious to do something," Bowers remarked. "He appears to try every possible expedient. His plans are good but the great difficulty is that our troops cannot be relied upon. The failure to take advantage of opportunities pains and chafes him beyond anything I have ever before known him to manifest." The best he could hope for was that the armies "may yet accidentally blunder into Richmond." Another staff officer agreed. "If we only had some of our old Western troops, with their own Generals to command them, down here just now, we could smash Lee most effectively," he declared.[12]

Grant struggled to hide his disappointment but was not always successful. Visiting City Point, John Eaton had a long talk with the general. He "listened to the story of his difficulties and disappointments, which seemed to me almost more than a man could bear," especially the failure to take Petersburg in June and the botched mine operation. Time and again something had gone wrong, and he could not conceal his frustration with the performance of some subordinates. He even reviewed his own actions. "I regret not having made better progress in whipping out the rebellion, but feel conscious of having done the best I know how," he confided to Daniel Ammen. "Several times we have had decisive victories within our grasp, but let them, through accident or fault, slip through our hands. . . . We will peg away, however, and end this matter, if our people at home will be but true to themselves." Others were more skeptical. "Things are looking blue now," observed Comstock. The soldiers were "not worth half what they were when we started on this campaign"; news from home, especially "a very strong peace feeling growing up at the north," cast doubts about the enforcement of the draft and the raising of more volunteers. "It is hard to foresee the future," he remarked.[13]

By the end of August numbers limited what Grant could achieve. The Army of the Potomac (minus the Sixth Corps) numbered under 29,000 effectives, while Butler's two corps added another 17,000. More men were needed to press the Confederates. "The South now have every man in the

wow,

ranks, including old men and little boys," he told Ammen. "They have no longer means to replace a man lost; whilst by enforcing the draft we have abundance of men. Give us half the men called for by the draft, and there will hardly be any resistance made." But that was precisely the problem. Many of the new recruits and conscripts were worthless as soldiers. He particularly despised the "bounty jumpers," who enlisted to collect the financial incentives offered, then looked to desert at the first chance, perhaps with an eye to repeating the whole process. "Of this class of recruits," he complained to Secretary of State William H. Seward, "we do not get one for every eight bounties paid to do good service."[14]

Grant refused to draw on an obvious potential source of manpower, rejecting calls to reopen prisoner exchanges, despite the growing outcry in the North against the suffering of Union captives in Confederate prison camps. He well knew what his decision meant for those half-starved Union soldiers who languished in Rebel prisons, but he also realized that to resume exchanges, whatever the short-term humanitarian consequences, would result in long-term tragedy — and it would betray those black soldiers who were not treated as prisoners of war if captured. "It is hard on our men held in Southern prisons not to exchange them but it is humanity to those left in the ranks to fight our battles," he explained. "Every man released, on parole or otherwise, becomes an active soldier against us at once"; should exchanges resume "we will have to fight on until the whole South is exterminated." He conveyed the same message to Seward: "We ought not to make a single exchange nor release a prisoner on any pretext whatever until the war closes. We have got to fight until the Military power of the South is exhausted and if we release or exchange prisoners captured it simply becomes a War of extermination."[15] ➙ war of exhaustion?

It was becoming a hard war for all concerned. Generals on both sides, unable to strike decisive blows at enemy armies, had taken to destroying homes and buildings. David Hunter had commenced such behavior when he put both the Virginia Military Institute and the home of Virginia governor John Letcher to the torch in June; the following month, Jubal Early retaliated by ordering his men to set fire to the Silver Spring home of the Blair family, currently the residence of Lincoln's postmaster general, Montgomery Blair. At the end of July, Confederate cavalry under John McCausland carried through on a threat to burn Chambersburg, Pennsylvania, when that town's citizens could not raise sufficient funds to meet a ransom demand. The cycle of retribution promised to become endless. After conferring with Stanton, Lincoln asked Grant to see if he could reach an agreement with Lee putting an end to such activities; Grant re-

plied that he believed the Confederates would not feel themselves bound
by such an agreement (as the experience with paroles and exchanges had
demonstrated). "On the whole," he suggested, "I think the best that can
be done is to publish a prohibitory order against burning private property
except where it is a Military necessity or in retaliation for like acts by the
enemy."[16]

Grant preferred turning up the pressure on the Confederates. Tired of
the activities of John S. Mosby and his partisan rangers in disrupting Union communication and supply lines and in picking off errant Yankee detachments, he directed Sheridan to execute any of Mosby's men who were
not in uniform when captured; he also suggested that the families of
Mosby's raiders be detained "as hostages for good conduct of Mosby and
his men." A cavalry division should strip Loudoun County of food, animals, and slaves and take as prisoners all adult males under fifty capable of
bearing arms. Later he modified these orders to allow for the compensation of loyal citizens and the exemption of Quakers from arrest. Although
eager to make sure the area "should not be capable of subsisting a hostile
Army," he added, "At the same time we want to inflict as little hardship
upon Union men as possible." One did not want to injure friends when
striking at the enemy; Grant was no advocate of indiscriminate warfare.
That he was in favor of harsh measures, however, was evident in a late August directive: "Do all the damage to rail-roads & crops you can. Carry off
stock of all discreptions and negroes so as to prevent further planting. If
the War is to last another year we want the Shenandoah Valley to remain a
barren waste."[17]

Although such measures intensified the war, they were no substitute for
the body blow Grant ached to deliver. His frustration began to take its toll,
and near the end of August he fell ill. "He feels languid and feeble and is
hardly able to keep about," observed Bowers, "yet he tends to business
promptly and his daily walk and conduct are unexceptional." But signs
of the political situation were ever present. "The rebellion is now fed by
the bickering and differences North," Grant noted. "The hope of a coun-
ter-revolution over the draft or the Presidential election keeps them together." At the end of the month the Democrats would meet to choose
their standard-bearer in the fall election. George B. McClellan was the obvious choice. Little Mac stood for the limited war for reunion that many of
Lincoln foes now charged the president with discarding in favor of emancipation; he also reminded voters that he, too, had laid siege to Richmond
once without incurring anywhere near the losses Grant had suffered. Butler went to New York amid rumors that he was still intriguing for the Democratic nomination or for some other presidential possibility. Several days

later Grant had a reminder of chances lost when he was interviewed by the court of inquiry convened to review the Crater debacle.

The arrival of Julia and the children for a short visit eased his anxiety somewhat. The family had rented a home in Burlington, New Jersey, near Philadelphia ("I have a horror of living in Washington and never intend to do it," Grant told Julia) to be closer to City Point. Horace Porter encountered him wrestling Fred and Buck; Grant got up, brushed off his pants, and remarked: "Ah, you know my weaknesses — my children and my horses." He needed the distraction. It was easier to tussle with his boys than it was to get things done at the front.[18]

On the evening of September 2, Grant opened a telegram from Washington bearing the news that advance elements of Sherman's army had entered Atlanta. Additional messages arriving the next day seemed to confirm this initial report, but everyone at headquarters remained cautious. "If this is but true," Comstock opined, "we can almost see the beginning of the end." Not until the evening of September 4 did definitive word finally arrive from Sherman via Washington: "Atlanta is ours, and fairly won." Immediately Grant directed that every battery fire a salute in honor of the victory. Throughout the night air the cannonade announced the news to Yank and Reb alike.[19]

Grant was gratified that at last his plan of sustained pressure against the enemy everywhere had finally paid off, but he recognized who deserved credit for the achievement. It was, he told Sherman, "the most gigantic undertaking given to any General in this War," and it was achieved "with a skill and ability that will be acknowledged in history as unsurpassed if not unequalled." Atlanta's fall rewarded the confidence he had shown in his subordinate's ability to exercise independent command — a quality he knew to be in short supply among his generals. "Our movements were co-operative but after starting each have done all that felt ourselves able to do," he told his father. The news proved welcome medicine. Before long his appetite had returned and he reported to Julia that he now felt "very strong."[20]

But it was no time to sit back and relax. Grant urged Sherman to push on. "As soon as your men are properly rested and preparations can be made it is desirable that another campaign should be commenced," he telegraphed. "We want to keep the enemy continually pressed to the end of the war. If we give him no peace whilst the war lasts the end cannot be distant." Two days later he sent Horace Porter to Sherman's headquarters to learn what his friend had in mind, building on previous conversations conducted by telegraph on how best to slice open the Confederate heart-

wants to know Sherm's future plans

land. Meanwhile he was working hard to improve his fortifications curling around Petersburg and Richmond so that he could reduce the number of men required to hold them; along with the arrival of reinforcements, this would allow him to mass larger assault forces "to make every blow struck more effective."[21]

Needing more men, Grant pushed again for an effective draft. Bounty-jumping volunteers were worthless; conscription would bring a better grade of recruit into the army. "We ought to have the whole number of men called for by the President in the shortest possible time," he told Stanton. "Prompt action in filling our Armies will have more effect upon the enemy than a victory over them. They profess to believe, and make their men believe, there is such a party North in favor of recognizing southern independence that the draft can not be enforced. Let them be undeceived."[22]

Grant even grew impatient with his favorite cavalryman, Phil Sheridan. Although he had put an end to Jubal Early's exploits north of the Potomac, Little Phil had done little else. After an initial advance southward through the Shenandoah past Winchester in August, he had pulled back, afraid that a reinforced Early would lash back. Grant kept a close eye on Confederate movements and notified Sheridan of information gathered from intelligence sources; he suggested that Sheridan draw on Washington for reinforcements, although he added that he was not explicitly ordering the cavalryman to move "because I believe you will allow no chance to escape which promises success."[23]

This faith proved short-lived, for Sheridan proved more cautious than Grant had anticipated. Growing unhappy, Lincoln asked Grant whether a quick concentration of forces under Sheridan might allow him to attack. Grant got the hint. Deciding to nudge the cavalryman forward, on September 15 he traveled to Sheridan's headquarters at Charlestown, West Virginia, to set things in motion. There would be no scheduled stop in Washington this time, for he feared that either Stanton or Halleck would undo whatever he proposed. In his pocket was a plan of operations for Sheridan, but when the two generals met on September 16, Sheridan, emboldened by information that Early had sent a division back to Lee, was ready with a plan of his own to attack the remaining Confederates, who were deployed outside Winchester, Virginia. Elated, Grant contented himself with urging Sheridan on. But his presence did not go unnoticed. "I hate to see that old cuss around," one soldier grumbled. "When that old cuss is around there's sure to be a big fight on hand."[24]

Grant knew as much — and he was confident of victory. Businessmen had expressed concern that unless traffic was restored along the Balti-

[handwritten: → does this factor into USG's strategy?]

more and Ohio Railroad and the Ohio and Chesapeake canal before the winter set in, there might be a shortage of coal to heat homes and offices in Washington, Baltimore, and nearby towns. Encountering the general on his way to Sheridan's headquarters, John W. Garrett, president of the railroad, had asked when traffic could resume. Grant promised an answer when he returned; days later, he informed Garrett that he could set his men to work on Wednesday, September 21, for by that time the road would be clear. The commanding general then swung north to Burlington, New Jersey, to visit Julia and the children. He wanted to see the house she had rented and discuss schools for the children (and to tell Jesse that yes, he did have to go to school). Curious onlookers grabbed the opportunity to catch a glimpse of the general. When he left the house on Sunday to return to City Point by way of Philadelphia and Baltimore, people bothered him the entire way. "It is but little pleasure now for me to travel," he told Julia.[25]

Arriving at City Point on the afternoon of September 19, Grant listened as officers recounted a raid by Confederate cavalry on the army's cattle stock that had taken place while he was gone. As he later remarked, only half in jest, it was going to be difficult to starve Lee's army if his own commissary provided food for the Confederates. He then told the officers that he had ordered Sheridan to "whip" Early. That language seemed lacking in military precision to one officer, who remarked: "I presume the actual form of the order was to move out and attack him."

"No, I mean just what I say," Grant replied. "I gave the order to whip him."[26]

The next morning the general attended to overdue correspondence and wrote a chatty letter to Julia as he awaited word from Sheridan. That afternoon the telegraph began clicking away. Sheridan reported that "after a most stubborn and sanguinary engagement" that lasted most of the day, he had "completely defeated" the foe at Winchester, capturing five cannon and about 2,500 men. Ecstatic, Grant fired off a telegram calling for Little Phil's promotion to brigadier general in the regular army; he told Sheridan that the army would celebrate with a hundred-gun salute, adding: "If practicable push your success and make all you can of it." Three days later the cavalryman did just that, scattering Early's rearguard at Fisher's Hill and earning yet another hundred-gun salute (the third in three weeks). "Keep at it and your work will cause the fall of Richmond," an enthused Grant telegraphed his general. However, Sheridan declined to advance on Charlottesville and the James River canal, passing up a chance to cut yet more supply lines to Richmond.[27] *[handwritten: — why?]*

[handwritten margin notes: Sheridan defeats Early; B. of Winchester; Fishers Hill]

Coming on the heels of the fall of Atlanta, Winchester and Fisher's Hill proved critical to Union fortunes in this election year. Early's withdrawal southward cut short any plans for a return visit by the Confederates to the outskirts of Washington. Grant was delighted. "The general is in good health & I never saw him in better spirits," staff officer George K. Leet reported. "He seems to think he has the rebs 'just where he wants them' now." If the Confederate presence in the Shenandoah Valley forced Grant to divert units intended for the Richmond-Petersburg front, depriving him of dearly needed manpower, it also allowed the Union commander to deliver a major blow against a portion of Lee's army outside the extensive defensive works that ringed those two cities by stretching Lee's lines to the breaking point. Grant was determined to make the most of his opportunity. "In a few more days more I [s]hall make another stir here," he told Julia, "and shall hope before many weeks to so wind up matters here that I will be able to spend at least a portion of my time at home."[28]

Again Grant resorted to the familiar ploy of alternating attacks on both sides of the James. Butler would lead two corps against Lee's fortifications north of the river; Meade would then sweep south around Petersburg. "The object of this movement is to surprise and capture Richmond if possible," Grant told Butler. "The prize sought is either Richmond or Petersburg or a position which will secure the fall of the latter." To avoid raising hopes he might not be able to satisfy, he did not share the details of the plan with his civil superiors; however, he confided to Julia on the eve of the operation that he was preparing to fight "another great battle."[29]

The movement commenced in the early morning hours of September 29. Accompanying Butler's two corps north of the James, Grant rode forward to examine a line of works captured by William Birney's brigade of black soldiers. "As soon as Grant was known to be approaching," one officer later recalled, "every man was on his feet & quiet, breathless quiet, prevailed. A cheer could never express what we felt." The reservations about using black units that had muddled the planning prior to the Crater had vanished. Learning that Edward O. C. Ord's corps had overrun Fort Harrison, Grant hurried over to investigate. Dismounting, he entered the fort, only to see dead and wounded men inside. As he made his way among them, he looked away from the sickening carnage, his pained expression noticeable to members of his staff, and fixed his gaze on the spires of Richmond. Perhaps this time . . . He sat down to write orders to the corps commanders to urge them onward. Shells exploded overhead; staff officers ducked or scrambled for cover. Grant just continued writing.[30]

At midday Grant returned to Deep Bottom to check on Meade's progress. There he opened a dispatch from Lincoln expressing concern about Sheridan's safety. Immediately he wired back: "I am taking steps to prevent Lee sending reinforcements to Early by attacking him here"; he estimated Butler's advance to be only six miles from Richmond. However, little more happened, and he tailored his assessment of the day's events to meet Lincoln's expectations. "I did not expect to carry Richmond," he wired Halleck, "but was in hopes of causing the enemy so to weaken the Garrison of Petersburg as to be able to carry that place. The great object however is to prevent the enemy sending reenforcements to Early."[31]

Grant was impressed by the day's gains. "The distance was too great to Richmond or it would have been taken," he wrote Julia. Now, of course, Lee would reinforce his left. It was time to counterpunch to the south. On the morning of September 30, Meade swung out and headed west toward the Southside Railroad, the last uninterrupted line out of Petersburg. Even a partial success would complicate Confederate efforts to draw supplies from the Weldon Railroad by wagon south of the Federal fortifications. "It seems to me the enemy must be weak enough at one or the other places to let us in," Grant speculated.[32]

It was a busy day. North of the James, Lee launched a counterattack to try to regain what he had lost, but Butler's men held their ground, while Meade made inroads against the Confederate right. Impressed, that evening Grant urged Meade to "hold on to what you have & be ready for an advance"; it was time to ascertain where Lee's weak point might be now. Once again, however, Confederate resistance stiffened. By October 1 the front had stabilized. Another offensive had come to an end. Richmond and Petersburg remained in enemy hands, to be sure, but at great cost; the noose was ever tighter.[33]

Immediately after the battle Grant struck a different sort of blow at Lee. The Confederate commander, concerned about the dwindling strength of the Army of Northern Virginia, contacted him about the possibility of exchanging prisoners captured during the recent offensive. With important state elections in the offing in several Northern states, perhaps he hoped to embarrass his foe by reviving the debate over prisoner exchange policy. This time, however, Grant outmaneuvered him. Reminding Lee that approximately one hundred of the Union soldiers captured during the last battle were black, he wanted to know "if you propose delivering these men the same as White soldiers." In his reply Lee tried to finesse the matter by saying that he was willing "to include all captured soldiers of the U. S. of whatever nation [or] Colour under my control," although "negroes belonging to our citizens are not Considered Subjects of exchange & were not included in my proposition." Grant rejected the offer, pointing out that "the Government is bound to secure to all persons received into her Armies the rights due to soldiers." There would be no exchange.[34]

slow going

As fall came, Meade and Butler continued to chip away at Lee's lines shielding Richmond and Petersburg; Sheridan had secured the Shenandoah. But this was not enough. Grant looked again to Sherman to provide the decisive blow. Atlanta was in Union hands; what next?

Plans for future operations became more complicated when Georgia unionist Joshua Hill floated a curious proposal before Sherman. What if Georgia's governor, Joseph E. Brown, decided to take his state out of the Confederacy and made separate terms with Union authorities? After all, Brown had already allowed members of his state militia to return home to help with the fall crops. Intrigued, Sherman informed Lincoln that "it would be a magnificent stroke of policy" if Brown followed through; in that case, "instead of desolating the land as we progress, I will keep our men to the high-roads and commons, and pay for the corn and meat we need and take." More skeptical, Grant worried about what Lincoln might do. "Please advise the President not to attempt to doctor up a state government for Georgia by the appointment of citizens in any capacity whatever," he asked Stanton. "Leave Sherman to treat on all questions in his own way the President reserving his power to approve or disapprove of his action." By month's end, he speculated to Julia that should Brown accede to the scheme, "it will be the end of rebellion, or nearly so that the rebelling will be by one portion of the South against the other." Nothing happened, although the notion that the president might trust his generals with delicate negotiations transcending their military authority raised interesting issues.[35]   *→ just a notion for now*

Grant and Sherman focused once more on military operations. Near the end of September Horace Porter returned to City Point armed with a letter from Sherman outlining a tempting plan. No sooner had Sherman taken Atlanta than he began to realize that his prize might become an albatross. Hood was now free to operate against the Union line of supply and communication that stretched back to Chattanooga along a single railroad. Anticipating where Hood might appear was a chancy business, and it would be difficult to strike him more than a glancing blow; it would be impossible to protect the entire line with sufficient force. Sherman's inability to dispose of the Army of Tennessee had come back to haunt him.

Sherman chose to make a virtue of necessity. An advance on the state capital at Milledgeville would force a choice between Augusta and Macon; should the enemy defend Macon, as he anticipated, he would then force a second choice between Augusta and Savannah. The more he exam-

strategy

ined his options "the more am I convinced that it would be wrong for me to penetrate much further into Georgia without an objective beyond." He would leave George H. Thomas with a sufficient force to keep an eye on Hood's still dangerous army, then set forth across Georgia, "breaking roads and doing irreparable damage" on the way to Savannah or Charleston, South Carolina. Perhaps Grant could arrange for another force to meet him on the coast.[36]

Originally Grant had wanted Sherman to follow up the capture of Atlanta with a thrust toward Mobile, where he could link up with Union forces near the city. However, the redeployment of possible reinforcements elsewhere to counter Confederate threats led him to consider an advance toward the Atlantic Ocean as another way to divide the Confederacy — but only after Sherman first disposed of Hood. Left to itself, the Army of Tennessee might well invade its namesake state. Grant also doubted that he could establish a beachhead along the coast to await Sherman's arrival. There were too many other demands for him to spare sufficient forces, despite repeated efforts to move more men to the front.[37]

Sherman, however, was now wedded to his idea. "I can make the march and make Georgia howl," he declared. Chasing Hood was a losing proposition. Grant, aware of reservations about the idea among his superiors, weighed the alternatives. "I am terribly bothered just at this time about matters in the West," he told Julia. At last he decided to trust Sherman once more, and on October 11 gave him the go-ahead (Sherman did not receive the telegram, for the lines were cut). The following day Grant instructed Sherman to destroy railroads and secure supplies and livestock as he went, and added that Sherman might absorb slaves encountered during his movement and arm the adult males with surplus or captured weapons: "Give them such organization as you can. They will be of some use." Such advice was wasted on Sherman, who had no time for the freedmen.[38]

Having approved Sherman's plan, Grant advocated it to Lincoln and Stanton, doing what he could to counter their skepticism. The president feared that "a mis step by Sherman might be fatal to his army"; however, those concerns were countered by the knowledge that on October 12 Republicans swept to victory in Ohio, Pennsylvania, and Indiana, all but guaranteeing his reelection. Grant was certain that Sherman and his men would be "hard to corner or capture"; he began making preparations to gather supplies to greet Sherman when he arrived on the seacoast.[39]

Rawlins opposed Sherman's plan, while Porter liked it: the two men took the lead in debating its wisdom. Usually Grant listened; once, however, the argument lasted so long that he retired to his tent, later emerging just long enough to declare, "Oh, do go to bed, all of you! You're keeping the whole camp awake." But Grant was torn, too. He still wished that Sherman would destroy Hood's army before setting out on a march lest the Confederate commander make mischief in the Union rear. Would Thomas be able to check Hood?[40] *→ if, in an alt. reality, Thomas did not, Sherman would have really made a bad more*

As Grant discussed with Sherman how best to destroy the Confederacy, he received a reminder of just why it needed to be destroyed. Rebel deserters informed Benjamin F. Butler that the Confederates were using black POWs as laborers on fortifications within the range of Union guns. Forwarding the information to Grant, Butler added that he planned to retaliate by using Confederate prisoners in like manner. Approving this response, Grant furnished Butler with the prisoners to make good his threat. *→ hard war   → to who*

Forcing captured black Union soldiers to erect fortifications in combat sectors was regrettable, to say the least. Lee scrambled to justify his action, composing a lengthy response explaining Confederate policy on the reenslavement of those blacks who had escaped their owners, joined the Union army, and then were captured — that "species of property," as he put it. One might have added that those blacks who were captured were lucky to be alive, in light of reports about how Confederates had treated blacks attempting to surrender at the Crater and elsewhere, but Lee, ever the gentleman, chose to overlook those transgressions. Instead, he admitted that whatever the rationale for Confederate policy, this deployment of the prisoners was due to an administrative mistake and none of the prisoners had been within range of Union fire. Left unmentioned was the pen large enough to hold one hundred prisoners opposite the Union artillery shelling the Confederate line at Dutch Gap.[41]

Casting aside Lee's lengthy essay — "I have nothing to do with the discussion of the slavery question" — Grant replied that it was his duty "to protect all persons received into the Army of the United States, regardless of color or nationality." Should the Confederates do otherwise, he would retaliate. Noting that the black POWs had been withdrawn from the front, Grant informed Lee that he would instruct Butler to do likewise with the Confederate prisoners under his control. Unlike Lincoln, who shrank away from retaliation after Confederates butchered black soldiers at Fort Pillow, Grant would stand by his men, whatever the cost. All in all, it was a remarkable act on the part of the former slaveholder.[42]

good of USG

As the military situation improved, so did Grant's personal circumstances. The general had not forgotten that less than four years ago he was struggling to make ends meet. During the war he had done whatever he could to save from his salary, for he never knew "when his fortunes might change and he be thrown out of office." That he said this in November 1863, when he held a commission as a major general in the regular army, suggests that it took a long time for him to understand that he had at last achieved some sort of financial security, for that rank would not expire with the end of the war. Grant welcomed the news that some of Philadelphia's leading citizens were raising funds to buy him a home; so did his boys. Burlington was a Democratic stronghold, and at times the Grant boys found the going tough, until Fred began to defend both the family honor and his younger brothers by thrashing those schoolmates who were (as little Jesse later put it) "Southern sympathizers."[43]

The wave of military successes contributed to the positive feeling around headquarters. The unassuming lieutenant general would sit outside his tent and converse with anyone, regardless of rank. As one officer put it, "Without lowering his manner to the level of familiarity, he put everyone at ease by his natural simplicity." Even a visit to headquarters by Stanton and the new treasury secretary, William P. Fessenden, passed off pleasantly, although Theodore Lyman grumbled that this was laying on the partisan politics a bit thick. When someone who had noticed that Grant served his guests meat and water asked about the simple fare, the general replied: "How could I permit a drop of liquor or wine in my camp, with all the newspaper slander I receive?" Those people who sought more elaborate meals and drink found them at newspaper correspondent Sylvanus Cadwallader's mess.[44]

Stanton's visit had a serious side. He wanted to discuss the situation in the Shenandoah Valley. Throughout October Sheridan had been working his way back north through the valley, burning as he went; he advocated withdrawing to a fortified line in the lower valley so that he could return units to the Richmond/Petersburg front. Grant reconsidered his initial desire that Sheridan advance toward the Virginia Central Railroad and the James River canal and contemplated the best use against Lee of the forces that would be freed up by Sheridan's proposal. Halleck urged establishment of a fortified base somewhere near Manassas Gap, east of the valley, to shield Washington. Stanton talked over these options with Grant, then returned to the capital to confer with Halleck and Sheridan who had left his command deployed along Cedar Creek, some twenty miles south of Winchester. The cavalryman prevailed in that conference, and he started back to his command on October 17, reaching Winchester the next evening.[45]

On the afternoon of October 20, just after Grant had concluded his discussion of the treatment of black POWs with Lee, a telegraph operator ran to Grant's tent, entered it, and handed the general a message. Staff officers wondered what was up. In a moment Grant emerged, dispatch in hand, and began to read. It was from Sheridan. Early had attacked the previous morning, driving back the Yankees. Sheridan, riding forward from Winchester, had encountered his men in retreat. "That's pretty bad, isn't it?" Grant remarked. Only the twinkle in his eyes gave away the rest of the story — for Sheridan had helped to rally his men, and in the afternoon they launched a counterattack that swept Early from the field. Out went orders for another hundred-gun salute.[46]

Cedar Creek was one of those battles that, while dramatic, was unnecessary, except insofar as it was much better to win than to lose it. Had the Confederates achieved a triumph on the eve of the October state elections a week earlier, it might have been worth something, but, short of the outright destruction of Sheridan's army, it was unlikely that a Rebel victory would have amounted to much in the long run. And yet the battle eclipsed the far more significant Union triumphs the previous month at Winchester and Fisher's Hill. Reporters knew that the romance and excitement of Sheridan's ride and the Yankee counterattack in the afternoon would be thrilling copy for Northern readers.

At this point Grant could have sat and waited for the November elections. There was no need to risk anything more against Lee. "We are busy doing nothing, positively nothing, and I confess to you that I see no prospect of our doing anything for some time to come," Bowers wrote just days after Cedar Creek. "Everything is at a deadlock." The army lacked the manpower to enable it to do anything more than to render its present position secure; reinforcements did not replace losses or compensate for expired enlistments. "Everything now hinges upon the elections."[47]

But Grant wanted to make one last push to stretch Lee to the breaking point. Meade would target another one of Lee's supply links — the Southside Railroad — while Butler's men would keep the Confederates occupied and distracted. However, Butler did not heed Grant's explicit instructions not to attack entrenched positions. His corps commanders turned the demonstration into an assault, serving only to lose men needlessly. The expedition south of Petersburg had an even worse result. Headquarters did not know that the Confederates had prepared fortified positions in the path of the Union advance. Of the three corps initially detailed to cooperate in the offensive, one and several divisions of another were reassigned to keep an eye on these lines, leaving Hancock's Second Corps (augmented by another division) to shoulder the burden of the offensive. Once more Grant came under fire as he observed Hancock's initial advance. A shell burst just beneath the neck of his mount, although horse and rider somehow escaped injury. Moments later the horse became tangled in downed telegraph wires, and Orville Babcock had to free the animal, as Grant cautioned him not to hurt his mount.[48]

Grant found the Confederates had positioned themselves to open fire on both flanks of the Second Corps as it advanced. If Hancock pressed forward, he might well suffer another costly setback. The presidential election was ten days off. It would be foolish to squander the political advantage gained by recent military triumphs. Grant ordered a withdrawal. It barely avoided disaster, as a Confederate attack almost cut off the Union line of retreat.[49]

Grant minimized the setback, and Northern newspapers gave little attention to it. "I will work this thing out all right yet," he told Julia. And yet it seemed to others that it was not his fault that he had not already worked it out. "He is very sanguine and confident though there has been so many of his plans ruined by subordinates that I sometimes wish he had different men under him," remarked Grenville Dodge, one of Grant's old Western generals, who visited City Point in October. "Three different times has Richmond and Petersburg been virtually in his hands and by some *unexcusable neglect* or *slowness* each time his plans were ruined and the *opportunity lost.* How Grant stands it I do not see." Too many officers offered uninspired leadership, merely going through the motions. And too many of them had one eye on the November contest, according to Dodge, who noted that many of the army's leaders were "McClellanized" and that Meade's headquarters was "a hot bed" of sentiment for the Democratic candidate.[50]

Yet it was not only in the Army of the Potomac that one found generals who lacked Grant's relentless determination. Even Phil Sheridan hesitated at critical moments. What had most impressed Grant about Sheridan's performance at Missionary Ridge some eleven months ago was the division commander's willingness to inflict more damage by pursuing a defeated enemy. After Cedar Creek, however, Sheridan seemed satisfied with what he had already won. Grant urged the cavalryman to launch a blow against the Virginia Central Railroad and the James River canal or to send men back to City Point. Sheridan chose the latter. That was not the answer Grant wanted. With Early's force reeling southward in disarray, now was the time to sever yet more of Lee's supply lines, rendering tenuous his links to the outside world as winter came. Yet when Sheridan again declined to advance toward the canal and railroad, Grant gave in.[51]

Grant's commitment to keep pushing forward meant that no victory was complete enough for him; there was always something more a general could do. However, the battlefield successes of the past two months bore fruit for the administration at the ballot box(Grant had done what Lincoln had hoped he would do. He had devised and executed a plan of operations that produced <u>decisive Union victories</u>, convincing Northern voters to register their approval of the administration at the polls.)Republican triumphs in mid-October contests indicated what was to come, and <u>Cedar Creek clinched the case for Lincoln's reelection</u>. As November began, one staff officer reported that Grant was "in good health and buoyant spirits." He could even afford to smile.[52]

On the evening of November 8, 1864, Grant and his staff gathered outside his headquarters cabin to await news of the presidential election returns. It was a momentous contest in more than one respect, for this time(soldiers would be allowed to cast their ballots while serving in the field.)Several states had made provisions for such voting; where no legislation had been forthcoming, as in Indiana, Lincoln had done what he could to secure furloughs for soldiers from those states. Grant remarked that the concept was "novel," but then so was the situation. "A very large proportion of the legal voters of the United States, are now under arms in the field, or in hospitals, or otherwise engaged in the Military service of the United States," he wrote Stanton. "They have left their homes temporarily, to sustain the cause of their country, in the hour of trial. In performing this sacred duty, <u>they should not be deprived of a most precious privilege</u>. They have as much right to demand that their votes shall be counted, in the choice of their rulers, as those citizens, who remain at home; Nay more, for they have sacrificed more for their country."(He promised to do all he could to make sure that they could cast their ballots freely and without interference; noting that the soldiers had access to newspapers and campaign literature, he opposed political speeches and canvassing.[53])

    <u>Grant did not cast a ballot</u>, but his preference for president was well known. He had repeatedly stated that only the hope of a Democratic victory kept alive the Confederacy's chances for victory. Nor would he hear of any midsummer efforts to have him run himself: when John Eaton raised the question, Grant pounded his chair as he exclaimed, "They can't do it! They can't compel me to do it!"(He believed that a Lincoln victory at the polls was as essential as military successes to the ultimate triumph of the cause.) He offered no objection to(Lincoln's use of their correspondence to counter charges that the chief executive had meddled in military affairs,)although he observed that for the president "to attempt to answer

all the charges the opposition will bring against him will be like setting a maiden to work to prove her chastity."[54]

As the returns came in over the wire, a telegraph operator handed them to Grant. He shook his head. It looked as if McClellan would win after all. Disheartened, staff officers grew even more depressed as Grant read more returns. Several officers went to bed shaking their heads in disgust; the general's staff was composed of Lincoln men, in contrast to the divided loyalties that were so painfully evident at several other headquarters. No one remembered the stunt he had pulled off when he read Sheridan's Cedar Creek dispatch. Not until after midnight did the general admit that every report he had received showed Lincoln in the lead, well on the way to winning a second term.[55] ⟶ *kind of mean*

The general characterized the result as a "a double victory"; that the election went off peacefully was "worth more to the country than a battle won." He hoped that the news "will prove a terrible damper to the Rebels." After all, Northern discord had long sustained Confederate hopes of victory. "If there was less clamer and dessenting in the North the rebellion would be much sooner put down," Grant wrote Julia several days later. "The hopes of the South are constantly fed by the sayings of our Northern people."[56]

Grant was a Lincoln man in large part because Lincoln had become a Grant man. The president well knew how much he owed his general for framing and implementing a master plan that finally produced a series of major victories; Grant had also deprived Lee of the ability to seize the initiative and gain any sort of dramatic triumph that would nullify the impact of Union gains elsewhere. He had done so while honoring political necessity, retaining generals whose performance hindered military operations, and wrestling with the officer corps of the Army of the Potomac. Not everyone, then or later, appreciated the magnitude of the accomplishment. One who did was William T. Sherman. "Like yourself you take the biggest load," he had told his friend back in April. If it fell to Sherman to strike the decisive blow, he knew that it was all part of the larger plan, which, as he later put it, "in its strategy, in its logistics, in its grand and minor tactics, has added new luster to the old science of war." Another who agreed was Abraham Lincoln. Acknowledging an audience that gathered at the White House on November 10 to celebrate his triumph, Lincoln closed his remarks by "asking three hearty cheers for our brave soldiers and seamen and their gallant and skilful commanders."[57] *Lincoln has become one of USG's supporters*

19

Give Him No Peace

●

DESPITE LINCOLN'S REELECTION, the war was far from over. At first glance, the task that remained might not seem to have posed much of a challenge for Grant. Freed of the constraints imposed on his operations by election-year politics, the general could now subdue the Confederacy in more deliberate fashion, and he would not have to weigh the political costs of seeking someone's removal from command. Nevertheless, Grant also knew that the way he ended the war would shape the peace that would follow. The conflict could grind on for several years; Confederate armies might dissolve into bands of hard-bitten guerrillas; refugees might seek sanctuary in Mexico and inaugurate endless border clashes. How one destroyed the Confederacy was as important as that it be destroyed.

First among the blows aimed at the Confederacy's destruction was Sherman's proposed march to the Atlantic coast. Grant addressed last-minute concerns about the operation that jeopardized its implementation. The threat originated from an unlikely source. John A. Rawlins, still insistent that Sherman should first confront and destroy John Bell Hood's Army of Tennessee, had left City Point at the end of October. His orders were to travel to Missouri to ensure that William S. Rosecrans complied with directives instructing him to funnel reinforcements to Nashville, where George H. Thomas was assembling a force to keep Hood in check. "I am satisfied on full and mature reflection that Sherman's idea of striking across for the sea coast is the best way to rid Ten. & Ky. of threatened danger and to make the war felt," Grant explained in his instructions to his chief of staff. Rawlins disagreed. His first stop was Washington, where he shared his reservations about Sherman's proposed movement with Lincoln and Stanton. By November 1 word arrived at headquarters of revived misgivings about the next move.[1] Puzzled at this last-minute hitch, Grant nevertheless decided to check one more time with Sherman: "Do you not think it advisable now that

390

[handwritten: the stubbornness could have made things turn out badly]

Hood has gone so far north, to entirely settle him before starting on your proposed campaign?" Sherman, set on his planned march, presented his case once more in a series of telegrams that reiterated the impossibility of holding Atlanta while going after Hood and highlighted the ample force that would stay behind. Grant, satisfied by the first message in this flurry of dispatches, flatly directed his friend to "go on as you propose." Nevertheless, the exchange allowed Sherman to wax eloquent about his plan. He had learned that Jefferson Davis had boasted of the Confederacy's ability to protect its people. Sherman was willing to put that claim to the test. "If we can march a well appointed Army right through his territory, it is a demonstration to the world, foreign and domestic, that we have a power which Davis cannot resist. This may not be war, but rather Statesmanship, nevertheless, it is overwhelming to my mind that there are thousands of people abroad and in the South who will reason thus — 'If the North can march an Army right through the South, it is proof positive that the North can prevail in this contest,' leaving only open the question of its willingness to use that power."[2]

Such reasoning echoed Grant's own belief that there were many ways to undermine Confederate military strength. In addition to the weakening of Confederate armies through open battle, the cessation of prisoner exchanges, the destruction of supply sources, and the severing of supply lines, he now looked to crack Confederate civilian morale, knowing that discouraged people at home would encourage soldiers at the front to desert. "I see no present reason for changing your plan," Grant wired Sherman on election eve. "Should any arise you will see it or if I do will inform you. I think everything here favorable now. Great good fortune attend you. I believe you will be eminently succesful and at worse can only make a march less fruitful of results than is hoped for." A week later Sherman commenced his march. Grant was confident it would work. "The Confederacy is a mere shell," he told a reporter. "I know it. I am sure of it. It is a hollow shell, and Sherman will prove it to you."[3]

[handwritten margin note: great point]

Grant also sought to take Virginia out of the war. He directed Sheridan to warn residents living just east of the Blue Ridge to transfer all of their livestock, harvest, and provisions north of the Potomac before "clearing out that country. . . . So long as the war lasts they must be prevented from raising another crop both there and as high up the valley as we can controll." As for Richmond and Petersburg, he preferred to wait until he had more men before making a move; anything now might "liberate to[o] much of a force to oppose Sherman with."[4]

In mid-November, with matters seemingly well in hand, Grant paid a

[handwritten: USG is holding many Confs in place for Sherman]

visit to Washington, with plans to see the family at Burlington. "Every thing is very quiet here," he told one correspondent, "and seems likely to remain so until I make it otherwise. The rebels are reinforcing to a conciderable extent by bringing in men who have heretofore been detailed in workshops &c. and by collecting old men and little boys. It is better that it should be so. When the job is done then it will be well done."[5]

Even away from City Point there was no rest for the commanding general. At Washington he countered an effort to replace Stanton with Butler; he also met with Alabama unionist J. J. Giers, who had some ideas about rousing opposition to Confederate authorities there; at Burlington he prodded Sheridan to take advantage of any changes on his front and kept a careful eye on enemy movements to make sure there was no concentration against Sherman's column. With the election over, he urged that several generals who had long annoyed him be mustered out of service, including Franz Sigel, John McClernand, and James Ledlie of Crater infamy; and that others, notably William S. Rosecrans, be relieved of command. Nor would he consider returning Nathaniel Banks to field command in Louisiana — and this time Lincoln heeded his wishes. And then there were the curious crowds, anxious for a look at the general. A family visit to New York was complicated when news leaked out of the general's arrival at Astor House. "Men and women mounted chairs and tables, and cheers and huzzahs were kept up at intervals the whole evening" during a ceremony in that hotel's dining room, Sylvanus Cadwallader later recalled. "It was all Grant, all the time." His attempt to take an anonymous stroll down the streets of Philadelphia in a faded blue army overcoat also failed. Policemen had to shield the general from people; when he attempted to escape by boarding a carriage, the throngs broke windows to get a better look. "It is a terrible bore to me that I cannot travel like a quiet citizen," he told Julia — although after months of worrying about public support for the war effort, he may have felt some sense of gratification as well.[6]

One encounter in particular must have moved him (although he did not mention it to Julia). While in New York, he paid a call on his old commanding officer, Winfield Scott. Twenty-five years ago, as a West Point plebe, he had first laid eyes on the general. "With his commanding figure, his quite colossal size and showy uniform, I thought him the finest specimen of manhood my eyes had ever beheld," he later recalled, "and the most to be envied." For a moment, Grant remembered, he had envisioned that one day he might stand in Scott's place. Now, in a sense, he was. Scott had been keeping close watch on the activities of his former lieutenant, passing along short notes and recoiling in astonishment at a rumor that he had spoken disparagingly of Grant. Not only had he spoken highly of Grant's service at Molino del Rey, Scott assured Elihu Washburne, but he had also told others that the new lieutenant general "had richly earned his present rank." Grant dismissed the story out of hand, remarking that if anything Scott's remarks about him had been "more flattering to me than I probably deserve." Scott added to that when he presented Grant with a copy of his newly published memoirs, bearing the inscription: "From the oldest to the ablest General in the world." High praise indeed— especially from someone who once counted Robert E. Lee as a prized staff officer.[7] *check out Scott's memoirs?*

On his return to City Point Grant began paying close attention to the movements of John Bell Hood. Instead of chasing Sherman through Georgia, the Confederate commander gathered the Army of Tennessee in north Alabama for a strike into its namesake state. "Do not let Hoods forces get off without punishment," Grant warned George H. Thomas, who was responsible for making sure the Confederates did not commit any mischief. Thomas, however, was not yet in a position to deal a telling blow. Long-promised reinforcements had yet to arrive; his cavalry required new mounts; some fifteen thousand soldiers had been discharged or had gone home to vote.[8] *what was holding them up?*

Grant looked to keep the pressure on elsewhere. He wanted to bolster his forces for a new strike against Richmond and Petersburg, and was delighted to learn that Lee, apparently fearing just such an operation, had not sent large reinforcements southward to check Sherman. Reports that the Confederates had chosen instead to strip their garrisons in North Carolina to concentrate against the Yankees in Georgia led him to prepare an expedition against Fort Fisher, which guarded Wilmington, the last major open Confederate port east of the Mississippi. Perhaps the depleted defenders might give way easily. The onset of winter weather did not mean an end to campaigning.[9] *strategy*

As December came, Union authorities grew concerned about Sherman's fate. Would he make it to safety? Where would he appear? And would Thomas be able to check Hood's army? At a time when Tennessee's military governor (and vice president–elect) Andrew Johnson was completing the restoration of loyal civil government in Tennessee while Union authorities wrestled with pacifying Kentuckians, a Confederate thrust through these two states would be disruptive. The devastating losses suffered by Hood on November 30 when he assailed a fortified Union posi- *was he on radio silence?*

look into

actually, this makes it kind of shocking that Army approved this plan - risky

B. of Franklin (Hood loss) gives little comfort to Feds

woah. telling

tion at Franklin, Tennessee, south of Thomas's main force at Nashville, gave little comfort to those far from the scene. In public Lincoln remained confident about the success of Sherman's expedition, reasoning that Grant knew what he was doing (although he struck from his annual message the remark that Grant believed "our cause could, if need be, survive the loss of the whole detached force"); he could tell a crowd, "We all know where he went in at, but I can't tell where he will come out at." In private, however, he worried a great deal about both Sherman and Thomas. "The President feels solicitous about the disposition of Thomas to lay in fortifications for an indefinite period," Stanton informed Grant. The secretary dismissed Thomas's explanation that his cavalry commander, none other than Grant's old staff officer James H. Wilson, still needed to secure sufficient mounts: "This looks like the McClellan & Rosecranz strategy of do nothing and let the Rebels raid the country. The President wishes you to consider the matter."[10]

rjlt. it's all up to Thomas while Sherm is away

The general-in-chief had already sent out telegrams looking for new sources of horseflesh and men; another one prodded Thomas: "If Hood is permitted to remain quietly about Nashville you will loose all the road back to Chattanooga and possibly have to abandon the line of the Tenn. Should he attack you it is all well but if he does not you should attack him before he fortifies." Two hours later, having learned of Lincoln's concern in the interim, he reiterated his impatience. Confident that Thomas could "force the enemy to retire or fight upon ground of your own choosing," he expressed disappointment that Thomas had not mounted a counteroffensive after checking Hood at Franklin. However, he admitted that "at this distance . . . I may err as to the best method of dealing with the enemy." Nevertheless, Thomas should now "put forth . . . every possible exertion" to destroy Hood. "Should you get him to retreating give him no peace."[11]

USG tries to get rein-forcements etc to Thomas

Grant should have heeded his own observation that perhaps the man on the scene knew better than he what to do. Thomas explained that once he received reinforcements and mounts for Wilson's cavalry, he would move out and deal a shattering blow to Hood's already wounded force. But that would take time; adding to Grant's skepticism were reports from Halleck and Stanton that much had been done to provide Thomas with men and horses.[12] → was much done?

Days passed. Anxious to do something, Grant investigated the possibility of swinging south and west of Petersburg once more; guessing that Sherman would appear at Savannah within a week, he updated his subordinate. Only a handful of cavalry had left Virginia to go south; the Confederate decision to strip the North Carolina coast of troops left Wilmington a tempting target. As to Thomas's <u>withdrawal</u> to the outskirts of Nashville, Grant admitted that it might have been justifiable, but added, "It did not look so however to me. . . . I hope yet Hood will be badly crippled if not destroyed."[13]

Under such circumstances — waiting for Sherman, prodding Admiral Porter and General Butler to move against Fort Fisher, renewing his call for Sheridan to cut the Virginia Central Railroad, hearing from Washington of the administration's anxiety — Grant wanted something done now. By December 5 he had heard nothing suggesting that Thomas had acted on the promise he had made three days earlier to attack Hood "in [a] few more days." Another dispatch went out from City Point. Wouldn't Wilson's cavalry be best employed keeping watch on <u>Nathan Bedford Forrest</u>? As for Hood, he "should be attacked where he is. Time strengthens him in all probability as much as it does you." Thomas, replying the next evening, assured Grant that Wilson was doing all he could to remount his cavalry, but that it would be unwise to attack before then. So much for a "few more days."[14]

In the past Grant had deferred when Sherman and Sheridan explained why they would not implement their superior's suggestions; whatever his reservations and second guesses, Grant trusted both men. He and Thomas shared no such bond of affection, respect, or trust. Furthermore, "Old Slow Trot" never displayed alacrity in assuming the offensive. At Chattanooga, he had moved slowly to comply with Grant's orders on the climactic day of the battle; he had done the same the following February when Grant had repeatedly ordered him to advance to hold in check troops that might threaten Sherman's raid against Meridian. Sherman's complaints of Thomas's lethargy in offensive operations confirmed Grant's suspicions. To make matters worse, telegrams from Washington indicated the impatience with which ranking officials awaited news of an attack. And Grant could never quite shake the memory of the cool reception he had received at Chattanooga in October 1863. Nearly fifty years later James H. Wilson would recall the reserve with which Thomas greeted Grant and the tinge of condescension with which he treated his superior officer.[15]

On December 6, Grant's patience ran out. Offering suggestions, no matter how strongly worded, had gotten nowhere; it was time to speak bluntly and directly. Not yet in possession of Thomas's report of the condition of his horsemen, he wired: "Attack Hood <u>at once</u> and wait no longer for a remount of your Cavalry. There is great danger of delay resulting in a campaign back to the Ohio river." Surely Hood was not content to remain sitting outside Nashville; the Confederates had come too far to retreat now. Thomas promptly replied that he would comply with Grant's directive, "though I believe it will be hazardous with the small force of cavalry now at my service." But no word of a battle reached either City Point or Washington. "Thomas seems unwilling to attack because it is hazardous as if all war was any thing but hazardous," Stanton fumed. "If he waits for Wilson to get ready, Gabriel will be blowing his last horn." Grant replied that if Thomas did not move "promptly" he should be replaced by John M. Schofield.[16]

By December 8 impatience had turned into panic. More than a few days had passed; Thomas had yet to attack. Surely Hood would take advantage of this golden opportunity to march north to the Ohio River. Calling for all available reinforcements to be sent to Nashville, Grant also inquired about the possibility of mobilizing short-term forces north of the Ohio. "If Thomas has not yet struck yet he ought to be ordered to hand over his command to Schofield," he added. "There is no better man to repel an attack than Thomas — but I fear he is too cautious to ever take the initiative."[17]

Halleck read the dispatch carefully, especially the request that Thomas "ought to be ordered" to relinquish his command. Unlike Stanton, he had sent no dispatches to City Point complaining about Thomas's failure to attack. He pointedly replied, "If you wish Genl Thomas relieved from command, give the order. No one here will, I think, interfere. The responsibility, however, will be yours, as no one here, so far as I am informed, wishes Genl Thomas' removal." In light of the tenor of Stanton's remarks, Grant must have been puzzled to read these words. What exactly was going on in Washington? For the moment, he pulled back: "I want Gen. Thomas reminded of the importance of immediate action. . . . I would not say relieve him until I hear further from him."[18]

Grant goaded Thomas again. He believed that the Confederates were trying to cross the Cumberland River on their way north. "Why not attack at once? By all means avoid the contingency of a footrace to see which, you or Hood, can beat to the Ohio. . . . Now is one of the farest opertunities ever presented of destroying one of the three Armies of the enemy. If destroyed he can never replace it. Use the means at your command and you can do this and cause a rejoicing that will resound from one end of the land to another."[19]

Within twenty-four hours, however, Grant concluded that Thomas had to go. He directed Halleck to place Schofield in command. The orders were on the verge of being transmitted from Washington when word arrived from Thomas containing new information. Halleck decided to hold on to the directive until Grant had a chance to digest this latest missive.[20]

Grant was not pleased with what he read. Just as Thomas was putting together the final touches for an attack, "a terrible storm of freezing rain" rendered his command immobile; he pledged to "make the attack immediately after" the storm broke. He added that Hood was indeed preparing to cross the Cumberland (confirming Grant's worst fears); he also let on that he had heard of Grant's dissatisfaction from Halleck himself. "I can only say I have done all in my power to prepare, and if you should deem it necessary to relieve me I shall submit without a murmur."[21]

Recalling his prediction that if Thomas delayed attacking, bad weather might intervene, Grant was disappointed at news of another delay. If Thomas was to be believed, the Rebels were readying their march to the Ohio. But nothing could be done about the weather. "Gen. Thomas has been urged in every way possible to attack the enemy even to the giving of a positive order," he told Halleck. "He did say he thought he would be able to attack on the 7th but did not do so nor has he given a reason for not doing it. I am very unwilling to do injustice to an officer who has done as much good service as Gen. Thomas has, however and will therefore suspend the order relieving him until it is seen whether he will do anything." And, in an awkward effort to repair relations with Thomas, Grant wired Nashville: "I have as much confidence in your conducting a battle rightly as I have in any other officer. But it has seemed to me that you have been slow and I have had no explaination of affairs to convince me otherwise." In light of the weather, however, he would suspend the order relieving him "until we should hear further. I hope most sincerely that there will be no necessity of repeating the order and that the facts will show that you have been right all the time."[22]

In these replies lay an explanation for Grant's evident impatience. Thomas had failed to satisfactorily explain his delay in attacking prior to the storm— a repeat of his grim silence at Orchard Knob on November 25, 1863. Was this another case of passive insubordination?

Forty-eight hours later, with no word from Nashville, Grant contacted Thomas again. "If you delay attack longer the mortifying spectacle will be witnessed of a Rebel Army moving for the Ohio River and you will be forced to act, accepting such weather as you find. Let there be no further delay." Thomas replied that evening that the storm had left "a perfect sheet of ice & sleet," rendering troop movement impossible. However, "Will obey the order as promptly as possible however much I may regret it as the attack will have to be made under every disadvantage." It would have been prudent for Thomas to have relayed these facts on his own instead of waiting for another prod from Grant; such failures to communicate eroded the commanding general's already weak faith in Thomas. It is not wise to try the patience of an impatient man.[23]

John A. Logan happened to be visiting City Point. Grant, who had a good deal of faith in the Illinois soldier-politician, decided that perhaps Logan would move where Thomas made excuses. He directed Logan to head to Nashville to relieve Thomas, but not to act if Thomas had taken the offensive. No sooner had Logan left, however, when Grant decided that perhaps he should oversee events personally. On the evening of December 14 he hastily left City Point. Reaching Washington the following morning, he conferred with Lincoln and Stanton. That evening, news came that the ice had melted and Thomas was on the move; a second telegram reported success on the battlefield. "Push the enemy now and give him no rest until he is entirely destroyed," Grant wired. Nothing should stop the offensive. "Much is now expected." Privately, he was relieved. "I guess we won't have to go to Nashville after all," he told his telegraph operator. "Thomas has licked Hood."[24]

With a command crisis averted, the general decided to swing by Burlington for a short visit with Julia and the children. Additional telegrams arrived that day and next, describing how Thomas's sledgehammer blows had shattered Hood's weary ranks, ending whatever threat there may have been to a final Rebel strike northward. Grant warmly congratulated Thomas, but urged him to complete the job by pursuing the fleeing Confederates. Logan, who had reached Louisville, returned to Washington. Meanwhile, at Richmond and Petersburg another salute — this time some two hundred guns — announced the victory. Perhaps the doubling of the traditional number of cannon was a measure of Grant's relief.[25]

Although hindsight makes Grant's treatment of Thomas seem unfair, even peevish, Grant's past experiences with Thomas underlay his concern. Although the results vindicated Thomas, he was able to crush Hood's force because the Confederate defenders were already battered, bruised, and struggling to survive after Franklin. Nevertheless, Grant did not extend to Thomas the same understanding and patience he had shown to Sherman and Sheridan, justifying later claims that personal antagonism shaped much of the ill temper displayed in the telegraphic exchanges during the two weeks preceding the battle. Halleck played a useful role in mediating several crucial communications; the president cannily remained aloof, leaving Stanton to voice the administration's anxiety.

Thomas also bore the brunt of Grant's frustration about several other operations. Launching an amphibious assault against Fort Fisher and Wilmington was proving difficult; efforts to set into motion the armies opposite Richmond and Petersburg failed to achieve much, and for several days Grant wondered about the fate of a Fifth Corps expedition against the Weldon Railroad. Nor would Sheridan accede to yet another request to rip up the Virginia Central. Such proposed movements belied later claims that even as Grant pressured Thomas to move he was content with doing nothing himself; they help explain his impatience all around. Passing through Washington on his return from Burlington, he stopped at the War Department. Awaiting him there was most welcome news: Sherman had appeared outside Savannah.

Back at City Point, exhausted by the tension of the past few weeks, Grant fell ill. Perhaps it was another one of those agonizing migraines that revealed the pressure under which he had been laboring. Abstaining from food and even his beloved cigars, he spent a whole day confined to his cot. He had never felt so poorly during the war, he wrote Julia: and "It will not do for me to get sick at this time when there is so much to do and when we have it in our hands to do so much toward the suppression of the rebellion."[26]

One reason for Grant's indisposition may have been the appearance of a delegation from the Joint Committee on the Conduct of the War to investigate what had happened at the Crater. Grant himself testified in support of Meade's management of the operation, blaming the division commanders for the disaster — although he also accepted responsibility for failing to insist that Ledlie, "the worst commander" in Burnside's corps, not spearhead the assault. Elsewhere he proved willing to second-guess the wisdom of the decision not to employ Edward Ferrero's black division to lead the attack, although he stood by Meade's determination not to do so. But it did little good to revisit past failures, especially to members of a committee who seemed determined to exonerate Burnside and his commanders.[27]

After the committee's departure, Grant's health improved. By Christmas Eve he was able to eat dinner. "I know how much there is dependent on me and will prove equal to the task," he told Julia. "I believe determination can do a great deal to sustain one and I have that quality certainly to its fullest extent." News from the front was also encouraging. "Every thing seems to be working well and I have great hope this will be the last Winter of the War." Christmas Day proved even more rewarding. Fred Grant arrived at City Point; so did news of the fall of Savannah. Properly pleased, Grant nevertheless noted the failure to capture the Confederate garrison. No victory was perfect.[28]

The misadventures of Ben Butler served as a reminder of what could still go wrong. By mid-December, after several frustrating delays, all was ready for the Fort Fisher expedition. Two of Butler's divisions would launch the attack under Godfrey Weitzel; Butler would help outfit the expedition, but Weitzel would work with David Porter in executing it. Inevitable delays followed; Grant, already worried about Thomas, was in no mood to tolerate Butler's dilatory behavior.

Before long the entire operation bore Butler's imprint. He became transfixed by the idea of loading up an old ship with gunpowder and putting it afloat outside Fort Fisher's walls in the hopes that by exploding the boat he could destroy the fort. Capturing the fort, Grant argued, was unnecessary. Once Weitzel had secured and fortified a beachhead a mile or so from the fort, Wilmington would be cut off from the sea. However, Grant failed to stop Butler's scheme, in part because Admiral Porter endorsed it; however, the general explicitly stated that the gunpowder boat was not a substitute for the original plan. Worse was Grant's acquiescence in Butler's insistence that he take charge of the expedition himself. By now Grant entertained serious doubts about Butler's military abilities; he had intended to have Weitzel direct the landing force. However, there seemed no easy way to prohibit Butler from exercising command should he choose to do so. At least Butler showed an eagerness to fight that Thomas seemingly lacked.[29]

The result was both predictable and ludicrous. The gunpowder boat proved an embarrassment, producing little more than a big noise and a spectacular explosion — fitting results in light of the identity of the project's originator. A naval cannonade on Christmas Eve failed to inflict much damage, and Butler's men had no sooner landed on Christmas Day than Butler decided to withdraw and return to Hampton Roads — a decision contrary to Grant's explicit instructions to secure and maintain a beachhead. Porter wailed loudly about what happened; Grant fumed, especially after Colonel Comstock made clear that Butler had grabbed humiliation from the jaws of victory. "The Wilmington expedition has proven a gross and culpable failure," Grant informed the president. Nothing had gone according to plan. "Who is to blame I hope will be known."[30]

It did not take long to answer that question. "Matters are in Train to oust Butler, but I fear the President's indecision," Marsena Patrick noted. Grant needed no more proof of the cost of Butler's incompetency, and with Lincoln safely reelected, he did not need to tolerate it any longer.

"Please hold on where you are for a few days," he told Porter, "and I will endeavor to be back again with an increased force and without the former Commander." He named Alfred H. Terry, one of Butler's corps commanders who had seen a great deal of service along the Atlantic coast, to head the new expedition; in his instructions he made it explicit that Terry and Porter should work in harness. But that solved only one problem; as Grant himself observed, he would have gone to Wilmington himself, but that would leave Butler in charge. As Terry prepared to depart Grant telegraphed Washington to request Butler's removal. "In my absence Gen. Butler necessarily commands," Grant reminded Stanton, "and there is a lack of confidence felt in his Military ability, making him an unsafe commander for a large Army. His administration of the affairs of his Department is also objectionable." On learning that the war secretary had left Washington to visit Sherman, Grant pressed the president to take "prompt action" on his request. He did.[31]

Butler left, but not before issuing a farewell order announcing that he had been relieved because he refused to sacrifice his men's lives needlessly ("The wasted blood of my men does not stain my garments"). If he had any dirt on Grant, one might think that now was the time to divulge it — although perhaps Butler knew that it is by threatening to reveal such secrets, not by actually sharing them, that one wields power. And two could play at that game. Grant not only called his bluff, but also had gathered information about affairs in Butler's command that cast a shadow on Butler's less than stainless integrity. But the main point — Butler's removal — was now achieved. As the commanding general later observed, "The failure at Fort Fisher was not without important and valuable results."[32]

So off went Butler to Lowell, Massachusetts, gone from the war but not from either politics or Grant's life. Meanwhile, Terry and Porter departed for Fort Fisher. Alerted to probable Union intentions, the Confederate defenders were ready. Nevertheless, the fort fell on January 15.[33]

Grant prepared to exploit Terry's success at the expense of George H. Thomas. His satisfaction at the outcome of Nashville soon dissipated. He delayed approving Thomas's promotion to major general in the regular army until he could assess "the extent of the damages done Hood"; not until a week after the battle did he give the go-ahead. Meanwhile he urged Thomas to keep up the pursuit. By year's end, however, whatever could be done had been done. Halleck, who had played a key role in saving Thomas from removal, now expressed dissatisfaction when Thomas proposed waiting until spring to resume offensive operations. Agreeing, Grant directed the transfer of John M. Schofield and the Twenty-third Corps to Annapolis with an eye to sending them on to North Carolina. He explained to Sherman that Thomas's behavior after Nashville "indicated a sluggishness" that suggested that he would not move again until spring. "He is possessed of excelle[n]t judgement, great coolness and honesty, but he is not good on a pursuit."[34]

The commanding general busied himself this winter shuffling subordinates. With Butler gone and Thomas reduced, he urged the dismissal of William S. Rosecrans, but had to be satisfied with his displacement from department command. He pushed for reorganizing what remained of the Army of the James into two corps, the Twenty-fourth and Twenty-fifth, the latter composed of black regiments. Edward O. C. Ord replaced Butler as army commander; John Gibbon headed the Twenty-fourth Corps, with Godfrey Weitzel leading the Twenty-fifth. The Army of the Potomac was still adjusting to the departure of Winfield Scott Hancock from the Second Corps in November; Andrew A. Humphreys, who had long thirsted to head a corps, replaced him, leaving none other than Gouverneur Warren as the army's senior corps commander. Finally, Grant secured Senate confirmation of Meade's long-overdue promotion to major general in the regular army. That Meade had not earned the laurels of a Sherman or a Sheridan was beside the point; Grant could overlook his subordinate's shortcomings, in large part because he appreciated the difficult circumstances under which Meade labored. "I defy any one to name a commander who could do more than he has done with the same chances," he told Washburne. Meade, who had grown frustrated over the delay and embittered over criticisms of his generalship, was laboring under great strain, for the general's son Sergeant was in failing health; thus Grant's lobbying was an act of compassion as well as recognition.[35]

Grant reserved his loudest praise for Sherman. He warmly congratulated his friend on his "most brilliant campaign," adding: "I never had a doubt of the result." In writing Jesse Grant, the commanding general was even more effusive. "Sherman has now demonstrated his great Capacity as a Soldier by his unequalled campaign through Georgia. I know him well as one of the greatest purest and best of men." Perhaps, he suggested, Jesse could pull strings to get up a fund to raise money to buy a house for the Shermans; when he learned that such a movement was already under way, he happily subscribed five hundred dollars. Even more pleasing was Sherman's graciousness in victory, especially toward Grant. The commanding general reciprocated the sentiment in a letter to Julia: "I am glad to say that I appreciated Sherman from the first feeling him to be what he has proven to the world he is."[36]

What next? At first Grant wanted Sherman to secure Savannah, then transfer his army via water north to Richmond and Petersburg. Sherman preferred replicating his march, this time through the Carolinas; Grant, who had learned that he lacked sufficient transports to carry Sherman's command northward, consented. By the time Sherman reached North Carolina, Grant reasoned, Wilmington should be in Union hands, and the two invading columns could link up. Either Lee would have to abandon Richmond to check Sherman or remain in his trenches, conceding what remained of the Confederate heartland to the Yankees. "My own opinion is that Lee is averse to going out of Va. and if the cause of the South is lost he wants Richmond to be the last place surrendered," Grant remarked. "If he has such views it may be well to indulge him until we get everything else in our hands."[37]

To achieve this objective, Grant continued to peel away units from Thomas. Now that he had remounted and refitted his cavalry, James H. Wilson was to strike southward into Alabama; A. J. Smith's Thirteenth Corps was to move via water to assist in the capture of Mobile. A smaller column of horsemen under George Stoneman was to rip up the rail lines in western North Carolina and southwest Virginia. These moves would slice up the Confederacy into ever smaller pieces.[38]

Even while waging relentless war, Grant — in the interests of humanity — was willing to let up in regard to exchanging prisoners. Once Confederate authorities abandoned their refusal to include black soldiers in exchanges, he endorsed their resumption and supported measures to ease the suffering of those who remained imprisoned. Had he been intent on grinding away at the Confederacy regardless of the cost, the observations he had offered in support of the no-exchange policy the previous fall would still have held. In facilitating efforts to provide relief for Union prisoners, he noted that he hoped to obtain a far better idea of the conditions they were forced to endure — information that might "at least have a most beneficial effect upon the public mind." However, he opposed proposals to allow Confederate prisoners to choose to remain in prison or to be enticed with bounties to enlist in the Union army. Better, he argued, for those prisoners who were most unhappy with the Confederacy to be exchanged first. If they wanted to fight for the Union, let them first go home, then take the oath of allegiance. He also directed that soldiers from areas already occupied by Union forces be given priority in exchanges, and indicated his preference that Confederate prisoners with old uniforms be exchanged before their comrades with new uniforms and blankets. He was determined to retain whatever edge he could gain, knowing full well that many of the Union prisoners would never return to active duty.[39]

The resumption of exchanges also promised to resolve a personal difficulty. John Dent, Grant's brother-in-law, had been seized by Confederate authorities while on a visit to a friend in Louisiana early in 1864. Confederate authorities had offered to exchange him that summer, but Grant refused, revealing his commitment to doing his duty. Not only would it be unfair to the Union soldiers languishing in prison to secure John's release, but as a civilian (and one in sympathy with the Confederacy), John should not have been imprisoned in the first place.[40]

Busy though he might be, Grant always had time for his wife and children. During the last week in December, his oldest son, Fred, visited headquarters and went on an ill-fated duck hunting expedition. Along with Grant's servant, Bill Barnes, Fred took off in a small boat, ready to bring down some game. Union pickets mistook his school uniform of gray trimmed with black for that of a Confederate soldier, and seized him as a spy. It was with some difficulty that Fred convinced his captors he was the general's son; in turn Grant teased him that he was lucky not to have been executed.[41]

As the new year began, Grant decided that he wanted Julia at his side. Leaving the children at Burlington under the watchful eye of her brother Fred's wife, she joined the general in a roomy cabin that had just been constructed for winter quarters. Although the structure was much smaller than Hardscrabble, Julia seemed fond of her new abode. "I am snugly nestled away in my husband's log cabin," she told a friend. "Headquarters can be as private as a home." She enjoyed the time she was able to spend with her husband, including long evening talks. "Am I not a happy woman?"[42]

The general's wife was a welcome presence at City Point. She looked after everyone, made sure that sick officers were fed their favorite foods, told the general to stand up straight for photographers, and lent a domestic air to headquarters. If nothing else, when she was there, Rawlins, always fearful about the general's vulnerability to liquor, could relax. It was obvious to everyone that the Grants enjoyed an affectionate relationship, judging by their conversations, expressions, and gestures; Horace Porter recalled how they would blush when staff officers entering the general's quarters would see the couple holding hands.[43]

Having Julia at the front meant exposing her to risk. In the early morning hours of January 24, the Grants awoke to the sound of someone knocking on the cabin door. An aide excitedly reported that several Confederate rams were coming down the James River, headed for City Point. Grant threw a coat over his pajamas, pulled on his boots, and began puffing away on a cigar "like a little steam engine" as he scribbled dispatch after dispatch. Julia appeared in the front room. "Will the ram shell the bluff?" she asked.

"Yes, of course."

"Then what should I do?" Julia inquired, a bit anxious. Suddenly Grant realized that it was not always a good idea to have his wife around. An aide volunteered to take her away, but it soon became evident that City Point was safe, and the Grants returned to bed. The Confederate opportunity to wreak havoc on both the Union supply depot and army headquarters dissipated when underwater obstructions severely damaged the rams; Grant made sure that there would be no second chance.[44]

Thoughts of homes past and future ran through the general's mind. Learning that White Haven was about to be auctioned for back taxes (including taxes never paid on property the colonel had given Julia, although he had never transferred deed to the land), Grant decided to buy the property — after it had first been sold to satisfy the tax debt. The general was not happy with the way John Dent, Julia's brother, had handled the land; he knew that he would never be repaid any money he loaned John to pay the taxes.[45]

Anxious as he was to take control of White Haven, Grant knew he no longer had to worry about securing a home for his family. The efforts of Philadelphia's finest citizens to raise enough funds to buy the Grants a house had paid off; the residence, fully furnished, was tendered to the general at the beginning of the new year. Grant was so moved that his eyes welled up as he accepted the gift. In formally acknowledging the gift of the house, he remarked, "I will not predict a day when we will have peace again, with a Union restored. But that that day will come is as sure as the rising of to-morrow's Sun. I have never doubted this in the darkest days of this dark and terrible rebellion.

"Until this happy day of peace does come my family will occupy and enjoy your magnificent present. But until that [day] I do not expect, nor desire, to see much of the enjoyments of a home fireside."[46]

Even as Grant looked for ways to close out the war on the battlefield, he was drawn into efforts to secure a negotiated peace. At the end of 1864 he welcomed a visit by Francis P. Blair, Sr. In talking with the aged politician, he may have learned about Blair's proposal that both sides agree to an armistice so that a combined Union-Confederate force could rescue Mexico from Maximilian's regime. Presumably, the bonds of military service forged in service against a common foe would provide the foundation for a negotiated peace looking toward reunion. Grant, who was growing con-

woah

cerned about securing the Mexican border to prevent the construction of an exile Confederate state favored ousting Maximilian. However, he said nothing about the Blair mission; at the time he was preoccupied with the Fort Fisher operation and Butler's removal. When Blair appeared once more at City Point a week later on his way to Richmond to present his proposal to Jefferson Davis, Grant invited him to stay at headquarters as his guest. Blair's scheme reminded Grant of another idea offered by Lew Wallace, who thought that with the proper enticement Confederates in western Texas would make common cause with their former enemies to drive the French from Mexico. Grant decided to let Wallace see what he could do.[47]

Returning from a trip to Wilmington, Grant learned that three gentlemen awaited safe passage through the lines in response to an offer of negotiations delivered by Blair to Jefferson Davis. Nor were these just any three gentlemen. Alexander H. Stephens, vice president of the Confederate States of America, headed the delegation. Accompanying him were former Supreme Court justice John A. Campbell and former senator Robert M. T. Hunter. The three envoys wanted to go to Washington to meet with Lincoln; Grant asked them to wait at City Point as his guests while he telegraphed Washington to request instructions.[48]

Unknown to Grant, Washington already knew of the commissioners' mission; Lincoln had empowered Major Thomas T. Eckert with instructions on whether to receive them. Had he known that, Grant would not have invited the trio to headquarters. But now they were there, and Eckert was on the way to meet them. Through Stanton, the president instructed Grant to continue to conduct military operations as if nothing was happening, and the general, concerned that the whole enterprise might be a ruse, directed his army commanders to be ready to move at a moment's notice. He said little to the commissioners, but observed that they seemed eager and sincere to reach some sort of peace settlement that embraced reunion. Whatever hopes had kindled inside him soon flickered, for when Eckert arrived on the afternoon of February 1, he prevented Grant from joining in a meeting with the commissioners.

At first it looked as if there would be no meeting. The commissioners would not accede to the president's preconditions of reunion, abolition, and an end to the conflict; they insisted that they had to comply with Davis's directive authorizing negotiations to achieve peace between "the two countries." The Confederates tried to bypass Eckert by appealing directly to Grant to allow them to go to Washington; the major blocked this effort at circumvention. The general was clearly unhappy. Eckert seemed so intent on following the letter of his instructions in his brusque manner that he overlooked the opportunity the commissioners presented. What harm could it do for Lincoln to meet with them? In turn, Grant prodded the commissioners, asking them if they could find it within themselves to soften the wording of their reply so as to open the door to future talks. The commissioners complied; Stephens, having expected to meet a blunt, rude soldier, was pleasantly surprised to find in Grant a reflective, intelligent, and shrewd gentleman.[49]

At 10:30 P.M. telegraph operators transmitted two messages from City Point to the War Department. One, from Eckert, relayed that the commissioners were willing to be flexible on the wording of an agreement to meet; the other, from Grant, conveyed the general's favorable impression of Stephens and Hunter and suggested that to pass up this opportunity might "have a bad influence." Lincoln later said that it was Grant's telegram that induced him to change his mind and decide to meet the commissioners; he cannily omitted Eckert's dispatch when he relayed the correspondence to the House of Representatives, preferring to emphasize Grant's agency in the proceedings. In the meantime he had secured congressional passage of the Thirteenth Amendment, abolishing slavery, which would strengthen his hand in any talks.[50]

Lincoln and Secretary of State William H. Seward met the three commissioners on a vessel at Hampton Roads, offshore Fort Monroe, on February 3. Several hours of negotiations proved fruitless, for the Confederate representatives refused to abandon their insistence on a tacit recognition of Confederate sovereignty, preferring to delay answering that question until later. Even Julia Grant was surprised by their stand. She had chatted with the commissioners, finding them reasonable men. Thus the news that the negotiations had fallen apart took her by surprise. She soon confronted Lincoln. "Why, Mr. President, are you not going to make terms with them? They are our own people, you know."

"Yes, I do not forget that," replied the president; he then took out a piece of paper and shared his proposal with the general's wife. Julia read the document with astonishment. "Why, what do they want? That paper is most liberal."

Lincoln smiled. "I thought when you understood the matter you would agree with us."[51]

"Every thing looks to me very favorable for a speedy termination of the war," Grant observed in mid-February. "The people of the South are ready for it if they can get clear of their leaders." Although he did not let up against the enemy while rumors of a negotiated peace filled the air, he preferred not to press forward too quickly until Sherman and Schofield were well along with their operations. He did not want Lee to abandon Richmond and Petersburg in a desperate effort to beat back those advances. "I shall necessarily have to take the odium of apparent inactivity," he told Stanton, "but if it results, as I expect it will, in the discomfiture of Lee's Army, I shall be satisfied." Lee played right into Grant's hands by remaining where he was; Grant would always wonder why his counterpart did not risk all on such a move, especially when the alternative almost certainly meant the ultimate defeat of the Confederacy. Although he knew that it appeared as if nothing was going on, he could even laugh about it. One day at headquarters, he noted that Rufus Ingalls had acquired a dog. Did his old West Point buddy intend to take it into Richmond? "I guess so," Ingalls replied. "He's a long-lived breed."[52]

Chipping away at his opponent, Grant directed Meade to lash out at Confederate resupply efforts via a wagon convoy from the Weldon Railroad north to Richmond and Petersburg. The Second Corps screened cavalry sent out for that purpose; it fended off Lee's effort to interrupt the raid. Grant applauded the result but told Meade to refrain from assaulting fortified positions. There was no need to take more losses; however, when Grant learned that Confederate forces were being shifted from the Shenandoah to the James, he once more urged Sheridan to strike the Virginia Central Railroad, only to learn that snow and low temperatures made such a movement impossible. Perhaps Grant had learned something from Nashville, but it is more likely he chose to give Sheridan what he had denied Thomas: time.[53]

Part of Grant's concern about the appearance of inactivity along the front was his awareness that the Joint Committee on the Conduct of the War was casting a critical eye on recent operations. Even now it was reviewing Butler's abortive attempt to take Fort Fisher in an effort to exonerate that general, who was a favorite with Radical Republicans. Always suspicious of the committee's activities, Meade concluded, "This is the beginning of a war on Grant." The general-in-chief received a request to testify; as he readied to depart for Washington, he got a look at the committee's just-released findings on the Crater, which absolved Burnside of charges of mismanagement while criticizing Meade, an old committee target. Such conclusions, Grant reassured Meade, "are not sustained by Knowledge of the facts nor by my evidence nor yours." Rather, the report embraced Burnside's understanding of events, "& to draw it mildly he had forgotten some of the facts."

In February Grant traveled to Washington to testify about Fort Fisher. Touring the Capitol, he found himself forced to put out his cigar before entering the Senate chamber; after he left, a senator joked that perhaps it was time to reconsider the wisdom of promoting such an unprepossessing figure. Things were not so pleasant when the general encountered the committee. The interrogation revealed the committee's determination to shield Butler; Grant stood his ground; then he fielded a series of inquiries about other matters, all previously raised by Butler, who was determined to enact revenge on his former chief. Committee members were in sympathy with Butler: one of them, Congressman George W. Julian of Indiana, claimed that Grant looked as if he had been drinking. Nothing Grant did could ever satisfy some people, especially those who seemed more adept at political warfare than military conflict.[54]

One would never have guessed from Julian's remark that things were going well for the Union war effort. Less than a week after Grant offered his testimony, Sherman entered Columbia, South Carolina; the Confederates also abandoned Charleston. Days later Schofield captured Wilmington. Grant paid a visit to the White House, where he and Lincoln looked over maps and discussed what to do next. "Everything looks like dissolution in the South," Grant observed. "A few days more of success with Sherman will put us where we can crow loud."[55]

Most encouraging was the growing desertion from Lee's ranks attrition need not be a bloody process. Grant was particularly impressed with the wholesale departure of a squad from South Carolina. Eager to see "the final overthrow of the rebellion," he predicted that Confederate armies would approach collapse in a matter of weeks. Still, he urged Edward R. S. Canby, in command of Union forces laying siege to Mobile, to outfit a column for an expedition into Alabama. "I feel a great anxiety to see the enemy entirely broken up in the west, whilst I believe it will be an easy job," he remarked. Delays would allow the Confederates to gather deserters and blacks in an effort to rebuild their forces.[56]

As February drew to a close Grant glimpsed yet another way to end the war. Edward O. C. Ord had met several times with Confederate general James Longstreet on the subject of exchanging prisoners, especially civilians held in custody — including Julia's brother John. Now Ord raised the possibility of a negotiated peace settlement growing out of a meeting between the commanding generals of both armies (Lee had been elevated to the position of general-in-chief earlier that month). Before long these discussions took some unconventional turns. After all, Longstreet was married to Julia Dent Grant's cousin, the former Louise Garland; he had been present at the Grant wedding. Might not the two women get together? Maybe they (and the generals) could succeed where the politicians had failed at Hampton Roads.

The proposal was curious, and yet the parties involved took it most seriously. Longstreet shared it with Davis, Lee, and other Confederate officials, including Secretary of War John C. Breckinridge, who was especially captivated by the roles assigned to Mrs. Grant and Mrs. Longstreet. A dispatch went out to Lynchburg, Virginia, directing Louise Longstreet to come to Richmond. In turn Ord assured Longstreet that Grant possessed the authority to enter into such negotiations: Longstreet relayed to his commander his belief that "General Grant will agree to take the matter up without requiring any principle as a basis further than the general principle of desiring to make peace upon terms which are equally honorable to both sides."[57]

Aware of these talks, Grant wondered what might develop. Ord reported Longstreet's belief that Jefferson Davis "was the obstacle to peace," for Lee "considered the cause of the South hopeless." If Longstreet was to be believed, Lee was looking for some way to force Davis to face the reality of defeat. Perhaps, by threatening to resign, the general could force the Confederate president to sue for peace based on reunion, compensation for freed slaves, and "an immediate share in the Gov't" for the former Confederates. Surely that was what Lincoln had contemplated at Hampton Roads. But why those terms were acceptable now and not before remained something of a mystery; equally unclear was what both Davis and Lee hoped to achieve through negotiations with Grant, who had already demonstrated that, whatever his personal interest in peace, he deferred to Lincoln on such matters.[58]

On March 3, Grant opened two dispatches from Lee that had been composed the previous day. The first message referred to the ongoing discussions about civilian prisoners; the second proved more momentous, for the Confederate general, interested in "the possibility of arriving at a satisfactory adjustment of the present unhappy difficulties by means of a military convention," and "[s]incerely desiring to leave nothing untried which may put an end to the calamities of war," wanted to meet Grant in the hope that the discussions might result in submitting "the subjects of controversy between the belligerents to a convention of the Kind mentioned," adding that he was authorized "to do whatever the result of the proposed interview may render necessary or advisable."[59]

In the present military situation, Lee's offer could only mean one thing: capitulation upon terms. And yet that was not what Lincoln had offered at Hampton Roads, for there the president had outlined surrender, reunion, and emancipation as preconditions to negotiating the way in which these ends were accomplished. Grant understood as much, and knew that he had no authority to enter into such talks. He may also have realized that

Ord had gone too far. Already he had quashed talk of a meeting between Julia Grant and Louise Longstreet, flatly putting an end to Julia's
entreaties to perform diplomatic service: "No, you must not. It is simply
absurd. The men have fought this war and the men will finish it." Nor
would Grant act on his own. Off went a telegram to Washington requesting instructions.[60] → good man

Early the next morning, March 4 — the same day Lincoln, sworn in for
a second term, would speak of his desire to make peace "with malice toward none; with charity for all" — Grant received his reply, signed by
Stanton:[61]

> The President directs me to say to you that he wishes you to have no con-
> ference with Gen Lee unless it be for the capitulation of Lees army, or on
> solely minor and purely military matters. He instructs me to say that you
> are not to decide, discuss, or confer upon any political question: such
> questions the President holds in his own hands; and will submit them
> to no military conferences or conventions — mean time you are to press
> to the utmost, your military advantages.

A second message revealed that Lincoln himself had composed the missive; Stanton also reprimanded Ord for discussing such subjects with
Longstreet in the first place.[62]

These replies were needlessly harsh. In forwarding Lee's request to
Washington, Grant had already shown he knew who was in charge. Moreover, he had been working for days on a possible attack to pin Lee's
army to prevent it from detaching forces southward to stop Sherman. Off
went a telegram to the war secretary that showed how much the general
smarted under the apparent rebuke. "I can assure you that no act of the
enemy will prevent me pressing all advantages gained to the utmost of my
ability," he told Stanton. "Neither will I under any circumstances exceed
my authority or in any way embarrass the Govt. It was because I had no
right to meet Gen. Lee on the subject proposed by him that I refered the
matter for instructions." He was tempted to add that it would also be
wrong for him to reject such proposals out of hand, for "Peace must Come
some day," but on reflection he struck the sentiment from his reply. Then
he told Lee that he lacked the authority to confer about matters beyond
his purview. The war would continue.[63]

The arrival of March meant that spring was not far away, bringing sunshine and dry roads that would offer Lee an opportunity to head for the
Carolinas. And there was no word from Sherman. "I feel no doubt of the

result with him," Grant explained, "but cut loose as he is I necessarily feel anxious." Not until midmonth did he learn that Sherman was in fine shape in North Carolina. Good news also came from Sheridan, who at long last moved southward to hit the Virginia Central line and the James River canal. At the same time Grant had to calm Stanton's jitters about the possibility of another Confederate thrust at Washington; he had to push both Thomas and Canby to get moving. At one point he considered replacing Canby, who was "slow beyond excuse" — words which he also used that month to describe Thomas. Anxious to make sure that Lee did not wriggle loose, he directed Meade to keep his men "in condition to be moved in the very shortest possible notice."[64]

The general-in-chief sent out telegrams; arranged for supplies; considered command issues; and juggled egos, hesitant subordinates, and worried superiors. He could take satisfaction in his accomplishments, notably when he received the medal Congress had ordered struck in celebration of his victories at Vicksburg and Chattanooga. He had to offer some remarks on accepting the medal and scribbled out a short reply, but he spoke so softly when reading it that few were able to make out what he said. Whatever anguish he felt at that moment was soon eclipsed when Julia suggested that the military band present start playing at what soon became an improvised ball. The general, much against his will, had to waltz across the floor, keeping time with the music as best he could. Had Lee only known, he might have traded weapons for musical instruments to keep his foe off balance.[65]

Yet March was also a sad month, for he learned of the death of his sister Clara, the second of his siblings to die during the war. Although Grant had been aware that she was seriously ill, her passing caught him unprepared, and it took some time for him to gather his thoughts and reply to his father's letter conveying the news. For now, at least, he found it easier to discuss other matters. "We are now having fine weather and I think will be able to wind up matters about Richmond soon," he told his father. "I am anxious to have Lee hold on where he is a short time longer so that I can get him in a position where he must loose a great portion of his Army. The rebellion has lost its vitality"; barring a catastrophe, "there will be no rebel Army of any great dimentions a few weeks hence." At the moment he was well, but he would welcome a break; "I hope it will come soon."

"My kindest regards to all at home. I shall expect to make you a visit the coming Summer."[66]

20

Ending the Matter

◉

SPRING BROUGHT BETTER WEATHER to central Virginia. The skies cleared, the rain let up, and temperatures rose. "The mud here at City Point is rapidly becoming dried up, an important event that it would be unexcusable not to mention," observed a Vermont private on March 24. "The streets are not only dry, but some of them are actually dusty." Stiff winds played havoc with hospital tents, but otherwise all was quiet. After dusk a steamboat, accompanied by a smaller vessel, drew up at the landing at City Point. Within minutes Ulysses and Julia Grant walked down to the landing. Waiting at the end of the gangplank was the president of the United States. After heartily shaking the general's hand, Abraham Lincoln escorted the couple onto the deck of the *River Queen* and into a cabin where Mary Todd Lincoln was waiting. He proposed that the two ladies get to know each other a little better while the two men went off to discuss matters.[1]

Although the president occasionally visited his generals at the front (this was his second trip to City Point), what made this trip unusual was that the Lincolns came at Grant's invitation. Julia had been reading newspaper accounts describing the president's tired features; she thought it would be wonderful if the president visited headquarters. At first Grant had brushed off these requests, noting that the president was free to come if he so desired; Julia countered that in the past such visits had been interpreted (not without some justification) as meddling by the chief executive. What clinched the matter was a remark from a new captain on the general's staff. Asked why the Lincolns did not come to City Point, Robert Todd Lincoln replied, "I supposed they would, if they were sure they would not be intruding."[2]

The captain's comment reflected the evolution of the relationship between the president and the general-in-chief. Once safely reelected, Lincoln could accede to some of Grant's requests that had once carried with them a considerable political price tag. Ben Butler was gone; while Nathaniel Banks might continue to serve as Lincoln's representative in Louisiana, he would never again command troops in the field. The two men even reached a reasonable compromise on William S. Rosecrans, shelving rather than dismissing him from the service. Finally the president bowed to Grant's wish to cease trading with the enemy.[3]

What had begun as a sometimes uneasy alliance now showed signs of blossoming into a true friendship. The general helped the president resolve a troublesome family matter of long standing when he allowed Robert Lincoln to assume a place on his staff with the rank of captain, even though some of Grant's own staff officers had held that rank (or less) for some time. In so doing, he enabled the president to deflect criticism about his son's failure to serve, gratify Robert's own desires, and quell Mary Lincoln's fears of losing yet another son. And the president could still call on the general to provide political protection. When the House of Representatives, suspicious of what had happened at Hampton Roads, requested Lincoln to turn over relevant correspondence, he asked Grant if he could include the general's dispatch asserting that to dismiss the commissioners without a hearing would "have a bad influence." The president wanted to explain his decision to meet the envoys as a response to that observation. "I think the dispatch does you credit," he explained, "while I do not see that it can embarrass you." Grant acceded to the request; Lincoln included the dispatch, while omitting one from Thomas Eckert. Sent at the same time as Grant's message, Eckert's telegram reported the commissioners' willingness to drop Jefferson Davis's call for negotiations between "two countries" to facilitate discussions toward "a just & honorable peace" — a message that shed additional light on the president's decision to travel to Hampton Roads. Better, Lincoln thought, to take cover behind the general's reputation by emphasizing Grant's message.[4]

Although Grant was doubtless glad to see the president, he had more important things on his mind. The good weather and dusty roads meant that at last Lee might try to extricate himself from Richmond and Petersburg. Although he had lost between six and seven thousand men to desertion over the past ten weeks, he could still count on about 50,000 soldiers (Grant had built up his numbers to nearly 113,000, but not all could be employed in offensive operations). Should the Confederate commander wriggle loose, he might still commit mischief, especially if he joined forces with Joseph E. Johnston's army in North Carolina where they could lash out at Sherman. Anticipating such a move, Grant urged Phil Sheridan to hurry his horsemen to the south side of the James as soon as possible, so that the cavalryman could sweep around the western edge of the enemy's fortifications and sever Lee's two remaining lifelines, the Southside and Danville railroads, and be in position to check a breakout attempt.)

This time Grant itched to play for high stakes. "When this movement commences I shall move out by my left with all the force I can, holding present entrenched lines," he told Sherman. "I shall start with no distinct view further than holding Lee's forces from following Sheridan. But I shall be along myself and will take advantage of any thing that turns up." Orders outlining these movements went out to Meade the morning of March 24. Most unusual was a directive urging commanders to react according to circumstances: "I would have it particularly enjoined upon Corps Commanders that in case of an attack from the enemy those not attacked are not to wait for orders from the commanding officer of the Army to which they belong, but that they will move promptly and notify the commander of their action. I would also enjoin the same action on the part of Division commanders when other parts of their Corps are engaged. In like manner I would urge the importance of following up a repulse of the enemy."5

(Expect the unexpected; hit hard; be alert; seize the initiative.) These were all sensible instructions, and Grant did not have to wait long to see them implemented. At dawn on March 25 word arrived at headquarters that (the Confederates had launched a major attack, overrunning Fort Stedman, east of Petersburg, just eight miles from City Point. Should the attackers hold on to their gains, Grant would have to shift forces to protect his supply depot, allowing Lee to escape.) Moreover, although Meade's headquarters was but a mile away from the front, Meade himself had spent the night at City Point with Lincoln, Grant, and Army of the James commander Edward O. C. Ord. It would be up to Ninth Corps chief John G. Parke to contain the Rebel advance. He did so: (the Union lines on either side of the breakthrough held firm, allowing him to mount a counterattack. Within hours the threat dissipated; the Confederates found themselves cut off and thousands surrendered.) Even the president took the event in stride, wiring Stanton at Washington: "Robert just now tells me there was a little rumpus up the line this morning, ending about where it began."6

Grant was pleased with the response of Parke and Second Corps commander Andrew A. Humphreys to the attack and their eagerness to strike back — qualities all too often in short supply in the recent past. That afternoon he invited the president to a review but a short distance from that morning's action. Mounting Jeff Davis, a black horse liberated from the plantation of its namesake, Lincoln found his legs dangling down the sides of the smallish mount; Grant made sure that next time the president would ride the general's favorite, Cincinnati, who at 17½ hands was well suited to the lanky chief executive. Riding to the front, the president and his general saw the aftermath of the attack, including the wounded, the dead, and the captured. Along for the ride were little Jesse Grant and the president's younger son, Tad. At one point Jesse's mount bolted; both his father and the president commenced pursuing horse and rider, until Grant decided that it would be better to let Jesse's horse run itself out (as it did, in a sense, by heading straight for a mule corral). The party even came under fire from a Confederate battery, forcing them to seek cover in a bombproof, the boys delighted by the racket.[7]

Another review, equally eventful in its own way, took place the next day, featuring Ord's army north of the James. Mrs. Lincoln and Mrs. Grant accompanied the party, seated in an ambulance especially outfitted for the purpose. The ride proved a bumpy one in more than one way. Mrs. Lincoln, already discomfited by the way that the wagon jostled the passengers, exploded when she saw Mrs. Ord riding alongside her husband. Grant's secretary Adam Badeau made things worse with an ill-timed remark; Julia tried to remedy the situation by having Mrs. Ord greet the ambulance. But Mary Todd Lincoln was not to be placated; later that afternoon she snapped at Ord when the general made an unfortunate comment about providing the president's wife with a mount that would remain by the side of the president. Horace Porter, who was present in the ambulance, later remarked that perhaps it was all due to the uncomfortable ride.[8]

Others knew better. Julia had already suffered under several of Mrs. Lincoln's outbursts, including an unseemly incident on the first evening of the Lincolns' visit. After the president had taken the general away to talk, Mrs. Grant started to sit down, only to be brought up short when Mrs. Lincoln remarked that Julia should wait to be asked to sit by the First Lady. Before long the coolness between the wives of the two most important men heading the Union war effort was painfully evident, although Julia tried to keep both the peace and her distance.[9]

Mary Todd Lincoln was not the only person fuming that day. Phil Sheridan, who had arrived at City Point early that morning, was peeved with Grant's instructions, which suggested that once Sheridan tore up the railroads west of Petersburg, he might lead his men south to meet Sherman. This would not do; the cavalryman wanted to be in at the kill. Learning of Sheridan's displeasure, Rawlins told him to talk to Grant. After hearing out his subordinate's protest, which was delivered in a voice so loud it did not require staff officers to go to the trouble of eavesdropping, Grant quietly told him that the instructions were worded for public consumption. If all went well, Sheridan would rejoin Grant's army after destroying the railroads; however, should the cavalryman find himself in trouble, it would look as if a juncture with Sherman was part of the plan.[10]

Another visitor arrived late in the afternoon of March 27. Now that his men had joined forces with John Schofield's column at Goldsboro, North Carolina, thus reestablishing his supply line, William T. Sherman took advantage of a pause for resting and refitting his command to run up to City Point. He wanted to have a quick meeting about the next — and perhaps the last — move. No sooner had his steamer docked than Sherman hurriedly strode forward across the gangplank toward his friend, who had come down the wharf. "How d'you do, Sherman!" "How are you, Grant!" They shook hands so warmly and heartily that Horace Porter recalled that it seemed like a reunion of schoolmates. Grant took Sherman up to greet Julia; pleased to see a captive audience, Sherman started describing his marches across the Confederate heartland with characteristic enthusiasm flavored with colorful language.[11]

After listening to Sherman's stories for an hour, Grant broke in to suggest that perhaps they should pay a visit to the president on the *River Queen*. It was a short and cordial conversation; the generals parted with the understanding that they were to return tomorrow for a more serious discussion. On their return, Julia asked them if they had seen Mrs. Lincoln. The two generals admitted they had not (Sherman confessed he did not know she was aboard), whereupon Julia playfully scolded the pair for their poor manners. Then it was time to talk over future military operations. Julia remained in the room writing letters. Her husband paused. "Sherman, do you think it is safe to let Mrs. Grant hear us?" After all, he added, women were known to spread stories. Taking the bait, Sherman began questioning Julia about the location of rivers, cities, and other geographic features, all of which Julia deliberately botched. The lighthearted fun was a momentary distraction from the grim business ahead. It also revealed how truly glad Grant and Sherman were to be together again, for despite frequent conversations over the wire and by dispatch, they had not seen each other for twelve months.[12] → *woah*

Not everything they discussed was frivolous. When Sherman had reached Savannah, Grant had contemplated bringing his army north to Virginia via water, only to discover that he lacked sufficient seaworthy transport for such a tremendous undertaking. That had led him to agree with Sherman's idea of marching north to Virginia through the Carolinas.

It had not been a demanding advance, although just a week ago Joe Johnston, having gathered a makeshift force out of what remained of the Army of Tennessee and other commands, had caused some tense moments when he hit Sherman's columns at Bentonville, North Carolina, only to withdraw once the Yankees arrived in force. Now, however, Grant's plan called for Sherman to keep the pressure on Johnston while the armies around Richmond took care of Lee on their own. It was as much a political as a military decision: Grant did not want to fuel existing sectional rivalries by giving the Westerners the opportunity to say that the Easterners could not close up Bobby Lee by themselves.[13]

The next morning, Grant, Sherman, and Admiral David D. Porter boarded the *River Queen* to meet with the president (but only after Grant and Sherman first inquired about Mrs. Lincoln — and learned that she was not well). Several observers had noted that during the past several days Lincoln had appeared anxious. Perhaps what he had seen at Fort Stedman sobered him as to what was to come next; doubtless some of his edginess was due to a lingering concern that Sherman had taken a risk in making his visit. Might not the Confederates try to take advantage of his absence? Sherman reassured him that he had left his command in good hands back in North Carolina, and that in any case he planned to depart shortly. Then Grant outlined his plan to flank Lee's right, which would cut off any chance of joining up with Johnston, and force him to come out and fight or starve. Meanwhile, Sherman would continue to move northward against Johnston. Lincoln's next question was in some sense a surprising reversal of previous conversations. Having for years urged his generals to keep after the enemy and be aggressive, the president now wondered whether Grant and Sherman could close out the war without spilling much more blood. Grant replied that what happened next depended in large part on how Lee and Johnston responded.

Sherman then changed the subject. What, he wanted to know, were Lincoln's thoughts about the end of the war? What should happen to Confederate leaders? How should Grant and he treat the defeated? Lincoln expressed his preference for lenient terms; he implied that it would be best if the Confederacy's civil leaders somehow left the country, thus avoiding capture and trial. Sherman peppered the president with question after question; Grant sat, smoked, and listened, gathering in everything, letting Sherman and Lincoln dominate the discussion. He was familiar with Lincoln's desire to "let 'em up easy"; earlier that week the president had observed, "Let them once surrender and reach their homes, they won't take up arms again. . . . Let them have their horses to plow with. . . . Give them the most liberal and honorable terms." Yet he may also have recalled that the president was not willing to allow his generals a free hand in such matters, although apparently he did not ask Lincoln to elaborate on the wording of his March 3 telegram directing Grant not to negotiate with Lee.[14]

Sherman was impressed by Lincoln's desire for leniency. Later he claimed that the president spoke in specific terms about the restoration of civil government, including the recognition of present state regimes until others could be constructed. Sherman also assumed that the generals would play a role in that process. Considering Lincoln's previous willingness to allow Sherman to confer with Joe Brown, perhaps this was understandable. Equally impressive was what Lincoln failed to say or do. Despite Gideon Welles's insistence that the president feared Grant and Sherman would impose harsh requirements, Lincoln refrained from dictating terms of surrender, resting content with sharing with his generals his thoughts on the matter — and only after Sherman had raised the subject in his barrage of questions. Gone was the anxiety that lurked behind his March 3 telegram to Grant about the proper scope of military authority; he treated Grant and Sherman as associates rather than agents of administration policy. He would leave it to the men in uniform to give voice to those sentiments in a written document. The wisdom of that decision would soon be put to the test.[15]

"Genl Grant is evidently preparing for something & is marshalling & preparing his troops for some movement, which is not yet disclosed. . . ." So wrote Robert E. Lee to his daughter on the very day that Lincoln was sharing with Grant and Sherman his desire that the war be brought to the close without another bloody battle. Lee was right. No sooner had Sherman left City Point than Grant issued final instructions outlining Sheridan's role in the forthcoming offensive. Nothing had changed in the aftermath of the abortive assault at Fort Stedman; the cavalryman was to sweep west, beyond Lee's right, and rip up his remaining railroad links. Two infantry corps would follow. If the Confederates failed to challenge the move, they were doomed; if they attacked, so much the better, for Grant was confident that he would prevail on an open field. "I mean to end the business here," he told Sheridan.[16]

The next morning, with his men in motion, Grant decided to leave for the front. He kissed Julia several times; Lincoln accompanied the general and his staff to the railroad station. Earlier, when the president had remarked that perhaps it was time for him to leave, Grant asked him to stay. After all, he added, in just a few days Lincoln might be able to visit Richmond.

At the station Lincoln shook Grant's hand; then he watched as the officers boarded the train. As the locomotive started to pull away, Grant and his staff raised their hats in salute to the president. Returning it, with voice nearly breaking, Lincoln, cried out, "Good-by, gentlemen. God bless you all! Remember, your success is my success!"[17]

As the train chugged toward the front, Grant sat down near the rear of the passenger car, lighted a cigar, and began discussing his plans. Aware of the president's anxiety, he remarked that he thought "we can send him some good news in a day or two." That seemed to be the purpose behind his initial dispatches to the president, which reported early progress as well as first contact with the enemy. But soon the news turned bad, as the sunny blue skies turned cloudy and gray, followed by heavy rain. That night and the next day a downpour turned the roads into mud, rendering movement slow and difficult. Efforts to build corduroy roads out of logs made some routes passable for horses, but it did not look good. Was it wise to proceed in such conditions?[18]

Grant was prepared to improvise in response to circumstances. On the evening of March 29 he directed Sheridan to abandon the thrust west to cut the rail lines. Instead, he was to ride around the Confederate right and into the enemy rear. "I now feel like ending the matter," he announced. But the bad weather forced him to reconsider that plan. Reports from the front led him to ponder for several hours the possibility of a frontal assault against what he was told were thinly held fortifications; by evening, however, he believed that the best opportunity to inflict damage was with Sheridan, Warren, and Humphreys against Lee's exposed right, which was attempting to check the flanking move. Orders went out to Sheridan directing the cavalryman to consolidate his gains to date and replenish his forage.

Hours later an unhappy Sheridan arrived at headquarters. Having regained some of the aggressiveness that seemed to have left him when he was an independent commander, he was determined to share his feelings with Grant. To anyone who would listen, he exclaimed, "I tell you, I'm ready to strike out tomorrow and go to smashing things." It would take but a wave of his hand to brush back the Confederate cavalry in his front; give him some infantry and he would roll up the enemy flank. Grant heard him out, then issued orders directing Sheridan to turn the enemy right the next morning with both his cavalry and the Fifth Corps. Should re-

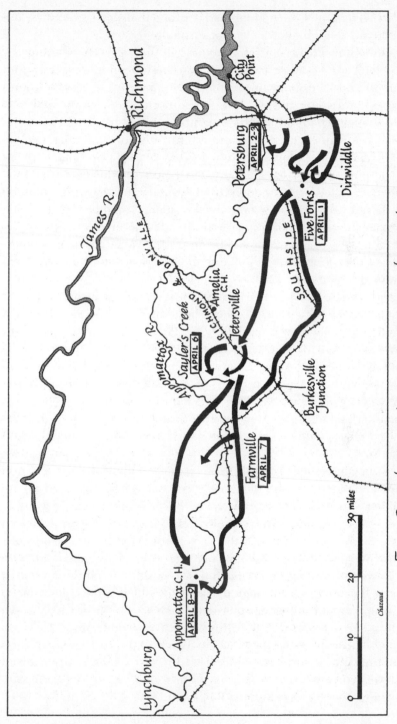

From Petersburg to Appomattox, March–April 1865

Richmond

City Point

James R.

Petersburg
APRIL 2–3

Dinwiddie

Five Forks
APRIL 1

SOUTHSIDE

Amelia C.H.

Jetersville

RICHMOND AND DANVILLE R.

Sayler's Creek
APRIL 6

Appomattox R.

Burkesville Junction

Farmville
APRIL 7

Appomattox C.H.
APRIL 8–9

Lynchburg

0   10   20   30 miles

Chazaud

ports arrive that the Confederates had thinned their lines to counter the move, then Grant would order a frontal assault.[19]

Grant was not sure what he wanted to do. If the object of the campaign was to capture Lee's entire army, then it was best to pin it in place around Richmond and Petersburg until Union columns cut off possible routes of escape to the south and west. One reason armies during the Civil War had done such a poor job of following up on initial battlefield successes was that commanders failed to plan for a pursuit prior to initiating combat. Defeated armies often proved amazingly resilient, and the delays in planning pursuits after engagements meant that by the time they were launched it was too late. Although Grant wanted to hit the Rebs out in the open, should Lee mass forces opposite Sheridan, it might prove tempting to overrun the thinly held trenches. In the case of an assault against Petersburg, the Rebels would have to be destroyed where they stood; otherwise, the Confederates might pull out and escape westward, leading to a difficult running pursuit with Lee in the lead.

Heavy fighting on March 31 complicated matters. Lee had gathered forces under George Pickett to check Sheridan, who soon found himself scrambling to hold on at Dinwiddie Court House. Warren's corps fought desperately to gain White Oak Road, a critical byway that linked Pickett's command to the rest of Lee's army. By noon the Rebel threat was contained, and in the afternoon portions of the road were secured — but not before Grant grumbled about Warren's handling of his men. The corps commander had struggled much of the day, and by evening he was doing about as well as could be expected: his track record was coming back to haunt him.[20]

By evening it seemed likely that the next day would bring decisive action on the Confederate right. Pulling his men back, Pickett fortified a position along a road juncture known as Five Forks. Uncomfortable with the prospect of commanding Warren but eager to attack, Sheridan requested that the Sixth Corps spearhead the movement. That proved impossible: Horatio Wright's Valley veterans were too far away, and redeployment westward would take too much time. "Besides," Grant pointed out, "Wright thinks he can go through the line where he is and it is advisable to have troops and a commander there who feels so. . . ." Instead, Sheridan would have to make do with the Fifth Corps. Grant understood the cavalryman's reluctance. What happened at White Oak Road served as a reminder that Warren's performance over the last year had been mixed at best; his run-in with Sheridan on the march from the Wilderness to Spotsylvania was still fresh in Little Phil's mind.[21]

April 1 promised to be a long day of anxious waiting at headquarters at Dabney's Mill, located just to the rear of the Union line along Ord's front, ten miles southwest of Petersburg. Nearly another dozen miles to the west, Sheridan was going into battle. With him was Horace Porter, sent by Grant to apprise the cavalryman of his superior's wishes and to keep headquarters informed. At last the Confederates would be caught out in the open. Grant dashed off a note to Julia, describing the situation. "I am feeling very well and full of confidence," he added.[22]

Yet Grant had felt the same way before, only to find his plans undone. Sheridan did not worry him, but the same could not be said of Warren. Grant knew that the two men did not get along and that Warren was prone to give orders his own peculiar interpretation, often leading to delays and disagreements. Lacking faith in Warren and anxious that a critical operation not be botched by inept leadership, Grant took an unusual step. Calling Orville Babcock over, he entrusted his aide with a private message for Sheridan, authorizing him to displace any officer whose performance hindered the progress of operations. This time Grant would not tolerate error.[23] *what's this mean?*

In midafternoon a message arrived from Porter. Dismounted Union cavalry had overwhelmed the Confederate defenses at Five Forks; infantry was getting into place to finish the job. "Our men have never fought better," the aide had scribbled. "All are in excellent spirits and anxious to go in." The Confederates appeared demoralized and defeated.[24]

Cheered by the news, Grant continued to manage operations by telegram, urging Meade to finalize preparations for an assault against the Petersburg fortifications and to shield Sheridan's strike force from counterattack. But he also knew that the promise of victory contained in Porter's message might dissolve. And so he waited. Dusk was approaching; Grant wrapped himself in a cavalry overcoat and joined his staff around a fire. Suddenly a horseman galloped up, shouting all the way. It was Porter. Jumping off his mount, the excited aide rushed to Grant, hugged him, and blurted out the news that Sheridan had smashed the Confederate lines. The Southside Railroad was doomed; so was the Confederate defense of Richmond and Petersburg. Staff members started shouting and celebrating.[25]

Recovering from the staff officer's enthusiastic embrace, Grant inquired about prisoners; Porter estimated that there were at least five thousand. Then Grant began writing out orders for a general assault early the next day. "Sheridan has captured every thing before him," he wired Meade. Now it was time to attack Petersburg. If the Rebs bolstered their

Meade

crumbling right, they would not have enough men left to hold on to their trenches for long. But this time there would be no <u>mindless</u> frontal assaults, no banging one's head against a brick wall. "Understand: I do not wish you to fight your way over difficult barriers, <u>against defended lines</u>," he instructed Ord. "I want you to see if the enemy is leaving and if so follow him up." Sheridan was to act as circumstances suggested, but Grant urged him to gain possession of the Southside Railroad.[26]

see p 423

Before long word arrived from Five Forks that the Fifth Corps was now under hard-bitten Charles Griffin. Sheridan, impatient with Warren for failing to deploy his divisions properly and in a timely manner, had taken Grant's hint. Seeing in the slightest delay the promise of procrastination, he relieved Warren of command. Grant sustained the decision. That there was something decidedly <u>unfair</u> about the whole business — Warren had worked hard all day to get his men into position — was lost in the larger message that this time generals would pay for their mistakes. Nearly a year of debating with his superiors and grumbling about the campaign had finally done in the senior corps commander in the Army of the Potomac. Not until midnight did the downcast Warren arrive at Meade's headquarters. He had every right to believe that Sheridan had acted hastily and unreasonably in this instance, but he was now suffering for past sins.[27]

Having put in place plans for an attack at 4 A.M., Grant tried to get some sleep. It had been a good day's work. Most rewarding was the confidence his corps commanders expressed about taking the works in their front. He had not seen such self-assurance in some time. All night cannons fired at Confederate positions to make sure that Lee could not concentrate his men for a counterattack against Sheridan. At dawn on April 2 a barrage announced the Union advance. A short time later the first dispatch announced that Wright's Sixth Corps had carried the center of the enemy line. Not long afterward John Parke reported that the Ninth Corps had achieved like results against Lee's left. After notifying Lincoln of the news, Grant rode toward the front, passing several columns of <u>prisoners</u> being herded to the rear. Union infantry, realizing <u>the end of months of trench warfare was in sight</u>, cheered.[28]

Grant conferred with Meade, <u>directing him to press the attack to cut off as many Confederates as possible.</u> Establishing headquarters on a knoll that offered a good view of the assault, he sat down under a tree. Couriers came and went, bringing reports of progress and carrying away instructions. Enemy artillery began dropping shells around the hill. Staff officers, betraying reasonable anxiety, urged the general to seek a safer position. "Well, they do seem to have the range on us," he finally conceded, and he moved to another spot.[29]

It was the moment Grant had waited a long time to see. The calm exterior masked the elation betrayed in a hastily drafted letter to Julia; even as he readied to close in for the kill, he wanted to share the moment with her. "I am now writing from far inside of what was the rebel fortifications this morning but what are ours now," he began, using prose that echoed his letters from Mexico. After detailing the news of captured cannons and prisoners, he added, "Altogether this has been one of the greatest victories of the war. Greatest because it is over what the rebels have always regarded as their most invincible Army and the one used for the defince of their capitol. We may have some more hard work but I hope not."[30]

By midafternoon the Confederate position was dissolving. Lee was already preparing to dash westward. Once more Grant started puffing and writing. Orders went out to start a pursuit and head off the enemy; so did a letter to City Point inviting Abraham Lincoln to pay headquarters in the field a visit. Rawlins knew why the good news kept coming: "Thank God, the Lieutenant General has commanded . . . himself and not permitted the spirit or, I might say, the genius of his orders, to be dampened by his subordinate commanders."[31]

Grant awoke on April 3 to the news that Petersburg had fallen. Eager to assess the situation, he hustled forward, and within hours the general-in-chief entered the city. As bullets whizzed down the streets, he huddled with Meade under cover of a house. Occasionally Grant peered around the corner and saw the bridges over the Appomattox filled with Confederates still making their escape. There was no artillery on hand to smash the span, but Grant confessed that in any case he "had not the heart to turn the artillery upon such a mass of defeated and fleeing men, and I hoped to capture them soon." He directed Sheridan to push on and block roads leading south. When Meade advocated pursuit across the river, Grant reminded him that the object now was to cut off Lee's line of retreat. The best way to do that was not to follow him, but to get ahead of him.[32]

Eventually the firing subsided, then ended altogether. Learning that Lincoln was on his way to join him, Grant waited at the residence of one Thomas Wallace on Market Street. Few white residents were visible to the headquarters group as they rode through the streets, although small groups of blacks cheered the sight of blue uniforms. Grant continued to issue orders, cigar in hand, just "as if the work before him was a mere matter of business in which he felt no particular enthusiasm or care." Before long the president arrived. Beaming and smiling, he greeted Grant with such enthusiasm that it looked as if he wanted to hug the general. "Do you know, general, I had sort of a sneaking idea all along that you intended to do something like this," he declared. Within minutes, however, he turned from what had been gained to the peace that was to come. Once more he shared with Grant his preferences for a lenient peace, aware now that Lee's surrender might not be far off. As the two men talked, blacks gathered to watch; some tried to sell Union officers Confederate money.[33]

Although anxious to leave Petersburg to direct the pursuit, Grant remained with Lincoln for nearly two hours, hoping that he could personally deliver to the president the news of Richmond's fall. Finally, he decided to make his way westward; hours later he opened the dispatch that announced the capture of the Confederate capital. Taking the news in stride, Grant merely remarked that he regretted being unable to share it personally with Lincoln. He left unsaid the observation that in the end it had been the Army of the James, not the Army of the Potomac, that entered the city, led by black soldiers. There was no talk of the conquering hero parading through the streets of the Rebel stronghold; Grant's true objective was not a place but a general and his army. But his note to Sherman reporting the events of the past three days revealed pride in what had been accomplished: "This Army has now won a most desicive Victory and followed the enemy. That is all it ever wanted to make it as good an Army as ever fought a battle."[34]

For the next forty-eight hours Grant and his men — at last they did seem to be *his* men — pressed westward, as Grant put it, "in the hope of overtaking or dispersing the remainder of Lee's army." His immediate target was Burkeville Junction; if he beat Lee there the door to North Carolina would slam shut. It would not be easy, for the Army of Northern Virginia could count about 55,000 men ready for action; Grant commenced the pursuit with some 75,000 men. Although Lee had gotten a head start, his retreat was delayed nearly a day when expected supplies did not show up at Amelia Court House. Here was the opportunity Grant sought; he wasted no time exploiting it, especially as his movements had left his men with a shorter distance to march to Burkeville Junction. Confident of the result, he informed Sherman early on the morning of April 5 that he believed Lee would next head for Danville. However, the Rebel army was dissolving: "If you can possibly do so push on from where you are and let us see if we cannot finish the job. . . . Rebel Armies are now the only strategic points to strike at." That day news came that Sheridan had checked the Confederate advance at Jetersville, blocking the road southward to Burkeville Junction and beyond. Infantry soon secured the position. The escape route to North Carolina was no more. Grant turned his attention to heading off the Confederate columns before they could reach the Blue Ridge Mountains. "Lee's Army is the objective point," he reminded Meade, "and to capture that is all we want."[35]

The soldiers knew that at last their hard work and sacrifice were about to pay off. They also knew who was responsible. Recognizing Grant as he rode past, the members of one regiment could not restrain themselves. "I thought the boys would split open they hallowed, cheered and made such a noise, threw caps at the horses & c.," one soldier noted. "Poor old Johnnie Rebs I think it will soon be all up with you."[36]

That evening Grant and his staff were on their way to Burkeville Junction when a rider dressed in gray pulled up (having just avoided being shot). He was a courier from Sheridan with a message expressing concern that Meade, who looked as if he was preparing for a major clash at Amelia Court House on the morrow, was insufficiently alert to the need to cut off Lee's retreat westward: "I wish you were here yourself. I feel confident of capturing the Army of Northern Virginia if we exert ourselves. I see no escape for Lee."[37]

It was some twenty miles to Jetersville, the route was wooded, and it was night. Enemy forces were in the vicinity: their campfires were visible in the distance through the trees. Nevertheless, Grant, perhaps recalling how confusion between Meade and Sheridan had led to a missed opportunity some eleven months before, decided that his presence was critical. He and his staff made their way through the darkness, reaching a small log cabin surrounded by a tobacco patch that served as Sheridan's headquarters at approximately 10:30 P.M. The cavalryman outlined the situation to Grant, boasting that he could capture the entire enemy force the next day. Grant demurred: Lee was wily enough to get away with some of his command. After issuing orders to Ord outlining the options for the morrow, Grant, tired by his trip, was prepared to call it a night; but nagging fears that Lee was making good his escape convinced him that rest was impossible until he and Sheridan conferred with Meade.

At midnight the three generals met. Anxious not to override Meade, Grant suggested that Meade make sure that Lee was in fact preparing to stand and fight it out before issuing instructions based on that assumption. Meade agreed, and changed his orders. Hours later information came that confirmed Sheridan's hunch that Lee was determined to keep moving. Rations awaited the Confederates at Farmville. The chase was on.[38]

April 6 was the third anniversary of Shiloh. Federal columns caught up with Lee's rear: the resulting firefight impeded Lee's march and stretched out his army still more, rendering it vulnerable to attack. Ord's lead elements nearly blocked Lee's line of march when they approached several bridges spanning the Appomattox River near Farmville. Although the Confederates drove off the enemy with heavy losses, the clash ate up more

⌐↳ to Conf, I assume

time. Finally, Sheridan pierced the Confederate column at Sayler's Creek, just east of Farmville, and ripped through the Rebels, capturing some 6,000 men and half a dozen generals, including Richard S. Ewell and Lee's son Custis. Only a brave stand by William Mahone's Virginians prevented the disintegration of the entire Army of Northern Virginia. In reporting the victory, Sheridan observed: "If the thing is pressed I think Lee will surrender."[39]

That night, as he set up headquarters at Burkeville Junction, Grant sensed that this time he would be able to press his advantage. "The troops are all pushing now though it is after night and they have had no rest for more than one week. The finest spirits prevails among the men and I believe that in three days more Lee will not have an army of 5,000 men to take out of Virginia, and no train or supplies." But it was not quite over yet. Lee had made it to Farmville, where rations awaited his hungry men. The Confederate commander next set his sights upon Appomattox Station, where supplies from Lynchburg would arrive. From there he might still turn south; just beyond Lynchburg the Blue Ridge beckoned. The next seventy-two hours would be crucial. "We have Lee's army pressed hard, his men scattering and going to their homes by the thousands," Grant telegraphed Sherman. "He is endeavoring to reach Danville where Davis and his cabinet have gone. I shall press the pursuit to the end. Push Johnston at the same time and let us finish up this job all at once."[40]

Grant was not the only person pondering how to end the war. A letter from Lincoln informed him that the president had been meeting with John A. Campbell, one of the three Confederate commissioners from the previous February, concerning an attempt to withdraw Virginia from the Confederacy. "I do not think anything will come of this," Lincoln observed; "but I have thought it best to notify you, so that if you see signs, you may understand them. From your recent despatches it seems that you are pretty effectually withdrawing the Virginia troops from opposition to the government." Then came the familiar refrain: "Nothing I have done, or probably shall do, is to delay, hinder, or interfere with you in your work." At the same time Grant learned that Richard S. Ewell had declared that the war was over, at least for Lee's army. It was time to make terms, the Confederate general believed, although he was not certain that Lee would do so without first consulting Jefferson Davis.[41]

On the morning of April 7 Grant headed toward Farmville. Morning rains promised to slow both armies' progress. Thinking that he would have to spend another dozen days or so in the field (he also wanted to help Sherman finish up Johnston), he sent word to City Point suggesting that Julia might want to return north. On horseback he passed by columns of soldiers, all cheering and shouting, the sounds of victory in the offing. This time they were determined to finish the job. Their general — for now Grant was clearly *their* general — acknowledged the cheers by doffing his hat. At noon he arrived in Farmville and established headquarters on the piazza of a brick hotel.[42] *USG is accompanying the troops on the Appx Camp's*

That afternoon, as Grant composed more dispatches directing his generals to close in on the fleeing foe, soldiers marching by cheered the small man in the muddy uniform puffing away at a cigar. Edward O. C. Ord and John Gibbon soon joined him. That morning Gibbon's Twenty-fourth Corps had punished the retreating Confederates, who were now pulling north of the Appomattox River, abandoning any hope of joining Johnston. Sheridan turned his columns toward Appomattox Station, eager to capture supplies waiting there for Lee: no doubt he would also encounter the advance elements of the Army of Northern Virginia. Repeated clashes hindered Lee's ability to pull away and head westward. As evening came, the men of the Sixth Corps, pressing forward, saw Grant, and staged a review of their own. With bonfires lighting the way, the soldiers marched past, some holding up torches, others cheering, with a band adding to the festivities, before nearly an entire division joined in singing "John Brown's Body."[43]

Inspiring as the evening doubtless was, Grant was not quite ready to celebrate. He discussed the situation with Ord and Gibbon and all agreed that the Confederates were in desperate straits. Sixth Corps commander Horatio Wright concurred, and relayed additional information about Ewell's belief that the game was up. Grant listened, pondered; at last he quietly remarked, "I have a great mind to summon Lee to surrender." Within minutes General Seth Williams, the longtime adjutant general of the Army of the Potomac, left the hotel, carrying the following dispatch:

Apl. 7, 1865

Gen. R. E. Lee
Comd.g C.S.A.
General,
The result of the last week must convince you of the hopelessness of further resistance on the part of the Army of Northern Va. in this struggle. I feel that it is so and regard it as my duty to shift from myself, the responsibility of any further effusion of blood, by asking of you the surrender of that portion of the C. S. Army known as the Army of Northern Va.

Very respectfully
your obt. svt
U. S. Grant
Lt. Gn

+ a little confusing

With Williams on his way, Grant decided to take a rest.[44]

Sometime after midnight Williams delivered Lee's rather curious response. The Confederate commander did not agree that further resistance was hopeless; however, as he shared Grant's wish "to avoid the useless effusion of blood," he asked his opponent to set forth terms.[45]

ie, paroled?

The battle of wills on paper had now been joined. Lee was still willing to fight to gain concessions from Grant. But Grant did not take the bait when he composed his response on the morning of April 8: "In reply I would say that *peace* being my great desire there is but one condition I would insist upon, namely: that the men and officers surrendered shall be disqualified for taking up arms again, against the Government of the United States, until properly exchanged." Aware that the major obstacle to an agreement might be Lee's pride, he added: "I will meet you or will designate Officers to meet any officers you may name for the same purpose, at any point agreeable to you, for the purpose of arranging definitely the terms upon which the surrender of the Army of N. Va. will be received." In allowing Lee to save face, Grant tried to ease him toward surrender. But that he was confident of the ultimate result was evident in a telegram to Stanton: "I feel very confidant of receiving the surrender of Lee and what remains of his army by to-morrow."[46]

April 8 proved to be another busy day. Informing Sheridan of his exchange with Lee, Grant predicted that the surrender might even happen sometime during the day. "We will push him until terms are agreed upon," he added. As he prodded his commanders forward, he received the following message from Lincoln: "Gen'l Sheridan says 'If the thing is pressed I think Lee will surrender.' Let the thing be pressed." Grant did so. Riding forward, he crossed the Appomattox and sought out Meade, whom he warmly greeted as "old fellow." By now both men were ailing: Meade was battling chills and fever, while Grant was falling victim to yet another migraine. The headquarters train was nowhere in sight, having been sent on to Appomattox Court House. Meade's staff, never too enthusiastic about their counterparts under Grant, had to share rations and blankets with the visitors.

Headquarters for the night was a white frame farmhouse. Grant was in bad shape. Hunger, anxiety, and exhaustion combined to produce a massive headache, and remedies featuring hot water and mustard plasters proved useless. Theodore Lyman noted that these episodes caused the general "fearful pain, such as almost overcomes even his iron stoicism." At least this time no one suggested that he partake of something stronger than coffee. News arrived from Sheridan that he had reached Appomat-

lol

tox Station, captured Lee's supply train, and checked the Confederate advance near Appomattox Court House. If the corps of Gibbon and Griffin could arrive soon, "we will, perhaps, finish the job in the morning. I do not think Lee means to surrender until compelled to do so."[47]

If the promise of finishing the job in the morning pleased Grant, the notion that Lee would not surrender until compelled to do so suggested that finishing the job might be bloody work. Grant's head continued to ache. To make matters worse, several officers had discovered a piano in the parlor and began plinking out some old favorites that provided an agonizing backbeat to the throbbing in the general's head. Finally someone got the message, and the music hour came to an end. In an effort to get some rest, Grant stretched out on a sofa.[48]

Sylvanus Cadwallader had just settled down for a good night's sleep on the parlor room floor when the sound of "jingling spurs and clanking saber" marked the arrival of a courier with a dispatch from Lee. Rawlins read it out loud to his chief. Lee still was not quite ready to give up: "To be frank, I do not think the emergency has arisen to call for the surrender" of his army; he now claimed that he was simply inquiring about what terms Grant would offer. However, "as the restoration of peace should be the sole object of all," Lee now proposed a meeting the next morning.[49]

What exactly the Confederate commander was thinking as he prepared this document remains a mystery. Any effort to revive the notion of a military convention floated last month was futile; Lee knew that Grant was not authorized to deal with such matters. Perhaps he thought he could still extract concessions. In any case he wanted to avoid the appearance of a surrender. Pride obscured his view of events; the letter seemed almost disingenuous.

Rawlins exploded. Lee was trying to twist words and bargain for something not offered. "'He don't think the emergency has arisen!' That's cool, but another falsehood. That emergency has been staring him in the face for forty-eight hours. If he hasn't seen it yet, we will soon bring it to his comprehension! He has to surrender. He shall surrender. By the eternal, it shall be surrender, and nothing else."

Likewise unhappy with Lee's dispatch, Grant nevertheless realized that his counterpart was having a difficult time accepting that the end was near. Certainly this game of thrust and parry was beginning to resemble the struggle over arranging terms to bury the dead and rescue the wounded after Cold Harbor. Perhaps Sheridan was right; Lee seemed intent on doing whatever he could to avoid surrender. The trick was to arrange the proper terms for a meeting and to compel Lee to attend, for Grant believed that once the two men met, Lee would capitulate.

The headache continued to pound away. Grant, wanting to make sure that he was thinking clearly when he composed his response, put off replying for the moment. But efforts to fall asleep for even a few hours proved futile, and Horace Porter found the general pacing the floor. Trying to find something to say, Porter remarked that good things followed Grant's headaches. Forcing a smile, Grant replied: "The best thing that could happen to me would be to get rid of the pain I am suffering."[50]

April 9 was Palm Sunday. After grabbing a cup of coffee at Meade's headquarters mess, Grant, still in excruciating pain, sat down to compose another letter to Lee. Aware that he risked another reprimand from Washington if he agreed to meet to discuss "the restoration of peace," he framed a response that specified that it was a surrender that they were discussing: "Your note of yesterday is received. As I have no authority to treat on the subject of peace the meeting proposed for 10 A.M. to-day could lead to no good. I will state however General that I am equally anxious for peace with yourself and the whole North entertains the same feeling. The terms upon which peace can be had are well understood. By the South laying down their Arms they will hasten that most desirable event, save thousands of human lives and hundreds of Millions of property not yet destroyed. Sincerely hoping that all our difficulties may be settled without the loss of another li[f]e . . ."[51]

After sending that message off to Lee, Grant and his staff set off to join Sheridan near Appomattox Court House. It was a rough cross-country ride through mud and clay — not exactly a tonic for Grant's migraine. At eleven o'clock the party halted to rest horses and riders. Staff officers looked up to see one of Meade's staff officers coming toward them. He reined in his mount, who was foaming from the hard ride, and thrust forward a sealed envelope. Inside was another message from Lee. Grant read it, handed it to Rawlins, and asked him to share its contents with everyone else. "There was no more expression in Grant's countenance than in a last year's bird nest," Cadwallader noted. "It was that of a Sphinx."[52]

Taking a deep breath, Rawlins began reading. "General: I received your note of this morning on the picket line, whither I had come to meet you, and ascertain definitely what terms were embraced in your proposal of yesterday with reference to the surrender of this army. I now ask an interview, in accordance with the offer contained in your letter of yesterday, for that purpose."

For a moment all was silent. An attempt to rouse a cheer brought a weak response. Dismounting, Grant composed his reply, accepting Lee's invitation; he would "push forward to the front for the purpose of meeting you." Handing it to Rawlins, he smiled. "How will that do, Rawlins?"

"I think *that* will do," replied the chief of staff. Orville Babcock was entrusted with delivering the dispatch.

The headache was gone.[53]

Early that afternoon Grant, accompanied by his staff, approached Appomattox Court House. Waiting for him were Phil Sheridan and Edward O. C. Ord. The generals exchanged greetings. In response to Grant's query about Lee's whereabouts, the cavalryman pointed to a brick two-story farmhouse just off the courthouse. Motioning for Sheridan and Ord to join him, Grant rode over to the house, the residence of Wilmer McLean. Dismounting, he handed Cincinnati's reins to an orderly, then walked up the white wooden steps, across the porch, and through the front door opened by Babcock. There, in a parlor to his left, sat Lee, accompanied by a single aide, Colonel Charles Marshall. The two generals shook hands; moments later several of Grant's staff officers and generals entered the room. Lee returned to his chair next to a marble-topped table near the front window. Grant pulled up a leather-backed desk chair and sat down.[54]

Everyone present, Grant included, immediately noticed the contrast presented by the two main actors in the room. Lee was outfitted in a beautiful dress uniform, rescued from headquarters baggage just before those wagons were abandoned. By his side was an elegant sword with a hilt wrapped in gilt wire, the gift of a Marylander. He had dressed for the occasion. Not so Grant. The wagon carrying his dress uniform and other equipment was nowhere to be found at the moment; Grant was wearing his field uniform, a private's blouse distinguished only by shoulder straps, each bearing the three stars of his rank. At his side was not a sword but his field glasses; his boots and portions of his uniform were caked with mud and red Virginia clay picked up during the morning's ride. Someone later remarked that the commanding general of the Armies of the United States "looked like a fly on a shoulder of beef."

Introductions having been made, everyone struggled with a situation that could not help but be awkward. Grant opened the discussion by talking about the old days in Mexico. He recalled that he had met Lee, then on Winfield Scott's staff; Lee vaguely recalled the encounter, but added that he had struggled to remember his foe's features. Grant watched his antagonist closely. "What General Lee's feelings were I do not know," he later reflected. "As he was a man of much dignity, with an impassible face, it was impossible to say whether he felt inwardly glad that the end had finally come, or felt sad over the result, and was too manly to show it." Grant's own jubilation on receiving Lee's letter that morning had subsided, and he admitted to being "sad and depressed." Perhaps chatting about Mexico would make things better.

Lee, however, wanted to get down to business. What terms would Grant offer? Simple, Grant replied; the Confederates would lay down their arms and go home as paroled prisoners, promising not to take up arms again until exchanged. Lee seemed satisfied; perhaps he was also relieved not to hear the words "unconditional surrender," although in fact what Grant proposed differed little from what had happened at Vicksburg. And unlike Pemberton or even Buckner, Lee seemed so resigned to the result that discussing terms was not difficult. It all came so easily that the conversation soon veered off the topic once more, almost as if what had happened came as an anticlimax. Once more Lee brought everyone back to the matter at hand by suggesting that Grant commit the terms to paper. Agreeing, Grant waited while his military secretary, Ely S. Parker, brought over both a small oval wooden table and a manifold order book, which would make three copies of the document. Then, cigar in mouth, puffing away, he leaned over, ready to write.

"When I put my pen to the paper I did not know the first word that I should make use of in writing the terms," Grant later recalled. "I only knew what was in my mind, and I wished to express it clearly, so that there could be no mistaking it." He was aware of Lincoln's wishes for a lenient peace; they accorded with his own. Rather than preparing some sort of elaborate preface, he outlined in simple language the process by which the officers and men of the Army of Northern Virginia would stack their arms and record their paroles. That done, he paused and pondered what to write next. For a moment he looked at Lee, his eyes coming to rest on that beautiful sword. There was no reason, he decided, to humiliate Lee by asking the Confederate general to hand over that ceremonial side arm as a trophy of war. Nor was there any need to deprive other officers of their side arms, horses, or baggage. Those items, he decided, would be excluded from the weapons and property to be turned over.

And then there was a final thought that had been taking shape in his mind for some time. It echoed the sentiments that had helped shape previous negotiations at Fort Donelson and Vicksburg, and one to which Lincoln had given voice during their conversations at City Point and Petersburg. It found expression in a simple sentence: "This done each officer and man will be allowed to return to their homes not to be disturbed by United States Authority so long as they observe their parole and the laws in force where they may reside."[55]

It may have taken only a score or so of seconds to compose this final sentence, but in that moment Grant took a chance, transcending the bounds of military authority in defining the consequences of the parole he was extending to Lee and his men. "Not to be disturbed by United States Authority so long as they observe their parole and the laws in force": no persecution and no prosecutions, no trials for treason, no reprisals, no revenge. Defeat was punishment enough. The sentence offered an olive branch to those who accepted it; it restrained those who wanted still more. It established a necessary (if not entirely sufficient) foundation for reconciliation and reunion. Having waged relentless war, Grant now endeavored to make sure that victory brought with it a peace worth winning.

With Parker at his side Grant reviewed what he had written, making several minor revisions and insertions; then Horace Porter handed the result to Lee. The Confederate commander cleared aside several books and a pair of candlesticks to make room for the order book, pulled out a pair of glasses, and began reading. Turning to the second page, he paused, then remarked that Grant omitted the word "exchanged" in the discussion of the terms of the parole. After borrowing Porter's pencil to mark where the word should be inserted, he resumed reading. Only when he came to the final two sentences did his face betray a mixture of relief and happiness, and even then it was barely discernible. Looking up, he remarked, "This will have a very happy effect upon my army."

Nevertheless, Lee raised a question. Not only officers but also enlisted men had furnished the army with their own personal horses. Would those men also be allowed to take their mounts home? At first Grant demurred, pointing out that the terms did not provide for it; Lee reluctantly acknowledged the fact. Indeed, Grant did not know that such was the case in the Confederate army, for in the United States Army the government provided the mounts. Quickly he reconsidered the matter. No, he would not alter the wording of the terms, but he would instruct the officers in charge of the formal surrender ceremony to allow anyone who claimed a horse or a mule to take the animals with them to help in the spring plowing . . . a decision he knew to be in accordance with Lincoln's wishes on the matter.

Relieved, even pleased, Lee relaxed ever so slightly. "This will have the best possible effect upon the men," he responded. "It will be very gratifying, and will do much toward conciliating our people." Then he handed the order book back to Grant, who proceeded to have a copy drawn up in ink (so nervous was Theodore Bowers about the task assigned to him that Parker eventually prepared the draft, using an inkstand borrowed from Colonel Marshall). Lee then directed Marshall to prepare a letter of acceptance, only to edit a stiffly worded draft in favor of simplicity. Marshall had to borrow paper from Parker to prepare a clean copy.

As these documents were being prepared, Grant introduced to Lee the numerous staff officers and generals who had congregated in the parlor. The Confederate commander promised to deliver the thousand or so prisoners in his possession, adding that he lacked rations not only for them but also for his entire force. He added that he had provided for a train filled with food to be sent from Lynchburg. When that train arrived, could he feed his men? Several officers stole a glance at Sheridan, who knew exactly what had happened to that train. Grant, not missing a beat, offered to send over rations for 25,000 men. Only then did the Union commander explain the reason for his unkempt appearance so that Lee would not take it as a sign of discourtesy.

It took several minutes to tie up several other loose ends; then, sometime before 4 P.M., Lee shook Grant's hand, bowed to the other officers present, and walked outside, with Marshall right behind. Within a minute he mounted his horse. Grant lifted his hat in salute, and the officers present followed suit. Lee returned the gesture and then rode away.

Although several generals stayed behind, eager to obtain, one way or another, mementos from the McLean House, Grant did not tarry long. After directing Parker to compose instructions for the officers who would be appointed to carry out the surrender, the general and the members of his staff rode to headquarters, which had been established within Sheridan's lines. The news of what had happened preceded them, and before long the sound of artillery salutes and wild cheering filled the air. The celebration soon ended, however, because Grant directed staff officers to tell his subordinates to stop the ruckus. They would not rub salt into the wounds of the defeated Confederates. "The war is over," he observed. "The Rebels are our countrymen again."[56]

It was left to someone else to remark that perhaps it would be a good idea to notify the authorities at Washington what had happened. Grant dismounted, sat on a large rock, and began scribbling a telegram to Stanton. "Gen. Lee surrendered the Army of Northern Va this afternoon on terms proposed by myself. The accompanying additional correspondence will show the conditions fully." No brag, no bluster, no stirring words . . . just a simple statement succinctly summarizing the day's events.

Minutes later the cavalcade arrived at camp. Dismounting, staff officers lingered by the commander, hoping to hear him reflect on what had just happened. But once more Grant's mind was elsewhere, wandering back to Mexico, as he recalled the antics of a rambunctious mule who had caused a young lieutenant and his friends no end of trouble. His old friends . . . our countrymen again.[57]

21

Peace

●

ALTHOUGH IT WAS RAINING when dawn broke over Appomattox Court House on April 10, by midmorning the skies had cleared. A staff officer notified Grant that a Confederate soldier was waiting to see him. But this was not just any soldier; it was one of Aunt Rachel's sons, Charley Tompkins. Perhaps the general smiled to himself as he recalled how, nearly four years ago, Aunt Rachel (Jesse's youngest sister) had declared that if the former captain enlisted to put down the rebellion, "the ties of consanguinity shall be forever severed." Obviously Charley didn't feel that way — at least not at the moment. Grant gave Charles a horse, fifty dollars, and a pass through the lines, and told him to go home.[1]

Grant then decided that he would like to talk to yet another Confederate. Accompanied by members of his staff, he rode out between the picket lines east of the courthouse proper, and then asked for Robert E. Lee to join him. Nearly an hour passed before Lee appeared. The two generals drew off to the side and commenced what soon became a curious conversation. Lee remarked that had the two generals met back in March, the war might have ended a month sooner. He freely admitted that the conflict was for all purposes over. Union forces might have to douse the remaining embers of resistance, but the Confederacy was effectively extinguished. He hoped, however, that the bloodshed was at an end, and "that everything would now be done to restore harmony and conciliate the people of the South."[2]

Grant saw here an opportunity to broaden the effect of the previous day's capitulation. Could not Lee convey his own sense of the futility of future fighting to his fellow Confederates? Could he not advise the generals remaining in the field to surrender? Lee demurred, claiming that he would have to first consult Jefferson Davis. When Grant urged him to do so, he replied that such an act would be beyond what he conceived to be his duties as a soldier. This was a puzzling explanation, for (as Lee had just admitted), in March he had been ready to discuss the possibility of peace

438

negotiations with the Confederate president (in ten days, he would advise Davis to sue for peace.) As the <u>commanding general of Confederate forces,</u> Lee was empowered to agree to a general surrender. But this he would not do at this time. Realizing that there was no sense in pressing the matter, *right* Grant let it drop.[3]

The two men reviewed details of the surrender, including the need to issue parole papers, Grant's promise to allow all Confederate soldiers to take their horses home with them, and transportation for other paroled Confederates. All this would be worked out by the three commissioners appointed by each general to establish procedures and implement the surrender — including the formal stacking of arms by the defeated Confederates over the next several days. Neither commander would be on the scene to witness those events, although (Grant had left instructions ensuring that the ceremony itself would be simple and spare the feelings of the defeated.[4])

Many Confederates were surprised and pleased by Grant's generous terms. "Judging from their hearty confessions of generous and liberal treatment by us," noted Sylvanus Cadwallader, "one would conclude they expected to have been chained together as felons to grace the triumphant march of our victorious general." Edward P. Alexander, Lee's artillery chief, concluded that "the exceedingly liberal treatment" contained in the terms "could only be ascribed to a policy of conciliation deliberately entered upon." The clause allowing soldiers to keep their horses was especially popular. Several Confederates told one of their captors "that if the government will only show the same spirit of kindness, and goodwill that the army has, all will soon be all right, and a real peace again extend over all the land."[5]

Grant sampled this attitude firsthand before he left Appomattox. After he concluded his discussion with Lee, he rode over to McLean's house once more. Soon James Longstreet, Henry Heth, and Cadmus Wilcox — all prewar friends — appeared, as did John B. Gordon, George E. Pickett, and some other officers. Gordon noted Grant's "modest demeanor," adding, "There was nothing in the expression of his face or in his language or general bearing which indicated exultation at the great victory he had won." Once more Grant's conversations wandered back to the years before the war. He was especially glad to see "Pete" Longstreet. Taking his friend (and fellow card player) by the arm, he said, "Pete, let's have another game of brag to recall the old days."[6]

Grant left Appomattox Court House at midday on April 10. He was eager to get back to Washington as soon as possible, not only to wind down the war program but also to oversee the final movements over the rest of the South. Some of the trip was through woods, with the general leading the way, picking his route around the trees. That evening, as the cavalcade stopped for the night at Prospect Station, they encountered Elihu B. Washburne, who had hurried down to Virginia in hopes of witnessing the last campaign. Grant was impressed by what he had seen that day. "If advantage is taken of the present feeling in the South," he wired Stanton, "I am greatly in hopes an early peace will be secured." It might even be advisable to extend the same terms he had given Lee to other Confederate forces still in the field.[7]

Reaching Burkeville Junction early on the afternoon of April 11, Grant and his staff boarded a train, and after a time-consuming journey arrived at City Point on the morning of April 12. There, in clear disregard of his suggestion that she return north, was Julia. She had waited up through the previous evening in anticipation of a grand celebration over dinner, only to turn in hours before the cavalcade finally appeared. Despite her exhaustion, she was happy to see her husband — and almost equally relieved that Mary Todd Lincoln had left with her husband several days before. The president's wife had not made life easy for Julia during Grant's absence. Once she had tried to embarrass her by asking what should be done with Jefferson Davis; Julia artfully replied that she would leave him "to the mercy of our always just and most gracious President." Miffed, Mrs. Lincoln shunned her; Julia had to visit Richmond by herself. Indignant that the president's wife had not invited her to a reception on the *River Queen,* Julia commandeered a band and embarked on her own inspection tour of Richmond via boat. As the vessel approached the *River Queen,* she requested that the band play "Now You'll Remember Me."[8]

Glad as Grant was to see his wife, the general did not want to dawdle. He rejected her pleas to visit Richmond, arguing that his presence "might lead to demonstrations which would only wound the feelings of the residents, and we ought not to do anything at such a time which would add to their sorrow." Better to return to Washington to see what was going on and to commence demobilization and cost-cutting. He placed Ord in charge of the former Confederate capital with instructions to do what he could to restore peace and good feeling among the city's inhabitants. Although staff officers who had seconded Julia's suggestion may have been disappointed, his gesture was appreciated by the staunch Rebel newspaper editor Edward A. Pollard, who noted that Grant "spared everything that might wound the feeling or imply the humiliation of a vanquished foe."[9]

After a day marked by yet another photographic session with Mathew Brady, the general, his wife, little Jesse, and several staff officers boarded a dispatch boat and headed out toward the James River. The vessel sliced up through the Chesapeake and the Potomac, arriving in Washington the following morning. After dropping Julia and Jesse off at Willard's, the general went on to the War Department to confer with Stanton about ending recruiting and reducing orders for munitions and supplies. Then it was on to the White House, where the president warmly greeted him. "General, I half suspected that movement of yours would end the business," he remarked, "and wanted to ask you, but did not like to." He was also delighted with the terms Grant had given Lee, believing that they established a solid foundation for reconciliation. John Gibbon, who supervised the formal surrender of the Army of Northern Virginia on April 12, confirmed this impression in a telegram to Grant on the same day, adding "that by announcing at once terms and a liberal merciful policy on the part of the Government we can once more have a happy united Country. I believe all reasoning men on both sides recognize the fact that slavery is dead."[10]

In later years people would describe how Northerners celebrated Grant's generous terms, but at the time they aroused debate. Some newspapers applauded the conditions of surrender. Grant's "noble spirit," according to one Washington journal, meant that "submission is restoration, amnesty, and peace." The *New York Times* argued that, although the surrender was primarily a military question, "the supplementary political task of completing a general measure of pacification is already simplified to a degree beyond a public anticipation." The conservative *New York Herald* was especially pleased. "By sending these soldiers home on parole Grant has provided for the immediate demoralization and dispersion of the rebel forces under Johnston . . . and has opened a way, broad and plain, for the reconstruction of the Union. Great as is Grant the general, he is equally matched by Grant the statesman and the diplomatist."[11]

But not everyone was overjoyed. "With a second reading of the matter came the American desire for details," editorialized the *Times*, "and to many the details were a cause of dissatisfaction. . . . It was very evident that a large number of our citizens would have been better satisfied if Grant had not allowed Lee and his men their parole." A *New York Tribune* correspondent claimed that the terms "are regarded with disgust and unqualified indignation by large numbers of the most sensible, loyal and influential citizens in this region"; the *Washington Star* reported that "a large number of officers, together with thousands of the men of this army, express their dissatisfaction." Ralph Waldo Emerson growled, "General Grant's terms certainly look a little too easy, as foreclosing any action hereafter to convict Lee of treason." The new vice president, Andrew Johnson, rushed to the White House to protest. For all the celebration, there still lurked a desire for vengeance, held in check only by the knowledge that Lincoln would stand by the surrender terms.[12]

On April 14, Grant attended a cabinet meeting. Discussion soon turned to reconstruction policy. With Lee's army disbanded, there remained no reason to work with the Virginia legislators, and so Lincoln had abandoned that idea. But the president, who professed himself not yet ready to decide what to do, instructed Stanton to distribute copies of a proposal on establishing temporary governments under military supervision, and then adjourned the meeting. As the cabinet members filed out of the room, Lincoln drew Grant aside. Mrs. Lincoln had made plans for the Lincolns and the Grants to attend Ford's Theater that night. Already the newspapers were publicizing the event. Would the Grants go?[13]

As Grant weighed the invitation, a message arrived from Julia. Spurred by news of the theater outing, she decided that she had suffered enough at the hands of Mary Lincoln: the note simply announced that she was taking Jesse home to Burlington that evening. Grant briefly pondered what to do. He had not seen his family in several weeks; like Julia, he also had no stomach for another encounter with Mrs. Lincoln. Just the previous evening, Grant had suffered Mrs. Lincoln's spite. The president had asked the general to accompany the First Lady on a tour of the illuminations around the city (Lincoln himself did not join them; Julia remained at the hotel with Jesse). Mrs. Lincoln grew resentful when she realized that the crowds lining the streets were cheering the general and not the president or his wife. A night at the theater was sure to produce the same results. Secretly relieved, Grant explained his wife's determination, adding that he would leave town with her. Lincoln, all too aware of the consequences of offending one's wife, accepted the general's regrets. That afternoon the Grants boarded the train for home. On their way to the station the general noted with some discomfort the prying eyes of a rider straining to look inside the carriage.[14]

The train arrived at Philadelphia; the Grants debarked to get something to eat. Several excited messengers sought out the general and thrust telegrams into his hands. Grant turned pale as he read the dispatches. Lincoln had been shot at the theater. He was dying. Secretary of State William H. Seward, already suffering from injuries received in a carriage accident, had also been attacked in his bed by a knife-wielding assailant.

Rumor had it that Vice President Johnson and Grant himself were also targeted for assassination. Julia later believed that a group of strangers who had observed her at lunch at Willard's that day included John Wilkes Booth. Grant wondered whether the man who had peered in the Grants' carriage that afternoon was none other than the president's assassin. Stoically he reviewed the messages. "Not a muscle of his face quivered or a line gave an indication of what he must have felt at that great crisis," one courier recalled. After making sure that Julia and Jesse were safe in Burlington, a deeply disturbed Grant returned to Washington early the next morning.[15]

In later years, Grant referred to April 14 as "the darkest day in my life." Just when peace seemed assured, the man perhaps best suited to realize it was gone. "I knew his goodness of heart, his generosity, his yielding disposition, his desire to have everybody happy," Grant later recalled, remembering "above all his desire to see all the people of the United States enter again upon the full privileges of citizenship with equality among all." Filled "with the gloomiest apprehension," he told Julia that Lincoln's death was "an irreparable loss to the South, which now needs so much both his tenderness and magnanimity." When Julia mentioned that Andrew Johnson would become president, Grant replied, "For some reason, I dread the change."[16]

The Tennessean's vehement denunciation of Confederates promised a much harsher treatment of the defeated than that envisioned by his predecessor, and years later the general remembered, "I felt that reconstruction had been set back, no telling how far." Having established a close working relationship with Lincoln, Grant now would have to cooperate with Johnson, whom he had encountered infrequently in Tennessee while Johnson was military governor.[17]

First, however, the general had to make sure that the violence at Ford's Theater was not part of a larger plot to subvert the government. Hastily he sent word to Ord, commanding at Richmond, to arrest John A. Campbell and others "who have not yet taken the oath of Allegiance" as well as "all paroled officers. . . . Extreme rigor will have to be observed whilst assassination remains the order of the day with the rebels." Aware of the implications of the order, Ord reminded Grant that Lee and his staff were among the paroled officers in Richmond. To arrest them would lead to more unrest. Campbell, still pursuing Lincoln's now-abandoned overtures to the Virginia legislature, had asked permission to go to Washington, which suggested that he was not part of any conspiracy. Agreeing, Grant rescinded the directive and soon rejected the notion that Lincoln's assassination was part of a widespread Confederate conspiracy.)He dismissed requests to seek lodging secure from potential assailants, telling his telegraph operator, "I guess, Beckwith, if they want me, they'll get me wherever I am." He chose to stay at Willard's.[18]

The commanding general also assisted in preparations for the late president's funeral. In the past, he had often ordered black regiments out on review for Lincoln, knowing how much interest the president took in their welfare. Now he asked Ord to send a black regiment to Washington for the ceremonies, a fitting symbol of Lincoln's legacy. On April 19 the general-in-chief attended the funeral service in the White House. He stood, alone, at the head of the catafalque, eyes welling with tears.[19]

not totally sweet-ing

The best way to remember Lincoln was to secure the peace that he had so ardently desired. But this was not going to be easy. Not all Republicans were grief-stricken by Lincoln's assassination. Several of them hoped Johnson's elevation to the presidency would enable them to overturn the terms agreed to at Appomattox — the first step in imposing a harsh peace. But severe measures would not produce a lasting peace, Grant told former Illinois senator Orville H. Browning. The policy outlined at Appomattox "was the true one," needing only to be complemented by a similar civil policy. Reconstruction would collapse if it "excluded more than half of the people of the South from participation."[20]

Grant soon became more optimistic. After conferring with Johnson, he concluded that maybe he could work with the Tennessean. "I have every reason to hope that in our new President we will find a man disposed and capable of conducting the government in its old channel," Grant told a St. Louis associate. "If so we may look for a speedy peace." Besides, he observed several days later, it was "unpatriotic at this time for professed lovers of this Country to express doubts of the capacity and integrity of our Chief Magistrate."[21]

On April 21, after seeing Lincoln's coffin placed aboard a train that would take the late president's body to Springfield, Illinois, for burial, Grant returned to headquarters. Although drained by the emotional demands of the past several days, he wanted to see if there was any news from North Carolina. Several days earlier, Sherman had telegraphed him that Joseph Johnston, having been informed of Lee's surrender, was willing to open negotiations. Sherman had assured Grant that he would offer Johnston the same terms Grant had given Lee and would "be careful not to complicate any points of civil policy."[22]

This promise proved short-lived. That afternoon Major Henry Hitchcock, one of Sherman's aides, arrived in Washington carrying a proposed agreement with Johnston and a cover letter, which Grant read first. Sherman explained that his proposal, if adopted, "will produce peace from the Potomac to the Rio Grande." Moreover, he said, "the point to which I attach the most importance, is that the dispersion and disbandment of these armies is done in such a manner as to prevent their breaking up into guerrilla bands." Grant approved these aims. But when he read the proposed settlement, he realized that his trusted subordinate had ranged far beyond the sphere of his competency in addressing civil as well as military questions. Under its terms, Confederate state officials and legislators, once they took the oath of allegiance, would be restored to power, pushing aside established provisional governments until the Supreme Court ruled which one was legitimate. Within weeks the civil courts would be in full operation, and most Southerners would resume their full civil and political rights. Having heard Lincoln's musings about what he would do to commence reconstruction, Sherman had undertaken to enact what he believed to be Lincoln's plan. Nothing was said about emancipation; indeed, in restoring to Southerners their "rights of person and property," one could argue that the agreement reinstated slavery.[23]

Grant was shocked. Only days before, Sherman had assured him that he would offer Johnston the same "magnanimous and liberal" terms Grant had given Lee. Far from avoiding issues of civil policy, Sherman had plunged right into them. Failing to find Stanton at the War Department, Grant hurriedly scribbled a note to the war secretary, remarking that Sherman's dispatches "are of such importance that I think immediate action should be taken on them." The president and cabinet should convene immediately.[24]

Cabinet members assembled at Johnson's temporary residence that evening to hear Grant read Sherman's proposal. Everyone immediately agreed that the terms should be rejected, but Stanton, Attorney General James Speed, and the president went on to denounce Sherman's actions as smacking of treason. This was too much for Grant. Sherman's terms were unacceptable and improper, but he was no traitor. At worst, he had broadly construed Lincoln's lenient sentiments expressed on the *River Queen* — a meeting at which neither Stanton nor Johnson had been present. When chaos threatened in the form of assassination and guerrilla war, Sherman understandably would seek ways to create a lasting peace and to restore order. At first Grant heatedly defended his subordinate; after calming down, he volunteered to notify Sherman personally that the agreement had been rejected. He could placate his irritable subordinate, bring him up to date on the new political environment in Washington, forestall a blunt rebuke, and oversee new negotiations. Johnson agreed. Within several hours, Grant, Hitchcock, and several staff officers were on their way to North Carolina. Grant, still smoldering, exclaimed, "It is infamous — infamous! After four years of such service as Sherman has done — that he should be used like this!"[25]

Before he left, Grant wrote Julia that he would not be able to return home for several days. Disturbed by the events of the past hours, he felt an increased sense of responsibility to see that what had been won in war was not now lost through miscalculation and malice. "I find my duties, anxieties, and the necessity for having all my wits about me increasing instead of diminishing. I have a Herculean task to perform and shall endeavor to do it, not to please any one, but for the interests of our great country that is now beginning to loom fair above all other countries, modern or ancient." He was trying awkwardly to link together his life, the outcome of the war, and the destiny of the republic. Somehow he had to make sure that the fruits of victory ennobled the nation. "That Nation, united, will have a strength that will enable it to dictate to all others, *conform to justice and right.* Power I think can go no further The moment conscience leaves, physical strength will avail nothing, in the long run." But who would protect that conscience?[26]

On his way to Sherman's headquarters, Grant stopped off at Fort Monroe to telegraph Halleck, now at Richmond, to set in motion Sheridan with his cavalry and some infantry. Should Johnston not submit to a new surrender agreement, Grant wanted to ensure that Union troops could surround and finish off the Confederates. No route would be left open for escape. Then he continued down to North Carolina, debarking at New Bern, where a surgeon noted that the general "had been dreadfully seasick and he looked sad and careworn." On April 24, Major Hitchcock entered Sherman's headquarters near Raleigh. Staff officers surrounded him, and one asked, "Well, major, do you bring peace or war?"

"I brought back General Grant."[27]

Sherman was not surprised when Grant told him that his agreement had been rejected. After reading the reaction of the Northern press to Lincoln's assassination, he had informed Johnston that it was unlikely their agreement would be approved. He was upset, however, when Grant showed him a copy of the March 3 telegram concerning the proper scope of military negotiations, remarking that if he had been aware of it he never would have concluded such an agreement. Instead, he had been guided not only by his impressions derived from the discussions aboard the *River Queen* but also by reports about Lincoln's dealings with Campbell and the Virginia legislature. He notified Johnston that the terms had been rejected. Hostilities would resume in forty-eight hours unless Johnston surrendered under the same terms Grant had offered Lee.[28]

Knowing that it was futile to continue fighting, Johnston assented to Sherman's proposition. On April 26 the two men signed a document identical in substance to the Appomattox agreement. After approving the result, Grant returned to Washington. He had been deeply impressed by what he had seen at Raleigh. "The people are anxious to see peace restored," he wrote Julia from Sherman's headquarters. "The suffering that must exist in the South the next year, even with the war ending now, will be beyond conception. People who talk now of further retaliation and punishment, except of the political leaders, either do not conceive of the suffering endured already or they are heartless and unfeeling." To a newspaper reporter, he described Southerners as "unfortunate, a desolated race" and added that "he would treat the masses of the South with kindness and humanity especially in view of the fact that they had been forced to obey their own desperate leaders." In early May he concluded, "Management is all that is now wanted to secure complete peace."[29]

First, however, Grant had to manage a conflict between Sherman and Stanton. Within hours of the April 21 meeting, rumors began circulating that impugned Sherman's motives; the next day, Stanton's account of the affair appeared in the morning papers. The war secretary not only rebuked Sherman for making such an agreement, but also insinuated that the general had succumbed to Confederate influences and might even have taken steps to help Jefferson Davis escape. Halleck compounded the problem by suggesting that Sherman's movements would allow Davis to escape with gold from the Confederate treasury. Sherman exploded. Over the next several weeks, the debate raged in the press as he engaged in fiery correspondence with both Stanton and Halleck. Grant, reluctantly, was in the middle.[30]

In Grant's eyes, both Stanton and Sherman had erred, and their fractious natures had exacerbated an already difficult situation. Sherman's telegram to Stanton announcing Grant's arrival at Raleigh had been a sign of what was to come. In it, Sherman had admitted his "folly in embracing in a military convention any civil matters" but added that "such is the nature of our situation that they seem inextricably united." Fair enough. But Sherman then added that Stanton himself had hinted that a quick peace might require "a little bending to policy" and that he believed that the new administration "has made a mistake." Stanton was no better. Later that day, the war secretary informed Grant that Sherman's proposal "meets with universal disapprobation. No one class or shade of opinion approves it. . . . The hope of the country is that you may repair the misfortune occasioned by Sherman's negotiations."[31]

The affair reminded Grant that his job was far from finished. The army would have to administer many aspects of whatever reconstruction policy was adopted. Sherman, Sheridan, and other soldiers looked to Grant to protect their interests and to present their views; Johnson, Stanton, and other politicians also leaned on him for support. Maryland Republican Henry Winter Davis questioned the president's reliance on Grant, "of whom he seemed not exactly to stand in awe of but anxious to conciliate rather than resolved to command." The nation's foremost hero still had much to do.[32]

During May, Grant commuted between Washington and his new home in Philadelphia; at home he did what he could via the telegraph, allowing him to avoid many visitors. Eventually, however, he brought Julia down with him, and the couple took up residence in Georgetown at Henry Halleck's house. Demobilization occupied much of his time; he played a supporting role in assisting Johnson to restore order throughout the South. Although he attended cabinet discussions on reconstruction policy, he preferred to speak only when others sought his opinion; then he shared his desire "to see something done to restore civil governments in those states" as soon as possible. However, Grant expected that any action undertaken now would be only a temporary expedient, for Congress would have the last say. In the interim, he told Sheridan, it would probably be best to divide the South into several military districts and supervise matters. The resulting quiet "would give the Southern people confidence, and encourage them to go to work, instead of distracting them with politics." When Johnson discussed a draft of an amnesty proclamation, Grant was more specific; he argued that Confederate generals, by virtue of their rank alone, should not be excluded from the general terms of the amnesty, and for some time he questioned the exclusion of Southerners owning $20,000 worth of property.[33]

In the midst of these deliberations the nation reserved a few days for celebration. On May 23 portions of the Army of the Potomac (the Second, Fifth, Ninth, and Cavalry Corps), joined by the Nineteenth Corps, marched down Pennsylvania Avenue and past a reviewing stand set up at the White House. It would not have been easy under any circumstances to organize such a spectacle, but complicating matters were signs of friction between the Eastern and Western armies, sometimes escalating to fistfights. These clashes, spurred in part by resentment over the harsh treatment accorded Sherman, demonstrated that Grant had been correct to consider sectional rivalries when he shaped his plans for the spring. The Easterners, firm in the belief that they had faced the best the Confederacy had to offer and had taken more than their share of losses, filed past in fine style. Since the days of McClellan the Army of the Potomac had been fond of such ceremonies. It was thus unfortunate that by the time Grant made his way over from headquarters to the reviewing stand in front of the White House, Meade, who headed the parade, had already passed; it did not matter that the president was also tardy. Late in the afternoon, after the conclusion of the ceremonies, Grant took a little ride up Pennsylvania Avenue. What remained of the crowds (as well as normal pedestrian traffic in a city teeming with visitors) cheered; he lifted his hat in return.[34]

The next day belonged to Sherman and his men. Present were veterans of the Vicksburg campaign, the Fifteenth and Seventeenth Corps; the lone representative of the Army of the Cumberland, the Fourteenth Corps; and the hybrid Twentieth Corps, a consolidation of the two corps that had traveled west after Chickamauga to help raise the siege of Chattanooga. Accompanying the corps were pack mules, wagons, and other oddities, lending a different flavor to the hard-marching Westerners (and by now even the men of the Twentieth Corps, although drawn from the East, had adopted many of their comrades' characteristics). Grant watched it all, with Julia and their son Jesse by his side. This time, however, some of the drama was reserved for the reviewing stand itself, for Sherman, still fuming, refused to shake Stanton's outstretched hand.[35]

Not everyone was there. The Army of the Potomac's Sixth Corps lingered in Virginia; so did portions of the Army of the James, including the all-black Twenty-fifth Corps. Except for some black pioneers from Sherman's army, no black units participated in the ceremonies, a pointed contrast to Grant's efforts to include black soldiers in Lincoln's funeral ceremonies. Most of the Army of the Cumberland, as well as several other commands, remained scattered throughout the Confederacy. Several prominent generals were absent, notably George Thomas and Phil Sheridan — the latter having been ordered to go to Texas to take charge of a new force forming on the Rio Grande.

On May 29, five days after the end of the review, Johnson formally commenced the reconstruction process by issuing two proclamations. The first announced his amnesty policy, complete with oath of allegiance and a list of "excepted classes," including generals, <u>West Point graduates</u>, men who had resigned army commissions to join the Confederacy, and individuals possessing $20,000 in taxable property — a sign that the president was not exactly Grant's pawn. The other proclamation outlined a process whereby civil government could be restored in North Carolina, featuring the appointment of a provisional governor and a call for a constitutional convention chosen by voters who had taken the amnesty oath and met the suffrage requirements of the prewar constitution — meaning <u>no black suffrage</u>. Military commanders were instructed to "aid and assist" the provisional governors and were admonished against "hindering, impeding, or discouraging the loyal people from the organization of a State government." In the following months, Johnson issued similar proclamations covering states that were not already operating under governments established during the Lincoln administration.[36]

With Johnson's policy now before the public, Grant decided to escape Washington for several weeks. First he visited New York, arriving on June 7. Making his way past a cheering crowd, he entered the Astor House, where some eleven years ago he had stayed while waiting for funds to return home after his resignation from the army. He shook hands and signed autographs for hours; as one paper put it, "he was shaken and bored, and bored and shaken." When a soldier on crutches dragged himself up to his commander and revealed that he had been struggling to secure a furlough, Grant immediately told Ely Parker to make one out. Later that day, at another function, the general listened as John A. Logan and Michigan senator Zachariah Chandler — the same Chandler who had once declared that young officers would not slip on the sidewalks of Detroit if they stayed sober — celebrated him as the savior of the Union. That evening he attended a New York rally at Cooper Union, arranged by New York War Democrats, to endorse Johnson's policy. One paper highlighted his "extreme modesty of demeanor" and "the quiet, natural gentleness which characterizes every movement." If at first glance Grant did not look the part of a great man (especially once he had exchanged his uniform for a brown coat and checked trousers), "his clear blue eyes, high forehead, and determined look speak plainly of his innate greatness."[37]

Grant received such an enthusiastic reception that he nearly defeated the purpose of the meeting. The crowd interrupted Daniel S. Dickinson's speech celebrating Johnson with cheers for Grant. Finally, the general left the hall, allowing Dickinson, Logan, and Frank Blair to continue extolling the chief executive. In light of later events, the resolutions presented at this meeting take on special interest: they included a call to enfranchise black soldiers and an endorsement of impartial suffrage. The *New York World,* a leading Democratic organ that would have been happy to record Grant's presence as indicative of his position, instead stressed the nonpolitical nature of Grant's reception. "In honoring General Grant," it asserted, "our people feel that they are honoring all that is best in themselves. . . . They endorse no political theory in this frank homage; they serve no political ambition in paying it."[38]

From New York Grant traveled to West Point, where he encountered Winfield Scott. The meeting was the fulfillment of a young plebe's prescient fantasy: Grant, the general-in-chief, was the center of attention for the cadets. Meeting the members of the graduating class, he said a few words to each of them. He then moved on to Chicago, where he attended a sanitary fair. Waiting for him there was Sherman. At one point the loyal lieutenant volunteered to offer the remarks his chief was reluctant to make, but Grant declined: "I never ask a soldier to do anything I cannot do myself." A feature of the fair was Grant's willingness to sacrifice one of his first war horses, a claybank named "Jack," to help raise funds through an auction. The general also learned a little about fair-weather friends when Governor Yates, who in 1863 had been prepared to throw his support behind John McClernand, now reminded everyone that he had signed Grant's commission as colonel.[39]

Throughout the spring Grant kept a careful eye on the South, looking for evidence of returning loyalty. From Richmond, Halleck kept him apprised of conditions in the former Confederate capital. "The rebel feeling in Va. is utterly dead and with proper management can never be revived," he observed, later adding that the best way to further Southern submission was to display lenience toward Robert E. Lee. Grant enthusiastically approved of conciliating the Confederate hero and welcomed reports that Lee was contemplating applying for pardon. "Although it will meet with opposition in the North to allow Lee the benefit of Amnesty," he told Halleck, "I think it would have the best possible effect towards restoring good feeling and peace in the South to have him come in. All the people except a few political leaders [in the] South will accept what ever he does as right and will be guided to a great extent by his example."[40]

Many Northerners disagreed. Some newspapers called on the government to try Lee for treason. The *New York Times* argued that "the terms granted to General Lee and his army cannot in the slightest degree affect their future responsibility to the civil authorities. Time only and the calm judgment of the American people will show what punishment is to be meted out to them." Ben Butler, eager to gain revenge for his removal by Grant, fueled the chief executive's desire to punish traitors, informing Johnson that the Appomattox agreement "was a purely military convention, and referred to military terms only. . . . As soon as these men cease to be prisoners of war, all supposed obligation to them will cease"; the general-in-chief "had no authority to grant amnesty or pardon." Attorney General Speed issued an opinion in late April narrowly defining the rights of Confederates who claimed residence in states that had not formally seceded, which led observers to claim that "the terms of the capitulation were strictly military." The distinguished legal theorist Francis Lieber also strictly construed the general's authority, although he wavered on the topic of Lee's vulnerability to a treason indictment.[41]

The debate escalated when federal judge John C. Underwood convened a grand jury in Norfolk, Virginia, at the end of May. Calling for Lee and other Confederate leaders to be indicted for treason, the judge characterized the Appomattox agreement as "a mere military arrangement" that had "no influence upon civil rights or the status of the persons involved." The grand jury, following Underwood's bidding, indicted Lee and a score of other prominent Confederates in early June. Coming on the heels of Johnson's May 29 proclamation outlining his amnesty policy, the news prompted the Confederate commander to ask for a pardon, not only to protect himself but also to set an example for others.[42]

Before submitting his application, Lee sought to find out how Grant would receive it, sending forth feelers through Ord and Senator Reverdy Johnson of Maryland. Speaking on behalf of Grant, who was still in New York, Rawlins assured Ord's contact, Rufus Ingalls, that Grant would "cheerfully" advise the president to pardon Lee. Several associates of the chief executive also told Ingalls that he would approve the Confederate general's request. Adam Badeau passed on similar assurances to Senator Johnson. On June 13 Lee forwarded his application for pardon to Grant, specifically asking whether the Appomattox terms protected him from Underwood's proceedings.[43]

Grant returned to Washington to find Lee's letter and application waiting for him. He endorsed both documents, urging that Lee be pardoned, defending the sanctity of the Appomattox terms, and asking the president to "quash" Underwood's actions. "Good faith as well as true policy dictates that we should observe the conditions of that convention," he argued, adding that the terms "met with the hearty approval of the President at the time, and of the people generally." On June 16, as Grant prepared to leave for the White House with the documents in hand, Badeau wrote James H. Wilson that all would be settled quickly. Not only did Grant believe that the terms Lee accepted at Appomattox precluded any treason trials, but also the president, according to Badeau, "is not at all vengeful or bitter towards the high officers of the late rebel army."44

Andrew Johnson had different ideas. Earlier that month, a Virginian seeking a pardon for George Pickett came away from the White House disappointed. Apparently the president "thought he would hold some of their principal leaders in suspense for some time," in part because he had accepted Butler's argument that the parole extended to Lee and his men applied only so long as they were prisoners of war. He presented the same case to Grant, arguing that Lee and other Rebel leaders had to face punishment. The general dissented. Johnson "might do as he pleased about civil rights, confiscation of property, and so on," but the Appomattox agreement had to be honored. Not only would legal proceedings prosecuting Lee for treason disrupt and possibly destroy the prospects for reconciliation, Grant insisted, but also they represented a breach of faith on the part of the government. To facilitate Lee's surrender, Grant had thought it wise to forbid reprisals. Otherwise, Lee's army would have dissolved into bands of outlaws and guerrillas, perpetuating the conflict. Furthermore, Lincoln had approved Grant's terms (albeit after the fact), and Johnson himself had endorsed them when he had ordered Grant to offer the same terms to Johnston.

The president persisted. "When can these men be tried?" he asked.

"Never," replied Grant, "unless they violate their paroles."

Both Grant and Johnson were stubborn men who held tightly to their convictions of right and wrong. The president was committed to punish treason; the general believed that to prosecute Lee would be a breach of faith. Finally, Grant played his last, most powerful card. He threatened to resign his commission if Johnson did not relent and honor the surrender terms. "And I will keep my word," he told his staff on his return to headquarters. "I will not stay in the army if they break the pledges I make."45

Realizing that without Grant's support his administration would be in serious trouble, Johnson backed down. On June 20 Attorney General Speed directed that the proceedings against Lee be dropped; immediately Grant notified Lee that the federal government would follow his interpretation of the surrender terms, thus shielding Lee from further prosecution.46

That same day Grant sat down to compose his official report of military operations during the closing year of the war. He was not thinking of the past and victories won, however, but of the need to secure the benefits of those victories in peace. For the past two months he had tried to balance leniency with his desire to smother the rebellion, rejecting both Johnson's desire for vengeance and Sherman's excessive generosity in his effort to rebuild a nation that would realize Lincoln's desire "to see all the people of the United States enter again upon the full privileges of citizenship with equality among all." What this nation needed now was statesmanship and compromise for the greater good, not further chaos and disruption.

Thus inspired, he drafted a report that said as much about peacemaking as it did about warmaking. "Lee's great influence throughout the whole South caused his example to be followed," resulting in "peace and quiet." If the Confederate leader had known at Appomattox that he would be tried for treason, "the surrender never would have taken place." Even though Grant advocated leniency toward the Confederacy's military leaders, he called for punishment of its political leaders, who were "guilty of the most heinous offenses known to our laws. Let them reap the fruit of their offenses." One could almost hear the echoes of the Grant of 1861 who had called for Jefferson Davis's execution. And he still worried that short-sighted politicians might fumble the opportunity now before them. The soldiers had "learned moderation and forgiveness"; could not the politicians do the same? He was not sure. After all, "those professedly loyal throughout the great conflict" were now "so differing in opinion as to what should be done in the great work of reconstruction as to endanger peace among friends. . . . Would it not be well for all to learn to yield enough of their individual views to the will of the majority to preserve a long and happy peace?"[47]

Then the general looked at what he had written. He felt uneasy about expressing such sentiments in an official report. After repeatedly insisting that military men should keep out of politics, here he was, violating his own maxim. Reluctantly, he decided to restrict himself to military matters in his report and omitted the passages quoted in the preceding paragraph. He could not justify getting involved in such issues. He had saved the Union. That was enough.

Afterword
Of Success, Fate, and Greatness

•

AS SUMMER CAME in 1865, Ulysses S. Grant could look back with satisfaction on a job well done. Whatever one might say about material resources and manpower, other generals working with similar advantages had not achieved what he had accomplished. Nor had he always possessed superior numbers and material during his campaigns in the West. Yet because of his leadership more than any other factor, the Union forces regained the Mississippi Valley and were ready to strike deep into the Confederate heartland as 1864 opened. In that most critical year, elevated to the position of general-in-chief, he devised an overall strategic approach utilizing those superior resources and manpower to crush the Confederacy in just under fifteen months through coordinated campaigns against enemy armies, resources, and morale. Battling the election year calendar, handcuffed by the political considerations of his superior, and facing Robert E. Lee in a titanic confrontation, he managed to nullify Lee, overcome the constraints of politics, and put into operation a plan that delivered military victories in time to secure Abraham Lincoln's reelection. He had then played the central role in closing out Confederate resistance while laying the foundation for national reconciliation. Although he had a lesser role in the destruction of slavery, he recognized the claims blacks placed on the national conscience by fighting for Union and freedom. No other Union general had done as much; it was a good question whether anyone else could have.

Time and again, Grant had faced adversity. Sometimes it came on the battlefield: the counterattack at Belmont, the breakout at Donelson, the surprise at Shiloh, the challenge of Vicksburg, the grapple in the Wilderness, the disasters at Cold Harbor and Petersburg, the stalemate of the summer of 1864. Sometimes it came from circumstances: separation from his wife and children, a continuing struggle with a reputation as a worthless alcoholic, an inability to make ends meet no matter how hard he tried. Sometimes it came from adversaries who wore the same uniform: Robert Buchanan, Halleck, Rosecrans, McClernand, and the officer corps of the Army of the Potomac. Sometimes it even came from Abraham Lincoln himself, as the president juggled political and military priorities, contemplated Grant's replacement, or worried about the general's political ambitions. And on occasion it came from his father-in-law or, most dauntingly, his own father. In each case he may have struggled, worried, even become discouraged and depressed — but he had prevailed.

The events of the past four years had purged many of the personal demons that had long eaten away at Grant's heart and soul. Foremost was that he could look his father straight in the eye. If he could not make Jesse Grant stop talking (no one could), at least his father was not berating him. He had succeeded on his own, with no help from home. When the old man sought to distribute his inheritance, Ulysses refused to take a share, replying that he had contributed nothing to it. Left unsaid was that he no longer needed it and was free to do as he pleased. He was being showered with gifts and money; the house in Philadelphia was to be the first of several he would receive in the next few years. Other soldiers might go back to the farm or the factory, but he would never work again behind the counter at the general store on Main Street in Galena.[1]

Jesse sought to capitalize on his son's fame not only because he could brag once more about "My Ulysses" but also because he hungered to line his pockets and enhance his own sense of self-importance. He still believed he knew what was best for his son, and never hesitated to tell others what he thought Ulysses would (and should) do. His overwhelming ego prevented him from realizing that he was now basking in reflected glory. Only Hannah seemed to share her son's ability to take matters in stride.

Nor was Grant going to have to endure the taunts of his father-in-law about Julia's misfortune in marrying an army officer of little promise. In a sense he had fulfilled his pledge to the Dent family slaves that he would liberate them if he ever got the chance. Thus he resolved the moral compromises he had made in marrying into a slaveholding family (although in truth many of the slaves apparently had liberated themselves by fleeing White Haven during the first year of the war). The end of slavery also completed the decline of Colonel Dent. His Yankee son-in-law had taken over as the family head, his achievements forever silencing the old man's carping about the inauspicious choice his favorite daughter had made. It would be left to Grant to save White Haven from falling into other hands. The "Colonel" might continue to drop comments about the mischievous

Yankees bent on malevolence and the wonders of the plantation South, but those remarks served only to amuse his son-in-law. The general outranked the colonel. - 101

Most of all, perhaps, he had at last proved Julia Grant right. She had always told people that her husband was destined for better things, that, sooner or later, he would justify her faith in him. Julia may not have been the perfect wife — even her husband would tease her about her laziness, her failure to write to him, and some of her other imperfections — but Ulysses Grant knew he was fortunate indeed. Julia had always been proud of him; she had always seen something in him that escaped others; she had given him the warm, loving family he had always wanted. And she gave him something else: unconditional love and confidence in his ultimate success. Once, when asked whether her husband would take Richmond, she replied: "Yes, before he gets through. Mr. Grant always was a very obstinate man." She was just as obstinate in her faith in him; he was determined not to let her down — and he had not.[2]

It had all been astonishing. The man who began the war working as a clerk in his father's general store ended it as the general-in-chief of the Armies of the United States, the American republic's foremost hero. How to explain what had happened? Was it dumb luck, chance, destiny, genius? A case of the right man in the right place at the right time? How could someone who had struggled so long and with such little success at fairly straightforward pursuits meet and beat the complex challenges of waging war? How to explain both the depths of defeat and the heights of triumph?

The answers are many, varied, and ultimately unsatisfactory. Grant did not look the part of a general or act as if he was a military genius; yet it is just as far-fetched to conclude that it was simply fate or fortune, that he had somehow blundered to a victory drenched in blood due to his clumsiness and ineptitude. He made mistakes, some of them serious; he sometimes misjudged fellow generals and opponents; his orders were not always the purported models of clarity his admirers described; he could be partial to friends and unfair to foes, especially those wearing the same uniform. Yet his understanding of the world around him and the challenges in front of him suggest that he was intelligent and insightful in remarkable ways. His unusual temperament and sense of self captivated, intrigued, and fascinated his close associates. Not everyone judged a general by his uniform; one newspaper concluded that "the qualities by which great things are accomplished . . . have no necessary connection with showy and superficial accomplishments." Yet even Grant later observed, "It is difficult to know what constitutes a great general."[3]

Critics made much of the claim that Grant was not a student of military history. When a committee of citizens from Boston, eager to furnish the general with a library for his new home, asked what he already had, they were shocked to learn that he did not own a single volume of military history. Yet that widely reported incident rendered a misleading picture. As a young officer he had pondered the plans of Winfield Scott, often second-guessing his superior; during the 1850s people listened to him analyze various campaigns in Europe. However, the lessons Grant derived from his study of military history were those of inspiration, not imitation. "I don't underrate the value of military knowledge," he later remarked, "but if men make war in slavish observance of rules, they will fail." If nothing else, he added, the conditions of warmaking in Europe and America differed greatly; while generals "were working out problems of an ideal character, problems that would have looked well on a blackboard, practical facts were neglected. To that extent I consider remembrances of old campaigns a disadvantage. Even Napoleon showed that, for my impression is that his first success came because he made war in his own way, and not in imitation of others. War is progressive, because all the instruments and elements of war are progressive." Vicksburg verified that conclusion, teaching him "that there are no fixed laws of war which are not subject to the conditions of the country, the climate, and the habits of the people."[4]

Realizing that "every war I knew anything about had made laws for itself," Grant came to understand that mapping out a plan of campaign was much like solving a mathematics problem. Time and again he sought to demystify the process of waging war. "The art of war is simple enough," he once observed. "Find out where your enemy is. Get at him as soon as you can. Strike at him as hard as you can and as often as you can, and keep moving on." By reducing strategy and operational planning to fundamental principles, he was able to solve problems on their merits, drawing on his experiences and the lessons of military history. Sometimes his comments misled observers into thinking that he was ignorant of his craft. "I don't believe in strategy, in the popular understanding of the term," he once declared, omitting to explain what he meant by public perceptions of strategy. "I believe in getting up just as close to the enemy and with just as little loss of life as possible." Such remarks conceal the extent to which he thought things through. Even so close a friend as Sherman did not come to grips with that truth. "My only points of doubt were as to your knowledge of grand strategy, and of books of science and history," he wrote Grant when his friend was elevated to lieutenant general in 1864; "but I confess your common-sense seems to have supplied all this."[5]

Common sense — time and again observers used this term to describe Grant's approach to generalship. There was no attempt to ape Napoleon or Wellington; no elaborate references to the exploits of legend; the general was just "a plain businessman of the republic" (an interesting choice of words, given Grant's experiences as a civilian) getting things done. "Dash is handsome, genius glorious," one officer remarked; "but modest, old fashioned, practical everyday sense is the trump, after all." Newspaper correspondent William Shanks agreed: "His wisdom is that which results from a combination of common sense trained to logical reflection with practical observation. He deals with all questions in a plain, business-like manner, and in a systematic style, which enables him to dispatch a great deal of business in a very short time."[6]

And yet it was more than that. In retrospect many of Grant's plans seem so obvious and straightforward that they appear to have been devoid of genius, and simple to plan and to execute. Critics wielding that greatest weapon of all armchair generals — hindsight — often insist that Grant should have done this, could have done that — as if drawing lines on a map were the equivalent of waging war. However, what is remarkable is how exceptional, how uncommon, common sense is in a general. If it is so common, why is it so rare? If it is so easy to be a general, why have so many others found it so difficult? Why did none of Grant's contemporaries do what he did? The Prussian military theorist Carl von Clausewitz once remarked that anyone who had never exercised high command might believe it would be easy: "Everything looks simple; the knowledge required does not look remarkable, the strategic options are so obvious that by comparison the simplest problem of higher mathematics has an impressive scientific dignity." However, he continued, while everything in war might look simple, "the simplest thing is difficult." Rarely did things turn out as a commander intended; human error, unanticipated responses, weather, terrain, chance — all made it difficult indeed. Moreover, as Clausewitz noted, the true sign of military genius was not the careful study of the rules laid down in past practice, but the quality of mind and imagination "which rises above all rules."[7]

Among those who grasped this point was John M. Schofield, who met Grant many times but never shared a field of battle with him. Noting that some people claimed Grant was a genius while others dismissed him as ordinary, Schofield argued that the "most extraordinary quality" of Grant's "extraordinary character . . . was its extreme simplicity — so extreme that many have entirely overlooked it in their search for some deeply hidden secret to account for so great a character, unmindful that simplicity is one of the most prominent attributes of greatness." In turn, what made him a great commander was the evolution of his military ability "as the result of his own experience and independent thought, — that is, the independent development of his own native military genius," something almost intuitive and having as much to do with temperament and character as with intelligence.[8]

Sherman understood. Of Grant he once said: "He does not know as much about books and strict military art and science as some others, but he possesses the last quality of great generalship; he knows, he *divines,* when the supreme hour has come in a campaign or battle, and always boldly seizes it." Sherman himself had seen this trait at Shiloh; he would see it again during the Vicksburg campaign; he recalled that Grant had realized the moment of crisis at Donelson. "When he begins a campaign, he fixes in his mind what is the true objective point, and abandons all minor ones. . . . If his plan works wrong, he is never disconcerted, but promptly devises a new one, and is sure he will win in the end." Confidence, flexibility, the ability to improvise in response to circumstances, the composure to remain cool under pressure — these were all qualities Grant possessed.[9]

Part of the planning process involved having other people share in working things through. Although people often wondered whether Grant was a good talker — he tended to open up only in the company of close associates and trusted friends — he was clearly a good listener. Many times he would sit silently as staff officers and subordinates discussed what to do. "General Grant had a wonderful power of drawing information from others in conversation without their being aware that they were imparting it," Ely Parker recalled. Another member of the staff, brother-in-law Fred Dent, agreed: "He was constantly questioning his officers on various points in a very modest way, and never saying much himself. In this way he formed his opinions of the men he had to deal with, and knew who could do certain work best."[10]

Sometimes his ability to listen misled even those close to him. A few years after the war Adam Badeau described these conversations at headquarters to his boarding house associate, Henry Adams. The general would sit, saying little: "For stretches of time, his mind seemed torpid. Rawlins and the others would systematically talk their ideas into it, for weeks, not directly but by discussion among themselves, in his presence. In the end, he would announce the idea as his own, without seeming conscious of the discussion; and would give the orders to carry it out with all the energy that belonged to his nature. They could never measure his character or be sure when he would act. They could never follow a mental process in his thought. They were not sure that he did think." As a result, some people believed that John Rawlins was the power behind Grant; others, including James H. Wilson, would claim to be the architect behind various plans. Unable to fathom how Grant thought things through, they preferred to pat themselves on the back, all the while assuming that simply by proposing ideas they should be recognized as true military geniuses. Badeau was more perceptive than he knew when he admitted "that neither he nor the rest of his staff knew why Grant succeeded; they believed in him because of his success."[11]

"He was a great man for details," Sherman noted. "He remembered the most minute details and watched every point." One of his soldiers in the Army of the Tennessee agreed: "He seems to always know merely by memory where every part of his entire army, even down to the smallest detachment or company, is or ought to be. He will ride along the long line of the army, apparently as an indifferent observer; yet he sees and notices everything. He seems to know and remember every regiment, and in fact every cannon, in his large army." An eye for ground, the imagination to get inside the mind of his foe, an awareness of the officers and men with whom he had to work, a sense of the ebb and flow of battle — Grant took it all in as he decided what to do on the battlefield, processing information so quickly that others thought his talents were instinctive and intuitive. Mortimer D. Leggett, who commanded a brigade under Grant in the West, observed that he was "remarkably quick in his comprehension and perception. He was a very accurate observer and a careful listener, and when he had the facts before him he was the quickest man to arrive at a conclusion that I have ever met."[12]

Moreover, once Grant made up his mind, he did not look back. He had a job to do, and he was bent on doing it. "One of his greatest traits was his perfect willingness to accept responsibility," M. Harrison Strong, who worked on the general's staff, observed. "He was perfectly sure of himself. There was no such thing as failure for him." Leggett declared that Grant's "confidence in his own judgment seemed unbounded." Moreover, it was contagious. "He inspired me with confidence," Phil Sheridan remarked; "he was so self-contained, and made you feel that there was a heap more in him than you had found out." That self-confidence bred a determination to persist and prevail. Even Lincoln glimpsed that. "The great thing about Grant, I take it, is his perfect coolness and persistency of purpose," he

once told the artist Frank Carpenter. "I judge he is not easily excited, —
which is a great element in an officer, — and he has the *grit* of a bull-dog!
Once let him get his 'teeth' *in,* and nothing can shake him off."[13]

Nor did Grant become discouraged when circumstances changed or
the unexpected occurred. Rather than throw up his hands and blast his
bad luck (or go searching for scapegoats) he took things as they presented themselves and adjusted. Leggett noted that "he showed wonderful resources and remarkable quickness in appreciating new facts and
modifying his plans accordingly, by being always ready to act at the very
moment of discovery." Others also commented on his flexibility. "When
Grant formed a plan of battle," General George Stannard later remarked,
"he took into consideration the fact that the position and strength of the
enemy might suddenly change during a battle, and he showed remarkable
quickness in appreciating new facts and changing his plans." Reporter
Shanks, who observed Grant in battle, agreed. "If one resource fails he has
another at hand. . . . He is not easily disheartened, but seems greatest in
disaster or when surrounded by difficulties."[14]

Grant's generalship was shaped as much by character as it was by intellect. Nowhere was this more evident than in his realization that he could
not control everything, that the unanticipated was part of the problem he
had to solve. Sherman marveled at this quality, sharing his wonderment in
typically blunt and brash fashion with James H. Wilson in late 1864: "Wilson, I am a damned sight smarter man than Grant; I know a great deal
more about war, military history, strategy, and grand tactics than he does; I
know more about organization, supply, and administration and about everything else than he does; but I'll tell you where he beats me and where
he beats the world. He don't care a damn for what the enemy does out of
his sight, but it scares me like hell!" Nor was that all. "I am more nervous
than he is. I am more likely to change my orders or to countermarch my
command than he is. He uses such information as he has according to his
best judgment; he issues his orders and does his level best to carry them
out without much reference to what is going on about him and, so far, experience seems to have fully justified him."[15]

Not everything could be explained by character. If Grant "aimed to
achieve results, caring little for the manner by which they were accomplished," as Sherman once observed, it was also true that Grant possessed certain talents of generalship.[16] He knew how to coordinate military movements across space and over time; in most cases his orders were
clear and direct; he drew on his training as a quartermaster and commissary officer to outfit and feed his command. He trained his men and

looked out for them, for that would build morale; aware of fluctuations in morale during combat, he acted accordingly. As a warrior defending a democratic republic, he understood the impact of public opinion on military operations and the pressures placed on generals to perform; in turn he knew how military successes inspired the folks at home. If he fell short in this regard, it was in failing to alter popular perceptions of victory and defeat so that people could have better appreciated his accomplishments during the spring and summer of 1864. And he comprehended the world of civil-military relations, enabling him to establish solid working relationships with civil superiors without falling prey to the temptations of political activity. He even applied these insights in attacking his foe. He struck at enemy logistics to deny resources to the Confederacy; he targeted enemy morale, whether by extending the olive branch or by striking hard at both soldiers and civilians; he worked to undermine public support for the Confederacy whenever possible.

He was less successful at shaking the perception that he was a ham-handed tactician who freely wasted the lives of his own men. This reputation was largely based on the pervasive impression of his generalship left by the 1864 campaign in Virginia. That during the Vicksburg and Chattanooga campaigns combined, Grant's forces suffered fewer losses than did Lee's troops at Gettysburg escaped most people's notice; that he was far more frugal with human life than his leading Confederate counterpart (Lee's losses in 1862 and 1863 help explain why he was in such dire need for men in 1864) is recognized by only a few. He preferred to take prisoners than to slay foes; he emphasized movement and logistics over slugging it out. Even his campaigns in Virginia show a general who (his own comments to the contrary notwithstanding) shifted units and probed for weaknesses, mixing assaults with marches, constantly seeking new approaches. If anything, he expected too much from the generals and soldiers under his command during his first months in the East, for the continuous fighting and costly warfare wore down his officers and men.

Those people who knew Grant well realized that he was not a blood-thirsty butcher. If he was realistic about the human cost of war, he was also saddened by it. "He always expressed a great aversion to war for its own sake," Ely Parker recalled; Fred Grant would later tell an audience that during the Vicksburg campaign his father's eyes "filled with tears" at seeing the wounded. "Stolid as Grant appeared to be," one officer noticed, "I have no doubt that he felt as deeply about the horrors of war as those who were more demonstrative." Twenty years after the end of the war, Grant confided to a physician "that the carnage in some of his engagements was a positive horror to him, and could be excused to his conscience only on the score of the awful necessity of the situation." Robert E. Lee might suggest that if war was not so terrible, people might grow "fond" of it; Grant never did. "It is at all times a sad and cruel business," he once remarked. "I hate war with all my heart, and nothing but imperative duty could induce me to engage in its work or witness its horrors." Others, like Sherman, might speak of war as a "game," but Grant took no joy in his profession. "I never went into a battle willingly or with enthusiasm," he later reflected. "I was always glad when a battle was over."[17]

Compiling and describing Grant's talents as a general, however, does not answer one of the riddles of Grant's life. For it is difficult to see what would have happened to him had the Civil War not come about when it did and found him in a situation where he was able to take advantage of it (as opposed to, say, a continued position in the regular army, which might have limited his options). True, the same could be said of most of the other men who made their reputations in four years of bloodshed, including Sherman, Lee, and Jackson. But somehow Grant's story still seems more difficult to comprehend than most. How is one to explain his rise to fame between 1861 and 1865 in light of what had preceded it? In 1861 very few people could have foreseen what lay in Grant's future; even those who had faith in his abilities were surprised by his success. How could someone who struggled to make ends meet despite repeated setbacks, who had proved himself simply inept in several lines of work, be the same man who accomplished such great feats on the battlefield?

Much of the contrast is more apparent than real. Grant had performed ably at West Point, although he was rarely challenged there; he had proven a courageous, resourceful junior officer during the Mexican-American War; he had wrestled with difficult problems (notably the crossing of the Isthmus) prior to his resignation from the Army. If his peers in the service did not think him extraordinary, at least they liked and respected him. Even the shadow cast over him by stories of his drinking need not have meant much, especially in a republic where so many famous people drank to excess. Grant's troubles, while they probably began in the humdrum life of the peacetime army after the Mexican conflict, became far more pronounced when he decided to leave the army and strike out on his own.

When Grant returned to civilian life, unfortunately he did not pursue his earlier ambition to become a college professor. Instead, his efforts to earn a living as a farmer were plagued by the same bad luck that dogged his attempts to make some extra money while he was on the West Coast. Market fluctuations (notably the Panic of 1857), his own poor health, and the difficult position in which he found himself, first at White Haven, then in St. Louis as a man whom everyone liked but could not embrace — a Northerner in a Southern city, with too many Southern connections to be trusted by Northerners — doomed all his efforts to make ends meet. (People interpreted his lack of success as evidence that he was a failure, whereas in truth circumstance, bad luck, inexperience, and economic conditions combined to thwart his attempts to make something of himself.) Except for his ill-fated stint as a realtor and debt collector, however, Grant could not be blamed for the result. No wonder he later observed, "Man proposes and God disposes," adding that "There are but few important events in the affairs of men brought about by their own choice." Julia understood: she told everyone who would listen that they would not always be in their present condition. That her husband persistently plugged away at various pursuits was the more telling personal trait; had he been able to escape his dependence on his father and father-in-law, he might have come into his own much earlier than he did. And, if he was frustrated and depressed by his failure to move ahead, he found comfort and joy in being with his wife and children. Bad as things might be in other ways, at least he was with them now.[18]

A careful observer watching the former army captain struggle to make his way in the world in the 1850s might have detected some of the very traits that would mark Grant's later military career. He often discussed military campaigns with insight and understanding; others remarked that he had a good grasp of politics and current affairs. Many people came away from a conversation with him impressed by what he had to say. If he had not yet encountered success, he revealed a resilience and determination in the face of frustration and failure. He never gave up; he just turned to something else, tried to be resourceful, never abandoning hope, always tackling whatever he needed to do (even if that meant working for his father). He was not afraid to fail; after a while, of course, what else did he have to lose? Nevertheless, the signs were there that in the right situation Grant could succeed, even if he was stymied at the moment.

The contrast becomes even less evident when one recalls that Grant's first years as a commander were not an unqualified success. He did a great deal of learning on the job. True, the exercise of command engaged him as perhaps nothing else ever did; reentry into the army could prove a liberating experience for someone eager to escape his dependence on others. Grant always recognized that he evolved as a commander. In 1864, having just accepted his third star, he admitted to a former member of his staff, "I think I should have failed in this position if I had come to it in the beginning, because I should not have had confidence enough." Later he would reflect that he had great compassion for George B. McClellan because of "the vast and cruel responsibility" that devolved on him so early in the conflict: "if he did not succeed, it was because the conditions of success were so trying." Had Little Mac "fought his way along and up" — as had Grant — "I have no reason to suppose that he would not have won as high a distinction as any of us." Perhaps he was not afraid of failure precisely because he had encountered setbacks so many times; perhaps he worried less about uncontrollable events precisely because he knew that he could not control them, and so there was no sense in worrying.[19]

The general who rose to prominence between 1861 and 1865 displayed the same basic traits of mind and character as did the young officer and retired army captain of the 1840s and 1850s. To be sure, he grew with experience, but the essential qualities were already in place. After Appomattox, however, there was no going back. He need not ever lack again for recognition; if he kept his position, he would be secure for the rest of his life. But the story was not over. "Though the war in which he has won his reputation is now ended," concluded correspondent Shanks, "the future has still much to do in establishing the position which Grant has to hold in history. Today he enjoys the confidence of his countrymen to a degree unknown to military leaders during the war. If ultimately successful in the end — if he directs his course through the mazes of the political campaign which has followed hard upon the close of the war as well as he has his military career, posterity will delight, and will find little difficulty, in tracing out a comparison between his character and that of the country's first great military leader. . . . [I]f he remains, as at present, aloft from politics and far above partisanism, General Grant, like Washington before him, will live forever in the memories of his countrymen as a good and honest man."[20]

NOTES
INDEX

Notes

●

The following abbreviations are used in the notes:

CHS Chicago Historical Society.

CWAL Roy P. Basler et al., eds., *The Collected Works of Abraham Lincoln*. New Brunswick: Rutgers University Press, 1953–55.

ISHL Illinois State Historical Library.

LC Library of Congress.

PMJDG John Y. Simon, ed., *The Personal Memoirs of Julia Dent Grant*. New York: G. P. Putnam's Sons, 1975.

PMUSG Ulysses S. Grant, *Personal Memoirs of U. S. Grant*. New York: Charles L. Webster, 1885–86.

PUSG John Y. Simon, et al., eds., *Papers of Ulysses S. Grant*, Vols., 1–22. Carbondale: Southern Illinois University Press, 1967–   .

OR *The War of the Rebellion: A Compilation of the Official Records of the Union and Confederate Armies*. Washington, D.C.: Government Printing Office, 1880–1901.

SCW Brooks D. Simpson and Jean V. Berlin, eds., *Sherman's Civil War: Selected Correspondence of William T. Sherman, 1860–1865*. Chapel Hill: University of North Carolina Press, 1999.

USGA Ulysses S. Grant Association, Southern Illinois University at Carbondale.

1. "My Ulysses"

1. Albert D. Richardson, *Personal History of Ulysses S. Grant* (Hartford, Conn.: American Publishing, 1868), 40–42; Lloyd Lewis, *Captain Sam Grant* (Boston: Little, Brown, 1950), 5–8; William S. McFeely, *Grant: A Biography* (New York: W. W. Norton, 1981), 3–6.

2. Lewis, *Captain Sam Grant*, 8–15.

3. Ibid., 16–17; Hamlin Garland, *Ulysses S. Grant: His Life and Character* (New York: Macmillan, 1920), 6.

4. Richardson, *Personal History*, 50–52.

5. Garland, *Grant*, 7.

6. Lewis, *Captain Sam Grant*, 26–27, 31–32; Richardson, *Personal History*, 56.

7. Richardson, *Personal History*, 56; Lewis, *Captain Sam Grant*, 34; Garland, *Grant*, 13–14.

8. *PMUSG*, 1:29–30.

9. Ibid., 1:30.

10. Lewis, *Captain Sam Grant*, 30, 33; Richardson, *Personal History*, 63; Geoffrey Perret, *Ulysses S. Grant: Soldier and President* (New York: Random House, 1997), 15; Clyde W. Park, "That Grant Boy" (Cincinnati: C. J. Krehbiel Co., 1957), 20.

11. Information about Georgetown from "Notes for a Short Tour of Historic Sites in Georgetown, Ohio" (pamphlet, n.p., n.d.) and visit in October 1998; Lewis, *Captain Sam Grant*, 27–30, 48.

12. Lewis, *Captain Sam Grant*, 27; Richardson, *Personal History*, 68; Garland, *Grant*, 3; Nancy Anderson and Dwight Anderson, *The Generals: Ulysses S. Grant and Robert E. Lee* (New York: A. A. Knopf, 1988), 23; Park, "That Grant Boy," 19.

13. Lewis, *Captain Sam Grant*, 37–38; Garland, *Grant*, 12–13; W. T. Galbreath interview, Hamlin Garland Papers, University of Southern California.

14. Park, "That Grant Boy," 35–36.

15. Garland, *Grant*, 10–11; George F. Shrady, *General Grant's Last Days* (New York: privately printed, 1908), 11.

16. Lewis, *Captain Sam Grant*, 42–46; Anderson and Anderson, *The Generals*, 22–23, 27; Garland, *Grant*, 15, 21.

17. Garland, *Grant*, 17–23.

18. Park, "That Grant Boy," 26; Lewis, *Captain Sam Grant*, 53–57; Richardson, *Personal History*, 75.

19. Lewis, *Captain Sam Grant*, 56–57; Richardson, *Personal History*, 70, 75–76.

20. Lewis, *Captain Sam Grant*, 58–59; Richardson, *Personal History*, 76; Garland, *Grant*, 31; *PMUSG*, 1:32.

21. *PMUSG*, 1:35; Lewis, *Captain Sam Grant*, 60–61; Frederick T. Dent interview, Hamlin Garland Papers, University of Southern California; Perret, *Grant*, 20. In later life Grant would say that he did not know what the *S* stood for, and early renditions of his full name were as likely to style him Ulysses Sydney Grant as Ulysses Simpson Grant. However, when Grant was baptized late in life, it was as Ulysses Simpson Grant.

22. Garland, *Grant*, 42.

23. Horace Porter, *Campaigning with Grant* (New York, 1897), 15; Lewis, *Captain Sam Grant*, 62–68, 72; William M. Lamers, *The Edge of Glory: A Biography of General William S. Rosecrans* (New York: Harcourt, Brace & World, 1961), 13; Richardson, *Personal History*, 90.

24. *PMUSG*, 1:38, 41–42.

25. Grant to R. McKinstry Griffith, September 22, 1839, *PUSG*, 1:4–7.

26. Ibid.; *PMUSG*, 1:38–39.

27. Lewis, *Captain Sam Grant*, 72–76; Porter, *Campaigning*, 342; John Eaton, *Grant, Lincoln, and the Freedmen* (New York: Longmans, Green, and Co., 1907), 256.

28. Porter, *Campaigning*, 342; *PMUSG*, 1:39–40; Lewis, *Captain Sam Grant*, 82; Richardson, *Personal History*, 92; James G. Wilson, *General Grant* (New York: D. Appleton, 1897), 40–41; Garland, *Grant*, 43.

29. Lewis, *Captain Sam Grant*, 84–85; Richardson, *Personal History*, 91; William C. Church, *Ulysses S. Grant and the Period of National Preservation and Reconstruction* (New York: G. P. Putnam's Sons, 1897), 20.

30. Lewis, *Captain Sam Grant*, 85–86.

31. Ibid., 87–90.

32. Ibid., 92–93; Wilson, *General Grant*, 33–34; Samuel G. French, *Two Wars: An Autobiography* (Nashville: Confederate Veteran, 1901), 14–15.

33. Lewis, *Captain Sam Grant*, 92–93; Perret, *Grant*, 33–35. Perret believes that the in-

cident with the horse cost Grant a commission in the Dragoons; he offers no evidence to support that conclusion.

34. Lewis, *Captain Sam Grant,* 94–95; Richardson, *Personal History,* 92–93.

35. *PMUSG,* 1:41–44. The boy, William H. Scott, later joined the Fifty-ninth Ohio Infantry; at Chattanooga Grant ordered that he be given a medical discharge after seeing him require two canes to walk. Park, "That Grant Boy," 45–46.

2. The Dashing Lieutenant

1. *PMJDG,* 34–37, 41–42.
2. Ibid., 34–36.
3. Ibid., 38–39, 47–48.
4. Lloyd Lewis, *Captain Sam Grant* (Boston: Little, Brown, 1950); 104–6; Ishbel Ross, *The General's Wife: The Life of Mrs. Ulysses S. Grant* (New York: Dodd, Mead, 1959), 4–5.
5. Lewis, *Captain Sam Grant,* 105–7; Ross, *The General's Wife,* 6.
6. Lewis, *Captain Sam Grant,* 107.
7. Ibid., 107–8; Ross, *The General's Wife,* 20.
8. *PMJDG,* 48–50.
9. *PMUSG,* 1:48.
10. Lewis, *Captain Sam Grant,* 110–12.
11. Grant to Mrs. George B. Bailey, June 6, 1844, *PUSG,* 1:28; Grant to Julia Dent, July 28, 1844, ibid., 1:31.
12. Grant to Julia Dent, August 31, September 7, 1844, ibid., 1:33–39.
13. Grant to Robert Hazlitt, December 1, 1844, ibid., 1:39; *PMUSG,* 1:57; Lewis, *Captain Sam Grant,* 119.
14. Grant to Julia Dent, January 12, 1845, *PUSG,* 1:40.
15. Lewis, *Captain Sam Grant,* 121; *PMJDG,* 51; Grant to Julia Dent, September 14, 1845, *PUSG,* 1:55; Ross, *The General's Wife,* 30.
16. Grant to Julia Dent, July 11, 17, 1845, *PUSG,* 1:50–53.
17. Grant to Julia Dent, July 6, 1845, ibid., 1:49; Lewis, *Captain Sam Grant,* 116, 123–24.
18. Grant to Julia Dent, September 14, 1845, *PUSG,* 1:53–55.
19. Grant to Julia Dent, October 10, [October], November 11, [November–December], 1845, ibid., 1:56–66.
20. Grant to Julia Dent, January 2, 1846, ibid., 1:66–68; Lewis, *Captain Sam Grant,* 125–30.
21. Grant to Julia Dent, January 2, January 12, February 5, and February 7, 1846, *PUSG,* 1:66–74.
22. Grant to Julia Dent, March 29, April 20, 1846, ibid., 1:76–82.

3. A Man of Fire

1. *PMUSG,* 1:53, 55, 68.
2. Grant to Julia Dent, May 3, 1846, *PUSG,* 1:83.
3. Albert D. Richardson, *Personal History of Ulysses S. Grant* (Hartford, Conn.: American Publishing, 1868), 104–5; *PMUSG,* 1:94–97.
4. *PMUSG,* 1:96–98; Grant to John W. Lowe, June 26, 1846, *PUSG,* 1:94–98.
5. Grant to Julia Dent, May 11, 1846, *PUSG,* 1:84–87.
6. Grant to John W. Lowe, June 26, 1846, ibid., 1:94–98.
7. Grant to Julia Dent, May 24 and June 5, 1846, ibid., 1:87–91.
8. Grant to Lowe, June 26, 1846, ibid., 1:97; Grant to Julia Dent, July 2 and 25, 1846,

ibid., 1:99–103. On attitudes toward Mexico, see Robert W. Johannsen, *To the Halls of the Montezumas: The Mexican War in the American Imagination* (New York: Oxford University Press, 1985), especially chapter 6; on the views of Grant's fellow officers on a number of topics, see Richard Bruce Winders, *Mr. Polk's Army: The American Military Experience in the Mexican War* (College Station: Texas A&M University Press, 1997).

9. Lloyd Lewis, *Captain Sam Grant* (Boston: Little, Brown, 1950), 152–53; *PMUSG*, 1:99–102.

10. Grant to Col. John Garland, [August 1846], *PUSG*, 1:106–7.

11. Grant to Julia Dent, August 14, September 6, 1846, ibid., 1:104–6, 108–9; *PMUSG*, 1:105–6.

12. Lewis, *Captain Sam Grant*, 175–78.

13. *PMUSG*, 1:113–17; Grant to Julia Dent, September 23, 1846, *PUSG*, 1:110–11.

14. Lewis, *Captain Sam Grant*, 185–86.

15. Grant to Julia Dent, September 6, 1846, *PUSG*, 1:109.

16. Grant to Julia Dent, October 3, 20, 1846, ibid., 1:112–15; Grant to James Hazlitt, November 23, 1846, Grant Papers, LC.

17. Grant to Julia Dent, November 7, 1846, *PUSG*, 1:117; Lewis, *Captain Sam Grant*, 183.

18. Grant to Mrs. Thomas L. Hamer, [December 1846], *PUSG*, 1:121 and note.

19. Grant to Maj. Gen. Thomas S. Jesup, January 31, 1847, ibid., 1:122–23.

20. Grant to Julia Dent, February 1, 1847, ibid., 1:123–24.

21. Lewis, *Captain Sam Grant*, 198–99.

22. Ibid., 202; Grant to Julia Dent, April 3, 1847, *PUSG*, 1:129–30.

23. Grant to Julia Dent, December 27, 1846, *PUSG*, 1:119; Lewis, *Captain Sam Grant*, 204–5.

24. Grant to ?, April 24, 1848, *PUSG*, 1:134; K. Jack Bauer, *The Mexican War, 1846–1848* (New York: Macmillan, 1974), 265–68.

25. Bauer, *The Mexican War*, 268–74; Grant to Julia Dent, February 25, April 24, 1847, *PUSG*, 1:127, 132; Grant to John W. Lowe, May 3, 1847, ibid., 1:135–37; Lewis, *Captain Sam Grant*, 219.

26. Grant, Endorsement, [April 1847], *PUSG*, 1:134–35.

27. Richardson, *Personal History*, 112; Lewis, *Captain Sam Grant*, 180.

28. Grant to Julia Dent, April 24, 1847, *PUSG*, 1:132–33.

29. Grant to John W. Lowe, May 3, 1847, ibid., 1:135–37; Hamlin Garland, *Ulysses S. Grant: His Life and Character* (New York: Macmillan, 1920), 100.

30. Grant to ?, [September 12, 1847], *PUSG*, 1:145; Lewis, *Captain Sam Grant*, 226–36; Bauer, *The Mexican War*, 291–301.

31. Grant to ?, [August 22, 1847], *PUSG*, 1:143–44; Lewis, *Captain Sam Grant*, 237–41; Richardson, *Personal History*, 121; Bauer, *The Mexican War*, 308–11.

32. Lewis, *Captain Sam Grant*, 249–51.

33. Ibid., 258–61.

34. Grant to Julia Dent, October 25, 1847, *PUSG*, 1:147.

35. Garland, *Grant*, 103–4; Richardson, *Personal History*, 126; Carl M. Becker, "Was Grant Drinking in Mexico?" *Bulletin of the Cincinnati Historical Society* 24 (January 1966):70–71.

36. Grant to Julia Dent, September 1847, January 9, 1848, and May 7, 1848, *PUSG* 1:147, 149, 155–57; Richardson, *Personal History*, 127; *PMUSG*, 1:175.

37. *PMUSG*, 1:180–81, 138–39.

38. Lewis, *Captain Sam Grant*, 269; Grant to Julia Dent, March 22, 1848, *PUSG*, 1:153. On military attitudes toward politics and politicians, see William B. Skelton, *An American Profession of Arms: The Army Officer Corps, 1784–1861* (Lawrence: University Press of Kansas, 1992), chapter 15.

39. Grant to Julia Dent, May 22, June 4, 1848, *PUSG,* 1:158–61; Grant, Statement, June 27, 1848, ibid., 1:162–63.

4. Forsaken

1. Lloyd Lewis, *Captain Sam Grant* (Boston: Little, Brown, 1950), 283; *PMJDG,* 54–55.

2. Lewis, *Captain Sam Grant,* 284; Grant to Julia Dent, August 7, 1848, *PUSG,* 1:163–64.

3. *PMJDG,* 56; Lewis, *Captain Sam Grant,* 283–85.

4. *PMJDG,* 56.

5. *PMUSG,* 58.

6. See letters in *PUSG,* 1:168–81; *PMJDG,* 59–61; Lewis, *Captain Sam Grant,* 288.

7. Grant to Julia Grant, April 27, May 20, and May 26, 1849, *PUSG* 1:184–89; *PMJDG,* 65; Albert D. Richardson, *Personal History of Ulysses S. Grant* (Hartford, Conn.: American Publishing, 1868), 132; Lewis, *Captain Sam Grant,* 289.

8. *PMJDG,* 66–67; Lewis, *Captain Sam Grant,* 289–91; James E. Pitman interview, William C. Church Papers, LC.

9. Grant to Maj. Oscar F. Winship, June 14, 1850, *PUSG,* 1:194.

10. Grant, Deposition, January 10, 1851, *PUSG,* 1:195; Richardson, *Personal History,* 134–35; *PMJDG,* 68–69.

11. Grant to Julia Grant, May 28, June 4, June 7, June 11, June 16, and June 22, 1851, *PUSG,* 1:202–12.

12. Grant to Julia Grant, June 29, July 3, and July 13, 1851, *PUSG,* 1:214–17, 219–20; Richardson, *Personal History,* 138.

13. Grant to Julia Grant, July 27, August 3, August 10, and August 17, 1851, *PUSG* 1:220–27.

14. Grant to Lt. Col. J. B. Grayson, November 12, 1851; Grant to Julia Grant, August 3, 1851; and Grant to Maj. Gen. Thomas S. Jesup, May 26, 1862, *PUSG,* 1:231–32, 223, 232; *PMJDG,* 69–71.

15. Grant to Julia Grant, June 20, July 1, and July 4, 1852, *PUSG,* 1:235–36, 242–46.

16. Grant to Julia Grant, July 5, 1852, ibid., 1:247.

17. Charles G. Ellington, *The Trial of U. S. Grant: The Pacific Coast Years, 1852–1854* (Glendale: Arthur H. Clark, 1987), 37–50, *PMUSG,* 1:195; William S. Lewis, "Reminiscences of Delia B. Sheffield," *Washington Historical Quarterly* 15 (January 1924):52.

18. Ellington, *The Trial of U. S. Grant,* 50–59.

19. Ibid., 59–70; Grant to Julia Grant, August 9, 1852, *PUSG,* 1:251–53.

20. Ellington, *The Trial of U. S. Grant,* 71–101; Lewis, *Captain Sam Grant,* 308–10.

21. Grant to Julia Grant, July 15, August 16, and August 20, 1852, *PUSG,* 1:248, 255–56, 257–58. Later, Grant inquired: "What does the S stand for in Ulys.'s name? in mine you know it does not stand for anything!" Grant to Julia Grant, March 31, 1853, ibid., 1:298.

22. Grant to Julia Grant, August 30, 1852, ibid., 1:258–60.

23. Grant to Julia Grant, August 16, December 3, and December 19, 1852, ibid., 1:255, 275, 278; Grant to Julia Grant, January 29, February 15, March 19, and June 15, 1853, ibid., 1:286, 289, 296, 301; Grant to Maj. Osborn Cross, July 25, 1853, ibid., 1:310.

24. Grant to Julia Grant, March 31, 1853, ibid., 1:297; Lewis, *Captain Sam Grant,* 315; Lewis, "Sheffield," 60–61; Ishbel Ross, *The General's Wife: The Life of Mrs. Ulysses S. Grant* (New York: Dodd, Mead, 1959), 72.

25. Grant to Julia Grant, December 19, 1852, *PUSG,* 1:277; Grant to Julia Grant, March 31, May 20, 1853, ibid., 1:298, 299; Richardson, *Personal History,* 145–46.

26. Robert MacFeely interview, Hamlin Garland Papers, University of Southern California; Ellington, *The Trial of U. S. Grant*, 166–70.

27. Ibid., 133; Richardson, *Personal History*, 146.

28. Ellington, *The Trial of U. S. Grant*, 148–52.

29. Grant to Julia Grant, February 2, 6, 1854, *PUSG*, 1:316–18, 320–22. Julia's letters did go astray; Grant found several of them at San Franscisco on his trip home. Julia Grant interview, Garland Papers, University of Southern California.

30. Ellington, *The Trial of U. S. Grant*, 151–53; Augustus Chetlain interview, Garland Papers, University of Southern California.

31. Grant to Julia Grant, March 6, 25, 1854, *PUSG*, 1:322–28; Ellington, *The Trial of U. S. Grant*, 157–58.

32. Grant to Julia Grant, March 25–April 3, 1854, *PUSG*, 1:326–28.

33. Grant to Col. Samuel Cooper (two letters), April 11, 1854, and Grant to 1st Lieut. Joseph B. Collins, April 11, 1854, ibid., 1:328–30. At a time when many army officers were resigning, Grant's act was not that unusual; see William B. Skelton, *An American Profession of Arms: The Army Officer Corps, 1784–1861* (Lawrence: University Press of Kansas, 1992), chapter 11.

34. Ellington, *The Trial of U. S. Grant*, 172, 178.

35. Ibid., chapter 6, offers an extended overview of the evidence on Grant's habits and his resignation.

36. Ibid., 151, 163–64; Grant to Julia Grant, May 2, 1854, *PUSG*, 1:332.

37. Richardson, *Personal History*, 149.

5. Hardscrabble

1. Lloyd Lewis, *Captain Sam Grant* (Boston: Little, Brown, 1950); 333–39; *PMJDG*, 71–73; Grant to Julia Grant, June 15, 1853, *PUSG*, 1:301.

2. Lewis, *Captain Sam Grant*, 333–36, 338–39.

3. Charles G. Ellington, *The Trial of U. S. Grant: The Pacific Coast Years, 1852–1854* (Glendale: Arthur H. Clark, 1987); 202; Hamlin Garland, *Ulysses S. Grant: His Life and Character* (New York: Macmillan, 1920), photograph between pages 132 and 133; *PMJDG*, 76.

4. *PMJDG*, 76.

5. Ibid.

6. Ibid.; Ishbel Ross, *The General's Wife: The Life of Mrs. Ulysses S. Grant* (New York: Dodd, Mead, 1959), 78; George B. Johnson interview, Hamlin Garland Papers, University of Southern California.

7. See *PUSG*, 1:427; Ross, *The General's Wife*, 80.

8. *PMJDG*, 78–79.

9. Ibid.; Grant to Jesse Grant, December 28, 1856, *PUSG*, 1:334–35.

10. Grant to Jesse Grant, February 7, 1857, ibid., 1:336–37.

11. Brooks D. Simpson, *Let Us Have Peace: Ulysses S. Grant and the Politics of War and Reconstruction, 1861–1868* (Chapel Hill: University of North Carolina Press, 1991), 4; Pamela K. Sanfilippo, "The Grants and White Haven: Essays on the People and Property" (draft of Historic Resource Study, National Park Service, 1999), 224–26, shows that the 1850 census reported a total of thirty slaves divided between White Haven and the St. Louis residence.

12. Garland, *Grant*, xxii; *New York Times*, July 24, 1885; Albert D. Richardson, *Personal History of Ulysses S. Grant* (Hartford, Conn.: American Publishing, 1868), 173; Lewis, *Captain Sam Grant*, 346.

13. On Julia's slaves, see Emma D. Casey, "When Grant Went A-Courtin'," Mis-

souri Historical Society, reprinted in *Ulysses S. Grant Association Newsletter* 6 (October 1968).

14. Grant to Mary Grant, September 7, 1858, *PUSG,* 1:343; Grant to Jesse Grant, October 1, 1858, ibid., 1:344; Ross, *The General's Wife,* 93.

15. *PMJDG,* 80.

16. Garland, *Grant,* xxii–xxiii.

17. Lewis, *Captain Sam Grant,* 364; *PMJDG,* 81; Richardson, *Personal History,* 162.

18. Richardson, *Personal History,* 162–63; Lewis, *Captain Sam Grant,* 365.

19. Lewis, *Captain Sam Grant,* 366; Grant to Jesse Grant, October 1, 1858, *PUSG,* 1:344.

20. Don Fehrenbacher, *The Dred Scott Case: Its Significance in American Law & Politics* (New York: Oxford University Press, 1978), 243–49.

21. Simpson, *Let Us Have Peace,* 7; Lewis, *Captain Sam Grant,* 369.

22. Simpson, *Let Us Have Peace,* 4; Fehrenbacher, *The Dred Scott Case,* 568.

23. Manumission of William Jones, [March 29, 1859], *PUSG,* 1:347.

24. Grant to Jesse Grant, August 20, September 23, 1859, ibid., 1:350–52; Simpson, *Let Us Have Peace,* 5–6.

25. Grant to Simpson Grant, October 24, 1859, and Grant to J. H. Lightner, February 13, 1860, *PUSG,* 1:353–55; Lewis, *Captain Sam Grant,* 371; *PMJDG,* 82.

26. Grant to Julia Grant, March 14, 1860, *PUSG,* 1:355–56.

27. *PMJDG,* 82–83.

28. Garland, *Grant,* 148.

29. *PMJDG,* 84–86; Jesse R. Grant, *In the Days of My Father General Grant* (New York: Harper and Brothers, 1925), 10–11.

30. Grant to Mr. Davis, August 7, 1860, *PUSG,* 1:357; Richardson, *Personal History,* 173; Lewis, *Captain Sam Grant,* 373, 376–77, 389–90; William H. Armstrong, *Warrior in Two Camps: Ely S. Parker, Union General and Seneca Chief* (Syracuse: Syracuse University Press, 1978), 50–51, 74.

31. Simpson, *Let Us Have Peace,* 8; John C. Smith, *Personal Recollections of General Ulysses S. Grant* (Chicago: n.p., 1904).

32. Simpson, *Let Us Have Peace,* 8.

33. *PMJDG,* 87; Grant to [?], [December 1860], *PUSG,* 1:359–60.

34. Richardson, *Personal History,* 176.

35. Simpson, *Let Us Have Peace,* 9.

36. Richardson, *Personal History,* 178–79; Lewis, *Captain Sam Grant,* 394–99.

37. Richardson, *Personal History,* 179.

6. Off to War

1. Lloyd Lewis, *Captain Sam Grant* (Boston: Little, Brown, 1950), 401.

2. Ibid., 401–3.

3. Grant to Frederick Dent, April 19, 1861, *PUSG,* 2:3–4.

4. Grant to Jesse Grant, April 21, 1861, ibid., 2:6–7.

5. Lewis, *Captain Sam Grant,* 409–17; *PUSG,* 2:15.

6. Lewis, *Captain Sam Grant,* 416–17; Grant to Mary Grant, April 29, 1861, *PUSG,* 2:13–14.

7. *PMUSG,* 1:233; Mason Brayman, "Recollections," Mason Brayman Papers, CHS; Grant to Julia Grant, May 1, 1861, *PUSG,* 2:15–16.

8. Grant to Julia Grant, May 1, 3, 1861, *PUSG,* 2:16,19; Grant to Jesse Grant, May 2, 6, 1861, ibid., 2:18, 21.

9. Grant to Julia Grant, May 1, 1861, ibid., 2:15–16.

10. Ibid.

11. Grant to Julia Grant, May 10, 15, 1861, ibid., 2:26–27, 30–31; *PMUSG,* 1:234–37.

12. Grant to Jesse Grant, May 6, 1861, *PUSG,* 2:20–22; Grant to Julia Grant, May 10, 1861, ibid., 2:26–28; see also Grant to Julia Grant, May 6, 1861, ibid., 2:23–24.

13. Lewis, *Captain Sam Grant,* 417–18; *PMUSG,* 1:239.

14. Grant to Col. Lorenzo Thomas, May 24, 1861, *PUSG,* 2:35–36; Grant to Jesse Grant, May 30, 1861, ibid., 2:37; Grant to Julia Grant, June 1, 6, and 10, 1861, ibid., 2:37–41; *PMUSG,* 1:241; John Russell Young, *Around the World with General Grant* (New York: American News, 1879), 2:214–15. There has been some discussion about McClellan's whereabouts at the time of Grant's visit; however, the general was evidently in town on the two days Grant visited (June 10 and 11; his June 10 letter to Julia speaks of visiting Cincinnati "to-day") before leaving on June 12. See *PUSG,* 2:41n. In *George B. McClellan and Civil War History: In the Shadow of Grant and Sherman* (Kent: Kent State University Press, 1998), 59–61, Thomas J. Rowland questions the story, but mistakenly claims that Grant visited Cincinnati June 11 and 12; McClellan's own account of a visit to Indianapolis requires substantiation.

15. Brayman, "Recollections," Brayman Papers, CHS.

16. See *PUSG,* 2:8.

17. Lewis, *Captain Sam Grant,* 423–27; on McClellan, see *PUSG,* 2:41.

18. Albert D. Richardson, *Personal History of Ulysses S. Grant* (Hartford, Conn.: American Publishing, 1868), 185; Lewis, *Captain Sam Grant,* 427–28; Bruce Catton, *Grant Moves South* (Boston: Little, Brown, 1960), 4.

19. See the series of orders in *PUSG,* 2:45–48; Lewis, *Captain Sam Grant,* 428.

20. Richardson, *Personal History,* 185–86; Catton, *Grant Moves South,* 7; Lewis, *Captain Sam Grant,* 428; details on Grant's uniform from *PUSG,* 2:44–45.

21. Grant to Julia Grant, June 26, 1861, *PUSG,* 2:50. See also James L. Crane, "Grant as a Colonel," *McClure's Magazine* 7 (June 1896):40–45.

22. Grant to Julia Grant, June 27/29, 1861 (and note), *PUSG,* 2:52–54; *PMUSG,* 1:245–46; Lewis, *Captain Sam Grant,* 429–30. Most previous narratives blur these various incidents into a single swearing-in ceremony; a careful reading of Grant's account, however, reveals that Grant put the Logan and McClernand speeches as "but a few days before the time set for mustering in the United States service."

23. Orders No. 17 (June 28, 1861), 18 (June 28, 1861), 19 (July 1, 1861), 22 (July 2, 1861), 23 (July 9, 1861), and 24 (July 9, 1861), *PUSG,* 2:55–57, 61–64; Grant to Julia Grant, July 7, 1861, ibid., 2:59; *PMUSG,* 1:246–47; Catton, *Grant Moves South,* 10–12; Kenneth P. Williams, *Lincoln Finds a General* (New York: Macmillan, 1949–59), 3:19.

24. *PMUSG,* 1:247–48; Grant to Julia Grant, July 13, 1861, *PUSG,* 2:69–70.

25. Grant to Julia Grant, July 13, 1861, *PUSG,* 2:69–70.

26. *PMUSG,* 1:248–50.

27. Ibid. Grant later observed that courage in battle "was a cultivated quality rather than an inherent trait," and that "a genuine scare was the first and best lesson." He added that "the courage that lasted was that which throughly appreciated danger and boldly faced it. He confessed to this as a personal experience." George F. Shrady, *General Grant's Last Days* (New York: privately printed, 1908), 44.

28. Grant to Julia Grant, July 19, 1861, *PUSG,* 2:72–73.

29. General Orders No. 1, Headquarters, Military District of Mexico, July 25, 1861, ibid., 2:74–75; *PMUSG,* 1:252.

30. Grant to Jesse Grant, August 3, 1861, *PUSG,* 2:80–81; Grant to Julia Grant, August 3, 1861, ibid., 2:83; *PMUSG,* 1:253. See Michael Fellman, *Inside War: The Guerrilla Conflict in Missouri during the American Civil War* (New York: Oxford University Press, 1989), for the fulfillment of Grant's prediction.

31. John Pope to Maj. Gen. John C. Frémont, August 5, 1861, *PUSG,* 2:86.

32. Grant to Julia Grant, August 10, 1861, ibid., 2:96–97.

33. Lewis, *Captain Sam Grant*, 380–81.

34. *PMUSG*, 1:254–56; Catton, *Grant Moves South*, 18; John M. Thayer, "Grant at Pilot Knob," *McClure's Magazine* 5 (October 1895): 434.

35. General Orders No. 9, August 9, 1861, *PUSG*, 2:88–89; Grant to Mary Grant, August 12, 1861, ibid., 2:105; Grant to Capt. John C. Kelton, August 12, 14, 15, 1861, ibid., 2:102, 111, 114; Grant to Maj. Warren E. McMackin, August 12, 1861, ibid., 2:104.

36. Thayer, "Grant at Pilot Knob," 436–37; Grant to Capt. Speed Butler, August 22, 23, 1861, *PUSG*, 2:128, 135–36; Grant to Capt. R. Chitwood, [August 25, 1861], ibid., 2:136; Grant to Col. William H. Worthington, August 26, 1861, ibid., 2:139–40. Mark Neely offers a somewhat different discussion of Grant's actions in *The Fate of Liberty: Abraham Lincoln and Civil Liberties* (New York: Oxford University Press, 1991), 33–34.

37. Grant to Butler, August 22, 23, and 26, 1861, *PUSG*, 2:128–29, 131, 138; Grant to Kelton, August 25, 1861 (two telegrams), ibid., 2:133–34.

38. Grant to Julia Grant, August 26, 29, 1861, ibid., 2:140–41, 148–49.

39. Grant to Kelton, August 30, 1861, ibid., 2:154–55; General Orders No. 1, August 30, 1861, ibid., 2:153–54.

40. Grant to Jesse Grant, August 31, 1861, ibid., 2:158; Grant to Brig. Gen. Benjamin Prentiss, September 2, 1861, ibid., 2:169–70.

41. Grant to Frémont, September 4, 5, 1861, ibid., 2:186, 190.

42. Grant to Julia Grant, September 8, 1861, ibid., 2:214; *PMUSG*, 1:265–66; Proclamation to the Citizens of Paducah, September 6, 1861, *PUSG*, 2:194; Grant to Brig. Gen. Eleazer A. Paine, September 6, 1861, ibid., 2:195.

43. Grant to Col. John Cook, September 12, 1861, ibid., 2:243–44; Brooks D. Simpson, *Let Us Have Peace: Ulysses S. Grant and the Politics of War and Reconstruction, 1861–1868* (Chapel Hill: University of North Carolina Press, 1991), 16.

7. What I Want Is to Advance

1. Grant to Mary Grant, September 11, 1861, *PUSG*, 2:237–38.

2. General Orders No. 11, District of Southeast Missouri, October 14, 1861, ibid., 3:38–39; Bruce Catton, *Grant Moves South* (Boston: Little, Brown, 1960), 63–64.

3. Elihu B. Washburne to Salmon P. Chase, October 31, 1861, *PUSG*, 3:98; Grant to Julia Grant, October 6, 1861, ibid., 3:23; Grant to Mary Grant, October 25, 1861, ibid., 3:75–77; Grant to Capt. Chauncey McKeever, September 26, 1861, ibid., 2:314–15; Grant to Brig. Gen. Charles F. Smith, September 11, 1861, ibid., 2:234; Grant to Julia Grant, September 8, 22, 1861, ibid., 2:214, 299–300; Grant to Mary Grant, September 25, 1861, ibid., 2:313; Catton, *Grant Moves South*, 65.

4. Grant to Maj. Gen. John C. Frémont, September 10, 12, 1861, ibid., 2:225, 242; Grant to Julia Grant, October 20, 1861, ibid., 3:63–64; *PMUSG*, 1:269; John H. Brinton, *Personal Memoirs of John H. Brinton* (New York: Neale Publishing, 1914), 37–38; Arthur L. Conger, *The Rise of U. S. Grant* (New York: Century Co., 1931), 77, 84; Kenneth P. Williams, *Lincoln Finds a General* (New York: Macmillan, 1949–59), 3:75.

5. McKeever to Grant, November 1, 2, 1861, *PUSG*, 3:143–44, 103; Grant to Col. Richard J. Oglesby, November 2, 3, 1861, ibid., 3:105, 108–9.

6. Grant to Smith, November 5, 1861, ibid., 3:114; Conger, *The Rise of U. S. Grant*, 85; Williams, *Lincoln Finds a General*, 3:76. The fullest study of the Belmont campaign is Nathaniel Cheairs Hughes, Jr., *The Battle of Belmont: Grant Strikes South* (Chapel Hill: University of North Carolina Press, 1991).

7. *PMUSG*, 1:271–72; Albert D. Richardson, *Personal History of Ulysses S. Grant* (Hartford, Conn.: American Publishing, 1868), 197–98; Williams, *Lincoln Finds a General*, 3:91. Much debate has surrounded Grant's intentions when he embarked for Belmont: a convenient summary is to be found in Hughes, *The Battle of Belmont*, 51–53. Several ac-

counts suggest that Grant had intended to initiate a full-scale combat all along. These include John Y. Simon, "Grant at Belmont," *Military Affairs* 45 (December 1981): 161–66, and James E. McGhee, "The Neophyte General: U. S. Grant and the Belmont Campaign," *Missouri Historical Review* 47 (July 1973): 465–83. These accounts overstate their case. Simon endeavors to show that an alleged telegram of November 5 cited in Grant's revised report of the Belmont operation was probably extrapolated by Grant's staff officers from the content of other dispatches of the same date. He fails, however, to cite the most persuasive evidence at hand — the text of Grant's dispatch to Smith, which says that he is acting "under the same instructions" issued on November 1 and 2. See *PUSG*, 3:103, 114, 143–44, 149–52. Less persuasive is Simon's contention that the message that Grant claimed he received early on the morning of November 7 was a product of Grant's imagination. Grant's memory on this point is specific; someone would well recall such a message at 2 A.M.; and the absence of a written dispatch overlooks that Grant never specified that he received a *written* message. Moreover, in light of what Grant and others in the Union high command thought was happening at Columbus (it was precisely the transfer of forces to Missouri that Grant's feint was designed to discourage), Grant's willingness to accept the report makes sense. See ibid., 3:146. One need not dismiss this report to conclude that Grant was spoiling for a fight at Belmont, for his November 5 dispatch to Smith explicitly states that Smith's advance toward Columbus, by holding Polk in place, "might enable me to drive those they now have out of Missouri." Ibid., 3:114.

8. Richardson, *Personal History*, 199–200.

9. Ibid., 202.

10. Hughes, *The Battle of Belmont*, 46–47, 60–177; Conger, *The Rise of U. S. Grant*, 109, offers another account of a sighting of Grant on the battlefield. Grant later told Julia that he thought about his family at this moment. See *PMJDG*, 93.

11. Hughes, *The Battle of Belmont*, 175, 178–208.

12. Grant to Jesse Grant, November 8, 1861, *PUSG*, 3:137; Grant to Elihu B. Washburne, November 20, 1861, ibid., 3:205.

13. William H. L. Wallace to Ann Wallace, November 14, 1861, Wallace-Dickey Papers, ISHL; Grant to Jesse Grant, November 27, 1861, *PUSG*, 3:227; Brooks D. Simpson, *Let Us Have Peace: Ulysses S. Grant and the Politics of War and Reconstruction, 1861–1868* (Chapel Hill: University of North Carolina Press, 1991); *PMUSG*, 1:443.

14. Maj. Gen. George B. McClellan to Maj. Gen. Henry W. Halleck, November 11, 1861, Stephen W. Sears, ed., *The Civil War Papers of George B. McClellan: Selected Correspondence, 1860–1865* (New York: Ticknor & Fields, 1989), 130–31; General Orders No. 3, Department of the Missouri, November 20, 1861, *PUSG*, 3:345; Grant to Col. John Cook, December 25, 1861, ibid., 3:342–43; Capt. William S. Hillyer to Col. Leonard F. Ross, January 5, 1862, ibid., 3:373–74.

15. Grant to Jesse Grant, November 27, 1861, *PUSG*, 3:226–27; Grant to CSA Maj. Gen. Leonidas Polk, December 5, 1861, ibid., 3:259; General Orders No. 3, District of Cairo, January 13, 1862, ibid., 4:45.

16. Grant to Maj. John Riggin, Jr., December 15, 1861, ibid., 3:292; Grant to Capt. John C. Kelton, January 2, 1862, ibid., 3:363; Grant to Ross, December 4, 1861, ibid., 3:258; Grant to Col. Thomas H. Cavanaugh, January 8, 1862, ibid., 4:13; Grant to Brig. Gen. Eleazer A. Paine, January 11, 1862, ibid., 4:32; Paine to Grant, January 12, 1862, and Grant to Paine, January 12, 1862, ibid., 4:40; Grant to Paine, January 19 and 23, 1862, ibid., 4:68–69, 93; see also Grant to Commanding Officer, Cape Girardeau, January 29, 1862, ibid., 4:109–10.

17. Grant to Brig. Gen. John A. McClernand, ibid., 3:184; Grant to Kelton, November 22, 1861, ibid., 3:212; General Orders No. 26, District of Cairo, December 28, 1861, ibid., 3:349–50.

18. Catton, *Grant Moves South*, 83–84; Simpson, *Let Us Have Peace*, 20; Conger, *The Rise of U. S. Grant*, 103–4; *Baltimore American*, February 7, 1887.

19. Richardson, *Personal History*, 207.

20. Grant to Washburne, November 20, 1861, *PUSG*, 3:204–5; General Orders No. 22, District of Cairo, December 23, 1861, ibid., 3:330–31; Grant to Kelton, November 21, December 25, 1861, ibid., 3:208–9, 341; McClellan to Grant, November 10, 1861, ibid., 3:161.

21. Grant to Jesse Grant, November 27, 29, 1861, ibid., 3:226–27, 238–39; Grant to Mary Grant, December 18, 1861, ibid., 3:308; *Davenport (Iowa) Democrat*, July 29, 1885.

22. Richardson, *Personal History*, 195.

23. *PMJDG*, 95–96; John Eaton, *Grant, Lincoln, and the Freedmen* (New York: Longmans, Green, and Co., 1007), 101–2. Kountz was not a witness to the events he purported to report, for he arrived at Cairo on December 19; his charges specified acts that allegedly took place nearly two weeks prior to his arrival. See *PUSG*, 2:321, 3:112.

24. Benjamin H. Campbell to Washburne, December 17, 1861, and John A. Rawlins to Washburne, December 30, 1861, Elihu B. Washburne Papers, LC; Richardson, *Personal History*, 195–96.

25. See the letters reprinted in *PUSG*, 4:118–19.

26. Grant to Kelton, January 14, 1862, *PUSG*, 4:53.

27. Grant to Kelton, November 21, 1861, ibid., 3:209; Grant to Montgomery C. Meigs, January 22, 1862, ibid., 4:79–80.

28. Charles C. Coffin to Henry Wilson, January 18, 1862, ibid., 4:4; Grant to McClernand, January 18, 1862, ibid., 4:67; Grant to Mary Grant, January 23, 1862, ibid., 2:96; Grant to Kelton, January 17, 1862, ibid., 4:63; Catton, *Grant Moves South*, 120–21.

29. Abraham Lincoln to Maj. Gen. Don Carlos Buell, January 7, 1862; Lincoln to McClellan, January 9, 1862; and Lincoln to Simon Cameron, January 10, 1862, *CWAL*, 5:91–92, 94, 95.

30. Williams, *Lincoln Finds a General*, 3:178–98, especially 185; Grant to Mary Grant, January 23, 1862, *PUSG*, 4:96. See also Benjamin Franklin Cooling, *Forts Henry and Donelson: The Key to the Confederate Heartland* (Knoxville: University of Tennessee Press, 1987).

31. Williams, *Lincoln Finds a General*, 3:179, 186; Conger, *The Rise of U. S. Grant*, 130–31.

32. Grant to Halleck, January 28, 29, 1862, *PUSG*, 4:99, 103–4; Halleck to Grant, January 30, 1862, ibid., 4:104. Williams, *Lincoln Finds a General*, 3:178–80, outlines Halleck's thinking at this time.

33. See the documents in *PUSG*, 4:110–16; on McClernand's dissatisfaction, see McClernand to John A. Logan, January 8, 1862, Logan Papers, LC. Grant did not forget those who talked about his drinking: see Silas Noble to Washburne, November 26, 1862, Washburne Papers, LC.

34. Catton, *Grant Moves South*, 138.

35. Conger, *The Rise of U. S. Grant*, 159; Brinton, *Personal Memoirs*, 130–31.

36. Grant to Julia Grant, February 4, 1862, *PUSG*, 4:149; District of Cairo, Field Orders No. 1, February 5, 1862, ibid., 4:150–51.

37. Conger, *The Rise of U. S. Grant*, 159; Grant to Halleck, February 6, 1862, *PUSG*, 4:155–58.

38. Richardson, *Personal History*, 217; Catton, *Grant Moves South*, 150–51.

39. Grant to Mary Grant, February 9, 1862, *PUSG*, 4:179–80; Grant to Flag Officer Andrew H. Foote, February 10, 1862, ibid., 4:182; Grant to McClernand, February 10, 1862, ibid., 4:183–84; Grant to Julia Grant, February 10, 14, 1862, ibid., 4:188, 211; Lew Wallace, *Lew Wallace: An Autobiography* (New York: Harper, 1906), 1:377; Richardson, *Personal History*, 217.

40. Catton, *Grant Moves South,* 153.

41. Ibid., 159; Grant to Julia Grant, February 14, 1862, *PUSG,* 4:211.

42. Williams, *Lincoln Finds a General,* 3:235–39; Cooling, *Forts Henry and Donelson,* 153–60; Conger, *The Rise of U. S. Grant,* 169, 172.

43. Grant to Brig. Gen. George W. Cullen, February 15, 1862, *PUSG,* 4:213.

44. Catton, *Grant Moves South,* 166–67; Lew Wallace, "The Capture of Fort Donelson," in Robert U. Johnson and Clarence C. Buel, eds., *Battles and Leaders of the Civil War* (New York: Century, 1887), 1:421–22: Cooling, *Forts Henry and Donelson,* 183–84.

45. Catton, *Grant Moves South,* 167–69; Cooling, *Forts Henry and Donelson,* 184.

46. Grant to Foote, February 15, 1862, *PUSG,* 4:214; Cooling, *Forts Henry and Donelson* 185. There has been debate about the sequence of events between the time Grant first learned of the Confederate attack and the Union counterattack. Several historians place Grant's letter to Foote much earlier in the engagement. However, its observations about the demoralization of enemy soldiers as well as his own suggest that it could have been written only after he visited his right flank.

47. Catton, *Grant Moves South,* 173.

48. Richardson, *Personal History,* 225–26; Brinton, *Personal Memoirs,* 129–30; Grant to Buckner, February 16, 1862, *PUSG,* 4:218.

49. Catton, *Grant Moves South,* 177–78.

8. *Under a Cloud*

1. Grant to Brig. Gen. George W. Cullum, February 19, 21, 1862, *PUSG,* 4:245, 257; Grant to Julia Grant, February 16, 1862, ibid., 4:229–30.

2. Bruce Catton, *Grant Moves South* (Boston: Little, Brown, 1960), 179–81; McPherson to Grant, February 21, 1862, *PUSG,* 4:222; Grant to Julia Grant, February 22, 1862, ibid., 4:271; J. R. Jones to Elihu Washburne, February 19, 1862, Washburne Papers, LC; William T. Sherman to John Sherman, February 23, 1862, *SCW,* 192.

3. General Orders No. 6, District of West Tennessee, February 21, 1862, *PUSG,* 4:253–54; Grant to Julia Grant, February 22, 24, 1862, ibid., 4:271, 284; Grant to Cullum, February 25, 1862, ibid., 4:287.

4. Grant to Julia Grant, February 26, 1862, ibid., 4:292–93; *Cincinnati Commercial,* February 22, 1862.

5. Grant to Cullum, February 28, 1862 (two letters), *PUSG,* 4:294–95, 296–97; Grant to Halleck (endorsement), March 1, 1862, ibid., 4:301; Grant to Capt. J. C. Kelton, February 28, March 1, 1862, ibid., 4:298–99, 304–5; Grant to Julia Grant, March 1, 1862, ibid., 4:305–6; Grant to Flag Officer Andrew H. Foote, March 3, 1862, ibid., 4:313–14; Catton, *Grant Moves South,* 190–93.

6. Ethan Allen Hitchcock, *Fifty Years in Camp and Field: The Diary of Major-General Ethan Allen Hitchcock, U.S.A.* (New York: G. P. Putnam's Sons, 1909), 434–35; *PUSG,* 4:197; Catton, *Grant Moves South,* 187; Kenneth P. Williams, *Lincoln Finds a General* (New York: Macmillan, 1949–59), 3:218. Arthur L. Conger, *The Rise of U. S. Grant* (New York: Century Co., 1931), 178–213, offers a good discussion of Halleck's behavior from the end of January to mid-March 1862.

7. Catton, *Grant Moves South,* 195; Conger, *The Rise of U. S. Grant,* 201.

8. Williams, *Lincoln Finds a General,* 3:303; Halleck to Grant, March 4, 1862, *PUSG,* 4:319; see ibid., 4:320, for the exchanges between McClellan and Halleck. In *Forty-Six Years in the Army* (New York: Century Co., 1897), 361, John M. Schofield insisted that Halleck hoped that in Grant's absence Smith would fight and win a battle, which would justify his promotion over Grant. According to Augustus W. Alexander, *Grant as a Soldier* (St. Louis: privately published, 1887), 69, on March 2 Halleck received an anonymous

letter containing allegations about Grant's intoxication. The report that Grant may have been drinking might have found its origins in a spell of illness; Cadwallader Washburn told his brother the congressman on March 3, 1862, that Grant "is quite ill this morning." See Washburn to Washburne, March 3, 1862, Elihu B. Washburne Papers, LC (Cadwallader Washburn omitted the "e" in rendering his name); Grant to Foote, March 3, 1862, *PUSG*, 4:313.

9. *PUSG*, 4:344; Grant to Halleck, March 5, 1862, ibid., 4:317–19; Grant to Julia Grant, March 5, 1862, ibid., 4:326–27; Catton, *Grant Moves South*, 207.

10. Grant to Halleck, March 7, 1862, *PUSG*, 4:331.

11. Halleck to Grant, March 8, 1862, ibid., 4:335; Grant to Halleck, March 9, 1862, ibid., 4:334; Halleck to Grant, March 6, 1862, ibid., 4:353; Grant to Halleck, March 13, 1862, ibid.; Catton, *Grant Moves South*, 204–5.

12. Cadwallader C. Washburn to Elihu B. Washburne, March 5, 1862, Washburne Papers, LC.

13. Cadwallader C. Washburn to Elihu B. Washburne, March 8, 1862, ibid.; J. Dana Webster to "Dear Annie," March 20, 1862, Horace White Papers, ISHL; Catton, *Grant Moves South*, 208–9.

14. Halleck to Grant, March 13, 1862, *PUSG*, 4:354. In later years, James H. Wilson tried to recover proof that Halleck had secured from Grant a pledge to abstain from alcohol. See Wilson to Grenville M. Dodge, November 8, 1904, and February 17, 1905, Wilson Papers, LC. No evidence of such a correspondence survives, nor does it comport with the correspondence that does survive.

15. Cadwallader C. Washburn to Elihu B. Washburne, March 7, 1862, and William R. Rowley to Washburne, March 14, 1862, Washburne Papers, LC; *PUSG*, 4:320–21; Grant to Halleck, March 21, 1862, ibid., 4:400–1; Conger, *The Rise of U. S. Grant*, 201, 211–12.

16. Grant to Julia Grant, March 1, 1862, *PUSG*, 4:306; Grant to Elihu B. Washburne, March 22, 1862, ibid., 4:409; Grant to Halleck, March 14, 24, 1862, ibid., 4:358–59; General Orders No. 21, March 15, 1862, ibid., 4:364; Conger, *The Rise of U. S. Grant*, 212; General Field Orders No. 16, February 16, 1862, *PUSG*, 4:219–20; Grant to Cullum, February 17, 1862, ibid., 4:233; General Orders No. 12, District of West Tennessee, February 25, 1862, ibid., 4:285; Grant to Col. William W. Lowe, March 15, 1862, ibid., 4:372–73; Grant to Col. Philip B. Fouke, March 16, 1862, ibid., 4:377; Grant to Halleck, March 18, 1862, ibid., 4:387; General Orders No. 24, District of West Tennessee, March 19, 1862, ibid., 4:390; Grant to Julia Grant, March 23, 1862, ibid., 4:412–13; Grant to Halleck, March 24, 1862, ibid., 4:414.

17. Brooks D. Simpson, *Let Us Have Peace: Ulysses S. Grant and the Politics of War and Reconstruction, 1861–1868* (Chapel Hill: University of North Carolina Press, 1991), 21; General Orders No. 21, District of West Tennessee, February 26, 1862, *PUSG*, 4:290–91.

18. General Orders No. 14, District of West Tennessee, February 26, 1862, *PUSG*, 4:290–91; General Orders No. 46, Department of the Missouri, February 22, 1862, ibid., 4:291; Grant to Washburne, March 22, 1862, ibid., 4:408–9.

19. Grant to Julia Grant, February 26, March 23, 1862, ibid., 4:292, 413.

20. Grant to Julia Grant, March 5, 23, 29, 1862, ibid., 4:326–27, 412–13, 443.

21. Grant to Cullum, February 19, 1862, ibid., 4:245; General Orders No. 7, District of West Tennessee, February 22, 1862, ibid., 4:265; Grant to Halleck, March 11, 1862, ibid., 4:341–42; Grant to Lowe, March 11, 1862, ibid., 4:346; Grant to Capt. Nathaniel H. McLean, March 15, 1862, ibid., 4:368; Grant to Julia Grant, March 18, 1862, ibid., 4:389.

22. Grant to Julia Grant, March 18, 1862, ibid., 4:389; see also Grant to Maj. Melancthon Smith, March 24, 1862, ibid., 4:417.

23. Grant to Sherman, March 17, 1862, ibid., 4:381; William H. L. Wallace to Ann Wallace, March 18, 1862, Wallace-Dickey Papers, ISHL; Rowley to Washburne, March 24, 1862, Washburne Papers, LC.

24. Sherman to Grant, February 15, 1862 (two letters), *PUSG*, 4:215–16. On Sherman, see John Marszalek, *Sherman: A Soldier's Passion for Order* (New York: The Free Press, 1993); Lloyd Lewis, *Sherman: Fighting Prophet* (Lincoln: University of Nebraska Press, 1993 [1932]); and Michael Fellman, *Citizen Sherman: A Life of William Tecumseh Sherman* (Lawrence: University Press of Kansas, 1997 [1995]).

25. Grant to Halleck, March 18, 1862, *PUSG*, 4:387.

26. Grant to McLean, March 20, 1862, ibid., 4:397; Grant to Halleck, March 21, 1862, ibid., 4:400; Catton, *Grant Moves South*, 212; Williams, *Lincoln Finds a General*, 3:329; Conger, *The Rise of U. S. Grant*, 216, 220, 222.

27. Grant to Sherman, March 17, 1862, *PUSG*, 4:382–83; Grant to Col. Marcellus M. Crocker, March 17, 1862, ibid., 4:384; General Orders No. 23, District of West Tennessee, March 18, 1862, ibid., 4:385–86; Grant to John A. McClernand, March 28, 1862, ibid., 4:437–38; Grant to Julia Grant, March 15, 29, 1862, ibid., 4:375, 443.

28. Grant to Sherman, April 4, 1862, and Grant to W. H. L. Wallace, April 4, 1862, *PUSG*, 5:9, 12; Grant to McLean, April 3, 1862, ibid., 5:3–4; Grant to Julia Grant, April 3, 1862, ibid., 5:7–8; Rowley to Sherman, July 12, 1881, Rowley Papers, ISHL.

29. Grant to Halleck, April 5, 1862 (two telegrams), *PUSG*, 4:13–14; Sherman to Grant, April 5, 1862, ibid., 4:14; Joshua T. Bradford, Diary, April 5, 1862, LC.

30. Grant to Don Carlos Buell, April 6, 1862, *PUSG*, 4:17; Grant to "Commanding General, Advance Forces," April 6, 1862, ibid., 4:18.

31. A. L. Chetlain to Washburne, May 24, 1862, Washburne Papers, LC; Catton, *Grant Moves South*, 226; Rowley to Sherman, July 12, 1881, Rowley Papers, ISHL.

32. Albert D. Richardson, *Personal History of Ulysses S. Grant* (Hartford, Conn.: American Publishing, 1868), 249; Douglas J. Putnam, "Reminiscences of the Battle of Shiloh," *Sketches of War History, 1861–1865: Military Order of the Loyal Legion of the United States, Ohio Commandery, Volume 3* (Cincinnati: Robert Clarke, 1890), 201.

33. Shelby Foote, *The Civil War: A Narrative* (New York: Random House, 1958–74), 1:336.

34. James Lee McDonough, *Shiloh — In Hell before Night* (Knoxville: University of Tennessee Press, 1997), 170–71.

35. William R. Rowley quoted Grant as saying on the morning of the engagement, "Wallace will soon be up and that will change the complexion of things, and in any event we can hold them by gradually drawing in our line until Buell gets up with his own forces." Sherman, July 12, 1881, Rowley Papers, ISHL.

36. Wiley Sword, *Shiloh: Bloody April* (New York: William Morrow, 1974), 360, 367–68; Richardson, *Personal History*, 251; Catton, *Grant Moves South*, 239–40. In light of Grant's well-known aversion to swearing, perhaps he was misquoted.

37. Foote, *The Civil War*, 1:343.

38. Catton, *Grant Moves South*, 241.

39. Ibid., 241–42.

40. Sword, *Shiloh: Bloody April*, 380; Richardson, *Personal History*, 253; William R. Rowley to E. Hempstead, April 19, 1862, Washburne Papers, LC; Grant to Buell, April 7, 8, 1862, *PUSG*, 5:21, 24.

41. Peter Cozzens and Robert I. Girardi, eds., *The Military Memoirs of General John Pope* (Chapel Hill: University of North Carolina, 1998), 64.

42. Halleck to Grant, April 9, 1862, *PUSG*, 5:20; General Orders No. 35, District of West Tennessee, April 9, 1862, ibid., 5:28–29; Halleck to wife, April 14, 1862, ibid., 5:48; General Orders No. 16, Department of the Mississippi, April 13, 1862, ibid., 5:48; Halleck to Grant, April 14, 1862, ibid., 5:48–49; General Orders No. 39, District of West Tennessee, April 17, 1862, ibid., 5:49; Special Field Orders No. 12, Department of the Mississippi, April 17, 1862, ibid., 5:49–50; Special Field Orders No. 21, Department of the Mississippi, April 22, 1862, ibid., 5:51; Special Field Orders No. 25, Department of

the Mississippi, April 23, 1862, ibid., 5:51–52; Halleck to Grant, April 28, 1862, ibid., 5:89; Grant to Julia Grant, April 30, 1862, ibid., 5:102; William Hemstreet, "Little Things About Big Generals," A. Noel Blakeman, ed., *Personal Recollections of the War of the Rebellion*, Third Series (New York: G. P. Putnam's Sons, 1907), 157.

43. Grant to Julia Grant, April 15, 1862, *PUSG*, 5:47; M. Smith to Washburne, April 22, 1862, Charles L. Stephenson to Washburne, April 19, 1862, and John E. Smith to Washburne, May 16, 1862, Washburne Papers, LC; Catton, *Grant Moves South*, 259; Rowley to E. Hempstead, April 19, 1862, and John E. Smith to Washburne, May 16, 1862, Washburne Papers, LC.

44. Rowley to Washburne, April 23, 1862, Washburne Papers, LC; William S. Hillyer to [?], April 21, 1862, *PUSG*, 5:79–80.

45. Hempstead to Washburne, April 23, 1862; Jesse Grant to Washburne, May 16, 1862; and Joseph Medill to Washburne, May 24, 1862, Washburne Papers, LC; Catton, *Grant Moves South*, 261.

46. Grant to Julia Grant, April 25, 30, 1862, *PUSG*, 5:72, 102–3.

47. Grant to George P. Ihrie, April 25, 1862, ibid., 5:73–74; Grant to Jesse Grant, April 26, 1862, ibid, 5:78–79.

48. See ibid., 5:78–83.

49. Grant to Julia Grant, May 4, 11, 1862, ibid., 5:110, 116.

50. Ibid., 4:344; Grant to Julia Grant, April 25, May 4, 1862, ibid., 5:72, 111.

51. Grant to Sherman, February 19, 1862, ibid., 4:249.

52. Grant to McLean, April 21, 1862, ibid., 5:63; Grant to Capt. Andrew C. Kemper, April 28, 1862, ibid., 5:89; ibid., 4:160; McClernand to Grant, March 6, 1862, ibid., 4:324.

53. *PMUSG*, 1:368; Grant to Julia Grant, April 15, 30, and May 13, 1862, *PUSG*, 5:47, 102, 118 Special Orders No. 35, Department of the Mississippi, April 30, 1862, ibid., 5:105; Halleck to Grant, April 30, 1862, ibid.

54. Grant to Halleck, May 11, 1862, *PUSG*, 5:114.

55. Grant to Julia Grant, May 11, 13, 20, 1862, ibid., 5:116, 117–18, 128; Grant to Washburne, May 14, 1862, ibid., 5:119–20; Richardson, *Personal History*, 258.

56. Halleck to Grant, May 12, 1862, *PUSG*, 5:115; Williams, *Lincoln Finds a General*, 3:410–11; McClernand to Washburne, July 9, 1862, Washburne Papers, LC.

57. *PMUSG*, 1: 376; Grant to Julia Grant, May 20, 1862, *PUSG*, 5:127; Cozzens and Girardi, *Military Memoirs of Pope*, 64–65, 90–91.

58. Marszalek, *Sherman*, 186; Grant to Washburne, June 1, 1862, *PUSG*, 5:136; *PMUSG*, 1:380–81.

59. Grant to Julia Grant, May 24, 1862, *PUSG*, 5:130; Grant to Rev. John H. Vincent, May 25, 862, ibid., 5:132; Rowley to Washburne, May 24, 1862, Washburne Papers, LC; Clark B. Lagow to Washburne, May 24, 1862, ibid.; *PMUSG*, 1:379; Catton, *Grant Moves South*, 271–73.

60. Grant to Julia Grant, May 31, 1862, *PUSG*, 5:134–35. Sherman later argued that Grant was headed out of the army altogether (see William T. Sherman, *Memoirs of W. T. Sherman* [New York: Appleton, 1875], 1:255), but that does not seem to be the case.

61. Grant to Julia Grant, June 3, 9, 1862, ibid., 5:137, 140–41; Grant to Washburne, June 19, 1862, ibid., 5:145; Sherman to Grant, June 6, 1862, *SCW*, 232–33. To his wife Sherman remarked, "He is not a brilliant man and has himself thoughtlessly used the press to give himself eclat in Illinois, but he is a good & brave soldier tried for years, is sober, very industrious, and as kind as a child. Yet he has been held up as careless, criminal, a drunkard, tyrant and every thing horrible." Sherman to Ellen Sherman, June 6, 1862, ibid., 236.

62. Grant to Julia Grant, June 3, 12, 1862, *PUSG*, 5:138, 142–43; Grant to Washburne, June 19, 1862, ibid., 5:146; Catton, *Grant Moves South*, 281.

63. Grant to Washburne, June 19, 1862, *PUSG,* 5:146.

64. Grant to Halleck, June 23, 24, 27, 1862, ibid., 5:147, 149, 165; General Orders No. 56, District of West Tennessee, June 24, 1862, ibid., 5:151; Special Orders No. 122, District of West Tennessee, June 28, 1862, ibid., 5:152; Grant to Hillyer, July 1, 1862, ibid., 5:181, and ibid., 5:181–82; General Orders No. 60, District of West Tennessee, July 3, 1862, ibid., 5:190–91.

65. See ibid., 5:192–93; Grant to Halleck, July 8[7], 1862, ibid., 5:199.

66. Catton, *Grant Moves South,* 287–88.

9. Enemies Front and Rear

1. *PUSG,* 5:230; Halleck to Grant, July 30, 1862, ibid., 5:255.

2. Grant to Halleck, July 19, 1862, ibid., 5:219; Grant to Jesse Grant, August 3, 1862, ibid., 5:263.

3. Washburne to Grant, July 25, 1862, ibid., 5:226.

4. Grant to Jesse Grant, August 3, 1862, ibid., 5:264; District of West Tennessee, General Orders No. 72, August 11, 1862, ibid., 5:273; Grant to Mary Grant, August 19, 1862, ibid., 5:310–11.

5. Brooks D. Simpson, *Let Us Have Peace: Ulysses S. Grant and the Politics of War and Reconstruction, 1861–1868* (Chapel Hill: University of North Carolina Press, 1991), 29; Grant to Halleck, August 9, 1862, *PUSG,* 5:278; Grant to Sherman, August 8, 1862, ibid., 5:274; Albert D. Richardson, *Personal History of Ulysses S. Grant* (Hartford, Conn.: American Publishing, 1868), 268. On escalation, see Mark Grimsley, *The Hard Hand of War: Union Military Policy toward Southern Civilians, 1861–1865* (Cambridge; Cambridge University Press, 1995) and Benjamin Franklin Cooling, *Fort Donelson's Legacy: War and Society in Kentucky and Tennessee, 1862–1863* (Knoxville: University of Tennessee Press, 1997).

6. Grant to Halleck, July 28, 1862, *PUSG,* 5:243; Grant to Mary Grant, August 19, 1862, ibid., 5:310–11; District of West Tennessee, General Orders No. 65, July 28, 1862, ibid., 247; Halleck to Grant, August 2, 1862, ibid., 5:244.

7. Sherman to Rawlins, July 30, 1862, ibid., 5:240; Grant to Chase, July 31, 1862, ibid., 5:255–56; District of West Tennessee, General Orders Nos. 64 and 69, July 25 and August 6, 1862, ibid., 5:238–39, 268; Grant to Brig. Gen. Isaac F. Quinby, July 26, 1862, ibid., 5:238; Grant to Halleck, July 30, 1862, ibid., 5:253.

8. Grant to Quinby, July 26, 1862, ibid., 5:238; Grant to Chase, July 31, 1862, ibid., 5:255–56; ibid., 5:238–41, 244.

9. Grant to Jesse Grant, August 3, 1862, ibid., 5:263–64.

10. Grant to Maj. Gen. Don C. Buell, August 12 and 13, 1862, ibid., 5:288, 290; Grant to Julia Grant, August 18, 22, 1862, ibid., 5:308, 328.

11. Grant to Julia Grant, September 14, 15, 1862, ibid., 6:43, 50–51.

12. Kenneth P. Williams, *Lincoln Finds a General* (New York: Macmillan, 1949–59), 4:72–75. The interpretation of this incident offered in Peter Cozzens, *The Darkest Days of the War: The Battles of Iuka & Corinth* (Chapel Hill: University of North Carolina Press, 1997), which claims that transmitting the dispatch to Price was Grant's idea, is contradicted by Ord to Leggett, September 19, 1862, *OR,* ser. 1, xvii, part 2, 229–30.

13. Ibid., 4:75–76, 77–79; Bruce Catton, *Grant Moves South* (Boston: Little, Brown, 1960), 311; Cozzens, *The Darkest Days of the War,* 77, 122, 128–29

14. Cozzens, *The Darkest Days of the War,* 72–73; Williams, *Lincoln Finds a General,* 4:75–79.

15. Grant to William S. Rosecrans, October 3, 1862, *PUSG,* 6:107.

16. Cozzens, *The Darkest Days of the War,* chapters 13–25; Grant to Halleck, October 5, 1862, *PUSG,* 6:118.

17. Halleck to Grant, October 8, 1862, *PUSG*, 6:130; Grant to Rosecrans, October 7, 1862, ibid., 6:131; Rosecrans to Grant, October 7, 9, 1862, ibid., 6:132, 142.

18. George G. Pride to Rawlins, October 16, 1862, ibid., 6:122; Lincoln to Grant, October 8, 1862, *CWAL*, 5:453; Grant to Mary Grant, October 16, 1862, *PUSG*, 6:155; Rosecrans to Grant, October 21, 1862, ibid., 6:164; *PMJDG*, 104.

19. Mortimer D. Leggett to Rawlins, October 19, 1862, *PUSG*, 6:166–67; William M. Lamers, *The Edge of Glory: A Biography of General William S. Rosecrans* (New York: Harcourt, Brace & World, 1961), 120–21, 172–73.

20. Grant to Rosecrans, October 23, 1862, *PUSG*, 6:182; Department of the Tennessee, General Orders No. 1, October 25, 1862, ibid., 6:186–87; Grant to Edward O. C. Ord, October 24, 1862, ibid., 6:184.

21. Grant to Julia Grant, September 15, 1862, ibid., 6:50; Grant to Jesse Grant, September 17, 1862, ibid., 6:61–62.

22. *PMJDG*, 105; Grant to Jesse Grant, November 23, 1862, *PUSG*, 6:344–45.

23. General Orders No. 1, Department of the Tennessee, October 25, 1862, *PUSG*, 6:186–87; Grant to Halleck, October 26, 1862, ibid., 6:199–201.

24. Grant to Halleck, November 2, 4, 1862, ibid., 6:243, 256.

25. Grant to Sherman, November 6, 1862, ibid., 6:262–63; Grant to Brig. Gen. Charles S. Hamilton, November 9, 1862, ibid., 6:285–86; Grant to Halleck, November 10, 1862, ibid., 6:288; Grant to Washburne, November 7, 1862, ibid., 6:273–74.

26. McClernand to Washburne, July 9, 1862, ibid., 5:331; Halleck to McClernand, August 20, 1862, ibid.; Grant to McClernand, August 25, 1862, ibid., 5:330.

27. Howard Beale, ed., *The Diary of Gideon Welles* (New York: W. W. Norton, 1960), 1:157 (October 1, 1862), 167 (October 10, 1862); David Donald, ed., *Inside Lincoln's Cabinet: The Civil War Diaries of Salmon P. Chase* (New York: Longmans, 1954), 161 (September 27, 1862); Catton, *Grant Moves South*, 325–27.

28. On the McClure account, see Brooks D. Simpson, "Alexander McClure on Lincoln and Grant: A Questionable Account," *Lincoln Herald* 95 (Fall 1993): 83–86; on the reports of drinking, see *PUSG*, 6:87–88. It is virtually impossible to determine whether Grant was drunk in St. Louis, although the person who observed that the general was "tight as a brick" was his friend Henry T. Blow, and Grant was accompanied by aide Clark B. Lagow, who was no stranger to the bottle — Rawlins believed that he was a bad influence on Grant.

29. Halleck to Grant, November 11, 1862, *PUSG*, 6:288; Grant to Sherman, November 10, 1862, ibid., 6:290–92; Halleck to Grant, November 15, 1862, ibid., 6:305.

30. Grant to Sherman, November 14, 1862, ibid., 6:310–12.

31. Porter described this encounter in his journal (Porter Papers, LC), 424–30, which in turn formed the basis of his *Incidents and Anecdotes of the Civil War* (New York: D. Appleton, 1885), 125–26 (he misdated it as happening in early December); Grant to Porter, November 22, 1862, *PUSG*, 6:340. Joseph Glatthaar, *Partners in Command: The Relationship between Leaders in the Civil War* (New York: The Free Press, 1994), chapter 6, offers an overview of the Grant-Porter relationship.

32. Grant to Sherman, November 14, 1862, *PUSG*, 6: 310–12; Grant to McPherson, November 21, 1862, ibid., 6:338.

33. Grant to Jesse Grant, November 23, 1862, ibid., 6:344–45.

34. Grant to Brig. Gen. Thomas A. Davies, October 30, 1862 (two letters), ibid., 6:225–26; General Orders No. 4, Department of the Tennessee, November 3, 1862, ibid., 6:252–53.

35. Special Field Orders No. 1, Department of the Tennessee, November 7, 1862, ibid., 6:266–67; Grant to Halleck, December 14, 1862, ibid., 7:29–30.

36. Simpson, *Let Us Have Peace*, 32–33.

37. Grant to Halleck, November 15, 1862, *PUSG*, 6:315; see ibid., 6:317.

38. Simpson, *Let Us Have Peace*, 31–32.

39. Grant to DuBois, December 9, 1862, *PUSG*, 7:8 and 9n; Grant to Mary Grant, December 15, 1862, ibid., 7:43–44; General Orders No. 11, Department of the Tennessee, December 17, 1862, ibid., 7:50.

40. Grant to Mary Grant, December 15, 1862, ibid., 7:43; Grant to Christopher P. Wolcott, December 17, 1862, ibid., 7:56–57.

41. See the discussion and documents in ibid., 7:53–56; *PMJDG*, 107. Frederick D. Grant later explained his father's decision to omit discussion of this incident in his *Memoirs* as due to the general's unwillingness to revisit his mistake: see Isaac Markens, "Lincoln and the Jews," *Publications of the American Jewish Historical Society* 17 (1909): 122. Thanks to Leah Berkowitz for bringing this to my attention.

42. Grant to Halleck, November 24, 1862, *PUSG*, 6:345–46; Halleck to Grant, November 23, 25, 1862, ibid., 6:346.

43. Grant to Mary Grant, December 15, 1862, ibid., 7:43–44.

44. Grant to Halleck, December 2, 3, and 5, 1862, ibid., 6:368, 371–72, 390; Grant to Sherman, December 2, 1862, ibid., 6:369; Grant to Halleck, December 8, 1862, ibid., 6:403; Grant to Sherman, December 8, 1862 (two letters), ibid., 6:404, 406–7.

45. See Glatthaar, *Partners in Command*, 166–68, for the origins of the Sherman-Porter relationship.

46. Grant to Halleck, December 14, 1862, *PUSG*, 7:28–32.

47. Halleck to Grant, December 9, 1862, ibid., 6:402; Grant to Halleck, December 9, 1862, ibid., 7:6; Grant to McClernand, December 18, 1862, ibid., 7:61–62.

48. Grant to James B. McPherson, December 18, 19, 1862, ibid., 7:63–64, 68–69; Grant to McClernand, December 28, 1862, ibid., 7:135–36.

49. Grant to McPherson, December 20, 1862, ibid., 7:79; *PMJDG*, 107.

50. Grant to Quinby, December 24, 1862, *PUSG*, 7:102; Grant to Hurlbut, December 25, 1862, ibid., 7:108; Grant to McClernand, December 25, 1862, ibid., 7:108–9; Grant to McPherson, December 31, 1862, ibid., 7:148; Grant to Hamilton, January 1, 1863, ibid, 7:156; Grant to Halleck, January 4, 9, 1863, ibid., 7:171, 204.

51. Grant to McClernand, January 10, 11, 1863, ibid., 7:207, 210–11; Grant to Halleck, January 11, 1863, and Halleck to Grant, January 12, 1863, ibid., 7:209–10; Rawlins to McClernand, January 12, 1863 (not sent), ibid., 7:210.

52. McClernand to Grant, January 11, 1863, ibid., 7:217; Grant to Halleck, January 13, 1863, ibid., 7:217; Grant to McClernand, January 13, 1863, ibid., 7:218–19; McClernand to Grant, January 16, 1863, ibid., 7:219; McClernand to Lincoln, January 16, 1863, Robert T. Lincoln Papers, LC.

53. Grant to McPherson, January 13, 1863, *PUSG*, 7:220; Grant to Halleck, January 14, 1863, ibid., 7:223; Grant to Silas Hudson, January 14, 1863, ibid., 7:224–25; Grant to Halleck, January 20, 1863, ibid., 7:233–34. James H. Wilson, *Under the Old Flag* (New York: D. Appleton, 1912), 1:148–49, offers background on a proposal to consolidate commands in the West.

54. J. Russell Jones to Washburne, January 17, 1863, Washburne Papers, LC; Grant to Julia Grant, January 28, 1863, *PUSG*, 7:253; Cadwallader C. Washburn to Washburne, January 28, 1863, Washburne Papers, LC.

10. Struggle and Scrutiny

1. Grant to Julia Grant, April 3, 1863, *PUSG*, 8:9; Grant to Porter, April 2, 1863, ibid., 8:3–4; Grant to Halleck, April 2, 1863, ibid., 8:5. Chester G. Hearn, *Admiral David Dixon Porter* (Annapolis: Naval Institute Press, 1996), offers useful information on naval activities along the Mississippi.

2. Grant to Porter, April 2, 1863; *PUSG*, 8:4; Grant to Halleck, April 2, 1863, ibid., 8:5; Grant to Julia Grant, April 3, 1863, ibid., 8:9.

3. J. Russell Jones to Elihu B. Washburne, January 28, 1863, Washburne Papers, LC; Sylvanus Cadwallader, *Three Years with Grant* (Lincoln: University of Nebraska Press, 1996 [1955]), 49–50; Grant to Julia Grant, January 28, 1863, *PUSG*, 7:253; Grant to Halleck, January 29, 31, 1863, ibid., 7:253–54; Grant to Hillyer, February 5, 1863, Hillyer Papers, University of Virginia.

4. McClernand to Grant, January 30, 1863, *PUSG*, 7:266–67.

5. Department of the Tennessee, General Orders No. 13, January 30, 1863, ibid., 7:265; McClernand to Grant, January 30, February 1, 1863, ibid., 8:265, 267; Grant to McClernand, January 31, 1863, ibid., 8:264; Grant to Col. John C. Kelton, February 1, 1863, ibid., 7:274; Kenneth P. Williams, *Lincoln Finds a General* (New York: Macmillan, 1949–59), 4:306–8.

6. Lincoln to McClernand, January 22, 1863, *CWAL*, 6:70; Wilson to Badeau, March 9, 1867, Wilson Papers, LC.

7. Grant to Julia Grant, January 31, 1863, *PUSG*, 7:270.

8. Grant to Kelton, February 4, 1863, ibid., 7:281.

9. Grant to William S. Hillyer, February 27, 1863, ibid., 7:368; Grant to Porter, January 30, 1863, ibid., 7:257; Grant to Kelton, February 4, 1863, ibid., 7:281.

10. Grant to McClernand, February 18, 1863, ibid., 7:340; Williams, *Lincoln Finds a General*, 4:318; Joseph Medill to Elihu B. Washburne, February 19, 1863, *PUSG*, 7:317–18.

11. Grant to Julia Grant, February 14, 1863, *PUSG*, 7:325; Grant to Stephen A. Hurlbut, February 13, 1863, ibid., 7:316; Shelby Foote, *The Civil War: A Narrative* (New York: Random House, 1958–74), 2:191.

12. Grant to Col. Robert C. Wood, March 6, 1863, *PUSG*, 7:391–92; Grant to Julia Grant, February 15, 1863, ibid., 7:331; Grant to Halleck, February 18, 1863, ibid., 7:339; Grant to William A. Hammond, March 12, 1863, ibid., 7:413–14; Williams, *Lincoln Finds a General*, 4:331; Olmsted to John Olmsted, April 1, 1863, Jane Turner Censer, ed., *The Papers of Frederick Law Olmsted, Volume IV: Defending the Union* (Baltimore: The Johns Hopkins University Press, 1986), 572.

13. Grant to James B. McPherson, February 5, 1863, *PUSG*, 7:285; Grant to Brig. Gen. John McArthur, February 8, 1863, ibid; John A. Rawlins to Capt. Asher R. Eddy, February 2, 1863, ibid., 7:319; Grant to Hillyer, February 27, 1863, ibid., 7:368; Grant to Salmon P. Chase, February 23, 1863, ibid., 7:352–53; Grant to Julia Grant, March 6, 1863, ibid., 7:396–97; Grant to Julia Grant, February 11, 1863, ibid., 7:311; Jesse Grant to Washburne, February 13, 1863, Lloyd Lewis–Bruce Catton Research Notes, USGA.

14. Albert D. Richardson, *Personal History of Ulysses S. Grant* (Hartford, Conn.: American Publishing, 1868), 295; Mary R. Livermore, *My Story of the War* (New York: Arno, 1972 [1889]), 316.

15. Lincoln to McClernand, January 22, 1863, *CWAL*, 6:70–71.

16. Porter Journal, 1:558–59, David D. Porter Papers, LC; Kountz to McClernand, February 25, 1863, McClernand Papers, ISHL; McClernand to Lincoln, March 15, 1863, and note by Kountz, *PUSG*, 7:275; the Rawlins-McClernand exchange is ibid.

17. Charles S. Hamilton to James R. Doolittle, February 11, 1863, *PUSG*, 7:308. In contrast, the previous fall Hamilton had declared: "Grant is the best man this war has produced yet, and he is the best abused man. He is cool & brave, is honest, and will do his duty, though daily slandered." Hamilton to "Dear sir," November 10, 1862, Lewis-Catton Research Notes, USGA.

18. On Halstead, see Donald W. Curl, *Murat Halstead and the* Cincinnati Commercial (Boca Raton: University Presses of Florida, 1980), 26–28; on Sherman and the *Herald* reporter, Thomas W. Knox, see John F. Marszalek, *Sherman's Other War: The General and the Civil War Press* (Memphis: Memphis State University Press, 1981), chapter 5; on McCullagh, see Cadwallader, *Three Years*, 113–15.

19. Catton, *Grant Moves South*, 395; Halstead to Chase, April 1, 1863, John Niven et

al., eds., *The Salmon P. Chase Papers* (Frederick, Md.: University Press of America, 1987 [microfilm]).

20. Chase to Lincoln, April 4 and 21, 1863, Niven, *Chase Papers;* O. W. Nixon to Chase, April 14, 1863, ibid.; Charles P. McIlvaine to Chase, April 21, 1863, ibid.; W. Rives to McClernand, April 13, 1863, McClernand Papers, ISHL.

21. Cadwallader C. Washburn to Elihu B. Washburne, April 11, 1863, Washburne Papers, LC; Livermore, *My Story of the War,* 309–11; Olmsted, "The Genesis of a Rumor," *The Nation,* April 23, 1868, 329–30. The evidence of an actual incident involving Grant is thin, but one letter alludes to a possible lapse from sobriety prior to the running of the batteries on April 16: see Edward D. Kittoe to James H. Wilson, July 15, 1885, Wilson Papers, LC.

22. Washburn to Washburne, March 16, 24, and 28, 1863, Washburne Papers, LC; Washburne to Chase, April 4, 1863, Niven, *Chase Papers;* Chase to Washburne, April 13, 1863, Washburne Papers, LC.

23. A. Schwartz to McClernand, April 4, 1863, McClernand Papers, ISHL; Lincoln to John A. Dix, January 29, 1863, *CWAL,* 6:83; Lincoln to "Whom it may concern," February 11, 1863, ibid., 6:100; draft order, February 17, 1863, ibid. Originally Lincoln had struggled to find a way to return Butler to New Orleans without offending Nathaniel Banks, who even at this early date was contemplating operations into Texas. See Lincoln to Banks, [January 23?], 1863, and Lincoln to Stanton, January 23, 1863, ibid., 6:73–74, 76–77. Grant's statement about Lincoln's constant support is in *PMUSG,* 1:460.

24. Charles A. Dana, *Recollections of the Civil War* (New York: Collier Books, 1963 [1898]), 41–43; Grant to Halleck, February 18, 1863, *PUSG,* 7:339; Grant to Edwin D. Judd, February 19, 1863, ibid., 7:343–44.

25. Grant to Washburne, February 15, 16, 1863, *PUSG,* 7:332–33; Grant to Halleck, February 18, 1863, ibid., 7:338–39.

26. Lincoln to Johnson, March 26, 1863, *CWAL,* 6:149–50.

27. Lincoln to Hurlbut, March 20 [25], 1863, ibid., 6:142; William Butler to Lincoln, April 9, 1863, which called Grant "the right man in the wrong place," Robert Todd Lincoln Papers, LC.

28. Halleck to Rosecrans, March 1, 1863, *OR,* ser. 1, 23 (pt. 2), 95; Halleck to Grant, March 20, 1863, *PUSG,* 7:401; Williams, *Lincoln Finds a General,* 4:333.

29. Grant to Halleck, March 6, 1863, *PUSG,* 7:401; Grant to Washburne, March 10, 1863, ibid., 7:409–10; Grant to James B. McPherson, February 5, March 16, 22, 1863, ibid., 7:284, 422, 453; Grant to Sherman, March 16, 1863 (two letters), ibid., 7:423–25; Grant to Sherman, March 22, 1863, ibid., 7:455–56; Grant to Banks, March 23, 1863, ibid., 7:445–47; Grant to Farragut, March 23, 1863, ibid., 7:458–59; Grant to Porter, March 23, 1863, ibid., 7:459–61.

30. Grant to Julia Grant, March 27, 1863, ibid., 7:479–80; Halleck to Grant, March 20, 1863, ibid., 7:401; Gaillard Hunt, *Israel, Elihu, and Cadwallader Washburn: A Chapter in American Biography* (New York: Macmillan, 1925), 341.

31. James R. Arnold, *Grant Wins the War: Decision at Vicksburg* (New York: John Wiley & Sons, 1997), 68; Halleck to Grant, April 2, 1863, *PUSG,* 7:428–29.

32. Grant to Porter, March 29, 1863, *PUSG,* 7:486; Porter to Grant, March 29, 1863, ibid., 7:486–87.

33. Porter to Grant, February 12, 1863, ibid., 7:346.

34. Grant to Hurlbut, February 13, 1863, ibid., 7:317; Grant to Hurlbut, March 9, 1863, ibid., 7:406–7; Grant to Hurlbut, April 3, 1863, ibid., 8:6.

35. Porter Journal, 1:557, 561, Porter Papers, LC.

36. Sherman to Thomas Ewing, Sr., March 7, 1863, *SCW,* 415; Sherman to Grant, April 7, 1863, *PUSG,* 8:32; Grant to Abraham Lincoln, April 12, 1863, ibid., 8:33;

Sherman to Rawlins, April 8, 1863, *SCW,* 443–44; Wilson to Badeau, March 30, 1867, Wilson Papers, LC.

37. Grant to Julia Grant, April 6, 1863, *PUSG,* 8:29–30.

38. Cadwallader, *Three Years,* 60–61; Dana, *Recollections,* 47–49; Sherman to John Sherman, April 10, 1863, *SCW,* 449–51.

39. Dana, *Recollections,* 50–51; Wilson to Badeau, March 22, 1867, Wilson Papers, LC.

40. Grant to Thomas W. Knox, April 6, 1863, *PUSG,* 8:30–31; Sherman to Grant, April 7, 1863, ibid., 8:32; Grant to Lincoln, April 12, 1863, ibid., 8:33; Rawlins to Hurlbut, April 8, 1863, ibid., 8:39; Grant to Napoleon Buford, April 8, 1863, ibid., 8:37; Grant to Hurlbut, April 9, 1863, ibid., 8:38–39.

41. Grant to Washburne, March 10, 1863, ibid., 7:409–10; Porter Journal, 1:621, Porter Papers, LC; Washburne to Lincoln, April 30, 1863, Robert Todd Lincoln Papers, LC. Actually, Cadwallader Washburn favored the new plan: see W. H. Morgan to Washburne, April 29, 1863, Washburne Papers, LC.

42. Halleck to Grant, March 30, 1863, *PUSG,* 7:93–94.

43. Grant to Steele, April 11, 1863, ibid., 8:49; General Orders No. 25, Department of the Tennessee, April 22, 1863, ibid., 8:94 (on dismissals and resignations see ibid.); Grant to Halleck, April 19, 1863, ibid., 8:91–92.

44. Williams, *Lincoln Finds a General,* 4:341; Porter Journal, 1:615–20, Porter Papers, LC (according to Porter, Thomas confided that he was authorized to remove Grant); Wilson to Badeau, March 22, 1867, Wilson Papers, LC; Grant to Halleck, April 12, 1863, *PUSG,* 8:54.

45. Grant to McClernand, April 11, 1863, *PUSG,* 8:47.

46. Dana, *Recollections,* 54–55; Frederick Grant in the *National Tribune,* January 20, 1887; James H. Wilson, *Under the Old Flag* (New York: D. Appleton, 1912), 1:163–64.

47. Grant to Rawlins, April 17, 1863, *PUSG,* 8:87–88; *PMUSG,* 1:466.

48. Earl S. Miers, *The Web of Victory: Grant at Vicksburg* (Baton Rouge: Louisiana State University Press, 1955), 144; *PMUSG,* 1:466–68; William E. Strong, "The Campaign against Vicksburg," *Military Essays and Recollections: Military Order of the Loyal Legion of the United States, Illinois Commandery* (Chicago: McClure, 1894), 2:316.

49. Richardson, *Personal History,* 302; *PMUSG,* 1:473; Catton, *Grant Moves South,* 420; Hearn, *Porter,* 221; Grant to Jesse Grant, April 21, 1863, *PUSG,* 7:109–10.

50. Grant to Sherman, April 27, 1863, *PUSG,* 7:130; Sherman to Ellen Ewing Sherman, April 23, 29, 1863, *SCW,* 455–57, 464–66.

51. Miers, *The Web of Victory,* 147; Grant to McClernand, April 27, 1863, *PUSG,* 7:126–27.

52. Grant to Julia Grant, April 28, 1863, *PUSG,* 7:132; *PMUSG,* 1:476.

53. Edwin Cole Bearss, *The Vicksburg Campaign* (Dayton: Morningside House, 1985–86), 2:317; *PMUSG,* 1:478.

54. *PMUSG,* 1:480–81.

11. Triumph at Vicksburg

1. Bruce Catton, *Grant Moves South* (Boston: Little, Brown, 1960), 428; Grant to Porter, May 1, 1863, *PUSG,* 8:138.

2. Adam Badeau, *Military History of U. S. Grant* (New York: D. Appleton, 1881), 1:208–9; *Chicago Tribune,* March 20, 1886; Edwin Cole Bearss, *The Vicksburg Campaign* (Dayton: Morningside House, 1985–86), 2:385, 398–99; Grant to Porter, May 1, 1863, *PUSG,* 8:139; Grant to McClernand, May 1, 1863, ibid., 8:140.

3. Bearss, *Vicksburg,* 2:410; Grant to Porter, May 2, 1863, *PUSG,* 8:142.

4. Bearss, *Vicksburg,* 2:412–13, 416, 421–23; Grant to Bowen, May 2, 1863, *PUSG,*

8:140–41; Badeau, *Military History,* 1:214; Kenneth P. Williams, *Lincoln Finds a General* (New York: Macmillan, 1949–59), 4:386; *PMUSG,* 325; Samuel H. M. Byers, *With Fire and Sword* (New York: The Neale Publishing Company, 1911), 65–66.

5. *PMUSG,* 1:407–10; Bearss, *Vicksburg,* 2:432–35; Grant to Sherman, May 3, 1863, *PUSG,* 8:151–52.

6. John Russell Young, *Around the World with General Grant* (New York: American News, 1879), 2:62; Washburne to Lincoln, May 1, 1863, Robert Todd Lincoln Papers, LC.

7. Grant to Halleck, May 3, 1863, *PUSG,* 8:143, 145–48 (two messages); Grant to Brig. Gen. J. C. Sullivan, May 3, 1863, ibid., 8:153; Grant to Julia Grant, May 3, 1863, ibid., 8:155.

8. Catton, *Grant Moves South,* 429; Grant to Sherman, May 4, 1863, *PUSG,* 8:158–59; Grant to William S. Hillyer, May 5, 1863, ibid., 8:162.

9. Bearss, *Vicksburg,* 2: 436; Grant to Halleck, May 6, 1863, *PUSG,* 8:169; McClernand to Grant, May 7, 1863, ibid., 8:173.

10. Grant to Hurlbut, May 6, 1863, *PUSG,* 8:170; Grant to Hillyer, May 7, 1863, ibid., 8:175. Grant to Sherman, May 9, 1863, ibid., 8:183–84.

11. Grant to Julia Grant, May 9, 1863, ibid., 8:189; Grant to Banks, May 10, 1863, ibid., 8:190.

12. Grant to McClernand, May 11, 1863, ibid., 8:197; Grant to McPherson, May 11, 1863, ibid., 8:200.

13. Grant to McClernand, May 12, 1863, ibid., 8:204–5; Grant to McPherson, May 12, 1863, ibid., 8:206; Bearss, *Vicksburg,* 2:511–13.

14. Bearss, *Vicksburg,* 2:546.

15. Catton, *Grant Moves South,* 441–42.

16. Johnston to Pemberton, May 13, 1863, *PUSG,* 8:214; Grant to McClernand, May 14, 1863, ibid., 8:215; Grant to Maj. Gen. Francis P. Blair, May 14, 1863, ibid., 8:213–14; Grant to Sherman, May 14, 1863, ibid., 8:218; Catton, *Grant Moves South,* 441–42; Albert D. Richardson, *Personal History of Ulysses S. Grant* (Hartford, Conn.: American Publishing, 1868), 315; Sylvanus Cadwallader, *Three Years with Grant* (Lincoln: University of Nebraska Press, 1996 [1955]), 75.

17. Bearss, *Vicksburg,* 2:550–52; Richardson, *Personal History,* 315.

18. Grant to McClernand, May 16, 1863, *PUSG,* 8:224; Grant to McPherson, May 16, 1863, ibid., 8:226; Grant to Sherman, May 16, 1863, ibid., 8:227–28; Bearss, *Vicksburg,* 2:579.

19. Grant to McClernand, May 16, 1863, *PUSG,* 8:224; McPherson to Grant, May 16, 1863, ibid., 8:22; Badeau, *Military History,* 1:261.

20. Grant to McClernand, May 16, 1863, *PUSG,* 8:226; Bearss, *Vicksburg,* 2:593.

21. Bearss, *Vicksburg,* 2:605, 607; Williams, *Lincoln Finds a General,* 4:378; Badeau, *Military History,* 1:264–65.

22. Grant to Sherman, May 16, 1863, *PUSG,* 8:228–29; *PMUSG,* 1:519–20.

23. *PMUSG,* 1:520–21; Richardson, *Personal History,* 319; Cadwallader, *Three Years,* 82.

24. Halleck to Grant, May 11, 1863, and Halleck to Banks, May 11, 1863, *PUSG,* 8:221. Later Grant recalled that he received these messages the following day, during the battle of Big Black River; however, both Badeau and Richardson place their receipt the previous evening. See *PMUSG,* 1:524–26; Richardson, *Personal History,* 319–20; Badeau, *Military History,* 1:273.

25. Bearss, *Vicksburg,* 2:654, 677; Richardson, *Personal History,* 320–21; Catton, *Grant Moves South,* 446.

26. Williams, *Lincoln Finds a General,* 4:382–83; Catton, *Grant Moves South,* 533–34. The accounts of Richardson and Badeau, previously cited, say that Halleck's message to Grant reached the latter on the night of May 16; this modifies (but does not essentially contradict) the conclusions of Williams and Catton.

27. Richardson, *Personal History*, 321; Lloyd Lewis, *Sherman: Fighting Prophet* (Lincoln: University of Nebraska Press, 1993 [1932]), 277.

28. Bearss, *Vicksburg*, 3: 753–73; Grant to Commanding Officer, Confederate Forces, May 21, 1863, *PUSG*, 8:243–44.

29. General Field Orders, May 21, 1863, *PUSG*, 8:246; *PMUSG*, 1:443.

30. Bearss, *Vicksburg*, 3:835–36, 859. McClernand later tried to explain away what he had done, but the fact remains that he had misrepresented (intentionally or inadvertently) his progress to Grant.

31. Ibid., 3:836–37.

32. Ibid., 3:860.

33. Grant to Porter, May 23, 1863, *PUSG*, 8:257; Banks to Grant, May 29, 1863, ibid., 0.271; Halleck to Grant, June 2, 1863, ibid., 8:283–84; Grant to Banks, May 31, 1863, ibid., 8:294–95; Catton, *Grant Moves South*, 459.

34. Grant to Brig. Gen. Peter J. Osterhaus, May 26, 1863, *PUSG*, 8:278; Grant to Col. A. K. Johnson, May 26, 1863, ibid., 8:280; Grant to Osterhaus, May 29, 1863, ibid., 8:291; Walter Lord, ed., *The Fremantle Diary* (Boston: Little, Brown, 1954), 98.

35. Grant to Halleck, May 24, 1863, *PUSG*, 8:261; Dana to Stanton, May 24, 1863, ibid., 8:255.

36. Grant to Porter, June 2, 1863, ibid., 8:299; Grant to Mower, June 2, 1863, ibid., 8:301.

37. Sherman to Grant, June 2, 1863, ibid., 8:300; Grant to Brig. Gen. Nathan Kimball, June 4, 5, 1863, ibid., 8:315, 316; Grant to McClernand, June 6, 1863, ibid., 321; Rawlins to Grant, June 6, 1863, ibid., 8:322–33; additional sources in ibid., 8:323–25; Cadwallader, *Three Years*, 102–111; Dana, *Recollections*, 90–91; Wilson, draft of Rawlins biography, 118, Wilson Papers, LC. I have explored the Yazoo incident in more detail in my introduction to Cadwallader, *Three Years*. The ways in which historians have adapted the conflicting accounts to construct an account of the matter is itself worthy of study.

38. Grant to Lorenzo Thomas, June 16, 1863, *PUSG*, 8:328; Bearss, *Vicksburg*, 3:1179–83.

39. Grant to Julia Grant, June 9 and 15, 1863, *PUSG*, 8:332, 376–77; Grant to Jesse Grant, June 15, 1863, ibid., 8:375–76; Grant to George G. Pride, June 15, 1863, ibid., 8:379; Catton, *Grant Moves South*, 460; Terrence J. Winschel, *Triumph and Defeat: The Vicksburg Campaign* (Mason City, Iowa: Savas Publishing, 1999), 135.

40. Catton, *Grant Moves South*, 390–91.

41. Ibid., 456–57.

42. Sherman to Grant, June 17, 1863, and McPherson to Grant, June 18, 1863, *PUSG*, 8:429–31; Bearss, *Vicksburg*, 3:878–79.

43. Catton, *Grant Moves South*, 467; Bearss, *Vicksburg*, 3:879–80.

44. McClernand to Grant, June 18, 1863; Grant to Halleck, June 19, 1863; Dana to Stanton, June 19, 1863, all *PUSG*, 8:385–86; Special Orders No. 165, Department of the Tennessee, June 19, 1863, ibid., 8:394.

45. Bearss, *Vicksburg*, 3:924; Grant to Sherman, June 23, 1863, *PUSG*, 8:411; Grant to Julia Grant, June 29, 1863, ibid., 8:444–45.

46. Grant to Taylor, June 22, 1863, *PUSG*, 8:400–01. Taylor himself reported that his men had "unfortunately" captured fifty black soldiers and two white officers. Bearss, *Vicksburg*, 3:1183, 1196–97.

47. Pemberton to Grant, July 3, 1863, and Grant to Pemberton, July 3, 1863, *PUSG*, 8:455. Phillip Thomas Taylor, *The Forgotten "Stonewall of the West": Major-General John Stevens Bowen* (Macon, Ga.: Mercer University Press, 1997) is a detailed biography.

48. Bearss, *Vicksburg*, 3:1285–87.

49. Ibid., 3:1287–88; William E. Strong, "The Campaign against Vicksburg," *Military Essays and Recollections: Military Order of the Loyal Legion of the United States, Illinois Commandery* (Chicago: McClure, 1894), 2:345–46; Arnold, *Grant Wins the War*, 295.

50. Catton, *Grant Moves South,* 472–76; Bearss, *Vicksburg,* 3:1291.

51. Bearss, *Vicksburg,* 3:1293–96; Richardson, *Personal History,* 334; David D. Porter, *Incidents and Anecdotes of the Civil War* (New York: D. Appleton, 1885), 201.

52. James R. Rusling, *Men and Things I Saw in Civil War Days* (New York: Eaton and Mains, 1899), 16–17.

53. Lincoln to John A. Dix, May 11, 1863, *CWAL,* 6:210; Lincoln to Hurlbut, May 22, 1863, ibid., 6:226; Lincoln to Isaac N. Arnold, May 26, 1863, ibid., 6:230; Lincoln to Grant, July 13, 1863, ibid., 6:326.

12. The Heights of Chattanooga

1. Special Orders No. 180, Department of the Tennessee, July 4, 1863, *PUSG,* 8:464; Grant to McPherson, July 5, 1863, ibid., 8:483; Grant to McPherson, July 7, 1863 (two letters), ibid., 9:3, 4; Grant to McPherson, July 8, 1863, ibid., 9:5.

2. Grant to Sherman, July 4, 1863, *PUSG,* 8:479; Grant to Maj. Gen. Francis J. Herron, July 9, 1863, ibid., 9:9; Grant to Maj. Gen. John M. Schofield, July 15,1863, ibid., 9:54; Grant to Lincoln, July 22, 1863, ibid., 9:97–99. The day after the fall of Vicksburg Grant (through Dana) requested instructions on what to do next; Charles A. Dana, *Recollections of the Civil War* (New York: Collier Books, 1963 [1898]), 105.

3. Virginia Laas, ed., *Wartime Washington: The Civil War Letters of Elizabeth Blair Lee* (Urbana: University of Illinois Press, 1991), 299.

4. Grant to Lorenzo Thomas, July 11, 1863, *PUSG,* 9:23–25; Grant to Brig. Gen. Elias S. Dennis, July 11, 1863, ibid., 9:39; Grant to Halleck, July 24, 1863, ibid., 9:110.

5. *PMJDG,* 120–21; Grant to Banks, July 10, 1863, *PUSG,* 9:17–18; Grant to Halleck, July 11, 18, 1863, ibid., 9:28, 70; Schofield to Grant, July 8, 1863, ibid., 9:56; Halleck to Grant, July 11, 22, 1863, ibid., 9:111–12, 71; Grant to Halleck, July 24, 1863, ibid., 9:108–11.

6. Grant to L. Thomas, July 19, 1863, *PUSG,* 9:78–79. For evidence of McClernand's public relations offensive with Washington authorities in the aftermath of his removal, see McClernand to Stanton, June 27, 1863; McClernand to Halleck, June 27, 1863; W. Rives to McClernand, June 28, 1863, all in McClernand Papers, ISHL.

7. Henry Wilson to Washburne, July 25, 1863, *PUSG,* 9:219; Dana to Washburne, August 29, 1863, ibid., 9:219; Grant to Lincoln, July 20, 1863, ibid., 9:80–81.

8. Lincoln to McClernand, August 12, 1863, *CWAL,* 6:383.

9. Chase to Grant, July 4, 1863, *PUSG,* 9:95–96; Grant to Dana, August 5, 1864, ibid., 9:145–47.

10. Lincoln to Grant, August 9, 1863, and Grant to Lincoln, August 23, 1863, *PUSG,* 9:195–97; Lincoln to Ambrose Burnside, July 27, 1863, *CWAL,* 6:350; Brooks D. Simpson, *Let Us Have Peace: Ulysses S. Grant and the Politics of War and Reconstruction, 1861–1868* (Chapel Hill: University of North Carolina Press, 1991), 45–46.

11. Grant to Frederick T. Dent, August 23, 1863, *PUSG,* 9:200–1; Grant to Ruel Hough et al., August 26, 1863, ibid., 9:202–3; Albert D. Richardson, *Personal History of Ulysses S. Grant* (Hartford, Conn.: American Publishing, 1868), 346–47; John Eaton, *Grant, Lincoln, and the Freedmen* (New York: Longmans, Green, 1907), 100.

12. Grant to Washburne, August 30, 1863, *PUSG,* 9:217–18.

13. Halleck to Grant, July 30, August 6, 1864, *PUSG,* 9:159; Bruce Catton, *Grant Takes Command* (Boston: Little, Brown, 1969), 13–14, 21–22; Banks to Grant, August 10, 1863, *PUSG,* 9:158–59. The account Grant gives of his interaction with Halleck over the virtues of a campaign against Mobile in *PMUSG,* 1:578–81, is misleading and shaped in large part by his later dismissiveness toward Halleck.

14. Catton, *Grant Takes Command,* 24–25; *PMUSG,* 1:581–82; Cadwallader C.

Washburn to Elihu B. Washburne, September 5, 1863, Washburne Papers, LC; Frank Parker, transcript of interview, Hamlin Garland Papers, University of Southern California.

15. Gaillard Hunt, *Israel, Elihu, and Cadwallader Washburn: A Chapter in American Biography* (New York: Macmillan, 1925), 342; William S. McFeely, *Grant: A Biography* (New York; W. W. Norton, 1981), 140–41; Catton, *Grant Takes Command*, 26–27, reviews most of the evidence in the matter; see also *PUSG*, 9:222–23.

16. Grant to Brig. Gen. Charles P. Stone, July 21, 1863, *PUSG*, 9:92; Grant to Charles W. Ford, July 28, 1863, ibid., 9:130–31; General Orders No. 50, Department of the Tennessee, [August 1, 1863], ibid., 9:133–34; Grant to Stephen A. Hurlbut, August 4, 1863, ibid., 9:139–40; Grant to Sherman, August 6, 1863, ibid., 9:155; Grant to Halleck, August 11, 1863, ibid., 9:173–74.

17. Grant to Brig. Gen. Marcellus M. Crocker, August 28, 1863, Ibid., 9:207–8, Grant to Halleck, August 31, 1863, ibid., 9:219–20.

18. Grant to Sherman, July 21, 1863, ibid., 9:89; Grant to Chase, July 21, 1863, ibid., 9:94–95; Grant to William P. Mellen, August 13, 1863, ibid., 9:177; Grant to Stanton, August 26, 1863, ibid., 9:201–2. Eventually Grant worked out a compromise with Mellen that restricted trade somewhat, although he continued to favor closing down the cotton trade. Grant to Chase, September 26, 1863, ibid., 9:241–42. For Grant's brother-in-law James Casey and Casey's brother Samuel, see *PUSG*, 9:245–46.

19. Grant to Halleck, September 19, 1863, ibid., 9:221–22.

20. Grant to Halleck, September 22, 25, 28, and 30, 1863, ibid., 9:229, 233, 238, 251–53; Grant to Col. John C. Kelton, September 25, 1863, ibid., 9:237–38; Grant to Sherman, September 30 and October 8, 1863, ibid., 9:255–56, 273.

21. Halleck to Lieut. Col. James H. Wilson, October 3, 1863, ibid., 9:276 and 277n; Grant to McPherson, October 10, 1863, ibid., 9:277–78; *PMJDG*, 123.

22. Rawlins to Mary Hurlbut, October 12, 14, 1863, *PUSG*, 9:281; Sherman to Grant, October 10, 15, 1863, ibid., 9:275, 282; Halleck to Grant, October 11, 1863, ibid., 9:253.

23. Halleck to Grant, October 16, 1863, ibid., 9:296

24. Wiley Sword, *Mountains Touched with Fire: Chattanooga Besieged, 1863* (New York: St. Martin's Press, 1995), 53.

25. Ibid., 53–54.

26. Stanton to Halleck, October 19, 1863, *PUSG*, 9:298; Grant to Thomas, October 19, 1863, ibid., 9:302; Sword, *Mountains Touched with Fire*, 53–54. Peter Cozzens, *The Shipwreck of Their Hopes: The Battles for Chattanooga* (Urbana: University of Illinois Press, 1994), 4–6, mistakenly places Grant and Stanton at Louisville on October 17.

27. Stanton to Halleck, October 19, 1863, *PUSG*, 9:298; Thomas to Grant, October 19, 1863, ibid., 9:302; ibid., 9:304; Andrew Johnson, "Remarks at Nashville," LeRoy P. Graf et al., eds., *The Papers of Andrew Johnson* (Knoxville: University of Tennessee Press, 1967–), 6:427–28; Sword, *Mountains Touched with Fire*, 56–57. Another observer noted that "Gen'l Grant is looking well but walks with a crutch and cane." Cyrus Dickey to Ann Wallace, October 17, 1863, Wallace-Dickey Papers, ISHL.

28. Catton, *Grant Takes Command*, 35–37; McFeely, *Grant*, 143.

29. Ibid., 37; John A. Carpenter, *Sword and Olive Branch: Oliver Otis Howard* (Pittsburgh: University of Pittsburgh Press, 1964), 59.

30. Catton, *Grant Takes Command*, 37–38.

31. Sword, *Mountains Touched with Fire*, 56.

32. Catton, *Grant Takes Command*, 40–41; Horace Porter, *Campaigning with Grant* (New York: Century Co., 1897), 1–8.

33. Edward D. Kittoe to Julia Grant, October 24, 1863, Grant Papers, LC.

34. Catton, *Grant Takes Command*, 44–46.

35. William F. Smith, *Autobiography of Major General William F. Smith*, ed. Herbert M.

Schiller (Dayton: Morningside House, 1990), 78; Sword, *Mountains Touched with Fire,* 60; Grant to Halleck, October 24, 1863, *PUSG,* 9:310–11; Grant to Sherman, October 24, 1863, ibid., 9:311–12.

36. Grant to Halleck, October 26, 1863, *PUSG,* 9:322; Dana to Stanton, October 29, 1863, ibid., 9:323.

37. Catton, *Grant Takes Command,* 56; Grant to Julia Grant, October 27, 1863, *PUSG,* 9:334; *PMUSG,* 421.

38. Grant to Halleck, October 28, 1863, *PUSG,* 9:335; Ephraim A. Wilson, *Memoirs (Memories) of the War* (Cleveland, 1893), 239, quoted in Lewis-Catton Notes, USGA.

39. Rawlins to Mary Hurlbut, October 27, 1863, Rawlins Papers, ISHL.

40. Grant to Burnside, October 20, November 3, 1863, *PUSG,* 9:305, 353.

41. Grant to Burnside, October 31, November 5, 1863, ibid., 9:343, 359; Smith, *Autobiography,* 78, 81–82.

42. Sword, *Mountains Touched with Fire,* 148–49; Grant to Burnside, November 7, 1863, *PUSG,* 9:368–69; Grant to Sherman, November 7, 1863, ibid., 9: 370; Grant to Thomas, November 7, 1863, ibid., 9:370–71.

43. William F. Smith, "Comments on General Grant's 'Chattanooga,'" Robert U. Johnson and Clarence C. Buel, eds., *Battles and Leaders of the Civil War* (New York: Century, 1887), 3:714–16; Smith, *Autobiography,* 78; Sword, *Mountains Touched with Fire,* 149–50; Grant to Burnside, November 8, 1863, *PUSG,* 9:374; Grant to Halleck, November 9, 1863, ibid., 9:377. In light of Smith's later efforts to shed responsibility for Grant's contemplated attack, it is interesting to note his admission that Grant's orders came "at my instigation."

44. Wilson to Adam Badeau, November 5–6, 1863, *PUSG,* 9:353; Grant to Sherman, November 11, 1863, *PUSG,* 9:380; Smith, *Autobiography,* 79; Cozzens, *The Shipwreck of Their Hopes,* 111; Sword, *Mountains Touched with Fire,* 151. When Wilson wrote of these gatherings later, he included Thomas as one of the guests, even though the context of his letter to Badeau makes it clear that Thomas was not at the gathering he described.

45. Grant to Julia Grant, November 2, 14, 1863, *PUSG,* 9:352, 395–97; Grant to Burnside, November 14, 1863, ibid., 9:391–92; William W. Smith Diary, November 13, 1863, ibid., 9:397–98; Rawlins to Washburne, November 14, 1863, Washburne Papers, LC.

46. Entry, November 14, 1863, William W. Smith Diary, LC.

47. Smith, *Autobiography,* 79; Grant to Halleck, November 15, 1863, *PUSG,* 9:399–400; Grant to Burnside, November 15, 1863, ibid., 9:401.

48. Catton, *Grant Takes Command,* 63–64; Cozzens, *The Shipwreck of Their Hopes,* 113.

49. Smith, *Autobiography,* 78–79; Grant to Halleck, November 16, 1863, *PUSG,* 9:404.

50. Rawlins to Mary Hurlbut, November 17, 1863, *PUSG,* 9:475; Rawlins to Grant, November 17, 1863, ibid., 9:475–76.

51. Ibid.; Entries, November 15, 16, 1863, William W. Smith Diary, LC; Catton, *Grant Takes Command,* 65–67. A comparison of several accounts of Chattanooga reveals confusion about dates — with interesting consequences. For example, James McDonough, who mischievously remarks, "It is impossible to know how frequently the Union commander was drinking at Chattanooga," attributes this episode to Grant's depression while waiting for Sherman to arrive — although Rawlins's letter clearly places the incident *after* Sherman returned to his command. McDonough, *Chattanooga,* 104. Among Grant's defenders, Bruce Catton misdates Rawlins's letters. The historians are not the only ones at fault. In his *Memoirs* Sherman says that he arrived at Chattanooga on November 14, then prints his report of the battle in which he states he arrived on November 15. Establishing what happened between November 14 and 17 also casts doubt on William F. Smith's insistence that Sherman and Grant shared a bottle on the evening of Sherman's arrival, resulting in Grant becoming intoxicated. Rawlins's letter refers to an incident on the night of November 16 (after Sherman had left and Hunter had arrived); Grant and Sherman (along with Howard and Thomas) talked long into the

night on November 15, the date of Sherman's arrival. The editor of Smith's *Autobiography,* much like Sherman, offers two dates for Sherman's arrival. It would have been hard to conceal Grant's condition from Hunter had he been as intoxicated as Smith suggests. See Smith, *Autobiography,* 79, 109.

52. Grant to J. Russell Jones, November 17, 1863, *PUSG,* 9:406; Grant to Thomas, November 18, 1863, ibid., 9:411–12; Grant to Col. John Riggin, [November 18, 1863], ibid., 9:413.

53. Cozzens, *Shipwreck of Their Hopes,* 122.

54. Grant to Burnside, November 15, 1863, *PUSG,* 9:405; Grant to Sherman, November 20, 1863, ibid., 9:421; Grant to Thomas, November 20, 1863, ibid., 9:423; Grant to Halleck, November 21, 1863, ibid., 9:425–26; Entry, November 18, 1863, William W. Smith Diary, LC; Catton, *Grant Takes Command,* 68, 70.

55. Grant to Halleck, November 21, 1863, *PUSG* 9:428, Grant to Sherman, November 22, 1863, ibid., 9:430–31.

56. Orlando B. Willcox to Halleck, November 22, 1863, and Grant to Halleck, November 23, 1863, ibid., 9:433–34; Sword, *Mountains Touched with Fire,* 163, 175–76. Grant's reply to Willcox contains a rare display of temper: "If you had shown half the willingness to sacrifice yourself and command at the start, you do in your dispatch, you might have rendered Burnside material aid. Now I judge you have got so far to the rear, you can do nothing for him." Grant to Willcox, November 23, 1863, ibid., 9:436–37.

57. Cozzens, *Shipwreck of Their Hopes,* 127–33; Montgomery Meigs, "Journal of the Battle of Chattanooga," November 23, 1863, Meigs Papers, LC; Meigs to Stanton, November 26, 1863, ibid.

58. Sword, *Mountains Touched with Fire,* 184.

59. Ibid., 195–98, 205–12.

60. Entry, November 24, 1864, William W. Smith Diary, LC; Sword, *Mountains Touched with Fire,* 224, 231; Cozzens, *Shipwreck of Their Hopes,* 200; Grant to Halleck, November 24, 1863, *PUSG,* 9:439–40; Grant to Thomas, November 24, 1863, ibid., 9:443.

61. Sherman to Grant, November 25, 1863, *PUSG,* 9:446; Cozzens, *Shipwreck of Their Hopes,* 200–10.

62. Sword, *Mountains Touched with Fire,* 259; Meigs, "Journal of the Battle of Chattanooga," November 25, 1863, Meigs Papers, LC; Hamlin Garland, *Ulysses S. Grant: His Life and Character* (New York: Macmillan, 1920), 249.

63. Contemporaries and historians have long debated Grant's intentions in ordering the assault on Missionary Ridge. Wiley Sword, James McDonough, and Peter Cozzens insist that all Grant had in mind was a demonstration designed to draw forces away from the Confederate right opposite Sherman; the assault force would stop after taking the rifle pits at the base of the ridge. Sword, *Mountains Touched with Fire,* 264–65; McDonough, *Chattanooga,* 163–64; Cozzens, *Shipwreck of Their Hopes,* 246–48, 259–60. These historians are doubtless correct in claiming that the only orders Grant issued to Thomas's commanders involved the rifle pits at the base of the ridge. However, other evidence contradicts the claim that Grant's *intentions* were limited to that goal. Grant's *Memoirs* offer a self-serving version of events; more telling is the account of Montgomery Meigs, who was present on Orchard Knob that afternoon, and who reported a conversation with Grant in which the general explained "it was contrary to orders, it was not his plan — he meant to form the lines and then prepare and launch columns of assault, but, as the men, carried away by their enthusiasm had gone so far, he would not order them back." Montgomery Meigs, "Journal of the Battle of Chattanooga," Meigs Papers, LC. One of the sources often used in support of the "unordered charge" thesis actually supports this interpretation, for when Absalom Baird asked James H. Wilson to clarify Grant's order, Wilson replied that it was "preparatory to a general assault"; see Cozzens, *Shipwreck of Their Hopes,* 260. Twenty-three years later, Wilson argued that

Grant's orders contemplated nothing more than carrying the rifle pits at the base of the ridge, although by then he was determined to denigrate Grant's accomplishments: Wilson to William F. Smith, September 20, 1886, Wilson Papers, LC. See also Sylvanus Cadwallader, *Three Years with Grant* (Lincoln: University of Nebraska Press, 1996 [1955]), 150–51; William A. Morgan, "Hazen's Brigade at Missionary Ridge," *War Talks in Kansas* (Kansas City, Mo.: Franklin Hudson, 1906), 273. Grant's concern was that the advance up the slope was impromptu and unorganized; just as he once thought that the ridge would be rendered vulnerable by Sherman's success, later he believed that Bragg's actions had made an attack feasible.

64. There are numerous accounts of what happened on Orchard Knob on the afternoon of November 25. Some featured Rawlins's outburst to underline how important he was to Grant; others asserted that Grant did not intend the assault column to take the crest of Missionary Ridge to strengthen the claim that the soldiers of the Army of the Cumberland took the initiative. These accounts assume that Grant's initial directives, issued to get things moving, constituted his entire plan. Overlooked is the degree to which these accounts reflect poorly on the performance of George H. Thomas and Gordon Granger. See Cozzens, *Shipwreck of Their Hopes*, 245–48, 282–83; Sword, *Mountains Touched with Fire*, 260–65, 280–81; Cadwallader, *Three Years*, 152–54; Steven E. Woodworth, *Six Armies in Tennessee: The Chickamauga and Chattanooga Campaigns* (Lincoln: University of Nebraska Press, 1998), 194–96.

65. McDonough, *Chattanooga*, 162; Garland, *Grant*, 249.

66. McDonough, *Chattanooga*, 179. In years to come veterans of the Army of the Cumberland would claim that they took matters into their own hands. The truth is more difficult to pin down, due to conflicting recollections about the exact wording of Grant's orders as relayed by staff officers and field commanders. Whatever the directive issued by Grant, several division and brigade commanders thought that the crest of the ridge was the ultimate target of the advance, and it was on their orders that the men ascended the ridge. See ibid., 178–80; Sword, *Mountains Touched with Fire*, 266–69, 277–80; Cozzens, *Shipwreck of Their Hopes*, 257–62; Catton, *Grant Takes Command*, 81–83.

67. Shelby Foote, *The Civil War: A Narrative* (New York: Random House, 1958–74), 2:854–55; Richardson, *Personal History*, 367; *National Tribune*, May 26, 1892; William F. G. Shanks, *Personal Recollections of Distinguished Generals* (New York: Harper and Brothers, 1866), 118; Meigs to Stanton, November 25, 1863, Meigs Papers, LC; Grant to Sherman, November 25, 1863, *PUSG*, 9:447.

68. Meigs to Stanton, November 25, 1863, Meigs Papers, LC; Garland, *Grant*, 251.

69. Grant to Halleck, November 25, 1863, *PUSG*, 9:449; Grant to Sherman, November 25, 1863, ibid., 9:451–52; Rawlins to Thomas, November 25, 1863, ibid., 9:448; Grant to Sherman, November 27, 1863, ibid., 9:456; Grant to Thomas, November 27, 1863, ibid., 9:457–58; Rawlins to Robert Byrd, November 29, 1863, ibid., 9:466; Entry, November 28, 1863, William W. Smith Diary, LC; Edward D. Kittoe to Washburne, December 9, 1863, Washburne Papers, LC; Lincoln to Grant, November 25, 1863, *CWAL*, 7:30. Cozzens, *The Shipwreck of Their Hopes*, 352–53, misconstrues Grant's reasoning concerning a pursuit by offering an incomplete version of his orders to Sherman.

70. Cozzens, *The Shipwreck of Their Hopes*, 386–88.

71. Lincoln to Grant, December 8, 1863, *CWAL*, 7:53.

72. Grant to John J. Speed, November 30, 1863, *PUSG*, 9:479–80; Grant to Washburne, December 2, 1863, ibid., 9:490–91; Grant to James B. McPherson, December 1, 1863, ibid., 9:480–81; Grant to Sherman, December 1, 1863, ibid., 9:481–82.

73. William H. Armstrong, *Warrior in Two Camps: Ely S. Parker, Union General and Seneca Chief* (Syracuse: Syracuse University Press, 1978), 90–91.

74. David Hunter to Stanton, December 14, 1863, *PUSG*, 9:476; Grant to Washburne, December 2, 1863, ibid., 9:490–91.

13. The Top Spot

1. Grant to McPherson, December 1, 1863, *PUSG*, 9:480–81; Grant to Sherman, December 1, 1863, ibid., 9:481–82; Grant to Halleck, December 7, 1863, ibid., 9:500–1; Halleck to Grant, December 17, 21, 1863, ibid., 9:501–2.

2. Charles A. Dana to Grant, December 21, 1863, ibid., 9:502.

3. Lincoln to Grant, December 8, 1863; Memorandum, December 7, 1863, John Nicolay Papers, LC.

4. *PUSG*, 9:503; *New York Herald*, December 8, 1863.

5. Washburne to Grant, January 24, 1864, *PUSG*, 9:522–23; *New York Herald*, December 9, 1863. As early as August 1863, in the aftermath of the fall of Vicksburg, there was talk of a Grant candidacy in 1864. See Jesse Fell to Lyman Trumbull, August 11, 1863, Trumbull Papers, LC.

6. *New York Herald*, December 15, 16, 17, 18, and 19, 1863.

7. Grant to Washburne, December 12, 1863, *PUSG*, 9:521–22; Grant to Barnabas Burns, December 17, 1863, ibid., 9:541.

8. *PMJDG*, 125; Grant to George H. Thomas, January 1, 19, 1864, *PUSG*, 10:3, 45–46; Grant to Julia Grant, January 2, 1864, ibid., 10:6–7.

9. James F. Rusling, *Men and Things I Saw in Civil War Days* (New York: Eaton and Mains, 1899), 135–37.

10. Grant to Halleck, January 8, 15, 1864, *PUSG*, 10:9–10, 14–17.

11. William F. Smith to Dana, January 15, 1864, and James H. Wilson to Dana, January 15, 1864, Stanton Papers, LC.

12. Grant to Sherman, January 15, 1864, *PUSG*, 10:19; Halleck to Grant, January 8, 17, 1864, ibid., 10:17–18, 23–24.

13. Halleck to Grant, January 8, 1864, ibid., 10:17–18; Grant to Halleck, January 19, 1864, ibid., 10:39–40. William Glenn Robertson, *Back Door to Richmond: The Bermuda Hundred Campaign, April–June 1864* (Baton Rouge, 1991 [1987]), highlights previous plans involving the James River.

14. Grant to Halleck, January 19, 1864, *PUSG*, 10:39–40; Grant to Thomas, January 19, 1864, ibid., 10:45–46. Grant shared his idea with John G. Foster on February 12, 1864: see Foster to Halleck, February 26, 1864, *OR*, ser. 1, 33:602–4.

15. Halleck to Grant, February 17, 1864, *PUSG*, 10:110–12.

16. Lincoln to Halleck, September 19, 1863, *CWAL*, 6:466–67.

17. Halleck to Grant, *PUSG*, 10:110–12.

18. Halleck to Grant, December 22, 1863, *PUSG*, 10:36; Grant to Henry Wilson, January 18, 1864, ibid., 10:35–36.

19. James H. Wilson to Grant, February 8, 1864, ibid., 10:37–38. In turn, William R. Rowley warned Washburne about Wilson: see Rowley to Washburne, February 17, 1864, Washburne Papers, LC.

20. Albert D. Richardson, *Personal History of Ulysses S. Grant* (Hartford, Conn.: American Publishing, 1868), 373; Grant to Morris, January 20, 1864, *PUSG*, 10:52–53.

21. Jesse R. Grant, *In the Days of My Father General Grant* (New York, 1925), 53–55; Morris to Grant, March 22, 1864, *PUSG*, 10:54; see the *Washington (D.C.) National Intelligencer*, March 21, 1864.

22. Washburne to Grant, January 24, 1864, *PUSG*, 9:522–23; Jones to Grant, January 14, 1864, ibid., 9:542–43; Michael Burlingame and John R. Turner Ettlinger, eds., *Inside Lincoln's White House: The Complete Civil War Diary of John Hay* (Carbondale: Southern Illinois University Press, 1997), 132–33; Rawlins to Washburne, January 20, 1864, *PUSG*, 9:543; John M. Palmer to Lyman Trumbull, January 24, 1864, Trumbull Papers, LC.

23. Grant to Halleck, January 17, 1864, *PUSG*, 10:48; *PMJDG*, 125–26; Grant to John

O'Fallon et al., January 27, 1864, *PUSG*, 10:69–70; see ibid., 10:70–71; Richardson, *Personal History*, 375–76; John M. Schofield, *Forty-Six Years in the Army* (New York: Century Co., 1897), 111. Jesse Grant, *In the Days of My Father*, 17, identifies the nurse as Julia.

24. *PMJDG*, 126–27.

25. Grant to Julia Grant, February 3, 10, 1864, *PUSG*, 10:76, 100; Grant to Jesse Grant, January 31, 1864, ibid., 10:75.

26. *New York Tribune*, February 2, 6, 10, 24, 26, 27, 1864.

27. Richardson, *Personal History*, 380–81; Brooks D. Simpson, *Let Us Have Peace: Ulysses S. Grant and the Politics of War and Reconstruction, 1861–1868* (Chapel Hill: University of North Carolina Press, 1991), 53–54; Virginia Laas, ed., *Wartime Washington: The Civil War Letters of Elizabeth Blair Lee* (Urbana: University of Illinois Press, 1991), 355.

28. Grant to Julia Grant, February 25, 1864, *PUSG*, 10:154–55; Grant to Daniel Ammen, February 16, 1864, ibid., 10:132–33; Grant to Jesse Grant, February 20, 1864, ibid., 10:148–49.

29. Grant to Sherman, March 4, 1864, ibid., 10:187–88.

30. Bruce Catton, *Grant Takes Command* (Boston: Little, Brown, 1969), 124–25; Shelby Foote, *The Civil War: A Narrative* (New York: Random House, 1958–74), 3:3–5; Noah Brooks, *Washington, D.C. in Lincoln's Time* (Chicago: Quadrangle, 1971), 134–35; *New York Tribune*, March 9, 1864; George R. Agassiz, ed., *Meade's Headquarters, 1863–1865: Letters of Colonel Theodore Lyman from The Wilderness to Appomattox* (Boston: Atlantic Monthly Press, 1922), 80.

31. Catton, *Grant Takes Command*, 125; John G. Nicolay, Notes, March 8, 1864, Nicolay Papers, LC.

32. *New York Herald*, March 12, 1864; Brooks, *Washington, D.C. in Lincoln's Time*, 135. See Brooks's original description in Michael Burlingame, ed., *Lincoln Observed: Civil War Dispatches of Noah Brooks* (Baltimore: Johns Hopkins University Press, 1998), 104.

33. Catton, *Grant Takes Command*, 126.

34. The remarks are in *PUSG*, 10:195; Helen Nicolay, *Lincoln's Secretary: A Biography of John G. Nicolay* (New York, Longmans, Green, 1949), 196; Catton, *Grant Takes Command*, 127. John Y. Simon asserts that Henry W. Halleck "forced Grant's hand" on assuming the position of general-in-chief by requesting to be relieved. However, Halleck's letter to Stanton of March 9, 1864, is a rather elaborate reminder *to Stanton and Lincoln* to issue the proper orders to announce Grant's elevation to the position of general-in-chief. That was done the next day and was announced in general orders on March 12. It was widely understood that Grant's promotion carried with it Halleck's displacement. The only negotiation in the process was that Grant would accept the rank (and position) contingent on an agreement to make his headquarters wherever he pleased. See Simon, "Grant, Lincoln, and Unconditional Surrender," in Gabor S. Boritt, ed., *Lincoln's Generals* (New York, 1994), 165; *PUSG*, 10:195–96.

35. Meade to wife, December 20, 1863, George Meade, ed., *The Life and Letters of George Gordon Meade* (New York: Charles Scribner's Sons, 1913), 2:162.

36. Meade to wife, March 8, 1864, ibid., 2:176.

37. *New York Tribune*, March 11, 1864; David S. Sparks, ed., *Inside Lincoln's Army: The Diary of Marsena Rudolph Patrick, Provost Marshal General, Army of the Potomac* (New York: Thomas Yoseloff, 1964), 347 (March 10, 1864); Noah Andre Trudeau, *Bloody Roads South: The Wilderness to Cold Harbor, May–June 1864* (Boston: Little, Brown, 1989), 8.

38. Meade to wife, March 10, 1864, Meade, *Life and Letters*, 2:177; Catton, *Grant Takes Command*, 131–32.

39. *PMUSG*, 2:116; Sparks, *Inside Lincoln's Army*, 347; Cyrus B. Comstock Diary, March 10 [11], 1864, Comstock Papers, LC; Meade to wife, March 14, 1864, Meade, *Life and Letters*, 2: 177–78.

40. Sherman to Grant, March 10, 1864, *PUSG*, 10:187–88.

41. Grenville M. Dodge, *Personal Recollections of President Abraham Lincoln, General Ulysses S. Grant, and General William T. Sherman* (Council Bluffs, Iowa, 1914), 70.

42. Grant to Nathaniel P. Banks, March 15, 1864, *PUSG*, 10:200–1.

43. John Marszalek, *Sherman: A Soldier's Passion for Order* (New York: The Free Press, 1993), 257; Grant to T. Lyle Dickey, March 15, 1864, *PUSG*, 10:208–9.

44. Sherman to Grant, March 10, 1864, *PUSG*, 10:187–88.

45. Catton, *Grant Takes Command*, 157–58; *PMJDG*, 128–29; *New York Herald*, March 21, 1864; Lloyd Lewis, *Sherman: Fighting Prophet* (Lincoln: University of Nebraska Press, 1993 [1932]), 345.

11. Planning the Grand Offensive

1. Bruce Catton, *Grant Takes Command* (Boston: Little, Brown, 1969), 137; Shelby Foote, *The Civil War: A Narrative* (New York: Random House, 1958–74), 3:8–9.

2. *New York Herald*, December 23, 1863, and April 2, 1864.

3. McClellan presented his plan to Lincoln in August 1861: see Stephen W. Sears, ed., *The Civil War Papers of George B. McClellan: Selected Correspondence, 1860–1865* (New York: Ticknor & Fields, 1989), 71–75; he modified it (to increase the emphasis on operations in Virginia) in a letter to Simon Cameron that October (ibid., 114–118).

4. Catton, *Grant Takes Command*, 151–52.

5. Ibid., 147; William Glenn Robertson, *Back Door to Richmond: The Bermuda Hundred Campaign, April–June 1864* (Baton Rouge, 1991 [1987]), 17–18. Butler had absorbed the thinking of others on this matter, including Samuel P. Heintzelman, a major general then residing at Columbus, Ohio, who had just written Butler about such a campaign.

6. Grant to Butler, April 2, 1864, *PUSG*, 10:245–47.

7. Butler to Grant, April 15, 1864; Grant to Butler, April 16, 1864, ibid., 10:292–93; Grant to Butler, April 19, 1864, ibid., 10:327–28; Robertson, *Back Door to Richmond*, 27–28.

8. Grant to Sherman, April 4, 1864, *PUSG*, 10:251–52; Grant to Sigel, April 4, 6, 12, and 15, 1864, ibid., 10:257–58, 264, 282, 286–87; Grant to Meade, April 9, 1864, ibid., 10:273–75.

9. Sherman to Grant, April 10, 1864, ibid., 10:253–54.

10. *PMUSG*, 2:143; Grant to Sherman, April 4, 1864, *PUSG*, 10:251–53. John Hay recorded Lincoln's comment: see Michael Burlingame and John R. Turner Ettlinger, eds., *Inside Lincoln's White House: The Complete Civil War Diary of John Hay* (Carbondale: Southern Illinois University Press, 1997), 194. T. Harry Williams spends an inordinate amount of space in attempting to prove that Grant's *Memoirs* were in error as to when Lincoln made this comment, a discussion based on the erroneous assumption that Grant and Lincoln last met at the end of April — for Grant was at that time in Culpeper (and had been there since mid-April). Although Grant passed through Washington on his visit to Burnside's command at Annapolis on April 13, his last prolonged stay in Washington was at the beginning of the month, at the time of his letter to Sherman. It is likely that Grant's last extended meeting with Lincoln about the spring campaign thus took place at that time, as he later stated in his *Memoirs*. See T. Harry Williams, *Lincoln and His Generals* (New York: Knopf, 1952), 308.

11. Catton, *Grant Takes Command*, 139, 145.

12. Ibid., 176–77.

13. Grant to Banks, March 15, 1864, *PUSG*, 10:200–1; Grant to Halleck, March 28, 1864, ibid., 10:232; Grant to Banks, March 31, 1864, ibid., 10:242–43; Grant to Banks, April 17, 1864, *PUSG*, 10:298. See Ludwell Johnson, *The Red River Campaign: Politics and Cotton in the Civil War* (Baltimore: The Johns Hopkins University Press, 1958), 40–48.

14. Banks to Grant, April 17, 18, 1864, *PUSG*, 10: 299–300; Grant to Halleck, April 22, 1864, ibid., 10:340; Halleck to Grant, April 26, 1864, ibid., 10:340–41.

15. Halleck to Grant, May 2, 1864, ibid., 10:375.

16. Hunter to Grant, April 28, May 2, 1864, ibid., 10:308; Grant to Halleck, April 25, 1864, ibid., 10:351–52.

17. Catton, *Grant Takes Command*, 138–39.

18. Dana to Stanton, July 13, 1863, Dana Papers, LC.

19. Catton, *Grant Takes Command*, 116–18; William H. Armstrong, *Warrior in Two Camps: Ely S. Parker, Union General and Seneca Chief* (Syracuse: Syracuse University Press, 1978), 82–87. Badeau had been considered for a staff slot the previous year, but he had been wounded at Port Hudson. Wilson had recommended Badeau's appointment; see *PUSG*, 10:161 n3.

20. Grant to Wilson, April 4, 1864, *PUSG*, 10:259; Theodore S. Bowers to Washburne, April 9, 1864; William R. Rowley to Washburne, April 10, 1864; and Ely S. Parker to Washburne, April 12, 1864, Washburne Papers, LC.

21. Rowley to Washburne, April 10, 1864, Washburne Papers, LC; Bruce Catton, *Grant Moves South* (Boston: Little, Brown, 1960), 395–96; Armstrong, *Warrior in Two Camps*, 99; Catton, *Grant Takes Command*, 115, 135–36.

22. Catton, *Grant Takes Command*, 115–16.

23. *PUSG*, 10:280.

24. *New York Herald*, March 18, 19, 1864; *New York Tribune*, May 6, 1864; *New York Times*, April 21, 1864. See Brooks D. Simpson, "Great Expectations: Ulysses S. Grant, the Northern Press, and the Opening of the Wilderness Campaign," in Gary W. Gallagher, ed., *The Wilderness Campaign* (Chapel Hill: University of North Carolina Press, 1997), 1–35.

25. *New York Herald*, March 10, 30, and April 1, 1864.

26. Charles K. Rogers to Elihu B. Washburne, April 15, 1864, Washburne Papers, LC. Herman Hattaway and Archer Jones, *How the North Won: A Military History of the Civil War* (Urbana: University of Illinois Press, 1983), chapters 15, 16, and 17, is extremely helpful for readers wanting an introduction to the main themes of the 1864 campaign.

27. Meade to wife, March 22, 24, 26, 27, and April 2, 1984, Meade, *Life and Letters*, 2:182, 183, 184, 187.

28. Meade to wife, April 13, 24, 1864, ibid., 2: 189, 191.

29. George R. Agassiz, ed., *Meade's Headquarters, 1863–1865: Letters of Colonel Theodore Lyman from The Wilderness to Appomattox* (Boston: Atlantic Monthly Press, 1922), 81; Allen Nevins, ed., *A Diary of Battle: The Personal Journals of Colonel Charles S. Wainwright, 1861–1865* (New York: Harcourt, Brace & World, 1962), 329 (March 10, 1864).

30. *New York Herald*, March 30, April 25, 1864; Rufus R. Dawes, *Service with the Sixth Wisconsin Volunteers* (Dayton: Morningside House, 1984 [1890]), 239, 241–42. Grant reviewed the Fifth Corps on March 29, the Sixth Corps on April 18, and the Second Corps on April 22.

31. Catton, *Grant Takes Command*, 155; Nevins, *A Diary of Battle*, 338–39 (March 31, 1864); Agassiz, *Meade's Headquarters*, 83–84; Robert Hunt Rhodes, ed., *All for the Union: The Civil War Diary and Letters of Elisha Hunt Rhodes* (Lincoln, R.I.: Andrew Mobray Inc., 1985), 134; Meade to wife, April 18, 1864, *Life and Letters*, 2:190.

32. Ed Malles, ed., *Bridge Building in Wartime: Colonel Wesley Brainerd's Memoir of the 50th New York Volunteer Engineers* (Knoxville: University of Tennessee Press, 1997), 198–99.

33. *New York Herald*, March 29, April 1, 1864; *New York Tribune*, March 25, April 30, 1864. Less ardently covered was Grant's encounter with the Ninth Corps on April 13 at Annapolis, but remarks show the same mix of disappointment and confidence. See Ste-

phen M. Weld, *War Diary and Letters of Stephen Minot Weld, 1861–1865* (Boston: Massachusetts Historical Society, 1979), 274; Jerome M. Loring, ed., *Civil War Letters of George Washington Whitman* (Durham: Duke University Press, 1975), 114.

34. Frank A. Burr, *The Life and Deeds of General U. S. Grant* (Philadelphia: National Publishing, 1885), 512; Peter S. Michie, ed., *The Life and Letters of Emory Upton* (New York: D. Appleton, 1885), 91; Worthington C. Ford, ed., *A Cycle of Adams Letters, 1861–1865* (Boston: Houghton Mifflin, 1920), 2:128.

35. Horace Porter, *Campaigning with Grant* (New York: Century Co., 1897), 341; Robert G. Carter, ed., *Four Brothers in Blue* (Austin, Texas: University Press of Texas, 1978 [1913]), 383; Bruce Catton, *A Stillness at Appomattox* (Garden City,. NY: Doubleday, 1954), 33–35, 84.

36. [Elihu B. Washburne (?)] to Charles K. Rogers, April 15, 1864, Charles K. Rogers Papers, LC.; Seth Eyland, *The Evolution of a Life* (New York, S. W. Green's Sons, 1884), 304–6.

37. Charles F. Adams, Jr., *Richard H. Dana: A Biography* (Boston: Houghton Mifflin, 1890), 2:271–72.

38. Brooks D. Simpson, *America's Civil War* (Wheeling, Ill.: Harlan Davidson, 1996), 93; Porter, *Campaigning,* 47.

39. Porter, *Campaigning,* 30; Grant to Julia Grant, April 17, 1864, *PUSG,* 10:315; Edward Hagerman, *The American Civil War and the Origins of Modern Warfare: Ideas, Organization, and Field Command* (Bloomington: Indiana University Press, 1988), chapter 10. In *PMUSG,* 2:141–42, Grant reported that his near-miss with Mosby happened on his return to Culpeper; the editorial note in *PUSG,* 10:316 n2, that the incident happened on May 4 (or that Grant said so in his memoirs) is in error.

40. Grant to Halleck, April 29, 1864, *PUSG,* 10:370–72.

41. *PMJDG,* 130–31; Grant to Julia Grant, April 24, 1864, *PUSG,* 10:350; Stanton Garner, *The Civil War World of Herman Melville* (Lawrence, KS, 1993), 326, 330; Grant to John E. Smith, April 26, 1864, *PUSG,* 10:356–57.

42. Grant to Julia Grant, April 27, 30, 1864, *PUSG,* 10:362–63, 377; Grant to Butler, April 28, 1864, ibid., 10:364.

43. Lincoln to Grant, April 30, 1864, ibid., 10:380.

44. Catton, *Grant Takes Command,* 147; Rosecrans to Grant, April 29, 1864, *PUSG,* 10:377; Grant to Rosecrans, April 30, 1864, ibid., 10:376; Grant to Rosecrans and Rosecrans to Grant, May 1, 1864, ibid., 10:382–83; Comstock Diary, May 1, 1864, Comstock Papers, LC.

45. Grant to Lincoln, May 1, 1864, *PUSG,* 10:380.

46. Porter, *Campaigning,* 36–37. On June 14, 1864, Porter recalled the conversation in a letter to his wife. Apprising her of the decision to cross the James, he observed: "This is all part of the original plan explained to me the day before we left Culpepper." Porter to wife, June 14, 1864, Porter Papers, LC.

47. Grant to Burnside, May 2, 1864, *PUSG,* 10:388–89; Grant to Julia Grant, May 2, 1864, *PUSG,* 10:394.

15. No Turning Back

1. Horace Porter, *Campaigning with Grant* (New York: Century Co., 1897), 41–43.

2. Gordon C. Rhea, *The Battle of the Wilderness, May 5–6, 1864* (Baton Rouge: Louisiana State University Press, 1994), 68.

3. George R. Agassiz, ed., *Meade's Headquarters, 1863–1865: Letters of Colonel Theodore Lyman from The Wilderness to Appomattox* (Boston: Atlantic Monthly Press, 1922), 87; Grant to Halleck, May 4, 1864, *PUSG,* 10:397.

4. Rhea, *Wilderness*, 91–93; Sylvanus Cadwallader, *Three Years with Grant* (Lincoln: University of Nebraska Press, 1996 [1955]), 175; Gaillard Hunt, *Israel, Elihu, and Cadwallader Washburn: A Chapter in American Biography* (New York: Macmillan, 1925), 208.

5. Hunt, *Israel, Elihu and Cadwallader Washburn*, 208; Grant to Meade, May 5, 1864, *PUSG*, 10:399; Porter, *Campaigning*, 47–48. See James F. Epperson, "The Chance Battle in the Wilderness," *Columbiad* 2 (Spring 1998):77–96, for a discussion of the origins of this clash.

6. Noah Andre Trudeau, *Bloody Roads South: The Wilderness to Cold Harbor, May–June 1864* (Boston: Little, Brown, 1989), 47.

7. Hunt, *Israel, Elihu, and Cadwallader Washburn*, 209; Frank A. Burr, *The Life and Deeds of General U. S. Grant* (Philadelphia: National Publishing, 1885), 56; Porter, *Campaigning*, 50–51. On Grant and the calming qualities of tobacco, see Oliver O. Howard and Ely S. Parker, "Some Reminiscences of Grant," *McClure's Magazine* 2 (May 1894): 533.

8. Hunt, *Israel, Elihu, and Cadwallader Washburn*, 209; Agassiz, *Meade's Headquarters*, 91; Bruce Catton, *A Stillness at Appomattox* (Garden City, N.Y.: Doubleday, 1954), 66.

9. Agassiz, *Meade's Headquarters*, 91; Trudeau, *Bloody Roads South*, 63; Bruce Catton, *Grant Takes Command* (Boston: Little, Brown, 1969), 205; Porter, *Campaigning*, 52. On the impact of cigars on Grant, see George F. Shrady, *General Grant's Last Days* (New York: privately printed, 1908), 15.

10. Trudeau, *Bloody Roads South*, 81; Porter, *Campaigning*, 54; Henry E. Wing, *When Lincoln Kissed Me* (New York: Eaton and Mains, 1913), 12–13. Geoffrey Perret, *Ulysses S. Grant: Soldier and President* (New York: Random House, 1997), erroneously places the Grant-Wing encounter on the evening of May 6.

11. Meade to Grant, May 5, 1864, and William R. Rowley to Meade, May 5, 1864, *PUSG*, 10: 400; Rhea, *Wilderness*, 266–67; Porter, *Campaigning*, 56–60; Albert D. Richardson, *Personal History of Ulysses S. Grant* (Hartford, Conn.: American Publishing, 1868), 395–96.

12. Trudeau, *Bloody Roads South*, 97, 108.

13. Porter, *Campaigning*, 63–67; Hunt, *Israel, Elihu, and Cadwallader Washburn*, 211–13. Another account that stresses Grant's calm demeanor is in Almon Clarke, "In the Immediate Rear: Experience and Observation of a Field Surgeon," *War Papers* (Milwaukee: Military Order of the Loyal League of the United States, Wisconsin, 1896), 2:92–93.

14. Trudeau, *Bloody Roads South*, 113; Grant to Edward Ferrero, May 6, 1864, *PUSG*, 10:403; *National Tribune*, June 10, 1886.

15. Porter, *Campaigning*, 69–70.

16. Adam Badeau, *Military History of U. S. Grant* (New York: D. Appleton, 1881), 2:127; Porter, *Campaigning*, 70.

17. Badeau, *Military History*, 2:126; Cadwallader, *Three Years*, 180–82; Richardson, *Personal History*, 398; James H. Wilson, *Under the Old Flag* (New York: D. Appleton, 1912), 1:389–90; Shelby Foote, *The Civil War: A Narrative* (New York: Random House, 1958–74), 3:186; Morris Schaff, *Battle of the Wilderness* (Boston: Houghton Mifflin, 1910), 327. Elihu Washburne's diary (*Hunt, Israel, Elihu, and Cadwallader Washburn*, 213) mentions that at some point Grant did leave his headquarters to assess the situation. As Horatio Wright later noted of Grant's demeanor, "He didn't seem to be a bit shaken; he was just the man we needed at the time." Wright interview, Hamlin Garland Papers, University of Southern California.

18. Grant to Halleck, May 6, 1864, *PUSG*, 10:400; Grant to Halleck, May 7, 1864, ibid., 10:405.

19. Agassiz, *Meade's Headquarters*, 102; Trudeau, *Bloody Roads South*, 123; Wilson, *Under the Old Flag*, 1:389.

20. Trudeau, *Bloody Roads South*, 124.

21. Burr, *Grant*, 59; William B. Lapham, *My Recollections of the War of the Rebellion* (Augusta, Maine: Burleigh and Flynt, 1892), 118–19; Robert Hunt Rhodes, ed., *All for the Union* (Lincoln, R.I.: Andrew Mobray Inc., 1985), 146 (May 7, 1864); Badeau, *Military History*, 2:135; Richardson, *Personal History*, 40; Porter, *Campaigning*, 79–82.

22. Wing, *When Lincoln Kissed Me*, 31–39.

23. Porter, *Campaigning*, 82.

24. Allen Nevins, ed., *A Diary of Battle: The Personal Journals of Colonel Charles S. Wainwright, 1861–1865* (New York: Harcourt, Brace & World, 1962), 359 (May 8, 1864).

25. Grant to Halleck, May 8, 1864, *PUSG*, 10:411.

26. Porter, *Campaigning*, 84.

27. Ibid.

28. Agassiz, *Meade's Headquarters*, 104–5; Cyrus B. Comstock Diary, May 8, 1864, Comstock Papers, LC; Henry J. Hunt, Journal, Petersburg Operations, May 8, 1864, Hunt Papers, LC; Gordon C. Rhea, *The Battles for Spotsylvania Court House and the Road to Yellow Tavern, May 7–12, 1864* (Baton Rouge: Louisiana State University Press), 86. On Spotsylvania, see also William D. Matter, *If It Takes All Summer: The Battle of Spotsylvania* (Chapel Hill: University of North Carolina Press, 1988), and the essays by Rhea, Matter, and Carol Reardon in Gary W. Gallagher, ed., *The Spotsylvania Campaign* (Chapel Hill: University of North Carolina Press, 1998).

29. Porter, *Campaigning*, 90.

30. Rhea, *Spotsylvania*, 96–101.

31. Agassiz, *Meade's Headquarters*, 100; Dana to Stanton, May 10, 1864, Dana Papers, LC. Dana reported some 27,621 in losses, although he added that this total was inflated due to a great deal of straggling.

32. Rhea, *Spotsylvania*, 108–112; Grant to Halleck, May 10, 1864, *PUSG*, 10:418–19.

33. Grant to Burnside, May 10, 1864, *PUSG*, 10:419–20.

34. Rhea, *Spotsylvania*, 174.

35. Ibid., 148; Charles C. Coffin, *Redeeming the Republic* (New York: Harper and Brothers, 1890), 112; Evan R. Jones, *Lincoln, Stanton, and Grant* (London: Frederick Warne & Co., 1875), 281; Porter, *Campaigning*, 96–97.

36. William H. Armstrong, *Warrior in Two Camps: Ely S. Parker, Union General and Seneca Chief* (Syracuse: Syracuse University Press, 1978), 98; Porter, *Campaigning*, 97–98; Grant to Stanton, May 11, 1864, and Grant to Halleck, May 11, 1864, *PUSG*, 10:422–23.

37. George Meade, ed., *The Life and Letters of George Gordon Meade* (New York: Charles Scribner's Sons, 1913), 2:194; Trudeau, *Bloody Roads South*, 162.

38. Rhea, *Spotsylvania*, 213.

39. Grant to Burnside, May 11, 1864, *PUSG*, 10:424–25; Grant to Meade, May 11, 1864, ibid., 10:427.

40. Agassiz, *Meade's Headquarters*, 110.

41. Francis A. Walker, *History of the Second Army Corps* (New York: Charles Scribner's Sons, 1887), 533 (Walker made the comment in the context of the June 16 assault on Petersburg, but offered it as a general observation); Francis C. Barlow, "Capture of the Salient May 12, 1864," *Papers of the Military Historical Society of Massachusetts* (Wilmington, N.C.: Broadfoot Publishing, 1989 [1905]), 4:246–47; Rhea, *Spotsylvania*, 224.

42. Porter, *Campaigning*, 104–5.

43. Grant to Burnside, May 12, 1864 (two messages), and Grant to Meade, same date, *PUSG*, 10:431–33; William Marvel, *Burnside* (Chapel Hill: University of North Carolina Press, 1991), 362–66.

44. Grant to Halleck, May 12, 1864, *PUSG*, 10:428.

45. Porter, *Campaigning*, 113–15.

46. Grant to Julia Grant, May 13, 1864, *PUSG*, 10:443–44.

47. James G. Smart, ed., *A Radical View: The "Agate" Dispatches of Whitelaw Reid, 1861–1865* (Memphis: Memphis State University Press, 1978), 2:156 (May 23, 1864); Comstock Diary, May 14, 1864, Comstock Papers, LC; Dana to Stanton, May 16, 1864, Dana Papers, LC; Trudeau, *Bloody Roads South*, 208; Meade, *Life and Letters*, 2:195. Others agreed that many of the men sent to Washington had minor wounds: Beman Gates, Rufus Dawes's father-in-law, noted on May 13 that the majority of the wounds suffered were slight. Dawes, *Service with the Sixth Wisconsin Volunteers*, 251.

48. Grant to Halleck, May 14, 1864, *PUSG*, 10:445. My thanks to Gordon Rhea for calling my attention to this movement.

49. Porter, *Campaigning*, 114–19; Trudeau, *Bloody Roads South*, 191.

50. Porter, *Campaigning*, 118–19; Grant to Halleck, May 16, 1864, *PUSG*, 10:451–52; Meade, *Life and Letters*, 2:196.

51. Rhodes, *All for the Union*, 153 (May 17, 1864); Meade, *Life and Letters*, 2:197; Porter, *Campaigning*, 123–24.

52. Halleck to Grant, May 17, 1864, *PUSG*, 10:460; Grant to Halleck, May 16, 1864, ibid., 10:452; Halleck to Grant, May 18, 1864, and Grant to Halleck, May 19, 1864, ibid., 10:470. On Butler's troubles, see Herbert M. Schiller, *The Bermuda Hundred Campaign* (Dayton: Morningside House, 1988).

53. Grant to Halleck, May 21, 22, 1864, *PUSG*, 10:475, 477.

54. Cadwallader, *Three Years*, 206; Porter, *Campaigning*, 137–39.

55. Comstock Diary, May 23, 1864, Comstock Papers, LC.

56. Grant to Halleck, May 24, 1864, *PUSG*, 10:483–84.

57. Agassiz, *Meade's Headquarters*, 123, 125–26.

58. J. Michael Miller, *The North Anna Campaign: "Even to Hell Itself," May 21–26, 1864* (Lynchburg, Va.: H. E. Howard, 1989), 10; Special Orders No. 25, May 24, 1864, *PUSG*, 10:486.

59. Porter, *Campaigning*, 147–49.

60. Grant to Burnside, May 24, 1864, *PUSG*, 10:484; Charles F. Adams, Jr., Diary, May 25, 1864, Adams Family Papers, Massachusetts Historical Society (microfilm); Grant to Halleck, May 25, 1864, ibid., 10:487–88; Miller, *The North Anna Campaign*, 130.

61. Miller, *The North Anna Campaign*, 130–31; Nevins, *A Diary of Battle*, 388; Porter, *Campaigning*, 145–46; Grant to Meade, May 25, 1864, *PUSG*, 10:488–89.

62. Porter, *Campaigning*, 161; Grant to Halleck, May 26, 1864, *PUSG*, 10:491.

63. Ed Malles, ed., *Bridge Building in Wartime: Colonel Wesley Brainerd's Memoir of the 50th New York Volunteer Engineers* (Knoxville: University of Tennessee Press, 1997), 230; Trudeau, *Bloody Roads South*, 245; Nevins, *A Diary of Battle*, 388; William T. Schoyer, ed., *The Road to Cold Harbor* (Pittsburgh: Clossum Press, 1986), 92.

64. Agassiz, *Meade's Headquarters*, 129–30.

65. Comstock Diary, May 28, 1864, Comstock Papers, LC; Agassiz, *Meade's Headquarters*, 131; Meade to wife, May 29, 1864, Meade, *Life and Letters*, 2:199.

66. Charles Francis Adams, Jr., to Charles Francis Adams, Sr., May 29, 1864, Worthington C. Ford, ed., *A Cycle of Adams Letters, 1861–1865* (Boston: Houghton Mifflin, 1920), 2:133–34.

67. Ibid., 2:131; Meade to wife, May 30, 1864, Meade, *Life and Letters*, 2:199.

16. A Very Tedious Job

1. See Brooks D. Simpson, "Great Expectations: Ulysses S. Grant, the Northern Press, and the Opening of the Wilderness Campaign," in Gary W. Gallagher, ed., *The Wilderness Campaign* (Chapel Hill: University of North Carolina Press, 1997), 1–35.

2. Donald B. Cole and John J. McDonough, eds., *Witness to the Young Republic: A Yankee's Journal, 1828–1870* (Hanover, N.H.: University Press of New England, 1989), 450 (May 22, 1864); Simpson, "Great Expectations," 28–29; Michael Burlingame, ed., *Lincoln Observed: Civil War Dispatches of Noah Brooks* (Baltimore: The Johns Hopkins University Press, 1998), 109; Howard Beale, ed., *The Diary of Gideon Welles* (New York: W. W. Norton, 1960), 2:44; Lincoln to Frederick A. Conkling et al., June 3, 1864, *CWAL*, 7:374.

3. Luther A. Rose Diary, May 31, 1864, Rose Papers, LC; Noah Andre Trudeau, *Bloody Roads South: The Wilderness to Cold Harbor, May–June 1864* (Boston: Little, Brown, 1989), 262–67.

4. Charles F. Adams, Jr., Diary, June 1, 1864, Adams Family Papers, Massachusetts Historical Society (microfilm); Trudeau, *Bloody Roads South*, 273.

5. George R. Agassiz, ed., *Meade's Headquarters, 1863–1865: Letters of Colonel Theodore Lyman from The Wilderness to Appomattox* (Boston: Atlantic Monthly Press, 1922), 138 (June 1, 1864); Trudeau, *Bloody Roads South*, 274; George Meade, ed., *The Life and Letters of George Gordon Meade* (New York: Charles Scribner's Sons, 1913), 2:200.

6. Horace Porter, *Campaigning with Grant* (New York: The Century Co., 1897), 164–65.

7. Louis J. Baltz III, *The Battle of Cold Harbor, May 27–June 13, 1864* (Lynchburg, Va.: H. E. Howard, 1994), 117–125.

8. Agassiz, *Meade's Headquarters*, 141.

9. William F. Smith, *Autobiography of Major General William F. Smith*, ed. Herbert M. Schiller (Dayton: Morningside House, 1990), 93; Theodore Lyman, "Operations of the Army of the Potomac, June 5–15, 1864," *Papers of the Military Historical Society of Massachusetts*, 15 vols. (Boston: Military Historical Society of Massachusetts, 1895–1918), 5:7; Porter, *Campaigning*, 174–75.

10. Grant to Meade, June 3, 1864, *PUSG*, 11:14.

11. Grant to Meade, June 3, 1864, ibid., 11:13; William W. Smith interview, Hamlin Garland Papers, University of Southern California; Porter, *Campaigning*, 175–78; Agassiz, *Meade's Headquarters*, 147 (June 3, 1864). Later messages from Dana to Stanton offered a more accurate and informed estimate of casualties, so that the authorities at Washington knew as of June 4 what had happened.

12. Meade, *Life and Letters*, 2:200; Allen Nevins, ed., *A Diary of Battle: The Personal Journals of Colonel Charles S. Wainwright, 1861–1865* (New York: Harcourt, Brace & World, 1962), 406.

13. William R. Rowley to Washburne, June 3, 4, 1864, Washburne Papers, LC; Meade, *Life and Letters*, 2:200; David S. Sparks, ed., *Inside Lincoln's Army: The Diary of Marsena Rudolph Patrick, Provost Marshal General, Army of the Potomac* (New York: Thomas Yoseloff, 1964), 380 (June 3, 1864); Agassiz, *Meade's Headquarters*, 147–48 (June 3, 1864); Nevins, *Diary of Battle*, 405–6.

14. Baltz, *Cold Harbor*, 174–79; Francis A. Walker, *History of the Second Army Corps* (New York: Charles Scribner's Sons, 1887), 517.

15. Grant to Ellen W. Grant, June 4, 1864, *PUSG*, 11:16; John Gibbon, *Personal Recollections of the Civil War* (Dayton: Morningside House, 1988 [1928]), 234–37.

16. Grant to Lee, June 5, 1864, *PUSG*, 11:17.

17. Lee to Grant, June 5, 1864, ibid., 11:17; Grant to Lee, June 6, 1864, and Lee to Grant, June 6, 1864, ibid., 11:22.

18. Grant to Lee, June 6, 1864, ibid., 11:22; Lee to Grant, June 6, 1864, ibid., 11:22–23; Grant to Lee, June 7, 1864, ibid., 11:26–27.

19. Bruce Catton, *Grant Takes Command* (Boston: Little, Brown, 1969), 271–72. Grant reprinted his side of the exchange in his *Memoirs,* summarizing Lee's responses, and remarked that by the time the cease-fire took place "all but two of the wounded had died." This oft-quoted estimate is not confirmed by various accounts of the cease-

fire, but that there were few wounded left seems apparent; moreover, Andrew A. Humphreys recalled that Union soldiers, by making "extraordinary efforts at night," had managed to recover most of the wounded in the days after the battle. *PMUSG*, 2:272–76; Andrew A. Humphreys, *The Virginia Campaign, 1864 and 1865* (New York: DaCapo, 1995 [1883]), 192; Walker, *History of the Second Corps*, 517–18.

20. Luther A. Rose Diary, June 3, 4, and 5, 1864, Rose Papers, LC; Meade to wife, June 5, 1864, Meade, *Life and Letters*, 2:201; Porter, *Campaigning*, 184–87.

21. Peter S. Michie, *The Life and Letters of Emory Upton* (New York: D. Appleton, 1885), 108–9. As Upton offered his comments in letters of June 4 and 5, many historians have understandably assumed that they describe what happened on June 3, although the June 5 letter specifically cites the action of June 1. See ibid., 106, which shows that Upton's brigade did not join in the June 3 assault.

22. Porter to wife, June 4, 1864, Porter Papers, LC.

23. Smith, *Autobiography*, 114; Trudeau, *Bloody Roads South*, 304–5; *PMUSG*, 2:276–77; James H. Wilson, *Under the Old Flag* (New York: D. Appleton, 1912), 1:443.

24. Orvil Grant to Charles H. Rogers, June 9, 1864, Rogers Papers, LC; Beale, *Diary of Welles*, 2:45, 46.

25. David W. Blight, ed., *When This Cruel War Is Over: The Civil War Letters of Charles Harvey Brewster* (Amherst: University of Massachusetts Press, 1992), 313; Nevins, *Diary of Battle*, 394, 407, 412; Meade, *Life and Letters*, 2:201.

26. Comstock Diary, June 5, 1864, Comstock Papers, LC; Grant to Halleck, June 5, 1864, *PUSG*, 11:19–20; Trudeau, *Bloody Roads South*, 301.

27. Grant to Halleck, May 30, 1864, *PUSG*, 10:496; Rawlins to Mary Rawlins, June 13, 1864, Wilson Papers, LC, observes: "From the commencement of this campaign General Grant has not deviated at all from his written plan, but has steadily pursued the line he then marked out."

28. Grant to Halleck, June 5, 1864, ibid., 11:19; Porter, *Campaigning*, 182–83.

29. Grant to Julia Grant, June 6, 1864, *PUSG*, 11:25.

30. Porter, *Campaigning*, 187–88; Comstock Diary, June 7–11, 1864, Comstock Papers, LC; Grant to Brig. Gen. John J. Abercrombie, June 7, 1864, *PUSG*, 11:28; Grant to Meade, June 8, 1864, ibid., 11:30–31; Grant to Washburne, June 9, 1864, ibid., 11:32.

31. Noah Andre Trudeau, *The Last Citadel: Petersburg, Virginia, June 1864–April 1865* (Boston: Little, Brown, 1991), 30. Rawlins noted that Grant regretted the degree to which Meade's contributions had been eclipsed. James H. Wilson, *The Life of John A. Rawlins* (New York: Neale Publishing, 1916), 229.

32. Catton, *Grant Takes Command*, 272–73; Sylvanus Cadwallader, *Three Years with Grant* (Lincoln: University of Nebraska Press, 1996 [1955]), 207; Sparks, *Inside Lincoln's Army*, 381. Crapsey was former Congressman Isaac N. Morris's nephew; see Grant to Morris, August 10, 1864, *PUSG*, 11:396–97.

33. Nevins, *Diary of Battle*, 409; *PMUSG*, 2:143–45; Cadwallader, *Three Years*, 211–12; Baltz, *Cold Harbor*, 201.

34. Meade to wife, June 12, 1864, Meade, *Life and Letters*, 2:203.

35. See William Glenn Robertson, *The Battle of Old Men and Young Boys, June 9, 1864* (Lynchburg, Va.: H. E. Howard, 1989).

36. Grant to Butler, June 11, 1864, and Grant to Meade, June 11, 1864, *PUSG*, 11:34–37.

37. Porter, *Campaigning*, 189–90; Porter to wife, June 14, 1864, Porter Papers, LC.

38. Agassiz, *Meade's Headquarters*, 156 (June 12, 1864).

39. Charles A. Page, *Letters of a War Correspondent* (Boston: L. C. Page, 1898); 110–11; Porter, *Campaigning*, 196–97.

40. Porter, *Campaigning*, 197–98; Grant to Halleck, June 14, 1864, *PUSG*, 11:45; Grant to Butler, June 14, 1864, ibid.; Dana to Stanton, June 15, 1864, *OR*, ser. 1, 40 (part 1): 19–20; Trudeau, *The Last Citadel*, 25.

41. Porter, *Campaigning*, 199–201; Grant to Butler, June 14, 15, 1864, *PUSG*, 11:46, 47. A detailed account of the operations of June 15–18 is Thomas J. Howe, *Wasted Valor: The Petersburg Campaign, June 15–18, 1864* (Lynchburg, Va.: H. E. Howard, 1988). Howe suggests that physical exhaustion and flawed leadership best explain the Union failure to take Petersburg. He discounts suggestions that soldiers were suffering from their memories of Cold Harbor. Nevertheless, the two corps that spearheaded the drive were the same ones that had suffered most at Petersburg, and Smith's cautious, careful behavior may have been in response to his Cold Harbor experience.

42. Grant to Butler and Smith, June 15, 1864, *PUSG*, 11:49; Grant to Butler, June 15, 1864, ibid., 11:51; Grant to Gibbon, June 15, 1864, ibid., 11:52–53; Grant to Hancock, June 15, 1864, ibid., 11:53; Walker, *History of the Second Corps*, 527.

43. Grant to Meade, June 16, 1864; Grant to Hancock, June 16, 1864; Grant to Burnside, June 16, 1864; Grant to Smith, June 16, 1864, all in *PUSG*, 11:60–61, 56, 64, Porter, *Campaigning*, 203–6; Agassiz, *Meade's Headquarters*, 164; Trudeau, *The Last Citadel*, 46; Walker, *History of the Second Corps*, 534.

44. Grant to Butler, June 16, 1864, *PUSG*, 11:57–58; Trudeau, *The Last Citadel*, 47–48; Agassiz, *Meade's Headquarters*, 166 (June 16, 1864).

45. Grant to Butler, June 17, 1864 (three dispatches), *PUSG*, 11:68–70; Comstock Diary, June 17, 1864, Comstock Papers, LC; Porter, *Campaigning*, 207; Agassiz, *Meade's Headquarters*, 170.

46. Nevins, *Diary of Battle*, 425.

47. Grant to Meade, June 18, 1864, *PUSG*, 11:78. See Brian Holden Reid, "Another Look at Grant's Crossing of the James, 1864," *Civil War History* 39 (December 1993):291–316.

48. Agassiz, *Meade's Headquarters*, 160; Meade, *Life and Letters*, 2:205–6; Comstock Diary, June 17, 18, 1864, Comstock Papers, LC. Meade later admitted that he had come up short during the initial attacks on Petersburg; see Agassiz, *Meade's Headquarters*, 224.

49. Charles F. Adams, Jr., to Charles F. Adams, Sr., June 19, 1864, Worthington C. Ford, ed., *A Cycle of Adams Letters, 1861–1865* (Boston: Houghton Mifflin, 1920), 2:154–55.

50. Smith to Butler, June 15, 1864, Smith, *Autobiography*, 154.

51. Charles F. Adams, Jr., to Charles F. Adams, Sr., June 19, 1864, Ford, *Cycle of Adams Letters*, 2:148–56.

52. Grant to Butler, June 20, 1864 (two letters), *PUSG*, 11:89, 91–92; Grant to Meade, June 20, 1864, ibid., 11:92–93.

53. Lincoln to Grant, June 15, 1864, *CWAL*, 7:393; Speech at Sanitary Fair, June 16, 1864, ibid., 7:395–96; Beale, *Diary of Welles*, 2:55 (June 20, 1864).

54. Horace Porter to wife, June 24, 1864, Porter Papers, LC; Dana to Stanton, June 21, 1864, *OR*, ser. 1, 40 (part 1): 27; Trudeau, *The Last Citadel*, 65–67; James G. Randall and Theodore C. Pease, *The Diary of Orville Hickman Browning* (Springfield, Ill.: Illinois State Historical Library, 1925–33), 1:673 (June 26, 1864); Porter, *Campaigning*, 217–23; Cadwallader, *Three Years*, 231–33; David Herbert Donald, *Lincoln* (New York: Simon and Schuster, 1995), 516.

55. Grant to Meade, June 21, 1864, *PUSG*, 11:101–2.

56. Comstock Diary, June 22, 1864, Comstock Papers, LC; Sparks, *Inside Lincoln's Army*, 388 (June 23, 1864); Nevins, *Diary of Battle*, 427; Grant to Halleck, June 24, 1864, *PUSG*, 11:123.

57. Comstock Diary, June 22, 1864, Comstock Papers, LC; Grant to Julia Grant, June 7, 1864, *PUSG*, 11:30.

58. Grant to Halleck, June 23, 1864, *PUSG*, 11:111–12; Agassiz, *Meade's Headquarters*, 179.

59. Dana to Stanton, July 1, 1864, *OR*, ser. 1, 40 (part 1): 28; Grant to Halleck, June 28, 1864, *PUSG*, 11:142–43; Grant to Meade, June 28, 1864, ibid., 11:144–45.

60. Burlingame, *Lincoln Observed,* 116; Charles F. Adams, Sr., to Charles F. Adams, Jr., June 24, 1864, Ford, *Cycle of Adams Letters,* 2:156–57.

61. Edward L. Cook to his parents, June 14, 1864, Cook Papers, University of California, Santa Barbara.

62. Grant to Julia Grant, June 22, 1864, *PUSG,* 11:110.

17. Summer of Discontent

1. Allan Nevins, ed., *A Diary of Battle: The Personal Journals of Colonel Charles S. Wainwright, 1861–1865* (New York: Harcourt, Brace & World, 1962), 431.

2. David S. Sparks, ed., *Inside Lincoln's Army: The Dairy of Marsena Rudolph Patrick, Provost Marshal General, Army of the Potomac* (New York: Thomas Yoseloff, 1964), 388, 393 (June 23, July 6, 1864); Bruce Catton, *A Stillness at Appomattox* (Garden City, N.Y.: Doubleday, 1953), 211.

3. George Agassiz, ed., *Meade's Headquarters, 1863–1865: Letters of Colonel Theodore Lyman from The Wilderness to Appomattox* (Boston: Atlantic Monthly Press, 1922), 175–76; Sparks, *Inside Lincoln's Army,* 381; Noah Andre Trudeau, *The Last Citadel: Petersburg, Virginia, June 1864–April 1865* (Boston: Little, Brown, 1991), 104; Comstock Diary, July 2, 1864, Comstock Papers, LC.

4. Comstock Diary, June 26, 1864, Comstock Papers, LC.

5. James H. Wilson, *Under the Old Flag* (New York: D. Appleton, 1912), 1:400.

6. Bruce Catton, *Grant Takes Command* (Boston: Little, Brown, 1969), 303.

7. Grant to Jones, July 5, 1864, *PUSG,* 11:175–76.

8. Agassiz, *Meade's Headquarters,* 179 (June 25, 1864); Sparks, *Inside Lincoln's Army,* 387 (June 23, 1864); Comstock Diary, June 28, 1864, Comstock Papers, LC; Horace Porter, *Campaigning with Grant* (New York: The Century Co., 1897), 231; William F. Smith, *Autobiography of Major General William F. Smith, 1861–1864,* ed. Herbert M. Schiller (Dayton: Morningside House, 1990), 109–10. On the liquor supply at Burnside's headquarters, see Nevins, *Diary of Battle,* 433.

9. Comstock Diary, June 29, 1864, Comstock Papers, LC (Comstock says nothing about the incident Smith described); Smith, *Autobiography,* 110–11. Rawlins told his wife: "The general was at the front today and I learn from one of his staff, he deviated from the only path he should ever travel, by taking a glass of liquor" — a far cry from Smith's story. Rawlins to Mary E. Rawlins, June 29, 1864, James H. Wilson Papers, LC.

10. Smith to Grant, July 2, 1864, *PUSG,* 11:163.

11. Grant to Halleck, July 1, 1864, ibid., 11:155–56.

12. Halleck to Grant, July 3, 1864, ibid., 11:156.

13. Grant to Halleck, July 6, 1864, ibid., 11:176.

14. Orville E. Babcock to William F. Smith, July 6, 1864, ibid., 11:165; Ely S. Parker to William R. Rowley, July 8, 1864, Rowley Papers, ISHL.

15. Sparks, *Inside Lincoln's Army,* 393–96; Comstock Diary, July 7, 1864, Comstock Papers, LC; Meade to wife, July 12, 1864, George Meade, ed., *The Life and Letters of George Gordon Meade* (New York: Scribner's, 1913), 2:212; John Gibbon, *Recollections of the Civil War* (Dayton: Morningside House, 1988 [1828]), 239.

16. Grant to Meade, June 28, 1864, *PUSG,* 11:145–46; see also ibid., 11:158–60 (the rumor of Swinton's return was erroneous). Several later accounts persisted in claiming that Meade as well as Hancock had not been informed of the plan to take Petersburg. See Francis A. Walker, *History of the Second Army Corps in the Army of the Potomac* (New York: Charles Scribner's Sons, 1887), 528, 531–32.

17. Sylvanus Cadwallader, *Three Years with Grant* (Lincoln: University of Nebraska Press, 1996 [1955]), 233–41.

18. See *PUSG*, 11:206; Stanton to Halleck, July 7, 1864, *OR*, ser. 1, 40 (part 3):59. For a curious interpretation of the change in the wording of the order, see T. Harry Williams, *Lincoln and His Generals* (New York: Knopf, 1952), 323–24.

19. Catton, *Grant Takes Command*, 26; Smith, *Autobiography*, 111–12.

20. Smith, *Autobiography*, 111–13; Comstock Diary, July 17, 1864, Comstock Papers, LC.

21. Butler to wife, July 10, 1864, *PUSG*, 11:206–7; Grant to Halleck, July 10, 1864, ibid., 11:205–6; William D. Mallam, "The Grant-Butler Relationship," *Mississippi Valley Historical Review* 41 (September 1954): 264. Halleck later claimed to Grant that he had drafted General Orders No. 225 "precisely to carry out your views," although that clearly was not the case. Halleck to Grant, July 12, 1864, *PUSG*, 11:234.

22. Grant to Halleck, July 3, 1864, *PUSG*, 11:166; Grant to Meade, July 3, 1864, ibid., 11:167–68; Grant to Halleck, July 4, 5, 1864, ibid., 11:169, 170; Sparks, *Inside Lincoln's Army*, 392; Comstock Diary, July 4, 5, 1864, Comstock Papers, LC. William B. Feis, "A Union Military Intelligence Failure: Jubal Early's Raid, June 12–July 14, 1864," *Civil War History* 36 (September 1990): 209–25, shows the difficulty Grant had in pinning down Early's location and intentions.

23. Grant to Meade, July 3, 8, 1864, *PUSG*, 11:168, 194; Comstock Diary, July 5, 1864, Comstock Papers, LC; Grant to Halleck, July 5, 9, 1864, *PUSG*, 11:170, 197; Meade to wife, July 12, 1864, Meade, *Life and Letters*, 2:211.

24. Comstock Diary, July 10, 1864, Comstock Papers, LC; Grant to Halleck, July 9, 1864, *PUSG*, 11:198–99; Lincoln to Grant, July 10, 1864, ibid., 11:199; Grant to Lincoln, July 10, 1864, ibid., 11:203.

25. Grant to Meade, July 11, 1864, *PUSG*, 11:218; Comstock Diary, July 12, 1864, Comstock Papers, LC; Porter, *Campaigning*, 238.

26. Ely S. Parker to William R. Rowley, July 11, 1864, Rowley Papers, ISHL; Grant to Halleck, July 12, 1864, *PUSG*, 11:221; Grant to Dana, July 13, 1864, ibid., 11:228; Dana to Rawlins, July 13, 1864, ibid., 11:231; Dana to Grant, July 12, 1864, ibid., 11:229–30; Catton, *Grant Takes Command*, 313–14. Lincoln held Halleck accountable for the failure to mount an energetic pursuit: Noah Brooks, *Washington, D.C. in Lincoln's Time* (Chicago: Quadrangle, 1971), 162.

27. Comstock Diary, July 15, 1864, Comstock Papers, LC. Albert Castel makes much of Grant's July 16 dispatch to Sherman warning of a possible transfer of Early's men to Georgia; however, in context, Grant's alarm soon subsided. Grant's interest in renewing operations against Petersburg at the end of the month argues against Castel's claim that this dispatch was "tantamount to a confession of failure in Virginia"; more likely it was framed in a moment of frustration, even panic. See Grant to Sherman, July 16, 1864, *PUSG*, 11:262–63: Castel, *Decision in the West: The Atlanta Campaign of 1864* (Lawrence: University Press of Kansas, 1992).

28. Comstock Diary, July 17, 1864, ibid.

29. Sparks, *Inside Lincoln's Army*, 401 (July 22, 1864); Comstock Diary, July 17, 1864, Comstock Papers, LC.

30. Smith, *Autobiography*, 116.

31. Ibid., 113–16; Sparks, *Inside Lincoln's Army*, 401–2 (July 22, 1864); Agassiz, *Meade's Headquarters*, 192–93 (July 20, 1864); Meade to wife, July 20, 1864, Meade, *Life and Letters*, 2:214. Even Sylvanus Cadwallader questioned the tale that Butler had blackmailed Grant: "His drinking habits were so well known, he might have defied everybody." Cadwallader to Wilson, September 17, 1904, Wilson Papers, LC. Smith wasted no time in spreading the blackmail story, both in correspondence and through aides: see Sparks, *Inside Lincoln's Army*, 415 (August 19, 1864).

32. Catton, *Grant Takes Command*, 335; Agassiz, *Meade's Headquarters*, 193; Rawlins to Mary E. Rawlins, July 19, 1864, Wilson Papers, LC. Smith himself referred to Grant's in-

clusion of the critical correspondence; see Smith, *Autobiography*, 115. James H. Wilson later explained to Smith that Grant observed that Smith was "at odds with too many men, and some whom I can't overthrow"; Wilson to Smith, August 4, 1864, Lloyd Lewis–Bruce Catton Research Notes, USGA.

33. Agassiz, *Meade's Headquarters*, 193; Sparks, *Inside Lincoln's Army*, 400, 402 (July 20, 24, 1864). Butler reportedly had been discussing the Democratic nomination for some time; see William F. Smith to Solomon Foot, July 30, 1864, in Smith, *Autobiography*, 115. General William T. H. Brooks had resigned his commission (and thus command of the Tenth Corps) during the Butler-Smith controversy. See *PUSG*, 11:181–82.

34. Sparks, *Inside Lincoln's Army*, 403–4 (July 27, 1864); Meade to wife, July 29, 1864, Meade, *Life and Letters*, 2:216–17; Catton, *Grant Takes Command*, 316–17.

35. Catton, *Grant Takes Command*, 317–18.

36. W. Springer Menge and J. August Shimrak, eds., *The Civil War Notebook of Daniel Chisholm* (New York: Orion Books, 1989), 123; Catton, *Grant Takes Command*, 306–7.

37. Comstock Diary, July 24, 1864, Comstock Papers, LC: *New York Times*, May 31, 1914; Porter, *Campaigning*, 244–45.

38. Sparks, *Inside Lincoln's Army*, 403–4 (July 27, 1864).

39. Walker, *History of the Second Corps*, 559.

40. Comstock Diary, July 27, 29, 1864, Comstock Papers, LC; Walker, *History of the Second Corps*, 564–65; Grant to Halleck, July 28, 1864, *PUSG*, 11:332–33.

41. Sparks, *Inside Lincoln's Army*, 404 (July 27, 1864); Michael A. Cavanaugh and William Marvel, *The Battle of the Crater: "The Horrid Pit"* (Lynchburg, Va.: H. E. Howard, 1989), 16–17.

42. Cavanaugh and Marvel, *Battle of the Crater*, 17–18.

43. Grant to Burnside, July 26, 1864, and Grant to Meade, July 26, 1864, *PUSG*, 11:320–22; Grant to Meade, July 29, 1864, ibid., 11:344; Cavanaugh and Marvel, *Battle of the Crater*, 19.

44. Agassiz, *Meade's Headquarters*, 102.

45. Cavanaugh and Marvel, *Battle of the Crater*, 21–23; *PMUSG*, 2:311; *OR*, ser. 1, 40 (part 1):43–46, 137.

46. Agassiz, *Meade's Headquarters*, 197–98.

47. Porter, *Campaigning*, 264–67.

48. Ibid., 267–68; Agassiz, *Meade's Headquarters*, 200–1; Comstock Diary, July 30, 1864, Comstock Papers, LC.

49. Sparks, *Inside Lincoln's Army*, 405; Capt. George K. Leet to Rowley, August 9, 1864, *PUSG*, 11:363; Agassiz, *Meade's Headquarters*, 199–201 (July 31, 1864); Comstock Diary, July 30, 1864, Comstock Papers, LC.

50. *PUSG*, 11:364. Much debate persists concerning the abatis and parapets. Although historians who look on Burnside with far more charity than is usually the case suggest that these obstacles were at best minimal and "disintegrated in a twinkling," other writers note that the obstacles seriously hampered the attackers. Cavanaugh and Marvel, *Battle of the Crater*, 42, 115; Warren Wilkenson, *Mother, May You Never See the Sights I Have Seen: The Fifty-seventh Massachusetts Veteran Volunteers in the Last Year of the War* (New York: Harper & Row, 1990), 247–48. Wilkenson's assessment that the failure to remove the obstacles hindered the initial stages of the attack appears persuasive.

51. Grant to Halleck, August 1, 1864, *PUSG*, 11:361; Adam Badeau, *Military History of U. S. Grant* (New York: D. Appleton, 1881), 2:486; Grant to Meade, July 30, 1864, *PUSG*, 11:353.

52. Sparks, *Inside Lincoln's Army*, 409–10 (August 5, 1864); Meade to wife, August 3, 1864, *Life and Letters*, 2:218–19; Agassiz, *Meade's Headquarters*, 204 (August 1, 1864). Among those misled by what happened at the meeting is John Y. Simon, who offers an unconvincing analysis in "Grant, Lincoln, and Unconditional Surrender," in Gabor

Boritt, ed., *Lincoln's Generals* (New York: Oxford University Press, 1994), 178–80. The meeting came about because Grant and Lincoln needed to converse directly about matters connected to the defense of Washington and operations against Early's force. That Grant did not mention the encounter in his memoirs may reflect not his embarrassment at the encounter (for he frankly discussed the muddled command situation) but two more mundane facts connected with the composition of his text: his health was failing during the preparation of the second volume; and one of the texts on which he placed much reliance, Badeau's *Military History,* likewise failed to mention it. Simon's account does not refer to the sources cited in this note, which offer a detailed discussion of what happened on July 31.

53. Grant to Halleck, August 1, 1864, *PUSG,* 11:358; see the exchange of correspondence with Grant, Halleck, and Lincoln in ibid., 11:359–60.

54. Grant to Meade, August 1, 1864, ibid., 11:369; Theodore S. Bowers to James H. Wilson, August 1, 2, 1864, ibid., 11:363; Sparks, *Inside Lincoln's Army,* 409 (August 4, 1864); Grant to Butler, August 4, 1864, *PUSG,* 11:374; Comstock Diary, August 4, 1864, Comstock Papers, LC; Wilson to William F. Smith, August 4, 1864, Wilson Papers, LC.

55. Grant to David Hunter, August 5, 1864, *PUSG,* 11:378; Comstock Diary, August 5, 1864, Comstock Papers, LC.

56. Grant to Sheridan, August 7, 1864, *PUSG,* 11:380; Porter, *Campaigning,* 271–72.

57. Bowers to Rowley, August 9, 1864, Rowley Papers, ISHL; *PMUSG,* 2:317.

58. Howard K. Beale, ed., *Diary of Gideon Welles* (New York: W. W. Norton, 1960), 2:92 (August 2, 1864).

18. Celebrations and Salutes

1. Theodore S. Bowers to William R. Rowley, August 9, 1864, Rowley Papers, ISHL; Sherman to Grant, August 7, 1864, *PUSG,* 11:381; George R. Agassiz, ed., *Meade's Headquarters, 1863–1865: Letters of Colonel Theodore Lyman from The Wilderness to Appomattox* (Boston: Atlantic Monthly Press, 1922), 210 (August 9, 1864).

2. Grant to Halleck, August 9, 11, 1864, *PUSG,* 11:384; Porter, *Campaigning,* 273–74. Porter's figures of killed and wounded are far lower than those reported by Grant.

3. Noah Andre Trudeau, *The Last Citadel: Petersburg, Virginia, June 1864–April 1865* (Boston: Little, Brown, 1991), 143–57; Grant to Butler, August 12, 1864, *PUSG,* 11:406–7; Grant to Maj. Gen. Winfield S. Hancock, August 13, 1864, ibid., 11:411–12; Grant to Sheridan, August 14, 1864, ibid., 11:420. William B. Feis, "Neutralizing the Valley: The Role of Military Intelligence in the Defeat of Jubal Early's Army of the Valley, 1864–1865," *Civil War History* 39 (September 1993):199–215, explores how Grant learned about Confederate troop movements in Virginia.

4. Trudeau, *The Last Citadel,* 160–73; Grant to Hancock and Butler, August 19, 1864, *PUSG,* 12:45.

5. Trudeau, *The Last Citadel,* 175–89; Meade to wife, August 26, 1864, George Meade, *The Life and Letters of George Gordon Meade* (New York: Charles Scribner's Sons, 1913), 2:225 (August 26, 1864).

6. James H. Wilson, *The Life of John A. Rawlins* (New York: Neale Publishing, 1916), 257 (Theodore S. Bowers to Rawlins, August 10, 1864); Halleck to Grant, August 11, 1864, *PUSG,* 11:424–25.

7. Grant to Halleck, August 15, 1864, *PUSG,* 11:424.

8. Lincoln to Grant, August 17, 1864, *CWAL,* 7:499; Porter, *Campaigning,* 279.

9. Bruce Catton, *Grant Takes Command* (Boston: Little, Brown, 1969), 348; Grant to Stanton, August 15, 1864, *PUSG,* 11:422; Leet to Rowley, August 20, 1864, Rowley Papers, ISHL.

10. David S. Sparks, ed., *Inside Lincoln's Army: The Diary of Marsena Rudolph Patrick, Provost Marshal General, Army of the Potomac* (New York: Thomas Yoseloff, 1964), 415 (August 18, 19, 1864); Catton, *Grant Takes Command,* 340–41.

11. Grant to Sherman, August 9, 1864, *PUSG,* 11:389; Grant to Halleck, August 10, 1864, ibid., 11:392–93; Grant to Washburne, August 16, 1864, ibid., 12:16–17.

12. Bowers quoted in Leet to Rowley, August 23, 1864, Rowley Papers, ISHL; Catton, *Grant Takes Command,* 365–66.

13. John Eaton, *Grant, Lincoln, and the Freedmen* (New York: Longmans, Green, 1907), 188–89; Grant to Daniel Ammen, August 18, 1864, *PUSG,* 12:35; Wilson, *Rawlins,* 258 (Bowers to Rawlins, August 21, 1864); Comstock Diary, August 20, 1864, Comstock Papers, LC.

14. Grant to Ammen, August 18, 1864, *PUSG,* 12:35–36; Grant to Seward, August 19, 1864, ibid., 12:37–38.

15. Catton, *Grant Takes Command,* 352; Grant to Butler, August 18, 1864, *PUSG,* 12:27; Grant to William H. Seward, August 19, 1864, ibid., 12:38.

16. Lincoln to Grant, August 14, 1864, and Grant to Lincoln, August 17, 1864, *PUSG,* 12:17–18. See Virginia Laas, ed., *Wartime Washington: The Civil War Letters of Elizabeth Blair Lee* (Urbana: University of Illinois Press, 1991), 420.

17. Grant to Sheridan, August 16, 1864 (two dispatches), *PUSG,* 12:13, 15; Grant to Sheridan, August 21, 26, and September 4, 1864, ibid., 12:63, 97, and 127. In early September Grant called for the prompt removal of General Eleazer A. Paine from command of the District of Western Kentucky. "He is not fit to have a command where there is a solitary family within his reach favorable to the Government," he informed Halleck; Paine's measures in disciplining the civilian population (including several executions without trial) were so extreme that while Grant observed that Paine might "do to put in an intensely disloyal district to scourge the people . . . even then it is doubtful whether it comes within the bounds of civilized warfare to use him." Grant to Halleck, September 4, 1864, ibid., 12:124.

18. Patrick, *Inside Lincoln's Army,* 417–18; Grant to Julia Grant, August 25, 1864, *PUSG,* 12:90–91; Wilson, *Rawlins,* 258 (Bowers to Rawlins, August 25, 1864); Grant to Ammen, August 18, 1864, *PUSG,* 12:36; Grant to Lincoln, August 29, 1864, ibid., 12:100–1; Comstock Diary, August 30, 1864, Comstock Papers, LC; Porter, *Campaigning,* 283. Grant's testimony before the Committee on the Conduct of the War concerning the Crater is in *PUSG,* 12:111–12.

19. Comstock Diary, September 3, 1864, Comstock Papers, LC; Porter, *Campaigning,* 285–86.

20. Grant to Sherman, September 12, 1864, *PUSG,* 12:155; Grant to Jesse Grant, September 5, 1864, ibid., 12:130; Grant to Julia Grant, September 5, 7, 1864, ibid., 12:130–31, 136.

21. Grant to Sherman, September 10, 1864, ibid., 12:144, 154–55; Grant to Sheridan, September 9, 1864, ibid., 12:139.

22. Grant to Stanton, September 13, 1864, ibid., 12:158–59.

23. Grant to Sheridan, September 8, 9, 1864, ibid., 12:137, 139.

24. Porter, *Campaigning,* 297–98; Catton, *Grant Takes Command,* 363.

25. Catton, *Grant Takes Command,* 363; Grant to Julia Grant, September 14, 20, 1864, *PUSG,* 12:166, 179–80; Grant to Halleck, September 17, 1864 (two telegrams), ibid., 12:171; *New York Tribune,* September 19, 1864.

26. Porter, *Campaigning,* 298.

27. Grant to Stanton, September 20, 1864, *PUSG,* 12:175; Grant to Sheridan, September 20, 1864, ibid., 12:177; Grant to Meade, September 23, 1864, ibid., 12:192; Grant to Sheridan, September 23, 26, 1864, ibid., 12:193, 208.

28. Leet to Rowley, September 23, 1864, Rowley Papers, ISHL; Grant to Julia Grant, September 25, 1864, *PUSG,* 12:206.

29. Grant to Butler, September 27, 1864, *PUSG,* 12:219–21; Grant to Meade, September 27, 1864, ibid., 12:222–23; Grant to Julia Grant, September 28, 1864, ibid., 12:228.

30. Richard J. Sommers, *Richmond Redeemed: The Siege at Petersburg* (Garden City, N.Y.: Doubleday & Co., 1981), 75; Porter, *Campaigning with Grant,* 301–2; *Burlington (Vermont) Free Press,* July 29, 1885. Porter also reports (300–1) that little Jesse Grant accompanied his father into action, but Grant's letters to Julia suggest that the general's youngest child was with his mother in New Jersey at this time: see Grant to Julia Grant, September 25, October 2, 1864, *PUSG,* 12:207, 262.

31. Porter, *Campaigning,* 302–3; Lincoln to Grant, September 29, 1864, *CWAL,* 8:29; Grant to Lincoln, September 29, 1864, *PUSG,* 12:228–29.

32. Grant to Julia Grant, September 29, 1864, *PUSG,* 12:241; Grant to Butler, September 29, 1864, ibid., 12:237; Grant to Meade, September 30, 1864, ibid., 12:247.

33. Grant to Meade, September 30, 1864, ibid., 12:249.

34. Brooks D. Simpson, *Let Us Have Peace: Ulysses S. Grant and the Politics of War and Reconstruction, 1861–1868* (Chapel Hill: University of North Carolina Press, 1991), 65.

35. William T. Sherman, *Memoirs of W. T. Sherman* (New York: Appleton, 1875), 2:137–40; Grant to Stanton, September 20, 1864, *PUSG,* 12:174–75; Grant to Julia Grant, September 30, 1864, ibid., 12:250–51.

36. Sherman to Grant, September 20, 1864, *PUSG,* 12:156–57; Sherman to Grant, October 1, 1864, ibid., 12:273–74.

37. Halleck to Grant, October 2, 1864, and Grant to Halleck, October 4, 1864, ibid., 12:272–75; Grant to Meade, October 3, 1864, ibid., 12:267; Grant to Sherman, October 11, 1864, ibid., 12:289–90; Comstock Diary, October 3, 6, 1864, Comstock Papers, LC. On the lost dispatch, see Porter, *Campaigning,* 316–18.

38. Sherman to Grant, October 9, 1864, *PUSG,* 12:291; Grant to Julia Grant, October 10, 1864, ibid., 12:284–85; Grant to Sherman, October 11, 12, 1864, ibid., 1:290, 298.

39. Stanton to Grant, October 12, 1864, ibid., 12:303; Grant to Stanton, October 13, 1864, ibid., 12:302–3; Grant to Halleck, October 13, 14, 1864, ibid., 12:304–5.

40. Porter, *Campaigning,* 314–18.

41. Lee to Grant, October 18, 1864, *PUSG,* 12:324–26; Simpson, *Let Us Have Peace,* 66. On the Crater see Bryce A. Suderow, "The Battle of the Crater: The Civil War's Worse Massacre," *Civil War History* 43 (September 1997):219–24.

42. Grant to Lee, October 20, 1864, *PUSG,* 12:323–24.

43. Entry, November 13, 1863, William W. Smith Diary, LC; Jesse Grant, *In the Days of My Father General Grant* (New York: Harper and Brothers, 1925), 21; *PMJDG,* 132.

44. Joseph P. Farley, *Three Rivers: The James, The Potomac, The Hudson* (New York: Neale Publishing, 1910), 88; Agassiz, *Meade's Headquarters,* 247–50; Porter, *Campaigning,* 304–6; Richard S. Cramer, ed., "An Artist's Close-up View of Lincoln, Grant, and Sherman," *U. S. Grant: An Appraisal and Six Vignettes* (Jamestown, Va.: Eastern Acorn Press, 1983), 25; Sylvanus Cadwallader, *Three Years with Grant* (Lincoln: University of Nebraska Press, 1996 [1955]), 223–25.

45. Philip H. Sheridan, *Personal Memoirs of P. H. Sheridan* (New York: Charles L. Webster, 1888), 2:53–67; Grant to Butler, October 3, 1864, *PUSG,* 12:266; Grant to Sheridan, October 3, 14, 1864, ibid., 12:268, 312; Grant to Halleck, October 11, 1864, ibid., 12:286.

46. Porter, *Campaigning,* 307–8.

47. Bowers to Rowley, October 22, 1864, Rowley Papers, ISHL.

48. Grant to Butler, October 20 (24?), 1864, *PUSG,* 12:331–32; Grant to Meade, October 24, 1864, ibid., 12:343–44; Comstock Diary, October 27, 1864, Comstock Papers, LC; Porter, *Campaigning,* 310–11; Francis A. Walker, *History of the Second Army Corps* (New York: Charles Scribner's Sons, 1887), 623–24.

49. Walker, *History of the Second Corps,* 625–38.

50. Grenville Dodge to Richard Oglesby, October 29, 1864, Oglesby Papers, ISHL; Catton, *Grant Takes Command*, 383.

51. Grant to Sheridan, October 21, 1864, ibid., 12:334; Sheridan to Grant, October 25, 1864, ibid., 12:335.

52. Leet to Rowley, November 1, 1864, Rowley Papers, ISHL.

53. Grant to Stanton, September 27, 1864, *PUSG*, 12:212–14.

54. Eaton, *Grant, Lincoln, and the Freedmen*, 190–91 (Eaton admitted later that he raised the issue at Lincoln's request); Grant to Washburne, September 21, 1864, *PUSG*, 12:185.

55. Michael R. Morgan, "From City Point to Appomattox with General Grant," *Journal of the Military Service Institution* 149 (September–October 1907), 234.

56. Grant to Julia Grant, November 9, 1864, *PUSG*, 12:398.

57. William T. Sherman, "The Grand Strategy of the Last Year of the War," Robert U. Johnson and Clarence C. Buel, eds., *Battles and Leaders of the Civil War* (New York: Century, 1887), 4:250; *CWAL*, 8:101.

19. Give Him No Peace

1. Grant to Halleck, October 27, 1864, *PUSG*, 12:354; Grant to Rawlins, October 29, 1864, ibid., 12:363–64; Adam Badeau, *Military History of U. S. Grant* (New York: D. Appleton, 1881), 3:156–57; James H. Wilson, *The Life of John A. Rawlins* (New York: Neale Publishing, 1916), 270, which shows that Rawlins traveled to Washington with Halleck.

2. Grant to Sherman, November 1, 1864, *PUSG*, 12:370–71. Grant to Sherman, November 2, 1864, ibid., 12:373; Sherman to Grant, November 6, 1864, ibid., 12:375.

3. Grant to Sherman, November 7, 1864, ibid., 12:394; *New York Times*, November 22, 1864.

4. Grant to Sheridan, November 9, 1864, *PUSG*, 12:397; Grant to Stanton, November 13, 1864, ibid., 12:413; Grant to Meade, November 15, 1864, ibid., 12:423.

5. Grant to J. Russell Jones, November 13, 1864, ibid., 12:415–16.

6. David S. Sparks, ed., *Inside Lincoln's Army: The Diary of Marsena Rudolph Patrick, Provost Marshal General, Army of the Potomac* (New York: Thomas Yoseloff, 1964), 442, 445; Grant to Sheridan, November 19, 1864, *PUSG*, 13:5; Grant to Rawlins, November 19, 1864, ibid., 13:10–12; Grant to Stanton, November 23, 1864, ibid., 13:16–17; Grant to Thomas, [November 23, 1864], ibid., 13:17–18; Grant to Halleck, November 25, 1864, ibid., 13:24–25; Grant to Julia Grant, November 25, 1864, ibid., 13:26–27; Sylvanus Cadwallader, *Three Years with Grant* (Lincoln: University of Nebraska Press, 1996 [1955]), 267–70. On Rosecrans, see also Rosecrans to Grant, February 18, 1865, *PUSG*, 13:29; on Banks, see Lincoln to Banks, December 2, 1864, *CWAL*, 8:131.

7. Stanton to Grant, May 12, 1864, *PUSG*, 10:435; Scott to Washburne, July 2, 1864, and Grant to Scott, July 23, 1864, ibid., 11:298–99; Albert D. Richardson, *Personal History of Ulysses S. Grant* (Hartford, Conn.: American Publishing, 1868), 445. Back in 1862 Scott had spoken highly of Grant; Gaillard Hunt, *Israel, Elihu, and Cadwallader Washburn: A Chapter in American Biography* (New York: Macmillan, 1925), 205.

8. Grant to Thomas, November 24, 1864, *PUSG*, 13:21, 24; Thomas to Grant, ibid., 13:24.

9. Grant to Meade, November 28, 1864, ibid., 13:30; Grant to Halleck, November 30, 1864, ibid., 13:34–35; Grant to David D. Porter, November 30, 1864, ibid., 13:36; Grant to Butler, November 30, 1864, ibid., 13:37; see also ibid., 13:39.

10. Lincoln, Annual Message, December 6, 1864, *CWAL*, 8:148; *New York Tribune*, De-

cember 8, 1864; Stanton to Grant, December 2, 1864, *PUSG*, 13:50. Stephen Z. Starr's "Grant and Thomas: December, 1864," presented to the Cincinnati Civil War Round Table in April 1961, is a rather passionate brief for Thomas and against Grant. I am indebted to David M. Smith for calling it to my attention.

11. Grant to Stanton, December 2, 1864 (two dispatches), *PUSG*, 13:49–50; Grant to Halleck, December 2, 1864, ibid., 13:51; Grant to Thomas, December 2, 1864 (two dispatches), ibid., 13:52–53. Badeau, *Military History*, 3:215–16, highlights the relationship between Grant's messages to Thomas and Stanton's December 2 wire.

12. Halleck to Grant, December 3, 1864, *PUSG*, 13:51; Halleck to Grant, December 5, 1864, ibid., 13:50; Thomas to Grant, December 2, 1864, ibid., 13:53–54.

13. Grant to Meade, December 3, 1864 (two dispatches), ibid., 13:55–56; Grant to Sherman, December 3, 1864, ibid., 13:56–57.

14. Grant to Butler, December 4, 1864, ibid., 13:61; Grant to Sheridan, December 4, 1864, ibid., 13:62; Grant to Meade, December 5, 1864, ibid., 13:64–65; Grant to Thomas, December 5, 1864, and Thomas to Grant, December 6, 1864, ibid., 13:67–68. Accounts of the Grant-Thomas exchanges prior to Nashville that defend Thomas assert that Grant was sitting inactive before Richmond and Petersburg at the same time he was urging Thomas to attack. An examination of Grant's correspondence reveals that the general-in-chief wanted action on several fronts, including Virginia.

15. James H. Wilson, *Under the Old Flag* (New York: D. Appleton, 1912), 1:274–76.

16. Grant to Thomas, December 6, 1864, *PUSG*, 13:77; Thomas to Grant, December 6, 1864, ibid., 13:77; Stanton to Grant, December 7, 1864, ibid., 13:79; Grant to Stanton, December 7, 1864, ibid., 13:78–79.

17. Grant to Halleck, December 8, 1864, ibid., 13:83.

18. Halleck to Grant, December 8, 1864, and Grant to Halleck, December 8, 1864, ibid., 13:84.

19. Grant to Thomas, December 8, 1864, ibid., 13:87–88.

20. Grant to Halleck, December 9, 1864, ibid., 13:90; Halleck to Grant, December 9, 1864, ibid., 13:90.

21. Thomas to Grant, December 9, 1864, ibid., 13:87–88.

22. Grant to Halleck, December 9, 1864, ibid., 13:90–91; Grant to Thomas, December 9, 1864, ibid., 13:96.

23. Grant to Thomas, December 11, 1864, and Thomas to Grant, December 11, 1864, ibid., 13:107.

24. See ibid., 13:128, Grant to Thomas, December 15, 1864, ibid., 13:124; David L. Wilson and John Y. Simon, eds., *Ulysses S. Grant: Essays and Documents* (Carbondale: Southern Illinois University Press, 1981), 118. For a different interpretation of the Grant-Thomas relationship, see Thomas B. Buell, *The Warrior Generals: Combat Leadership in the Civil War* (New York: Crown, 1997).

25. Grant to Logan, December 17, 1864, *PUSG*, 13:127; Grant to Thomas, December 18, 1864, ibid., 13:134. When Lincoln heard of the action on December 15, he betrayed a hint of his own impatience in observing to Thomas: "You have made a magnificent beginning. A grand consummation is within your easy reach. Do not let it slip." Lincoln to Thomas, December 16, 1864, *CWAL*, 8:169.

26. Grant to Julia Grant, December 20, 22, 1864, *PUSG*, 13:149, 152–53.

27. Grant to Meade, December 19, 1864, ibid., 13:135–36; also ibid., 13:138–42.

28. Grant to Julia Grant, December 24, 1864, ibid., 13:163; Grant to Stanton, December 25, 1864, ibid; Grant to Julia Grant, December 26, 1864, ibid., 13:167–68.

29. *PMUSG*, 2:387–91.

30. Ibid., 2:391–95; Grant to Lincoln, December 28, 1864, *PUSG*, 13:177–78.

31. David S. Sparks, ed., *Inside Lincoln's Army: The Diary of Marsena Rudolph Patrick, Provost Marshal General, Army of the Potomac* (New York: Thomas Yoseloff, 1964), 454;

Grant to Porter, December 30, 1864, *PUSG*, 13:190; Grant to Stanton, December 30, 1864, ibid., 13:183–84; Grant to Stanton, January 2, 1865, ibid., 13:204–5; Grant to Terry, January 3, 1865, ibid., 13:219; Grant to Stanton, January 4, 1865, ibid., 13:223; Grant to Lincoln, January 6, 1865, ibid., 13:223.

32. Edward O. C. Ord to Grant, January 11, 1865, *PUSG*, 13:224; Grant to Daniel Ammen, February 4, 1865, ibid., 13:366.

33. For a discussion of the January operation, see Rowena Reed, *Combined Operations in the Civil War* (Annapolis: U.S. Naval Institute Press, 1978), 355–83.

34. Grant to Stanton, December 20, 23, 1864, *PUSG*, 13:143–44; Grant to Thomas, December 22, 1864, ibid., 13:151; Halleck to Grant, December 30, 1864, ibid., 13:188; Grant to Halleck, January 7, 1865, ibid., 13:245; Grant to Sherman, January 21, 1865, ibid., 13:291–92; S. S. Cox to Manton Marble, January 12, 1865, Marble Papers, LC.

35. Grant to Stanton, [January 1–3, 1865], *PUSG*, 13:199–200; Grant to Washburne, January 23, 1865, ibid., 13:299; Meade to wife, January 10, 1865, George Meade, ed., *The Life and Letters of George Gordon Meade* (New York: Charles Scribner's Sons, 1913), 2: 255; Meade to Henry A. Cram, January 21, 1865, ibid., 2:256–57; Meade to wife, February 2, 1865, ibid., 2:260. Sergeant Meade died February 21, 1865.

36. Grant to Sherman, December 18, 1864, *PUSG*, 13:129–30; Grant to Jesse Grant, December 20, 1864, ibid., 13:148–49; Grant to H. H. Hunter et al., December 22, 1864, ibid., 13:153–54; Grant to Julia Grant, January 1, 1865, ibid., 13:203.

37. Grant to Sherman, December 18, 27, 1864, ibid., 13:129–30, 168–70.

38. Grant to Halleck, January 18, 1865, ibid., 13:273; Grant to Thomas, January 31, 1865, ibid., 13:342–44.

39. Grant to E. D. Townsend, December 31, 1864, ibid., 13:195; Grant to Halleck, December 31, 1864, ibid., 13:196, Grant to Ethan A. Hitchcock, February 16, 1865, ibid., 13:431; Grant to Halleck, February 18, 1865, ibid., 13:439–40; Grant to Stanton, February 19, 1865, ibid., 13:444–45.

40. Grant to Lieut. Col. Charles E. Fuller, July 16, 1864, ibid., 11:265; *PMJDG*, 138.

41. Horace Porter, *Campaigning with Grant* (New York: The Century Co., 1897), 365–66; *PMJDG*, 135.

42. Julia Grant to Lillian Rogers, February 7, 1865, Grant Papers, LC, quoted in Geoffrey Perret, *Ulysses S. Grant: Soldier and President* (New York: Random House, 1997), 349.

43. Porter, *Campaigning*, 284–85; Albert D. Richardson, *Personal History of Ulysses S. Grant* (Hartford, Conn.: American Publishing, 1868), 445; *PMJDG*, 135; on the Grants and the photographer, see the sketch in the Charles W. Reed Papers, LC.

44. *PMJDG*, 136–37; Grant to Stanton, January 24, 1865, *PUSG*, 13:303; Grant to Washburne, January 24, 1865, ibid., 13:321; Porter, *Campaigning*, 376–80.

45. See *PUSG*, 13:260–62.

46. Grant to George H. Stuart et al., January 4, 1865, ibid., 13:234; George H. Stuart, *The Life of George H. Stuart* (Philadelphia: J. M. Stoddart, 1890), 183.

47. See *PUSG*, 13:209–10; Grant to Irvin McDowell, January 8, 1865, ibid., 13:250–51; Grant to Blair, January 8, 1865, ibid., 13:254–55; on Wallace, see ibid., 13:282–90.

48. On Grant and the Hampton Roads Conference, see Howard C. Westwood, "The Signing Wire Conspiracy: Manipulation of Men and Measures for Peace," *Civil War Times Illustrated* 19 (December 1980):30–35; Brooks D. Simpson, *Let Us Have Peace: Ulysses S. Grant and the Politics of War and Reconstruction, 1861–1868* (Chapel Hill: University of North Carolina Press, 1991), 72–75; Grant to Lincoln, January 31, 1865, *PUSG*, 13:333–34.

49. Simpson, *Let Us Have Peace*, 73–74; Porter, *Campaigning*, 384–85.

50. Grant to Stanton, February 1, 1865, *PUSG*, 13:345–46; see *CWAL*, 8: 281–82.

51. *PMJDG*, 137–38.

52. Grant to Isaac N. Morris, February 15, 1865, *PUSG*, 13:429; Grant to Stanton, February 4, 1865, ibid., 13:362; *New York Tribune*, August 5, 1885; Porter, *Campaigning*, 330–31.

53. Grant to Meade, February 4, 1865, *PUSG*, 13:365; Grant to Meade, February 6, 1865, ibid., 13:382; Grant to Sheridan, February 8, 13, 20, 1865, ibid., 13:394, 395, 457–58.

54. Meade to wife, January 14, 1865, Meade, *Life and Letters*, 2:256; Grant to Meade, February 9, 1865, *PUSG*, 13:399; Grant's testimony is ibid., 13:400–12; William F. G. Shanks, *Personal Recollections of Distinguished Generals* (New York: Harper and Brothers, 1866), 116, 121; Bruce Tap, *Over Lincoln's Shoulder: The Committee on the Conduct of the War* (Lawrence: University Press of Kansas, 1998), 234–42.

55. Charles Royster, *The Destructive War: William Tecumseh Sherman, Stonewall Jackson, and the Americans* (New York: Knopf, 1991), 3–4; Grant to Washburne, February 23, 1865, *PUSG*, 13:30–31.

56. Grant to Edward D. Kittoe, ibid., 14:42–43; Grant to E. R. S. Canby, February 27, 1865, ibid., 14:61–63.

57. Simpson, *Let Us Have Peace*, 75–76; Porter, *Campaigning*, 391–92.

58. See Ord's comments, *PUSG*, 14:63–64.

59. Lee to Grant, March 2, 1865 (two letters), ibid., 14:99.

60. *PMJDG*, 140–41; Grant to Stanton, March 3, 1865, *PUSG*, 14:90–91.

61. Stanton to Grant, March 3, 1865, *PUSG*, 14:91 (first message).

62. Stanton to Grant, March 3, 1865, *PUSG*, 14:91 (second message).

63. Grant to Stanton, March 4, 1865, and Grant to Lee, March 4, 1865, *PUSG*, 14:100, 98–99; Porter, *Campaigning*, 390.

64. Grant to Charles W. Ford, March 1, 1865, *PUSG*, 14:79–80; Grant to Meade and Ord, March 14, 1864, ibid., 14:161–62; Grant to Stanton, March 2, 1865 (three dispatches), ibid., 14:81–84; Grant to Stanton, March 14, 1865, ibid., 14:156; Grant to Meade, March 14, 1865, ibid., 14:159. Grant's letter to Sherman of March 16, 1865 (ibid., 14:172–75), contains a summary of his frustrations.

65. Ibid., 14:131–32; Porter, *Campaigning*, 393–94.

66. Grant to Jesse Grant, March 19, 1865, *PUSG*, 14:186–87.

20. Ending the Matter

1. Allan Nevins, ed., *A Diary of Battle: The Personal Journals of Colonel Charles S. Wainwright, 1861–1865* (New York: Harcourt, Brace and World, 1962), 501; Emil and Ruth Rosenblatt, eds., *Hard Marching Every Day: The Civil War Letters of Private Wilbur Fisk, 1861–1865* (Lawrence: University Press of Kansas, 1992), 317; *PMJDG*, 142.

2. *PMJDG*, 141–42.

3. Lincoln to Grant, March 8, 1865, *CWAL*, 8:343–44.

4. Grant to Lincoln, January 21, 1865, *PUSG*, 13:281; Lincoln to Grant, February 8, 1865, ibid., 13:347. Lincoln's assessment of Grant's role in bringing about the Hampton Roads conference differs from that offered by John Y. Simon in "Grant, Lincoln, and Unconditional Surrender," in Gabor S. Boritt, ed., *Lincoln's Generals* (New York: Oxford University Press, 1994), 190–92.

5. *PMUSG*, 2:424–25; Grant to Sheridan, March 19, 1865, *PUSG*, 14:182–83; Grant to Sheridan, March 21, 1865, ibid., 14:195–96; Grant to Sherman, March 22, 1865, ibid., 14:202–4; Grant to Meade, March 24, 1865, ibid., 14:211–14. The desertion estimate is derived from John Horn, *The Petersburg Campaign* (Conshocken, Pa.: Combined Books, 1993), 217–18.

6. *PMUSG*, 2: 431–34; Horace Porter, *Campaigning with Grant* (New York: The Century Co., 1897), 404–6; Lincoln to Stanton, March 25, 1865, *CWAL*, 8:373.

7. Grant to Meade, March 25, 1865, *PUSG*, 14:223; Lincoln to Stanton, March 25, 1865, *CWAL*, 8:374; Jesse R. Grant, *In the Days of My Father General Grant* (New York: Harper & Brothers, 1925), 23–27; William H. Crook, *Across Five Administrations* (compiled and edited by Margarita S. Gerry; New York: Harper and Brothers, 1915), 42–43.

8. Porter, *Campaigning*, 412–15; *PMJDG*, 146–47; Adam Badeau, *Grant in Peace* (Hartford: S. S. Scranton, 1887), 356–59.

9. Badeau, *Grant in Peace*, 356–57, 362; *PMJDG*, 142.

10. Porter, *Campaigning*, 411–12.

11. Ibid., 417–18.

12. Ibid., 420–21; *PMJDG*, 135.

13. Albert D. Richardson, *Personal History of Ulysses S. Grant* (Hartford, Conn.: American Publishing, 1868), 457; Porter, *Campaigning*, 450–51.

14. Brooks D. Simpson, *Let Us Have Peace: Ulysses S. Grant and the Politics of War and Reconstruction, 1861–1868* (Chapel Hill: University of North Carolina Press, 1991), 78.

15. William T. Sherman, *Memoirs of W. T. Sherman* (New York: D. Appleton, 1875), 2:325–31.

16. Lee to Agnes Lee, March 28, 1865, Clifford Dowdey and Louis H. Manarin, eds., *The Wartime Papers of Robert E. Lee* (New York: DaCapo, 1987), 919; Grant to Sheridan, March 28, 1865, *PUSG*, 14:241; John Russell Young, *Around the World with General Grant* (New York: American News, 1879), 2:357; Adam Badeau, *Military History of U. S. Grant* (New York: D. Appleton, 1881), 3:451.

17. Michael Burlingame, ed., *Lincoln Observed: Civil War Dispatches of Noah Brooks* (Baltimore: The Johns Hopkins University Press, 1998), 180; Porter, *Campaigning*, 425–26.

18. Porter, *Campaigning*, 426–28; Grant to Lincoln, March 29, 1865 (two telegrams), *PUSG*, 14:248; Grant to Julia Grant, March 30, 1865, ibid., 14:272–73.

19. Grant to Sheridan, March 29, 1865, *PUSG*, 14:253–54; Grant to Meade, March 30, 1865 (three messages), ibid., 14:260–63; Grant to Sheridan, March 30, 1865, ibid., 14:270; Badeau, *Military History*, 3:455–56; Porter, *Campaigning*, 428–29.

20. Grant to Meade, March 31, 1865, *PUSG*, 14:274–75.

21. Sheridan to Grant, March 31, 1865, and Grant to Sheridan, same date, ibid., 14:287–88.

22. Porter, *Campaigning*, 434; Grant to Julia Grant, April 1, 1865, *PUSG*, 14:310–11.

23. Porter, *Campaigning*, 435.

24. Porter to Rawlins, April 1, 1865, *PUSG*, 14:295.

25. Porter, *Campaigning*, 442–43.

26. Ibid., 442–43; Grant to Meade, April 1, 1865 (three telegrams), *PUSG*, 14:297–99; Grant to Ord, April 1, 1865, ibid., 14:303; Grant to Sheridan, April 1, 1865, ibid., 14:306.

27. George R. Agassiz, ed., *Meade's Headquarters, 1863–1865: Letters of Theodore Lyman from The Wilderness to Appomattox* (Boston: Atlantic Monthly Press, 1922), 333–34. Stephen W. Sears offers an overview of the Sheridan-Warren controversy in *Controversies and Commanders: Dispatches from the Army of the Potomac* (Boston: Houghton Mifflin, 1999).

28. Porter, *Campaigning*, 444–46.

29. Ibid., 446–47.

30. Grant to Julia Grant, April 2, 1865, *PUSG*, 14:330.

31. Porter, *Campaigning*, 447–48; Grant to Bowers, April 2, 1865, *PUSG*, 14:327; James H. Wilson, *The Life of John A. Rawlins* (New York: Neale Publishing, 1916), 316.

32. Grant to Sheridan, April 3, 1865, *PUSG*, 14:336; *PMUSG*, 2:454–56.

33. Grant to Sheridan, April 3, 1865, *PUSG*, 14:336; Catton, *Stillness at Appomattox*, 364; Porter, *Campaigning*, 449–51; Agassiz, *Meade's Headquarters*, 340–41; Crook, *Across Five Administrations*, 30.

34. Porter, *Campaigning*, 452; Grant to Sherman, April 3, 1865, *PUSG*, 14:339.

35. Grant to Stanton, April 4, 1865, *PUSG*, 14:343; Grant to Sherman, April 5, 1865, ibid., 14:352; Grant to Meade, April 5, 1865, ibid., 14:350. For campaign strengths and losses, see Christopher M. Calkins, *From Petersburg to Appomattox* (Farmville: The Farmville Herald, 1983), 44.

36. W. Springer Menge and J. August Shimrak, eds., *The Civil War Notebook of Daniel Chisholm* (New York: Orion Books, 1989), 75.

37. Porter, *Campaigning*, 453–54.

38. Ibid., 454–56; Bruce Catton, *Grant Takes Command* (Boston: Little, Brown, 1909), 452–53; Sylvanus Cadwallader, *Three Years with Grant* (Lincoln: University of Nebraska Press, 1996 [1955]), 313; Badeau, *Military History*, 3:563–64; *PMUSG*, 2:469; Young, *Around the World with General Grant*, 2:302–3. In *Meade at Gettysburg* (Norman: University of Oklahoma Press, 1960), 325, Freeman Cleaves rather weakly asserts that the meeting between Grant, Meade, and Sheridan did not take place, although he offers nothing to challenge the accounts of Badeau, Grant, Porter, and Sheridan.

39. Sheridan to Grant, April 6, 1865, *PUSG*, 14:358.

40. Grant to Theodore S. Bowers, April 6, 1865, ibid., 14:359–60; Grant to Sherman, April 6, 1865, ibid., 14:359.

41. Cadwallader, *Three Years*, 315; Lincoln to Grant, April 6, 1865, *CWAL*, 8:388; *PMUSG*, 2:477–78.

42. Grant to Julia Grant, April 7, 1865, *PUSG*, 14:366; Porter, *Campaigning*, 457–58.

43. Porter, *Campaigning*, 458–59.

44. Grant to Lee, April 7, 1865, *PUSG*, 14:361; Porter, *Campaigning*, 459–60; John Gibbon, *Recollections of the Civil War* (Dayton: Morningside House, 1988 [1928]), 304–7; Frank P. Cauble, *The Surrender Proceedings: April 9, 1865, Appomattox Court House* (Lynchburg, Va.: H. E. Howard, 1987), 2.

45. Lee to Grant, April 7, 1865, *PUSG*, 14:361.

46. Grant to Lee, April 8, 1865, ibid., 14:367; Grant to Stanton, April 8, 1865, ibid.

47. Grant to Sheridan, April 8, 1865, and Sheridan to Grant, April 8, 1865, ibid., 14:369; Lincoln to Grant, April 7, 1865, *CWAL*, 8:392; Agassiz, *Meade's Headquarters*, 354.

48. Cadwallader, *Three Years*, 317.

49. Ibid., 317–18; Lee to Grant, April 8, 1865, *PUSG*, 14:367.

50. Cadwallader, *Three Years*, 318–20; Porter, *Campaigning*, 462–64.

51. Grant to Lee, April 9, 1865, *PUSG*, 14:371; Porter, *Campaigning*, 464–65.

52. Cadwallader, *Three Years*, 322.

53. Ibid., 322–323; Lee to Grant, April 9, 1865, *PUSG*, 14:373; Grant to Lee, April 9, 1865, ibid., 14:372–73; Porter, *Campaigning*, 468; *PMUSG*, 2:485.

54. The following account of the events that took place on the afternoon of April 9, 1865, in Wilmer McLean's parlor is drawn from the following sources: *PMUSG*, 2:488–95; Porter, *Campaigning*, 472–86; Cauble, *The Surrender Proceedings*, 47–59, 119; Badeau to Wilson, May 27, 1865, Wilson Papers, LC; "Ely S. Parker's Narrative," Grant Papers, LC; Orville E. Babcock's account of the surrender c. 1877, Grant Papers, CHS; Catton, *Grant Takes Command*, 463–67.

55. Grant to Lee, April 9, 1865, *PUSG*, 14:373–74.

56. Porter, *Campaigning*, 486; Badeau, *Military History*, 3:608.

57. Grant to Stanton, April 9, 1865, *PUSG*, 14:375; Porter, *Campaigning*, 488–89; Badeau, *Military History*, 3:608–9.

21. Peace

1. Albert D. Richardson, *Personal History of Ulysses S. Grant* (Hartford, Conn.: American Publishing, 1868), 488; see *PUSG*, 2:15.

2. Horace Porter, *Campaigning with Grant* (New York: Century Co., 1897), 489–90; Sylvanus Cadwallader, *Three Years with Grant* (Lincoln: University of Nebraska Press, 1996 [1955]), 334; Adam Badeau, *Military History of U. S. Grant* (New York: D. Appleton, 1881), 3:610–11.

3. For Lee's actions in February and March, see Douglas S. Freeman, *Lee* (New York: Scribner's, 1933–37), 4:2–10.

4. *PMUSG*, 2:497; John Russell Young, *Around the World with General Grant* (New York: American News, 1879), 2:458; Freeman, *Lee*, 4:8–9; Charles A. Dana to Edwin M. Stanton, April 12, 1865, *OR*, 46 (part 3):716–17.

5. Cadwallader, *Three Years*, 333; Gary W. Gallagher, ed., *Fighting for the Confederacy: The Personal Recollections of General Edward Porter Alexander* (Chapel Hill: University of North Carolina Press, 1989), 540; Allan Nevins, ed., *A Diary of Battle: The Personal Journals of Colonel Charles S. Wainwright, 1861–1865* (New York: Harcourt, Brace & World, 1962), 523.

6. Porter, *Campaigning*, 491–92; Frank A. Burr, *The Life and Deeds of General U. S. Grant* (Philadelphia: National Publishing, 1885), 813; Badeau, *Military History*, 3:611–13; Longstreet in the *New York Times*, July 24, 1885.

7. Chris M. Calkins, *The Final Bivouac: The Surrender Parade at Appomattox and the Disbanding of the Armies, April 10–May 20, 1865* (Lynchburg, Va.: H. E. Howard, 1988), 16; Richardson, *Personal History*, 489; Grant to Stanton, April 10, 1865, *PUSG*, 15:379, 380 (two telegrams).

8. *PMJDG*, 149–51.

9. Ibid., 153; Porter, *Campaigning*, 493–94; Edward Pollard, *The Lost Cause* (New York: E. B. Treat and Co., 1867), 712.

10. David S. Sparks, ed., *Inside Lincoln's Army: The Diary of Marsena Rudolph Patrick, Provost Marshal General, Army of the Potomac* (New York: Thomas Yoseloff, 1964), 494 (April 13, 1865); Young, *Around the World with General Grant*, 2:356; David D. Porter, *Incidents and Anecdotes of the Civil War* (New York: D. Appleton, 1885), 314; William T. Sherman, *Memoirs of W. T. Sherman* (New York: Appleton, 1875), 2:329; Gibbon to Grant, April 13, 1865, *PUSG*, 14:384; James G. Randall and Richard N. Current, *Lincoln: The Last Full Measure* (New York: Dodd, Mead, 1955), 351–52.

11. *Washington (DC) Intelligencer*, April 14, 1865; *New York Times*, April 12, 14, 1865; *New York Herald*, April 11, 12, 15, 1865.

12. *New York Times*, April 11, 1865; *Washington (DC) Star*, April 13, 1865; *New York Herald*, April 14, 1865, citing the *New York Tribune;* Len Gougeon, *Virtue's Hero: Emerson, Antislavery, and Reform* (Athens: University of Georgia Press, 1990), 314; Hans L. Trefousse, *Andrew Johnson: A Biography* (New York: W. W. Norton, 1989), 192.

13. Howard K. Beale, ed., *The Diary of Gideon Welles* (New York: W. W. Norton, 1960), 2:280–83 (April 14, 1865); Bruce Catton, *Grant Takes Command* (Boston: Little, Brown, 1969), 474.

14. *PMJDG*, 154–56; Catton, *Grant Takes Command*, 474; Porter, *Campaigning*, 498–99; Hamilton Fish Diary, December 12, 1869, Fish Papers, LC.

15. *PMJDG*, 156–57; Charles E. Bolles, "General Grant and the News of Mr. Lincoln's Death," *Century Magazine* 40 (June 1890):309–10; Jesse R. Grant, *In the Days of My Father General Grant* (New York: Harper and Brothers, 1925), 37–38; *New York Sun*, April 27, 1913.

16. Young, *Around the World*, 2:355; *PMUSG*, 2:509; *PMJDG*, 156.

17. *PMUSG*, 2:509.

18. Grant to Ord, April 15, 1865 (two messages), and Ord to Grant, same date, *PUSG*, 14:391–92.

19. Catton, *Grant Takes Command*, 478–79; Theodore S. Bowers to Ord, April 16, 1865, Grant Papers, LC; Brooks D. Simpson, *Let Us Have Peace: Ulysses S. Grant and the Politics of War and Reconstruction, 1861–1868* (Chapel Hill: University of North Carolina Press, 1991), 93.

20. James G. Randall and Theodore C. Pease, *The Diary of Orville Hickman Browning* (Springfield, Ill.: Illinois State Historical Library, 1925–33), 2:22 (April 18, 1865).

21. Grant to Charles W. Ford, April 17, 1865, *PUSG*, 14:405; Grant to Silas A. Hudson, April 21, 1865, ibid., 14:429–30.

22. Sherman to Grant, April 15, 1865, *SCW*, 862.

23. Sherman to Grant, April 18, 1865, ibid., 863–65.

24. Sherman to Grant, April 12, 1865, ibid., 859; Grant to Stanton, April 21, 1865, *PUSG*, 14:423.

25. Simpson, *Let Us Have Peace*, 96–97; Beale, *Diary of Welles*, 2:294–95; Badeau, *Grant in Peace*, 120.

26. Grant to Julia Grant, April 21, 1865, *PUSG*, 14:428–29.

27. Daniel Hand, "Reminiscences of an Army Surgeon," in Edward D. Neill et al., eds, *Glimpses of the Nation's Struggle* (St. Paul, Minn.: St. Paul Book and Stationery, 1887–1906), 1:306; Henry Hitchcock, *Marching with Sherman* (Lincoln: University of Nebraska Press, 1995 [1927]), 309.

28. Grant to Stanton, April 24, 1865, *PUSG*, 14:431–32; *New York Herald*, April 30, 1865; Catton, *Grant Takes Command*, 486–87.

29. Grant to Julia Grant, April 25, 1865, *PUSG*, 14:433; *New York Tribune*, May 3, 1865; Grant to Julia, May 9, 1865, *PUSG*, 15:30.

30. Beale, *Diary of Welles*, 2:295 (April 22, 23, 1865); Sherman to Grant, April 28, 1865, *SCW*, 880–82; John Marszalek, *Sherman: A Soldier's Passion for Order* (New York: The Free Press, 1993), 349–54.

31. Sherman to Stanton, April 25, 1865, *SCW*, 878; Stanton to Grant, April 25, 1865, *PUSG*, 14:432.

32. John Niven, *Gideon Welles: Lincoln's Secretary of the Navy* (New York: Oxford University Press, 1973), 501.

33. *PMJDG*, 158; Grant to Jesse Grant, May 6, 1865, *PUSG*, 15:23; Grant to Halleck, May 18, 1865, ibid., 15:52; Grant to Washburne, May 21, 1865, ibid., 15:85–86; ibid., 17:210–32; Philip H. Sheridan, *Personal Memoirs of P. H. Sheridan* (New York: Charles L. Webster, 1888), 2:209.

34. *New York Times*, May 24, 1865.

35. *PMJDG*, 159; Grant, *In the Days of My Father*, 43; Sherman, *Memoirs*, 2:376–77.

36. The proclamations appear in Edward McPherson, *The Political History of the United States of America during the Period of Reconstruction* (New York: Negro Universities Press, 1969 [1875]), 9–12.

37. Hamlin Garland, *Ulysses S. Grant: His Life and Character* (New York: Macmillan, 1920), 325–27; William S. McFeely, *Grant: A Biography* (New York: W. W. Norton, 1981), 233; *New York Times*, June 8, 1865.

38. *New York World*, June 8, 1865.

39. *New York Times*, June 9, 1865; *Chicago Tribune*, June 12, 1865; Grant to Ellen E. Sherman, May 31, 1865, *PUSG*, 15:117; Garland, *Grant*, 327–29.

40. Halleck to Grant, April 29, 1865, Grant Papers, LC; Halleck to Grant, May 5, 1865, *PUSG*, 15:7, and Grant to Halleck, May 6, 1865, ibid., 15:11.

41. *New York Times*, April 19, 26, June 4, 17, 1865; Butler to Johnson, April 25, 1865, Johnson Papers, LC.

42. Freeman, *Lee*, 4:202–3; *New York Tribune*, June 5, 1865; *New York World*, June 12, 1865; *New Orleans Tribune*, June 25, 1865.

43. Badeau, *Grant in Peace*, 25–26; Bernarr Cresap, *Appomattox Commander: The Story of General E. O. C. Ord* (San Diego: A. S. Barnes, 1981), 228; Lee to Grant, June 13, 1865, Grant Papers, ISHL.

44. Grant, endorsement of June 16, 1865, on Robert E. Lee to Grant, June 13, 1865, Grant Papers, ISHL; Badeau to Wilson, June 16, 1865, James H. Wilson Papers, LC; Simpson, *Let Us Have Peace*, 107.

45. Randall and Pease, *Diary of Browning*, 2:32 (June 7, 1865); Badeau, *Grant in Peace*, 26; McPherson, *Political History*, 299–300.

46. Badeau, *Grant in Peace*, 26; Grant to Lee, June 20, 1865, *PUSG*, 15:210–11; Speed to Lucius Chandler, June 20, 1865, Record Group 60, Department of Justice, Letters Sent, NA.

47. Grant, draft of report to Edwin M. Stanton, June 20, 1865, *PUSG*, 15:164–206.

Afterword: Of Success, Fate, and Greatness

1. Albert D. Richardson, *Personal History of Ulysses S. Grant* (Hartford, Conn.: American Publishing, 1868), 170.

2. Ibid., 388.

3. *New York World*, April 26, 1865; John Russell Young, *Around the World with General Grant* (New York: American News, 1879), 2:351–52.

4. Young, *Around the World with General Grant*, 2:352–53, 625.

5. Ibid., 2:615; John H. Brinton, *Personal Memoirs of John H. Brinton* (New York: Neale Publishing, 1914), 239; T. Harry Williams, *McClellan, Sherman, and Grant* (New Brunswick: Rutgers University Press, 1962), 105; John L. Ringwalt, *Anecdotes of General Ulysses S. Grant* (Philadelphia: J. B. Lippincott, 1886), 43; Sherman to Grant, March 10, 1864, *SCW*, 603.

6. Williams, *McClellan, Sherman, and Grant*, 85; William F. G. Shanks, *Personal Recollections of Distinguished Generals* (New York: Harper and Brothers, 1866), 98, 103–4.

7. Carl von Clausewitz, *On War* (Princeton: Princeton University Press, 1976), 119, 136.

8. John M. Schofield, *Forty-Six Years in the Army* (New York: Century Co., 1897), 524, 544.

9. James F. Rusling, *Men and Things I Saw in Civil War Days* (New York: Eaton and Mains, 1899), 146.

10. Parker's comments are in the Grant family scrapbooks, Grant Papers, LC; *National Tribune*, February 6, 1886.

11. Henry Adams, *The Education of Henry Adams* (Boston: Houghton Mifflin, 1973 [1918], 264; James H. Wilson, *Under the Old Flag* (New York: D. Appleton and Co., 1912), 1:156–60. Along with Sylvanus Cadwallader, Wilson was the originator, not of the plan to take Vicksburg (as he liked to believe) but of the legend that Rawlins was the brains of the Grant-Rawlins partnership.

12. *New York Tribune*, August 2, 1885; Albert O. Marshall, *Army Life* (Joliet, Ill.: Chicago Legal News Co., 1883), 275; *Cleveland (Ohio) Leader*, July 31, 1885.

13. M. Harrison Strong interview, Hamlin Garland Papers, University of Southern California; *Cleveland (Ohio) Leader*, July 31, 1885; *National Tribune*, December 10, 1885; Francis B. Carpenter, *The Inner Life of Abraham Lincoln: Six Months at the White House* (Boston: Houghton, Osgood, and Co., 1880), 283.

14. *Cleveland (Ohio) Leader*, July 31, 1885; *Burlington (Vermont) Free Press*, July 29, 1885; Shanks, *Recollections*, 98, 103–4.

15. Wilson, *Under the Old Flag,* 2:17.

16. William T. Sherman, "An Address on Grant," in James G. Wilson and Titus M. Coan, eds., *Personal Recollections of the War of the Rebellion* (New York: Military Order of the Loyal Legion of the United States, New York Chapter, 1891), 111.

17. Ely S. Parker, "The Character of Grant," Wilson and Coan, *Personal Recollections of the War of the Rebellion,* 347; Frederick D. Grant, "A Boy's Experience at Vicksburg," in A. Noel Blakeman, ed., *Personal Recollections of the War of the Rebellion,* Third Series (New York: G. P. Putnam's Sons, 1907), 96; Frank Harrison, *Anecdotes and Reminiscences of Gen'l U. S. Grant* (New York: NY Cheap Publishing Co., 1885), 8; George F. Shrady, *General Grant's Last Days* (New York: privately printed, 1908), 13; *New York Star,* January 13, 1886; Young, *Around the World with General Grant,* 2:451.

18. *PMUSG,* 1:7; *St. Louis Republican,* July 24, 1885.

19. Ibid., 2:216–17; *Cincinnati Commercial,* January 27, 1869 (interview with William S. Hillyer).

20. Shanks, *Recollections,* 127.

Index

●

298
287 also 261
see p. 234 358